American Experiences

American Experiences

READINGS IN AMERICAN HISTORY

Volume I   To 1877

Sixth Edition

Randy Roberts
Purdue University

James S. Olson
Sam Houston State University

PEARSON
Longman

New York San Francisco Boston
London Toronto Sydney Tokyo Singapore Madrid
Mexico City Munich Paris Cape Town Hong Kong Montreal

Vice President and Publisher: Priscilla McGeehon
Executive Marketing Manager: Sue Westmoreland
Production Manager: Denise Phillip
Project Coordination, Text Design, and Electronic Page Makeup: Shepherd Incorporated
Cover Design Manager: John Callahan
Cover Designer: John Callahan
Cover Image: Michael Staats
Photo Researcher: Photosearch, Inc.
Senior Manufacturing Buyer: Alfred C. Dorsey
Printer and Binder: Hamilton Printing
Cover Printer: Phoenix Color Corporation

For permission to use copyrighted material, grateful acknowledgment is made to the copyright holders on p.415, which are hereby made part of this copyright page.

Library of Congress Cataloging-in-Publication Data

Constructing the American past : a source book of a people's history / [edited by] Elliott J.
   Gorn, Randy Roberts, Terry D. Bilhartz.—5th ed.
      p. cm.
   Includes bibliographical references and indexes.
   ISBN 0-321-21642-3 (v. 1)—ISBN 0-321-21641-5 (v. 2)
    1. United States—History—Sources. I. Gorn, Elliott J., 1951– II. Roberts, Randy, 1951–
   III. Bilhartz, Terry D.

   E173.C69 2004
   973—dc22   2004052998

Please visit our website at http://www.ablongman.com

ISBN 0-321-21644-X

1 2 3 4 5 6 7 8 9 10—HT—07 06 05 04

To Our Families

Contents

Preface

American History instructors enjoy talking about the grand sweep of the American past. Many note the development of unique traditions such as the American political tradition and the American diplomatic tradition. They employ the article *the* so often that they depict history as a seamless garment and Americans as all cut from the same fabric. Nothing could be further from the truth. America is a diverse country, and its population is the most ethnically varied in the world—white and black, Indian and Chicano, rich and poor, male and female. No single tradition can encompass this variety. *American Experiences* shows the complexity and richness of the nation's past by focusing on the people—how they coped with, adjusted to, or rebelled against America. The readings examine these people as they worked and played, fought and made love, lived and died.

We designed *American Experiences* as a supplement to the standard textbooks used in college survey classes in American History. Unlike other readers, it covers ground not usually found in textbooks. For example, instead of a discussion on the War of 1812, it has an article about dying of breast cancer in 1811. In short, it presents different slants on standard and not-so-standard topics.

We have tested each essay in classrooms so that *American Experiences* reflects not only our interest in social history but also student interests in American history in general. We have selected essays that are readable, interesting, and that illustrate important aspects of America's past. For example, to show the nature of the class system in the South and to introduce the topic of southern values, we selected one essay on gambling and horse racing in the Old South and another on gouging matches in the southern backcountry. As an introduction to the conventional discussion of Jacksonian Democracy, it includes an article about the advent of surgical anesthesia and what type of person should be entitled to it. Each essay, then, serves at least two purposes: to tell a particular story well, and to help illuminate the social or political landscape of America.

This reader presents a balanced picture of the experiences of Americans. The characters in these volumes are not exclusively white males from the Northeast, whose eyes are continually focused on Boston, New York, and Washington. Although their stories are certainly important, so too are the stories of blacks adjusting with dignity to a barbarous labor system, Chicanos coming to terms with Anglo society, and women striving for increased opportunities in a society restricted by gender. We have looked at all of these stories and, in doing so, we have assumed that Americans express themselves in a variety of ways, through work, sex, and games, as well as politics and diplomacy.

Changes to the Sixth Edition

During the past four years, we have solicited a variety of opinions, from colleagues and students, about the selections for Volume 1 of *American Experiences*. Based on that feedback, we have made a number of changes in the sixth edition, always with the intent of selecting articles that undergraduate students will find interesting and informative. The new articles for the first volume of this edition are:

- Peggy Robbins, "The Devil in Salem"
- Phyllis Lee Levin, "Founding Mother: Abigail Adams"
- Uzal W. Ent, "On the Shores of Tripoli"
- Randy Roberts and James S. Olson, "In Search of Davy's Grave"
- Martin S. Pernick, "Anesthesia and the Politics of Pain"
- Benjamin Reiss, "P. T. Barnum, Joice Heth, and Antebellum Spectacles of Race"
- Joseph T. Glatthar, "The Common Soldier's Gettysburg Campaign"
- Allen W. Trelease, "Knights of the Rising Sun"

American Experiences is divided into standard chronological and topical parts. Each part is introduced by a brief discussion of the major themes of the period or topic. In turn, each selection is preceded by a short discussion of how it fits into the part's general theme. We employed this method to give students some guidance through the complexity of the American experience. At the conclusion of each selection is a series of study questions and a brief bibliographic essay. These are intended to further the usefulness of *American Experiences* for students as well as teachers.

We would like to acknowledge the help of our reviewers and thank them for their efforts: Anna Bates, Aquinas College; Paul E. Doutrich, York College of Pennsylvania; Steve Goodson, State University of West Georgia; Cheryl T. Kalny, St. Norbert College; Dennis Lythgoe, University of Utah; Timothy R. Mahoney, University of Nebraska; Marc Maltby, Owensboro Community and Technical College; Constance M. McGovern, Frostburg State University; Johnny S. Moore, Radford University; Susan E. Myers-Shirk, Middle Tennessee State University; Richard Pate, Danville Area Community College.

Randy Roberts
James S. Olson

American Experiences

New England Life

John Winthrop, the first governor of the Puritan settlement of Massachusetts Bay, was charged with a sense of mission. He and his Puritan followers braved the North Atlantic to establish a society in which the will of God would be observed completely. Aboard the flagship *Arbella* in April 1630, Winthrop explained their "errand into the wilderness." They were a unique people, for they had been given "a special commission" by God, and "He looks to have it strictly observed in every article." By working together, defeating selfishness, and keeping the Lord foremost in their thoughts, they would help create a kingdom of God on earth and blaze a trail for the future of all people. As Winthrop said, "Wee shall be as a City upon a Hill, the eies of all people are upon us."

The Puritans' Lord was a stern master, and their religion was as uncompromising as the cold rocky shores of New England. At the heart of Puritanism was the doctrine of predestination. Since humanity was too sinful to deserve salvation, God simply gave the gift of salvation to select individuals, while condemning the rest to eternal damnation. There was nothing an individual could do to alter this decision. Nor could an individual ever know absolutely if he or she was saved or damned.

The ultimate mystery of predestination created an underlying tension in Puritan society. Puritans searched constantly for some sign that they had received God's gift of salvation. In their diaries, they scrutinized their actions and thoughts, examining their lives for evidence of the sin that was inherent in all people. Puritans believed that sin could be as passive as an envious thought or as active as a violent deed. Occasionally, however, they found reason for hope.

The Puritans' deep religious belief influenced every aspect of their lives. They believed that God and the devil intervened constantly in daily affairs. The devil lurked in the New England forests and the Indian tribes, and stood ready to claim those with weak hearts and bodies. In addition, God punished those who disobeyed His laws. A bolt of lightning or debilitating disease might very well be a sign of God's disfavor. The epidemic diseases that devastated the Indians were, in the Puritan mind, afflictions imposed by God.

Nevertheless, the Puritans should not be viewed as one-dimensional people. Their sins, excesses, and great accomplishments were the actions of humans. The following selections of essays present the world of the Puritans at its best and worst. The common thread in these essays is the Puritans' commitment to their religion and the way in which they used that religion to interpret and determine the course of their lives. Ultimately, the history of American Puritanism is the unfolding of a religious idea.

Not all of New England was Puritan, however. As the northern colonies matured, many people moved away from the stern religion of the earliest settlers. Some were more recent immigrants who had never followed the Puritan faith; others were children or grandchildren of Puritans in whose hearts the fire of faith did not burn as strongly. Certainly Boston and Massachusetts Bay retained something of its Puritan heritage, but its economic position in the British empire also exerted a powerful influence. By the eighteenth century, images of zealous Puritans and shrewd Yankees mixed to form the popular conception of the New Englander. If Sunday remained God's day, trade and commerce ruled the rest of the week. Tied to England and the West Indies by economic bonds, Boston—like Philadelphia and Charles Town—became part of the Atlantic community.

READING 1

God . . . Would Destroy Them, and Give Their Country to Another People . . .

Alfred W. Crosby, Jr.

In 1616 or 1617, several years before the Pilgrims and later the Puritans ever arrived in Massachusetts, the local Indians suffered from catastrophic epidemics of disease, probably from a malignant form of typhus left behind by some sick Europeans whose ships anchored temporarily along the coast as a refuge from bad weather. The Indians had no immunities. They had been separated geographically from the European and Asian landmasses for thousands of years, leaving them unprepared for the variety of diseases the Europeans brought—typhus, bubonic plague, smallpox, chicken pox, mumps, measles, influenza, diphtheria, and a host of other maladies. Europeans, with their dense urban populations and wide variety of domesticated animals, had already accumulated the necessary immunities. But the illnesses spread like a wildfire through the Indian villages, devastating whole tribes and whole regions, depopulating the area as Indians either died or fled. European germs were far more important than European weapons in explaining how so few conquered so many in the New World.

Indians found the plagues profoundly disturbing—a series of events inconsistent with their worldview. For them, disease was simply a manifestation of spiritual imbalances, which could be cured by medicine men who understood the balances of nature and the human psyche. When their own healers failed to stem the plagues, the Indians lost not only their lives but their faith and vision as well. Puritans interpreted the plague as the punishment of God. Indian idolatry could not be tolerated, and since they would not repent, God poured out his wrath upon them. In the process of destroying the Indians, God also gave "their country to another people"—the Puritans.

In December of 1620, a group of English dissenters who "knew they were pilgrimes," in the words of William Bradford, stepped ashore on the southern coast of Massachusetts at the site of the Wampanoag Indian village of Pawtuxet. The village was empty, abandoned long enough for the grasses and weeds to have taken over the cornfields, but not long enough for the trees to have returned. The Pilgrims occupied the lonely place and called it Plymouth.

It was pestilence that had cleared the way for this tiny foothold in New England, and the shadow of death would be a major factor in giving the settlement form and substance in the months ahead.

New England Indians and European fishermen and traders had been in intermittent contact for a century, and it was inevitable that more than otter skins, beaver pelts, knives, and kettles would be exchanged. Disease was among the commodities, and in this trade the Indians would come off second best. Europe, with ancient contact by land and new ones by sea with the chief disease communities of the world, and with her relatively dense populations of often hungry and always filthy people, had all the advantages of her disadvantages: an arsenal of diseases.

Europe was in the midst of a golden age for infectious disease organisms, an era ushered in by the Black Death in the fourteenth century. To such old regulars as smallpox and consumption were added such new, or newly recognized, diseases as plague, typhus, and syphilis. Bubonic plague, the greatest killer of them all, smoldered continually and broke out periodically in consuming epidemics. Early in 1617 southeast gales drove whales ashore in the Netherlands. The fearful thought them a portent of plague, and sure enough, by August the plague was general throughout the land. London had full-scale epidemics of that killer in 1603 and again in 1625,

"God . . . Would Destroy Them, and Give Their Country to Another People . . ." by Alfred W. Crosby in *American Heritage* 29 (October/November 1978), pp. 39–43. Reprinted by permission of American Heritage Magazine, a division of Forbes Inc., © Forbes Inc., 1978.

and the plague—or something very like it—soon made its presence felt among the Indians of the Northeast coast of America. Innocent of immunity or experience, the Indians were helpless.

As Indian tempers rose, respect for Europeans fell in the second decade of the seventeenth century, particularly after the kidnaping of Indians for purposes of slavery began. Sometime in that period, a French ship was wrecked on the shores of Massachusetts, and some of the crew escaped alive. Possibly in retaliation for a recent kidnaping raid by whites, the Indians eventually killed all but three or four, whom they reduced to slavery. According to what the Indians told the Pilgrims, one of these captives, angry and helpless, had struck at his captors with words, telling them that "God was angry with them for their wickedness, and would destroy them, and give their country to another people, that should not live as beasts as they did but should be clothed. . . ." The Indians laughed at him, saying that they were so numerous that the white man's god could not kill them. He answered "that though they were never so many, God had many ways to destroy them that they knew not." Within a year or so an epidemic struck the coast of New England, devastating the tribes like an autumnal nor'easter raking leaves from the trees.

When did this pestilence first appear in New England? Probably no earlier than 1616 and no later than 1617, and it lasted until at least 1619. What vessel brought it? It is improbable that we will ever know. What was the disease? Another difficult question. We know it lasted through winters, which suggests that it wasn't a mosquito-borne disease, like yellow fever. We know that the few Europeans who actually saw its victims did not identify it as smallpox, measles, mumps, chicken pox, or any of Europe's common diseases, which they certainly would have recognized. We know it spread along the coast no farther southwest than Narragansett Bay, nor farther northeast than the Kennebec River or possibly Penobscot Bay, nor did it penetrate inland more than twenty or thirty miles. The narrow geographical limitations of the epidemic suggest that the disease was not one of the breath-borne maladies, like smallpox or measles, which normally surge across vast areas. A flea- or louse-borne disease like typhus or plague seems more likely.

We know that the disease produced spots on its victims' skins; and we know by hearsay that some Englishmen in New England at the peak of the epidemic slept in huts with dead and dying Indians, but that not one of these whites fell ill or even so much as "felt their heads to ache while they stayed there." Spots certainly suggest typhus. The Europeans' freedom from infection suggests some disease so common in Europe that they all had acquired immunity to it at home, or that they didn't stay around long enough to get a proper dose of the disease—or that the account is in part or whole false.

Most of the seventeenth-century chroniclers called the disease the plague. "Plague" was and is a word often used to mean any pestilence, but these chroniclers often called it *the* plague." Captain Thomas Dermer, one of the few Europeans actually to see Indians who were freshly recovering from the experience, called their infection in 1619 "the Plague, for wee might perceive the sores of some that had escaped, who described the spots of such as usually died."

Plague is certainly capable of doing what this pestilence did, and Europeans certainly knew it well enough to recognize it by sight or description. And it is true that plague was well established in Western Europe in the early years of the seventeenth century. Like some kinds of typhus, it is a disease carried by rats and their attendant vermin, rats which swarmed in the holds of the sailing vessels of that era. The disease travels readily by ship, as the European colonists in America knew. Many Britons fell ill and died on the vessels of the Third Supply sailing to Virginia in 1609, and a rumor was that one of the vessels had plague on board. In the 1660's, during London's last great siege of plague, Virginians fled from their ports for fear of the disease coming across on the ships from England.

Fear was justified because ship rats were coming across and establishing beachheads in America. Captain John Smith tells us that they already

numbered in the thousands in Jamestown in 1609, when the rats almost starved out the colony by eating its stores of food. They were present and prospering in New England by at least the 1660's, and probably a great deal earlier. It is likely that they found living in the layered bark walls of the Indian wigwams warm and comfortable, and the Indian food-storage practices and eating habits conducive to good diet. Once the rats were established, the transfer of their plague-ridden fleas to the Indians would have been almost automatic and perhaps not even noticed by the new hosts. Body lice were even more common among New England Indians than among white settlers, and the natives commonly passed the time by picking lice and killing them between their teeth.

It is disturbing, though, to those who diagnose the pestilence as plague, that Dermer described its chief signs as sores and spots, rather than the terrible buboes or boils of the groin and armpits that are impossible to overlook in typical victims of the plague. And it is even more odd that the plague-infected fleas did not establish themselves and their bacilli permanently among the wild rodents of New England, as they did in those of the western United States at the end of the nineteenth century. A diagnosis of typhus is tempting, but the historian is reluctant to contradict first-hand witnesses.

Whether plague or typhus, the disease went through the Indians like fire. Almost all the seventeenth-century writers say it killed nine of ten and even nineteen of twenty of the Indians it touched—an incredible mortality rate. But if it was, indeed, plague, it could well have killed that proportion. In the fourteenth century, plague killed one-third of all the people in Europe and a much higher percentage than that in many towns and districts. Further, the Indians knew nothing of the principle of contagion and had an ancient custom of visiting the sick, jamming into extremely hot little huts with them, assuring maximum dispersal of the illness. Their methods of treating illness, which usually featured a stay in a sweatbox, followed by immersion in the nearest cold pond or river, would have been a dreadful trauma for a person with a high fever, and a fine way to encourage pneumonic complications. Consider, too, that the epidemic could not have failed to disrupt food-procurement patterns, as women lay too ill to tend the corn and the men too weak to hunt. Starvation often gleans what epidemic disease has missed. Consider, finally, that after the Indians realized the full extent of the disease, some of them, at least, ran away and left the sick and convalescent to die of neglect. In short, one does not necessarily have to accept a 90 percent death rate for a given village or area in order to accept a 90 percent depopulation rate.

It is undeniable that the pestilence largely emptied the Indian villages of coastal New England by 1619. That year, Thomas Dermer found "ancient plantations, not long since populous, now utterly void; in other places a remnant remains, but not free of sickness."

In 1621 a party of Pilgrims went to visit Massasoit, the most powerful Wampanoag sachem, at his summer quarters on a river about fifteen miles from Plymouth. They saw the remnants of many villages and former Indian cornfields along both sides of the river grown up in weeds higher than a man's head: "Thousands of men have lived there, which died in a great plague not long since: and pity it was and is to see so many goodly fields, and so well seated, without men to dress and manure the same."

Near Boston Bay, Thomas Morton saw even more vivid indications of the plague: "For in a place where many inhabited, there hath been but one left alive, to tell what became of the rest, the living being (as it seemed) not able to bury the dead, they were left for Crowes, kites and vermin to prey upon. And the bones and skulls upon the severall places of their habitations, made such a spectacle after my coming into those partes, that as I travailed in that Forrest, nere the Massachusets, it seemed to mee a new found Golgotha."

What destroyed Indian bodies also undermined Indian religion—the Indian's entire view of the universe and of himself. Disease was always considered a manifestation of spiritual influences, and the power of the powwows (medicine men) to direct and cure disease was central to the In-

dian religion. Later in the century we hear of powwows being hounded, punished, and even killed for failing to produce promised cures. What was the impact when hundreds, even thousands, died under the hands of leaders whose chief distinction was their ability to cure? Many of the powwows themselves, in constant contact with the sick they sought to cure, must have died. What was the impact of this final and irrevocable defeat of these priestly physicians?

What seemed cosmically appalling to the Indians was interpreted as clear proof of God's love by the Pilgrims—a divine intercession that revealed itself from the beginning. They had planned to settle in the Hudson River area or thereabouts, but the master of the *Mayflower* deposited them on the coast of New England. His inability or refusal to take them where they wanted to go proved a bit of luck—"God out-shoots Satan oftentimes in his own bow"—for the lands about the Hudson's mouth, though more attractive because more fertile than Plymouth's, were "then abounding with a multitude of pernicious savages. . . ." God had directed the Pilgrims to a coast His plague had cleared of such savages: "whereby he made way for the carrying of his good purpose in promulgating his gospel. . . ." There were no Indians at Plymouth and none for eight or ten miles, and yet it had recently been a village of Wampanoags who had, over the years, cut away the tough climax growth of forest to plant corn. When the weak and hungry Colonists went out to plant in the following spring, all they had to do was to clear out the weeds. Death, it seemed obvious, was God's handyman and the Pilgrim's friend.

The wind of pestilence did more than merely clear a safe place for the Pilgrims to settle; in the long run, it enabled that settlement not only to survive, but to take root and, in the end, to prosper with a minimum of native resistance. The natives of coastal Massachusetts were fewer in number than in a very long time, possibly than in several thousand years, but there were still quite enough of them to wipe out the few Europeans from the *Mayflower,* and they

had reason to hate whites. In addition to kid-
napings, Europeans—English, the Indians told
Dermer—recently had lured a number of
Wampanoags on board their ship and had then
"made great slaughter of them with their murderers (small ship's cannon). . . . " When a
party of Pilgrims visited the next tribe to the
south, the Nausets, in 1621, they met an old
woman who broke "forth into great passion,
weeping and crying excessively." She had lost
three of her sons to kidnapers, and now was
without comfort in her old age. A Wampanoag
said that the Nausets had killed three English in-
terlopers in the summer of 1620.

Half the English at Plymouth died of malnutri-
tion, exhaustion, and exposure that first winter.
Indian anger and Indian power could have made
Plymouth one of the lost colonies, like the one
Columbus left behind on La Española in 1493 or
Sir Walter Raleigh's Roanoke colony of the 1580's.

At some time during this low ebb of Pilgrim history the powwows gathered in the fastnesses of a
swamp, where, for three days, they "did curse and
execrate" the newcomers to destroy them or drive
them away. It almost worked: at times the number
of English healthy enough to offer any real help to
the sick and, if necessary, any real resistance to attackers was as low as six or seven. But in the end
the Indian's gods failed, and the English survived,
"having borne this affliction with much patience,
being upheld by the Lord."

What held the Indians back from physical attack? They had the strength and motive, and
bloody precedent had been set by both whites
and Indians. The answer must be fear. The coastal
Indians may have been second only to the Pilgrims in New England as believers in the power of
the white man's god. A visitor to Plymouth in
1621 wrote that the plague had sapped
Wampanoag courage, as well as the tribe's numbers: "their countenance is dejected, and they
seem as a people affrighted." They were coming
to the English settlement in great numbers every
day, "and might in one hour have made a dispatch
of us, yet such a fear was upon them, as that they
never offered us the least injury in word or deed."

*Tisquantum ("Squanto") taught the Pilgrims how
to plant and grow corn.*

Direct relations between the Wampanoags
and the Pilgrims began in March of 1621, approximately three months after the English arrival. An Indian walked out of the woods and
through the fields and into Plymouth. He was
Samoset, who spoke some English, having
learned it from English fishermen on the coast of
Maine. He asked for beer, and received "strong
water," biscuit, butter, cheese, pudding, and a
piece of duck. It was he who told the Pilgrims the
old Indian name for their village and explained
what had happened to its original inhabitants. A
few days later he returned with the individual
whom the Pilgrims would soon rank as "a special
instrument sent of God for their good beyond
their expectation." The man was Squanto, a Pawtuxet who had been kidnaped, had escaped in
Spain, and had lived in Cornhill, London, before
making his way back to America.

An hour later the sachem, Massasoit, walked
in with a train of sixty men. If he had come to
fight, he could have swept Plymouth out of existence, but he came in peace, and what amounts

to a nonaggression and mutual defense pact was soon agreed upon—the Treaty of Plymouth. Massasoit, wrote Edward Winslow in his first-person account of that day in March, "hath a potent adversary, the Narrohigansets (Narragansets), that are at war with him, against whom he thinks we may be some strength to him, for our peeces are terrible unto them."

In the eyes of the native people of New England, the whites possessed a greater potency, a greater mana, than any Indian people. Nothing could be more immediately impressive than firearms, which made clouds of smoke and a sound like the nearest of thunderclaps and killed at a distance of many paces. And what could seem more logical but to see a similarity between the muskets and cannon, which reached out invisibly and tore bodies, and the plague, which reached out invisibly and corrupted bodies? In the 1580's, Indians in the vicinity of Roanoke had blamed the epidemic then raging on "invisible bullets" that the whites could shoot any distance desired; and it is quite likely that Massasoit and his followers had a similar interpretation of their experience with epidemic disease. No wonder the mighty sachem literally trembled as he sat beside the governor of Plymouth that day in March of 1621.

The following year, the Pilgrims learned that Squanto, taking advantage of his position as go-between for the Indians and English, had been telling the former that he had such control over the latter that he could persuade them to unleash the plague again, if he wished. He tried to use this claim of immense power to persuade the Wampanoags to shift their allegiance from Massasoit to himself. It was a game which nearly cost the schemer his life, and he had to spend the rest of his days living with the Pilgrims.

He told the Indians that the plague was buried under the storehouse in Plymouth, where, interestingly enough, the Pilgrims did have something buried: their reserve kegs of gunpowder. He told the Wampanoags that the English could send the plague forth to destroy whomever they wished, while not stirring a foot from home. When, in May of 1622, the Pilgrims dug up some of the gunpowder kegs, another Wampanoag, understandably disturbed, asked the English if they did, indeed, have the plague at their beck and call. The answer he got was as honest a one as could be expected from a seventeenth-century Christian: "No; but the God of the English has it in store, and could send it at his pleasure, to the destruction of his or our enemies." Not long after, Massasoit asked Governor William Bradford if "he would let out the plague to destroy the Sachem, and his men, who were his enemies, promising that he himself, and all his posterity, would be their everlasting friends, so great an opinion he had of the English."

Those enemies were the Narragansets, whose presence was the greatest immediate threat to Plymouth, and whose fear of the Englishmen's power was Plymouth's (and the Wampanoags') best shield. In the late fall of 1621 Canonicus, the Narragansets' greatest sachem, sent a bundle of arrows wrapped in a snakeskin to Squanto at Plymouth. Squanto was not present when they arrived, for which the messenger who brought the bundle was visibly thankful, and he departed "with all expedition." When Squanto returned and examined Canonicus' package, he explained that it signified a threat and a challenge to the new colony. The governor, who as a European of the Reformation era knew as much of threat and challenge as any Indian, stuffed the skin with gunpowder and shot, and sent it back to Canonicus. The great and terrible sachem refused to accept it, would not touch the powder and shot, nor suffer the bundle to remain in Narraganset country. The sinister package, "having been posted from place to place a long time, at length came whole back again." The plague perhaps had taught the Indian the principle of contagion.

Disease, real and imagined, remained a crucial element in English-Indian relations for at least the next two years, and seemingly always to the advantage of the English. In 1622 and 1623 the Pilgrims were still so incompetent at living in America that only the abundance of shellfish and corn obtained from the Indians kept them from starvation: a dangerous situation, because by then the Indians' fear of and respect for the whites were declining. As one Pilgrim chronicler put it, the Indians "began again to cast forth many insulting speeches, glorying in our weakness, and giving out how easy it would be ere long to cut us off. Now also Massassowat [Massasoit] seemed to frown on us, and neither came or sent to us as formerly." A letter arrived from Jamestown far to the south in Virginia telling of how the Indians had risen there, killing hundreds of the colonists. In the summer of 1622 a band of ne'er-do-well English settled at Wessagusset (Weymouth), not far from Plymouth, and after begging food from the impoverished Pilgrims, set about stealing it from the Indians. That fall Squanto, the almost indispensable man in the Pilgrims' dealings with the Indians, fell ill on a trip to collect corn from the natives. After fever and nosebleeds he died, asking the governor to pray for him "that he might go to the Englishman's God in heaven. . . . "

The Indians, apparently with the Massachusetts tribe in the lead, began to plot to exterminate the Wessagusset settlement. They were less intolerant of the Plymouth than the Wessagusset people, but their plan was to destroy the Pilgrims, as well, for fear that the latter would take revenge for the murder of any English. The scheme never got beyond the talking stage. Why weren't the Indians able to organize themselves and take the action they planned? Pilgrims collecting corn from the Massachusetts in the latter part of 1622 learned of a "great sickness" among them "not unlike the plague, if not the same." Soon after, Wampanoag women bringing corn to Plymouth were struck with a "great sickness," and the English were obliged to carry much of the corn home on their own backs.

Disease or, at least, bodily malfunction most dramatically affected New England history in 1623 when Massasoit developed a massive case of constipation. In March the news arrived in Plymouth that Massasoit was close to death and that a Dutch vessel had grounded on the sands right in front of his current home. The English knew of the Indian custom that any and all friends must visit the ill, especially the very ill, and they also wanted to meet with the stranded Dutch; so a small party set out from Plymouth for the sachem's sickbed. The Pilgrims found the Dutch afloat and gone, and Massasoit's dwelling jammed to bursting with well-wishers and powwows "making such a hellish noise, as it distempered us that were well, and therefore unlike to ease him that was sick."

Edward Winslow undertook the sachem's case and managed to get between his teeth "a confection of many comfortable conserves, on the point of my knife. . . . " He then washed out his patient's mouth, put him on a light diet, and soon his bowels were functioning again. The Englishman had, with the simplest of Hippocratic remedies, apparently saved the life of the most powerful man in the immediate environs of Plymouth. For the next day or so Winslow was kept busy going from one to another of the sachem's sick or allegedly sick followers, doling out smidgens of his confection and receiving "many joyful thanks." In an era which was, for the Indians, one of almost incomprehensible mortality, Winslow had succeeded where all the powwows had failed in thwarting the influences drawing Massasoit toward death. The English could not only persuade a profoundly malevolent god to kill, but also *not* to kill.

The most important immediate product of Massasoit's recovery was his gratitude. He revealed the details of the Indian plot against Wessagusset and Plymouth, a plot involving most of the larger tribes within two or three days' travel of Plymouth, and even the Indians of Capawack (Martha's Vineyard). He said he had been asked to join when he was sick, but had refused for himself and his people. The Pilgrims probably had already heard rumors of the plot, and the sachem's story was confirmed by Phineas Pratt, one of the ne'er-do-wells from Wessagusset, who made his way by fleetness of foot and luck through hostile Indians to Plymouth.

Captain Miles Standish sailed to Boston Bay with a small group of armed men, tiny in number but gigantic in the power the Indians thought they possessed. They killed five or so of the alleged leaders of the plot and returned home with the head of one of them. The remnants of the

Wessagusset colony were swept together and brought to Plymouth, where in time most of them made the decision to go back to Europe as hands on the vessels fishing along the Maine coast. The Indian head was set up at Plymouth fort as a visual aid to Indian education.

The Indian plan to wipe out the white colonies fell to pieces. Members of the several tribes within striking distance of Plymouth "forsook their houses, running to and fro like men distracted, living in swamps and other desert places, and so brought manifold diseases amongst themselves, whereof very many are dead. . . ." Ianough, sachem of the Massachusets, said "the God of the English was offended with them, and would destroy them in his anger. . . ." The Pilgrims noted smugly that the mortality rate among their opponents was, indeed, high, and "neither is there any likelihood it will easily cease; because

through fear they set little or no corn, which is the staff of life, and without which they cannot long preserve health and strength."

By 1622 or so the very last cases of the plague had occurred in New England—if indeed these were examples of plague and not of misdiagnosis—and the only remains of the great pestilence were disarticulating bones lost in fallen walls of rotting bark that had once been homes. But it had done its work. In 1625 the Pilgrims, for the first time, raised enough corn to fill their own stomachs *and* trade with the Indians. The Pilgrims had survived and were getting stronger, thanks more to biology than religion, despite Pilgrim preconceptions, but Thomas Morton nevertheless was reminded of a line from Exodus: "By little and little (saith God of old to his people) will I drive them out from before thee; till thou be increased, and inherit the land."

Study Questions

1. Why does Crosby think typhus was one of the diseases that struck the Indians? What other disease might have been responsible for the epidemics?

2. How were the Pilgrims viewed by their Indian neighbors?

3. How did Indians react when their own healers could not cure the diseases?

4. How did the Pilgrims regard the Indians of New England?

5. Who was Samoset? Squanto? Massasoit?

6. What Indian practices actually made the epidemics worse?

7. Why did the Indian plan to wipe out the Pilgrim settlement fail to materialize?

Bibliography

For a look at Native America on the eve of the arrival of Europeans, see Stuart J. Fiedel, *Prehistory of the Americas* (1992) and Brian M. Fagan, *Great Journey: The Peopling of Ancient America* (1987). The catastrophic impact of European diseases on the indigenous peoples of the New World is the subject of Russell Thornton's *American Indian Holocaust and Survival: A Population History since 1492* (1987) and Alfred W. Crosby's *The Columbian Exchange: Biological and Cultural Consequences of 1492* (1972). Also see Crosby's *Biological Imperialism: The Biological*

Expansion of Europe, 1250-1600 (1990). For specific descriptions of Indian-European relations, see Gary B. Nash, *Red, White, and Black* (1992) and John Demos, *The Unredeemed Captive: A Family Story from Early America* (1994). New England is the focus of Neal Salisbury, *Manitou and Providence: Indians, Europeans, and the Making of New England* (1982). Also see Francis Jennings, *The Invasion of America: Indians, Colonialism, and the Cant of Conquest* (1975). Daniel K. Richter's *Facing East from Indian Country: A Native History of Early America* (2001) takes an insightful look at how Indian peoples adjusted and adapted to the arrival of Europeans in United States history.

READING 2

★ ★ ★

Deficient Husbands: Manhood, Sexual Incapacity, and Male Marital Sexuality in Seventeenth-Century New England

Thomas A. Foster

Nearly four centuries after the Separatists first arrived in Plymouth and the Puritans in Massachusetts Bay, their tug on American culture remains strong. Over time, Americans erroneously came to the conclusion that Puritans were narrow-minded bigots intent on banning natural sexual pleasures. H. L. Mencken best captured that feeling when he defined Puritanism as "the haunting fear that someone, somewhere, may be happy." In a 1942 essay entitled "The Puritans and Sex," historian Edmund Morgan dispelled the notion that Puritans were responsible for America's sexual neuroses. He made it clear that Puritans, though opposed to sexual relations outside the bonds of marriage, viewed sex in marriage as a wholesome, healthy, and natural human activity, sanctioned by God. The Puritans were not nearly as inhibited as many Americans thought them to be, and they did understand that humans were often morally weak. In the following essay, historian Thomas A. Foster examines the problem of male impotency and the Puritan reaction to it.

Historians of sex and sexuality have for the most part argued that the seventeenth-century view of intimate relations can best be understood within the framework of an ideology of reproduction, rather than as part of a discourse of sexuality. Puritan New England was a society in which sexual unions were, in the words of one historian, "dominated by a reproductive imperative." Two elements demonstrate this obligation: Puritan community leaders urged the fledgling society to reproduce itself, and all nonprocreative sexual acts were, therefore, criminalized. Similarly, seventeenth-century sex acts conform to what other historians have termed a "reproductive matrix," whereby sex, even though "a joy within marriage," remained centrally "for the purposes of procreation." Sex was therefore both marital and procreative. From this perspective, seventeenth-century New Englanders understood sex only as distinct, unrelated acts, either marital and reproductive or transgressive, rather than as part of an integrated sexual identity. Moreover, because Puritans did not understand same-sex and transgressive sex acts as components of a more general sexual identity, a discourse of sexuality did not exist in the seventeenth century.

. . . Because of the seventeenth-century emphasis on marital pleasure as well as fertility, marriage was an important institution for the elaboration of ideas about male sexuality. Furthermore, the seventeenth-century discourse on marriage and sex yielded a category of sexually deficient men against which to posit a normative masculine ideal. John Demos, like others writing about impotence in Puritan New England, assumes that, to the extent that Puritans viewed impotence as a social problem, they did so because it interfered with procreative sex. Writing about impotence as grounds for divorce, Demos concedes that, although "the reasoning behind this is nowhere made explicit . . . most likely it reflected the felt

necessity that a marriage produce children." But evidence shows Puritan rationales for making sexual incapacity grounds for divorce and suggests an equal if not paramount emphasis on the sexual coupling of husband and wife.

Historians have established that manhood in seventeenth-century New England rested in large part on the social and political role of husband and head of household. As Demos and others have pointed out, male-headed households were the building blocks with which Puritan communities were constructed and understood as "little commonwealths," models for authority relations in the larger society. In its emphasis on sexuality, this article does not dispute the importance of the patriarchal role; it examines that role's sexual component and the connections between sex and manhood in seventeenth-century New England. Sexual incapacity had serious repercussions for manhood because, as grounds for divorce, it could prevent men from fully performing their role as head of household, husband, and father. . . .

Given the Puritan view of marriage as a civil contract rather than a sacrament, Massachusetts and Connecticut had the most liberal divorce laws of all the British mainland colonies. Both granted divorce on the grounds of male sexual incapacity, as did the colonies of New Haven and Plymouth before their respective mergers with Connecticut and Massachusetts in 1665 and 1691. The divorce cases discussed below are from 1639 to 1711, roughly the period during which the seventeenth-century Massachusetts and Connecticut county court systems dealt with divorce. Although New Haven alone had codified divorce statutes, little difference existed between the two court systems' handling of petitions for divorces based on male sexual incapacity.

Although the most frequently used legal grounds for divorce in seventeenth-century New England were desertion and bigamy or adultery, about one in six divorce petitions filed by women involved charges of male sexual incapacity. Owing to the loss and incompleteness of records, it is difficult to estimate with accuracy the number of divorce cases involving incapacity charges,

Thomas A. Foster, "Deficient Husbands: Manhood, Sexual Incapacity, and Male Marital Sexuality in Seventeenth-Century New England," *William and Mary Quarterly,* 56 (October 1999), 723–45.

but, of the roughly eighty petitions from wives in Connecticut, New Haven, Plymouth, and Massachusetts Bay Colonies, fourteen involve charges of male sexual incapacity. Of these petitions, six resulted in annulments, four in separations, two were rejected, and the results of the remaining two are unknown. It is always risky to extrapolate from court cases, but they afford glimpses of communal norms and even behaviors. Some extant divorce records contain rich testimony, not only by divorcing husbands and wives but also by kinfolk and neighbors, that reveals popular as well as legal attitudes toward male sexual incapacity. Thus, although the number of cases is small, statements of witnesses point to a larger network of participants and to standards of male sexual performance and manhood.

Important to an understanding of early modern marital sexuality is the contemporary medical belief that conception was possible only when intercourse resulted in orgasm for both partners. At the time of orgasm, both men and women produced "seed" that had to mix together for generation to occur. "The Instruments of Generation are two sorts," explained Nicholas Culpeper in his *Directory for Midwives,* which circulated widely throughout the colonies; "*Male and Female . . . the Operation is by Action and Passion,* the Agent is the *Seed.*" A discussion of how the sex of the child is determined offers similar evidence of the two-seed model. "If the Mans Seed be strongest, a Male is conceived; if the Womans, a Female." Thus, this view held that female as well as male orgasm was necessary for reproduction. As *The Compleat Practice of Physick,* which Culpeper translated and coauthored with Abdiah Cole and William Rowland, explains, "Her womb, skipping as it were for joy . . . poured forth in that pang of Pleasure" the female seed needed for reproduction. Much of the early sex, marriage, and reproduction literature likewise stressed the importance of male and female orgasm. The clitoris, explained Culpeper, "represents the Yard of a man, and suffers erection and falling as that doth; this is that which causeth Lust in women, and gives delight in Copulation, for without this a

woman neither desires Copulation, or hath pleasure in it, or conceives by it." Whether the literature of the period emphasized pleasure because of its link to procreation or its strengthening of the spousal bond is nearly impossible to disentangle. Most important, procreative sex was pleasure-based sex according to the two-orgasm model of reproduction. In other words, male reproductive capabilities considered the ability of a husband to satisfy his wife sexually. Sexual pleasure and reproduction were fused together in the literature reaching colonial New England and elsewhere.

In many instances, moreover, advice manual writers downplayed the reproductive element of marital sexual relations and highlighted sexual pleasure in its own right. William Gouge, a Puritan rector and author of *Domesticall Duties,* a seventeenth-century advice book on marriage, delivered his popular text as a series of sermons in London before it was published and read in the colonies. Gouge argued that divorce in cases of female infertility should not be granted because sexual fulfillment was still possible for both partners. But male impotence, he wrote, should remain grounds for divorce, because it entirely prohibited sexual intercourse. He separated sex from procreation within marriage by arguing that conception was not the only purpose of intercourse, writing in one section entitled "Of Barrennesse, That It Hindereth Not Marriage" that, "though procreation of children be one end of marriage, yet it is not the only end."

This stress on the marital duty to provide sexual pleasure was not limited to sex and marriage manuals. At least one legal statute also contained such distinctions. In New Haven, where every family received a published copy of the colony's codified laws, the divorce statute explicitly emphasized both procreation and sexual pleasure by making grounds for divorce not only a husband's inability to impregnate a "woman fit to bear Children" but also his inability to have intercourse with any wife "needing and requiring conjugall duty, and due benevolence from her husband." Thus, the statute anticipated the position of women past childbearing age, and in any instance allowed a woman to make her case for divorce not only on grounds that she was deprived of children but of sexual pleasure (which the phrase "due benevolence" signified) as well.

Lay individuals believed in the importance of sexual satisfaction for women as well as men. John Dunton, a prolific London bookseller and publisher, heard about the divorce case of Bostonian Ann Perry while traveling in New England and included mention of it in his *Letters from New-England:* "Women are of the same Species and Composition with our selves, and have their Natural Inclinations as well as we. The Institution of Marriage has some Regards to the lawful Pleasures of Sense, with reference to them, as well as to our selves; and when they Suffer a disappointment of this Nature, why shou'd they be reckon'd Impudent, if they but complain?" Such statements underscore the argument that sexual pleasure, or pleasures of "sense," as Dunton phrases it, was important. No mention is made of a woman's expectations of having children, nor is her unhappiness attributed to the couple's infertility. The focus is on pleasure, not procreation. Jane Sharp, who wrote *The Midwives Book,* the only guide for midwives and "child-bearing women" authored by a woman before the 1730s, goes one step further, presenting sexual pleasure as a core element of love: "Lies the chief pleasure of loves delight in Copulation; and indeed were not the pleasure transcendently ravishing us, a man or woman would hardly ever die for love."

In such passages from both New England and London, sexual pleasure is an end in itself—within marriage at least. To acknowledge this opinion widens our perspective on seventeenth-century views of sex and of male sexual incapacity in particular. Although seventeenth-century New Englanders held strong beliefs about the importance of reproduction, they subscribed to an allied and separable appreciation for sexual relations between husbands and wives. Within this matrix, sexual incapacity was not solely an obstacle to reproduction but to the giving and receiving of "due benevolence."

Seventeenth-century English advice literature dealing with male sexual incapacity also contained well-developed discussions of the healthy male sexual body, discussions that, in turn, linked the normatively desirable male body to more general standards of manhood. As such works associated both fertility and the ability to provide sexual pleasure in marriage with specific kinds of male bodies, bodily pleasures, and character types, they tentatively mapped out what can be called an early discourse of male sexuality.

The marriage and reproduction literature defined with precision the boundaries of normalcy for the male sexual body. Thus, when English sex and marriage manuals advised women how to select husbands who could provide them with children, they associated male reproductive potential with certain male body types. *Aristoteles Master-Piece,* anonymously published in 1684 and one of the most popular English sex manuals of the period, describes the appearance of fertile men of "even temper," stating that a man who was "corpulent, having little Hair, a well coloured Face, and a handsome Body . . . is most like to be Fruitful." The book, according to Roger Thompson and David D. Hall, was "frequently mentioned in cases involving sexual offenses in the Middlesex County (Mass.) Court records for the seventeenth century." A translation of Nicholas Fontanus's medical text on women, *The Womans Doctour,* associated male fertility with ideals of strength and musculature: "The man ought to be of a strong constitution, well set, full of *muscles,* and neither too slender, nor too thick." Marriage sermons, when discussing deserving husbands, placed a similar premium on the male body. "Thou lovest thine husband because he is a proper man, and hath an active and able body, is of good health, wit, [and] carriage," read one example.

In conformity with an approach that used specific features of the body as indicators of general states of health, the advice literature also held that the size and shape of men's genitalia were excellent indicators of sexual drive and reproductive capacity. Thus, Jane Sharp insisted that a "yard" of "moderate size" was most likely to "cary the Seed home to the place it should do." She also singled out men whose "stones" (testes) "are longer and harder." Such men, being "prone to venery," were considered potent and, therefore, good husbands. Even body hair, and genital hair in particular, had significance as an indicator of a man's sexual drive. Philip Barrough's medical text, *The Method of Physick,* for example, included detailed discussions of the amount, texture, and color of men's pubic hair. He associated "black" and "abundant" hair with "hot distemper," asserting that men with curly hair were "lascivious and ready to carnal lust" and, thus, virile partners. Fortunately, such men were also "soon satiate[d] and filled" and, therefore, could be expected to perform within the bounds of what was considered to be healthy sexual moderation. Conversely, the medical literature's focus on bodies and its repetitive rehearsal of the details of genital anatomy produced portraits of men who would have made for poor marital partners: men whose bodies were desexualized. Thus, according to Barrough, men who were "by the parts about the stones being bald and without hair" were "not desirous to and prone to carnall lust." And men whose "yards" were considered to be too short for fertilization to occur Barrough called "half-geldings," or near eunuchs. In so doing, he implied that they were less than men. One seventeenth-century variant on the meaning of "eunuch" was "emasculation."

The medical and other advice literature not only used the anatomy of the male genitalia as an indicator of the general health and vigor of the male body, including reproductive potential, but it also linked sexual anatomy and general body morphology to emotional disposition, to temperament and qualities of character. The testes, according to Culpeper, "add heat, strength and courage to the Body, and that appears, because Eunuchs are neither so strong, hot, nor valiant as other men." Men with bodies "hard, thin, and lean, hairy and the hairs . . . black curled," observed medical text author John Archer, were "angry persons . . . lovers of Brawlings, . . . [who] desire few things." Archer posited connections between body type and emotions, derived actions from such emo-

tions, and identified a general disposition of character, that is, a lack of desire for material things. Male emotions, in this case anger or combativeness, were associated not with experience or education, but with sexual bodies. Fontanus defined normalcy by contrasting barren men with "hairy men, that have testicles of an indifferent size, and a well concocted seed" and who were thereby "cheerfull [and] affable." Similarly, men of moderate temperament, who according to *Aristoteles Master-Piece* were the most "fruitful," were "ignorant, good natured, [and] sweet voyced."

By the same token, a cluster of undesirable physical and emotional characteristics singled out sexually incapacitated men. "Weakly Men get most Girls, if they get any Children at all," wrote Culpeper. Men of a "cold Constitution," those with lesser virility or potency than men of a "hot" temper, and impotent men in particular had bodies "white, fat, slow, soft and bald . . . [and] a narrow breast without hair," wrote John Archer. "Easily hurt by cold things," these men lacked strength and hardiness. Here again, the writer associated specific features of the sexually incapacitated man's body, including pallor, hairlessness, and softness, with the lack of power, speed, and endurance—that is, with bodily attributes that had sexual implications but that were, when present, also esteemed general qualities in the seventeenth-century male. In the same vein, Fontanus wrote that barren men are not only "commonly beardless" but also "slow in imagination, and dull in practice . . . they sit like images, and are sad, and insociable." Fontanus's coupling of the inability to reproduce with specific qualities of temperament and social behaviors has important implications. Through their use of typologies, with ancillary attention to detailed descriptions of bodies and characters, the authors of such literature created the category of the sexually incapable man. Their works describe body types and emotional temperament. Readers find that sexually incapacitated men are sad, dimwitted, and ineffectual in social settings as well as in the marital bedroom. The blending of sexual capacity with social capabilities is significant in that it points to the production of ideals of manhood that are closely associated with standards of male sexuality.

Impotence, therefore, meant more than simply sexual incapability. The ability to function sexually and the value placed on reproduction cast impotent men in a negative light. Seventeenth-century definitions of the word "impotence" highlight the relationship between male sexual dysfunctioning and more general male character flaws. All the various definitions of impotence point to notions of weakness, deficiency, or powerlessness. Seventeenth-century meanings touching on various aspects of power include "want of strength or power to perform anything; utter inability or weakness; helplessness," and "wholly lacking sexual power." The word also had specific character associations. Impotence could mean "not master of oneself; unable to restrain oneself" and was "frequently used to denote moral weakness, inability to follow virtuous courses or to resist temptation." These definitions taken together indicate that impotence meant more than simply sexual incapacity. Manhood incorporated strength, power, mastery, and morality, whereas impotence signified the absence of these qualities and, thereby, the erosion of manliness.

In divorce petitions, lay standards of sexual manliness establish links between manhood and sexual capability similar to those found in contemporary household advice literature. The Puritan courts, where popular views and ideas from medical treatises circulated, provide a good place to highlight this similarity. Scholars of the early courts are unanimous in emphasizing the informal nature of Puritan court proceedings: their reliance on substantive notions of justice and morality rather than legal precedent and formal adherence to procedure. Given the informality of the courts, the incompleteness of legal codes, and the lack of formal training for judges and clerks, the records, as Mary Beth Norton notes, "supply a treasure trove of information about colonists' assumptions, attitudes, and behavior." The court proceedings of the seventeenth century, Cornelia Hughes Dayton demonstrates, were markedly different from those of the eighteenth century.

Seventeenth-century courts exhibited a "collective commitment to upholding a God-fearing society" and resisted the "technicalities of English common law practice." One result was that women's presence in the colonial courts of the seventeenth century was far greater than it would be in the more formalized proceedings of the eighteenth century. Puritan courts were marked by an absence of lawyers and a presence of lay judges, clerks, and "experts," who, in the divorce cases in this study, appear as midwives, physicians, and community members who were often called upon to give depositions.

"Proof" of a man's incapacity was varied. In many cases, the courts employed male examiners. Nathaniel Clarke, who was one of the secretaries to Plymouth's Court of Assistants, which had jurisdiction over divorce cases in that colony, challenged his wife's charge of impotence. As a result, the court ordered "that his Body be viewed by some persons skilful and judicious" and chose three physicians to give their "judgment" with Nathaniel "shewing himself unto them." Similarly, when Mary Halloway complained that her husband "is not in a capacity to performe or affoard unto her . . . that corporal communion" to which she was entitled, the court "appointed some to viewe the body" of John Halloway. Examinations also took place in the case of Hugh Drury, whose "manhood" was "referred to further search & tryall."

As marriages were part of communal life, so, too, were marital problems. Impotence was not a private charge kept secret. In court proceedings, family members often testified and brought charges to the courts on behalf of the women suing for divorce. John Uffoot's impotence was "confirmed by his father." Mary White's mother brought the charges "in behalf of her daughter" against Elias White in "regard to his insufficiency." Zacheus Curtis, father of Mary Heard, complained to the court "in behalf of his daughter . . . asking for a separation on the grounds of insufficiency." Community members could also be involved in ridiculing sexually incapable men. One wife whose husband was the brunt of com-

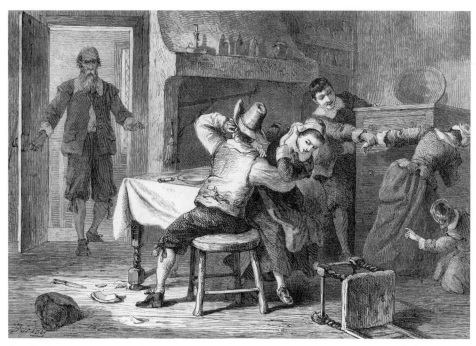

"Frolic in a Puritan Farmhouse": man entering on two "frolicking" young couples.

munity gossip encountered a man who "offered to put his hands under coats & sayd he came of a woman & knew what belonged to a woman & because her husband was not able to give her a great belly he would help him." As Mary Beth Norton points out, husbands were, as in this case, often the real object of insults hurled at their wives.

A detailed look at one case, the divorce hearings triggered by Mary Drury's charge of impotence against her husband, Hugh, will illustrate the heavy involvement of community and family in divorce hearings. The charges of impotence, even when a divorce was not granted, could involve the wider community's judging a man's sexual capabilities and his fitness as a husband. The case also reveals that proceedings involve an emphasis on dissatisfaction with husbandly performance. These sexual failings are, in turn, bound up with a husband's character flaws as friend and head of household. Most important, Mary Drury was fifty-four years old when she petitioned the court, well past childbearing years by seventeenth-century, as well as modern, under-

standings. Her case is an instance where the sexual coupling of husband and wife was not tied to procreation.

No fewer than fourteen community members gave depositions in the Drury case. Statements came from Hugh's first wife's family, church members, and from friends of Hugh's first and second wife as well as from Hugh and Mary themselves. The couple's marital problems were public long before any court proceedings began, as deacon Henry Allen and church member Abel Porter indicate when testifying that "Brother Drury did in the oppen Congregation declare his willingnes to live with his wife as A husband ought to live with his wife." (By the time of the divorce proceedings, Mary Drury had already begun living separately from her husband.) Hugh's specific sexual failings were also widely known to be at the core of the couple's problems, as is evidenced by testimony: "At another meeting with four of the Brethren at goodman Daws his house [Hugh] did promis that if shee would com to him Again what was Amiss in him should bee mended."

Five brothers of Hugh's first wife testified to the contrary that they had never known of any problems between Hugh and their sister Lidia: "In all the discours private or bublick [sic] that ever wee had with our dear sister Drury. wee never understood any such thing from her as now our loveing Brother Drury is charged with since her death. Neither did wee ever perceiv any dissatisfaction in any kind from our dear sister Concerning her loveing husband." The brothers took it for granted that they would have known of the couple's sexual problems had there been any. Their statements also reveal the emphasis placed on satisfaction in marital relations. That they never detected their sister's "dissatisfaction" was "proof" that Hugh was not impotent. Lidia's sisters were also aware of the intimate details of the marriage, "haveing many times secret Discours with our dear and loveing sister." Indeed, they were privy to information of a kind "as is not meet heer to be inserted." And they, too, stressed sexual pleasure. Not only had they never heard a word about impotence ("we never understood from her any such thing" as Drury was now "charged with"); they declared flatly that she did "take full content and satisfaction in [him]."

But, in the statements of the church deacons, such information was not limited to family members. Lydia Chevers testified that she knew of Hugh's sexual problems and that his first wife had told her that Hugh "went to England to gett helpe but Could Gett none." Information concerning Lidia's resignation to Hugh's sexual inability came from a woman who at one time had asked if her not feeling well was the result of a pregnancy: "She said I was a simple woman for my thoughts. . . . she said she never was with child since she had her son John; & said alas my husband hath had a great weaknes upon him along time. . . . As for children, I thank the Lord I am content with my portion." According to this testimony, had Lidia not been content with one son, or had she been more unhappy with her relationship with Hugh, he might have found himself in court on impotence charges decades earlier. Lidia's reported reference to Hugh's impotence as his

"great weaknes," with its hint of general as well as specific incapacity, and her apparent resignation to it ("alas") at least suggests that the neighbor, like the authors of the advice literature, associated sexual incapacity with a more general lack of strength and power.

Mary, Hugh's second wife, explicitly associated her husband's sexual incapacity with other failures as a husband. She complained that not only was he "under Some inability of Body"; he was "unkind" and in "noe ways hath Caryed himselfe toawrds [sic] her as a Friend much Lesse a husband." Although Lidia found Hugh's "weakness" tolerable, Mary considered his inability to perform sexually, together with his "unkind" carriage toward her, as a failure to meet her expectations of a dutiful man and husband. She called him her "pretended husband," filed for divorce, and thereby left a permanent record of attitudes toward sexual incapacity and manhood.

The final deposition of the Drury case also underscores the extent to which manhood was associated with sexual performance. Mary was not granted her divorce, and the divorce records include a "Certificate for Hugh Drury's manhood"—granted on the basis of evidence presented by those who believed Hugh to be fully capable of sexual intercourse, evidence that successfully rebutted the incapacity charges brought by Mary. The substitution of the word "manhood" for "sexually able husband" indicates that seventeenth-century New Englanders believed sexual ability to be a strong enough indicator of manhood to make the terms synonymous.

Such evidence is not limited to the Drury case. Testimony from the divorce records for the Bostonians Edward and Anna Lane make similar substitutions. In 1658, the Court of Assistants granted the couple a divorce, having found Edward "deficient in performing the duty of a husband" by his own admission. Some time after the divorce was granted, desiring to be remarried, the couple continued to attempt sexual relations. In one instance, Anna's grandmother, when escorted out of the couple's presence by a sexual adviser, was told to "let them alone" so that Anna could "try him for he is a man." By dropping the qualifier "sexually capable" and simply implying it in the definition of "man," such statements indicate the importance of sexual performance to manhood. Apparently believing Edward to be cured of his sexual infirmity, the couple then presented themselves before the court late in 1659 and asked to be remarried. An observer recalled that Anna agreed to the second marriage because "she was sattisfied in his sufficiency as a man."

Indeed, men who married knowing they were impotent committed a kind of fraud, or misrepresentation, of their manliness. In her petition for divorce, Anna Lane states clearly that she had been duped by her husband: "Your petitioner hath bin deceived in contract of marriage with Mr. Edward Lane, to whom (upon an essentiall mistake) shee gave her selfe as wife, and hath not bin wanting in the duty of that relation, expecting the performance of an husband on his part, wherein he hath been from first to last altogether deficient." A successful charge of impotence carried with it a serious social burden. Impotent men could not marry again and therefore could not assume the conventional prerogatives of a male head of household. Thus, when Mary White sued for divorce, the court granted an annulment permitting her "to marry another man." Her former husband, Elias, on the other hand, would risk a fine if he were to marry and once again be brought before the court on similar charges.

In the case of John Uffoot, charged with fornication with his father's servant, the court found him guilty and expected the couple to marry. But it considered the matter only after it had cleared up a confusion surrounding his earlier divorce. His former wife had successfully sued him on the grounds of impotence (supported by her plea that it was a "piteous case that she must live with one she never did love"), stating "now it is a strange thing, that after all this he should miscary in this manner." The court needed to decide that annulment had been granted in error or that Uffoot was merely taking advantage of the servant's pregnancy to marry again. Although the servant, Martha Netleton, supported Uffoot's claim that he

fathered her child, the court held "some suspitions that she hath caryed it ill w[i]th come other p[er]son." In the interest of creating stable households, and given the testimony of friends and neighbors who convinced the court that Uffoot, contrary to New Haven's divorce statute, had been divorced for partner-specific, or temporary, impotence, the court ordered his former wife to pay back the thirty pounds that the court had fined Uffoot for "wrong done by him to her, which now appears otherwise," and then ordered him to marry Martha Netleton.

Thomas Rolinson, divorced for being "impotent," was later sued by his former wife's new husband, William Beale. Included in Beale's list of grievances was "wrong done his wife under pretence of marriage." The Beales had been the subject of scorn and harassment for years. The focus of much of it was on Martha's earlier divorce. Martha eventually brought defamation charges against a neighbor for "railing speeches and reproachful words." Mistress Hollingworth had "called her baud, said she lived in adultery and had two husbands, having been divorce[d] from an honest man." As Mary Beth Norton writes, even though the courts had granted the divorce, neighbors "did not concur with that judgment" and considered Rolinson an "honest man," rather than one who had deceived Martha in marriage.

Because of the long-term consequences of a successful charge of sexual incapacity, community members sometimes took a skeptical view of the women who brought these charges. In his commentary on a Boston divorce case of 1655, George Cartwright, one of the king's commissioners for New England, satirized at women's expense both the medical literature's attention to anatomical detail and popular understandings that equated a husband's virility and capacity to satisfy his wife with his physical endowments. Noting tartly of the divorce proceedings that three doctors had "carefully taken the dimensions, and are to be witnesses to-morrow. . . . It will be worth the knowing what or how much is necessary for a holy sister." Although John Dunton himself argued that women's sexual needs were similar to men's, in his commentary on the Boston Perry divorce case he felt it necessary to begin by responding to the perceived general charge, "In All such Cases the good Wives are loaded with Impudence." Clearly, in many instances women bore the brunt of male insecurities about masculinity.

A variety of ailments or problems could serve as grounds for challenging a man's role as a husband. Divorce could be sought whatever the cause of the sexual dysfunction, including congenital malformation, temporary sexual dysfunction, injury, marital discord, and even bewitchment. Men could be challenged in their role as husband, father, and head of household with the sudden slip of a jagged piece of wood, a fall on a farm tool, or any other serious injury to their genitals. Hugh Drury had been married previously for more than thirty years and was sixty-five years old when his second wife, age fifty-four, attempted to divorce him; during the proceedings, a neighbor testified that Hugh Drury had confessed that he "got a hurt with a great peece of timber" some time after the birth of his first child.

Ralph Ellenwood, whose marriage was annulled because of his "insufficiency," complained of the effect of witches on his sexual capabilities. In a statement presumably referring to the cause of his sexual problems, Mary Houghton, an unidentified member of the household, testified that, "in his house one night," when she "sat up later than usual, he said he thought there were witches not far off." Perhaps the court's inclination to grant annulment was enhanced by Katheren Ellenwood's plea that "she was very young and would rather die than live with this man." Witchcraft was long thought to be a cause of impotence, and witches were believed to have a variety of ways of inducing it. Some cast spells that caused men to see their wives as hideous and undesirable and thus disabled for intercourse. All such spells centered on the relationship between the imagination and sexual performance.

Witchcraft aside, popular writings stressed the influence of imagination on successful sexual performance and conception. "Among things un-

natural," and therefore to be guarded against, were excessive "passions of the mind." "In the time of copulation, avoid passions, anger, sadness, [and] fear," advised Nicholas Culpeper. Although this understanding typically applied to wives as well as husbands, for men imagination prevented both the ability to penetrate as well as to fertilize. Medical knowledge connected inability to become erect for intercourse with problems of imagination, desire, or failure to maintain attention and manage emotions.

The court cases reflect this widely held view that men were expected to clear their minds and focus on their duty as husbands. In the case of Elias and Mary White, the court initially did not see fit to grant the divorce in March 1663 and instead "advised them to a more loving & suitable cohabitation one with the other & that all due phisicall meanes may be used." At that hearing, two of Elias's Marblehead friends testified that they had asked him if, "when he lay with his wife . . . there were any motion in him." Elias's reply implies that his problem was pressure to perform for his wife. He responded, "Yea fower or five hours together but when . . . [I] turned to her it was gone again." Similarly, Mary Heard contended that her husband John was unable to become erect, stating, "His yard Is as weake as a pece of fleshe without bone or sinnow," and she was careful to add, "I have beine helpful to him as many times as I could and nevere refuused but when the Custom of a woman was upon mee." Although Mary claimed that her husband was incapable of erections, testimony from community member John Byxbe Junear indicated the problem might be their particular union. Junear "heard that john heards wife hade saide that he had no strenth in his previ memburs. He aske ed him to let him se them which he died and it stood steife." Unlike the Elias White case, where a friend's testimony reveals partner-specific impotence, Heard's friend, Junear, "asked him if it stoode so strong when he was with his wife and he said yese and further saith not." Although the he-said, she-said testimony caused the court to reject the case, the following year Mary Heard, her husband's having "left her contrary to court's order," was "granted a divorce on the grounds of insufficiency," and not abandonment. Marital discord might also have aggravated John Uffoot's problems. In his testimony, Uffoot stated that he felt "wronged" by his wife. He had been divorced for "insufficiency," he explained, which "in . . . time he hoped . . . might [have] appeare[d] otherwise," if his wife had "caryed . . . toward him as she ought." Men were expected to control discouraging thoughts and potentially disruptive powers of the imagination while performing their marital duty. Inability to do so was a source of sexual problems and was itself symptomatic of the erosion of manly self-mastery.

Aristoteles Master-Piece echoed the view that mutually satisfactory sexual relations were the husband's responsibility: "When the Husband cometh into the Wives Chamber, he must entertain her with all kind of dalliance, wanton behaviour, and allurements to Venery . . . he must cherish, embrace, and tickle her . . . intermixing more wanton Kisses with wanton Words and Speeches." Although it verges on titillating seduction, the imagery emphasizes the role of the husband as master of sexual ceremonies in the bedroom. Bringing appropriate pleasures to his wife, at the right time, was necessary not only for reproduction but for the cohesion of their marriage. A man who did not follow such advice was shirking his responsibility, according to this popular text. For the implications, consider Gouge, author of *Domesticall Duties,* who argued that men who failed sexually "are to be accounted *impotent,* and in that respect unable to performe the essentiall duties of mariage. . . . By those signes of impotencie God sheweth that he calleth them to live single." The impotent man, subject to divorce, fines, and punishment, "ought not to seeke after marriage."

All the divorce records use language that equates the sexual failings of a man with failure in his most important role, husband. Divorce records use the terms "office" and "duty" to indicate a man's sexual responsibility and "insufficiency," "inability to perform," and "incapacity" to point out his failure to shoulder such responsi-

bility. Seventeenth-century meanings of "insufficiency" included "inadequacy, inability to fulfill requirements," "lacking in what is necessary or requisite," and "wanting in strength or stability." Divorce cases based on charges of male sexual incapacity illuminate what it meant for a man to be "insufficient," "deficient," or "impotent"—all words that focus on the absence of male power and strength, sexual power and performance. In the Whites' case, for example, the records charge that Elias White could not "performe the duty or office of husband to [his wife]." Similarly, John Halloway was taken to the Connecticut Court of Assistants by his wife, Mary, who stated that he was "not in a capacity to perform that duty which relation requires to his sayd wife." In Plymouth, Captain John Williams's wife accused John of "refuysing to perform marriage duty unto her," a charge he eventually declared was the result of his "insufficiency for converse with women." When combined with the basic assumption that it was the male head's responsibility to ensure orderly relations within his household and that the stability of the larger commonwealth rested substantially on his ability to do so, the premium on sexual pleasure in marriage enhanced the view that sexual performance and provision of pleasure was a male "duty" and an "office" and, thus, had a social and political dimension.

Sexually incapable men, men who could not live up to the "office" of husband, not only left women unsatisfied, marriage unions incomplete, and families childless; they also placed their wives in a position vulnerable to sin. Many believed that sexual coupling was an important component of companionate marriage, in part because they saw women as naturally passionate and incapable of self-regulation. Without sexual fulfillment in marriage, women tended to commit sexual transgression. Therefore, men who could not please their wives could not properly care for their subordinates. In her plea for divorce from a husband who had abandoned her, Elizabeth Jerrad of Hartford blamed her husband's absence on her sexual transgressions with other men and included this defense in her request for divorce. The court

recorded that they "release her from her matrimo-
niall tye to the sayd Robert Jarrad that so she may
allso be freed from such temptation as hath occasioned her gross & scandolouse fall into the sinn of
uncleaness." Zacheus Curtis, on behalf of his
daughter, Mary, pleaded with the court to dissolve
her marriage to impotent John Heard, stating, "I
Bee Sech this Honrd Coure to Consider of ye Great
temtations of satan that shee Lyed under in this
Condition." Likewise, Sarah Doorman complained
that her husband's sexual inability robbed her of
the benefit of "the avoiding of fornication and preventing of incontinency." Gouge's *Domesticall
Duties* similarly exclaimed that when husbands
and wives "rob each other of that due benevolence . . . they expose themselves to the devils
snares." "To avoid fornication," advised Gouge,
"render due benevolence." Marital sexual pleasure
could "keep men and women from adulterie."
Richard Allestree's popular work, *The Whole Duty
of Man,* declared that one of the "ends of Marriage" was "the avoiding of Fornication."

Gouge explained the phrase "due benevolence"
as follows: sexual intercourse was "benevolence"
because it "must be performed with good will and
delight, willingly, readily and cheerfully," and it
was "due" because it was a marital obligation. He
continued, "Impotent persons cannot yeeld due
benevolence; but such as are barren may." The
issue here was, not sterility or barrenness, but impotence, the failure to provide sexual pleasure or
"benevolence." New Haven, with its codified divorce law, specified the importance of "due benevolence" and upheld its necessity in practice. The
colonial divorce statute read in part: "If any man
marrying a woman . . . needing and requiring
. . . due benevolence . . . and satisfyingly proved,
That the husband, neither at the time of marriage,
nor since is like to be able to perform or afford the
same . . . every such marriage shall by the Court
of Magistrates, be declared voyd, and a nullity, the
woman freed from all conjugall relation to that
man." This stipulation was clearly enforced in the
case of John Doorman of New Haven. The court
granted Sarah her divorce after establishing that
John was "wholly disabled to perform conjugall
duties to her, or grant her due benevolence."

Impotence was not grounds for divorce only
because of "the felt necessity that a marriage produce children" but because sexual intercourse
was necessary for the maintenance of the marital
union as well. Although fifty-four-year-old Mary
Drury was not granted an annulment, her petition and lengthy trial point to the importance, for
authorities and lay persons, of sexual pleasure
distinguished from its reproductive function.
This distinction, in turn, reveals the importance
of male sexual performance in the role of husband and head of household. When the courts rejected petitions, they did so, not because they
found a woman's claims of dissatisfaction irrelevant, but because they did not find her convincing. The divorce cases presented here reveal that
popular notions of male sexual incapacity linked
male sexual capability with larger features of per-
sonhood and masculinity.

Analysis of male sexual incapacity in
seventeenth-century New England confirms that a
discourse of sexuality did flourish despite heavily
circumscribed norms of sexual behavior. Therefore, to characterize the seventeenth-century
Anglo-American understanding of sexuality as one
centered around an "ideology of reproduction"
overemphasizes the reproductive element of sexuality found in both official statements and practice. That the official discussion of sexual pleasure
was normatively linked to reproduction and was
confined to the marital realm did not prohibit a
seventeenth-century understanding of pleasure-
based sexual relations. After all, courts grappled
with the issue of male sexual performance, as did
medical literature in London and New England,
thereby reflecting and shaping the popular understanding that not only healthy marital unions but
also reproduction itself *required* sexual pleasure.
In the seventeenth century, the stress was on sexual duty and benevolence, understood, in part, as
the capacity to provide pleasure. This stress on
sexual duty and mutual pleasure waned in the
eighteenth century. In its place appeared a more
one-sided, and more privatized, emphasis on male
pleasure, accompanied, as Mary Fissell and others
point out, by a cultural construction of the female
body as a passive instrument of men's pleasure.

Study Questions

1. According to Puritan beliefs, what was the purpose of sexual relations between husband and wife? How did Puritans view nonprocreative sexual acts? Why?

2. Did Puritans believe that sexual relations ought to be pleasurable to both partners? Why?

3. Given Puritan beliefs about marital relations, why was male impotency, or "sexual incapacity," viewed as a serious problem?

4. Why was male sexual incapacity grounds for divorce? How common was it for a Puritan woman to seek a divorce because of her husband's impotency?

5. Describe Puritan culture's ideal body type for a man. What type of men were deemed to be the most fertile?

6. How did Puritan courts confirm truthfulness of a wife's accusation that her husband was impotent?

Bibliography

The history of sexuality is among the most innovative dimensions of American historiography. Edmund Morgan's pioneering essay "The Puritans and Sex," *New England Quarterly* (1942), remains a very interesting read for undergraduate students. Merrill D. Smith's *Sex and Sexuality in Early America* (1998) is equally compelling, as is his *Breaking the Bonds: Marital Discord in Pennsylvania, 1730–1830* (1991). Among the best studies of gender in early America are Laura Ulrich Thatcher, *Good Wives: Image and Reality in the Lives of Women in Northern New England, 1650–1750* (1982) and Kathleen Brown, *Good Wives, Nasty Wenches, and Anxious Patriarchs: Gender, Race, and Power in Colonial Virginia* (1996). Also see Nancy F. Cott, *The Bonds of Womanhood: "Women's Sphere" in New England, 1780–1835* (1977) and Lyle Koehler, *A Search for Power: The "Weaker" Sex in Seventeenth-Century New England* (1980).

READING 3

Taking the Trade: Abortion and Gender Relations in an Eighteenth-Century New England Village

Cornelia Hughes Dayton

Abortion generates today perhaps the most convulsive debate in American politics, a "right or wrong" issue which seems to defy compromise. Pro-choice and right-to-life advocates cite the Constitution and the Bill of Rights to support their arguments, and political discourse has fallen victim to shrill hyperbole. Abortion is nothing new in American society, although the disagreements over it have steadily become more intense. Just like twenty-first century Americans, eighteenth-century Puritans had to deal with the problem of unwanted pregnancies, and one option open to them was abortion. In the following essay, historian Cornelia Hughes Dayton describes an abortion that took place in 1742 in northeastern Connecticut. Because Sarah Grosvenor died from the side effects of the abortion, the case had political, social, and legal ramifications that revealed much about gender relations.

In 1742 in the village of Pomfret, perched in the hills of northeastern Connecticut, nineteen-year-old Sarah Grosvenor and twenty-seven-year-old Amasa Sessions became involved in a liaison that led to pregnancy, abortion, and death. Both were from prominent yeoman families, and neither a marriage between them nor an arrangement for the support of their illegitimate child would have been an unusual event for mid-eighteenth-century New England. Amasa Sessions chose a different course; in consultation with John Hallowell, a self-proclaimed "practitioner of physick," he coerced his lover into taking an abortifacient. Within two months, Sarah fell ill. Unbeknownst to all but Amasa, Sarah, Sarah's sister Zerviah, and her cousin Hannah, Hallowell made an attempt to "Remove her Conseption" by a "manual opperation." Two days later Sarah miscarried, and her two young relatives secretly buried the fetus in the woods. Over the next month, Sarah struggled against a "Malignant fever" and was attended by several physicians, but on September 14, 1742, she died. . . .

The Narrative

. . . The chronicle opens in late July 1742 when Zerviah Grosvenor, aged twenty-one, finally prevailed upon her younger sister to admit that she was pregnant. In tears, Sarah explained that she had not told Zerviah sooner because "she had been taking [the] trade to remove it." "Trade" was used in this period to signify stuff or goods, often in the deprecatory sense of rubbish and trash. The *Oxford English Dictionary* confirms that in some parts of England and New England the word was used to refer to medicine. In Pomfret trade meant a particular type of medicine, an abortifacient, thus a substance that might be regarded as "bad" medicine, as rubbish, unsafe and associated with destruction. What is notable is that Sarah

Cornelia Hughes Dayton, "Taking the Trade: Abortion and Gender Relations in an Eighteenth-Century New England Village," *William and Mary Quarterly,* 48 (January 1991), 19–50.

and Zerviah, and neighboring young people who also used the word, had no need to explain to one another the meaning of "taking the trade." Perhaps only a few New Englanders knew how to prepare an abortifacient or knew of books that would give them recipes, but many more, especially young women who lived with the fear of becoming pregnant before marriage, were familiar with at least the *idea* of taking an abortifacient.

Sarah probably began taking the trade in mid-May when she was already three-and-a-half-months pregnant. It was brought to her in the form of a powder by Amasa. Sarah understood clearly that her lover had obtained the concoction "from docter hollowel," who conveyed "directions" for her doses through Amasa. Zerviah deposed later that Sarah had been "loath to Take" the drug and "Thot it an Evil," probably because at three and a half months she anticipated quickening, the time from which she knew the law counted abortion an "unlawful measure." At the outset, Sarah argued in vain with Amasa against his proposed "Method." Later, during June and July, she sometimes "neglected" to take the doses he left for her, but, with mounting urgency, Amasa and the doctor pressed her to comply. "It was necessary," Amasa explained in late July, that she take "more, or [else] they were afraid She would be greatly hurt by what was already done." To calm her worries, he assured her that "there was no life [left] in the Child" and that the potion "would not hurt her." Apparently, the men hoped that a few more doses would provoke a miscarriage, thereby expelling the dead fetus and restoring Sarah's body to its natural balance of humors.

Presumably, Hallowell decided to operate in early August because Sarah's pregnancy was increasingly visible, and he guessed that she was not going to miscarry. An operation in which the fetus would be removed or punctured was now the only certain way to terminate the pregnancy secretly. To avoid the scrutiny of Sarah's parents, Hallowell resorted to a plan he had used once before in arranging a private examination of Sarah. Early one afternoon he arrived at the house of John Grosvenor and begged for a room as "he was weary and wanted Rest." John, Sarah's thirty-one-year-old first cousin, lived with his wife, Hannah, and their young children in a homestead only a short walk down the hill but out of sight of Sarah's father's house. While John and Hannah were busy, the physician sent one of the little children to fetch Sarah.

The narrative of Sarah's fateful meeting with Hallowell that August afternoon is best told in the words of one of the deponents. Abigail Nightingale had married and moved to Pomfret two years earlier, and by 1742 she had become Sarah's close friend. Several weeks after the operation, Sarah attempted to relieve her own "Distress of mind" by confiding the details of her shocking experience to Abigail. Unconnected to the Grosvenor or Sessions families by kinship, and without any other apparent stake in the legal uses of her testimony, Abigail can probably be trusted as a fairly accurate paraphraser of Sarah's words. If so, we have here an unparalleled eyewitness account of an eighteenth-century abortion attempt.

This is how Abigail recollected Sarah's deathbed story:

On [Sarah's] going down [to her cousin John's], [Hallowell] said he wanted to Speake with her alone; and then they two went into a Room together; and then sd. Hallowell told her it was necessary that something more should be done or else she would Certainly die; to which she replyed that she was afraid they had done too much already, and then he told her that there was one thing more that could easily be done, and she asking him what it was; he said he could easily deliver her. but she said she was afraid there was life in the Child, then he asked her how long she had felt it; and she replyed about a fortnight; then he said that was impossible or could not be or ever would; for that the trade she had taken had or would prevent it: and that the alteration she felt Was owing to what she had taken. And he farther told her that he verily thought that the Child grew to her body to the Bigness of his hand, or else it would have Come away before that time. and

that it would never Come away, but Certainly Kill her, unless other Means were used. On which she yielded to his making an Attempt to take it away; charging him that if he could percieve that there was life in it he would not proceed on any Account. And then the Doctor openning his portmantua took an Instrument out of it and Laid it on the Bed, and she asking him what it was for, he replyed that it was to make way; and that then he tryed to remove the Child for Some time in vain putting her to the Utmost Distress, and that at Last she observed he trembled and immediately perceived a Strange alteration in her body and thought a bone of the Child was broken; on which she desired him (as she said) to Call in some body, for that she feared she was a dying, and instantly swooned away.

With Sarah's faint, Abigail's account broke off, but within minutes others, who would testify later, stepped into the room. Hallowell reacted to Sarah's swoon by unfastening the door and calling in Hannah, the young mistress of the house, and Zerviah, who had followed her sister there. Cold water and "a bottle of drops" were brought to keep Sarah from fainting again, while Hallowell explained to the "much Surprized" women that "he had been making an Attempt" to deliver Sarah. Despite their protests, he then "used a further force upon her" but did not succeed in "Tak[ing] the Child . . . away." Some days later Hallowell told a Pomfret man that in this effort "to distroy hir conception" he had "either knipt or Squeisd the head of the Conception." At the time of the attempt, Hallowell explained to the women that he "had done so much to her, as would Cause the Birth of the Child in a Little time." Just before sunset, he packed up his portmanteau and went to a nearby tavern, where Amasa was waiting "to hear [the outcome of] the event." Meanwhile, Sarah, weak-kneed and in pain, leaned on the arm of her sister as the young women managed to make their way home in the twilight.

After his attempted "force," Hallowell fades from the scene, while Zerviah and Hannah Grosvenor become the key figures. About two days after enduring the operation, Sarah began to experience contractions. Zerviah ran to get Hannah, telling her "she Tho't . . . Sarah would be quickly delivered." They returned to find Sarah, who was alone "in her Father's Chamber," just delivered and rising from the chamber pot. In the pot was "an Untimely birth"—a "Child [that] did not Appear to have any Life In it." To Hannah, it "Seemed by The Scent . . . That it had been hurt and was decaying," while Zerviah later remembered it as "a perfect Child," even "a pritty child." Determined to keep the event "as private as they Could," the two women helped Sarah back to bed, and then "wr[ap]ed . . . up" the fetus, carried it to the woods on the edge of the farmstead, and there "Buried it in the Bushes."

On learning that Sarah had finally miscarried and that the event had evidently been kept hidden from Sarah's parents, Amasa and Hallowell may have congratulated themselves on the success of their operation. However, about ten days after the miscarriage, Sarah grew feverish and weak. Her parents consulted two college-educated physicians who hailed from outside the Pomfret area. Their visits did little good, nor were Sarah's symptoms—fever, delirium, convulsions—relieved by a visit from Hallowell, whom Amasa "fetcht" to Sarah's bedside. In the end, Hallowell, who had decided to move from nearby Killingly to more distant Providence, washed his hands of the case. A few days before Sarah died, her cousin John "went after" Hallowell, whether to bring him back or to express his rage, we do not know. Hallowell predicted "that She woul[d] not live."

Silence seems to have settled on the Grosvenor house and its neighborhood after Sarah's death on September 14. It was two and a half years later that rumors about a murderous abortion spread through and beyond Pomfret village, prompting legal investigation. The silence, the gap between event and prosecution, the passivity of Sarah's parents—all lend mystery to the narrative. But despite its ellipses, the Grosvenor case provides us with an unusual set of details about one young couple's extreme response to the common problem of failed courtship and illegitimacy. To gain insight into both the mysteries and the extremities of the Grosvenor-Sessions case, we need to look more closely at Pomfret, at the two families centrally involved, and at clues to the motivations of the principal participants. Our abortion tale, it turns out, holds beneath its surface a complex trail of evidence about generational conflict and troubled relations between men and women.

The Pomfret Players

In 1742 the town of Pomfret had been settled for just over forty years. Within its central neighborhood and in homesteads scattered over rugged, wooded hillsides lived probably no more than 270 men, women, and children. During the founding decades, the fathers of Sarah and Amasa ranked among the ten leading householders; Leicester Grosvenor and Nathaniel Sessions were chosen often to fill important local offices.

Grosvenor, the older of the two by seven years, had inherited standing and a choice farmstead from his father, one of the original six purchasers of the Pomfret territory. When the town was incorporated in 1714, he was elected a militia officer and one of the first selectmen. He was returned to the latter post nineteen times and eventually rose to the highest elective position—that of captain—in the local trainband. Concurrently, he was appointed many times throughout the 1710s and 1720s to ad hoc town committees, often alongside Nathaniel Sessions. But unlike Sessions, Grosvenor went on to serve at the colony level. Pomfret freemen chose him to represent them at ten General Assembly sessions between 1726 and 1744. Finally, in the 1730s, when he was in his late fifties, the legislature appointed him a justice of the peace for Windham County. Thus, until his retirement in 1748 at age seventy-four, his house would have served as the venue for petty trials, hearings, and recordings of documents. After retiring from public office, Grosvenor lived another eleven years, leaving behind in 1759 an estate worth over £600.

Nathaniel Sessions managed a sizable farm and ran one of Pomfret's taverns at the family homestead. Town meetings were sometimes held there. Sessions was chosen constable in 1714 and rose from ensign to lieutenant in the militia—always a step behind Leicester Grosvenor. He could take pride in one exceptional distinction redounding to the family honor: in 1737 his son Darius became only the second Pomfret resident to graduate from Yale College, and before Sessions died at ninety-one he saw Darius elected assistant and then deputy governor of Rhode Island.

The records are silent as to whether Sessions and his family resented the Grosvenors, who must have been perceived in town as more prominent, or whether the two families—who sat in adjoining private pews in the meetinghouse—enjoyed a close relationship that went sour for some reason *before* the affair between Sarah and Amasa. Instead, the signs (such as the cooperative public work of the two fathers, the visits back and forth between the Grosvenor and Sessions girls) point to a long-standing friendship and dense web of interchanges between the families. Indeed, courtship and marriage between a Sessions son and a Grosvenor daughter would hardly have been surprising.

What went wrong in the affair between Sarah and Amasa is not clear. Sarah's sisters and cousins knew that "Amasy" "made Sure to" Sarah, and they gave no indication of disapproving. The few who guessed at Sarah's condition in the summer of 1742 were not so much surprised that she was pregnant as that the couple "did not marry." It was evidently routine in this New England village, as in others, for courting couples to post banns for their nuptials soon after the woman discovered that she was pregnant.

Amasa offered different answers among his Pomfret peers to explain his failure to marry his lover. When Zerviah Grosvenor told Amasa that he and Sarah "had better Marry," he responded, "That would not do," for "he was afraid of his Parents . . . [who would] always make their lives [at home] uncomfortable." Later, Abigail Nightingale heard rumors that Amasa was resorting to the standard excuse of men wishing to avoid a shotgun marriage—denying that the child was his. Hallowell, with whom Amasa may have been honest, claimed "the Reason that they did not marry" was "that Sessions Did not Love her well a nough for [he] saith he did not believe it was his son and if he Could Cause her to gitt Red of it he would not Go near her again." Showing yet another face to a Grosvenor kinsman after Sarah's death, Amasa repented his actions and extravagantly claimed he would "give All he had" to "bring Sarah . . . To life again . . . and have her as his wife."

The unusual feature of Amasa's behavior was not his unwillingness to marry Sarah, but his determination to terminate her pregnancy before it showed. Increasing numbers of young men in eighteenth-century New England weathered the temporary obloquy of abandoning a pregnant lover in order to prolong their bachelorhood or marry someone else. What drove Amasa, and an ostensibly reluctant Sarah, to resort to abortion? Was it fear of their fathers? Nathaniel Sessions had chosen Amasa as the son who would remain on the family farm and care for his parents in their old age. An ill-timed marriage could have disrupted these plans and threatened Amasa's inheritance. For his part, Leicester Grosvenor may have made it clear to his daughter that he would be greatly displeased at her marrying before she reached a certain age or until her older sister wed. Rigid piety, an authoritarian nature, an intense concern with being seen as a good household governor—any of these traits in Leicester Grosvenor or Nathaniel Sessions could have colored Amasa's decisions.

Perhaps it was not family relations that proved the catalyst but Amasa's acquaintance with a medical man who boasted about a powder more effective than the herbal remedies that were part of women's lore. Hallowell himself had fathered an illegitimate child fifteen years earlier, and he may have encouraged a rakish attitude in Amasa, beguiling the younger man with the promise of dissociating sex from its possible consequences. Or the explanation may have been that classic one: another woman. Two years after Sarah's death,

Amasa married Hannah Miller of Rehoboth, Massachusetts. Perhaps in early 1742 he was already making trips to the town just east of Providence to see his future wife.

What should we make of Sarah's role in the scheme? It is possible that she no longer loved Amasa and was as eager as he to forestall external pressures toward a quick marriage. However, Zerviah swore that on one occasion before the operation Amasa reluctantly agreed to post banns for their nuptials and that Sarah did not object. *If* Sarah was a willing and active participant in the abortion plot all along, then by 1745 her female kin and friends had fabricated and rehearsed a careful and seamless story to preserve the memory of the dead girl untarnished.

In the portrait drawn by her friends, Sarah reacted to her pregnancy and to Amasa's plan first by arguing and finally by doing her utmost to protect her lover. She may have wished to marry Amasa, yet she did not insist on it or bring in older family members to negotiate with him and his parents. Abigail Nightingale insisted that Sarah accepted Amasa's recalcitrance and only pleaded with him that they not "go on to add sin to sin." Privately, she urged Amasa that there was an alternative to taking the trade—a way that would enable him to keep his role hidden and prevent the couple from committing a "Last transgression [that] would be worse then the first." Sarah told him that "she was willing to take the sin and shame to her self, and to be obliged never to tell whose Child it was, and that she did not doubt but that if she humbled her self on her Knees to her Father he would take her and her Child home." Her lover, afraid that his identity would become known, vetoed her proposal.

According to the Pomfret women's reconstruction, abortion was not a freely chosen and defiant act for Sarah. Against her own desires, she reluctantly consented in taking the trade only because Amasa "So very earnestly perswaided her." In fact, she had claimed to her friends that she was coerced; he "would take no denyal." Sarah's confidantes presented her as being aware of her options, shrinking from abortion as an unnatural and immoral deed, and yet finally choosing the strategy consistent with her lover's vision of what would best protect their futures. Thus, if Amasa's hubris was extreme, so too was Sarah's internalization of those strains of thought in her culture that taught women to make themselves pleasing and obedient to men.

While we cannot be sure that the deponents' picture of Sarah's initial recoil and reluctant submission to the abortion plot was entirely accurate, it is clear that once she was caught up in the plan she extracted a pledge of silence from all her confidantes. Near her death, before telling Abigail about the operation, she "insist[ed] on . . . [her friend's] never discovering the Matter" to anyone. Clearly, she had earlier bound Zerviah and Hannah on their honor not to tell their elders. Reluctant when faced with the abortionist's powder, Sarah became a leading co-conspirator when alone with her female friends.

One of the most remarkable aspects of the Grosvenor-Sessions case is Sarah and Amasa's success in keeping their parents in the dark, at least until her final illness. If by July Sarah's sisters grew suspicious that Sarah was "with child," what explains the failure of her parents to observe her pregnancy and to intervene and uncover the abortion scheme? Were they negligent, preoccupied with other matters, or willfully blind? Most mysterious is the role of forty-eight-year-old Rebecca Grosvenor, Grosvenor's second wife and Sarah's stepmother since 1729. Rebecca is mentioned only once in the depositions, and she was not summoned as a witness in the 1745–1747 investigations into Sarah's death. Even if some extraordinary circumstance—an invalid condition or an implacable hatred between Sarah and her stepmother—explains Rebecca's abdication of her role as guardian, Sarah had two widowed aunts living in or near her household. These matrons, experienced in childbirth matters and concerned for the family reputation, were just the sort of older women who traditionally watched and advised young women entering courtship.

In terms of who knew what, the events of summer 1742 in Pomfret apparently unfolded in two stages. The first stretched from Sarah's discovery of her pregnancy by early May to some point in late August after her miscarriage. In this period a determined, collective effort by Sarah and Amasa and their friends kept their elders in the dark. When Sarah fell seriously ill from the aftereffects of the abortion attempt and miscarriage, rumors of the young people's secret activities reached Leicester Grosvenor's neighbors and even one of the doctors he had called in. It is difficult to escape the conclusion that by Sarah's death in mid-September her father and stepmother had learned of the steps that had precipitated her mortal condition and kept silent for reasons of their own.

Except for Hallowell, the circle of intimates entrusted by Amasa and Sarah with their scheme consisted of young adults ranging in age from nineteen to thirty-three. Born between about 1710 and 1725, these young people had grown up just as the town attracted enough settlers to support a church, militia, and local market. They were second-generation Pomfret residents who shared the generational identity that came with sitting side by side through long worship services, attending school, playing, and working together at children's tasks. By 1740, these sisters, brothers, cousins, courting couples, and neighbors, in their visits from house to house—sometimes in their own households, sometimes at their parents'—had managed to create a world of talk and socializing that was largely exempt from parental supervision. In Pomfret in 1742 it was this group of young people in their twenties and early thirties, *not* the cluster of Grosvenor matrons over forty-five, who monitored Sarah's courtship, attempted to get Amasa to marry his lover, privately investigated the activities and motives of Amasa and Hallowell, and, belatedly, spoke out publicly to help Connecticut juries decide who should be blamed for Sarah's death.

That Leicester Grosvenor made no public move to punish those around him and that he avoided giving testimony when legal proceedings commenced are intriguing clues to social changes underway in New England villages in the mid-eighteenth century. Local leaders like Grosvenor,

along with the respectable yeomen whom he represented in public office, were increasingly withdrawing delicate family problems from the purview of their communities. Slander, illegitimacy, and feuds among neighbors came infrequently to local courts by mid-century, indicating male householders' growing preference for handling such matters privately. Wealthy and ambitious families adopted this ethic of privacy at the same time that they became caught up in elaborating their material worlds by adding rooms and acquiring luxury goods. The "good feather bed" with all of its furniture that Grosvenor bequeathed to his one unmarried daughter was but one of many marks of status by which the Grosvenors differentiated themselves from their Pomfret neighbors. But all the fine accoutrements in the world would not excuse Justice Grosvenor from his obligation to govern his household effectively. Mortified no doubt at his inability to monitor the young people in his extended family, he responded, ironically, by extending their conspiracy of silence. The best way for him to shield the family name from scandal and protect his political reputation in the county and colony was to keep the story of Sarah's abortion out of the courts.

The Doctor

John Hallowell's status as an outsider in Pomfret and his dangerous, secret alliance with the town's young adults may have shaped his destiny as the one conspirator sentenced to suffer at the whipping post. Although the physician had been involved in shady dealings before 1742, he had managed to win the trust of many patients and a respectable social standing. Tracking down his history in northeastern Connecticut tells us something of the uncertainty surrounding personal and professional identity before the advent of police records and medical licensing boards. It also gives us an all-too-rare glimpse into the fashion in which an eighteenth-century country doctor tried to make his way in the world.

Hallowell's earliest brushes with the law came in the 1720s. In 1725 he purchased land in

Killingly, a Connecticut town just north of Pomfret and bordering both Massachusetts and Rhode Island. Newly married, he was probably in his twenties at the time. Seven months before his wife gave birth to their first child, a sixteen-year-old Killingly woman charged Hallowell with fathering her illegitimate child. Using the alias Nicholas Hallaway, he fled to southeastern Connecticut, where he lived as a "transient" for three months. He was arrested and settled the case by admitting to paternity and agreeing to contribute to the child's maintenance for four years.

Hallowell resumed his life in Killingly. Two years later, now referred to as "Dr.," he was arrested again; this time the charge was counterfeiting. Hallowell and several confederates were hauled before the governor and council for questioning and then put on trial before the Superior Court. Although many Killingly witnesses testified to the team's suspect activities in a woodland shelter, the charges against Hallowell were dropped when a key informer failed to appear in court.

Hallowell thus escaped conviction on a serious felony charge, but he had been tainted by stories linking him to the criminal subculture of transient, disorderly, greedy, and manually skilled men who typically made up gangs of counterfeiters in eighteenth-century New England. After 1727 Hallowell may have given up dabbling in money-making schemes and turned to earning his livelihood chiefly from his medical practice. Like two-thirds of the male medical practitioners in colonial New England, he probably did not have college or apprentice training, but his skill, or charm, was not therefore necessarily less than that of any one of his peers who might have inherited a library of books and a fund of knowledge from a physician father. All colonial practitioners, as Richard D. Brown reminds us, mixed learned practices with home or folk remedies, and no doctor had access to safe, reliable pharmacological preparations or antiseptic surgical procedures.

In the years immediately following the counterfeiting charge, Hallowell appears to have made several deliberate moves to portray himself as a sober neighbor and reliable physician. At about the time of his second marriage, in 1729, he became a more frequent attendant at the Killingly meetinghouse, where he renewed his covenant and presented his first two children for baptism. He also threw himself into the land and credit markets of northeastern Connecticut, establishing himself as a physician who was also an enterprising yeoman and a frequent litigant.

These activities had dual implications. On the one hand, they suggest that Hallowell epitomized the eighteenth-century Yankee citizen—a man as comfortable in the courtroom and counting-house as at a patient's bedside; a man of restless energy, not content to limit his scope to his fields and village; a practical, ambitious man with a shrewd eye for a good deal. On the other hand, Hallowell's losses to Boston creditors, his constant efforts to collect debts, and his farflung practice raise questions about the nature of his activities and medical practice. He evidently had clients not just in towns across northeastern Connecticut but also in neighboring Massachusetts and Rhode Island. Perhaps rural practitioners normally traveled extensively, spending many nights away from their wives and children. It is also possible, however, either that Hallowell was forced to travel because established doctors from leading families had monopolized the local practice or that he chose to recruit patients in Providence and other towns as a cover for illicit activities. Despite his land speculations and his frequent resort to litigation, Hallowell was losing money. In the sixteen years before 1742, his creditors secured judgments against him for a total of £1,060, while he was able to collect only £700 in debts. The disjunction between his ambition and actual material gains may have led Hallowell in middle age to renew his illicit money-making schemes. By supplying young men with potent abortifacients and dabbling in schemes to counterfeit New England's paper money, he betrayed the very gentlemen whose respect, credit, and society he sought.

What is most intriguing about Hallowell was his ability to ingratiate himself throughout his life with elite men whose reputations were unblemished by scandal. Despite the rumors that must have circulated about his early sexual dalliance, counterfeiting activities, suspect medical remedies, heavy debts, and shady business transactions, leading ministers, merchants, and magistrates welcomed him into their houses. In Pomfret such acceptance took its most dramatic form in September 1739 when Hallowell was admitted along with thirty-five other original covenanters to the first private library association in eastern Connecticut. Gathering in the house of Pomfret's respected, conservative minister, Ebenezer Williams, the members pledged sums for the purchase of "useful and profitable English books." In the company of the region's scholars, clergy, and "gentlemen," along with a few yeomen—all "warm friends of learning and literature"—Hallowell marked himself off from the more modest subscribers by joining with thirteen prominent and wealthy signers to pledge a sum exceeding £15.

Lacking college degree and family pedigree, Hallowell traded on his profession and his charm to gain acceptability with the elite. In August 1742 he shrewdly removed himself from the Pomfret scene, just before Sarah Grosvenor's death. In that month he moved, possibly without his wife and children, to Providence, where he had many connections. Within five years, Hallowell had so insinuated himself with town leaders such as Stephen Hopkins that fourteen of them petitioned for mitigation of what they saw as the misguided sentence imposed on him in the Grosvenor case.

Hallowell's capacity for landing on his feet, despite persistent brushes with scandal, debt, and the law, suggests that we should look at the fluidity of New England's eighteenth-century elite in new ways. What bound sons of old New England families, learned men, and upwardly mobile merchants and professionals in an expanded elite may partly have been a reshaped, largely unspoken set of values shared by men. We know that the archetype for white New England women as sexual beings was changing from carnal Eve to resisting Pamela and that the calculus of accountability for seduction was shifting blame solely to women.

But the simultaneous metamorphosis in cultural images and values defining manhood in the early and mid-eighteenth century has not been studied. The scattered evidence we do have suggests that, increasingly, for men in the more secular and anglicized culture of New England, the lines between legitimate and illegitimate sexuality, between sanctioned and shady business dealings, and between speaking the truth and protecting family honor blurred. Hallowell's acceptability to men like minister Ebenezer Williams and merchant Stephen Hopkins hints at how changing sexual and moral standards shaped the economic and social alliances made by New England's male leadership in the 1700s.

Women's Talk and Men's Talk

If age played a major role in determining who knew the truth about Sarah Grosvenor's illness, gender affected how the conspiring young adults responded to Sarah's impending death and how they weighed the issue of blame. Our last glimpse into the social world of eighteenth-century Pomfret looks at the different ways in which women and men reconstructed their roles in the events of 1742.

An inward gaze, a strong consciousness of sin and guilt, a desire to avoid conflict and achieve reconciliation, a need to confess—these are the impulses expressed in women's intimate talk in the weeks before Sarah died. The central female characters in the plot, Sarah and Zerviah Grosvenor, lived for six weeks with the daily fear that their parents or aunts might detect Sarah's condition or their covert comings and goings. Deposing three years later, Zerviah represented the sisters as suffering under an intensifying sense of complicity as they had passed through two stages of involvement in the concealment plan. At first, they were passive players, submitting to the hands of men. But once Hallowell declared that he had done all he could, they were left to salvage the conspiracy by enduring the terrors of a first delivery alone, knowing that their failure to call in the older women of the family resembled the decision made by women who committed infanticide. While the pain and shock of miscarrying a five-and-one-half-month fetus through a possibly lacerated vagina may have been the experience that later most grieved Sarah, Zerviah would be haunted particularly by her stealthy venture into the woods with Hannah to bury the shrouded evidence of miscarriage.

The Grosvenor sisters later recalled that they had regarded the first stage of the scheme—taking the trade—as "a Sin" and "an Evil" not so much because it was intended to end the life of a fetus as because it entailed a protracted set of actions, worse than a single lie, to cover up an initial transgression: fornication. According to their religion and the traditions of their New England culture, Sarah and Zerviah knew that the proper response to the sin of "uncleanness" (especially when it led to its visible manifestation, pregnancy) was to confess, seeking to allay God's wrath and cleanse oneself and one's community. Dire were the consequences of hiding a grave sin, so the logic and folklore of religion warned. Having piled one covert act upon another, all in defiance of her parents, each sister wondered if she had not ventured beyond the pale, forsaking God and in turn being forsaken.

Within hours after the burial, Zerviah ran in a frenzy to Alexander Sessions's house and blurted out an account of her sister's "Untimely birth" and the burying of the fetus. While Alexander and Silence Sessions wondered if Zerviah was "in her right mind" and supposed she was having "a very bad fit," we might judge that she was in shock—horrified and confused by what she had done, fearful of retribution, and torn between the pragmatic strategy of silence and an intense spiritual longing to confess. Silence took her aside and demanded, "how could you do it?—I could not!" Zerviah, in despair, replied, "I don't Know; the Devil was in us." Hers was the characteristic refuge of the defiant sinner: Satan made her do it.

Sarah's descent into despondency, according to the portrait drawn in the women's depositions, was not so immediate. In the week following the miscarriage she recovered enough to be up and about the house. Then the fever came on. Bedridden for weeks, yet still lucid, she exhibited such "great Concern of mind" that Abigail, alone with her, felt compelled to ask her "what was the Matter." "Full of Sorrow" and "in a very affectionate Manner," Sarah replied by asking her friend "whether [she] thought her Sins would ever be pardoned?" Abigail's answer blended a reassuringly familiar exhortation to repent with an awareness that Sarah might have stepped beyond the possibility of salvation. "I answered that I hoped she had not Sinned the unpardonable Sin [that of renouncing Christ], but with true and hearty repentance hoped she would find forgiveness." On this occasion, and at least once more, Sarah responded to the call for repentance by pouring out her troubled heart to Abigail—as we have seen—confessing her version of the story in a torrent of words.

Thus, visions of judgment and of their personal accountability to God haunted Sarah and Zerviah during the waning days of summer—or so their female friends later contended. Caught between the traditional religious ethic of confession, recently renewed in revivals across New England, and the newer, status-driven cultural pressure to keep moral missteps private, the Grosvenor women declined to take up roles as accusers. By focusing on their own actions, they rejected a portrait of themselves as helpless victims, yet they also ceded to their male kin responsibility for assessing blame and mediating between the public interest in seeing justice done and the private interests of the Grosvenor family. Finally, by trying to keep the conspiracy of silence intact and by allowing Amasa frequent visits to her bedside to lament his role and his delusion by Hallowell, Sarah at once endorsed a policy of private repentance and forgiveness *and* indicated that she wished her lover to be spared eventual public retribution for her death.

Talk among the men of Pomfret in the weeks preceding and following Sarah's death centered on more secular concerns than the preoccupation with sin and God's anger that ran through the women's conversations. Neither Hallowell nor

Sessions expressed any guilt or sense of sin, as far as the record shows, *until* Sarah was diagnosed as mortally ill. Indeed, their initial accounts of the plot took the form of braggadocio, with Amasa (according to Hallowell) casting himself as the rake who could "gitt Red" of his child and look elsewhere for female companionship, and Hallowell boasting of his abortionist's surgical technique to Sarah's cousin Ebenezer. Later, anticipating popular censure and possible prosecution, each man "Tried to Cast it" on the other. The physician insisted that "He did not do any thing but What Sessions Importuned him to Do," while Amasa exclaimed "That he could freely be Strip[p]ed naked provided he could bring Sarah . . . To life again . . . but Doct Hollowell had Deluded him, and Destroyed her." While this sort of denial and buck-passing seems very human, it was the antithesis of the New England way—a religious way of life that made confession its central motif. The Grosvenor-Sessions case is one illustration among many of how New England women continued to measure themselves by "the moral allegory of repentance and confession" while men, at least when presenting themselves before legal authorities, adopted secular voices and learned self-interested strategies.

For the Grosvenor men—at least the cluster of Sarah's cousins living near her—the key issue was not exposing sin but protecting the family's reputation. In the weeks before Sarah died, her cousins John and Ebenezer each attempted to investigate and sort out the roles and motives of Amasa Sessions and John Hallowell in the scheme to conceal Sarah's pregnancy. Grilled in August by Ebenezer about Sarah's condition, Hallowell revealed that "Sessions had bin Interseeding with him to Remove her Conseption." On another occasion, when John Grosvenor demanded that he justify his actions, Hallowell was more specific. He "[did] with her [Sarah] as he did . . . because Sessions Came to him and was So very earnest . . . and offered him five pounds if he would do it." "But," Hallowell boasted, "he would have twenty of[f] of him before he had done." John persisted: did Amasa know that Hallowell was attempting a man-

ual abortion at John's house on that day in early August? Hallowell replied that Amasa "knew before he did anything and was at Mr. Waldo's [a Pomfret tavernkeeper] to hear the event."

John and Ebenezer, deposing three or four years after these events, did not mention having thrown questions at Amasa Sessions at the time, nor did they explain why they did not act immediately to have charges brought against the two conspirators. Perhaps these young householders were loath to move against a male peer and childhood friend. More likely, they kept their information to themselves to protect John's wife, Hannah, and their cousin Zerviah from prosecution as accessories. They may also have acted, in league with their uncle Leicester, out of a larger concern for keeping the family name out of the courts. Finally, it is probable that the male cousins, partly because of their own complicity and partly because they may have believed that Sarah had consented to the abortion, simply did not think that Amasa's and Hallowell's actions added up to the murder of their relative.

Three years later, yet another Grosvenor cousin intervened, expressing himself much more vehemently than John or Ebenezer ever had. In 1742, John Shaw at age thirty-eight may have been perceived by the younger Grosvenors as too old—too close to the age when men took public office and served as grand jurors—to be trusted with their secret. Shaw seems to have known nothing of Sarah's taking the trade or having a miscarriage until 1745 when "the Storys" suddenly surfaced. Then Hannah and Zerviah gave him a truncated account. Shaw reacted with rage, realizing that Sarah had died not of natural causes but from "what Hollowell had done," and he set out to wring the truth from the doctor. Several times he sought out Hallowell in Rhode Island to tell him that "I could not look upon him otherwise Than [as] a Bad man Since he had Destroyed my Kinswoman." When Hallowell countered that "Amasa Sessions . . . was the Occasion of it," Shaw's fury grew. "I Told him he was like old Mother Eve When She said The Serpent beguild her; . . . [and] I Told him in my Mind he Deserved to dye for it."

Questioning Amasa, Shaw was quick to accept his protestations of sincere regret and his insistence that Hallowell had "Deluded" him. Shaw concluded that Amasa had never "Importuned [Hallowell] . . . to lay hands on her" (that is, to perform the manual abortion). Forged in the men's talk about the Grosvenor-Sessions case in 1745 and 1746 appears to have been a consensus that, while Amasa Sessions was somewhat blameworthy "as concerned in it," it was only Hallowell—the outsider, the man easily labeled a quack—who deserved to be branded "a Man of Death." Nevertheless, it was the stories of *both* men and women that ensured the fulfillment of a doctor's warning to Hallowell in the Leicester Grosvenor house just before Sarah died: "The Hand of Justice [will] Take hold of [you] sooner or Later."

The Law

The hand of justice reached out to catch John Hallowell in November 1745. The warrants issued for the apprehension and examination of suspects that autumn gave no indication of a single informer or highly placed magistrate who had triggered the prosecution so long after the events. Witnesses referred to "those Stories Concerning Amasa Sessions and Sarah Grosvenor" that had begun to circulate beyond the inner circle of Pomfret initiates in the summer of 1745. *Something* had caused Zerviah and Hannah Grosvenor to break their silence. Zerviah provided the key to the puzzle, as she alone had been present at the crucial series of incidents leading to Sarah's death. The only surviving account of Zerviah's belated conversion from silence to public confession comes from the stories told by Pomfret residents into the nineteenth century. In Ellen Larned's melodramatic prose, the "whispered" tale recounted Zerviah's increasing discomfort thus: "Night after night, in her solitary chamber, the surviving sister was awakened by the rattling of the rings on which her bed-curtains were suspended, a ghostly knell continuing and intensifying till she was convinced of its preternatural origin; and at length, in response to her

agonized entreaties, the spirit of her dead sister made known to her, 'That she could not rest in her grave till her crime was made public.' "

Embellished as this tale undoubtedly is, we should not dismiss it out of hand as a Victorian ghost story. In early modern English culture, belief persisted in both apparitions and the supernatural power of the guiltless victim to return and expose her murderer. Zerviah in 1742 already fretted over her sin as an accomplice, yet she kept her pledge of silence to her sister. It is certainly conceivable that, after a lapse of three years, she could no longer bear the pressure of hiding the acts that she increasingly believed amounted to the murder of her sister and an unborn child. Whether Zerviah's sudden outburst of talk in 1745 came about at the urging of some Pomfret confidante, or perhaps under the influence of the revivals then sweeping Windham County churches, or indeed because of her belief in nightly visitations by her dead sister's spirit, we simply cannot know.

The Pomfret meetinghouse was the site of the first public legal hearing into the facts behind Sarah Grosvenor's death. We can imagine that townsfolk crowded the pews over the course of two November days to watch two prominent county magistrates examine a string of witnesses before pronouncing their preliminary judgment. The evidence, they concluded, was sufficient to bind four people over for trial at the Superior Court: Hallowell, who in their opinion was "Guilty of murdering Sarah," along with Amasa Sessions, Zerviah Grosvenor, and Hannah Grosvenor as accessories to that murder. The inclusion of Zerviah and Hannah may have been a ploy to pressure these crucial, possibly still reluctant, witnesses to testify for the crown. When Joseph Fowler, the king's attorney, prepared a formal indictment in the case eleven months later, he dropped all charges against Zerviah and Hannah. Rather than stand trial, the two women traveled frequently during 1746 and 1747 to the county seat to give evidence against Sessions and Hallowell.

The criminal process recommenced in September 1746. A grand jury empaneled by the Superior Court at its Windham session first rejected a presentment against Hallowell for murdering Sarah "by his Wicked and Diabolical practice." Fowler, recognizing that the capital charges of murder and accessory to murder against Hallowell and Sessions were going to fail before jurors, changed his tack. He presented the grand jury with a joint indictment against the two men not for outright murder but for endangering Sarah's health by trying to "procure an Abortion" with medicines and "a violent manual opperation"; this time the jurors endorsed the bill. When the Superior Court trial opened in November, two attorneys for the defendants managed to persuade the judges that the indictment was faulty on technical grounds. However, upon the advice of the king's attorney that there "appear reasons vehemently to suspect" the two men "Guilty of Sundry Heinous Offenses" at Pomfret four years earlier, the justices agreed to bind them over to answer charges in March 1747.

Fowler next moved to bring separate indictments against Hallowell and Sessions for the "highhanded misdemeanour" of endeavoring to destroy Sarah's health "and the fruit of her womb." This wording echoed the English common law designation of abortion as a misdemeanor, not a felony or capital crime. A newly empaneled grand jury of eighteen county yeomen made what turned out to be the pivotal decision in getting a conviction: they returned a true bill against Hallowell and rejected a similarly worded bill against Sessions. Only Hallowell, "the notorious physician," would go to trial.

On March 20, 1747, John Hallowell stepped before the bar for the final time to answer for the death of Sarah Grosvenor. He maintained his innocence, the case went to a trial jury of twelve men, and they returned with a guilty verdict. The Superior Court judges, who had discretion to choose any penalty less than death, pronounced a severe sentence of public shaming and corporal punishment. Hallowell was to be paraded to the town gallows, made to stand there before the public for two hours "with a rope visibly hanging about his neck," and then endure a public whipping of twenty-nine lashes "on the naked back."

Before the authorities could carry out this sentence, Hallowell escaped and fled to Rhode Island. From Providence seven months after his trial, he audaciously petitioned the Connecticut General Assembly for a mitigated sentence, presenting himself as a destitute "Exile." As previously noted, fourteen respected male citizens of Providence took up his cause, arguing that this valued doctor had been convicted by prejudiced witnesses and hearsay evidence and asserting that corporal punishment was unwarranted in a misdemeanor case. While the Connecticut legislators rejected these petitions, the language used by Hallowell and his Rhode Island patrons is yet another marker of the distance separating many educated New England men at mid-century from their more God-fearing predecessors. Never mentioning the words "sin" or "repentance," the Providence men wrote that Hallowell was justified in escaping the lash since "every Person is prompted [by the natural Law of Self-Preservation] to avoid Pain and Misery."

In the series of indictments against Hallowell and Sessions, the central legal question became who had directly caused Sarah's death. To the farmers in their forties and fifties who sat as jurors, Hallowell clearly deserved punishment. By recklessly endangering Sarah's life he had abused the trust that heads of household placed in him as a physician. Moreover, he had conspired with the younger generation to keep their dangerous activities secret from their parents and elders.

Several rationales could have been behind the Windham jurors' conclusion that Amasa Sessions ought to be spared the lash. Legally, they could distinguish him from Hallowell as not being *directly* responsible for Sarah's death. Along with Sarah's male kin, they dismissed the evidence that Amasa had instigated the scheme, employed Hallowell, and monitored all of his activities. Perhaps they saw him as a native son who deserved the chance to prove himself mature and responsible. They may have excused his actions as nothing more than a misguided effort to cast off an unwanted lover. Rather than acknowledge that a culture that excused male sexual irresponsibility was responsible for Sarah's death, the Grosvenor family, the Pomfret community, and the jury men of the county persuaded themselves that Sessions had been ignorant of the potentially deadly consequences of his actions.

Memory and History

No family-feud, no endless round of recriminations followed the many months of deposing and attending trials that engaged the Grosvenor and Sessions clans in 1746 and 1747. Indeed, as Sarah and Amasa's generation matured, the ties between the two families thickened. In 1748 Zerviah married a man whose family homestead adjoined the farm of Amasa's father. Twenty years later, when the aging Sessions patriarch wrote his will, Zerviah and her husband were at his elbow to witness the solemn document. Amasa, who would inherit "the Whole of the Farm," was doubtless present also. Within another decade, the third generation came of age, and despite the painful memories of Sarah's death that must have lingered in the minds of her now middle-aged siblings, a marriage directly joining the two families finally took place. In 1775 Amasa's third son, and namesake, married sixteen-year-old Esther Grosvenor, daughter of Sarah's brother, Leicester, Jr.

It is clear that the Grosvenor clan was not willing to break ranks with their respectable yeoman neighbors and heap blame on the Sessions family for Sarah's death. It would, however, be fascinating to know what women in Pomfret and other Windham County towns had to say about the outcome of the legal proceedings in 1747. Did they concur with the jurors that Hallowell was the prime culprit, or did they, unlike Sarah Grosvenor, direct their ire more concertedly at

Amasa, insisting that he too was "a Bad man?" Several decades later, middle-class New England women would organize against the sexual double standard. However, Amasa's future career tells us that female piety in the 1740s did not instruct Windham County women to expel the newly married, thirty-two-year-old man from their homes.

Amasa, as he grew into middle age in Pomfret, easily replicated his father's status. He served as militia captain in the Seven Years' War, prospered in farming, fathered ten children, and lived fifty-seven years beyond Sarah Grosvenor. His handsome gravestone, inscribed with a long verse, stands but twenty-five feet from the simpler stone erected in 1742 for Sarah.

After his death, male kin remembered Amasa fondly; nephews and grandsons recalled him as a "favorite" relative, "remarkably capable" in his prime and "very corpulent" in old age. Moreover, local story-telling tradition and the published history of the region, which made such a spectacular ghost story out of Sarah's abortion and death, preserved Amasa Sessions's reputation unsullied: the *name* of Sarah's lover was left out of the tale.

If Sarah Grosvenor's life is a cautionary tale in any sense for us in the late twentieth century, it is as a reminder of the historically distinctive ways in which socialized gender roles, community and class solidarity, and legal culture combine in each set of generations to excuse or make invisible certain abuses and crimes against women. The form in which Sarah Grosvenor's death became local history reminds us of how the excuses and erasures of one generation not unwittingly become embedded in the narratives and memories of the next cultural era.

Study Questions

1. Why did Amasa Sessions want Sarah to have an abortion? Were his motives any different from those of many contemporary men whose lovers become pregnant? Why or why not?

2. What evidence suggests that Sarah was not a willing participant in the abortion?

3. Why did a code of silence prevail in the community concerning Sarah's death?

4. Describe the role of John Hallowell in the death of Sarah Grosvenor. What type of reputation did Hallowell have?

5. How did religious beliefs influence the decision-making process of Sarah and her sister?

6. How did the discourse of men and women in Pomfret differ concerning Sarah's death?

7. Why did Zerviah Grosvenor finally bring the case to public attention?

Bibliography

For a general look at the history of abortion in early American history, see Harold Rosen, ed., *Abortion in America: Medical, Psychiatric, Legal, Anthropological, and Religious Considerations* (1967) and James C. Mohr, *Abortion in America: The Origins and Evolution of National Policy, 1800–1900* (1978). Also see Michael Grossberg, *Governing the Hearth: Law and the Family in Nineteenth-Century America* (1985). For general attitudes about sexuality and abortion in Puritan New England, see Roger Thompson, *Sex in Middlesex: Popular Mores in a Massachusetts County, 1649–1699* (1986) and Lyle Koehler, *A Search for Power: The "Weaker Sex" in Seventeenth-Century New England* (1980). Audrey Eccles's *Obstetrics and Gynecology in Tudor and Stuart England* (1982) is also valuable. Also see Kathleen Brown, *Good Wives, Nasty Wenches, and Anxious Patriarchs: Gender, Race, and Power in Colonial Virginia* (1996) and Daniel Scott Smith and Michael S. Hindus, "Premarital Pregnancy in America, 1640–1971," *Journal of Interdisciplinary History* (1975).

READING 4

The Devil in Salem

Peggy Robbins

Most of the "facts" of the Salem witchcraft trials and executions are known. The trouble started in the cold winter of 1691–1692, and by the end of the summer, nineteen people were adjudged to be witches and hanged. What is difficult to determine is why the trials ever took place. Certainly the belief in witchcraft was nearly universal in seventeenth-century New England, and perhaps a few of the people executed had even practiced witchcraft. But the vast majority were as innocent as Sarah Good, whose last words to her minister were, "I am no more a witch than you are a wizard, and if you take away my life, God will give you blood to drink." For more than a century, historians have debated the cause of the outbreak. Many have blamed the young women who set the dreadful events into motion. Others have stressed the community conflicts within Salem and the general social and religious tension created by an expanding society and declining religiosity. In the following essay, historian Peggy Robbins describes and interprets the witchcraft trials of 1692.

Hysteria or demonic possession? Whatever the case, Salem, Massachusetts endured in 1692 a gothic nightmare of fear that saw over 200 convicted of witchcraft, and sent twenty poor souls to meet their master, in Heaven or Hell.

It is difficult for the modern mind to understand how the barbaric Massachusetts witch hunts of the late 17th century could have occurred in America, and it is easy to suppose that the shocking accounts of citizens sent to the gallows for the practice of witchcraft have been exaggerated in their telling and retelling. But records reveal, with facts all too plain, that in Salem Village and its vicinity in 1692, alone, 170 "witches" were imprisoned, and twenty of them were put to death, nineteen on the gallows and one by being pressed under heavy weights until dead.

The Salem witch trials became the most celebrated of all witch hunts even though the number of people who suffered during the Salem hysteria was small in comparison with the thousands who were persecuted in Europe in such outbreaks during the late Middle Ages.

The Massachusetts Bay Colony, from its first settlement, was a likely place for belief in witchcraft as the means by which Satan, through the use of human beings, carried on his war against Heaven. The England from which the colonists emigrated had witnessed, during the decade prior to the 1620 landing at Plymouth, the trial of the Lancashire witches, with ten of the accused sent to the gallows. James I, King of England from 1603 to 1625, had written for the enlightenment of his subjects a treatise on witchcraft called *Demonologie* which served to increase the general fear of witches. Typical of the "investigations" James I reported was one having to do with the cause of tempests which beset his bride on her voyage from Denmark; he found that several hundred witches had taken to sea in a sieve from Leith and caused the storms.

New England in the 17th century was a religious community of fanatically rigid Calvinists.

Peggy Robbins, "The Devil in Salem," *American History Illustrated*, 6 (December 1971), 4–9, 44–48.

The unknown was categorized as evil and the Devil's power was reckoned to be as strong as God's. Massachusetts Bay settlers were largely Puritans who considered the Devil their particular, personal enemy; since their religion was the true one, it was the one Satan was most anxious to destroy. Doctors, judges, schoolmasters, and particularly ministers, as well as the less learned among the Puritans, were strong believers in witchcraft. Even the most minor occurence was attributed to witchery: if a farmer's cow failed to give milk, or his horse went lame, or his well dried up, it was a witch's doing; if a housewife couldn't get the butter to come, a witch was controlling the churning; if a horse's mane was found tangled, it had been knotted by a witch who had used it as a stirrup to mount for a stolen ride to a witches' Sabbath (a gathering at which witches got instructions from their master, the Devil). The Puritan culture, with its strict, tedious, repressed way of life, in which even Christmas and Mardi Gras were labeled "pagan festivities" and fiercely forbidden, lent itself to the stimulating, unrestrained belief in witchcraft and monotony-breaking witch hunts.

The first recorded American witch hanging was in Boston in 1648. Little is known of the circumstances. In 1656, a quarrelsome Boston widow named Anne Hibbins who was "possessed of preternatural knowledge" was executed as a witch. In 1663, in Hartford, Connecticut, Rebecca Greensmith, who "confessed that she had familiarity with the Devil, which had frequent use of her body," and her husband Nathaniel were hanged; they had been arrested after being "called out against by a person esteemed pious while suffering a violent public fit." As the years passed, a few other accusations of witchcraft in New England resulted in the hanging of "the Devil's advocates."

Then, in 1688, in Boston, the four children of a sober, pious mason named John Goodwin began having strange fits. As the Reverend Cotton Mather, the highly esteemed young minister of Boston's Second Church, later described their symptoms in his *Memorable Providences* "Sometimes they would be deaf, sometimes dumb, and

A mansion home, built in 1668, in Salem, Massachusetts.

sometimes blind, and often all this at once. One while their tongues would be drawn down their throats; another while they would be pulled out upon their chins to prodigious length. They would have their mouths opened into such a wideness that their jaws went out of joint, and then they would clap together again with a force like that of a strong spring-lock. The same would happen to their shoulder-blades, and their elbows, and hand-wrists. . . . They would make most piteous outcries that they were cut with knives, and struck with blows that they could not bear. . . . Their heads would be twisted almost around, . . . they would roar exceedingly. Thus they lay some weeks most pitiful spectacles."

The oldest Goodwin child, a teen-age girl, had had a quarrel over some laundry with a slovenly, vile-tongued Irish washerwoman named Glover,

and the Goodwins' neighbors began to remember that "the late husband of Goodwife Glover said she was such a scandalous old woman she was undoubtedly a witch." ("Goodwife," often shortened to "Goody," and "Goodman" were much-used forms of address at this period.)

John Goodwin called in Cotton Mather and three other clergymen, who held a day of prayer and fasting in the Goodwin house. It wasn't the first time Mather had "wrestled with the Devil" in "a case of possession, when Satan had entered a human body and spoke through it." In his sermons—he called one "Discourse on Witchcraft"—he told of his bouts with the Devil, often quoting the evil one's exact words, and his congregation thought him a very brave man for personally battling Satan.

After the day with the ministers, the youngest Goodwin child recovered, but the other three continued to be "so seized by the Devil they could not look upon the Bible or the Catechism." Goodwin entered a complaint against Mrs. Glover with the magistrates, and she was arrested and brought to trial under the law making witchcraft a capital offense. She "gave a wretched account of herself," received the sentence of death, and was hanged as a witch.

The oldest Goodwin child continued to be "spelled, bewitched," and Cotton Mather, who was 26 at the time, took her into his home so that he might closely observe her as part of his study of witchcraft. Less than a year later he published his book on witchcraft in general and the Goodwin case in particular. It was a fast best-seller throughout Massachusetts.

At this time there lived in Boston a 36-year-old merchant, Samuel Parris. Parris had studied theology at Harvard but, before completing the course, left to become a trader in the West Indies. Upon returning to Massachusetts he tried a merchant's career, but was not successful in business. In 1689 he decided to return to the ministry; he was unable, however, to find an opening in Boston, where the churches wanted graduate theologians. Finally, late in 1689, Parris accepted a call to the little hamlet north of Boston called Salem Village, which could not afford a regular minister.

Mr. Parris' small library, when he moved with his family from Boston to Salem Village (now Danvers), included a copy of Cotton Mather's book about witchcraft, and Puritan children were encouraged to read everything written by both Cotton and his father, Increase Mather, the president of Harvard University. The latter in 1684 had written a book against witchcraft— against its practice and against permitting it to go unpunished, not against believing in it. It is quite probable that Parris' family, including the younger members, had witnessed the hanging of Goodwife Glover in Boston. Puritans didn't approve of children witnessing frivolous activity but sanctioned their attendance at such "corrective procedures" as hangings.

Preacher Parris' household in Salem Village in early 1692 included his withdrawn, meek wife; his gentle, obedient, 9-year-old daughter Elizabeth, called Betty, who was subject to sudden weeping spells; his 11-year-old niece, Abigail Williams, a self-satisfied, restive child bold enough to engage in lusty talk about the Devil; and two slaves Parris had brought from Barbados—John, and his consort Tituba, both Carib Indians.

The aging Tituba was not an enthusiastic worker, but she liked taking care of the children, and she spent much of her time in the parsonage kitchen telling them stories of magic and showing them fortune-telling tricks, with both the slave and the children being careful that the Parrises knew nothing of their talk. Sometime during the cold, gloomy January of 1692, other girls, most of them older than Betty and Abigail, began joining Tituba and her two charges in the Parris kitchen. The young visitors had no trouble getting permission from their parents to visit the parsonage, and, if their elders were aware of the time they spent with Tituba, it must have been assumed the sessions were concerned with cooking and housework. Several of the older girls who worked as servants in Salem Village homes managed to slip by the parsonage for a few exciting moments while on errands.

Tituba's fortune-telling began with palm-reading and continued with involved, mysterious machinations by which the girls supposedly could divine the occupations of their future husbands, and the like. It was later divulged that the two slaves at one point, to break the spell of an unidentified witch, prepared a witch cake of rye meal mixed with the children's urine, baked it and fed it to a particular dog, the belief being that the dog was a "familiar," a messenger servant assigned to a witch by the Devil. Obviously, the secret experimentation with magic and superstition in the Parris kitchen was no light matter. There is little doubt that it was there, in the parsonage, that the girls' inherent Calvinist fears of the unknown were sparked into a flame, a flame that lit the stage for the terrible Salem witch hunts.

In February, Betty Parris and Abigail Williams began to have hysterical fits, behaving very much as the Goodwin children had four years earlier in

Boston. Soon their friends were similarly affected. Ann Putnam, the daughter of the village's prosperous and highly respected Sergeant Thomas Putnam, a tense 12-year-old who had been one of the most determined of the delvers into the occult under Tituba, was the first to follow Betty and Abigail "into horrible bewitchment." There is indication that Ann's mother was the one adult who knew of Tituba's kitchen magic; one account claims Mrs. Putnam, a sickly woman troubled by dreams, sent Ann to Tituba for dream interpretation. Ann was joined in bewitchment by Mercy Lewis, the sly, untidy, 19-year-old maid servant in the Putnam household.

The Reverend Mr. Parris was baffled and distressed by the affliction of his daughter and niece. When prayer and fasting failed to help them, he called in Salem Village's only doctor, William Griggs. The doctor watched the pair twisting and jerking and listened to their piercing gobberish; he pronounced sadly, "The evil hand is upon them," adding, it being the work of the Devil, that he was powerless to help them. Summoned by Sergeant Putnam to see Ann and Mercy, he repeated the diagnosis: The girls had been afflicted by witchcraft.

Word of this sped through Salem Village and by the next day others were having fits: 16-year-old Mary Walcott, a neighbor of the Parrises; 20-year-old Mary Warren, maidservant to John and Elizabeth Proctor; and 17-year-old Elizabeth Hubbard, niece of Mrs. Griggs, who lived and worked in the doctor's household. Other girls joined the number of afflicted as the days passed. All evidenced "possession" in the same general pattern, which included convulsions, contortions, hysterics, barking, periodic blindness, and complaints of being struck, cut, and bitten.

Today, nearly three centuries later, educated opinions are in complete disagreement as to whether these girls were "caught up in histrionics" and faking symptoms of madness or had actually become mentally ill. One chronicler of the Salem story says that, if Thomas Putnam and Samuel Parris had just given the girls in their households sound spankings, the witchcraft persecutions would never have taken place. Others insist this view makes the girls far more gifted at acting than could have possibly been the case; their behavior was not fraudulent but pathological. It is well to remember there is great witchcraft power in a society that believes in witchcraft.

As soon as the girls were pronounced bewitched, all Salem Village sought to know who the witches were. Under constant badgering, sick little Betty Parris sobbed out something about Tituba; the older girls finally admitted a little about her kitchen magic, and the first witch had been pinpointed. But the girls were uneasy that Tituba was being blamed, although the slave cleverly admitted everything, apparently instinctively aware that confessed witches, for whom there might be salvation, were seldom hanged. The afflicted ones cried that Tituba was not alone in practicing witchcraft and they named two other witches, Sarah Good and Sarah Osburn. Sarah Good was a shiftless, dirty, pipe-smoking tramp who wandered with her ragged children from door to door, begging, and who was suspected of stealing when turned away. Well-to-do Sarah Osburn had been considered respectable, but she was a cross, strange woman, and she had not been inside Samuel Parris' church in a year.

Four "yeomen of Salem Village in the County of Essex," one of whom was Thomas Putnam, appeared before the local magistrates and swore out warrants for the arrest of the three accused women on suspicion of witchcraft. Mrs. Osburn was in bed, ill, when arrested and had to be supported even to stand. They were taken to the nearest prison—there was none in Salem Village—and there they were examined for "witches teats from which Satan sucks blood" and "Devil's marks," accepted evidence of guilt. Tituba was found to have "Devils scars" but the examiners were undecided about the moles on the other two. The three were left in leg chains.

On March 1, 1692, a preliminary examination of the women was made in an improvised courtroom in the village church by magistrates Jonathan Corwin and John Hathorne (great-great-grandfather of Nathaniel, who added a "w" to his name), who had been sent from Salem Town, a much larger community a few miles from Salem Village. Neither of these men had any legal training. Professional lawyers were generally disregarded in the colony and at no time did attorneys figure in the proceedings nor did anyone suggest that an accused witch might have the right of counsel.

With the Reverend Mr. Parris assisting the magistrates, the accused were questioned before a throng that filled every inch of the meeting-house and included all the afflicted girls, who were lined up on the front bench. Both Sarah Good and Sarah Osburn claimed innocence—Mrs. Good defiantly, Mrs. Osburn weakly—but what they tried to say was lost in the screams and noisy movements of the girls, who accused them to their faces. Sarah Good's husband William testified that he had "been afraid she was a witch" and had seen "a strange tit or wart" on her body. Dorcas Good, Sarah's 5-year-old daughter, was encouraged to testify against her; the child declared that her mother had familiars: "three birds, one black, one yellow, and these birds hurt children and afflict people."

As the questioning of Tituba began, the girls became motionless and quiet, hanging on her every word—possibly terrified that she might reveal their part in the experimentation with forbidden magic and make them objects of suspicion.

But Tituba didn't incriminate any of them. She knew what the people of Salem Village wanted to hear, and she told it to them, picking up and enlarging upon each suggestion made by her questioners. Yes, she said, she'd been bidden by the Devil to serve him. Goody Osburn and Goody Good and some other unidentified women had hurt the little girls and Tituba had been made to hurt them, too, although she hadn't wanted to. And there was an evil man from Boston, tall and with white hair, who had a book with nine witch names in it, but she could not tell whose names they were because she could not read. Tituba had been made to see red cats and rats, and huge dogs and hogs, and to listen to them talk, and she had been forced to serve them. She had been to many witches' Sabbaths, flying through the sky with the man from Boston, a hog, two cats, and a yellow, woman-headed dog, the last of which was Goody

Osburn's familiar. One of Sarah Good's familiars was a wolf and Tituba had seen Witch Good set the wolf on Elizabeth Hubbard.

Apparently enjoying the rapt attention of the crowd, over whom she was exercising a positive spell, the old slave confessed for three days. Of the small number who doubted the truth of her tale, only a few dared make even mild issue of it—and they were soon sorry. There was a general consensus that anyone expressing skepticism of witchcraft was hiding something and was a witch himself.

The slave John, during Tituba's testimony, succumbed to complete demoniac possession, having roaring fits before witnesses at Ingersoll's Inn across from the meeting-house—thus landing himself in the category of the victims rather than the guilty.

On March 7, the magistrates sent the three women, the first lot of history's "Salem witches," to Boston to be imprisoned until their trial. Two months later, Sarah Osburn died in prison. Sometime during that period, a tiny baby belonging to Sarah Good also died in prison; the records do not tell whether it was born prior to, or during, Mrs. Good's imprisonment.

The jailing of the three witches did not ease the girls' affliction nor lighten their fits. In addition, several married women, including Ann Putnam's mother, began having hysterical seizures. Led by Ann Putnam and Abigail Williams, the afflicted cried out periodically against others of Salem Village: farm woman Martha Corey, who had laughed at the girls' antics as "put-ons"; 71-year-old, deeply pious Rebecca Nurse, whose family had been in a prolonged quarrel with Samuel Parris over a land boundary; little Dorcas Good, who, the girls said, had bitten them; Elizabeth and John Proctor, after John had punished the Proctors' maidservant, Mary Warren, for crying out against Rebecca Nurse; Bridget Bishop, who operated a tavern with a bad reputation; Abigail Hobbs, who "lived like a gypsy"; 80-year-old Giles Corey, Martha's husband; the Reverend George Burroughs, a former minister at Salem, who once bested Ann Putnam's uncle in a lawsuit; and many others. At each examination there were witnesses who testified the accused one was "queer" or "practiseth tricks" or the like, and in each case the girls went into fits. As an example, while Mrs. Corey was before the magistrates, Abigail Williams jumped up, pointed to the rafter overhead, and screamed, "Suffer to look! There sits Goody Corey on the beam suckling a yellow bird betwixt her fingers!"

In April, Hathorne and Corwin were joined in conducting the examinations by four additional magistrates, including Samuel Sewall of Boston and Thomas Danforth, the colony's deputy governor, who served as presiding magistrate. But this resulted in little change in the examining procedure.

At the examination of Elizabeth and John Proctor, Ann Putnam threw herself on the floor and pleaded pathetically that they be made to stop tormenting her. Judge Sewall wrote in his diary, after referring to this scene, "'Twas awful to see how the afflicted persons were agitated." Then, later, he added in the margin, as if remorsefully, "Alas, alas, alas!"

The arrest of 70-year-old John Alden, son of Priscilla and John, as Tituba's "tall man from Boston," added to the excitment in Salem. After fifteen weeks in prison, John Alden managed to escape; he stayed far away until the witch hysteria subsided.

During May 1692, the witch hunts were extended to the villages surrounding Salem, and the jails in all of them grew full. The prisoners, from little Dorcas Good to the several aged and infirm, were forced to exist under such conditions that they grew thin and dirty, with wild, matted hair and sullen eyes—they looked like witches!

There had been no formal trials because there was no legally constituted court to try them. But Sir William Phips, the new royal governor, had arrived in Boston on May 14, and he issued a commission for a Court of Oyer and Terminer to be held in Salem Town, appointing the judges on May 27. The seven judges included Samuel Sewall and three others from Boston, John Richards, William Sergeant, and Wait Winthrop; Bartholomew Gedney from Salem; Nathaniel Saltonstall

from Haverhill; and the new deputy governor, William Stoughton, the presiding justice, from Dorchester.

The court opened in the solidly packed courthouse in Salem Town on the morning of June 2, with Bridget Bishop the first to face the judges—and the assembled afflicted girls. Witnesses testified the tavernkeeper, filthy now in the red dress once considered offensively flashy, had a "preternatural teat" on her body and that she had wrought mischief upon her neighbors even as her "disembodied shape" had tormented the girls. She was sentenced to be "hanged by the neck until dead" on the tenth of June, and on that day the sheriff took her in a cart to Salem's Gallows Hill and so hanged her.

The procedure in the Bishop trial, as well as future trials, was little different from the preliminary examinations: in general, convictions were obtained on the old evidence and the continuing afflictions of the girls. There was a jury, but the judges, and particularly the merciless Chief Justice Stoughton, were all-supreme. Cotton Mather, in his account of the Bishop trial, said, "There was little occasion to prove the witchcraft, it being evident and notorious to all beholders."

A heavily controlling feature in convicting the "witches" was the fact that the Court of Oyer and Terminer had decided to accept "spectral evidence," testimony that an accused had appeared as a "shape" or apparition of some sort rather than her recognizable bodily person, just as had been done in the preliminary examinations. Much of the evidence against all the accused was spectral evidence.

Before the second session of the court, Judge Saltonstall, who was troubled about the kind of evidence being accepted, resigned from the court. Although he did so quietly, his reason must have been suspected because some of the afflicted girls promptly claimed to have been tormented by his "shape," which acted mysteriously. Saltonstall hurried to Haverhill, far removed from the witchcraft scene, and stayed there, but he took to drinking heavily—so heavily that Samuel Sewall, hearing about it, wrote him reprovingly.

His place on the court was filled by Jonathan Corwin, who had helped hold the first examinations and voiced no complaint about the acceptance of spectral evidence.

When the second court session ended on June 30, all five who had been tried—Sarah Good, Rebecca Nurse, Susanna Martin, Elizabeth Howe, Sarah Wildes—had been condemned to die on July 19. At the gallows that day, the Reverend Nicholas Noyes told Sarah Good she would do well to confess because she knew she was a witch. Her reply was loud enough for all the crowd on Gallows Hill to hear, "You are a liar! I am no more a witch than you are a wizard, and if you take away my life God will give you blood to drink!" Tradition has it that, many years later, Noyes choked to death on his own blood.

The third court session, on August 5, again condemned all who were tried—John and Elizabeth Proctor, John Willard, George Jacobs, Martha Carrier, and George Burroughs—but Elizabeth Proctor, pregnant, was given a stay of execution until after the baby's birth. The other five made the trip to Gallows Hill on August 19. Burroughs, speaking from the scaffold ladder, repeated the Lord's Prayer, which no servant of Satan was supposed to be able to do, but it didn't save him.

Cotton Mather, present at the hanging, was having ever stronger doubts about accepting spectral evidence. He had earlier written Judge John Richards, "Do not lay more stress upon pure Spectre evidence than it will bear—It is very certain that the Devills have sometimes represented the shapes of persons not only innocent, but also very vertuous."

On September 9, the court condemned six witches, and on September 17, nine more. Of these fifteen, eight whom preacher Noyes called "firebrands of Hell" were hanged on September 22—Martha Corey, Mary Easty, Alice Parker, Ann Pudeator, Margaret Scott, Wilmot Reed, Samuel Wardwell, and Mary Parker. One of the others escaped, one was pregnant, and five confessed in time to be reprieved. Some fifty-five of those who had confessed earlier, including Tituba, had not been scheduled for trial but were still in prison with those protesting innocence.

Giles Corey was also brought before the court on September 17. When asked how he pleaded, he refused to utter a word. Under law, a man who "stood mute" could not be tried; he could, however, be subjected to *peine forte et dure*—tortured. Corey was taken to a public lot and laid on the ground, and heavy stones were piled on his chest. With each addition of more weight, he was coaxed to answer to his indictment. He moaned, but said not a word. It took Giles Corey two terrible days to die.

Corey's dramatic protest against witch hunting, added to the uneasiness about accepting spectral evidence which had been steadily building, particularly since the execution of the Reverend Mr. Burroughs, began to still the witchcraft hysteria. Lady Phips, the governor's wife, publicly stated the witchcraft trials were a disgrace to the colony. Then the girls cried out against her, and Sir William, furious, called a halt to the court sessions. On October 29, 1692, he issued an order dissolving the Special Court of Oyer and Terminer.

But there was still the problem of the accused who were in jail and who, by law, had to be tried—some 140; an undetermined number had died in jail. Governor Phips appointed another court which began meeting in Salem in January 1693; it did not admit spectral evidence and, in a series of trials, found no one guilty. In May, Sir William, disgusted with the whole affair, issued a proclamation releasing all accused witches from jail. His action brought loud protest from some of the Puritan ministers, but it ended the Salem witch hunts. Twenty had been put to death, others had died of ill treatment, and many, like little Dorcas Good, had minds and bodies permanently injured by their ordeals. The property of all the accused had been seized at the time of their arrest and few of the victims were able to recover anything.

Parris, who was held responsible by many for the Devil's work in Salem, was ousted from the

Salem Village church; he and his family afterward wandered from one small parish to another.

In 1696, a document signed by twelve of the men who had served as jurors in some of the witchcraft cases was presented to the public. It concluded, "We do therefore hereby signify to all in general, and to the surviving sufferers in special, our deep sense of, and sorrow for, our errors, in acting on such evidence to the condemning of any person; and do hereby declare that we justly fear that we were sadly deluded and mistaken. . . . We do heartily ask forgiveness of you all. . . ."

On January 14, 1697, which had been declared a day of prayer and fasting in repentance of sins in the whole of Massachusetts Bay, Samuel Sewall publicly acknowledged personal guilt for his actions as a judge of the witchcraft trials and asked for the forgiveness of God and man. He stood before the congregation of Boston's Third Church while the minister read his statement of deep repentance. But he did not stop there; during his long life, on the anniversary of the fast day, he did penance. As late as 1720, after reading a passage in a New England history about the Salem trials, he wrote in his diary, "The good and gracious God be pleased to save New England and me and my family!" With the exception of Nathaniel Saltonstall, who had early run from the Salem court, Sewall was the only judge at the trials who admitted error.

Of the afflicted girls, Ann Putnam was the only one to express remorse for her actions, so far as is known. In August 1706, Ann, a semi-invalid who was only 26 but who looked much older and had less than ten years of life remaining, "made public confession." Head bowed, she stood in the Salem Village church while the minister read the long confession she had written. She claimed to have acted "not out of anger, malice or ill will," but because of being deluded by Satan. Her confession ended, "I desire to lie in the dust and earnestly beg forgiveness of God and from all those whom I have given just cause of sorrow and offense, whose relatives were taken away and accused."

On January 15, 1697, the day after the Massachusetts fast day, Cotton Mather wrote in his diary that he had been "afflicted last night with discouraging thoughts, as if unavoidable marks of the Divine Displeasure must overtake my family for my not appearing with vigor enough to stop the proceedings of the judges when the inextricable storm from the invisible world assaulted the country. . . ." The Puritans had not reversed their position as to belief in witchcraft; they had just rejected spectral evidence as a means for catching witches.

Study Questions

1. Why was the Massachusetts Bay Colony a likely place for belief in witchcraft?

2. Since educated opinions are still in disagreement about the source of the girls' behavior, do you feel that their behavior was more fraudulent or pathological? Why?

3. What was Tituba's alleged role in the bewitchments?

4. What was "spectral" evidence? How was it used in the trials? Would it be admitted in a court of law today? Why or why not?

5. Were the accused and the convicted only older women? Were they all hanged? Explain.

6. Why are some historical events referred to as "modern-day witch-hunts"? Can you provide an example?

Bibliography

The Salem witchcraft trials remain the single most studied event in colonial history. Certainly, the drama of the events accounts for much of the scholarly interest. However, of equal importance is the fact that the documentation produced by the trials provides the historian with a comprehensive view of Salem society. For students interested in these sources, Paul Boyer and Stephen Nissenbaum, eds., *The Salem Witchcraft Papers: Verbatim Transcripts of the Legal Documents of the Salem Witchcraft Outbreak of 1692,* three volumes (1977) is an ideal starting place. The first significant history of the event is Charles W. Upham, *Salem Witchcraft,* two volumes (1867). Marion Starkey's *The Devil in Massachusetts* (1949) is a very readable description. The number of first-rate scholarly analyses of the trials is remarkable, including Chadwick Hansen, *Witchcraft at Salem* (1969); Paul Boyer and Stephen Nissenbaum, *Salem Possessed: The Social Origins of Witchcraft* (1974); John P. Demos, *Entertaining Satan: Witchcraft and the Culture of Early New England* (1982); Frances Hill, *The Delusion of Satan: The Full Story of the Salem Witchcraft Trials* (1997); Peter Charles Hoffer, *The Devil's Disciples: Makers of the Salem Witchcraft Trials* (1996); and Mary Beth Norton, *In the Devil's Snare: The Salem Witchcraft Crisis of 1692* (2002).

READING 5

Under the Banner of King Death: The Social World of the Anglo-American Pirates, 1716 to 1726

Marcus Rediker

We tend to think of Puritans as ascetics who rejected material goods, yet nothing could be further from the truth. It is true Puritans were opposed to luxury and gluttony, but they had no problem with the creature comforts earned by "honeste industrie" and the pursuit of a "godly calling." Puritans realized early on, however, that New England's rocky soil meant many in the community would not be pursuing their "calling," nor earning disposable income, as grain farmers. Nevertheless, forests and grasslands were plentiful in New England, and by the late 1600s processing lumber, raising livestock, and building ships anchored a healthy regional economy that enabled Puritans to become major players in the mercantile networks of the Atlantic basin. In what became known as the "triangular trade," New England merchants exchanged lumber, cattle, and rum for slaves and manufactured goods in all three of the major trading areas on the Atlantic rim—the Gold Coast of Africa, London, and the West Indies.

New England's success in the "triangular trade" during the seventeenth and eighteenth centuries would not have been possible without the direct or implicit protection of an assertive and expansive mother England and her Royal Navy. American merchants from all regions were grateful for the protection and grew increasingly patriotic when British military power saved the colonies from foreign invasion during the era's numerous intercontinental conflicts. Still, membership in a mercantile empire automatically involved colonists directly in England's wars with European rivals France and Spain, making American merchants the target not only of the navies of opposing powers, but of privateers attacking British trade networks and colonial outposts while the Royal Navy was busy elsewhere. Of course, some American sea captains used periods of warfare as an excuse to become pirates themselves and raid enemy shipping.

Marcus Rediker's "Under the Banner of King Death" picks up the tale of the Atlantic pirates just as England and her American colonies were emerging scarred but victorious from twenty-five years of warfare with France and Spain, warfare sparked by England's "Glorious Revolution" (1688). In the Treaty of Utrecht (1713), which ended the conflict, the combatants made a peace that lasted for a generation and gave England commercial and colonial supremacy in the Atlantic basin. Yet, ironically, the end of war made the pirate threat to the British empire's Atlantic commerce temporarily worse, as disaffected and embittered British sailors mustered out of the peace-time fleet and turned to privateering as an easy way to use their naval skills for profit as well as revenge against cruel masters.

Ten years of pursuit by the Royal Navy, along with trials and public mass hangings in the port cities of the American colonies, finally crushed the pirate threat. But, as Rediker shows, this tale of warfare on the high seas is only part of the story. He demonstrates that pirate crews were as much a part of the Atlantic mercantile world as Puritan merchants and British men-of-war. Moreover, pirate crews were just as jealously protective of their "rights"—and just as skeptical of despotic royal authority—as the British Parliamentarians and American colonists who ousted the Catholic absolutist James II and his colonial officers in the Revolution of 1688. Rediker's pirates, of course, mostly opted out of leading a traditional life under the post-revolutionary British government. Yet, as you read Rediker's article, keep in mind that the social code of the pirates' shadow world had much in common with the strident anti-authoritarianism of American colonists, and that communities of disaffected sailors extended to all of the major port cities of the British empire in the 1700s, including those like Boston and New York which would become hotbeds of rebellion during America's revolutionary era.

Writing to the Board of Trade in 1724, Governor Alexander Spotswood of Virginia lamented his lack of "some safe opportunity to get home" to London. He insisted that he would travel only in a well-armed man-of-war.

Your Lordships will easily conceive my Meaning when you reflect on the Vigorous part I've acted to suppress Pirates: and if those barbarous Wretches can be moved to cut off the Nose & Ears of a Master for but correcting his own Sailors, what inhuman treatment must I expect, should I fall within their power, who have been markt as the principle object of their vengeance, for cutting off their arch Pirate Thatch [Teach, also known as Blackbeard], with all his grand Designs, & making so many of their Fraternity to swing in the open air of Virginia.

Spotswood knew these pirates well. He had authorized the expedition that returned to Virginia boasting Blackbeard's head as a trophy. He had done his share to see that many pirates swung on Virginia gallows. He knew that pirates had a fondness for revenge, that they often punished ship captains for "correcting" their crews, and that a kind of "fraternity" prevailed among them. He had good reason to fear them.

The Anglo-American pirates active between 1716 and 1726 occupied a grand position in the long history of robbery at sea. Their numbers, near five thousand, were extraordinary, and their plunderings were exceptional in both volume and value. Spotswood and other officials and merchants produced a plentiful body of written testimony on pirates and their ways, but historians, though long fascinated by sea-rovers, have not used this material to full advantage. This essay explores the social and cultural dimensions of

Marcus Rediker, " 'Under the Banner of King Death': The Social World of Anglo-American Pirates, 1716 to 1726," *William and Mary Quarterly*, 3d Ser., 38 (April 1981) 203-27. Reprinted by permission of the Omohundro Institute of Early American History and Culture.

piracy, focusing on pirates' experience, the organization of their ships, and their social relations and consciousness, with observations on the social and economic context of the crime and its culture. Piracy represented crime on a massive scale—crime as a way of life voluntarily chosen, for the most part, by large numbers of men and directly challenging the ways of the society from which the pirates excepted themselves. The main intent of this essay is to see how piracy looked from the inside and to examine the kinds of social order that pirates forged beyond the reach of traditional authority. Beneath the Jolly Roger, "the banner of King Death," a new social world took shape once pirates had, as one of them put it, "the choice in themselves."

Contemporary estimates of the pirate population during the period under consideration placed the number between one and two thousand at any one time. This range seems generally accurate. From records that describe the activities of pirate ships and from reports or projections of crew sizes, it appears that eighteen to twenty-four hundred Anglo-American pirates were active between 1716 and 1718, fifteen hundred to two thousand between 1719 and 1722, and one thousand to fifteen hundred declining to fewer than two hundred between 1723 and 1726. In the only estimate we have from the other side of the law, a band of pirates in 1716 claimed that there were "30 Company of them," or roughly twenty-four hundred men, around the world. In all, some forty-five to fifty-five hundred men went, as they called it, "upon the account."

These sea-robbers followed lucrative trade and, like their predecessors, sought bases for their depredations in the Caribbean Sea and the Indian Ocean. The Bahama Islands, no longer defended or governed by the crown, began in 1716 to attract pirates by the hundreds. By 1718 a torrent of complaints moved George I to commission Woodes Rogers to lead an expedition to bring the islands under control. Rogers's efforts largely succeeded, and pirates scattered to the unpeopled inlets of the Carolinas and to Africa. They had frequented African shores as early as 1691; by

1718, Madagascar served as both an entrepôt for booty and as a spot for temporary settlement. At the mouth of the Sierra Leone River on Africa's western coast pirates stopped off for "whoring and drinking" and to unload goods. Theaters of operation among pirates shifted, however, according to the policing designs of the Royal Navy. Pirates favored the Caribbean because of its shallow waters and numerous unsettled cays, but generally, as one pirate noted, these rovers were "dispers't into several parts of the World." Sea-robbers sought and usually found bases near major trade routes, as distant as possible from the powers of the state.

Almost all pirates had labored as merchant seamen, Royal Navy sailors, or privateersmen. The vast majority came from captured merchantmen as volunteers, for reasons suggested by Dr. Samuel Johnson's observation that "no man will be a sailor who has contrivance enough to get himself into a jail; for being in a ship is being in jail with the chance of being drowned. . . . A man in jail has more room, better food, and commonly better company." Merchant seamen got a hard, close look at death: disease and accidents were commonplace in their occupation, rations were often meager, and discipline was brutal. Each ship was "a little kingdom" whose captain held a near-absolute power which he often abused. Peacetime wages for sailors were consistently low between 1643 and 1797; fraud and irregularities in the distribution of pay were general. A prime purpose of eighteenth-century maritime laws was "to assure a ready supply of cheap, docile labor." Merchant seamen also had to contend with impressment as practiced by the Royal Navy.

Some pirates had served in the navy where conditions aboard ship were no less harsh. Food supplies often ran short, wages were low, mortality was high, discipline severe, and desertion consequently chronic. As one officer reported, the navy had trouble fighting pirates because the king's ships were "so much disabled by sickness, death, and desertion of their seamen." In 1722 the crown sent the *Weymouth* and the *Swallow* in

Blackbeard (Edward Teach) was killed in 1718 by a royal navy ship.

search of a pirate convoy. Royal surgeon John Atkins, noting that merchant seamen were frequently pressed, underlined precisely what these sailors had to fear when he recorded that the "*Weymouth,* who brought out of *England* a Compliment [*sic*] of 240 Men," had "at the end of the Voyage 280 dead upon her Books." Epidemics, consumption, and scurvy raged on royal ships, and the men were "caught in a machine from which there was no escape, bar desertion, incapacitation, or death."

Pirates who had served on privateering vessels knew well that this employment was far less onerous than on merchant or naval ships: food was usually more plentiful, the pay considerably higher, and the work shifts generally shorter. Even so, owing to rigid discipline and to other grievances, mutinies were not uncommon. On Woodes Rogers's spectacularly successful privateering expedition of 1708–1711, Peter Clark was thrown into irons for wishing himself "aboard a Pirate" and saying that "he should be glad that an Enemy, who could over-power us, was a-long-side of us."

Whether from the merchant service, the navy, or the privateering enterprise, pirates necessarily came from seafaring employments. Piracy emphatically was not an option open to landlubbers since sea-robbers "entertain'd so contemptible a Notion of Landmen." Men who became pirates were grimly familiar with the rigors of life at sea and with a single-sex community of work.

Ages are known for 117 pirates active between 1716 and 1726. The range was seventeen to fifty years, the mean 27.4, and the median 27; the twenty-to-twenty-four and the twenty-five-to-twenty-nine age categories had the highest concentrations, with 39 and 37 men respectively. Significantly, 59.3 percent were aged twenty-five or older. Given the high mortality rates within the occupations from which pirates came, these ages were advanced. Though evidence is sketchy, most pirates seem not to have been bound to land and home by familial ties or obligations. Wives and children are rarely mentioned in the records of trials of pirates, and pirate vessels, to forestall desertion, often would "take no Married Man." Almost without exception, pirates came from the lowest social classes. They were, as a royal official condescendingly observed, "desperate Rogues" who could have little hope in life ashore. These traits served as bases of unity when men of the sea decided, in search of something better, to become pirates.

These characteristics had a vital bearing on the ways pirates organized their daily activities. Contemporaries who claimed that pirates had "no regular command among them" mistook a different social order—different from the ordering of merchant, naval, and privateering vessels—for disorder. This social order, articulated in the organization of the pirate ship, was conceived and deliberately constructed by the pirates themselves. Its hallmark was a rough, improvised, but effective egalitarianism that placed authority in the collective hands of the crew.

A striking uniformity of rules and customs prevailed aboard pirate ships, each of which functioned under the terms of written articles, a compact drawn up at the beginning of a voyage or upon election of a new captain, and agreed to by the crew. By these articles crews allocated authority, distributed plunder, and enforced discipline. These arrangements made the captain the creature of his crew. Demanding someone both bold of temper and skilled in navigation, the men elected their captain. They gave him few privileges: he "or any other Officer is allowed no more [food] than another man, nay, the Captain cannot keep his Cabbin to himself." A merchant captain held captive by pirates noted with displeasure that crew members slept on the ship wherever they pleased, "the Captain himself not being allowed a Bed." The crew granted the captain unquestioned authority "in fighting, chasing, or being chased," but "in all other Matters whatsoever" he was "governed by a Majority." As the majority elected, so it could depose. Captains were snatched from their positions for cowardice, cruelty, or refusing "to take and plunder English Vessels." One captain incurred the class-conscious wrath of his crew for being too "Gentleman-like." Occasionally, a despotic captain was summarily executed. As pirate Francis Kennedy explained, most sea-robbers, "having suffered formerly from the ill-treatment of their officers, provided carefully against any such evil" once they arranged their own command.

To prevent the misuse of authority, countervailing powers were designated for the quartermaster, who was elected to protect "the Interest of the Crew." His tasks were to adjudicate minor disputes, distribute food and money, and in some instances to lead attacks on prize vessels. He served as a "civil Magistrate" and dispensed necessaries "with an Equality to them all." The quartermaster often became the captain of a captured ship when the captor was overcrowded or divided by discord. This containment of authority within a dual executive was a distinctive feature of social organization among pirates.

The decisions that had the greatest bearing on the welfare of the crew were generally reserved to the council, a body usually including every man on the ship. The council determined such matters as where the best prizes could be taken and how disruptive dissension was to be resolved. Some crews continually used the council, "carrying every thing by a majority of votes"; others set up the council as a court. The decisions made by this body constituted the highest authority on a pirate ship: even the boldest captain dared not challenge a council's mandate.

The distribution of plunder was regulated explicitly by the ship's articles, which allocated booty according to skills and duties. Captain and quartermaster received between one and one-half and two shares; gunners, boatswains, mates, carpenters, and doctors, one and one-quarter or one and one-half; all others got one share each. This pay system represented a radical departure from practices in the merchant service, Royal Navy, or privateering. It leveled an elaborate hierarchy of pay ranks and decisively reduced the disparity between the top and bottom of the scale. Indeed, this must have been one of the most egalitarian plans for the disposition of resources to be found anywhere in the early eighteenth century. The scheme indicates that pirates did not consider themselves wage laborers but rather risk-sharing partners. If, as a noted historian of piracy, Philip Gosse, has suggested, "the pick of all seamen were pirates," the equitable distribution of plunder and the conception of the partnership may be understood as the work of men who valued and respected the skills of their comrades. But not all booty was dispensed this way. A portion went into a "common fund" to provide for the men who sustained injury of lasting effect. The loss of eyesight or any appendage merited compensation. By this welfare system pirates attempted to guard against debilities caused by accidents, to protect skills, and to promote loyalty within the group.

The articles also regulated discipline aboard ship, though "discipline" is perhaps a misnomer for a rule system that left large ranges of behavior uncontrolled. Less arbitrary than that of the merchant service and less codified than that of the navy, discipline among pirates always depended on a collective sense of transgression. Many misdeeds were accorded "what Punishment the Captain and Majority of the Company shall think fit," and it is noteworthy that pirates did not often resort to the whip. Their discipline, if no less severe in certain cases, was generally tolerant of behavior that provoked punishment in other maritime occupations. Three major methods of discipline were employed, all conditioned by the fact that pirate ships were crowded: an average crew numbered near eighty on a 250-ton vessel. The articles of Bartholomew Roberts's ship revealed one tactic for maintaining order: "No striking one another on board, but every Man's Quarrels to be ended on Shore at Sword and Pistol." Antagonists were to fight a duel with pistols, but if both their first shots missed, then with swords, and the first to draw blood was declared the victor. By taking such conflicts off the ship (and symbolically off the sea), this practice promoted harmony in the crowded quarters below decks. The ideal of harmony was also reflected when, in an often-used disciplinary action, pirates made a crew member the "Governor of an Island." Men who were incorrigibly disruptive or who transgressed important rules were marooned. For defrauding his mates by taking more than a proper share of plunder, for deserting or malingering during battle, for keeping secrets from the crew, or for stealing, a pirate risked being deposited "where he was sure to encounter Hardships." The ultimate method of maintaining order was execution. This penalty was exacted for bringing on board "a Boy or a Woman" or for meddling with a "prudent Woman" on a prize ship, but was most commonly invoked to punish a captain who abused his authority.

Some crews attempted to circumvent disciplinary problems by taking "no Body against their Wills." By the same logic, they would keep no unwilling person. The confession of pirate Edward Davis in 1718 indicates that oaths of honor were used to cement the loyalty of new members: "at first the old Pirates were a little shy of the new ones, . . . yet in a short time the *New Men* being sworn to be faithful, and not to cheat the Company to the Value of a *Piece of Eight,* they all consulted and acted together with great unanimity, and no distinction was made between *Old* and *New.*" Yet for all their efforts to blunt the cutting edge of authority and to maintain harmony and cohesion, conflict could not always be contained. Occasionally, upon election of a new captain, men who favored other leadership drew up new articles and sailed away from their former mates. The social organization constructed by pirates, although flexible, was unable to accommodate severe, sustained conflict. The egalitarian and collective exercise of authority by pirates had both negative and positive effects. Although it produced a chronic instability, it also guaranteed continuity: the very process by which new crews were established helped to ensure a social uniformity and, as we shall see, a consciousness of kind among pirates.

One important mechanism in this continuity can be seen by charting the connections among pirate crews. The accompanying diagram [Figure 5.1, see p. 58], arranged according to vessel captaincy, demonstrates that by splintering, by sailing in consorts, or by other associations, roughly thirty-six hundred pirates—more than 70 percent of all those active between 1716 and 1726—fit into two main lines of genealogical descent. Captain Benjamin Hornigold and the pirate rendezvous in the Bahamas stood at the origin of an intricate lineage that ended with the hanging of John Phillips's crew in June 1724. The second line, spawned in the chance meeting of the lately mutinous crews of George Lowther and Edward Low in 1722, culminated in the executions of William Fly and his men in July 1726. It was primarily within and through this network that the social organization of the pirate ship took on its significance, transmitting and preserving customs and meanings, and helping to structure and perpetuate the pirates' social world.

Pirates constructed that world in defiant contradistinction to the ways of the world they left behind, in particular to its salient figures of power, the merchant captain and the royal official, and to

the system of authority those figures represented and enforced. When eight pirates were tried in Boston in 1718, merchant captain Thomas Checkley told of the capture of his ship by pirates who "pretended," he said, "to be Robbin Hoods Men." Eric Hobsbawm has defined social banditry as a "universal and virtually unchanging phenomenon," an "endemic peasant protest against oppression and poverty: a cry for vengeance on the rich and the oppressors." Its goal is "a traditional world in which men are justly dealt with, not a new and perfect world"; Hobsbawm calls its advocates "revolutionary traditionalists." Pirates, of course, were not peasants, but they fit Hobsbawm's formulation in every other respect. Of special importance was their "cry for vengeance."

Spotswood told no more than the simple truth when he expressed his fear of pirate vengeance, for the very names of pirate ships made the same threat. Edward Teach, whom Spotswood's men cut off, called his vessel *Queen Anne's Revenge;* other notorious craft were Stede Bonnet's *Revenge* and John Cole's *New York Revenge's Revenge.* The foremost target of vengeance was the merchant captain. Frequently, "in a far distant latitude," as one seaman put it, "unlimited power, bad views, ill nature and ill principles all concur[red]" in a ship's commander. This was a man "past all restraint," who often made life miserable for his crew. Spotswood also noted how pirates avenged the captain's "correcting" of his sailors. In 1722, merchant captains Isham Randolph, Constantine Cane, and William Halladay petitioned Spotswood "in behalf of themselves and other Masters of Ships" for "some certain method . . . for punishing mutinous & disobedient Seamen." They explained that captains faced great danger "in case of meeting with Pyrates, where we are sure to suffer all the tortures w[hi]ch such an abandoned crew can invent, upon the least intimation of our Striking any of our men."

Upon seizing a merchantman, pirates often administered the "Distribution of Justice," "enquiring into the Manner of the Commander's Behaviour to their Men, and those, against whom Complaint was made" were "whipp'd and pickled." In 1724, merchant captain Richard Hawkins

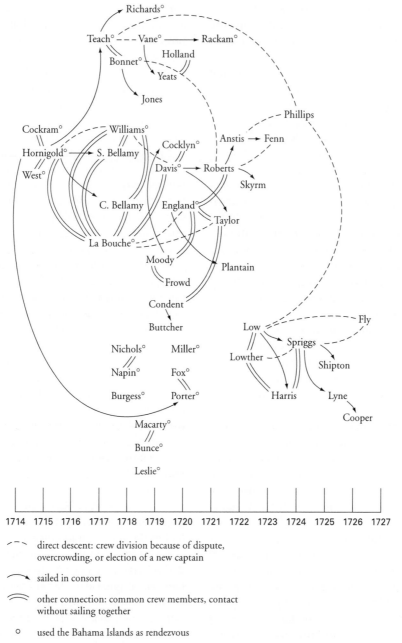

Figure 5.1 *Connections Among Anglo-American Pirate Crews, 1714 to 1726*

1714 1715 1716 1717 1718 1719 1720 1721 1722 1723 1724 1725 1726 1727

- - - direct descent: crew division because of dispute, overcrowding, or election of a new captain

⌒ sailed in consort

⌒⌒ other connection: common crew members, contact without sailing together

° used the Bahama Islands as rendezvous

described another form of retribution, a torture known as the "Sweat": "Between decks they stick Candles round the Mizen-Mast, and about twenty-five men surround it with Points of Swords, Penknives, Compasses, Forks, Etc. in each of their hands: *Culprit* enters the Circle; the Violin plays a merry Jig; and he must run for about ten Minutes, while each man runs his Instrument into his Posteriors." Many captured captains were "barbarously used," and some were summarily executed. Pirate Philip Lyne carried this vengeance to its bloodiest extremity, confessing when apprehended in 1726 that "during the time of his Piracy" he "had killed 37 Masters of Vessels."

Still, the punishment of captains was not indiscriminate, for a captain who had been "an honest Fellow that never abused any Sailors" was often rewarded by pirates. The best description of pirates' notions of justice comes from merchant captain William Snelgrave's account of his capture in 1719. On April 1, Snelgrave's ship was seized by Thomas Cocklyn's crew of rovers at the mouth of the Sierra Leone River. Cocklyn was soon joined by men captained by Oliver LaBouche and Howell Davis, and Snelgrave spent the next thirty days among two hundred forty pirates.

The capture was effected when twelve pirates in a small boat came alongside Snelgrave's ship, which was manned by forty-five sailors. Snelgrave ordered his crew to arms; though they refused, the pirate quartermaster, infuriated by the command, drew a pistol. He then, Snelgrave testified, "with the but-end endeavoured to beat out my Brains," until "some of my People . . . cried out aloud 'For God sake don't kill our Captain, for we never were with a better Man.' " The quartermaster, Snelgrave noted, "told me, 'my Life was safe provided none of my People complained against me.' I replied, 'I was sure none of them could.' "

Snelgrave was taken to Cocklyn, who told him, "I am sorry you have met with bad usage after Quarter given, but 'tis the Fortune of War sometimes. . . . [I]f you tell the truth, and your Men make no Complaints against you, you shall be kindly used." Howell Davis, commander of the largest of the pirate ships, reprimanded Cocklyn's men for their roughness and, by Snelgrave's account, expressed himself "ashamed to hear how I had been used by them. That they should remember their reasons for going a pirating were to revenge themselves on base Merchants and cruel commanders of Ships. . . . [N]o one of my People, even those that had entered with them gave me the least ill-character. . . . [I]t was plain they loved me."

Snelgrave's character proved so respectable that the pirates proposed to give him a captured ship with full cargo and to sell the goods for him. Then they would capture a Portuguese slaver, sell the slaves, and give the proceeds to Snelgrave so that he could "return with a large sum of Money to London, and bid the Merchants defiance." The proposal was "unanimously approved" by the pirates, but fearing a charge of complicity, Snelgrave hesitated to accept it. Davis then interceded, saying that he favored "allowing every Body to go to the Devil in their own way" and that he knew that Snelgrave feared for "his Reputation." The refusal was graciously accepted, Snelgrave claiming that "the Tide being turned, they were as kind to me, as they had been at first severe."

Snelgrave related another revealing episode. While he remained in pirate hands, a decrepit schooner belonging to the Royal African Company sailed into the Sierra Leone and was taken by his captors. Simon Jones, a member of Cocklyn's crew, urged his mates to burn the ship since he had been poorly treated while in the company's employ. The pirates were about to do so when another of them, James Stubbs, protested that such action would only "serve the Company's interests" since the ship was worth but little. He also pointed out that "the poor People that now belong to her, and have been on so long a voyage, will lose their Wages, which I am sure is Three times the Value of the Vessel." The pirates concurred and returned the ship to its crew, who "came safe home to England in it." Captain Snelgrave also returned to England soon after this incident, but eleven of his seamen remained behind as pirates.

Snelgrave seems to have been an exceptionally decent captain. Pirates like Howell Davis claimed that abusive treatment by masters of merchant-men contributed mightily to their willingness to become searobbers. John Archer, whose career as a pirate dated from 1718 when he sailed with Edward Teach, uttered a final protest before his execution in 1724: "I could wish that Masters of Vessels would not use their Men with so much Severity, as many of them do, which exposes us to great Temptations." William Fly, facing the gallows for murder and piracy in 1726, angrily said, "I can't charge myself,—I shan't own myself Guilty of any Murder,—Our Captain and his Mate used us Barbarously. We poor Men can't have Justice done us. There is nothing said to our Commanders, let them never so much abuse us, and use us like Dogs." To pirates revenge was justice; punishment was meted out to barbarous captains, as befitted the captains' crimes.

Sea-robbers who fell into the hands of the state received the full force of penalties for crimes against property. The official view of piracy as crime was outlined in 1718 by Vice-Admiralty Judge Nicholas Trott in his charge to the jury in the trial of Stede Bonnet and thirty-three members of his crew at Charleston, South Carolina. Declaring that "the Sea was given by God for the use of Men, and is subject to Dominion and Property, as well as the Land," Trott observed of the accused that "the Law of Nations never granted to them a Power to change the Right of Property." Pirates on trial were denied benefit of clergy, were "called *Hostis Humani Generis,* with whom neither Faith nor Oath" were to be kept, and were regarded as *Brutes, and Beasts of Prey.*" Turning from the jury to the accused, Trott circumspectly surmised that "no further Good or Benefit can be expected from you but by the Example of your Deaths."

The insistence on obtaining this final benefit locked royal officials and pirates into a system of reciprocal terrorism. As royal authorities offered bounties for captured pirates, so too did pirates "offer any price" for certain officials. In Virginia in 1720 one of six pirates facing the gallows "called for a Bottle of Wine, and taking a Glass of it, he Drank Damnation to the Governour and Confu-

sion to the Colony, which the rest pledged." Not to be outdone, Governor Spotswood thought it "necessary for the greater Terrour to hang up four of them in Chains." Pirates demonstrated disdain for state authority when George I extended general pardons for piracy in 1717 and 1718. Some accepted the grace but refused to reform; others "seem'd to slight it," and the most defiant "used the King's Proclamation with great contempt, and tore it into pieces." One pirate crew downed its punch proclaiming, "Curse the King and all the Higher Powers." The social relations of piracy were marked by vigorous, often violent, antipathy toward traditional authority.

At the Charleston trial over which Trott presided, Richard Allen, attorney general of South Carolina, told the jury that "pirates prey upon all Mankind, their own Species and Fellow-Creatures without Distinction of Nations or Religions." Allen was mistaken in one significant point: pirates did not prey on one another. Rather, they consistently expressed in numerous and subtle ways a highly developed consciousness of kind. Here we turn from the external social relations of piracy to the internal, in order to examine this consciousness of kind—in a sense, a strategy for survival—and the collectivistic ethos it expressed.

Pirates showed recurrent willingness to join forces at sea and in port. In April 1719, when Howell Davis and crew sailed into the Sierra Leone River, the pirates captained by Thomas Cocklyn were wary until they saw on the approaching ship "her Black Flag," then "immediately they were easy in their minds, and a little time after" the crews "saluted one another with their Cannon." Other crews exchanged similar greetings and, like Davis and Cocklyn who combined their powers, frequently invoked an unwritten code of hospitality to forge spontaneous alliances.

This communitarian urge was perhaps most evident in the pirate strongholds of Madagascar and Sierra Leone. Sea-robbers occasionally chose more sedentary lifeways on various thinly populated islands, and they contributed a notorious number of men to the community of logwood cutters at the Bay of Campeachy in the Gulf of

Mexico. In 1718 a royal official complained of a "nest of pirates" in the Bahamas "who already esteem themselves a community, and to have one common interest."

To perpetuate such community it was necessary to minimize conflict not only on each ship but also among separate bands of pirates. Indeed, one of the strongest indicators of consciousness of kind lies in the manifest absence of discord between different pirate crews. To some extent this was even a transnational matter: French and Anglo-American pirates usually cooperated peaceably, only occasionally exchanging cannon fire. Anglo-American crews consistently refused to attack one another.

In no way was the pirate sense of fraternity, which Spotswood and others noted, more forcefully expressed than in the threats and acts of revenge taken by pirates. Theirs was truly a case of hanging together or being hanged separately. In April 1717, the pirate ship *Whidah* was wrecked near Boston. Most of its crew perished; the survivors were jailed. In July, Thomas Fox, a Boston ship captain, was taken by pirates who "Questioned him whether anything was done to the Pyrates in Boston Goall," promising "that if the Prisoners Suffered they would Kill every Body they took belonging to New England." Shortly after this incident, Teach's sea-rovers captured a merchant vessel and, "because she belonged to Boston, [Teach] alledging the People of Boston had hanged some of the Pirates, so burnt her." Teach declared that all Boston ships deserved a similar fate. Charles Vane, reputedly a most fearsome pirate, "would give no quarter to the Bermudians" and punished them and "cut away their masts upon account of one Thomas Brown who was (some time) detain'd in these Islands upon suspicion of piracy." Brown apparently had plans to sail as Vane's consort until foiled by his capture.

In September 1720, pirates captained by Bartholomew Roberts "openly and in the daytime burnt and destroyed . . . vessels in the Road of Basseterre [St. Kitts] and had the audaciousness to insult H. M. Fort," avenging the execution of "their comrades at Nevis." Roberts then sent word to the

governor that "they would Come and Burn the Town [Sandy Point] about his Ears for hanging the Pyrates there." In 1721, Spotswood relayed information to the Council of Trade and Plantations that Roberts "said he expected to be joined by another ship and would then visit Virginia, and avenge the pirates who have been executed here." The credibility of the threat was confirmed by the unanimous resolution of the Virginia Executive Council that "the Country be put into an immediate posture of Defense." Lookouts and beacons were quickly provided, and communications with neighboring colonies effected. "Near 60 Cannon," Spotswood later reported, were "mounted on sundry Substantial Batteries."

In 1723 pirate captain Francis Spriggs vowed to find a Captain Moore "and put him to death for being the cause of the death of [pirate] Lowther," and, shortly after, similarly pledged to go "in quest of Captain Solgard," who had overpowered a pirate ship commanded by Charles Harris. In January 1724, Lieutenant Governor Charles Hope of Bermuda wrote to the Board of Trade that he found it difficult to procure trial evidence against pirates because residents "feared that this very execution wou'd make our vessels fare the worse for it, when they happen'd to fall into pirate hands."

Pirates also affirmed their unity symbolically. Some evidence indicates that sea-robbers may have had a sense of belonging to a separate, in some manner exclusive, speech community. Philip Ashton, who spent sixteen months among pirates in 1722, noted that "according to the Pirates usual Custom, and *in their proper Dialect,* asked me, If I would sign their Articles." Many sources suggest that cursing, swearing, and blaspheming may have been defining traits of this style of speech. For example, near the Sierra Leone River a British official named Plunkett pretended to cooperate with, but then attacked, the pirates with Bartholomew Roberts. Plunkett was captured, and Roberts

upon the first sight of Plunkett swore at him like any Devil, for his Irish Impudence in daring to resist him. Old Plunkett, finding he had

*got into bad Company, fell a swearing and
cursing as fast or faster than Roberts; which
made the rest of the Pirates laugh heartily, desiring Roberts to sit down and hold his Peace,
for he had no Share in the Pallaver with Plunkett at all. So that by meer Dint of Cursing and
Damning, Old Plunkett . . . sav'd his life.*

Admittedly we can see only outlines here, but it
appears that the symbolic connectedness, the
consciousness of kind, extended into the domain of language.

Certainly the best known symbol of piracy is
the flag, the Jolly Roger. Less known and appreci-
ated is the fact that the flag was very widely used:
no fewer, and probably a great many more, than
two thousand five hundred men sailed under it.
So general an adoption indicates an advanced
state of group identification. The Jolly Roger was
described as a "black Ensign, in the Middle of
which is a large white Skeleton with a Dart in one
hand striking a bleeding Heart, and in the other an
Hour Glass." Although there was considerable
variation in particulars among these flags, there
was also a general uniformity of chosen images.
The flag background was black, adorned with
white representational figures. The most common symbol was the human skull, or "death's
head," sometimes isolated but more frequently
the most prominent feature of an entire skeleton.
Other recurring items were a weapon—cutlass,
sword, or dart—and an hour glass.

The flag was intended to terrify the pirates'
prey, but its triad of interlocking symbols—death,
violence, limited time—simultaneously pointed to
meaningful parts of the seaman's experience, and
eloquently bespoke the pirates' own consciousness of themselves as preyed upon in turn. Pirates
seized the symbol of mortality from ship captains
who used the skull "as a marginal sign in their logs
to indicate the record of a death." Seamen who became pirates escaped from one closed system only
to find themselves encased in another. But as
pirates—and only as pirates—these men were
able to fight back beneath the somber colors of
"King Death" against those captains, merchants,

and officials who waved banners of authority.
Moreover, pirates self-righteously perceived their
situation and the excesses of these powerful figures through a collectivistic ethos that had been
forged in the struggles for survival.

The self-righteousness of pirates was strongly
linked to the "traditional world in which men are
justly dealt with," as described by Hobsbawm. It
found expression in their social rules, their egalitarian social organization, and their notions of revenge and justice. By walking "to the Gallows
without a Tear," by calling themselves "Honest
Men" and "Gentlemen," and by speaking self-
servingly but proudly of their "Conscience" and
"Honor," pirates flaunted their certitude. When,
in 1720, ruling groups concluded that "nothing
but force will subdue them," many pirates responded by intensifying their commitment. It was
observed of Edward Low's crew in 1724 that they
"swear, with the most direful Imprecations, that if
ever they should find themselves overpower'd
they would immediately blow their ship up rather
than suffer themselves to be hang'd like Dogs."
These sea-robbers would not "do Jolly Roger the
Disgrace to be struck."

This consciousness of kind among pirates manifested itself in an elaborate social code. Through
rule, custom, and symbol the code prescribed
specific behavioral standards intended to preserve the social world that pirates built for themselves. As the examples of revenge reveal, royal
officials recognized the threat of the pirates'
alternative order. Some authorities feared that pirates might "set up a sort of Commonwealth"—
a correct designation—in uninhabited regions,
since "no Power in those Parts of the World
could have been able to dispute it with them."
But the consciousness of kind never took national shape, and piracy was soon suppressed.
We now turn to the general social and economic
context of the crime and its culture.

Contemporary observers seem to have attributed the rise of piracy to the demobilizing of the
Royal Navy at the end of the War of the Spanish
Succession. A group of Virginia merchants, for instance, wrote to the Admiralty in 1713, setting

forth "the apprehensions they have of Pyrates molesting their trade in the time of Peace." The navy plunged from 49,860 men at the end of the war to 13,475 just two years later, and only by 1740 did it increase to as many as 30,000 again. At the same time, the expiration of privateering licenses—bills of marque—added to the number of seamen loose and looking for work in the port cities of the empire. Such underemployment contributed significantly to the rise of piracy, but it is not a sufficient explanation since, as already noted, the vast majority of those who became pirates were working in the merchant service at the moment of their joining. The surplus of labor at the end of the war had jarring social effects. It produced an immediate contraction of wages; merchant seamen who made 45-50 shillings per month in 1708 made only half that amount in 1713. It provoked greater competition for seafaring jobs, favorable to the hiring of older, more experienced seamen. And it would, over time, affect the social conditions and relations of life at sea, cutting back material benefits and hardening discipline. War years, despite their dangers, provided seafarers with tangible benefits. The Anglo-American seamen of 1713 had performed wartime labor for twenty of the previous twenty-five years, and for eleven years consecutively. But conditions did not worsen immediately after the war. As Ralph Davis explains, "the years 1713-1715 saw—as did immediate post-war years throughout the eighteenth century—the shifting of heaped-up surpluses of colonial goods, the movement of great quantities of English goods to colonial and other markets, and a general filling in of stocks of imported goods which had been allowed to run down." This small-scale boom gave employment to some of the seamen who had been dropped from naval rolls. But by late 1715, a slump in trade began, to last into the 1730s. All of these difficulties were exacerbated by the century-long trend in which "life on board [a merchant] ship was carried on amid a discipline which grew harsher with the passage of time." Many seamen knew that things had once been different and, for many, decisively better.

By 1726, the menace of piracy had been effectively suppressed by governmental action. Circumstantial factors do not account for its demise. The number of men in the Royal Navy did increase from 6,298 in 1725 to 16,872 in 1726, and again to 20,697 in 1727. This increase probably had some bearing on the declining numbers of sea-robbers. Yet some 20,000 sailors had been in the navy in 1719 and 1720, years when pirates were numerous. In addition, seafaring wages only twice rose above 24-25 shillings per month between 1713 and the mid-1730s: there were temporary increases to 30 shillings in 1718 and 1727. Conditions of life at sea probably did not change appreciably until war broke out in 1739.

The pardons offered to pirates in 1717 and 1718 largely failed to rid the sea of robbers. Since the graces specified that only crimes committed at certain times and in particular regions would be forgiven, many pirates saw enormous latitude for official trickery and refused to surrender. Moreover, accepting and abiding by the rules of the pardon would have meant for most men a return to the dismal conditions they had escaped. Their tactic failing, royal officials intensified the naval campaign against piracy—with great and gruesome effect. Corpses dangled in chains in British ports around the world "as a Spectacle for the Warning of others." No fewer than four hundred, and probably five to six hundred, Anglo-American pirates were executed between 1716 and 1726. The campaign to cleanse the seas was supported by clergymen, royal officials, and publicists who sought through sermons, proclamations, pamphlets and the newspaper press to create an image of the pirate that would legitimate his extermination. Piracy had always depended in some measure on the rumors and tales of its successes, especially among seamen and dealers in stolen cargo. In 1722 and 1723, after a spate of hangings and verbal chastisements, the pirate population began to decline. By 1726, only a handful of the fraternity remained.

Finally, pirates themselves unwittingly took a hand in their own destruction. From the outset, theirs had been a fragile social group. They produced nothing and were economically parasitic on the mercantile system. And they were widely dispersed, virtually without geographic boundaries. Try as they might, they were unable to create reliable mechanisms through which they could either replenish their ranks or mobilize their collective strength. These deficiencies of social organization made them, in the long run, easy prey.

We see in the end that the pirate was, perhaps above all else, an unremarkable man caught in harsh, often deadly circumstances. Wealth he surely desired, but a strong social logic informed both his motivation and his behavior. Emerging from lower-class backgrounds and maritime employments, and loosed from familial bonds, pirates developed common symbols and standards of conduct. They forged spontaneous alliances, refused to fight each other, swore to avenge injury to their own kind, and even retired to pirate communities. They erected their own ideal of justice, insisted upon an egalitarian, if unstable, form of social organization, and defined themselves against other social groups and types. So, too, did they perceive many of their activities as ethical and justified, not unlike the eighteenth-century crowds described by Edward Thompson. But pirates, experienced as cooperative seafaring laborers and no longer disciplined by law, were both familiar with the workings of an international market economy and little affected by the uncertainties of economic change. Perhaps their dual relationship to the mode of production as free wage laborers and members of a criminal subculture gave pirates the perspective and resources to fight back against brutal and unjust authority, and to construct a new social order where King Death would not reign supreme. This was probably a contradictory pursuit: for many, piracy, as strategy of survival, was ill-fated.

Piracy, in the end, offers us an extraordinary opportunity. Here we can see how a sizeable group of Anglo-Americans—poor men in canvas jackets and tarred breeches—constructed a social world where they had "the choice in themselves." Theirs was truly a culture of masterless men: Pirates were as far removed from traditional authority as any men could be in the early eighteenth century. Beyond the church, beyond the family, beyond disciplinary labor, and using the sea to distance themselves from the powers of the state, they carried out a strange experiment. The social constellation of piracy, in particular the complex consciousness and egalitarian impulses that developed once the shackles were off, might provide valuable clarification of more general social and cultural patterns among the laboring poor. Here we can see aspirations and achievements that under normal circumstances would have been heavily muted, if not rendered imperceptible, by the power relationships of everyday life.

Study Questions

1. Why did many sailors find piracy an appealing substitute for more legitimate employment?

2. What social class were most pirates drawn from and why does Rediker think this is important?

3. How did self-governance in the pirate communities compare with the exercise of authority on British men-of-war or merchant vessels? What function did the "ship's articles" and the "council" serve?

4. What treatment did captured ship masters receive, and how did pirates determine punishment for such captives?

5. What were the usual symbols on the "Jolly Roger," and what did they mean to the pirates and their prey?

6. What conditions after the end of the War of the Spanish Succession contributed to an increase in piracy in the Atlantic?

Bibliography

Marcus Rediker expands on his own story here in *Between the Devil and Deep Blue Sea: Merchant Seamen, Pirates, and the Anglo-American Maritime World, 1700-1750* (1989). Good sources for the history of piracy include Hugh F. Rankin, *The Golden Age of Piracy* (1969); Neville Williams, *Captains Outrageous: Seven Centuries of Piracy* (1961); and the popular history by Patrick Pringle, *Jolly Roger* (1953). Also see Hans Turley, *Rum, Sodomy, and the Lash: Pirates, Sexuality, and Masculinity* (1999) and David Cordingly, *Under the Black Flag: The Romance and the Reality of Life Among the Pirates* (1996). For a comprehensive reference work, see David Marley, *Pirates and Privateers of the Americas* (1994). The best recent study of the New England economy in the Puritan era is Stephen Innes, *Creating the Commonwealth: The Economic Culture of Puritan New England* (1995). For a larger portrait of the American colonial economy in general, see John J. McCusker and Russell R. Menard, *The Economy of British North America, 1607-1789,* rev. ed. (1991); and for the American colonial economy in an imperial context see Michael Kammen, *Empire and Interest: The American Colonies and the Politics of Mercantilism* (1970); also Richard R. Johnson, *Adjustment to Empire: The New England Colonies, 1675-1715* (1981); and finally Ian K. Steele, *The English Atlantic, 1675-1740: Communication and Community* (1986).

2

★ ★ ★

Southern Life

The Southern colonies differed markedly from the New England colonies. Colonial Virginia, for example, never enjoyed the remarkable demographic stability of colonial Massachusetts Bay. Most of the people who traveled to Virginia during the seventeenth century were young, unmarried male servants—indeed, before 1640 males outnumbered females by a ratio of 6 to 1. In addition, the humid lowlands of the Chesapeake fostered high mortality rates. During the seventeenth century, the average life expectancy for Chesapeake males was about forty-three, and for females it was even lower. Only 50 percent of the children born in the region lived past the age of twenty, and many of the survivors suffered illnesses that left them too weak for strenuous labor.

The most obvious result of this demographic nightmare was a severe labor shortage. English immigration to the South simply did not satisfy the labor needs. As a result, colonial planters began to import black Africans as early as 1619. The question of whether these unwilling emigrants were chattel slaves or free servants fulfilling an indentureship remained in doubt for some years, but certainly by 1700 white planters had developed the institution of slavery. This peculiar institution was far more than an economic arrangement; it had a psychological effect on everyone who lived close to its dominion.

More than demographics and slavery separated the Southern colonies from the New England colonies. The first settlers who landed in Jamestown were not concerned with the impurities in the Anglican Church. Instead, they worried about their own economic futures. Most longed to become wealthy—and the faster the better. They were worldly men in search of worldly success. The majority readily accepted not only the Anglican Church but also the English class structure. Their goal was to move up the pyramid, not to level it.

With very few exceptions, their dreams of easy prosperity vanished before the hardships of Southern existence. Indians, swamps, diseases, and backbreaking labor were formidable foes. Men who possessed stronger bodies, quicker minds, or larger bank accounts advanced by buying land and growing tobacco. Their society was bru-

tally competitive and early success was no guarantee of lasting success. But by the 1650s a real colonial aristocracy had begun to emerge. The great Chesapeake families—the Byrds, Carters, Masons, and Burwells—commenced their domination of society and politics.

Without losing their competitive urges, the leaders of the major families began to cooperate to preserve and perpetuate their wealth and status. They intermarried, awarded themselves military titles, and dominated the colonial assemblies throughout the south. By the eighteenth century such bodies as Virginia's House of Burgesses began to resemble a gathering of cousins. Not surprisingly, as the gentry consolidated its control over all aspects of colonial society, it became increasingly more difficult for the ordinary man to rise into the ruling class. This development, however, created few problems. Not many people in the colonial South questioned deferential attitudes.

READING 6

Englishmen and Africans

Winthrop Jordan

The institution of chattel slavery developed gradually in the British seaboard colonies. The first Africans landed in Virginia in 1619, but over the next forty years relatively few others followed. By 1660 only about fifteen hundred blacks lived in Virginia, and their status was unclear. White planters regarded some as slaves, others as indentured servants. But as the black population grew after 1660 and the demand for a steady labor force became critical, white planters adopted the institution of chattel slavery.

Planters masked the economic foundations of slavery with a rhetoric that emphasized humanitarianism and Christianity. As Winthrop D. Jordan emphasizes in his National Book Award-winning study, *White Over Black: American Attitudes Toward the Negro, 1550-1812,* from their first meeting, Englishmen viewed Africans as a strange and disturbing people. The Africans' color, religion, and social behavior upset Englishmen. This early form of prejudice laid the intellectual groundwork for later justifications of slavery.

The institution of slavery influenced the development of the entire South and left deep psychological scars both on whites and blacks. In the following essay Jordan discusses the initial English attitude toward Africans.

When the Atlantic nations of Europe began expanding overseas in the sixteenth century, Portugal led the way to Africa and to the east while Spain founded a great empire in America. It was not until the reign of Queen Elizabeth that Englishmen came to realize that overseas exploration and plantations could bring home wealth, power, glory, and fascinating information. By the early years of the seventeenth century Englishmen had developed a taste for empire and for tales of adventure and discovery. More than is usual in human affairs, one man, the great chronicler Richard Hakluyt, had roused enthusiasm for western planting and had stirred the nation with his monumental compilation, *The Principal Navigations, Voyages, Traffiques and Discoveries of the English Nation.* Here was a work to widen a people's horizons. Its exhilarating accounts of voyages to all quarters of the globe constituted a national hymn, a scientific treatise, a sermon, and an adventure story.

English voyagers did not touch upon the shores of West Africa until after 1550, nearly a century after Prince Henry the Navigator had mounted the sustained Portuguese thrust southward for a water passage to the Orient. Usually Englishmen came to Africa to trade goods *with* the natives. The earliest English descriptions of West Africa were written by adventurous traders, men who had no special interest in converting the natives or, except for the famous Hawkins voyages in the 1560s, in otherwise laying hands on them. Extensive English participation in the slave trade did not develop until well into the seventeenth century. Initially English contact with Africans did not take place primarily in a context which prejudged the Negro as a slave, at least not as a slave of Englishmen. Rather, Englishmen met Africans merely as another sort of men.

Englishmen found the peoples of Africa very different from themselves. "Negroes" looked different to Englishmen; their religion was unChristian; their manner of living was anything but English; they seemed to be a particularly libidinous sort of people. All these clusters of perceptions were related to each other, though they may be spread apart for inspection, and they were related also to the circumstances of contact in Africa, to previously accumulated traditions concerning that strange and distant continent, and to certain special qualities of English society on the eve of its expansion into the New World.

The Blackness Without

For Englishmen, the most arresting characteristic of the newly discovered African was his color. Travelers rarely failed to comment upon it; indeed when describing Africans they frequently began with complexion and then moved on to dress (or, as they saw, lack of it) and manners. At Cape Verde, "These people are all blacke, and are called Negroes, without any apparell, saving before their privities." Robert Baker's narrative poem recounting his two voyages to the West African coast in 1562 and 1563 introduced the people he saw with these engaging lines:

> *And entering in [a river], we see*
> *   a number of blacke soules,*
> *Whose likelinesse seem'd men to be,*
> *   but all as blacke as coles.*
> *Their Captain comes to me*
> *   as naked as my naile,*
> *Not having witte or honestie*
> *   to cover once his taile.*

Englishmen actually described Negroes as *black*—an exaggerated term which in itself suggests that the Negro's complexion had powerful impact upon their perceptions. Even the peoples of northern Africa seemed so dark that Englishmen tended to call them "black" and let further refinements go by the board. In Shakespeare's day, the Moors, including Othello, were commonly portrayed as pitchy black and the terms

From "Fruits of Passion" by Winthrop Jordan in *White Over Black: American Attitudes Toward the Negro, 1550-1812.* Copyright © 1968 by the University of North Carolina Press. Reprinted by permission.

Moor and *Negro* were used almost interchangeably. With curious inconsistency, however, Englishmen recognized that Africans south of the Sahara were not at all the same people as the much more familiar Moors. Sometimes they referred to West Africans as "black Moors" to distinguish them from the peoples of North Africa.

The powerful impact which the Negro's color made upon Englishmen must have been partly owing to suddenness of contact. Though the Bible as well as the arts and literature of antiquity and the Middle Ages offered some slight introduction to the "Ethiope," England's immediate acquaintance with "black"-skinned peoples came with relative rapidity. People much darker than Englishmen were not entirely unfamiliar, but really "black" men were virtually unknown except as vaguely referred to in the hazy literature about the sub-Sahara which had filtered down from antiquity. Native West Africans probably first appeared in London in 1554; in that year five "Negroes," as one trader reported, were taken to England, "kept till they could speak the language," and then brought back again "to be a helpe to Englishmen" who were engaged in trade with Africans on the coast. Hakluyt's later discussion of these Africans suggests that these "black Moors" were a novelty to Englishmen. In this respect the English experience was markedly different from that of the Spanish and Portuguese who for centuries had been in close contact with North Africa and had actually been invaded and subjected by people both darker and more "highly civilized" than themselves. The impact of the Negro's color was the more powerful upon Englishmen, moreover, because England's principal contact with Africans came in West Africa and the Congo, which meant that one of the lightest-skinned of the earth's peoples suddenly came face to face with one of the darkest.

In England perhaps more than in southern Europe, the concept of blackness was loaded with intense meaning. Long before they found that some men were black, Englishmen found in the idea of blackness a way of expressing some of their most ingrained values. No other color except white conveyed so much emotional impact. As described by the *Oxford English Dictionary,* the meaning of *black* before the sixteenth century included, "Deeply stained with dirt; soiled, dirty, foul. . . . Having dark or deadly purposes, malignant; pertaining to or involving death, deadly; baneful, disastrous, sinister. . . . Foul, iniquitous, atrocious, horrible, wicked. . . . Indicating disgrace, censure, liability to punishment, etc." Black was an emotionally partisan color, the handmaid and symbol of baseness and evil, a sign of danger and repulsion.

Embedded in the concept of blackness was its direct opposite—whiteness. No other colors so clearly implied opposition, "beinge coloures utterlye contrary":

Everye white will have its blacke,
And every sweete its sowre.

White and black connoted purity and filthiness, virginity and sin, virtue and baseness, beauty and ugliness, beneficence and evil, God and the devil. Whiteness, moreover, carried a special significance for Elizabethan Englishmen: it was, particularly when complemented by red, the color of perfect human beauty, especially *female* beauty. This ideal was already centuries old in Elizabeth's time, and their fair Queen was its very embodiment: her cheeks were "roses in a bed of lillies." (Elizabeth was naturally pale but like many ladies then and since she freshened her "lillies" at the cosmetic table.) An adoring nation knew precisely what a beautiful Queen looked like.

Her cheeke, her chinne, her neck, her
  nose,
This was a lillye, that was a rose;
Her bosome, sleeke as Paris plaster,
Held upp twoo bowles of Alabaster.

By contrast, the Negro was ugly, by reason of his color and also his "horrid Curles" and "disfigured" lips and nose. A century later blackness still required apology: one of the earliest attempts to delineate the West African as a heroic character, the popular story *Oroonoko* (1688), presented Negroes as capable of blushing and turning pale. It was important, if incalculably so, that English discovery of black Africans came at a time when the accepted English standard of ideal beauty was a fair complexion of rose and white. Negroes seemed the very picture of perverse negation.

From the first, however, many English observers displayed a certain sophistication about the Negro's color. Despite an ethnocentric tendency to find blackness repulsive, many writers were fully aware that Africans themselves might have different tastes. As early as 1621 one writer told of the "Jetty coloured" Negroes, "Who in their native beauty most delight,/And in contempt doe paint the Divell white"; this assertion became almost a commonplace. Many accounts of Africa reported explicitly that the Negro's preference in colors was inverse to the European's. Even the Negro's features were conceded to be appealing to Negroes.

The Causes of Complexion

Black human beings were not only startling but extremely puzzling. The complexion of Africans posed problems about its nature, especially its permanence and utility, its cause and origin, and its significance. Although these were rather separate questions, there was a pronounced tendency among Englishmen and other Europeans to formulate the problem in terms of causation alone. If the cause of human blackness could be explained, then its nature and significance would follow.

Not that the problem was completely novel. The ancient Greeks had touched upon it. The story of Phaëton's driving the chariot sun wildly through the heavens apparently served as an explanation for the Ethiopian's blackness even before written records, and traces of this ancient fable were still drifting about during the seventeenth century. Ptolemy had made the important suggestion that the Negro's blackness and woolly hair were caused by exposure to the hot sun and had pointed out that people in northern climates were white and those in temperate areas an intermediate color. Before the sixteenth century, though, the question of the Negro's color can hardly be said to have drawn the attention of Englishmen or indeed of Europeans generally.

The discovery of West Africa and the development of Negro slavery made the question far more urgent. The range of possible answers was rigidly restricted, however, by the virtually universal assumption, dictated by church and Scripture, that all mankind stemmed from a single source. Indeed it is impossible fully to understand the various efforts at explaining the Negro's complexion without bearing in mind the strength of the tradition which in 1614 made the chronicler, the Reverend Samuel Purchas, proclaim vehemently: "the tawney Moore, blacke Negro, duskie Libyan, ash-coloured Indian, olive-coloured American, should with the whiter European become one *sheep-fold,* under *one great Sheepheard . . .* without any more distinction of Colour, Nation, Language, Sexe, Condition, all may bee One in him that is One. . . ."

In general, the most satisfactory answer to the problem was some sort of reference to the action of the sun, whether the sun was assumed to have scorched the skin, drawn the bile, or blackened the blood. People living on the line had obviously been getting too much of it; after all, even Englishmen were darkened by a little exposure. How much more, then, with the Negroes who were "so scorched and vexed with the heat of the sunne, that in many places they curse it when it riseth." This association of the Negro's color with the sun became a commonplace in Elizabethan literature; as Shakespeare's Prince of Morocco apologized, "Mislike me not for my complexion,/The shadow'd livery of the burnish'd sun,/To whom I am a neighbour and near bred."

Unfortunately this theory ran headlong into a stubborn fact of nature which simply could not be overridden: if the equatorial inhabitants of Africa were blackened by the sun, why not the people living on the same line in America? Logic required them to be the same color. Yet by the middle of the sixteenth century it was becoming perfectly apparent that the Indians living in the hottest regions of the New World could by no stretch of the imagination be described as black. They were "olive" or "tawny," and moreover they had long hair rather than the curious "wool" of Negroes. Clearly the method of accounting for human complexion by latitude just did not work. The worst of it was that the formula did not seem altogether wrong, since it was apparent that in general men in hot climates tended to be darker than in cold ones.

Another difficulty with the climatic explanation of skin color arose as lengthening experience provided more knowledge about Negroes. If the heat of the sun caused the Negro's blackness, then his removal to cold northerly countries ought to result in his losing it; even if he did not himself surrender his peculiar color, surely his descendants must. By mid-seventeenth century it was becoming increasingly apparent that this expectation was ill founded: Negroes in Europe and northern America were simply not whitening up very noticeably.

From the beginning, in fact, some Englishmen were certain that the Negro's blackness was permanent and innate and that no amount of cold was going to alter it. There was good authority in Jeremiah 13:23; "Can the Ethiopian change his skin/or the leopard his spots?" Elizabethan dramatists used the stock expression "to wash in Ethiop white" as indicating sheer impossibility. In 1578 a voyager and speculative geographer, George Best, announced that the blackness of Negroes "proceedeth of some naturall infection of the first inhabitants of that country, and so all the whole progenie of them descended, are still polluted with the same blot of infection." An essayist in 1695 declared firmly, "A negroe will always be a negroe, carry him to Greenland, give him chalk, feed and manage him never so many ways."

There was an alternative to the naturalistic explanations of the Negro's blackness. Some writers felt that God's curse on Ham (Cham), or upon his son Canaan, and all their descendants was entirely sufficient to account for the color of Negroes. This could be an appealing explanation, especially for men like George Best who wished to

stress the "natural infection" of blackness and for those who hoped to incorporate the Negro's complexion securely within the accepted history of mankind. The original story in Genesis 9 and 10 was that after the Flood, Ham had looked upon his father's "nakedness" as Noah lay drunk in the tent, but the other two sons, Shem and Japheth, had covered their father without looking upon him; when Noah awoke he cursed Canaan, son of Ham, saying that he would be a "servant of servants" unto his brothers. Given this text, the question becomes why a tale which logically implied slavery but absolutely nothing about skin color should have become a popular explanation of the Negro's blackness. The matter is puzzling, but probably, over the very long run, the story was supported by the ancient association of heat with sensuality and by the fact that some sub-Saharan Africans had been enslaved by Europeans since ancient times. In addition, the extraordinary persistence of the tale in the face of centuries of constant refutation was probably sustained by a feeling that blackness could scarcely be anything *but* a curse and by the common need to confirm the facts of nature by specific reference to Scripture. In contrast to the climatic theory, God's curse provided a satisfying purposiveness which the sun's scorching heat could not match until the eighteenth century.

In the long run, of course, the Negro's color attained greatest significance not as a scientific problem but as a social fact. Englishmen found blackness in human beings a peculiar and important point of difference. The African's color set him radically *apart* from Englishmen. But then, distant Africa had been known to Christians for ages as a land of men radically different in religion.

Defective Religion

While distinctive appearance set Africans apart in a novel way, their religious condition distinguished them in a more familiar manner. Englishmen and Christians everywhere were sufficiently acquainted with the concept of heathenism that they confronted its living representatives without puzzlement. Certainly the rather sudden discovery that the world was teeming with heathen people made for heightened vividness and urgency in a long-standing problem; but it was the fact that this problem was already well formulated long before contact with Africa which proved important in shaping English reaction to the Negro's defective religious condition.

In one sense heathenism was less a "problem" for Christians than an exercise in self-definition: the heathen condition defined by negation the proper Christian life. In another sense, the presence of heathenism in the world constituted an imperative to intensification of religious commitment. From its origin Christianity was a universalist, proselytizing religion, and the sacred and secular histories of Christianity made manifest the necessity of bringing non-Christians into the fold. For Englishmen, then, the heathenism of Negroes was at once a counter-image of their own religion and a summons to eradicate an important distinction between the two peoples. Yet the interaction of these two facets of the concept of heathenism made for a peculiar difficulty: On the one hand, to act upon the felt necessity of converting Africans would have been to eradicate the point of distinction which Englishmen found most familiar and most readily comprehensible. Yet if they did not act upon this necessity, continued heathenism among Negroes would remain an unwelcome reminder to Englishmen that they were not meeting their obligations to their own faith— nor to the benighted Negroes. Englishmen resolved this implicit dilemma by doing nothing.

Considering the strength of the Christian tradition, it is almost startling that Englishmen failed to respond to the discovery of heathenism in Africa with at least the rudiments of a campaign for conversion. Although the impulse to spread Christianity seems to have been weaker in Englishmen than, say, in the Catholic Portuguese, it cannot be said that Englishmen were indifferent to the obligation imposed upon them by the overseas discoveries of the sixteenth century. While they were badly out of practice at the business of conversion (again in contrast to the Portuguese) and

while they had never before been faced with the practical difficulties involved in Christianizing entire continents, they nonetheless were able to contemplate with equanimity and even eagerness the prospect of converting the heathen. Indeed they went so far as to conclude that converting the natives in America was sufficiently important to demand English settlement there. As it turned out, the well-publicized English program for converting Indians produced very meager results, but the avowed intentions certainly were genuine. It was in marked contrast, therefore, that Englishmen did not avow similar intentions concerning Africans until the late eighteenth century. Fully as much as with skin color, though less consciously, Englishmen distinguished between the heathenisms of Indians and of Negroes.

It is not easy to account for the distinction which Englishmen made. On the basis of the travelers' reports there was no reason for Englishmen to suppose Indians inherently superior to Negroes as candidates for conversion. But America was not Africa. Englishmen contemplated settling in America, where voyagers had established the King's claim and where supposedly the climate was temperate; in contrast, Englishmen did not envision settlement in Africa, which had quickly gained notoriety as a graveyard for Europeans and where the Portuguese had been first on the scene. Certainly these very different circumstances meant that Englishmen confronted Negroes and Indians in radically different social contexts and that Englishmen would find it far easier to contemplate converting Indians than Negroes. Yet it remains difficult to see why Negroes were not included, at least as a secondary target. The fact that English contact with Africans so frequently occurred in a context of slave dealing does not entirely explain the omission of Negroes, since in that same context the Portuguese and Spanish did sometimes attempt to minister to the souls of Africans and since Englishmen in America enslaved Indians when good occasion arose. Given these circumstances, it is hard to escape the conclusion that the distinction which Englishmen made as to conversion was at least in some small measure modeled after the difference they saw in skin color.

The most important aspect of English reaction to African heathenism was that Englishmen evidently did not regard it as separable from the Negro's other attributes. Heathenism was treated not so much as a specifically religious defect but as one manifestation of a general refusal to measure up to proper standards, as a failure to be English or even civilized. There was every reason for Englishmen to fuse the various attributes they found in Africans. During the first century of English contact with Africa, Protestant Christianity was an important element in English patriotism; especially during the struggle against Spain the Elizabethan's special Christianity was interwoven into his conception of his own nationality, and he was therefore inclined to regard the Negroes' lack of true religion as part of theirs. Being a Christian was not merely a matter of subscribing to certain doctrines; it was a quality inherent in oneself and in one's society. It was interconnected with all the other attributes of normal and proper men: as one of the earliest English travelers described Africans, they were "a people of beastly living, without a God, lawe, religion, or common wealth"—which was to say that Negroes were not Englishmen. Far from isolating African heathenism as a separate characteristic, English travelers sometimes linked it explicitly with blackness and savagery.

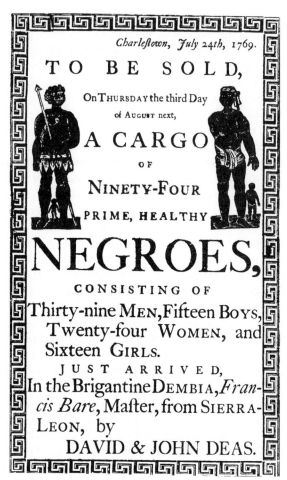

A notice announcing the arrival of slaves to be sold at an auction in Charleston, South Carolina.

Savage Behavior

The condition of savagery—the failure to be civilized—set Negroes apart from Englishmen in an ill-defined but crucial fashion. Africans were *different* from Englishmen in so many ways: in their clothing, housing, farming, warfare, language, government, morals, and (not least important) in their table manners. To judge from the comments of voyagers, Englishmen had an unquenchable thirst for the details of savage life. Englishmen were, indeed, enormously curious about their rapidly expanding world, and it is scarcely surprising that they should have taken an

interest in reports about cosmetic mutilation, polygamy, infanticide, ritual murder, and the like. In addition, reports about "savages" began arriving at a time when Englishmen very much needed to be able to translate their apprehensive interest in an uncontrollable world out of medieval religious terms. The discovery of savages overseas enabled them to make this translation easily, to move from miracles to verifiable monstrosities, from heaven to earth.

As with skin color, English reporting of African customs was partly an exercise in self-inspection by means of comparison. The necessity of continuously measuring African practices with an English yardstick of course tended to emphasize the differences between the two groups, but it also made for heightened sensitivity to instances of similarity. Thus the Englishman's ethnocentrism tended to distort his perception of African culture in two opposite directions. While it led him to emphasize differences and to condemn deviations from the English norm, it led him also to seek out similarities. Particularly, Englishmen were inclined to see the structures of African societies as analogous to their own, complete with kings, counselors, gentlemen, and the baser sort. Here especially they found Africans like themselves, partly because they knew no other way to describe any society and partly because there was actually good basis for such a view of the social organization of West African communities.

Despite the fascination and self-instruction Englishmen derived from discussing the savage behavior of Africans, they never felt that savagery was as important a quality in Africans as it was in the American Indians. As was the case with heathenism, contrasting social contexts played an important role in shaping the English response to savagery in the two peoples. Inevitably, the savagery of the Indians assumed a special significance in the minds of those actively engaged in a program of planting civilization in the American wilderness. The case with the African was different; the English errand into Africa was not a new or a perfect community but a business trip. No hope was entertained for civilizing the Negro's steaming continent, and Englishmen therefore lacked compelling reason to develop a program for remodeling the African natives.

From the beginning, also, the importance of the Negro's savagery was muted by the Negro's color. Englishmen could go a long way toward expressing their sense of being different from Africans merely by calling them "black." By contrast, the aboriginals in America did not have the appearance of being radically distinct from Europeans except in religion and savage behavior. English voyages placed much less emphasis upon the Indian's color than upon the Negro's, and

they never permitted the Indian's physiognomy to distract their attention from what they regarded as his essential quality, his savagery.

It would be a mistake, however, to slight the importance of what was seen as the African's savagery, since it fascinated Englishmen from the very first. English observers in West Africa were sometimes so profoundly impressed by the Negro's behavior that they resorted to a powerful metaphor with which to express their own sense of difference from him. They knew perfectly well that Negroes were men, yet they frequently described the Africans as "brutish" or "bestial" or "beastly." The supposed hideous tortures, cannibalism, rapacious warfare, revolting diet (and so forth page after page) seemed somehow to place the Negro among the beasts. The eventual circumstances of the Englishman's contact with Africans served to strengthen this feeling. *Slave* traders in Africa necessarily handled Negroes the same way men in England handled beasts, herding and examining and buying, as with any other animals which were products of commerce.

The Apes of Africa

If Negroes were likened to beasts, there was in Africa a beast which was likened to men. It was a strange and eventually tragic happenstance of nature that Africa was the habitat of the animal which in appearance most resembles man. The animal called "orang-outang" by contemporaries (actually the chimpanzee) was native to those parts of western Africa where the early slave trade was heavily concentrated. Though Englishmen were acquainted (for the most part vicariously) with monkeys and baboons, they were unfamiliar with tail-less apes who walked about like men. Accordingly, it happened that Englishmen were introduced to the anthropoid apes and to Negroes at the same time and in the same place. The startlingly human appearance and movements of the "ape"—a generic term though often used as a synonym for the "orang-outang"—aroused some curious speculations.

In large measure these speculations derived from traditions which had been accumulating in Western culture since ancient times. Medieval books on animals contained rosters of strange creatures who in one way or another seemed disturbingly to resemble men. There were the *simia* and the *cynocephali* and the *satyri* and the others, all variously described and related to one another, all jumbled in a characteristic blend of ancient reports and medieval morality. The confusion was not easily nor rapidly dispelled, and many of the traditions established by this literature were very much alive during the seventeenth century.

The section on apes in Edward Topsell's *Historie of Foure-Footed Beastes* (1607) serves to illustrate how certain seemingly trivial traditions and associations persisted in such form that they were bound to affect the way in which Englishmen would perceive the inhabitants of Africa. Above all, according to Topsell, "apes" were venerous. The red apes were "so venerous that they will ravish their Women." Baboons were "as lustful and venerous as goats"; a baboon which had been "brought to the French king . . . above all loved the companie of women, and young maidens; his genitall member was greater than might match the quantity of his other parts." Pictures of two varieties of apes, a "Satyre" and an "Ægopithecus," graphically emphasize the "virile member."

In addition to stressing the "lustful disposition" of the ape kind, Topsell's compilation contained suggestions concerning the character of simian facial features. "Men that have low and flat nostrils," readers were told in the section on apes, "are Libidinous as Apes that attempt women. . . ." There also seemed to be some connection between apes and devils. In a not altogether successful attempt to distinguish the "Satyre-apes" from the mythical creatures of that name, Topsell straightened everything out by explaining that it was "probable, that Devils take not any dænomination or shape from Satyres, but rather the Apes themselves from Devils whome they resemble, for there are many things common to the Satyre-apes and devilish Satyres." Association of apes and/or satyrs with devils was common in England: the inner logic of this association derived from uneasiness concerning the ape's "indecent likenesse and imitation of man"; it revolved around evil and sexual sin; and, rather tenuously, it connected apes with blackness.

Given this tradition and the coincidence of contact, it was virtually inevitable that Englishmen should discern similarity between the manlike beasts and the beastlike men of Africa. A few commentators went so far as to suggest that Negroes had sprung from the generation of apekind or that apes were themselves the offspring of Negroes and some unknown African beast. These contentions were squarely in line with the ancient tradition that Africa was a land "bringing dailie foorth newe monsters" because, as Aristotle himself had suggested, many different species came into proximity at the scarce watering places. Jean Bodin, the famous sixteenth-century French political theorist, summarized this wisdom of the ages with the categorical remark that "promiscuous coition of men and animals took place, wherefore the regions of Africa produced for us so many monsters." Despite all these monsters out of Africa, the notion that Negroes stemmed from beasts in a literal sense was not widely believed. It simply floated about, available, later, for anyone who wanted it.

Far more common and persistent was the notion that there sometimes occurred "a beastly copulation or conjuncture" between apes and Negroes, and especially that apes were inclined wantonly to attack Negro women. The very explicit idea that apes assaulted female human beings was not new; Africans were merely being asked to demonstrate what Europeans had known for centuries. As late as the 1730s a well-traveled, well-educated, and intelligent naval surgeon, John Atkins, was not at all certain that the stories were false: "At some Places the *Negroes* have been suspected of Bestiality with them [apes and monkeys], and by the Boldness and Affection they are known under some Circumstances to express to our Females; the Ignorance and Stupidity on the other side, to guide or control Lust; but more from the near resemblance [of apes] . . . to the Human Species would tempt one to suspect the Fact."

By the time Atkins addressed himself to this evidently fascinating problem, some of the confusion arising from the resemblance of apes to men had been dispelled. In 1699 the web of legend and unverified fact was disentangled by Edward Tyson, whose comparative study of a young "orang-outang" was a masterwork of critical scientific investigation. Throughout his dissection of the chimpanzee, Tyson meticulously compared the animal with human beings in every anatomical detail, and he established beyond question both the close relationship and the non-identity of ape and man. Here was a step forward; the question of the ape's proper place in nature was now grounded upon much firmer knowledge of the facts. Despite their scientific importance, Tyson's conclusions did nothing to weaken the vigorous tradition which linked the Negro with the ape. The supposed affinity between apes and men had as frequently been expressed in sexual as in anatomical terms, and his findings did not effectively rule out the possibility of unnatural sexual unions. Tyson himself remarked that organs were especially given to venery.

The sexual association of apes with Negroes had an inner logic which kept it alive: sexual union seemed to prove a certain affinity without going so far as to indicate actual identity—which was what Englishmen really thought was the case. By forging a sexual link between Negroes and apes, furthermore, Englishmen were able to give vent to their feeling that Negroes were a lewd, lascivious, and wanton people.

Libidinous Men

Undertones of sexuality run throughout many English accounts of West Africa. To liken Africans—and human beings—to beasts was to stress the animal within the man. Indeed the sexual connotations embodied in the terms *bestial* and *beastly* were considerably stronger in Elizabethan English than they are today, and when the Elizabethan traveler pinned these epithets upon the behavior of Africans he was more frequently registering a sense of sexual shock than describing swinish manners.

Lecherousness among Africans was at times for Englishmen merely another attribute which one would expect to find among heathen, savage, beastlike men. One commentator's remarks made evident how closely interrelated all these attributes were in the minds of Englishmen: "They have no knowledge of God . . . they are very greedie eaters, and no lesse drinkers, and very lecherous, and theevish, and much addicted to uncleanenesse: one man hath as many wives as hee is able to keepe and maintaine." Sexuality was what one expected of savages.

Clearly, however, the association of Africans with potent sexuality represented more than an incidental appendage to the concept of savagery. Long before the first English contact with West Africa, the inhabitants of virtually the entire continent stood confirmed in European literature as lustful and venerous. About 1526 Leo Africanus (a Spanish Moroccan Moor converted to Christianity) supplied an influential description of the little-known lands of "Barbary," "Libya," "Numedia," and "Land of Negroes"; and Leo was as explicit as he was imaginative. In the English translation (1600) readers were informed concerning the "Negroes" that "there is no Nation under Heaven more prone to Venery." Leo disclosed that "the Negroes . . . leade a beastly kind of life, being utterly destitute of the use of reason, of dexteritie of wit, and of all arts. Yea, they so behave themselves, as if they had continually lived in a Forrest among wild beasts. They have great swarmes of Harlots among them; whereupon a man may easily conjecture their manner of living." Nor was Leo Africanus the only scholar to elaborate upon the ancient classical sources concerning Africa. In a highly eclectic work first published in 1566, Jean Bodin sifted the writings of ancient authorities and concluded that heat and lust went hand in hand and that "in Ethiopia . . . the race of men is very keen and lustful." Bodin announced in a thoroughly characteristic sentence, "Ptolemy reported that on account of southern sensuality Venus chiefly is worshiped in

Africa and that the constellation of Scorpion, which pertains to the pudenda, dominates that continent."

Depiction of the Negro as a lustful creature was not radically new, therefore, when Englishmen first met Africans face to face. Seizing upon and reconfirming these long-standing and apparently common notions, Elizabethan travelers and literati dwelt explicitly with ease upon the especial sexuality of Africans. Othello's embraces were "the gross clasps of a lascivious Moor." Francis Bacon's *New Atlantis* (1624) referred to "an holy hermit" who "desired to see the Spirit of Fornication; and there appeared to him a little foul ugly Æthiop." Negro men, reported a seventeenth-century traveler, sported "large Propagators." In 1623 Richard Jobson, a sympathetic observer, reported that Mandingo men were "furnisht with such members as are after a sort burthensome unto them." Another commentator thought Negroes "very lustful and impudent, especially, when they come to hide their nakedness, (for a *Negroes* hiding his Members, their extraordinary greatness) is a token of their Lust, and therefore much troubled with the Pox." By the eighteenth century a report on the sexual aggressiveness of African women was virtually required of European commentators. By then, of course, with many Englishmen actively participating in the slave trade, there were pressures making for descriptions of "hot constitution'd Ladies" possessed of a "temper hot and lascivious, making no scruple to prostitute themselves to the *Europeans* for a very slender profit, so great is their inclination to white men."

While the animus underlying these and similar remarks becomes sufficiently obvious once Englishmen began active participation in the slave trade, it is less easy to see why Englishmen should have fastened upon Negroes a pronounced sexuality virtually upon first sight. The ancient notions distilled by Bodin and Leo Africanus must have helped pattern initial English perceptions. Yet clearly there was something in English culture working in this direction. It is certain that the presumption of powerful sexuality in black men was far from being an incidental or casual association

in the minds of Englishmen. How very deeply this association operated is obvious in *Othello,* a drama which loses most of its power and several of its central points if it is read with the assumption that because the black man was the hero English audiences were indifferent to his blackness. Shakespeare was writing both *about* and *to* his countrymen's feelings concerning physical distinctions between peoples; the play is shot through with the language of blackness and sex. Iago goes out of his way to talk about his own motives: "I hate the Moor/And it is thought abroad that twixt my sheets/He has done my office." Later, he becomes more direct, "For that I do suspect the lusty Moor hath leaped into my seat." It was upon this so obviously absurd suspicion that Iago based his resolve to "turn her virtue into pitch." Such was his success, of course, that Othello finally rushes off "to furnish me with some means of death for the fair devil." With this contorted denomination of Desdemona, Othello unwittingly revealed how deeply Iago's promptings about Desdemona's "own clime, complexion, and degree" had eaten into his consciousness. Othello was driven into accepting the premise that the physical distinction *matters:* "For she had eyes," he has to reassure himself, "and chose me." Then, as his suspicions give way to certainty, he equates her character with his own complexion:

> *Her name, that was as fresh,*
>   *As Dian's visage, is now begrim'd*
>   *and black*
>   *As mine own face.*

This important aspect of Iago's triumph over the noble Moor was a subtly inverted reflection of the propositions which Iago, hidden in darkness, worked upon the fair lady's father. No one knew better than Iago how to play upon hidden strings of emotion. Not content with the straight-forward crudity that "your daughter and the Moor are now making the beast with two backs," Iago told the agitated Brabantio that "an old black ram/Is tupping your white ewe" and alluded politely to "your daughter cover'd with a Barbary horse."

This was not merely the language of (as we say) a "dirty" mind: it was the integrated imagery of blackness and whiteness, of Africa, of the sexuality of beasts and the bestiality of sex. And of course Iago was entirely successful in persuading Brabantio, who had initially welcomed Othello into his house, that the marriage was "against all rules of nature." Eventually Brabantio came to demand of Othello what could have brought a girl "so tender, fair, and happy"

> *To incur a general mock*
> *Run from her guardage to the sooty*
> *bosom*
> *Of such a thing as thou.*

Altogether a curious way for a senator to address a successful general.

These and similar remarks in the play *Othello* suggest that Shakespeare and his audiences were not totally indifferent to the sexual union of "black" men and "white" women. Shakespeare did not condemn such union; rather, he played upon an inner theme of black and white sexuality, showing how the poisonous mind of a white man perverted and destroyed the noblest of loves by means of bringing to the surface (from the darkness, whence Iago spoke) the lurking shadows of animal sex to assault the whiteness of chastity. Never did "dirty" words more dramatically "blacken" a "fair" name. At the play's climax, standing stunned by the realization that the wife he has murdered was innocent, Othello groans to Emilia, "Twas I that killed her"; and Emilia responds with a torrent of condemnation: "O! the more angel she,/And you the blacker devil." Of Desdemona: "She was too fond of her filthy bargain." To Othello: "O gull! O dolt!/As ignorant as dirt!" Shakespeare's genius lay precisely in juxtaposing these two pairs: inner blackness and inner whiteness. The drama meant little if his audiences had felt no response to this cross-inversion and to the deeply turbulent double meaning of black *over* white.

It required a very great dramatist to expose some of the more inward biocultural values which led—or drove—Englishmen to accept readily the notion that Negroes were peculiarly sexual men. Probably these values and the ancient reputation of Africa upon which they built were of primary importance in determining the response of Englishmen to Africans. Whatever the importance of biologic elements in these values—whatever the effects of long northern nights, of living in a cool climate, of possessing light-colored bodies which excreted contrasting lumps of darkness—these values by Shakespeare's time were interlocked with English history and culture and, more immediately, with the circumstances of contact with Africans and the social upheaval of Tudor England.

Study Questions

1. How might the sixteenth century define "black"? How did their concept of blackness influence their attitude toward Africans?

2. What different theories were advanced to explain the reasons why Africans were black? What do these theories indicate about the attitude of the English toward the Africans?

3. How did Africans' behavior and customs reinforce English prejudice?

4. How did Englishmen interpret African sexual behavior? Did their interpretation strengthen or weaken their prejudice toward Africans?

5. How did the formation of prejudice lead to the development of slavery?

Bibliography

Historians have written more about slavery than any other aspect of Southern life. Those interested in the origins of slavery should read Winthrop Jordan, *White Over Black: American Attitudes Toward the Negro, 1550–1812* (1968); David B. Davis, *The Problem of Slavery in Western Culture* (1966); and Oscar and Mary Handlin, "The Origins of the Southern Labor System," *William and Mary Quarterly,* 3rd Ser., 7 (1950). To gauge the severity of slavery in the United States, historians have taken a comparative approach. Frank Tannenbaum, *Slave and Citizen: The Negro in the Americas* (1947), began the debate over theory and practice of slavery. Other important studies in this field are H. S. Klein, *Slavery in the Americas: A Comparative Study of Virginia and Cuba* (1967); Carl N. Degler, *Neither Black nor White: Slavery and Race Relations in Brazil and the United States* (1971); and Philip D. Curtin, *The Atlantic Slave Trade: A Census* (1969). For the life of a slave, see Alan Kulikoff, *Tobacco and Slaves: The Development of Southern Cultures in the Chesapeake, 1680–1800* (1986); John B. Boles, *Black Southerners, 1619–1869* (1984); and Betty Wood, *Slavery in Colonial Georgia, 1730–1775* (1984). For the best recent work on slavery, see Ira Berlin, *Many Thousands Gone: The First Two Centuries of Slavery* (1998) and John Thornton, *Africa and Africans in the Making of the Atlantic World, 1400–1800* (1998). For issues of race and sexuality, see Kathleen Brown, *Good Wives, Nasty Wenches, and Anxious Patriarchs: Gender, Race, and Power in Colonial Virginia* (1996).

READING 7

Treatment of the Slaves

Alexander Falconbridge

The first African slaves were seized by the Portuguese to supply labor for their Brazilian sugar plantations. Late in the seventeenth century, after tobacco and sugar plantations were well established in North America, the Caribbean, and Brazil, the English created the Royal African Company. From that time until its demise in the nineteenth century, the slave trade was dominated by the British. It was, in the words of one European trader, "a dreadful business." As many as one-fourth of the slaves never survived the trip to the New World. Because perhaps 10 million slaves were taken from Africa to all the colonies in the Western Hemisphere between 1600 and 1830, it can safely be assumed that 2.5 million of them died along the way.

There were three stages to the enslavement of Africans. First, the slaves were captured by other Africans. Second, the African captors transported the newly acquired slaves from the interior of their countries to coastal exchange posts where European traders purchased them with rum, cotton cloth, guns, gunpowder, cowrie shells, brass rings, and pig iron. Finally, there was the third stage, the "Middle Passage" across the Atlantic to the New World. Hundreds of slaves were crowded into the dark, damp holds of slave ships for months at a time, with little exercise, subsistence diets, and no sanitary facilities. The mortality rate from flu, dysentery, pleurisy, pneumonia, and smallpox was devastating. In the following account, Alexander Falconbridge, a physician aboard a slave ship describes the horrors of the middle passage.

As soon as the wretched Africans, purchased at the fairs, fall into the hands of the black traders, they experience an earnest[1] of those dreadful sufferings which they are doomed in future to undergo. And there is not the least room to doubt, but that even before they can reach the fairs, great numbers perish from cruel usage, want of food, travelling through inhospitable deserts, and so forth. They are brought from the places where they are purchased . . . in canoes; at the bottom of which they lie, having their hands tied with a kind of willow twigs, and a strict watch is kept over them. Their usage in other respects, during the time of the passage, which generally lasts several days, is equally cruel. Their allowance of food is so scanty that it is barely sufficient to support nature. They are, besides, much exposed to the violent rains which frequently fall here, being covered only with mats that afford but a slight defence; and as there is usually water at the bottom of the canoes, from their leaking, they are scarcely ever dry.

Nor do these unhappy beings, after they become the property of the Europeans (from whom, as a more civilized people, more humanity might naturally be expected), find their situation in the least amended. Their treatment is not less rigorous. The men negroes, on being brought aboard the ship, are immediately fastened together, two and two, by hand-cuffs on their wrists, and by irons rivetted on their legs. They are then sent down between the decks and placed in an apartment partitioned off for that purpose. The women likewise are placed in a separate apartment between decks, but without being ironed. And an adjoining room, on the same deck, is besides appointed for the boys. Thus are they all placed in different apartments.

But at the same time, they are frequently stowed so close, as to admit of no other posture than lying on their sides. Neither will the height between decks, unless directly under the grating, permit them the indulgence of an erect posture; especially where there are platforms, which is generally the case. These platforms are a kind of shelf, about eight or nine feet in breadth, extending from the side of the ship towards the centre. They are placed nearly midway between the decks, at the distance of two or three feet from each deck. Upon these the negroes are stowed in the same manner as they are on the deck underneath.

In each of the apartments are placed three or four large buckets, of a conical form, being near two feet in diameter at the bottom, and only one foot at the top, and in depth about twenty-eight inches; to which, when necessary, the negroes have recourse. It often happens, that those who are placed at a distance from the buckets, in endeavouring to get to them, tumble over their companions, in consequence of their being shackled. These accidents, although unavoidable, are productive of continual quarrels, in which some of them are always bruised. In this distressed situation, unable to proceed, and prevented from getting to the tubs, they desist from the attempt; and, as the necessities of nature are not to be repelled, ease themselves as they lie. This becomes a fresh source of boils and disturbances, and tends to render the condition of the poor captive wretches still more uncomfortable. The nuisance arising from these circumstances, is not unfrequently increased by the tubs being much too small for the purpose intended, and their being usually emptied but once every day. The rule for doing this, however, varies in different ships, according to the attention paid to the health and convenience of the slaves by the captain.

About eight o'clock in the morning the negroes are generally brought upon deck. Their irons being examined, a long chain, which is locked to a ring-bolt, fixed in the deck, is run through the rings of the shackles of the men, and then locked to another ring-bolt, fixed also in the deck. By this means fifty or sixty, and sometimes more, are fastened to one chain, in order to prevent them from rising, or endeavouring to escape. If the weather proves favourable, they are permit-

---

[1]*Foretaste.*
Alexander Falconbridge, "Treatment of the Slaves," *An Account of the Slave Trade on the Coast of Africa.* London: 1788.

ted to remain in that situation till four or five in the afternoon, when they are disengaged from the chain, and sent down.

The diet of the negroes, while on board, consists chiefly of horse-beans, boiled to the consistence of a pulp; of boiled yams and rice, and sometimes of a small quantity of beef or pork. The latter are frequently taken from the provisions laid in for the sailors. They sometimes make use of a sauce, composed of palm-oil, mixed with flour, water, and pepper, which the sailors call slabber-sauce. Yams are the favourite food of the Eboe, or Bight negroes; and rice or corn, of those from the Gold and Windward Coasts, each preferring the produce of their native soil.

In their own country, the negroes in general live on animal food and fish, with roots, yams, and Indian corn. The horse-beans and rice, with which they are fed aboard ship, are chiefly taken from Europe. The latter, indeed, is sometimes purchased on the coast, being far superior to any other.

The Gold Coast negroes scarcely ever refuse any food that is offered them, and they generally eat larger quantities of whatever is placed before them, than any other species of negroes, whom they likewise excel in strength of body and mind. Most of the slaves have such an aversion to the horse-beans that unless they are narrowly watched, when fed upon deck, they will throw them overboard, or in each other's faces when they quarrel.

They are commonly fed twice a day, about eight o'clock in the morning and four in the afternoon. In most ships they are only fed with their own food once a day. Their food is served up to them in tubs, about the size of a small water bucket. They are placed round these tubs in companies of ten to each tub, out of which they feed themselves with wooden spoons. These they soon lose, and when they are not allowed others, they feed themselves with their hands. In favourable weather they are fed upon deck, but in bad weather their food is given them below. Numberless quarrels take place among them during their meals; more especially when they are put upon short allowance, which frequently happens, if the passage from the coast of Guinea to

the West-India islands, proves of unusual length. In that case, the weak are obliged to be content with a very scanty portion. Their allowance of water is about half a pint each at every meal. It is handed round in a bucket and given to each negroe in a pannekin; a small utensil with a strait handle, somewhat similar to a sauceboat. However, when the ships approach the islands with a favourable breeze, they are no longer restricted.

Upon the negroes refusing to take sustenance, I have seen coals of fire, glowing hot, put on a shovel, and placed so near their lips, as to scorch and burn them. And this has been accompanied with threats, of forcing them to swallow the coals, if they any longer persisted in refusing to eat. These means have generally had the desired effect. I have also been credibly informed, that a certain captain in the slave trade, poured melted lead on such of the negroes as obstinately refused their food.

Exercise being deemed necessary for the preservation of their health, they are sometimes obliged to dance, when the weather will permit their coming on deck. If they go about it reluctantly, or do not move with agility, they are flogged; a person standing by them all the time with a cat-o'-nine-tails in his hand for that purpose. Their musick, upon these occasions, consists of a drum, sometimes with only one head, and when that is worn out, they do not scruple to make use of the bottom of one of the tubs before described. The poor wretches are frequently compelled to sing also; but when they do so, their songs are generally, as may naturally be expected, melancholy lamentations of their exile from their native country.

The women are furnished with beads for the purpose of affording them some diversion. But this end is generally defeated by the squabbles which are occasioned, in consequence of their stealing them from each other.

On board some ships, the common sailors are allowed to have intercourse with such of the black women whose consent they can procure. And some of them have been known to take the inconstancy of their paramours so much to heart, as to leap overboard and drown themselves. The

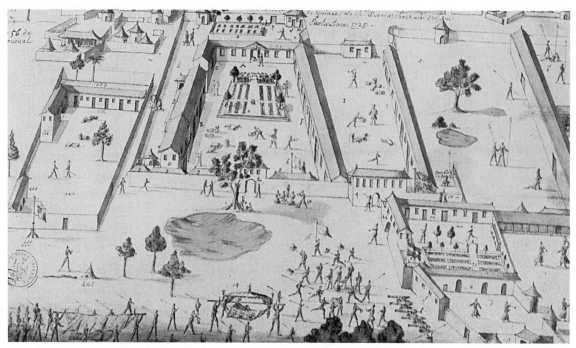

European slave traders built compounds on the African coast. Each compound served a different European company.

officers are permitted to indulge their passions among them at pleasure and sometimes are guilty of such brutal excesses as disgrace human nature.

The hardships and inconveniences suffered by the negroes during the passage are scarcely to be enumerated or conceived. They are far more violently affected by the sea-sickness than the Europeans. It frequently terminates in death, especially among the women. But the exclusion of the fresh air is among the most intolerable. For the purpose of admitting this needful refreshment, most of the ships in the slave-trade are provided, between the decks, with five or six air-ports on each side of the ship, of about six inches in length, and four in breadth; in addition to which, some few ships, but not one in twenty, have what they denominate wind-sails. But whenever the sea is rough, and the rain heavy, it becomes necessary to shut these, and every other conveyance by which the air is admitted. The fresh air being

thus excluded, the negroes rooms very soon grow intolerably hot. The confined air, rendered noxious by the effluvia exhaled from their bodies and by being repeatedly breathed, soon produces fevers and fluxes, which generally carries off great numbers of them.

During the voyages I made, I was frequently a witness to the fatal effects of this exclusion of the fresh air. I will give one instance, as it serves to convey some idea, though a very faint one, of the sufferings of those unhappy beings whom we wantonly drag from their native country and doom to perpetual labour and captivity. Some wet and blowing weather having occasioned the port-holes to be shut, and the grating to be covered, fluxes and fevers among the negroes ensued. While they were in this situation, my profession requiring it, I frequently went down among them, till at length their apartments became so extremely hot, as to be only sufferable for a very short time. But the excessive heat was not the only thing that rendered their situation intolerable. The deck, that is, the floor of their rooms, was so covered with the blood and mucus which had proceeded from them in consequence of the flux, that it resembled a slaughter-house. It is not in the power of the human imagination to picture to itself a situation more dreadful or disgusting. Numbers of the slaves having fainted, they were carried upon deck, where several of them died, and the rest were, with great difficulty, restored. It had nearly proved fatal to me also. The climate was too warm to admit the wearing of any clothing but a shirt, and that I had pulled off before I went down; notwithstanding which, by only continuing among them for about a quarter of an hour, I was so overcome with the heat, stench, and foul air that I had nearly fainted; and it was not without assistance that I soon after fell sick of the same disorder, from which I did not recover for several months.

A circumstance of this kind, sometimes repeatedly happens in the course of a voyage; and often to a greater degree than what was just been described; particularly when the slaves are much crowded, which was not the case at that time, the ship having more than a hundred short of the number she was to have taken in.

This devastation, great as it was, some few years ago was greatly exceeded on board a Liverpool ship. I shall particularize the circumstances of it, as a more glaring instance of an insatiable thirst for gain, or of less attention to the lives and happiness even of that despised and oppressed race of mortals, the fable inhabitants of Africa, perhaps was never exceeded; though indeed several similar instances have been known.

This ship, though a much smaller ship than that in which the event I have just mentioned happened, took on board at Bonny, at least six hundred negroes; but according to the information of the black traders, from whom I received the intelligence immediately after the ship failed, they amounted to near seven hundred. By purchasing so great a number, the slaves were so crowded, that they were even obliged to lie one upon another. This occasioned such a mortality among them, that, without meeting with unusual bad weather, or having a longer voyage than common, nearly one half of them died before the ship arrived in the West Indies.

That the publick may be able to form some idea of the almost incredible small space into which so large a number of negroes were crammed, the following particulars of this ship are given. According to Liverpool custom she measured 235 tons. Her width across the beam, 25 feet. Length between the decks, 92 feet, which was divided into four rooms, thus:

Store room, in which there were not any negroes placed	<u>15 feet</u>

Negroes' rooms:	
men's room	about 45 feet
women's ditto	about 10 feet
boys' ditto	about 22 feet
Total room for negroes	<u>77 feet</u>

Exclusive of the platform before described, from 8 to 9 feet in breadth, and equal in length to that of the rooms.

It may be worthy of remark, that the ships in this trade, are usually fitted out to receive only one third women negroes, or perhaps a smaller number, which the dimensions of the room allotted for them, above given, plainly shew, but in a great disproportion.

One would naturally suppose, that an attention to their own interest, would prompt the owners of the Guinea ships not to suffer the captains to take on board a greater number of negroes than the ship would allow room sufficient for them to lie with ease to themselves, or, at least, without rubbing against each other. However that may be, a more striking instance than the above, of avarice, completely and deservedly disappointed, was surely never displayed; for there is little room to doubt, but that in consequence of the expected premium usually allowed to the captains, of 61 per cent sterling on the produce of the negroes, this vessel was so thronged as to occasion such a heavy loss.

The place allotted for the sick negroes is under the half deck, where they lie on the bare planks. By this means, those who are emaciated, frequently have their skin, and even their flesh, entirely rubbed off, by the motion of the ship, from the prominent parts of the shoulders, elbows, and hips, so as to render the bones in those parts quite bare. And some of them, by constantly lying in the blood and mucus, that had flowed from those afflicted with the flux, and which, as before observed, is generally so violent as to prevent their being kept clean, have their flesh much sooner rubbed off, than those who have only to contend with the mere friction of the ship. The excruciating pain which the poor sufferers feel from being obliged to continue in such a dreadful situation, frequently for several weeks, in case they happen to live so long, is not to be conceived or described. Few, indeed, are ever able to withstand the fatal effects of it. The utmost skill of the surgeon is here ineffectual. If plaisters be applied, they are soon displaced by the friction of the ship; and when bandages are used, the negroes very soon take them off, and appropriate them to other purposes.

The surgeon, upon going between decks, in the morning, to examine the situation of the slaves, frequently finds several dead; and among the men, sometimes a dead and living negro fastened by their irons together. When this is the case, they are brought upon the deck, and being laid in the grating, the living negroe is disengaged, and the dead one is thrown overboard.

It may not be improper here to remark, that the surgeons employed in the Guinea trade are generally driven to engage in so disagreeable an employ by the confined state of their finances. An exertion of the greatest skill and attention could afford the diseased negroes little relief, so long as the causes of their diseases, namely, the breathing of a putrid atmosphere, and wallowing in their own excrements, remain. When once the fever and dysentery get to any height at sea, a cure is scarcely ever effected.

Almost the only means by which the surgeon can render himself useful to the slaves is by seeing that their food is properly cooked and distributed among them. It is true, when they arrive near the markets for which they are destined, care is taken to polish them for sale, by an application of the lunar caustic to such as are afflicted with the yaws. This, however, affords but a temporary relief, as the disease most assuredly breaks out, whenever the patient is put upon a vegetable diet.

It has been asserted, in favour of the captains in this trade, that the sick slaves are usually fed from their tables. The great number generally ill at a time, proves the falsity of such an assertion. Were even a captain disposed to do this, how could he feed half the slaves in the ship from his own table? For it is well known, that more than half are often sick at a time. Two or three perhaps may be fed.

The loss of slaves, through mortality arising from the causes just mentioned, is frequently very considerable. In the voyage lately referred to (not the Liverpool ship before-mentioned) one hundred and five, out of three hundred and eighty, died in the passage. A proportion seemingly very great, but by no means uncommon. One half, sometimes two thirds, and even beyond that, have been known to perish. Before we left Bonny River, no less than fifteen died of fevers and dysenteries occasioned by their confinement. On the Windward Coast, where slaves are procured more slowly, very few die, in proportion to the numbers which die at Bonny, and at Old and New Calabar, where they are obtained much faster; the latter being of a more delicate make and habit.

The havock made among the seamen engaged in this destructive commerce will be noticed in another part; and will be found to make no inconsiderable addition to the unnecessary waste of life just represented.

As very few of the negroes can so far brook the loss of their liberty and the hardships they endure as to bear them with any degree of patience, they are ever upon the watch to take advantage of the least negligence in their oppressors. Insurrections are frequently the consequence; which are seldom suppressed without much bloodshed. Sometimes these are successful, and the whole ship's company is cut off. They are likewise always ready to seize every opportunity for committing some act of desperation to free themselves from their miserable state; and not withstanding the restraints under which they are laid, they often succeed.

While a ship, to which I belonged, lay in a Bonny River, one evening, a short time before our departure, a lot of negroes, consisting of about ten, was brought on board; when one of them, in a favourable moment, forced his way through the net-work on the larboard side of the vessel, jumped overboard, and was supposed to have been devoured by the sharks.

During the time we were there, fifteen negroes belonging to a vessel from Liverpool, found means to throw themselves into the river; very few were saved; and the residue fell a sacrifice to the sharks. A similar instance took place in a French ship while we lay there.

Circumstances of this kind are very frequent. On the coast of Angola, at the River Ambris, the following incident happened: During the time of our residing on shore, we erected a tent to shelter ourselves from the weather. After having been there several weeks and being unable to purchase the number of slaves we wanted, through the opposition of another English slave vessel, we determined to leave the place. The night before our departure, the tent was struck; which was no sooner perceived by some of the negroe women on board, than it was considered as a prelude to our sailing; and about eighteen of them, when they were sent between decks, threw themselves into the sea through one of the gun ports; the ship carrying guns between decks. They were all of them, however, excepting one, soon picked up; and that which was missing, was, not long after, taken about a mile from the shore.

I once knew a negroe woman, too sensible of her woes, who pined for a considerable time, and was taken ill of a fever and dysentery; when declaring it to be her determination to die, she refused all food and medical aid, and, in about a fortnight after, expired. On being thrown overboard, her body was instantly torn to pieces by the sharks.

The following circumstance also came within my knowledge. A young female negroe, falling into a desponding way, it was judged necessary, in order to attempt her recovery, to send her on shore, to the hut of one of the black traders. Elevated with the prospect of regaining her liberty by this unexpected step, she soon recovered her usual cheerfulness; but hearing, by accident, that it was intended to take her on board the ship again, the poor young creature hung herself.

. . . I saw a middle aged stout woman, who had been brought down from a fair the preceding day, chained to the post of a black trader's door, in a state of furious insanity. On board a ship in Bonny River, I saw a young negroe woman chained to the deck, who had lost her senses, soon after she was purchased and taken on board. In a former voyage, on board a ship to which I belonged, we were obliged to confine a female negroe, of about twenty-three years of age, on her becoming a lunatic. She was afterwards sold during one of her lucid intervals.

One morning, upon examining the place allotted for the sick negroes, I perceived that one of them, who was so emaciated as scarcely to be able to walk, was missing, and was convinced that he must have gone overboard in the night, probably to put a more expeditious period to his sufferings. And, to conclude on this subject, I could not help being sensibly affected, on a former voyage, at observing with what apparent eagerness a black woman seized some dirt from off an African yam, and put it into her mouth; seeming to rejoice at the opportunity of possessing some of her native earth.

From these instances I think it may be clearly deduced, that the unhappy Africans are not bereft of the finer feelings but have a strong attachment to their native country, together with a just sense of the value of liberty. And the situation of the miserable beings above described, more forcibly urge the necessity of abolishing a trade which is the source of such evils, than the most eloquent harangue or persuasive arguments could do.

Study Questions

1. What was Falconbridge's general opinion about the morality of the slave trade? Did he feel guilty about the role he played in the traffic?

2. What was the greatest threat to the health of the slaves on the slave ship?

3. Why did the slave traders bring the slaves up on deck periodically and have them dance?

4. Describe the general living arrangements among the Africans being transported across the Atlantic Ocean.

5. Why was disease so rampant on the slave ships?

Bibliography

For general histories of the Atlantic slave trade, see Phillip D. Curtin, *The Atlantic Slave Trade: A Census* (1969); Basil Davidson, *Black Mother: The Years of the African Slave Trade* (1961); Daniel Mannix and Malcolm Cowley, *Black Cargoes: A History of the Atlantic Slave Trade, 1518-1865* (1962); James Pope-Hennessey, *Sin of the Fathers: A Study of the Atlantic Slave Trade, 1441-1807* (1968); and James A. Rawley, *The Transatlantic Slave Trade* (1981). For the impact of the slave trade on regional politics and society in West Africa, see David Birmingham, *Trade and Conflict in Angola, 1483-1790* (1966); K. Y. Daaku, *Trade and Politics on the Gold Coast, 1600-1720: A Study of the African Reaction to European Trade* (1970); and Karl Polanyi, *Dahomey and the Slave Trade* (1966). The best study of the Royal African Company is Kenneth Davies, *The Royal African Company* (1957). For the death rate among slaves being transported to the New World, see Raymond L. Cohn and Richard A. Jensen, "Mortality Rates and the Slave Trade," *Essays in Economic and Business History* (1981), and Phillip D. Curtin, "Epidemiology and the Slave Trade," *Political Science Quarterly* (June 1968). For a more recent look at the Atlantic slave trade, see David Northrup, ed., *The Atlantic Slave Trade* (1994) and Edward Reynolds, *Stand in the Storm: A History of the Atlantic Slave Trade* (1985). Also see Ira Berlin, *Many Thousands Gone: The First Two Centuries of Slavery* (1998) and John Thornton, *Africa and Africans in the Making of the Atlantic World, 1400-1800* (1998).

READING 8

Horses and Gentlemen

T. H. Breen

Traditional lines between history and the social sciences, and history and the humanities, have largely melted in the past generation. Historians have employed sociological, psychological, and anthropological theories and techniques to better uncover the richness of the past. In the following essay, T. H. Breen demonstrates in an exciting and provocative fashion the uses of anthropological techniques for the historian. Breen particularly was influenced by the ground-breaking work of anthropologist Clifford Geertz, who used cockfighting as a text for interpreting Balinese society. In "Notes on the Balinese Cockfight," Geertz writes, "In the cockfight . . . the Balinese forms and discovers his temperament and his society's temper at the same time."

Breen is interested in the temperament of the aristocratic Virginian and the temper of his society. In horse racing, a passion for the wealthy of Virginia, he hoped to expose the core values of colonial society. As he illustrates, horse racing involved more than simply wagering money, creating excitement, and aping English aristocratic manners: "By promoting horse racing the great planters legitimized the cultural values which racing symbolized—materialism, individualism, and competitiveness. . . . The wild sprint down the dirt track served the interests of Virginia's gentlemen better than they imagined."

In the fall of 1686 Durand of Dauphiné, a French Huguenot, visited the capital of colonial Virginia. Durand regularly recorded in a journal what he saw and heard, providing one of the few firsthand accounts of late seventeenth-century Virginia society that has survived to the present day. When he arrived in Jamestown the House of Burgesses was in session. "I saw there fine-looking men," he noted, "sitting in judgment booted and with belted sword." But to Durand's surprise, several of these Virginia gentlemen "started gambling" soon after dinner, and it was not until midnight that one of the players noticed the Frenchman patiently waiting for the contest to end. The Virginian—obviously a veteran of long nights at the gaming table—advised Durand to go to bed. " 'For,' said he, 'it is quite possible that we shall be here all night,' and in truth I found them still playing the next morning."

The event Durand witnessed was not unusual. In late seventeenth- and early eighteenth-century Virginia, gentlemen spent a good deal of time gambling. During this period, in fact, competitive gaming involving high stakes became a distinguishing characteristic of gentry culture. Whenever the great planters congregated, someone inevitably produced a deck of cards, a pair of dice, or a backgammon board; and quarter-horse racing was a regular event throughout the colony. Indeed, these men hazarded money and tobacco on almost any proposition in which there was an element of chance. Robert Beverley, a member of one of Virginia's most prominent families, made a wager "with the gentlemen of the country" that if he could produce seven hundred gallons of wine on his own plantation, they would pay him the handsome sum of one thousand guineas. Another leading planter offered six-to-one odds that Alexander Spotswood could not procure a commission as the colony's governor. And in 1671

T. H. Breen "Horses and Gentlemen: The Cultural Significance of Gambling among the Gentry of Virginia" *William and Mary Quarterly,* 3d Ser., 34 (April 1977) pp. 239–57. Reprinted by permission of the author and the Omohundro Institute of Early American History and Culture.

one disgruntled gentleman asked a court of law to award him his winnings from a bet concerning "a Servant maid." The case of this suspect-sounding wager—unfortunately not described in greater detail—dragged on until the colony's highest court ordered the loser to pay the victor a thousand pounds of tobacco.

The great planters' passion for gambling, especially on quarter-horse racing, coincided with a period of far-reaching social change in Virginia. Before the mid-1680s constant political unrest, servant risings both real and threatened, plant-cutting riots, and even a full-scale civil war had plagued the colony. But by the end of the century Virginia had achieved internal peace. Several elements contributed to the growth of social tranquility. First, by 1700 the ruling gentry were united as they had never been before. The great planters of the seventeenth century had been for the most part aggressive English immigrants. They fought among themselves for political and social dominance, and during Bacon's Rebellion in 1676 various factions within the gentry attempted to settle their differences on the battlefield. By the end of the century, however, a sizable percentage of the Virginia gentry, perhaps a majority, had been born in the colony. The members of this native-born elite—one historian calls them a "creole elite"—cooperated more frequently in political affairs than had their immigrant fathers. They found it necessary to unite in resistance against a series of interfering royal governors such as Thomas Lord Culpeper, Francis Nicholson, and Alexander Spotswood. After Bacon's Rebellion the leading planters—the kind of men whom Durand watched gamble the night away—successfully consolidated their control over Virginia's civil, military, and ecclesiastical institutions. They monopolized the most important offices; they patented the best lands.

A second and even more far-reaching element in the creation of this remarkable solidarity among the gentry was the shifting racial composition of the plantation labor force. Before the 1680s the planters had relied on large numbers of white indentured servants to cultivate Virginia's sole export crop, tobacco. These impoverished, often desperate servants disputed their masters' authority and on several occasions resisted colonial rulers with force of arms. In part because of their dissatisfaction with the indenture system, and in part because changes in the international slave trade made it easier and cheaper for Virginians to purchase black laborers, the major planters increasingly turned to Africans. The blacks' cultural disorientation made them less difficult to control than the white servants. Large-scale collective violence such as Bacon's Rebellion and the 1682 plant-cutting riots consequently declined markedly. By the beginning of the eighteenth century Virginia had been transformed into a relatively peaceful, biracial society in which a few planters exercised almost unchallenged hegemony over both their slaves and their poorer white neighbors.

The growth of gambling among the great planters during a period of significant social change raises important questions not only about gentry values but also about the social structure of late seventeenth-century Virginia. Why did gambling, involving high stakes, become so popular among the gentlemen at precisely this time? Did it reflect gentry values or have symbolic connotations for the people living in this society? Did this activity serve a social function, contributing in some manner to the maintenance of group cohesion? Why did quarter-horse racing, in particular, become a gentry sport? And finally, did public displays such as this somehow reinforce the great planters' social and political dominance?

In part, of course, gentlemen laid wagers on women and horses simply because they enjoyed the excitement of competition. Gambling was a recreation, like a good meal among friends or a leisurely hunt in the woods—a pleasant pastime when hard-working planters got together. Another equally acceptable explanation for the gentry's fondness for gambling might be the transplanting of English social mores. Certainly, the upper classes in the mother country loved betting for high stakes, and it is possible that the all-night card games and the frequent horse races were

staged attempts by a provincial gentry to transform itself into a genuine landed aristocracy. While both views possess merit, neither is entirely satisfactory. The great planters of Virginia presumably could have favored less risky forms of competition. Moreover, even though several planters deliberately emulated English social styles, the widespread popularity of gambling among the gentry indicates that this type of behavior may have had deeper, more complex cultural roots than either of these explanations would suggest.

In many societies competitive gaming is a device by which the participants transform abstract cultural values into observable social behavior. In his now-classic analysis of the Balinese cockfight Clifford Geertz describes contests for extremely high stakes as intense social dramas. These battles not only involve the honor of important villagers and their kin groups but also reflect in symbolic form the entire Balinese social structure. Far from being a simple pastime, betting on cocks turns out to be an expression of the way Balinese perceive social reality. The rules of the fight, the patterns of wagering, the reactions of winners and losers—all these elements help us to understand more profoundly the totality of Balinese culture.

The Virginia case is analogous to the Balinese. When the great planter staked his money and tobacco on a favorite horse or spurred a sprinter to victory, he displayed some of the central elements of gentry culture—its competitiveness, individualism, and materialism. In fact, competitive gaming was for many gentlemen a means of translating a particular set of values into action, a mechanism for expressing a loose but deeply felt bundle of ideas and assumptions about the nature of society. The quarter-horse races of Virginia were intense contests involving personal honor, elaborate rules, heavy betting, and wide community interest; and just as the cockfight opens up hidden dimensions of Balinese culture, gentry gambling offers an opportunity to improve our understanding of the complex interplay between cultural values and social behavior in Virginia.

Gambling reflected core elements of late seventeenth- and early eighteenth-century gentry values. From diaries, letters, and travel accounts we discover that despite their occasional cooperation in political affairs, Virginia gentlemen placed extreme emphasis upon personal independence. This concern may in part have been the product of the colony's peculiar settlement patterns. The great planters required immense tracts of fresh land for their tobacco. Often thousands of acres in size, their plantations were scattered over a broad area from the Potomac River to the James. The dispersed planters lived in their "Great Houses" with their families and slaves, and though they saw friends from time to time, they led for the most part isolated, routine lives. An English visitor in 1686 noted with obvious disapproval that "their Plantations run over vast Tracts of Ground . . . whereby the Country is thinly inhabited; the Living solitary and unsociable." Some planters were uncomfortably aware of the problems created by physical isolation. William Fitzhugh, for example, admitted to a correspondent in the mother country, "Society that is good and ingenious is very scarce, and seldom to be come at except in books."

Yet despite such apparent cultural privation, Fitzhugh and his contemporaries refused to alter their life styles in any way that might compromise their freedom of action. They assumed it their right to give commands, and in the ordering of daily plantation affairs they rarely tolerated outside interference. Some of these planters even saw themselves as law-givers out of the Old Testament. In 1726 William Byrd II explained that "like one of the Patriarchs, I have my Flocks and my Herds, my Bondmen and Bondwomen, and every Soart of Trade amongst my own Servants, so that I live in a kind of Independence every one but Providence." Perhaps Byrd exaggerated for literary effect, but forty years earlier Durand had observed, "There are no lords [in Virginia], but each is sovereign on his own plantation." Whatever the origins of this independent spirit, it bred excessive individualism in a wide range of social activities. While these powerful gentlemen sometimes

NOTICE is hereby given,

THAT on Thursday and Friday, the 30th and 31st Days of this Instant *May* will be Run for at *John Conner's* in *Anne Arundel* County, the Sum of Ten Pounds Currency, the First Day : And on the following Day, will be Run for at the same Place, the Sum of Five Pounds Currency : By any Horse, Mare, or Gelding, *(Old Ranter* and *Limber Sides* excepted); to carry 115 Pounds, three Heats, the Course two Miles.

The Horses, &c. to be Entered with *John Conner*, before 10 o'Clock in the Forenoon of each Day of Running : paying Entrance-Money, 15 s. the first Day ; and 10 s. the Day following.

A notice of a horse race in Anne Arundel County, Maryland, as seen in the Maryland Gazette, May 17, 1745.

worked together to achieve specific political and economic ends, they bristled at the least hint of constraint. Andrew Burnaby later noted that "the public or political character of the Virginians corresponds with their private one: they are haughty and jealous of their liberties, impatient of restraint, and can scarcely bear the thought of being controuled by any superior power."

The gentry expressed this uncompromising individualism in aggressive competitiveness, engaging in a constant struggle against real and imagined rivals to obtain more lands, additional patronage, and high tobacco prices. Indeed, competition was a major factor shaping the character of face-to-face relationships among the colony's gentlemen, and when the stakes were high the planters were not particular about the methods they employed to gain victory. In large part, the goal of the competition within the gentry group was to improve social position by increasing wealth.

Some gentlemen believed that personal honor was at stake as well. Robert "King" Carter, by all accounts the most successful planter of his generation, expressed his anxiety about losing out to another Virginian in a competitive market situation. "In discourse with Colonel Byrd, Mr. Armistead, and a great many others," he explained, "I understand you [an English merchant] had sold their tobaccos in round parcels and at good rates. I cannot allow myself to come behind any of these gentlemen in the planter's trade." Carter's pain arose not so much from the lower price he had received as from the public knowledge that he had been bested by respected peers. He believed he had lost face. This kind of intense competition was sparked, especially among the less affluent members of the gentry, by a dread of slipping into the ranks of what one eighteenth-century Virginia historian called the "common Planters." Gov. Francis Nicholson, an acerbic English placeman, declared that the ordinary sort of planters knew full well "from whence these mighty dons derive their originals." The governor touched a nerve; the efforts of "these mighty dons" to outdo one another were almost certainly motivated by a desire to disguise their "originals," to demonstrate anew through competitive encounters that they could legitimately claim gentility.

Another fact of Virginia gentry culture was materialism. This certainly does not mean that the great planters lacked spiritual concerns. Religion played a vital role in the lives of men like Robert Carter and William Byrd II. Nevertheless, piety was largely a private matter. In public these men determined social standing not by a man's religiosity or philosophic knowledge but by his visible estate—his lands, slaves, buildings, even by the quality of his garments. When John Bartram, one of America's first botanists, set off in 1737 to visit two of Virginia's most influential planters, a London friend advised him to purchase a new set of clothes, "for though I should not esteem thee less, to come to me in what dress thou will—yet these Virginians are a very gentle, well-dressed people—and look, perhaps, more at a man's outside than his inside." This perception of gentry values was accurate. Fitzhugh's desire to maintain outward appearances drove him to collect a stock of monogrammed silver plates and to import at great expense a well-crafted, though not very practical, English carriage. One even finds hints that the difficulty of preserving the image of material success weighed heavily upon some planters. When he described local Indian customs in 1705, Robert Beverley noted that native Americans lived an easy, happy existence "without toiling and perplexing their mind for Riches, which other people often trouble themselves to provide for uncertain and ungrateful Heirs."

The gentry were acutely sensitive to the element of chance in human affairs, and this sensitivity influenced their attitudes toward other men and society. Virginians knew from bitter experience that despite the best-laid plans, nothing in their lives was certain. Slaves suddenly sickened and died. English patrons forgot to help their American friends. Tobacco prices fell without warning. Cargo ships sank. Storms and droughts ruined the crops. The list was endless. Fitzhugh warned an English correspondent to think twice before allowing a son to become a Virginia planter, for even "if the best husbandry and the greatest forecast and skill were used, yet ill luck at Sea, a fall of a Market, or twenty other accidents may ruin and overthrow the best Industry." Other planters, even those who had risen to the top of colonial society, longed for greater security. "I could wish," declared William Byrd I in 1685, "wee had Some more certain Commodity [than tobacco] to rely on but see no hopes of itt." However desirable such certainty may have appeared, the planters always put their labor and money into tobacco, hoping for a run of luck. One simply learned to live with chance. In 1710 William Byrd II confided in his secret diary, "I dreamed last night . . . that I won a tunfull of money and might win more if I had ventured."

Gaming relationships reflected these strands of gentry culture. In fact, gambling in Virginia was a ritual activity. It was a form of repetitive, patterned behavior that not only corresponded closely to the gentry's values and assumptions but also symbolized the realities of everyday planter life. This congruence between actions and belief, between form and experience, helps to account for the popularity of betting contests. The wager, whether over cards or horses, brought together in a single, focused act the great planter's competitiveness, independence, and materialism, as well as the element of chance. It represented a social agreement in which each individual was free to determine how he would play, and the gentleman who accepted a challenge risked losing his material possessions as well as his personal honor.

The favorite household or tavern contests during this period included cards, backgammon, billiards, nine-pins, and dice. The great planters preferred card games that demanded skill as well as luck. Put, piquet, and whist provided the necessary challenge, and Virginia gentlemen—Durand's hosts, for example—regularly played these games for small sums of money and tobacco. These activities brought men together, stimulated conversation, and furnished a harmless outlet for aggressive drives. They did not, however, become for the gentry a form of intense, symbolic play such as the cockfight in Bali. William Byrd II once cheated his wife in a game of piquet, something he would never have dared to do among his peers at Williamsburg. By and large, he showed little emotional involvement in these types of household gambling. The exception here proves the rule. After an unusually large loss at the gaming tables of Williamsburg, Byrd drew a pointed finger in the margin of his secret diary and swore a "solemn resolution never at once to lose more than 50 shillings and to spend less time in gaming, and I beg the God Almighty to give me grace to keep so good a resolution . . ." Byrd's reformation was short-lived, for within a few days he dispassionately noted losing another four pounds at piquet.

Horse racing generated far greater interest among the gentry than did the household games. Indeed for the great planters and the many others who came to watch, these contests were preeminently a social drama. To appreciate the importance of racing in seventeenth-century Virginia, we must understand the cultural significance of horses. By the turn of the century possession of one of these animals had become a social necessity. Without a horse, a planter felt despised, an object of ridicule. Owning even a slow-footed saddle horse made the common planter more of a man in his own eyes as well as in those of his neighbors; he was reluctant to venture forth on foot for fear of making an adverse impression. As the Rev. Hugh Jones explained in 1724, "Almost every ordinary Person keeps a Horse; and I have known some to spend the Morning in ranging several Miles in the Woods to find and catch their Horses only to ride two or three Miles to Church, to the Court-House, or to a Horse-Race, where they generally appoint to meet upon Business." Such behavior seems a waste of time and energy only to one who does not comprehend the symbolic importance which the Virginians attached to their horses. A horse was an extension of its owner; indeed, a man was only as good as his horse. Because of the horse's cultural significance, the gentry attempted to set its horsemanship apart from that of the common planters. Gentlemen took better care of their animals, and, according to John Clayton, who visited Virginia in 1688, they developed a distinctive riding style. "They ride pretty sharply," Clayton reported; "a Planter's Pace is a Proverb, which is a good sharp hand-Gallop." A fast-rising cloud of dust far down a Virginia road probably alerted the common planter that he was about to encounter a social superior.

The contest that generated the greatest interest among the gentry was the quarter-horse race, an all-out sprint by two horses over a quarter-mile dirt track. The great planters dominated these events. In the records of the country courts—our most important source of information about specific races—we find the names of some of the colony's most prominent planter families—Randolph, Eppes, Jefferson, Swan, Kenner, Hardiman, Parker, Cocke, Batte, Harwick (Hardidge), Youle (Yowell), and Washington. Members of the House of Burgesses, including its powerful speaker, William Randolph, were frequently mentioned in the contests that came before the courts. On at least one occasion the Rev. James Blair, Virginia's most eminent clergyman and a founder of the College of William and Mary, gave testimony in a suit arising from a race run between Capt. William Soane and Robert Napier. The tenacity with which the gentry pursued these cases, almost continuations of the race itself, suggests that victory was no less sweet when it was gained in court.

Many elements contributed to the exclusion of lower social groups from these contests. Because of the sheer size of wagers, poor freemen and common planters could not have participated regularly. Certainly, the members of the Accomack County Court were embarrassed to discover that one Thomas Davis, "a very poore Man," had lost 500 pounds of tobacco or a cow and calf in a horse race with an adolescent named Mr. John Andrews. Recognizing that Davis bore "a great charge of wife and Children," the justices withheld final judgment until the governor had an opportunity to rule on the legality of the wager. The Accomack court noted somewhat gratuitously that if the governor declared the action unlawful, it would fine Davis five days' work on a public bridge. In such cases country justices ordinarily made no comment upon a plaintiff's or defendant's financial condition, assuming, no doubt, that most people involved in racing were capable of meeting their gaming obligations.

The gentry actively enforced its exclusive control over quarter-horse racing. When James Bullocke, a York County tailor, challenged Mr. Mathew Slader to a race in 1674, the county court informed Bullocke that it was "contrary to Law for a Labourer to make a race being a Sport for Gentlemen" and fined the presumptuous tailor two hundred pounds of tobacco and cask. Additional evidence of exclusiveness is found in early eighteenth-century Hanover County. In one of the earliest issues of the colony's first newspaper, the *Virginia Gazette,* an advertisement appeared announcing that "some merry-dispos'd gentlemen" in Hanover planned to celebrate St. Andrew's Day with a race for quarter-milers. The Hanover gentlemen explained in a later, fuller description that "all Persons resorting there are desir'd to behave themselves with Decency and Sobriety, the Subscribers being resolv'd to discountenance all Immorality with the utmost Rigour." The purpose of these contests was to furnish the county's "considerable Number of Gentlemen, Merchants, and credible Planters" an opportunity for "cultivating Friendship." Less affluent persons apparently were welcome to watch the proceedings provided they acted like gentlemen.

In most match races the planter rode his own horse, and the exclusiveness of these contests meant that racing created intensely competitive confrontations. There were two ways to set up a

challenge. The first was a regularly scheduled affair usually held on Saturday afternoon. By 1700 there were at least a dozen tracks, important enough to be known by name, scattered through the counties of the Northern Neck and the James River valley. The records are filled with references to contests held at such places as Smith's Field, Coan Race Course, Devil's Field, Yeocomico, and Varina. No doubt, many races also occurred on nameless country roads or convenient pastures. On the appointed day the planter simply appeared at the race track and waited for a likely challenge. We know from a dispute heard before the Westmoreland County Court in 1693 that John Gardner boldly "Challeng'd all the horses then upon the ground to run with any of them for a thousand pounds of Tobo and twenty shillings in money." A second type of contest was a more spontaneous challenge. When gentlemen congregated over a jug of hard cider or peach brandy, the talk frequently turned to horses. The owners presumably bragged about the superior speed of their animals, and if one planter called another's bluff, the men cried out "done, and done," marched to the nearest field, and there discovered whose horse was in fact the swifter.

Regardless of the outcome, quarter-horse races in Virginia were exciting spectacles. The crowds of onlookers seem often to have been fairly large, as common planters, even servants, flocked to the tracks to watch the gentry challenge one another for what must have seemed immense amounts of money and tobacco. One witness before a Westmoreland County Court reported in 1674 that Mr. Stone and Mr. Youle had run a challenge for £10 sterling "in sight of many people." Attendance at race days was sizable enough to support a brisk trade in cider and brandy. In 1714 the Richmond County Court fined several men for peddling liquors "by Retaile in the Race Ground." Judging from the popularity of horses throughout planter society, it seems probable that the people who attended these events dreamed of one day riding a local champion such as Prince or Smoaker.

The magnitude of gentry betting indicates that racing must have deeply involved the planter's self-esteem. Wagering took place on two levels. The contestants themselves made a wager on the outcome, a main bet usually described in a written statement. In addition, side wagers were sometimes negotiated between spectators or between a contestant and spectator. Of the two, the main bet was far the more significant. From accounts of disputed races reaching the county courts we know that gentlemen frequently risked very large sums. The most extravagant contest of the period was a race run between John Baker and John Haynie in Northumberland County in 1693, in which the two men wagered 4,000 pounds of tobacco and 40 shillings sterling on the speed of their sprinters, Prince and Smoaker. Some races involved only twenty or thirty shillings, but a substantial number were run for several pounds sterling and hundreds of pounds of tobacco. While few, if any, of the seventeenth-century gentlemen were what we would call gambling addicts, their betting habits seem irrational even by the more prudential standards of their own day: in conducting normal business transactions, for example, they would never have placed so much money in such jeopardy.

To appreciate the large size of these bets we must interpret them within the context of Virginia's economy. Between 1660 and 1720 a planter could anticipate receiving about ten shillings per hundredweight of tobacco. Since the average grower seldom harvested more than 1,500 pounds of tobacco a year per man, he probably never enjoyed an annual income from tobacco in excess of eight pounds sterling. For most Virginians the conversion of tobacco into sterling occurred only in the neat columns of account books. They themselves seldom had coins in their pockets. Specie was extremely scarce, and planters ordinarily paid their taxes and conducted business transactions with tobacco notes—written promises to deliver to the bearer a designated amount of tobacco. The great preponderance of seventeenth-century planters were quite poor, and even the great planters estimated their income in hundreds, not thousands, of pounds sterling. Fitzhugh, one of the wealthier men of his

generation, described his financial situation in detail. "Thus I have given you some particulars," he wrote in 1686, "which I thus deduce, the yearly Crops of corn and Tobo, together with the surplusage of meat more than will serve the family's use, will amount annually to 60,000lb. Tobo. wch. at 10 shilling per Ct. is 300 £ annum." These facts reveal that the Baker-Haynie bet—to take a notable example—amounted to approximately £22 sterling, more than 7 percent of Fitzhugh's annual cash return. It is therefore not surprising that the common planters seldom took part in quarter-horse racing: this wager alone amounted to approximately three times the income they could expect to receive in a good year. Even a modest wager of a pound or two sterling represented a substantial risk.

Gentlemen sealed these gaming relationships with a formal agreement, either a written statement laying out the terms of the contest or a declaration before a disinterested third party of the nature of the wager. In either case the participants carefully stipulated what rules would be in effect. Sometimes the written agreements were quite elaborate. In 1698, for example, Richard Ward and John Steward, Jr., "Covenanted and agreed" to race at a quarter-mile track in Henrico County known as Ware. Ward's mount was to enjoy a ten-yard handicap, and if it crossed the finish line within five lengths of Steward's horse, Ward would win five pounds sterling; if Steward's obviously superior animal won by a greater distance, Ward promised to pay six pounds sterling. In another contest William Eppes and Stephen Cocke asked William Randolph to witness an agreement for a ten-shilling race: "Each horse was to keep his path, they not being to crosse unlesse Stephen Cocke could gett the other Riders Path at the start at two or three Jumps."

Virginia's county courts treated race covenants as binding legal contracts. If a gentleman failed to fulfill the agreement, the other party had legitimate grounds to sue; and the county justices' first consideration during a trial was whether the planters had properly recorded their agreement. The Henrico court summarily dismissed one gambling suit because "noe Money was stacked down nor Contract in writing made [,] one of wch in such cases is by the law required." Because any race might generate legal proceedings, it was necessary to have a number of people present at the track not only to assist in the running of the contest but also to act as witnessess if anything went wrong. The two riders normally appointed an official starter, several judges, and someone to hold the stakes.

Almost all of the agreements included a promise to ride a fair race. Thus two men in 1698 insisted upon "fair Rideing"; another pair pledged "they would run fair horseman's play." By such agreements the planters waived their customary right to jostle, whip, or knee an opponent, or to attempt to unseat him. During the last decades of the seventeenth century the gentry apparently attempted to substitute riding skill and strategy for physical violence. The demand for "fair Rideing" also suggests that the earliest races in Virginia were wild, no-holds-barred affairs that afforded contestants ample opportunity to vent their aggressions.

The intense desire to win sometimes undermined a gentleman's written promise to run a fair race. When the stakes were large, emotions ran high. One man complained in a York County court that an opponent had interfered with his horse in the middle of the race, "by meanes whereof the s[ai]d Plaintiff lost the said Race." Joseph Humphrey told a Northumberland County court that he would surely have come in first in a challenge for 1,500 pounds of tobacco had not Capt. Rodham Kenner (a future member of the House of Burgesses) "held the defendt horses bridle in running his race." Other riders testified that they had been "Josselled" while the race was in progress. An unusual case of interference grew out of a 1694 race which Rodham Kenner rode against John Hartly for one pound sterling and 575 pounds of tobacco. In a Westmoreland County court Hartly explained that after a fair start and without using "whipp or Spurr" he found himself "a great distance" in front of Kenner. But as Hartly neared the finish line, Kenner's brother, Richard, suddenly jumped onto the track

and "did hollow and shout and wave his hat over his head in the plts [plaintiff's] horse's face." The animal panicked, ran outside the posts marking the finish line, and lost the race. After a lengthy trial a Westmoreland jury decided that Richard Kenner "did no foule play in his hollowing and waveing his hatt." What exactly occurred during this race remains a mystery, but since no one denied that Richard acted very strangely, it seems likely that the Kenner brothers were persuasive as well as powerful.

Planters who lost large wagers because an opponent jostled or "hollowed" them off the track were understandably angry. Yet instead of challenging the other party to a duel or allowing gaming relationships to degenerate into blood feuds, the disappointed horsemen invariably took their complaints to the courts. Such behavior indicated not only that the gentlemen trusted the colony's formal legal system—after all, members of their group controlled it—but also that they were willing to place institutional limitations on their own competitiveness. Gentlemen who felt they had been cheated or abused at the track immediately collected witnessess and brought suit before the nearest county court. The legal machinery available to the aggrieved gambler was complex; and no matter how unhappy he may have been with the final verdict, he could rarely claim that the system had denied due process.

The plaintiff brought charges before a group of justices of the peace sitting as a county court; if these men found sufficient grounds for a suit, the parties—in the language of seventeenth-century Virginia—could "put themselves upon the country." In other words, they could ask that a jury of twelve substantial freeholders to hear the evidence and decide whether the race had in fact been fairly run. If the sums involved were high enough, either party could appeal a local decision to the colony's general court, a body consisting of the governor and his council. Several men who hotly insisted that they had been wronged followed this path. For example, Joseph Humphrey, loser in a race for 1,500 pounds of tobacco, stamped out of a Northumberland County court, demanding a stop to "farther proceedings in the Common Law till a hearing in Chancery." Since most of the General Court records for the seventeenth century were destroyed during the Civil War, it is impossible to follow these cases beyond the county level. It is apparent from the existing documents, however, that all the men involved in these race controversies took their responsibilities seriously, and there is no indication that the gentry regarded the resolution of a gambling dispute as less important than proving a will or punishing a criminal. It seems unlikely that the colony's courts would have adopted such an indulgent attitude toward racing had these contests not in some way served a significant social function for the gentry.

Competitive activities such as quarter-horse racing served social as well as symbolic functions. As we have seen, gambling reflected core elements of the culture of late seventeenth-century Virginia. Indeed, if it had not done so, horse racing would not have become so popular among the colony's gentlemen. These contests also helped the gentry to maintain group cohesion during a period of rapid social change. After 1680 the great planters do not appear to have become significantly less competitive, less individualistic, or less materialistic than their predecessors had been. But while the values persisted, the forms in which they were expressed changed. During the last decades of the century unprecedented external pressures, both political and economic, coupled with a major shift in the composition of the colony's labor force, caused the Virginia gentry to communicate these values in ways that would not lead to deadly physical violence or spark an eruption of blood feuding. The members of the native-born elite, anxious to preserve their autonomy over local affairs, sought to avoid the kinds of divisions within their ranks that had contributed to the outbreak of Bacon's Rebellion. They found it increasingly necessary to cooperate against meddling royal governors. Moreover, such earlier unrest among the colony's plantation workers as Bacon's Rebellion and the plant-cutting riots had impressed upon the great planters the need to present a common face to their dependent laborers, especially to the growing number of black slaves who seemed more and more menacing as the years passed.

Gaming relationships were one of several ways by which the planters, no doubt unconsciously, preserved class cohesion. By wagering on cards and horses they openly expressed their extreme competitiveness, winning temporary emblematic victories over their rivals without thereby threatening the social tranquility of Virginia. These nonlethal competitive devices, similar in form to what social anthropologists have termed "joking relationships," were a kind of functional alliance developed by the participants themselves to reduce dangerous, but often inevitable, social tensions.

Without rigid social stratification racing would have lost much of its significance for the gentry. Participation in these contests publicly identified a person as a member of an elite group. Great planters raced against their social peers. They certainly had no interest in competing with social inferiors, for in this kind of relationship victory carried no positive meaning: the winner gained neither honor nor respect. By the same token, defeat by someone like James Bullocke, the tailor from York, was painful, and to avoid such incidents gentlemen rarely allowed poorer whites to enter their gaming relationships—particularly the heavy betting on quarter horses. The common planters certainly gambled among themselves. Even the slaves may have laid wagers. But when the gentry competed for high stakes, they kept their inferiors at a distance, as spectators but never players.

The exclusiveness of horse racing strengthened the gentry's cultural dominance. By promoting these public displays the great planters legitimized the cultural values which racing symbolized—materialism, individualism, and competitiveness. These colorful, exclusive contests helped persuade subordinate white groups that gentry culture was desirable, something worth emulating; and it is not surprising that people who conceded the superiority of this culture readily accepted the gentry's right to rule. The wild sprint down a dirt tract served the interests of Virginia's gentlemen better than they imagined.

Study Questions

1. Breen notes that the "great planter's passion for gaming . . . coincided with a period of far-reaching social change in Virginia." How was Virginia changing?

2. Why did the Virginia gentry feel the need to display solidarity in the face of their social and economic inferiors? Why were members of the gentry reluctant to compete against social inferiors?

3. How important was excitement in work and play for the Virginia gentry?

4. What were the "core values" of Virginia society, and how did gambling illustrate those values?

5. What does Breen mean by the "role of chance" in colonial Virginia?

6. How did a member of the Virginia gentry view his best horse as an extension of himself? What were the symbolic aspects of horse racing in colonial Virginia?

7. How do sports and games illustrate the "core values" of American society?

Bibliography

Clifford Geertz's masterful essay "Deep Play: Notes on the Balinese Cockfight," *Daedalus,* 101 (1972) demonstrates the relationship between how people play and how they live. Recently sports historians have continued Geertz's line of investigation. They have shown that sports and games play important roles in society. Benjamin G. Rader, *American Sports: From the Age of Folk Games to the Age of Spectators* (1983) presents a balanced and insightful overview of the subject.

Several historians have studied English sports and pastimes of the seventeenth and eighteenth centuries. Among the better studies are Roger Longrigg, *The English Squire and His Sport* (1977); Patricia Ann Lee, "Play and the English Gentleman in the Early Seventeenth Century," *Historian,* 31 (1969); Dennis Brailsford, *Sport and Society: Elizabeth to Queen Anne* (1969); Robert W. Malcolmson, *Popular Recreations in English Society, 1700–1850* (1980); and E. P. Thompson, "Patrician Society, Plebian Culture," *Journal of Social History,* 7 (1974). For American attitudes toward sports and games see Winton V. Salberg, *Redeem the Times: The Puritan Sabbath in Early America* (1977); Nancy L. Struna, "Sport and Societal Values: Massachusetts Bay," *Quest,* 27 (1977); and C. Robert Barnett, "Recreational Patterns of the Colonial Virginia Aristocrat," *Journal of the West Virginia Historical Association,* 2 (1978). The evolution of Southern society can be studied in Allan Kulikoff, *Tobacco and Slaves* (1987); Rhys Isaac, *The Transformation of Virginia, 1740–1790* (1982); and Mechal Sobel, *The World They Made Together* (1987). Also see James Horn, *Adapting to a New World: English Society in the Seventeenth-Century Chesapeake* (1994) and Philip D. Morgan, *The Slave Counterpart: Black Culture in the Eighteenth-Century Chesapeake and Low Country* (1998).

READING 9

The Planter's Wife: The Experience of White Women in Seventeenth-Century Maryland

Lois Green Carr and Lorena S. Walsh

By any standard, life in seventeenth-century Maryland was a mean, brutal affair. Men and women lived long periods in indentured servitude, married late, lost most of their children to early deaths, and died young themselves. Without the steady influx of new immigrants, the Maryland population would not have been self-sustaining. And yet, the immigrants kept coming, drawn to the New World by the abundance of land and the chance to reinvent themselves. For women in seventeenth-century Maryland, life was even more problematic. They also had to deal with the fluctuations of the tobacco economy, epidemic disease, high rates of death during childbirth, sexual abuse, and a legal system that was biased against them. In the following essay, historians Lois Green Carr and Lorena S. Walsh describe the world of the "planter's wife."

Four facts were basic to all human experience in seventeenth-century Maryland. First, for most of the period the great majority of inhabitants had been born in what we now call Britain. Population increase in Maryland did not result primarily from births in the colony before the late 1680s and did not produce a predominantly native population of adults before the first decade of the eighteenth century. Second, immigrant men could not expect to live beyond age forty-three, and 70 percent would die before age fifty. Women may have had even shorter lives. Third, perhaps 85 percent of the immigrants, and practically all the unmarried immigrant women, arrived as indentured servants and consequently married late. Family groups were never predominant in the immigration to Maryland and were a significant part for only a brief time at mid-century. Fourth, many more men than women immigrated during the whole period. These facts—immigrant predominance, early death, late marriage, and sexual imbalance—created circumstances of social and demographic disruption that deeply affected family and community life.

We need to assess the effects of this disruption on the experience of women in seventeenth-century Maryland. Were women degraded by the hazards of servitude in a society in which everyone had left community and kin behind and in which women were in short supply? Were traditional restraints on social conduct weakened? If so, were women more exploited or more independent and powerful than women who remained in England? Did any differences from English experience which we can observe in the experience of Maryland women survive the transformation from an immigrant to a predominantly native-born society with its own kinship networks and community traditions? The tentative argument put forward here is that the answer to all these questions is Yes. There were degrading

aspects of servitude, although these probably did not characterize the lot of most women; there were fewer restraints on social conduct, especially in courtship than in England; women were less protected but also more powerful than those who remained at home; and at least some of these changes survived the appearance in Maryland of New World creole communities. However, these issues are far from settled, and we shall offer some suggestions as to how they might be further pursued.

Maryland was settled in 1634, but in 1650 there were probably no more than six hundred persons and fewer than two hundred adult women in the province. After that time population growth was steady; in 1704 a census listed 30,437 white persons, of whom 7,163 were adult women. Thus in discussing the experience of white women in seventeenth-century Maryland we are dealing basically with the second half of the century.

Marylanders of that period did not leave letters and diaries to record their New World experience or their relationships to one another. Nevertheless, they left trails in the public records that give us clues. Immigrant lists kept in England and documents of the Maryland courts offer quantifiable evidence about the kinds of people who came and some of the problems they faced in making a new life. Especially valuable are the probate court records. Estate inventories reveal the kinds of activities carried on in the house and on the farm, and wills, which are usually the only personal statements that remain for any man or woman, show something of personal attitudes. This essay relies on the most useful of the immigrant lists and all surviving Maryland court records, but concentrates especially on the surviving records of the lower Western Shore, an early-settled area highly suitable for tobacco. Most of this region comprised four counties: St. Mary's, Calvert, Charles, and Prince George's (formed in 1696 from Calvert and Charles). Inventories from all four counties, wills from St. Mary's and Charles, and court proceedings from Charles and Prince George's provide the major data.

Because immigrants predominated, who they were determined much about the character of

Lois Green Carr and Lorena S. Walsh, "The Planter's Wife: The Experience of White Women in Seventeenth-Century Maryland," *William and Mary Quarterly,* 34 (October 1977), 542–70.

Maryland society. The best information so far available comes from lists of indentured servants who left the ports of London, Bristol, and Liverpool. These lists vary in quality, but at the very least they distinguish immigrants by sex and general destination. A place of residence in England is usually given, although it may not represent the emigrant's place of origin; and age and occupation are often noted. These lists reveal several characteristics of immigrants to the Chesapeake and, by inference, to Maryland.

Servants who arrived under indenture included yeomen, husbandmen, farm laborers, artisans, and small tradesmen, as well as many untrained to any special skill. They were young: over half of the men on the London lists of 1683–1684 were aged eighteen to twenty-two. They were seldom under seventeen or over twenty-eight. The women were a little older; the great majority were between eighteen and twenty-five, and half were aged twenty to twenty-two. Most servants contracted for four or five years service although those under fifteen were to serve at least seven years. These youthful immigrants represented a wide range of English society. All were seeking opportunities they had not found at home.

However, many immigrants—perhaps about half—did not leave England with indentures but paid for their passage by serving according to the custom of the country. Less is known about their social characteristics, but some inferences are possible. From 1661, customary service was set by Maryland laws that required four-year (later five-year) terms for men and women who were twenty-two years or over at arrival and longer terms for those who were younger. A requirement of these laws enables us to determine something about age at arrival of servants who came without indentures. A planter who wished to obtain more than four or five years of service had to take his servant before the county court to have his or her age judged and a written record made. Servants aged over twenty-one were not often registered, there being no incentive for a master to pay court fees for those who would serve the minimum term. Nevertheless, a comparison of

the ages of servants under twenty-two recorded in Charles County, 1658–1689, with those under twenty-two on the London list is revealing. Of Charles County male servants (N = 363), 77.1 percent were aged seventeen or under whereas on the London list (N = 196), 77.6 percent were eighteen or over. Women registered in Charles County court were somewhat older than the men, but among those under twenty-two (N = 107), 5.5 percent were aged twenty-one, whereas on the London list (N = 69), 46.4 percent had reached this age. Evidently, some immigrants who served by custom were younger than those who came indentured, and this age difference probably characterized the two groups as a whole. Servants who were not only very young but had arrived without the protection of a written contract were possibly of lower social origins than were servants who came under indenture. The absence of skills among Charles County servants who served by custom supports this supposition.

Whatever their status, one fact about immigrant women is certain: many fewer came than men. Immigrant lists, headright lists, and itemizations of servants in inventories show severe imbalance. On a London immigrant list of 1634–1635 men outnumbered women six to one. From the 1650s at least until the 1680s most sources show a ratio of three to one. From then on, all sources show some, but not great, improvement. Among immigrants from Liverpool over the years 1697–1707 the ratio was just under two and one half to one.

Why did not more women come? Presumably, fewer wished to leave family and community to venture into a wilderness. But perhaps more important, women were not as desirable as men to merchants and planters who were making fortunes raising and marketing tobacco, a crop that requires large amounts of labor. The gradual improvement in the sex ratio among servants toward the end of the century may have been the result of a change in recruiting the needed labor. In the late 1660s the supply of young men willing to emigrate stopped increasing sufficiently to meet the labor demands of a growing Chesapeake population. Merchants who recruited servants for planters turned to other sources, and among these sources were women. They did not crowd the ships arriving in the Chesapeake, but their numbers did increase.

To ask the question another way, why did women come? Doubtless, most came to get a husband, an objective virtually certain of success in a land where women were so far outnumbered. The promotional literature, furthermore, painted bright pictures of the life that awaited men and women once out of their time; and various studies suggest that for a while, at least, the promoters were not being entirely fanciful. Until the 1660s, and to a less degree the 1680s, the expanding economy of Maryland and Virginia offered opportunities well beyond those available in England to men without capital and to the women who became their wives.

Nevertheless, the hazards were also great, and the greatest was untimely death. Newcomers promptly became ill, probably with malaria, and many died. What proportion survived is unclear; so far no one has devised a way of measuring it. Recurrent malaria made the woman who survived seasoning less able to withstand other diseases, especially dysentery and influenza. She was especially vulnerable when pregnant. Expectation of life for everyone was low in the Chesapeake, but especially so for women. A woman who had immigrated to Maryland took an extra risk, though perhaps a risk not greater than she might have suffered by moving from her village to London instead.

The majority of women who survived seasoning paid their transportation costs by working for a four- or five-year term of service. The kind of work depended on the status of the family they served. A female servant of a small planter—who through about the 1670s might have had a servant—probably worked at the hoe. Such a man could not afford to buy labor that would not help with the cash crop. In wealthy families women probably were household servants, although some are occasionally listed in inventories of well-to-do planters as living on the quarters—that is, on plantations other than the dwelling plantation. Such women saved men the jobs of preparing food and washing linen but doubtless also worked in the fields. In middling households experience must have varied. Where the number of people to feed and wash for was large, female servants would have had little time to tend the crops.

Tracts that promoted immigration to the Chesapeake region asserted that female servants did not labor in the fields, except "nasty" wenches not fit for other tasks. This implies that most immigrant women expected, or at least hoped, to avoid heavy field work, which English women—at least those above the cottager's status—did not do. What proportion of female servants in Maryland found themselves demeaned by this unaccustomed labor is impossible to say, but this must have been the fate of some. A study of the distribution of female servants among wealthy groups in Maryland might shed some light on this question. Nevertheless, we still would not know whether those purchased by the poor or sent to work on a quarter were women whose previous experience suited them for field labor.

An additional risk for the woman who came as a servant was the possibility of bearing a bastard. At least 20 percent of the female servants who came to Charles County between 1658 and 1705 were presented to the county court for this cause. A servant woman could not marry unless someone was willing to pay her master for the term she had left to serve. If a man made her pregnant, she could not marry him unless he could buy her time. Once a woman became free, however, marriage was clearly the usual solution. Only a handful of free women were presented in Charles County for bastardy between 1658 and 1705. Since few free women remained either single or widowed for long, not many were subject to the risk. The hazard of bearing a bastard was a hazard of being a servant.

This high rate of illegitimate pregnancies among servants raises lurid questions. Did men import women for sexual exploitation? Does John Barth's *Whore of Dorset* have a basis outside his fertile imagination? In our opinion, the answers are clearly No. Servants were economic investments on the part of planters who needed labor. A female servant in a household where there were unmarried men must have both provided and faced temptation, for the pressures were great in a society in which men outnumbered women by three to one. Nevertheless, the servant woman was in the household to work—to help feed and clothe the family and make tobacco. She was not primarily a concubine.

This point could be established more firmly if we knew more about the fathers of the bastards. Often the culprits were fellow servants or men recently freed but too poor to purchase the woman's remaining time. Sometimes the master was clearly at fault. But often the father is not identified. Some masters surely did exploit their female servants sexually. Nevertheless, masters were infrequently accused of fathering their servants' bastards, and those found guilty were punished as severely as were other men. Community mores did not sanction their misconduct.

A female servant paid dearly for the fault of unmarried pregnancy. She was heavily fined, and if no one would pay her fine, she was whipped. Furthermore, she served an extra twelve to twenty-four months to repay her master for the "trouble of his house" and labor lost, and the fathers often did not share in this payment of damages. On top of all, she might lose the child after weaning unless by then she had become free, for the courts bound out bastard children at very early ages.

English life probably did not offer a comparable hazard to young unmarried female servants. No figures are available to show rates of illegitimacy among those who were subject to the risk, but the female servant was less restricted in England than in the Chesapeake. She did not owe anyone for passage across the Atlantic; hence it was easier for her to marry, supposing she happened to become pregnant while in service. Perhaps, furthermore, her temptations were fewer. She was not 3,000 miles from home and friends, and she lived in a society in which there was no shortage of women. Bastards were born in En-

gland in the seventeenth century, but surely not to as many as one-fifth of the female servants.

Some women escaped all or part of their servitude because prospective husbands purchased the remainder of their time. At least one promotional pamphlet published in the 1660s described such purchases as likely, but how often they actually occurred is difficult to determine. Suggestive is a 20 percent difference between the sex ratios found in a Maryland headright sample, 1658–1681, and among servants listed in lower Western Shore inventories for 1658–1679. Some of the discrepancy must reflect the fact that male servants were younger than female servants and therefore served longer terms; hence they had a greater chance of appearing in an inventory. But part of the discrepancy doubtless follows from the purchase of women for wives. Before 1660, when sex ratios were even more unbalanced and the expanding economy enabled men to establish themselves more quickly, even more women may have married before their terms were finished.

Were women sold for wives against their wills? No record says so, but nothing restricted a man from selling his servant to whomever he wished. Perhaps some women were forced into such marriages or accepted them as the least evil. But the man who could afford to purchase a wife—especially a new arrival—was usually already an established landowner. Probably most servant women saw an opportunity in such a marriage. In addition, the shortage of labor gave women some bargaining power. Many masters must have been ready to refuse to sell a woman who was unwilling to marry a would-be purchaser.

If a woman's time was not purchased by a prospective husband, she was virtually certain to find a husband once she was free. Those famous spinsters, Margaret and Mary Brent, were probably almost unique in seventeenth-century Maryland. In the four counties of the lower Western Shore only two of the women who left a probate inventory before the eighteenth century are known to have died single. Comely or homely, strong or weak, any young woman was too valuable to be overlooked, and most could find a man with prospects.

The woman who immigrated to Maryland, survived seasoning and service, and gained her freedom became a planter's wife. She had considerable liberty in making her choice. There were men aplenty, and no fathers or brothers were hovering to monitor her behavior or disapprove her preference. This is the modern way of looking at her situation, of course. Perhaps she missed the protection of a father, a guardian, or kinfolk, and the participation in her decision of a community to which she felt ties. There is some evidence that the absence of kin and the pressures of the sex ratio created conditions of sexual freedom in courtship that were not customary in England. A register of marriages and births for seventeenth-century Somerset County shows that about one-third of the immigrant women whose marriages are recorded were pregnant at the time of the ceremony—nearly twice the rate in English parishes. There is no indication of community objection to this freedom so long as marriage took place. No presentments for bridal pregnancy were made in any of the Maryland courts.

The planter's wife was likely to be in her mid-twenties at marriage. An estimate of minimum age at marriage for servant women can be made from lists of indentured servants who left London over the years 1683–1684 and from age judgments in Maryland county court records. If we assume that the 112 female indentured servants going to Maryland and Virginia whose ages are given in the London lists served full four-year terms, then only 1.8 percent married before age twenty, but 68 percent after age twenty-four. Similarly, if the 141 women whose ages were judged in Charles County between 1666 and 1705 served out their terms according to the custom of the country, none married before age twenty-two, and half were twenty-five or over. When adjustments are made for the ages at which wives may have been purchased, the figures drop, but even so the majority of women waited until at least age twenty-four to marry. Actual age at marriage in Maryland can be found for few seventeenth-century female immigrants, but observations for Charles and Somerset counties place the mean age at about twenty-five.

Because of the age at which an immigrant woman married, the number of children she would bear her husband was small. She had lost up to ten years of her childbearing life—the possibility of perhaps four or five children, given the usual rhythm of childbearing. At the same time, high mortality would reduce both the number of children she would bear over the rest of her life and the number who would live. One partner to a marriage was likely to die within seven years, and the chances were only one in three that a marriage would last ten years. In these circumstances, most women would not bear more than three or four children—not counting those stillborn—to any one husband, plus a posthumous child were she the survivor. The best estimates suggest that nearly a quarter, perhaps more, of the children born alive died during their first year and that 40 to 55 percent would not live to see age twenty. Consequently, one of her children would probably die in infancy, and another one or two would fail to reach adulthood. Wills left in St. Mary's County during the seventeenth century show the results. In 105 families over the years 1660 to 1680 only twelve parents left more than three children behind them, including those conceived but not yet born. The average number was 2.3, nearly always minors, some of whom might die before reaching adulthood.

For the immigrant woman, then, one of the major facts of life was that although she might bear a child about every two years, nearly half would not reach maturity. The social implications of this fact are far-reaching. Because she married late in her childbearing years and because so many of her children would die young, the number who would reach marriageable age might not replace, or might only barely replace, her and her husband or husbands as child-producing members of the society. Consequently, so long as immigrants were heavily predominant in the adult female population, Maryland could not grow much by natural increase. It remained a land of newcomers.

This fact was fundamental to the character of seventeenth-century Maryland society, although its implications have yet to be fully explored. Settlers came from all parts of England and hence from differing traditions—in types of agriculture, forms of landholding and estate management, kinds of building construction, customary contributions to community needs, and family arrangements, including the role of women. The necessities of life in the Chesapeake required all immigrants to make adaptations. But until the native-born became predominant, a securely established Maryland tradition would not guide or restrict the newcomers.

If the immigrant woman had remained in England, she would probably have married at about the same age or perhaps a little later. But the social consequences of marriage at these ages in most parts of England were probably different. More children may have lived to maturity, and even where mortality was as high newcomers are not likely to have been the main source of population growth. The locally born would still dominate the community, its social organization, and its traditions. However, where there were exceptions, as perhaps in London, late age at marriage, combined with high mortality and heavy immigration, may have had consequences in some ways similar to those we have found in Maryland.

A hazard of marriage for seventeenth-century women everywhere was death in childbirth, but this hazard may have been greater than usual in the Chesapeake. Whereas in most societies women tend to outlive men, in this malaria-ridden area it is probable that men outlived women. Hazards of childbirth provide the likely reason that Chesapeake women died so young. Once a woman in the Chesapeake reached forty-five, she tended to outlive men who reached the same age. Darrett and Anita Rutman have found malaria a probable cause of an exceptionally high death rate among pregnant women, who are, it appears, peculiarly vulnerable to that disease.

This argument, however, suggests that immigrant women may have lived longer than their native-born daughters, although among men the opposite was true. Life tables created for men in Maryland show that those native-born who survived to age twenty could expect a life span three to ten years longer than that of immigrants, depending upon the region where they lived. The reason for the improvement was doubtless immunities to local diseases developed in childhood. A native woman developed these immunities, but, as we shall see, she also married earlier than immigrant women usually could and hence had more children. Thus she was more exposed to the hazards of childbirth and may have died a little sooner. Unfortunately, the life tables for immigrant women that would settle this question have so far proved impossible to construct.

However long they lived, immigrant women in Maryland tended to outlive their husbands—in Charles County, for example, by a ratio of two to one. This was possible, despite the fact that women were younger than men at death, because women were also younger than men at marriage. Some women were widowed with no living children, but most were left responsible for two or three. These were often tiny, and nearly always not yet sixteen.

This fact had drastic consequences, given the physical circumstances of life. People lived at a distance from one another, not even in villages, much less towns. The widow had left her kin 3,000 miles across an ocean, and her husband's family was also there. She would have to feed her children and make her own tobacco crop. Though neighbors might help, heavy labor would be required of her if she had no servants, until—what admittedly was usually not difficult—she acquired a new husband.

In this situation dying husbands were understandably anxious about the welfare of their families. Their wills reflected their feelings and tell something of how they regarded their wives. In St. Mary's and Charles counties during the seventeenth century, little more than one-quarter of the men left their widows with no more than the dower the law required—one-third of his land for her life, plus outright ownership of one-third of his personal property. (See Table 1.) If there were no children, a man almost always left his widow his whole estate. Otherwise there were a variety of arrangements. (See Table 2.)

During the 1660s, when testators begin to appear in quantity, nearly a fifth of the men who had children left all to their wives, trusting them to see that the children received fair portions. Thus in 1663 John Shircliffe willed his whole estate to his wife "towards the maintenance of herself and my children into whose tender care I do Commend them Desireing to see them brought up in the fear of God and the Catholick Religion and Chargeing them to be Dutiful and obedient to her." As the century progressed, husbands tended instead to give the wife all or a major part of the estate for her life, and to designate how it should be distributed after her death. Either way, the husband put great trust in his widow, considering that he knew she was bound to remarry. Only a handful of men left estates to their wives only for their term of widowhood or until the children came of age. When a man did not leave his wife a life estate, he often gave her land outright or more than her dower third of his movable property. Such bequests were at the expense of his children and showed his concern that his widow should have a maintenance which young children could not supply.

A husband usually made his wife his executor and thus responsible for paying his debts and preserving the estate. Only 11 percent deprived their wives of such powers. In many instances, however, men also appointed overseers to assist their wives and to see that their children were not abused or their property embezzled. Danger lay in the fact that a second husband acquired control of all his wife's property, including her life estate in the property of his predecessor. Over half

TABLE 1   Bequests of Husbands to Wives, St. Mary's and Charles Counties, Maryland, 1640 to 1710

		Dower or Less	
	N	N	%
1640s	6	2	34
1650s	24	7	29
1660s	65	18	28
1670s	86	21	24
1680s	64	17	27
1690s	83	23	28
1700s	74	25	34
Totals	402	113	28

Source: Wills, 1-XIV, Hall of Records, Annapolis, Md.

TABLE 2   Bequests of Husbands to Wives with Children, St. Mary's and Charles Counties, Maryland, 1640 to 1710

	N	All Estate		All or Dwelling Plantation for Life		All or Dwelling Plantation for Widowhood		All or Dwelling Plantation for Minority of Child		More than Dower in Other Form		Dower or Less or Unknown	
	N	N	%	N	%	N	%	N	%	N	%	N	%
1640s	3	1	33	33								2	67
1650s	16	1	6	2	13	1	6	1	6	4	25	7	44
1660s	45	8	18	8	18	2	4	3	7	9	20	15	33
1670s	61	4	7	21	34	2	3	3	5	13	21	18	30
1680s	52	5	10	19	37	2	4	2	4	11	21	13	25
1690s	69	1	1	31	45	7	10	2	3	10	14	18	26
1700s	62			20	32	6	10	2	3	14	23	20	32
Totals	308	20	6	101	33	20	6	13	4	61	20	93	30

Source: Wills, I-XIV

of the husbands who died in the 1650s and 1660s appointed overseers to ensure that their wills were followed. Some trusted to the overseers' "Care and good Conscience for the good of my widow and fatherless children." Others more explicitly made overseers responsible for seeing that "my said child . . . and the other [expected child] (when pleases God to send it) may have their right Proportion of my Said Estate and that the said Children may be bred up Chiefly in the fear of God." A few men—but remarkably few—authorized overseers to remove children from households of stepfathers who abused them or wasted their property. On the whole, the absence of such provisions for the protection of the children points to the husband's overriding concern for the welfare of his widow and to his confidence in her management, regardless of the certainty of her remarriage. Evidently, in the politics of family life women enjoyed great respect.

We have implied that this respect was a product of the experience of immigrants in the Chesapeake. Might it have been instead a reflection of English culture? Little work is yet in print that allows comparison of the provisions for Maryland widows with those made for the widows of English farmers. Possibly, Maryland husbands were making traditional wills which could have been written in the communities they left behind. However, Margaret Spufford's recent study of three Cambridgeshire villages in the late sixteenth century and early seventeenth century suggests a different pattern. In one of these villages, Chippenham, women usually did receive a life interest in the property, but in the other two they did not. If the children were all minors, the widow controlled the property until the oldest son came of age, and then only if she did not remarry. In the majority of cases adult sons were given control of the property with instructions for the support of their mothers. Spufford suggests that the pattern found in Chippenham must have been very exceptional. On the basis of village censuses in six other counties, dating from 1624 to 1724, which show only 3 percent of widowed people heading households that included a married child, she argues that if widows commonly controlled the farm, a higher proportion should have headed such households. However, she also argues that widows with an interest in land would not long remain unmarried. If so, the low percentage may be deceptive. More direct work with wills needs to be done before we can be sure that Maryland husbands and fathers gave their widows greater control of property and family than did their English counterparts.

Maryland men trusted their widows, but this is not to say that many did not express great anxiety about the future of their children. They asked both wives and overseers to see that the children received "some learning." Robert Sly made his wife sole guardian of his children but admonished her "to take due Care that they be brought up in the true fear of God and instructed in such Literature as may tend to their improvement." Widowers, whose children would be left without any parent, were often the most explicit in prescribing their upbringing. Robert Cole, a middling planter, directed that his children "have such Education in Learning as [to] write and read and Cast accompt I mean my three Sonnes my two daughters to learn to read and sew with their needle and all of them to be keept from Idleness but not to be kept as Comon Servants." John Lawson required his executors to see that his two daughters be reared together, receive learning and sewing instruction, and be "brought up to huswifery." Often present was the fear that orphaned children would be treated as servants and trained only to work in the fields. With stepfathers in mind, many fathers provided that their sons should be independent before the usual age of majority, which for girls was sixteen but for men twenty-one. Sometimes fathers willed that their sons should inherit when they were as young as sixteen, though more often eighteen. The sons could then escape an incompatible stepfather, who could no longer exploit their labor or property. If a son was already close to age sixteen, the father might bind him to his mother until he reached majority or his mother died, whichever came first. If she lived, she could watch out for his welfare, and his labor could contribute to her support. If she died, he and his property would be free from a stepfather's control.

What happened to widows and children if a man died without leaving a will? There was great need for some community institution that could protect children left fatherless or parentless in a society where they usually had no other kin. By the 1660s the probate court and county orphans' courts were supplying this need. If a man left a widow, the probate court—in Maryland a central government agency—usually appointed her or her new husband administrator of the estate with power to pay its creditors under court supervision. Probate procedures provided a large measure of protection. These required an inventory of the movable property and careful accounting of all disbursements, whether or not a man had left a will. William Hollis of Baltimore County, for example, had three stepfathers in seven years, and only the care of the judge of probate prevented the third stepfather from paying the debts of the second with goods that had belonged to William's father. As the judge remarked, William had "an uncareful mother."

Once the property of an intestate had been fully accounted and creditors paid, the county courts appointed a guardian who took charge of the property and gave bond to the children with sureties that he or she would not waste it. If the mother were living, she could be the guardian, or if she had remarried, her new husband would act. Through most of the century bond was waived in these circumstances, but from the 1690s security was required of all guardians, even of mothers. Thereafter the courts might actually take away an orphan's property from a widow or stepfather if she or he could not find sureties—that is, neighbors who judged the parent responsible and hence were willing to risk their own property as security. Children without any parents were assigned new families, who at all times found surety if there were property to manage. If the orphans inherited land, English common law allowed them to choose guardians for themselves at age fourteen—another escape hatch for children in

conflict with stepparents. Orphans who had no property, or whose property was insufficient to provide an income that could maintain them, were expected to work for their guardians in return for their maintenance. Every year the county courts were expected to check on the welfare of orphans of intestate parents and remove them or their property from guardians who abused them or misused their estates. From 1681, Maryland law required that a special jury be impaneled once a year to report neighborhood knowledge of mistreatment of orphans and hear complaints.

This form of community surveillance of widows and orphans proved quite effective. In 1696 the assembly declared that orphans of intestates were often better cared for than orphans of testators. From that time forward, orphans' courts were charged with supervision of all orphans and were soon given powers to remove any guardians who were shown false to their trusts, regardless of the arrangements laid down in a will. The assumption was that the deceased parent's main concern was the welfare of the child, and that the orphans' court, as "father to us poor orphans," should implement the parent's intent. In actual fact, the courts never removed children—as opposed to their property—from a household in which the mother was living, except to apprentice them at the mother's request. These powers were mainly exercised over guardians of orphans both of whose parents were dead. The community as well as the husband believed the mother most capable of nurturing his children.

Remarriage was the usual and often the immediate solution for a woman who had lost her husband. The shortage of women made any woman eligible to marry again, and the difficulties of raising a family while running a plantation must have made remarriage necessary for widows who had no son old enough to make tobacco. One indication of the high incidence of remarriage is the fact that there were only sixty women, almost all of them widows, among the 1,735 people who left probate inventories in four southern Maryland counties over the second half of the century. Most other women must have died while married and therefore legally without property to put through probate.

One result of remarriage was the development of complex family structures. Men found themselves responsible for stepchildren as well as their own offspring, and children acquired half-sisters and half-brothers. Sometimes a woman married a second husband who himself had been previously married, and both brought children of former spouses to the new marriage. They then produced children of their own. The possibilities for conflict over the upbringing of children are evident, and crowded living conditions, found even in the households of the wealthy, must have added to family tensions. Luckily, the children of the family very often had the same mother. In Charles County, at least, widows took new husbands three times more often than widowers took new wives. The role of the mother in managing the relationships of half-brothers and half-sisters or stepfathers and stepchildren must have been critical to family harmony.

Early death in this immigrant population thus had broad effects on Maryland society in the seventeenth century. It produced what we might call a pattern of serial polyandry, which enabled more men to marry and to father families than the sex ratios otherwise would have permitted. It produced thousands of orphaned children who had no kin to maintain them or preserve their property, and thus gave rise to an institution almost unknown in England, the orphans' court, which was charged with their protection. And early death, by creating families in which the mother was the unifying element, may have increased her authority within the household.

When the immigrant woman married her first husband, there was usually no property settlement involved, since she was unlikely to have any dowry. But her remarriage was another matter. At the very least, she owned or had a life interest in a third of her former husband's estate. She needed also to think of her children's interests. If she remarried, she would lose control of the property. Consequently, property settlements occasionally appear in the seventeenth-century court records between widows and their future husbands. Sometimes she and her intended signed an agreement whereby he relinquished his rights to the use of her children's portions. Sometimes he deeded to her property which she could dispose of at her pleasure. Whether any of these agreements or gifts would have survived a test in court is unknown. We have not yet found any challenged. Generally speaking, the formal marriage settlements of English law, which bypassed the legal difficulties of the married woman's inability to make a contract with her husband, were not adopted by immigrants, most of whom probably came from levels of English society that did not use these legal formalities.

The wife's dower rights in her husband's estate were a recognition of her role in contributing to his prosperity, whether by the property she had brought to the marriage or by the labor she performed in his household. A woman newly freed from servitude would not bring property, but the benefits of her labor would be great. A man not yet prosperous enough to own a servant might need his wife's help in the fields as well as in the house, especially if he were paying rent or still paying for land. Moreover, food preparation was so time-consuming that even if she worked only at household duties, she saved him time he needed for making tobacco and corn. The corn, for example, had to be pounded in the mortar or ground in a hand-mill before it could be used to make bread, for there were very few water mills in seventeenth-century Maryland. The wife probably raised vegetables in a kitchen garden; she also milked the cows and made butter and cheese, which might produce a salable surplus. She washed the clothes, and made them if she had the skill. When there were servants to do field work, the wife undoubtedly spent her time entirely in such household tasks. A contract of 1681 expressed such a division of labor. Nicholas Maniere agreed to live on a plantation with his wife and child and a servant. Nicholas and the servant were to work the land; his wife was to "Dresse the Victualls milk the Cowes wash for the servants and Doe allthings necessary for a woman to doe upon the s[ai]d plantation."

We have suggested that wives did field work; the suggestion is supported by occasional direct references in the court records. Mary Castleton, for example, told the judge of probate that "her husband late Deceased in his Life time had Little to sustaine himselfe and Children but what was produced out of ye ground by ye hard Labour of her the said Mary." Household inventories provide indirect evidence. Before about 1680 those of poor men and even middling planters on Maryland's lower Western Shore—the bottom two-thirds of the married decedents—show few signs of household industry, such as appear in equivalent English estates. Sheep and woolcards, flax and hackles, and spinning wheels all were a rarity, and such things as candle molds were nonexistent. Women in these households must have been busy at other work. In households with bound labor the wife doubtless was fully occupied preparing food and washing clothes for family and hands. But the wife in a household too poor to afford bound labor—the bottom fifth of the married decedent group—might well tend tobacco when she could. Eventually, the profits of her labor might enable the family to buy a servant, making greater profits possible. From such beginnings many families climbed the economic ladder in seventeenth-century Maryland.

The proportion of servantless households must have been larger than is suggested by the inventories of the dead, since young men were less likely to die than old men and had had less time to accumulate property. Well over a fifth of the households of married men on the lower Western Shore may have had no bound labor. Not every wife in such households would necessarily work at the hoe—saved from it by upbringing, ill-health, or the presence of small children who needed her care—but many women performed such work. A lease of 1691, for example, specified that the lessee could farm the amount of land which "he his wife and children can tend."

Stagnation of the tobacco economy, beginning about 1680, produced changes that had some effect on women's economic role. As shown by inventories of the lower Western Shore, home in-dustry increased, especially at the upper ranges of the economic spectrum. In these households women were spinning yarn and knitting it into clothing. The increase in such activity was far less in the households of the bottom fifth, where changes of a different kind may have increased the pressures to grow tobacco. Fewer men at this level could now purchase land, and a portion of their crop went for rent. At this level, more wives than before may have been helping to produce tobacco when they could. And by this time they were often helping as a matter of survival, not as a means of improving the family position.

So far we have considered primarily the experience of immigrant women. What of their daughters? How were their lives affected by the demographic stresses of Chesapeake society?

One of the most important points in which the experience of daughters differed from that of their mothers was the age at which they married. In this woman-short world, the mothers had married as soon as they were eligible, but they had not usually become eligible until they were mature women in their middle twenties. Their daughters were much younger at marriage. A vital register kept in Somerset County shows that some girls married at age twelve and that the mean age at marriage for those born before 1670 was sixteen and a half years.

Were some of these girls actually child brides? It seems unlikely that girls were married before they had become capable of bearing children. Culturally, such a practice would fly in the face of English, indeed Western European, precedent, nobility excepted. Nevertheless, the number of girls who married before age sixteen, the legal age of inheritance for girls, is astonishing. Their English counterparts ordinarily did not marry until their mid- to late twenties or early thirties. In other parts of the Chesapeake, historians have found somewhat higher ages at marriage than appear in Somerset, but everywhere in seventeenth-century Maryland and Virginia most native-born women married before they reached age twenty-one. Were such early marriages a result of the absence of fathers? Evidently not. In Somerset

County, the fathers of very young brides—those under sixteen—were usually living. Evidently, guardians were unlikely to allow such marriages, and this fact suggests that they were not entirely approved. But the shortage of women imposed strong pressures to marry as early as possible.

Not only did native girls marry early, but many of them were pregnant before the ceremony. Bridal pregnancy among native-born women was not as common as among immigrants. Nevertheless, in seventeenth-century Somerset County 20 percent of native brides bore children within eight and one half months of marriage. This was a somewhat higher percentage than has been reported from seventeenth-century English parishes.

These facts suggest considerable freedom for girls in selecting a husband. Almost any girl must have had more than one suitor, and evidently many had freedom to spend time with a suitor in a fashion that allowed her to become pregnant. We might suppose that such pregnancies were not incurred until after the couple had become betrothed, and that they were consequently an allowable part of courtship, were it not that girls whose fathers were living were usually not the culprits. In Somerset, at least, only 10 percent of the brides with fathers living were pregnant, in contrast to 30 percent of those who were orphans. Since there was only about one year's difference between the mean ages at which orphan and non-orphan girls married, parental supervision rather than age seems to have been the main factor in the differing bridal pregnancy rates.

Native girls married young and bore children young; hence they had more children than immigrant women. This fact ultimately changed the composition of the Maryland population. Native-born females began to have enough children to enable couples to replace themselves. These children, furthermore, were divided about evenly between males and females. By the mid-1680s, in all probability, the population thus began to grow through reproductive increase, and sexual imbalance began to decline. In 1704 the native-born preponderated in the Maryland assembly for the first time and by then were becoming predominant in the adult population as a whole.

This appearance of a native population was bringing alterations in family life, especially for widows and orphaned minors. They were acquiring kin. St. Mary's and Charles counties wills demonstrate the change. (See Table 3.) Before 1680, when nearly all those who died and left families had been immigrants, three-quarters of the men and women who left widows and/or minor children made no mention in their wills of any other kin in Maryland. In the first decade of the eighteenth century, among native-born testators, nearly three-fifths mention other kin, and if we add information from sources other than wills—other probate records, land records, vital registers, and so on—at least 70 percent are found to have had such local connections. This development of local family ties must have been one of the most important events of early Maryland history.

Historians have only recently begun to explore the consequences of the shift from an immigrant to a predominantly native population. We would like to suggest some changes in the position of women that may have resulted from this transition. It is already known that as sexual imbalance disappeared, age at first marriage rose, but it remained lower than it had been for immigrants over the second half of the seventeenth century. At the same time, life expectancy improved, at least for men. The results were longer marriages and more children who reached maturity. In St. Mary's County after 1700, dying men far more often than earlier left children of age to maintain their widows, and widows may have felt less inclination and had less opportunity to remarry.

We may speculate on the social consequences of such changes. More fathers were still alive when their daughters married, and hence would have been able to exercise control over the selection of their sons-in-law. What in the seventeenth century may have been a period of comparative independence for women, both immigrant and native, may have given way to a return to more traditional European social controls over the creation of new families. If so, we might see the results in a decline in bridal pregnancy and perhaps a decline in bastardy.

TABLE 3   Resident Kin of Testate Men and Women Who Left Minor Children, St Mary's and Charles Counties 1640 to 1710

	Families N	No Kin % Families	Only Wife % Families	Grown Child % Families	Other Kin % Families
			A.		
1640–1669	95	23	43	11	23
1670–1679	76	17	50	7	26
1700–1710	71	6	35[a]	25	34[b]
			B.		
1700–1710					
Immigrant	41	10	37	37	17
Native	30		33[c]	10	57[d]

Notes: [a] If information found in other records is included, the percentage is 30.

[b] If information found in other records is included the percentage is 39.

[c] If information found in other records is included the percentage is 20.

[d] If information found in other records is included the percentage is 70. For a discussion of wills as a reliable source for discovery of kin, see n. 78. Only 8 testators were natives of Maryland before 1680s; hence no effort has been made to distinguish them from immigrants.

Source: Wills, I–XIV.

We may also find the wife losing ground in the household's polity, although her economic importance probably remained unimpaired. Indeed, she must have been far more likely than a seventeenth-century immigrant woman to bring property to her marriage. But several changes may have caused women to play a smaller role than before in household decision making. Women became proportionately more numerous and may have lost bargaining power. Furthermore, as marriages lasted longer, the proportion of households full of stepchildren and half-brothers and half-sisters united primarily by the mother must have diminished. Finally, when husbands died, more widows would have had children old enough to maintain them and any minor brothers and sisters. There would be less need for women to play a controlling role, as well as less incentive for their husbands to grant it. The provincial marriage of the eighteenth century may have more closely resembled that of England than did the immigrant marriage of the seventeenth century.

If this change occurred, we should find symptoms to measure. There should be fewer gifts from husbands to wives of property put at the wife's disposal. Husbands should less frequently make bequests to wives that provided them with property beyond their dower. A wife might even be restricted to less than her dower, although the law allowed her to choose her dower instead of a bequest. At the same time, children should be commanded to maintain their mothers.

However, St. Mary's County wills do not show these symptoms. (See Table 4.) True, wives occasionally were willed less than their dower, an arrangement that was rare in the wills examined for the period before 1710. But there was no overall decrease in bequests to wives of property beyond their dower, nor was there a tendency to confine the wife's interest to the term of her widowhood or the minority of the oldest son. Children were not exhorted to help their mothers or give them living space. Widows evidently received at least enough property to maintain themselves, and husbands saw no need to ensure the help of children in managing it. Possibly, then, women did not lose ground, or at least not all ground, within the family polity. The demographic disruption of New World settlement may have given women power which they were able

TABLE 4 Bequests of Husbands to Wives with Children, St. Mary's County, Maryland, 1710 to 1776

	N	All Estate	All or Dwelling Plantation for Life	All or Dwelling Plantation for Widowhood	All or Dwelling Plantation for Minority of Child	More than Dower in Other Form	Dower or Less or Unknown	Maintenance or House Room
		%	%	%	%	%	%	%
1710-1714	13	0	46	0	0	23	31	0
1715-1719	25	4	24	4	0	28	36	4
1720-1724	31	10	42	0	0	28	23	3
1725-1729	34	3	29	0	0	24	41	3
1730-1734	31	6	16	13	0	29	35	0
1735-1739	27	0	37	4	4	19	37	0
1740-1744	35	0	40	0	3	23	34	0
1745-1749	39	3	31	8	0	31	28	0
1750-1754	43	2	35	7	0	16	40	0
1755-1759	34	3	41	3	0	41	12	0
1760-1764	48	2	46	10	2	13	27	0
1765-1769	45	4	27	11	2	18	33	4
1770-1774	46	4	26	7	0	37	26	0
1775-1776	19	5	32	26	0	5	32	0
Totals	470	3	33	7	1	24	31	1

Source: Wills, XIV–XLI.

to keep even after sex ratios became balanced and traditional family networks appeared. Immigrant mothers may have bequeathed their daughters a legacy of independence which they in turn handed down, despite pressures toward more traditional behavior.

. . . Should research in other areas of the Chesapeake fail to find women enjoying the status they achieved on the lower Western Shore of Maryland, then our arguments would have to be revised.

Work is also needed that will enable historians to compare conditions in Maryland with those in other colonies. Richard S. Dunn's study of the British West Indies also shows demographic disruption. When the status of wives is studied, it should prove similar to that of Maryland women. In contrast were demographic conditions in New England, where immigrants came in family groups, major immigration had ceased by the mid-seventeenth century, sex ratios balanced early, and mortality was low. Under these conditions, demographic disruption must have been both less severe and less prolonged. If New England women achieved status similar to that suggested for women in the Chesapeake, that fact will have to be explained. The dynamics might prove to have been different; or a dynamic we have not identified, common to both areas, might turn out to have been the primary engine of change. And, if women in England shared the status—which we doubt—conditions in the New World may have had secondary importance. The Maryland data establish persuasive grounds for a hypothesis, but the evidence is not all in.

Study Questions

1. What are the four basic facts common "to all human experience in seventeenth-century Maryland"?

2. How did the predominance of immigrants, early death, late marriage, and gender imbalance affect the lives of women in seventeenth-century Maryland?

3. In what ways did indentured servitude affect women's lives?

4. Did women find it easy or difficult in seventeenth-century Maryland to marry?

5. Why did relatively few women immigrate into seventeenth-century Maryland?

6. Describe the typical planter's wife.

7. Describe the life span for men and women in seventeenth-century Maryland and explain any differences.

8. What special challenges did widows and orphans face?

9. What impact did the shift from an immigrant to a predominantly native population have on seventeenth-century Maryland women?

Bibliography

For life in the seventeenth-century South, see Thad W. Tate and David L. Ammerman, eds., *The Chesapeake in the Seventeenth Century* (1979) and Gloria L. Main, *Tobacco Colony: Life in Early Maryland, 1650–1720* (1982). Carville Earle's *The Evolution of a Tidewater Settlement System: All Hallow's Parish, Maryland,*

1650-1783 (1975) is an outstanding example of local history that reveals larger issues. For race relations, see Edmund Morgan, *American Slavery, American Freedom* (1975) and Wesley F. Craven, *White, Red, and Black: The Seventeenth Century Virginian* (1971). Also see Allan Kulikoff, *Tobacco and Slaves* (1987); Rhys Isaac, *The Transformation of Virginia, 1740-1790* (1982); and Mechal Sobel, *The World They Made Together* (1987). Also see Darrett B. Rutman and Anita H. Rutman, *A Place in Time: Middlesex, Virginia, 1650-1750* (1984). For especially relevant recent scholarship, see Deborah Meyers, *Common Whores, Vertuous Women, and Loveing Wives: Free Will Christian Women in Colonial Maryland* (2003).

The Revolutionary Generation

When Thomas Jefferson proclaimed in the Declaration of Independence that people had the right to dissolve their government when it ceased to protect their "unalienable rights," he helped set in motion a crusade against European imperialism that lasted well into the twentieth century. Beginning with the "shot heard round the world" at Lexington, Massachusetts on April 19, 1775, colonial rebellions swept through Latin America early in the nineteenth century and through Africa and Asia in the twentieth century. By 1776, after nearly 170 years in the New World, the American colonists were ready for independence. With an English heritage and experience from trial and error, they had developed a political culture that emphasized localism, representative government, popular sovereignty, and individual rights. They had also acquired an American identity clearly distinguishing them from their English cousins. When the French and Indian War initiated changes in British imperial policy, colonists rebelled in a desperate and ultimately successful attempt to preserve a moral order.

But the destruction of one set of political relationships did not automatically create new ones. In the summer of 1776, the Second Continental Congress was a government without constitutional authority. The colonies were at best a loose alliance of competing states with limited resources, trying to make war against a major world power. The war also revealed strains between the rich and poor. The Continental army, for example, was periodically weakened by the struggles for power between well-to-do officers and enlisted men, as well as by the lack of support from civilians and politicians. The colonists triumphed by winning the war in the court of world opinion and by draining England of its financial and emotional resources. Their first attempt at constitution making, the Articles of Confederation, ended in failure. Although that government managed to bring the Revolution to a successful conclusion, Americans realized that a central government had to be able to support itself economically and maintain public

order. When Shays's Rebellion in 1786 raised doubts about the latter, the Founding Fathers gathered in Philadelphia in the summer of 1787 to try again.

They were eminently successful. The Constitution was a model political document, even though it represented the vested interests of a conservative minority. After its ratification in 1788, the Constitution became the symbol of the new republic. Americans considered themselves a free people blessed with a fundamental consensus about politics and power. They took their place among independent nations of the world confident that God had destined them for greatness.

Life was not easy. Older rivalries between the lower and upper classes, as well as between the seaboard region and the frontier, still manifested themselves. In 1794, a rebellion of poor farmers in western Pennsylvania challenged the authority of the new government. There were also political tensions within the ruling elite. During the 1790s a two-party system gradually emerged in the United States. George Washington, Alexander Hamilton, and John Adams led the Federalist Party, and Thomas Jefferson and James Madison headed the Democratic-Republicans. Both parties struggled for power throughout the 1790s and early 1800s. Despite the challenges, the new nation survived.

READING 10

But a Common Man:
Daniel Boone

John Mack Faragher

For generations historians portrayed Anglo-Americans' drive westward as the spread of civilization. These historians perceived a neat frontier line. On one side of the line were the fruits of European society—Christianity, refined behavior, written records, and rule by law. On the other side lurked danger and savagery—untamed lands, wild animals, and blood-thirsty Indians. Today no serious historian would ascribe to such glib and misleading stereotypes. The neat frontier line never existed; complex Native American and European civilizations flourished throughout America, mixing with each other in an area best described as a "middle ground" to create new hybrid cultures. In the late eighteenth and early nineteenth centuries the middle ground was the huge territory between the Appalachian Mountains and the Mississippi River. There Native Americans and European Americans negotiated and traded, formed alliances, and fought battles. Each took and gave, influencing and being influenced by the other. Hunters from both cultures dressed in composite European and Indian styles—moccasins, linen or deerskin hunting shirts, often even breechcloths. Like the Native Americans, European-American hunters wore their hair long and swept it back with bear grease; like the English and French Americans, Native Americans prized European rifles and iron goods. Both groups valued freedom and independence and were loyal to their families and clans.

The most famous European American of the middle ground was Daniel Boone, a Quaker born in Pennsylvania who drifted steadily westward. A man full of contradictions, whose fame grew even after he died, Boone's life demonstrated the dangers and joys of the middle ground. A man who had a deep respect for Native Americans, he nevertheless epitomized the movement of people that ultimately destroyed a way of life.

During the years preceding Daniel Boone's death in 1820 at age nearly eighty-six, a stream of visitors beat a path to the door of the woodsman's Missouri home—"induced by curiosity to visit this extraordinary person."

"Seeing strangers approaching," the aged frontiersman would, as his son Nathan re-called, "take his cane and walk off to avoid them," but if cornered, he usually agreed to talk. "Though at first reserved and barely answering questions," remembered one such visitor, Boone "soon became communicative, warmed up, and became animated in narrating his early adventures in the West."

"Many heroic actions and chivalrous adventures are related of me," the modest living legend would declare, "yet I have been but a common man."

Both extraordinary and common—this is but one of many paradoxes that distinguish the life and character of Daniel Boone, the prototype in American lore of the wilderness-ranging frontiersman. Contradictions—both within Boone himself and between the man and the legend that grew to overshadow him—abound:

Within his own lifetime Boone was elevated to near-mythic stature as a renowned hunter and Indian fighter. Yet he had been raised to honor a code of Quaker tolerance, and he objected to his notoriety for Indian-killing.

Boone was a devoted son, husband, and father, and throughout his life he treasured a close-knit community of kith and kin. Yet he often left home and family for months (even years) at a stretch to hunt and trap in the solitude of the western forests—in the process acquiring a reputation as a "natural man" of the woods or misanthrope who longed for "elbow room."

Boone was a courageous frontier leader of the American Revolution; yet many fellow officers and soldiers suspected him of harboring loyalty to

the crown and treasonous sympathy for England's Native American allies.

And, though Boone described himself as a simple woodsman, in midlife he strove mightily to transform himself into a man of property and standing.

These contradictions may be explained in part both by the scanty documentary record of the frontiersman's life and by the extent to which the real Boone quickly became obscured by folklore and legend. Fundamentally, however, the complexity the Boone's character itself was what allowed Americans to imagine him as in so many guises.

The quintessential frontier hero was born on October 22, 1734 in a log house in the upper Schuylkill River valley of Pennsylvania. The son of English Quaker emigrants—Squire and Sarah Morgan Boone—he grew up surrounded by family. The farm of his father was bounded by the land of Daniel's aunts and uncles, and nearby was the stone house and gristmill of his grandfather, the patriarch of the clan and local justice of the peace. The Boones were prominent members of the Society of Friends in the township of Exeter, and Squire was an overseer of the brown-stone meeting house, situated on land donated by the family. Here Daniel was, in the words of his son Nathan, "reared under the peaceful influence of the Quaker faith."

Family stories depict a happy household that included eleven rambunctious children. Sixth-born Daniel was responsible for his share of pranks—including dismantling meddlesome neighbors' wagons and hanging the wheels from barn roofs or treetops.

When Squire Boone felt compelled to discipline his boys for such misdeeds, his policy was to beat them only until their first cry, then put down his rod to reason with them, Quaker fashion. But the technique never worked with Daniel, who always endured his punishment in silence. One old tale has Squire "wishing to gain his point in government," appealing to Daniel: " 'Canst thou not beg?' But he could not beg, leaving his anxious parent to close the matter at his pleasure."

Thus the stubborn youth missed the opportunity for his father's embrace—an estrangement

"But A Common Man" by John Mack Faragher. This article is reprinted from the November/December 1992 issue, Volume XXVII/No. 5, pp. 28–37, 66–70, 73 of *American History Illustrated* with the permission of Cowles History Group, Inc. Copyright *American History Illustrated* magazine.

that in later years would haunt him. After Squire's death in 1765, Daniel frequently dreamed of his father. On several occasions he imagined an angry confrontation with no reconciliation; disaster, he told his children later, invariably followed these visions.

Daniel came by his independent streak quite naturally; his father was equally stubborn and headstrong. In 1747 the Exeter Quaker meeting reprimanded Squire for allowing his eldest son to marry a "worldling"—the second instance in which one of his children had wed outside the circle of Friends. Previously the senior Boone had promised "to be more careful for the future," but this time he was defiant. After repeated attempts to bring Squire "to a Sense of his Error," the meeting finally expelled him.

Squire Boone's withdrawal from the central institution of community life surely wrought considerable conflict for Daniel, who continued to attend Quaker meetings with his mother. But Squire's defiance encouraged Daniel's own quest for independence. Boone once professed that he had "always loved God ever since I recollect," but after his youth he never again joined a church.

In addition to raising a large brood of children, Daniel's Welsh mother Sarah Morgan Boone managed the family garden, hen house, and dairy. One of Boone's fondest memories of his childhood was of spending each "grass season" with her at a distant pasture, tending the cows while she milked and churned, then listening to her sing before the open fire. He fashioned a wooden shaft that he called his "herdsman's club," and with it killed small game for their supper.

Those memorable sojourns molded Boone's life course. His "love for the wilderness and hunter's life," Daniel later stated, began with "being a herdsman and thus being so much in the woods." Growing increasingly fond of solitude he took to remaining at the meadow after his mother returned home with her season's bounty of butter and cheese.

When Boone was twelve or thirteen, his father gave him a "short rifle gun." Roaming pasture and wood, the youth developed into an excellent marksman. It was common for him to be gone for several days, then to appear at the cabin door with meat enough to supply the family for a week. Thus did the strapping boy find resolution for his adolescent tensions, spending less time at home where the strong wills of father and son collided, and more time in the woods, a domain he identified with his beloved mother.

In those years, the Pennsylvania backcountry was the most peaceful of North American frontiers. Quaker authorities organized no militia or army, negotiated with indigenous peoples over the titles to land, and promised natives "the full and free privileges and Immunities of all the Said Laws as any other Inhabitants." Attracted by these policies, a number of Native American groups, whose homelands had been disrupted by the reverberating effects of colonization, relocated to Penn's Woods. Numerous communities of Delawares, Shawnees, and other native peoples settled within twenty or thirty miles of the Boone farm. Grandfather Boone often befriended native hunters who passed through the neighborhood, and Daniel had ample opportunity to see and meet the peoples of many tribes.

In this mixed cultural world young Boone found his teachers in woodcraft—both Europeans and Native Americans—who instructed him in the hunting way of life. On the frontier, males of both native and European cultures sought meat, hides, and furs for subsistence and trade, while the women raised corn and tended hogs and cattle. The American long rifle, developed by the German gunsmiths of southeastern Pennsylvania, served both cultures as well, as did native calls, disguises, decoys, surrounds, and fire hunts. Hunters adopted a composite of frontier clothing: deerskin moccasins, breechclouts, and leggings in combination with linen hunting shirts and beaver hats. Although some Americans wore fur caps, Boone despised their uncouth look and always stuck with his Quaker-style beaver.

Boone made this way of life his own during his youth in Pennsylvania, growing in his understanding of the ways of the woods and native culture. But he retained a Quaker approach: "Always

Portrait of Daniel Boone.

height, with broad shoulders and chest, muscular arms, and thick legs. A friend later described him as "a sort of pony-built man," a bit undersized but as strong as a horse. He bore pronounced facial features: a high forehead and heavy brow, prominent cheekbones, a tight wide mouth, and long, slender nose. He inherited his father's penetrating blue-gray eyes and ruddy complexion, but had his mother's dark hair, which he always kept "plaited and clubbed" in Native American fashion.

Within a year or two, the Boones were plowing the red clay at the Forks of the Yadkin River in North Carolina. But this agrarian life held few attractions for Daniel. "He never took any delight in farming," recalled a nephew, and Boone himself admitted to his children that while working his father's fields he would pray for rain, and if the storms came, he grabbed his rifle and headed for the woods—"and though the rain would cease in an hour, yet he was so fond of gunning, he would be sure to remain out till evening."

By age eighteen Boone had become a professional hunter, and during the next several years he established a reputation as a marksman. Legend claims that Bear Creek on the Yadkin took its name from the season Daniel shot ninety-nine bears along its waters; he and a companion also are credited with once downing thirty deer between sunup and sundown. The young woodsman competed eagerly at shooting matches, always scoring and sometimes employing his favorite trick shot in which he used only one of his powerful arms to support and fire his long rifle. Then, as one woman recalled, he would strut before the other competitors, "pat them on the shoulders, and tell them they couldn't shoot up to Boone."

When war threatened between England and France, twenty-year-old Boone signed on as a teamster with a military company headed north to join British General Edward Braddock. On July 9, 1755, near present Pittsburgh, French and Native American forces ambushed Braddock's column, killing or wounding more than nine hundred of the nearly fourteen hundred British and American troops. Steadying his team at the rear, Boone heard the cry of battle and saw men falling;

meet [Indians] frankly and fearlessly," he advised, and "by kind acts and just treatment, keep on the friendly side of them." This simple code of conduct, he declared, insured that when forced to "seek refuge with my deadliest foes and trust to their magniminity," his native hosts would be "kind and generous in their intercourse with me."

In 1750, soon after his expulsion from the meeting, Squire Boone moved his family south, seeking good land on which to settle his children and grandchildren. Daniel acted as hunter and guide as the family followed the Virginia Road down the Shenandoah Valley, the first of many highways that would lead Americans to the beckoning western country.

Daniel by now had nearly attained his adult stature and physique—five-feet-eight-inches in with the panicked retreat of the survivors he jumped onto his lead horse, slashed its harness free, and galloped away in terror.

An equally perilous encounter took place only a day or two later, when Boone made his way back alone to his Quaker relations in Exeter. As the woodsman crossed the bridge over the gorge of the Juniata River, a big, inebriated Native American suddenly confronted him. "He drew his knife on me," Boone remembered years later, "flourishing it over his head, boasting that he had killed many a Long Knife, and would kill some more on his way home." Unable to avoid a fight as the man lurched toward him, Boone drove his shoulder under his assailant's ribs, catapulting him off his feet and over the side of the bridge to the jagged rocks forty feet below.

Boone related this tale to an admiring group of visitors shortly before his death. In truth, he complained of his reputation as an Indian fighter, "I never killed but three," of which the man lying dead on the rocks was the first. "I am very sorry to say that I ever killed any," he said, "for they have always been kinder to me than the whites."

In the summer of 1756, the year following his return from the war, Boone began to court his future bride. Although no likeness of Rebecca Bryan Boone exists, contemporary descriptions endow her with jet-black hair and dark, penetrating eyes. Rebecca made her first appearance in Boone folklore as "a buxom daughter," and one of her nephews called her "a rather over common sized woman." In fact, in midlife Rebecca stood nearly as tall and broad as her husband, and she could handle a gun or an axe as well as many men. Yet Boone always called her "my little girl," reflecting back, perhaps, on his first sight of her when she was scarcely fifteen.

Boone likely won his future bride's devotion in part through his wit. In one family tale, Daniel, in order to demonstrate his skills as a provider, brings a deer to Rebecca's house. He dresses the carcass outdoors while she cooks him a first meal at the hearth. Without thought, the young hunter then joins the family at the table, his shirt still bloody from his task. The daughters of the rela-

tively well-to-do Bryans ridicule the suitor for this social blunder, but according to the story Boone quickly evens the score by examining his cup and declaring, "You, like me hunting shirt, have missed many a good washing."

Daniel was twenty-one and Rebecca seventeen when the couple married in August 1756. When they took up residence in a cabin owned by Daniel's father, Rebecca found herself mistress of a household that included two of Boone's orphaned nephews. The couple's firstborn, a son, arrived nine months later.[1]

For the first seventeen years of their lives together, the Boones lived in obscurity in the Yadkin valley of North Carolina. To support his growing family, Boone intensified his hunting and trapping, each winter going on a "long hunt" for deerskins and beaver pelts, and gradually shifting his range westward to the Blue Ridge mountains and the valleys beyond. Frequently he was joined by other men from the Yadkin country, but Boone preferred hunting by himself. He would construct a little "half-faced camp"—a three-sided shanty covered with brush, with the open end facing the campfire—and there take his evening meals. He usually carried a Bible, or a book of history (which he loved), or *Gulliver's Travels* (his favorite), to read by the firelight. Then he bedded down on a cushion of hemlock or dried leaves, his feet toward the fire to prevent the rheumatism that constantly plagued old hunters, leaving his moccasins tied to his gun, which stood primed and ready.

Boone's love of solitude later was criticized as evidence of an antisocial nature. The woodsman's family responded defensively. "His wanderings were from duty," declared a niece after his death; "no man loved society better, nor was more ardently attached to his family." Rebecca, eulogized

---

[1]During the first quarter-century of the couple's marriage, Rebecca delivered ten children—six sons and four daughters. When the oldest children married, they often lived in Rebecca's household, adding grandchildren to the brood already in her care. And, following the death of Rebecca's widowed brother, the Boones also adopted and raised six more nephews and nieces.

a granddaughter, was "the Companion of his toils, Pleasures, Sorrows for more than a half century," and Daniel "hardly Could live without her."

But outside the family others wondered why, if Boone could not live without Rebecca, he insisted on roaming away from her and the children for such long periods. After Daniel completed the spring plowing, it was Rebecca and the children who cropped the farm while he hunted. His neighbors whispered that Boone "wouldn't live at home" because he "didn't live happily with his family, [and] didn't like to work."

This gossip found a focus in an oft-repeated story that during one of Boone's long absences Rebecca bore an illegitimate child. When the woodsman returns home, so goes the tale, Rebecca meets him at the cabin door, weeping. "What's the matter," asks Boone. "You were gone so long," she replies, "[that] we had supposed you dead." In her sorrow Rebecca has found company with another man, and now there is a new baby in the house. "Oh well," Boone is said to have responded after a pause, "the race will be continued."

But that is only part of the confession: Rebecca admits that the baby's father is Boone's own brother—he "looked so much like Daniel," she confesses, that she "couldn't help it." This revelation, too, Boone is said to have taken in stride: "So much the better. It's all in the family."

The story cannot be taken as gospel, but combined with other circumstantial evidence it lends credence to the speculation that the Boones' daughter Jemima was conceived in 1762, when Daniel was absent on a two-year hunting and exploring expedition. This and other versions of the tale charitably conclude not by slandering the character of either Rebecca or Daniel, but instead by sympathizing with the plight of frontier women and by portraying Boone as a man of deliberation, slow to anger and ready to forgive.

In 1769, when Boone was in his mid-thirties, he led five other hunters across the Appalachian Mountains and into present-day Kentucky. In the Yadkin valley, as one of Boone's nephews put it, "game [had begun] to be scarce and harder to take." Like other hunter/farmers of his time and

place, Boone required a freehold of fertile land large enough to settle his children and near enough to rich hunting territory to enable him to make his living. This long hunt, then, was also a land hunt.

After crossing the mountain barrier, Boone climbed a hill and "saw with pleasure the beautiful level of Kentucke," a fertile land of cane and clover, with forests where "we found everywhere abundance of wild beasts of every sort." It was exactly the kind of place for which he had been searching.

From their very first movement into Kentucky, however, the hunters were opposed by the Shawnees, who after their sojourn in Pennsylvania had returned West to farming communities north of the Ohio River. A Shawnee party discovered Boone and his companions with a six-months' accumulation of deerskins and confiscated the entire cache, as well as their horses and supplies. Probably because of Boone's straightforward manner, the Shawnees released the intruders unharmed, but left them with a warning: "Now brothers, go home and stay there. Don't come here any more, for this is the Indians' hunting ground, and all the animals, skins, and furs are ours. And if you are so foolish as to venture here again, you may be sure the wasps and yellow-jackets will sting you severely."

Boone ignored the admonition. Instead, he and his brother-in-law pursued the natives and stole back their horses—only to be recaptured. Finally they succeeded in escaping, but several weeks later Boone's companion disappeared, presumably the victim of native retribution.

Still Boone refused to leave Kentucky. Joined by his younger brother Squire Boone, Jr., the woodsman hunted and explored the region until the spring of 1771. But during their return east the brothers were overwhelmed by yet another party of Native Americans, who again relieved the hapless hunters of their catch.

Despite these setbacks, Boone returned to Kentucky during the winter of 1772–73. This time he found that he was not the only white visitor. Virginia land speculators had dispatched agents to survey large parcels along the Ohio River, and at least two parties found their way to the Kentucky River country where Boone had established his base camp. No white American, however, knew the region as well as Boone. When he recrossed the mountains in the spring, he knew that a western land rush was imminent, and he resolved that his family would be among the first settlers.

The following fall of 1773, Boone led the first attempt to plant an American settlement in Kentucky. The party of forty or fifty immigrants, including Rebecca and the children, brother Squire's family, and several members of the Bryan clan, traveled by pack train over the roughest of mountain trails. They got only as far as the white-cliffed eastern entrance to the Cumberland Gap, where natives ambushed the men herding cattle at the rear of the march, killing six, including the Boones' oldest son James, only sixteen.

Boone "felt worse than ever in his life," and the attack "discouraged the whole company." Concluding that it was too dangerous to proceed, the pioneers retreated back to the settlements of southwest Virginia. The encounter was the opening shot of what became known as Lord Dunmore's War, during which Boone distinguished himself as a popular leader of the Virginia defense against Mingo and Shawnee attacks.

A published report of the incident at the Cumberland Gap marked the first time Boone's name appeared in print. Soon it would be linked indelibly with the American struggle to wrest Kentucky from the Shawnees, a war that would continue for more than twenty years and claim the lives of thousands on both sides—including Boone's second-born son Israel, another of his brothers, and many kinfolk, neighbors, and comrades. It was the single bloodiest phase in the three-century campaign for the conquest of North America.

Despite his deep personal losses, Boone never demonized his Native American opponents. He later characterized the origins of the conflict with candor: "We Virginians had for some time been waging a war of intrusion upon them. I, amongst the rest, rambled through the woods in pursuit of their race, as I now would follow the tracks of a ravenous animal." For their part, according to

Boone, the natives "saw the approaching hour when the Long Knife would dispossess them of their desirable habitations," and they "determined utterly to extirpate the whites out of Kentucke." In Boone's view, war came not because Americans and Indians were so alien, but because the two races were competing for the same resources.

By the end of Lord Dunmore's War, Boone's name was well known all along the southern Appalachian frontier. Thus, when Richard Henderson, a North Carolina land speculator, organized a company to purchase from the Cherokees their rights to Kentucky, it was natural that he would ask Boone to direct the marking of a road over the mountains and the fortification of a town site. In exchange, Boone was to have his choice of two thousand acres of Kentucky land.

At Sycamore Shoals in March 1775, Henderson's "Transylvania Company" and a contingent of Cherokees negotiated the purchase of twenty million acres. Before Boone left the treaty grounds to begin marking the path later known as the Wilderness Road, the old Cherokee chief Oconostota took him aside. "Brother," he said, grasping Boone's hand, "we have given you a fine land, but I believe you will have much trouble in settling it." The chief's words proved prophetic.

Trouble began soon after the roadmakers hacked a trace over the mountains. As they slept in their camp south of the Kentucky River, Native Americans fired on them, killing two men and wounding another.

Boone dashed off a message to Henderson, still east of the mountains with the main party. "The people are very uneasy, but are willing to stay and venture their lives with you," he wrote. "Now is the time to flusterate [the Indians'] intentions . . . and keep the country, whilst we are in it. If we give way to them now, it will ever be the case."

The dauntless frontiersman then led his men the final fifteen miles to a broad floodplain along the south side of the Kentucky River, where they established the settlement of Boonesborough. "It was owing to Boone's confidence in us, and the people's in him," Henderson later wrote, "that a stand was ever attempted."

Boone remained through the summer to begin construction of a fort, then returned east to bring his family over the mountains. "My wife and daughter," he declared with pride, were "the first white women that ever stood on the banks of Kentucke river."

With his family settled at Boonesborough, the woodsman had invested his all in the founding of an American community in Kentucky. By the end of 1775, a stream of settlers filed more than nine hundred claims to the land of the bluegrass, and Boonesborough was one of several expanding population centers. Henderson's Transylvania Company, however, soon disappeared, its title to the land (along with Boone's promised two thousand acres) ruled invalid by the government of Virginia, which assumed jurisdiction.

The Shawnees and Mingos continued to harass the settlement during the next year. The culmination of these raids came in July 1776 when five natives kidnapped Boone's thirteen-year-old daughter Jemima and two other girls. Boone, after two days of trailing the kidnappers, led an ambush of their camp that brilliantly succeeded in rescuing the girls unharmed. This dramatic episode, which James Fenimore Cooper later immortalized in *The Last of the Mohicans,* marked the *summum bonum* of Boone's reputation among his contemporaries.

With the American Revolution now under way in the east, the British engaged the western Indians in a strategy designed to demoralize the border settlements. Hard-hit by war parties, Kentucky settlers abandoned their outlying farms and sought refuge within Boonesborough's rough fortifications, swelling the population.

Forced to remain within the log walls, Boonesborough's inhabitants ran dangerously low on food by late 1777. The gravest problem was that they were "almost destitute of the necessary article of salt" required for preserving game. The supply was so exhausted by January 1778 that Boone was forced to risk leaving Boonesborough dangerously undermanned while he led a party of men to the springs on the Licking River to make salt.

Thus began the most controversial episode of Boone's life. While hunting to supply the saltmak-

ers, he was captured by a large Shawnee war party, and to divert the natives' attention from the weakened settlement, agreed to surrender his twenty-nine men. They were taken to the Shawnee town of Chillicothe, north of the Ohio River.

About half of the Americans ended up as prisoners of the British, where they endured great suffering—some toiling at forced labor, others rotting in damp dungeons until the end of the Revolution. The rest, including Boone, were adopted into Shawnee families. Boone became *Sheltowee,* "Big Turtle," the son of Blackfish, a chief of the Chillicothe Shawnees.

Because of his familiarity with native ways, Boone, unlike most of his men, took well to life at Chillicothe. His apparent pleasure with his lot baffled many of the other white captives; but it was all part of his plan, he later explained: "always appearing as chearful and satisfied as possible," watching all the while for an opportunity to escape.

The stories that Boone later told his family about his captivity, however, suggest there was more to it than that. He became very attached to Blackfish and his family, who were "friendly and sociable and kind to him." Blackfish addressed Boone as "my son," and Boone described his native father as "one of Nature's noblemen."

Boone "completely deceived Blackfish and his simple-hearted people," doing everything he could to win their confidence. Gradually their trust increased to the point where Boone was allowed to hunt, and he was able to secrete a small cache of ammunition in the fold of his hunting shirt.

But Boone also deceived his own men, who suspected him of treason. Boone had consulted with the British commander, hunted with the Shawnee warriors, even lived in the lodge of Blackfish himself. When one of the saltmakers escaped and reached an American settlement, he claimed that "Boone was a Tory, and had surrendered them all up to the British, and taken the oath of allegiance to the British at Detroit."

In fact, some of Rebecca's people were Loyalists; this only aggravated Boone's cause. Tormented by gossip and fearing that her husband had been killed, in May she took the children back to North Carolina. When Boone finally made a heroic escape from the Shawnees in June 1778, he arrived at Boonesborough to find his family gone and the settlers sullen and suspicious.

He brought news that the Shawnees were planning a massive attack against the outpost. Whatever the settlers' feelings about him, he declared, they "must make what preperration they could" for "the Indeans would certainly be their in a few Days." When Blackfish's army of four hundred arrived, all Boonesborough watched suspiciously from the walls as Boone went out to parley with his Shawnee "father." Their apparently warm reunion panicked the settlers, who feared that Boone "intended to surrender the fort." Instead, he reported that Blackfish had proposed negotiations to avoid bloodshed. Stalling for time while awaiting reinforcements, the Kentuckians agreed to the proposal. Adopting a ruse similar to that employed by Boone at Chillicothe, they agreed to recognize the Ohio as a boundary, and both sides promised "allegiance to the King of Great Britain." Although "we could not avoid suspicions of the savages," as Boone put it, "the articles were formally agreed to and signed" with a good deal of ceremony. But neither the whites nor the Shawnees trusted their opponents, and both had instructed their marksmen to fire at the first sign of trouble. As the ceremony concluded, a scuffle broke out; in the ensuing confusion riflemen opened fire. The Kentucky negotiators succeeded in reaching the cover of the fort, and the siege of Boonesborough began.

Lasting eleven days, this battle has taken its place in American history as a classic confrontation between Indians and Americans. The Shawnees made several attempts to storm the walls, and failing this began to dig a tunnel to undermine the fort. On what became the final night of the siege, the Shawnees set up an intense barrage of covering fire as warriors ran forward with torches in an attempt to burn the walls. But this tactic cost them enormous casualties, and a heavy rain late in the evening put out the fires and collapsed their tunnel. Accepting failure, the Shawnees slipped away under night's cover; the siege had cost them thirty-seven men to two Kentuckians killed.

Boone was then charged with treason, and a formal court-martial produced testimony that the frontiersman "was in favour of the British government; all his conduct proved it." Boone repeated his explanation that he had surrendered his men to protect Boonesborough, where "the fort was in bad order and the Indeans would take it easy." The panel quickly rendered its verdict: "The court Marshall Deseded in Boon's favour," wrote an observer, "and they at that time advanced Boon to a Major."

Boone clearly not only had been acquitted but vindicated. Nevertheless, a whispered debate, of which he was painfully aware, continued for years. One Boonesborough woman, who admitted that she could "never bear an Indian's presence," gossiped that the Shawnees surrounding the fort had called often for Boone, and he "would rise up, and go out freely to and among the Indians; did so repeatedly." For her, it was Boone's obvious ease with the Shawnees that made him suspect. "Boone was willing and wished to surrender," she believed, and she taught her children that "Boone never deserved any thing of the country."

Boone, always hypersensitive to criticism, felt crushed by the mere fact of the accusations. After the siege, he never lived at Boonesborough again. "I am a Woodsman," Boone once wrote. When it came to money, he professed to be "ignorant [of] how to acquire it, except from the chase or by the regular fruits of honest industry." But after the Revolution, when all of Kentucky came down with the fever of land speculation, he put all his effort into becoming a successful businessman. In 1783 Boone moved his family to the port of Limestone on the Ohio, where he kept a tavern, a store, and a warehouse, and engaged in river commerce. Putting to good use his knowledge of geography, he became one of the busiest of Kentucky surveyors. Without proper training or tools, men like Boone "shingled" tracts of land one atop the other in a confusing maze that kept generations of attorneys well fed. But he brought to his business dealings the same frank and open manner that made him a popular leader. "Sorry to here of the Dath of your brother," he wrote one of his clients, "however We must submit to providence, and provide for the Living, and talk of our Lands."

All the wealth he could accumulate he invested in land. It was an enterprise not a little like gambling, and for Boone and other small investors this was a game in which the house enjoyed an extraordinary advantage. A man risked his capital not at the close of the round, when title was granted, but at the opening bid, when he procured land certificates or warrants. Boone's total investment in warrants, certificates, and rights purchased from individuals during the 1780s was in the range of seven to ten thousand pounds. These entitled him to make entries on thousands of acres of land. An entry, however, was merely a claim on a particular tract and had to be defended through a torturous process of official survey and grant of patent. Were other claimants to demonstrate prior rights, or superior surveys shingling his tract, the entry was lost and with it the investment.

During the mid-1780s, according to Nathan Boone, his father "thought himself worth a fortune in the wild lands of the country." Public records indicate that Boone filed claims to at least thirty-nine thousand acres, which qualified him as one of the largest resident land speculators in Kentucky. His strategy was to enter all the claims he could afford, reasoning that this would offer him the best insurance against caveats, challenges, and failures. In fact, though many of the claims failed to prove up, his entries resulted in the eventual granting to him of more than twelve thousand acres. This certainly was not the record of a man ignorant of the means of acquiring property. Boone knew what he was doing, though things did not turn out the way he planned.

"Little by little," said Nathan of his father, "his wealth melted away," the result of a number of factors. One of Boone's first priorities was to provide for his children, and while this cost him land, it certainly cannot be counted a loss. But Boone was as trusting as he was generous, and he often suffered as a result. "So confiding" was Boone, said Nathan, that he once stood as security for the five-hundred-pound debt of a man with whom he did business, then thought nothing of loaning him a horse, saddle, and bridle, and his only male slave, never considering that the man would use them to abscond. But he did, and Boone not only lost his property but had to pay off the obligation.

Boone lacked the ruthless instincts that speculation demanded. For him business obligations were personal matters, and doing the right thing frequently meant taking a financial loss. When he sold land, he usually bonded it against challenge, pledging to "forever Defend the land and premises hereby bargained." Unfortunately, many of his claims were faulty, and as a nephew put it. "Boone's honour compel'd him to pay up his bond while he owned one acre of land."

But these factors were really incidental to the failure of Boone's investment strategy itself. In the heavily speculative environment of Kentucky, Virginia decided to assess not merely lands held under title but land claims as well, and thus Boone's property taxes reflected a valuation of tens of thousands of acres. In order to hold onto his most valuable entries, he began to sell perfected titles to other tracts, often "for a trifle." In this manner Boone disposed of most of the land granted to him. Eventually he even began to sell his entries. In some cases, where his entries were threatened by shingled claims, he sold his interest at deep discount to speculators endeavoring to buy up all the competing claims. The failure of many of these claims meant that Boone frequently had to make good the losses, further increasing his need for cash. The speculative structure Boone had built soon collapsed of its own weight.

His entrance into the speculative world of business, Boone later said, "plunged him into difficulty" with the law, and legal matters soon began to consume most of his time and drive him to distraction. "I am to pay a Large sum of money at Cort on tusday Next," Boone wrote one of his clients, "I hope you will Come Down and satel on Monday Next at my house as I am very on well myself." From 1786 to 1789 he was a party to at least ten lawsuits. Men sued him for faulty surveys, for failed claims, for breech of contract, for the debts of his own and for the debts of others for whom he had posted bond. He lost most of these cases.

Authorities also called on Boone to testify in numerous other suits, usually asking him, as the surveyor, to identify corner trees or landmarks. The record books of Kentucky counties are filled with Boone depositions, and when one reviews the numerous cases it is easy to understand why his patience was tried. At the end of his testimony, the lawyer for the opposing side usually asked whether or not Boone stood to benefit by the outcome of the case. It was one of those proforma legal questions, but he always took it as an insinuation about his character. Was it not the case that the defendant had paid him a certain sum of money for his testimony, one lawyer inquired. He had "not received one shilling," Boone replied angrily, "nor was never offered any sum." Will you gain if the land claimed in this entry is saved, asked another lawyer. "Not a farthing!" Boone shot back. His testimony inevitably enraged those who lost their claims as a result, and Boone again began to fear the resentments of his neighbors. He told his children that his life had been threatened a number of times, and fearing assassination he hesitated to travel alone through the country. "Even in time of peace," he said sadly, "his own Kentucky was as dangerous to him as in time of Indian dangers."

In 1799 Boone and most of his clan left the United States to settle in Missouri, where the Spanish governor had promised him a large estate.[2] There Boone served as "syndic" of the Femme Osage district, and played a mediating role in the transition to American power after the purchase of Louisiana.

But as had been his misfortune in Kentucky in 1809 the federal commission appointed to consider the validity of the Spanish grants rejected his

title. At seventy-five, "Unable to call a single acre his own," he wrote, Boone was once again "a wanderer in the world."

Boone first had achieved fame as the result of a narrative written by John Filson in 1784, in which the Kentucky promoter portrayed the woodsman as a triumphant hero. Later folklore dwelt on the resulting paradoxes in the woodsman's situation. As Boone prepares for his final departure from Kentucky, relates one such story, he goes to a young neighbor to say goodbye. "Where in the world are you going and what for?" asks his shocked friend. "To some point beyond the bounds of civilization and spend the remnant of my days in the woods," answers Boone. "For all my privations and toils I thought I was entitled to a home for my family," but "another bought the land over my head." He offers these parting words of wisdom: "I have lived to learn that your boasted civilization is nothing more than improved ways to overreach your neighbor." Boone throws his arms about his friend's neck and weeps like a child, then departs, leading Rebecca and their youngest son Nathan on horseback, in a scene reminiscent of the flight of Joseph and Mary into the wilderness.

Congress in fact later confirmed Boone's Missouri title; his children possessed fine farms of their own; and he spent his declining years in reasonable comfort. But the folklore struck at an essential truth. While the image of the poor pioneer "unable to call a single acre his own" may not have fit Boone's case precisely, it applied full well to many of his contemporaries. Many of the Kentucky settlers failed to prove their land claims, and by the 1790s fewer than half of the households in the Bluegrass owned land. Boone's troubles were taken to stand for the experience of his fellow pioneers. He had attempted to make the transition from frontier to plantation, moving away from his past as a woodsman and hunter, but he did not have the temperament. And so in his last quarter-century, he returned to hunting and trapping.

Many tales were told about Boone's final move back to the life of the woods. In one, as he moves

---

[2]As they departed, the sheriff of Fayette County was attempting to serve Boone with an arrest warrant for his failure to appear in a suit against him for six thousand pounds; at the same moment, the Kentucky assembly named a new county in Boone's honor.

down the Ohio toward Missouri, someone asks what had induced him to leave "so rich and flourishing a country as his dear Kentucky, which he discovered and had helped to win from the Indians," "Too crowded," Boone exclaims, "too crowded—I want more elbow room!" In another, set in Missouri, Boone tells a traveler that "I wanted to go where I would not be around so much by neabors," but that in Missouri "I am too much crowded." Well, how close are your neighbors, the man inquires, and he is incredulous at Boone's reply. Only twenty miles away!

Such stories angered Boone. "Nothing embitters my old age," he told a visitor, like "the circulation of absurd stories that I retire as civilization advances, that I shun the white men and seek the Indians, and that now even when old, I wish to retire beyond the second Alleganies." Indeed, there is frequently a double edge to the folklore of Boone's wanderlust, for while it celebrates migration, the very essence of American pioneering, it also raises questions about his social commitments. Boone "did not stay one plase long [enough] to get acquainted," declared one of his Kentucky neighbors; he "always lived in a world of his own." The settlers depended upon mutual assistance for survival and mistrusted men who refused to be neighborly.

A few years after Boone's death, Kentucky frontiersman Simon Kenton was asked for his reaction to debunking views of his old friend. Kenton was a quick-tempered man, but resigned to the inevitability of revisionist opinions, he summed up his feelings with a rhetorical shrug of his shoulders: "They may say what they please of Daniel Boone."

By considering Boone's life and legend, Americans have always sought to learn something of themselves. Boone was a woodsman, a man who loved the wilderness and sought a place to hunt and live at ease—but he also was a trailblazer who opened the way for thousands to follow. He was a husband and father devoted to his family—but also a man who craved solitude. He was a man who loved and respected Native Americans and hated violence—but also one who rose to fame as the leader of a war of dispossession. He was a man of contradictions—extraordinary, "but a common man."

Study Questions

1. What paradoxes and contradictions are contained in the life of Daniel Boone and the legend of Daniel Boone? How are the life and legend similar and different?

2. How did European American and Native American cultures mix on the frontier? How would you characterize Boone's relationships with the Native Americans of Pennsylvania, Virginia, North Carolina, and Kentucky? What did Boone believe was the origin of the hostility between Native Americans and Anglo-American settlers?

3. What was life on the frontier like for Rebecca Bryan Boone? How did men and women divide work on the frontier?

4. What characterized the Revolutionary warfare on the frontier? How did the war strain relations between the new settlers and Native Americans? How did the war alter Boone's reputation?

5. How did Boone make and lose a paper fortune in land?

Bibliography

The best study of Daniel Boone's life and times is John Mack Faragher, *Daniel Boone: The Life and Legend of an American Pioneer* (1992). Much of what we know of Boone comes from John Filson, *The Discovery, Settlement, and Present State of Kentucke* (1784), which has been reprinted in numerous versions. Boone was essentially a man of the "middle ground" where Native American and European peoples and cultures mixed and created original forms. A fine study of this "middle ground" is Richard White, *The Middle Ground: Indians, Empire, and Republics in the Great Lakes Region, 1650–1815* (1991). Also see Terry G. Jordan and Matti Kaups, *The American Backwoods Frontier: An Ethnic and Ecological Interpretation* (1989) and Francis Jennings, *Empire of Fortune: Crowns, Colonies, & Tribes in the Seven Years War in America* (1988). For information on the backwoods during the Revolutionary War, see Jack M. Sosin, *The Revolutionary Frontier, 1763–1783* (1967). For the development of the West in the American imagination, a fine starting point is Henry Nash Smith, *Virgin Land: The American West as Symbol and Myth* (1950). For the most recent biography of Daniel Boone, see Michael Lofaro, *Daniel Boone: An American Life* (2003).

READING 11

Founding Mother: Abigail Adams

Phyllis Lee Levin

If George Washington is the "father of the United States," then Abigail Adams is certainly the mother. The devoted wife of President John Adams and mother of President John Quincy Adams, she spent much of her life (1744–1818) in the vortex of American politics. A proponent of American independence, women's rights, and abolition, her political sensibilities always hearkened to the future, not the past, and she had no reluctance about pressing those views on her husband, who had the power to do something about them. John and Abigail spent much of their marriage apart. As a revolutionary activist, diplomat, vice president, and president, he lived for long stretches in London, New York, Paris, Philadelphia, and Washington, D.C., while she tended the family and the family farm in Quincy, Massachusetts. They sustained and nourished their marriage over the years with thousands of letters. In the following essay, biographer Phyllis Lee Levin puts those letters to good use. From the spring of 1775 to the summer of 1776, when her husband was a member of the Second Continental Congress and pushing the thirteen colonies toward independence, Abigail passionately expressed her own opinions, which her husband took very seriously. The following essay by Phyllis Lee Levin describes that time in their lives.

Abigail's correspondence with John in the last days of 1775 and the spring of 1776 delineates with amazing intensity the agonizing issues crucial to the construction of what she called the "Great Empire." Her decision, arrived at with the greatest deliberation possible, was absolutely clear-cut. She might have been pounding her fist on her desk as she wrote. As staunch a "delegate" as America would ever nurture, her farewell to England was unequivocal: "Let us separate, they are unworthy to be our Breathren. Let us renounce them and instead of suplications as formerly for their prosperity and happiness, Let us beseach the almighty to blast their counsels and bring to Nought all their devices."

Her problem was not with the decision to reach for Independence, but how to arrive at this desperately desired goal with thought and in peaceful order. In her opinion, "ten thousand Difficulties" were bound to arise; the reins of government had been slackened for so long she feared the people would not quietly submit to the restraints necessary for the peace and security of the community. Intermittently, consoling herself that "great difficulties may be surmounted, by patience and perseverance," she worried that "if we separate from Brittain, what Code of Laws will be established. How shall we be governed so as to retain our Liberties? Can any government be free which is not administered by general stated Laws? Who shall frame these Laws? Who will give them force and energy?"

Abigail, wandering about her "Labyrinth of perplexities," was preoccupied not only with the form of government, but just as much with the form of the governors. In one of her most anxious moments of skepticism, she said she was more and more convinced that man was a dangerous creature and that power, whether vested in many or few, was "ever grasping." She had reached the opinion, she continued, that "great fish swallow up the small," and that he who most championed the rights of the people, when vested with power, was as eager after the prerogatives of government. As for those who favored ancient customs and regulations, they made her more anxious for the fate of the monarchy or democracy, or whatever was to take place. Witheringly, she dismissed these people as "a little of the Spanel kind. Tho so often spurned still to fawn argues a meanness of Spirit that as an individual I disclaim, and would rather endure any hardships than submit to it."

In her exhaustive examination of the components of the future "Empire," Abigail was not about to overlook economic as well as legislative questions. "As I have been desired to mention to you some things I shall not omit them," she wrote John, by way of attracting his attention to her thoughts about a tax on liquor. As it was, with Massachusetts paying the tax—while the other colonies paid little or none—trade was drawn away from her state. And though she foresaw objections to her plan, she thought all the colonies ought to be taxed, not only in the interests of fairer trade, but because, she said, "too frequent use of Spirit endangers the well being of Society."

Another issue, called to John's attention by Abigail, concerned the loss of silver and gold that was poured into the West Indies in payment for molasses, coffee, sugar, and other commodities. As a result of this daily occurrence, Abigail could tell John that a dollar in silver was a great rarity, and that traders would give a hundred pounds of paper for ninety of silver, or about that proportion. Abigail's remedy was ingenuous: "If any trade is alloud to the West Indias would it not be better to carry some commodity of our own produce in exchange?"

Communication between Abigail and John was by no means one-sided at this time. His wish was equal to hers to share a "compleat History from the Beginning to the End of the Journey." What he had no time to write about, he promised to tell her at a future time. Guarded though he was— "Pimps destroy all freedom of Correspondence," he wrote—he seemed, nevertheless, to write amply about the climate, food, characters, and work he encountered in Philadelphia. "No Mortal Tale could equal it," he insisted, mincing no

---

Phyllis Lee Kevin, *Abigail Adams: A Biography* (1992), pp. 74–92.

numerous Tribes of Indians to negotiate with, a standing Army of Twenty seven Thousand Men to raise, pay, victual, and officer, I really shall pity 50 or 60 Men.

After an unexpected visit home—contrary to his earlier word, he had requested leave on December 8 because he was "worn down with long and uninterrupted Labour"—John took his seat in Congress two months later, on Friday, February 9. Once again the established routine was observed, with John packing newspapers and pamphlets along with his letters, which were more reticent and less frequent, but, if anything, more eagerly sought by Abigail. On February 18, 1776, he wrote of sending her a recently published pamphlet he thought written in "Vindication of Doctrines" to which they were both committed. The pamphlet, Thomas Paine's *Common Sense: Addressed lot the Inhabitants of America,* published anonymously, was significant to Abigail and John on several counts.

At the time of the publication of *Common Sense,* on January 10, 1776, Independence was still a matter of theory and even dispute, though John saw "no Prospect, no Probability no Possibility" for an alternative. He could only despise credulous minds that expected an honorable peace. He detested the hypocritical hearts, he said, that pretended to expect it, when in truth they did not. The pamphlet, which included fifty pages of "simple facts, plain arguments, and common sense," according to its author—"conceived to challenge even the warmest advocate of reconciliation to show a single advantage that America could reap by being connected with Great Britain"—added another block of votes, or would when it achieved its full readership, to the cause of Independence.

Abigail agreed. She was much obliged for the pamphlet, though its author was unknown to her at the time. It was highly prized around Boston, she said, and carried conviction wherever it was read, and she tried to spread it around as much as she could. "Everyone assents to the weighty truths it contains," she said, and she could only wish it could gain credit enough in John's assembly, to be

words about "the Fidgets, the Whims, the Caprice, the Vanity, the Superstition, the Irritability of some of us. . . . "

In spite of the complexities of the gathered assembly, John was intrigued from the beginning by such prospects as establishing monetary and postal systems, and consideration of Dr. Franklin's draft of the "Articles of Confederation and Perpetual Union." Alternately burdened and inspired, John defined for Abigail the breathtaking scope of the work ahead:

The Business I have had upon my Mind has been as great and important as can be intrusted to [One] Man, and the Difficulty and Intricacy of it is prodigious. When 50 or 60 Men have a Constitution to form for a great Empire, at the same Time that they have a Country of fifteen hundred Miles extent to fortify, Millions to arm and train, a Naval Power to begin, an extensive Commerce to regulate, "carried speadily into Execution." Her personal assessment was a complete endorsement:

I am charmed with the Sentiments of Common Sense; and wonder how an honest Heart, one who wishes the welfare of their country, and the happiness of posterity can hesitate one moment at adopting them; I want to know how those Sentiments are received in Congress? I dare say their would be no difficulty in procuring a vote and instructions from all the Assemblies in New England for independancy. I most sincerely wish that now in the Lucky Minuet it might be done.

A few weeks later, on March 19, John answered Abigail's query on how Congress felt about *Common Sense.*

Sensible Men think there are some Whims, some Sophisms, some artful Addresses to superstitious Notions, some keen attempts upon the Passions, in this Pamphlet. But all agree there is a great deal of good sense, delivered in a clear, simple, concise and nervous Style. . . . His Sentiments of the Abilities of America, and of the Difficulty of a Reconciliation with G.B. are generally approved. But his Notions, and Plans of Continental Government are not much applauded. Indeed this Writer has a better Hand at pulling down than building.

John added one other stunning bit of information to his provocative appraisal—there were many who thought *he* was the author of the pamphlet, an opinion he could not accept as a compliment. While he could not have written anything in so "manly and striking a style," he flattered himself, he said, that he should have made a "more respectable figure as an Architect." And further, the writer seemed to him to have "very inadequate Ideas of what is proper and necessary to be done, in order to form Constitutions for single Colonies, as well as a great Model of Union for the whole."

For the time being, John's differences with the author of *Common Sense,* the Englishman Thomas Paine, were entirely intellectual. Paine, who would be known variously as "pamphleteer laureate" of America, propagandist, opportunist, meddler, and gadfly, was introduced to the colonies by Benjamin Franklin as an "ingenious worthy young man"; his recognition by Thomas Jefferson would one day imperil the latter's friendship with John, and therefore with Abigail. A Quaker, a student of Newtonian science, the son of a corset maker, Paine was said by the painter John Trumbull to be a dull companion until after a bottle, which helped him talk, to everyone's surprise, like an "oracle."

The complexities of Thomas Paine's personality and contribution were, however, for the spring of 1776, future history. But John was stirred to write an anonymous reply, called *Thought on Government,* to what he thought were Paine's naïve notions about prospective new governments in America. *Thoughts* (published in Philadelphia by John Dunlap on April 22, 1776), synthesized John's lengthy studies of British law, of the principles of Aristotle and Plato, of Livy and Cicero, of Sidney, Harrington, and Locke. It concluded that all men by nature were equal, that kings had only delegated authority. *Thoughts* concentrated on the goals of American Independence as John saw them: "The happiness of society is the end of government . . . the happiness of the individual is the end of man . . . the form of government which communicates ease, comfort, security, or in one word, happiness, to the greatest number of persons, and in the greatest degree is the best. . . . " As a representative assembly, John envisioned one "in a miniature an exact portrait of the people at large. It should think, feel, reason, and act like them."

On May 9, Abigail commented on *Thoughts,* which she had received two days before its publication date.

Upon reading it I some how or other felt an uncommon affection for it; I could not help thinking it was a near relation of a very intimate Friend of mine. If I am mistaken in its descent, I know it has a near affinity to the

Sentiments of that person, and tho I cannot pretend to be an adept in the art of Government; yet it looks rational that a Government of Good Laws well administered should carry with them the fairest prospect of happiness to a community, as well as to individuals.

By the end of May, in response to Abigail, John maintained a modest or perhaps apologetic stance on the subject of *Thoughts.* It was best to say little about it, he cautioned Abigail. It was a "hasty hurried Thing of no great Consequence, calculated for a Meridian at a great Distance from N. England." It had one merit that he had to acknowledge: if it had done no good, it would do no harm, he said, and did accomplish something. It set people thinking. Since the publication of the letter, the "Manufactory of Governments" had been as much talked of "as that of salt Petre was before."

In the third week of February 1776, Abigail explained to John that she had not written because she had nothing worth saying. Except for the burning of some houses on Dorchester Neck, it had been a "dead calm of dull repose." It was true that preparations were increasing, that something great, something "terible" was predicted daily. On Saturday evening, March 2, she seemed almost despondent: "It has been said to morrow and to morrow for this month, but when the dreadful to morrow will be I know not." She had to stop writing at this point; her house was shaking. She ran to her door to learn from a passerby that the army had begun to fire, and the remaining militia was ordered to report within forty-eight hours. There was no sleep for Abigail that night. And if there was none for her, free of guilt for whatever was to happen—and she did presume that something would take place—she could hardly think that the "misirible wretches," the "procurers of this Dreadfull Scene," would rest easy, burdened with the "load of guilt" they bore upon their souls.

That Saturday night Abigail's pen kept pace with the cannonfire, as did her heartbeat, she assured John. Sunday was fairly quiet, but she was apprehensive. On Monday, the militia marched past her house at 3 p.m. (though they did not have to report until 8 p.m.), fortified with three days' provisions. She had climbed the giant slabs of stone to the top of Penn's Hill to look across the harbor, awed by the meaning of the evening's sights and sounds of shells and cannon, meant to harass the enemy and divert their attention from the plans to fortify Dorchester Neck. "The sound I think is one of the Grandest in Nature and is of the true Species of the Sublime. Tis now an incessant Roar. But O the fatal Ideas which are connected with the sound. How many of our dear country men must fall?"

What happened to Dorchester Hill mattered crucially. The only hill not fortified by the British, it was mounted with cannon that General Knox and his men had hauled hundreds of miles, over ice and snow and frozen rivers, 43 cannon and 16 mortars, 5,500 pounds in all, from Fort Ticonderoga. There was hope that the British, who had made Bunker's Hill impregnable, would be vanquished—a hope miraculously fulfilled, with the evening's help of a wild storm. By six o'clock on Tuesday morning, March 5, all was quiet, and Dorchester Hill was considered the colony's once more.

By Sunday, March 17, Abigail finally had a subject "worth writing upon." She proudly informed John of movements among the "Ministerial Troops," and that General William Howe, possibly sensing he had been outmaneuvered, thought Boston's troops had done more work in one night than the British had done in three months. She did not think this a bit of exaggeration, considering that two forts and long breastworks had sprung up almost instantly, besides a number of barracks, and that in the dark, foggy evening, an estimated four thousand men had dedicated themselves to backbreaking work with "good Hearts."

The enemy was quitting at last, and Abigail thought the American generals could say with Caesar, "veni vidi et vici." Monday, March 18, was a fine, quiet night—no alarms, no cannons—an ideal time to mull things over. Abigail was frankly amazed by General Howe's decision, on March 7, to evacuate Boston, leaving behind such a harbor, such fortifications, such entrenchments. Most of all, she could not comprehend his reason for leaving the Americans in "peaceable" possession of a town that hadn't cost them a drop, let alone the river, of the blood they had anticipated losing. By March 26, Howe, all his troops, and 1,000 Loyalists would set sail for Halifax. "Shurely it is the Lords doing and it is Marvelous in our Eyes," she said contentedly. "Every foot of Ground which they obtain now they must fight for, and may they purchase it at a Bunker Hill price," she told John.

Abigail confronted the changing aspect of the war with guarded elation. She was relieved that Boston was not destroyed, and hoped it would be so secured and guarded as to baffle all future attempts against it. Still, she did not see that the enemy quitting Boston was the solution to the problem; rather, "tis only lifting the burden from one shoulder to the other which perhaps is less able or less willing to support it." She sensed some "very important Crisis" near at hand:

Perhaps providence sees it necessary in order to answer important ends and designs that the Seal of War should be changed from this to the Southern colonies that each may have a proper sympathy for the others, and unite in a separation. The Refuge of the Believer amidst all the afflictive dispensations of providence, is that the Lord Reigneth, and that he can restrain the Arm of Man.

Just two weeks made the most extraordinary difference in Abigail's outlook. Like a butterfly freed from an intolerable cocoon, on winged spirits, Abigail soared to heights of optimism at which she could not help but marvel. "I feel a gaieti de Coar [*sic*] to which before I was a stranger," she said, almost bemused by her findings that the sun looked brighter to her, birds sang more melodiously, nature put on a more "cheerful countanance." She felt a temporary peace with the world and even a tentative sense of security—as though she and all those about her "might sit under our own vine and eat the good of the land." It had all been so different under the British, she wrote: "We knew not then whether we could plant or sow with safety, whether when we had told we could reap the fruits of our own industry, whether we could rest in our own Cottages,

or whether we should not be driven from the sea coasts to seek shelter in the wilderness. . . ."

Under the now more promising circumstances, Abigail could think about reclaiming the house in Boston. Because she was afraid of smallpox, she sent someone else to inspect it. To her relief, she learned it was very dirty but not damaged, the way General John Burgoyne, that man of "dark" designs and "Horrible wickedness," had left Samuel Quincy's house. There, it was reported by a neighbor, mahogany tables had been ruined by hacking raw meat on their surfaces, and superb damask curtains and cushions had been exposed to the rain as if they had no value at all. Abigail, elated at the prospect of retrieving her household, regarded it as a new acquisition that she could not have realistically valued at a single shilling just weeks before, and could, "with pleasure," have seen it go up in flames in the colony's cause.

Also in the interests of the cause, Abigail continued to make soap, manufacture clothing for her family ("which would else be naked"), and considered experimenting with saltpeter. She had recently seen a small manuscript describing the proportions for the various sorts of powder fit for cannon, small arms, and pistols, and would have it transcribed, she wrote to John, if it was of any "Service" down his way. Though it seemed at times as if all of Abigail's energies were confined to practical and immediate issues, such was hardly the case.

Abigail remained consistent in her pursuit of Independence; her bold concept of its horizons was singular. By March 31, 1776, in a letter to John, she had launched, unwittingly, the timeless campaign for women's rights. Accustomed to John's "indulgence," she had always written truthfully her thoughts about people, speeches—"tis a heavy unelegant verbose performance," she reported about one that did not strike her fancy at all—and places. "Tis a liberty I take with you," she admitted to John. Risking his finding her "saucy," Abigail proceeded:

I long to hear that you have declared an independency—and by the way in the new Code of Laws which I suppose it will be necessary for you to make I desire you would Remember the

Ladies, and be more generous and favourable to them than your ancestors. Do not put such unlimited power into the hands of the Husbands. Remember all Men would be tyrants if they could. If perticuliar care and attention is not paid to the Ladies we are determined to foment a Rebellion, and will not hold ourselves bound by any Laws in which we have no voice, or Representation. . . . That your Sex are Naturally Tyrannical is a Truth so thoroughly established as to admit of no dispute, but such of you as wish to be happy willingly give up the harsh title of Master for the more tender and endearing one of Friend. Why then, not put it out of the power of the vicious and the Lawless to use us with cruelty and indignity with impunity. Men of Sense in all Ages abhor those customs which treat us only as the vassals of your sex. Regard us then as Beings placed by providence under your protection and in immitation of the Supreme Being make use of that power only for our happiness.

The breadth of Abigail's concept was undoubtedly enhanced by the mounting possibilities of its realization. Still, the subject was of continuing interest to her, and she had already alerted John to the universality of her views of independence. She had written to him in September, 1774, of a cumbersome situation in which Negroes agreed to fight for the Governor if he would arm them and then liberate them if his side won. "You know my mind upon this Subject," she had said, "I wish most sincerely there was not a slave in the province. It allways appeared a most iniquitious Scheme to me—fight ourselves for what we are daily robbing and plundering from those who have as good a right to freedom as we have."

Again, in the summer of 1775, Abigail intimated a sense of deprivation regarding the subject of Independence, but this time in a highly personal way. She and her sister, Mary Cranch, had driven their chaise eleven miles to Dedham to hear the Reverend Jason Haven, and to spend time with Mrs. Samuel Adams. In reporting the pleasant events of July 25, Abigail referred to

Mrs. Adams as her "name sake and Sister Delegate," living with "patience, perseverance and fortitude" in a little country cottage. Somewhat defensively, Abigail explained the honorific she conferred on Elizabeth Adams: "Why should we not assume your titles when we give you up our names."

John, who fretted about finding a way for two "friendly Souls" to "converse" together, although the bodies were four hundred miles apart, appeared to experience no difficulty unburdening himself as to precisely what he thought about Abigail's letter, with its brave declaration of independence for the ladies. While excusing the brevity of his letters because of the "critical State of Things and the Multiplicity of Avocations," he responded, on April 14, in ample detail, more indulgently than condescendingly:

As to your extraordinary Code or Laws, I cannot but laugh. We have been told that our Struggle has loosened the bands of Government every where. That Children and Apprentices were disobedient—that schools and Colledges were grown turbulent—that Indians slighted their Guardians and Negroes grew insolent to their Masters. But your Letter was the first Intimation that another Tribe more numerous and powerful than all the rest were grown discontented.—This is rather too coarse a Compliment but you are so saucy, I won't blot it out.

Having acknowledged Abigail's argument on behalf of her sex, John, by way of an elaborate and affectionate rebuttal, insisted that Abigail overstated her case and that it was really the men, rather than the women, who were threatened. To enforce his point, he even left out the onerous word.

Depend upon it, We know better than to repeal our Masculine systems. Altho they are in full Force, you know they are little more than Theory. We dare not exert our Power in its full Latitude. We are obliged to go fair, and softly, and in Practice you know We are the subjects. We have only the Name of Masters, and rather

*than give up this, which would compleatly sub-
ject Us to the Despotism of the Peticoat, I hope
General Washington, and all our brave Heroes
would fight. I am sure every good Politician
would plot, as long as he would against Despotism, Empire, Monarchy, Aristocracy, Oli-
garchy, or Ochlocracy,—A fine Story indeed. I
begin to think the Ministry as deep as they are
wicked. After stirring up Tories, Landjobbers,
Trimmers, Bigots, Canadians, Indians, Negroes,
Hanoverians, Hessians, Russians, Irish Roman
Catholicks, Scotch Renegadoes, at last they
have stimulated them to demand new Priv-
iledges and threaten to rebell.*

Either Abigail had received no response from
John as yet, or she chose to ignore it, in her determination to make her thesis emphatic. She
had rephrased her initial pronouncement in her
letter of May 7, but the message was whole, and
almost threatening:

*I cannot say that I think you very generous to
the Ladies, for whilst you are proclaiming
peace and good will to Men, Emancipating all
Nations, you insist upon retaining an absolute
power over Wives. But you must remember
that Arbitrary power is like most other things
which are very hard, very liable to be broken—
and notwithstanding all your wise Laws and
Maxims we have it in our power not only to
free ourselves but to subdue our Masters, and
without violence throw both your natural and
legal authority at our feet*

   *"Charm by accepting, by submitting
   sway
   yet have our Humour most when we
   obey."*

One person with whom Abigail discussed thoroughly the subject of women's independence,
and her exchange with John, was Mercy Warren.
The two women's correspondence was already a
thriving success. No matter how careworn she
was, no matter how she might complain of the

"multiplicity" of concerns, Abigail always rallied.
"Let your letters be of the journal kind," she enthusiastically urged Mercy. "I could participate in
your amusements, in your pleasures, and in your
sentiments which would greatly gratify me, and I
should collect the best of inteligence."

True to character, then, Abigail interrupted her
preoccupation with her family, farm, country, and
particularly her thoughts on the ramifications of
independence long enough, in the spring of 1776,
to inquire about a recent resident of Boston. "How
do you like Mrs. Washington?" she asked Mercy.
"Any other person you have seen, and *noticed*
should be glad of your opinion," she added.

Mercy responded obligingly. She would endeavor to gratify her friend, as her "Curiosity seems
to be awake with Regard to the Company I keep
and the Manner of spending my time." She had met
with Mrs. Washington in Cambridge one April
morning at eleven o'clock, as well as with her son
and his wife. She had been received with that

*politness and Respect shewn in a first interview
among the well bred and with the Ease and Cor-
diallity of Friendship of a much Earlier date. . . .
If you wish to hear more of this Ladys Character
I will tell you I think the Complacency of her
Manners speaks at once the Benevolence of her
Heart, and her affability, Candor and Gentle-
ness Quallify her to soften the hours of private
Life or to sweeten the Cares of the Hero and
smooth the Rugged scenes of War.*

Mercy seemed equally impressed by John
Parke Custis, whom she described as "A sensible
Modest agreable young Man." His wife, Eleanor
Custis, received a more equivocal tribute:

*His Lady a Daughter of Coll. Calvert of Mari-
land, appears to be of an Engaging Disposition
but of so Exstrem Delicate a Constitution that
it Deprives her as well as her Friends of part of
the pleasure which I am perswaded would Result from her Conversation did she Enjoy a
Greater share of Health. She is pretty, Genteel,
Easey and Agreable, but a kind of Languor*

*about her prevents her being so sociable as
some Ladies. Yet it is Evident it is not owing to
that want of Vivacity which Renders youth
agreable, but to a want of health which a Little
Clouds her spirits.*

As a result of Mercy's account of the members
of the Washington family, Abigail said she should
"most certainly" be tempted (if coveting her
neighbor's goods was not prohibited by sacred
law), to envy her friend the happy talent she
possessed—"above the rest of her Sex"—of
adorning with her pen even trivial occurrences,
as well as dignifying the most important.

Abigail's compliment, one of many she bestowed on Mercy, was returned in kind and quantity. Furthermore, however much they deferred
to one another, however much Mercy insisted
she fell short of Abigail "in many Female accomplishments," she did believe they were on equal
footing in one quality. She was speaking of curiosity, consigned to them "so Generously" by the
other sex for no other reason, she supposed, but
that men had opportunities of indulging their "inquisitive Humour to the utmost in the Great
school of the World," while women, on the other
hand, were confined to the "Narrower Circle of
Domestic Care." But Mercy insisted she was not
defeated on this score. It afforded them "yet one
Advantage peculiar to ourselves," she told Abigail
with mischievous pleasure:

*If the Mental Faculties of the Female are not
improved it may be Concealed in the Obscure
Retreats of the Bed Chamber or the kitchen
which she is not often Necessitated to Leave.
Whereas Man is Generally Called out to the full
display of his Abilities but how often do they
Exhibit the most Mortifying instances of Neglected Opportunities and their Minds appear
Not with standing the Advantages of what is
Called a Liberal Education, as Barren of Culture and as Void of Every useful acquirement
as the most Triffling untutored Girl.*

Given their special relationship, their binding
persuasions, Abigail was at ease discussing her re-

cent exchange with John. On April 27, 1776 Abigail confided to Mercy that John had been "very
sausy" to her in return for a "List of Female Grievances" she had transmitted to him. She thought
she would ask Mercy to join her in a petition to
Congress, as it was very probable that their wise
statesmen would erect a new government and
form a new code of laws. "I ventured to speak a
word in behalf of our Sex," she explained to her
friend, "who are rather hardly dealt with by the
Laws of England which gives such unlimited
power to the Husband to use his wife Ill." Repeating her extraordinary plan to establish some
laws in favor of women on "just and Liberal prin-
cipals," she also mentioned John's wishfully con-
ciliatory reply. "So I have help'd the Sex abundantly," she had concluded.

On the whole, Abigail was probably more effective than she realized. On May 26, in a letter
to Brigadier General Joseph Palmer, Mr. Cranch's
brother-in-law, John discussed his ideals of government and who had the right to vote, and
under what circumstances. He was certain in
theory that the only moral foundation of government was the consent of the people; his
question was to what extent this principle could
be carried out. "Shall we say, that every Individual of the Community, old and young, male and
female, as well as rich and poor, must consent
. . . to every act of Legislation?" And if this was
impossible, as he judged Palmer would say, then
what about the "Right of Man to govern women
without their consent," John probed, or the
"Right of the Old to bind the young without
theirs?"

John labored specifically over his presumption
that Palmer would exclude women from voting
because it was the obligation of the minority to
obey and because their delicacy rendered them
unfit for the hardy enterprises of war, as well as
for the cares of state, and besides, nature had
made them "fittest" for domestic cares. "But will
not these reasons apply to others?" John insisted.

Men who were destitute of property, for example, were also too infrequently associated with
public affairs, too dependent upon other men, to
have a will of their own. If, therefore, every man

was given a vote without regard to property ownership, then, by the same reasoning, ought not women and children be entitled to vote? After all, he reasoned, men who were destitute of property were "to all intents and purposes" as much dependent on others to feed, clothe, and employ them as women were "upon their husbands, or children on their parents."

It is impossible to disassociate John's final paragraph to the general from Abigail's threatened rebellion. It was as though he had her letter open before him when he wrote: "Depend on it, Sir, it is dangerous to open so fruitfull a source of Controversy and altercation, as would be opened by attempting to alter the Qualifications of Voters. There will be no end to it—New claims will arise—Women will demand a Vote. . . ."

Just two months after the evacuation from Boston, Abigail's silken spirits were frayed by impatience and disappointment. Parliament had passed the American Prohibitory Act as of December 22, 1775, declaring all American ships and goods subject to British seizure, an act John regarded as "the last Stretch of Oppression." He assured Abigail that they were "hastening rapidly to great Events," but hardly rapidly enough for her. In her opinion, the eyes of their rulers were closed, and a lethargy had seized almost every member. She feared that a fatal sense of security had taken possession: "Whilst the Building is on flame they tremble at the expence of water to quench it," she complained to John. She was distressed that Boston's Harbor lay unprotected: "Tis a Maxim of state That power and Liberty are like Heat and moisture; where they are well mixt every thing prospers, where they are single, they are destructive."

By May 9, Abigail could at last report the awakening of "the Spirit of fortification." Fort Hill, the Castle, and Dorchester Point were almost completed; a committee had been sent down to Nantasket; orders had been given to protect Moon and George's Island. Still, a government of more stability was much wanted in the colony; people were waiting expectantly for direction from Congress. As she was already inclined to making "Maxims of State," she added another. It was possible, she said, "that a people may let a king fall, yet still remain a people, but if a king let his people slip from him, he is no longer a king."

John's letter of May 17 bolstered Abigail's hope for decisive action. Great Britain, he reported, had "at last" driven America to the final step, "a compleat Separation from her, a total absolute Independence, not only of her Parliament but of her Crown, for such is the Amount of the Resolve of the 15th." John was referring to the preamble, adopted on May 15, to a resolution voted after a debate of May 10, recommending to the assemblies and conventions of the individual colonies that they "adopt such government as shall, in the Opinion of the Representatives of the People, best conduce to the Happiness and Safety of their Constituents in particular, and America in general." Though ostensibly the work of a committee of three, including Edward Rutledge and Richard Henry Lee, the preamble was written by John, whose strong recommendation for separation from Great Britain was objected to by conservatives as "a Machine to fabricate independence."

John was not unaware of his responsibility. He was also humbled by his decisive role:

When I consider the great Events which are passed, and those greater which are rapidly advancing, and that I may have been instrumental of touching some Springs, and turning some small Wheels, which have had and will have such Effects, I feel an Awe upon my Mind, which is not easily described.

Despite the particular "Flickerings of Parties," he was optimistic about the future. He had reason to believe that any colony that assumed a government "under the People" would never give it up. With vision, he realized that "there is something very unnatural and odious in a Government 1,000 Leagues off. An whole Government of our own Choice, managed by Persons whom we love, revere, and can confide in, has charms in it for which Men Will fight."

Abigail, too, was vigorously persistent in the belief in eventual Independence, even as she allowed that the "dissagreable News" from Quebec was a "great damper" to their spirits. "But shall we receive good and not Evil?" she reasoned. At a time like this, she relied on the wisdom of one of John's favorite writers, Maximilien de Béthune, the Duc de Sully. The seventeenth-century Frenchman had taught Abigail the importance, "in bold and difficult enterprizes," of subduing one obstacle at a time, and of not being "deprest by their Greatness and their Number." Paraphrasing Béthune, Abigail's message to John was decisive and hopeful:

We ought never to despair of what has been once accomplished. How many things have the Idea of imposible been annexed to, that have become easy to those who knew how to take advantage of Time, opportunity, lucky Moments, the Faults of others, different dispositions and an infinite Number of other circumstances.

Furthermore, it was a sincere wish, she admitted, that they might be fortunate enough to have the "Spirit of Sully animaeting our counsels."

Abigail was able to write, on May 27, "My Heart is as light as a feather and my Spirits are dancing." She had received John's "fine" parcel of letters, a "feast" for her. She was also pleased that she had been able to hire a "Negro fellow" for six months, at ten pounds less than she had expected to pay, and that her farmhand Belcher was "exceeding assiduous" (and should he "purloin a little" she would look the other way). She even managed, on June 17, to spend "a remarkable day"—her first away from Braintree since John's departure—at Plymouth. There, with her sister Betsy, and with Mercy, she had been entertained aboard the brig *Defence,* where she had admired its captain, learned of its nine sea engagements, viewed a mock engagement, sipped tea, and observed dancing on the quarterdeck to violin and flute music. Her departure with her party at day's end was heralded by gunfire—an honor that Abigail said she could have dispensed with "readily."

Having enjoyed one excursion, Abigail planned another, of a drastically different sort. Anxious over the disastrous news from Canada that smallpox had been one of the main reasons for the precipitous retreat from Quebec ("The Small Pox is ten times more terrible than Britons, Canadians and Indians together," John said), Abigail made definitive plans to remedy her family's vulnerability. On July 7 she invited John Thaxter—he had always expressed a desire to have the smallpox with her family—to join her the following Thursday. Those in her party would include the Cranches and their children, her sister Betsy, Cotton Tufts, Jr., a maid, and an elderly nurse.

If Thaxter chose to enter as part of the family, at the cost of eighteen shillings weekly, he also needed to be prepared to pay his doctor for inoculation—a guinea per week was the cost, she had heard. She promised to find a bed and a bedstead for him, but said she would appreciate his bringing along two pairs of sheets and a counterpane. She was also taking a cow, hay, and wood from Braintree. If all went well, they might return in three weeks. "If you conclude to go, be at our House a wednesday Night," she added.

When word of Abigail's plans reached John, he wrote back almost immediately to tell her that he was happy to find her "resolved" to be with the children in the first group of patients to be received by Dr. Thomas Bulfinch. It was not until Sunday, July 14, however, that Abigail was able to reply—her eyes were so badly inflamed—to comment on the "Spirit of inoculation" that pervaded the town and every house in it, drawing not less than thirty people from Braintree to Boston.

That Sunday, Abigail felt well enough not only to write about family news, but to pay attention to the world beyond her sickbed. She could report that she was not only recovering, but actually happy. John's letters never failed to give her pleasure, whatever the subject. But these, dated July 3 and 4, that "heightened" the prospect of the future happiness and glory of her country, were especially prized. They brought her the momentous news she longed for. On July 3, John had written from Philadelphia:

Yesterday the greatest Question was decided, which ever was debated in America, and a greater perhaps, never was or will be decided among Men. A Resolution was passed without one dissenting Colony "that these united Colonies, are, and of right ought to be free and independent States, and as such, they have, and of Right ought to have full Power to make War, conclude Peace, establish Commerce, and to do all the other Acts and Things, which other States may rightfully do."

He also promised Abigail: "You will see in a few days a Declaration setting forth the Causes, which have impell'd Us to this mighty Revolution, and the Reasons which will justify it, in the Sight of God and Man. A Plan of Confederation will be taken up in a few days."

John's obvious elation over the news of independence dispelled tedium, discomfort, even doubts, momentarily. Acknowledging his inadequacies, proud of his responsibilities, humbly determined to do as well as he could, and make "Industry supply, in some degree the place of Abilities and Experience," he was inspired by the achievement.

When I look back to the Year 1761, and recollect the Argument concerning Writs of Assistance, in the Superior Court, which I have hitherto considered as the Commencement of the Controversy, between Great Britain and America, and run through the whole Period from that Time to this, and recollect the series of political Events, the Chain of Causes and Effects, I am surprised at the Suddenness, as well as Greatness of this Revolution. Britain has been fill'd with Folly, and America with Wisdom, at least this is my Judgment.—Time must determine. It is the Will of Heaven, that the two Countries should be sundered forever.

At this moment of euphoria, even as he wistfully considered that an earlier Declaration would have advanced foreign alliances and might have achieved possession of Quebec, John recognized the positive values in the delay. Waiting had, in his opinion,

"gradually and at last totally extinguished" hopes for reconciliation. Time had allowed for the "whole" people to consider maturely the "great Question of Independence," and to ripen their judgments, dissipate their fears, and "allure their Hopes," so that they had adopted it as their own act. He concluded, "This will cement the Union, and avoid those Heats and perhaps Convulsions which might have been occasioned by such a Declaration Six Months ago."

Having yearned and worked for the concept of Independence, John understood its startling significance and envisioned its enduring brilliance.

The Second Day[1] of July 1776, will be the most memorable Epocha, in the History of America.— I am apt to believe that it will be celebrated, by succeeding Generations, as the great anniversary Festival. It ought to be commemorated, as the Day of Deliverance by solemn Acts of Devotion to God Almighty. It ought to be solemnized with Pomp and Parade, with Shews, Games, Sports, Guns, Bells, Bonfires and Illuminations from one End of this Continent to the other from this Time forward forever more.

The significance of the Declaration, so grandly defined, did not obliterate knowledge of its price. John was full of apprehension. The new governments would require a "Purification" from their vices and an "Augmentation" of their virtues, or there would be no blessings. The people, too, presented problems. As they were extremely addicted to "Corruption and Venality," he would submit all his hopes and fears to an "overruling Providence, in which, unfashionable as the Faith may be," he believed firmly. He hoped Abigail's brother and his would serve their country "at this critical Period of its Distress." His words were both ominous and splendid at once as he wrote Abigail:

You will think me transported with Enthusiasm but I am not. I am well aware of the Toil

---

[1]July 2 was the day Congress actually voted for Independence.

and Blood and Treasure, that it will cost Us to maintain this Declaration, and support and defend these States.—Yet through all the Gloom I can see the Rays of ravishing Light and Glory. I can see that the End is more than worth all the Means. And that Posterity will tryumph in that Days Transaction, even although We should rue it, which I trust in God We shall not.

With the Declaration, Abigail seemed to forget the eye inflammation that had prevented her from writing to John for nearly a month. The news seemed to soothe her many cares, particularly over her children's recovery from their inoculations. She was thrilled not only by the actual event, but by the fact that a person "so nearly connected" with her had the honor of being a "principal actor" in laying a foundation for her country's "future greatness. May the foundation of our new constitution, be justice, Truth and Righteousness," she wrote to John. Craving permanence, she added: "Like the wise Mans house may it be founded upon those Rocks and then neither storms or tempests will overthrow it."

Abigail did not speak of John's coming home, and she promised to write very often. She asked to be informed "constantly" of every important transaction. And she reaffirmed his place in her life. All expressions of tenderness were invaluable, each a "cordial" to her heart. Unimportant as they might be to the rest of the world, to her, she emphasized, "they are *every Thing.*"

Study Questions

1. Describe Abigail Adams's position on the question of independence. Would you consider her a moderate or a radical on the question of separating from the British Empire? Why?

2. Assuming independence succeeded, what concerns did she express about any new government that would replace the British empire? How did she feel about relevant economic issues?

3. How did John and Abigail feel about Thomas Paine's pamphlet *Common Sense*?

4. Describe the battle of Dorchester Hill. Why was it important to Abigail?

5. Describe her feelings about women's rights.

6. What non-political news did she convey to her husband in 1775–1776?

Bibliography

For a look at the role of women in fomenting and shaping the American Revolution, see Linda K. Kerber, *Women of the Republic: Intellect and Ideology in Revolutionary America* (1980); and Richard Brookhiser, *America's First Dynasty: The Adamses, 1735-1918* (2002). For a highly readable biography of John Adams, see David G. McCullough, *John Adams* (2001). In *First Thoughts: The Life and Letters of Abigail Adams* (1998), Edith Belle Gilles has written a biography of Abigail Adams and compiled her letters. For biographies of Abigail Adams, see Phyllis Lee Levin, *Abigail Adams: A Biography* (1987); Edith Belle Gelles, *Portia: The World of Abigail Adams* (1992); and Lynn Withay, *Dearest Friend: A Life of Abigail Adams* (1981).

READING 12

★ ★ ★

Wounded and Presumed Dead: Dying of Breast Cancer in Early America

James S. Olson

The half-century between the end of the French and Indian War in 1763 and the outbreak of the War of 1812 was an extraordinary period in American history. The Founding Fathers unleashed the American Revolution, declaring their independence from Great Britain, and then won a military victory in the War for American Independence. They wrote the Constitution and the Bill of Rights, launched a new government, and developed a two-party system that has governed the United States ever since. Few people in the history of the world have lived through such dangerous and propitious times and accomplished so much. But while they were dealing with revolution, war, and nation building, they also had private lives and all of the personal challenges that go along with raising a family and making a living. John Adams—the first vice president and the second president of the United States—and his wife Abigail established what remains today one of the most distinguished families in American history. Their children brought them great joy. But as in all families, joy is often mixed with tragedy. In the essay below, historian James S. Olson describes how breast cancer ultimately killed their only daughter Nabby and how the family dealt with her illness.

It was just a tiny dimple. On a man's chin it would have looked rugged and distinguished. On a woman's cheek it might have been called a "beauty mark." But this was a different dimple, a killer dimple. It was on her left breast and "Nabby" Smith wondered what it was. She had never noticed it before, nor had her husband William. Perhaps it was just another physical sign of age, they thought, an indicator that she was not a young woman anymore. It was a sign, to be sure, but not of old age. The dimple was as much a symbol of premature death as a skull and crossbones, and within a few years, it would turn Nabby into a virtual skeleton before killing her in pain-wracked stupor. Actually, the dimple itself was not really the problem. Beneath the dimple, buried an inch below the skin, a small malignant tumor was attaching itself to surface tissues and drawing them in, like a sinking ship pulling water down in its own whirlpool. It was 1808 and Nabby was forty-four years old. She had a husband and three children, but she did not have much of a life left.

At first Nabby did not give it much thought, only noticing it now and then when she bathed or dressed in the morning. Nor did she talk about it. Nabby Smith was a shy and somewhat withdrawn woman, quiet and cautious in the expression of ideas, more comfortable with people who guarded their feelings than with those who exposed them. She blushed easily and rarely laughed out loud, allowing only a demure, half-smile to crease her face when she was amused. She had a pleasant disposition and a mellow temperament, both of which endeared her to family and friends. Nabby was a beautiful woman, blessed with long, red hair, a round face, deep-blue eyes, and a creamy, porcelain complexion. She commanded respect, not because of an aggressive personality but simply because of the quality of her mind and a powerful sense of personal dignity.

At least some of that dignity came from her background. Nabby Smith was a member of one of the most distinguished families in the United States. She was born in Quincy, Massachusetts, in 1766. Her parents named her Abigail Adams. They began calling her "Nabby" when she was little. Nabby had an extraordinary childhood. Her father was John Adams, the future president of the United States, and her mother was Abigail Adams, the most prominent woman in early American society. Her little brother John Quincy was destined to become president of the United States. From the time of her birth, Nabby's parents were busily engaged in colonial politics and eventually played leading roles in the American Revolution and the War for American Independence. They raised her on a steady diet of dinner table and parlor political talk— animated discussions of freedom, liberty, rights, despotism, war, and foreign policy. Nabby absorbed it all; political philosophy in her family was not a mere abstraction. Her position in the family was secure.

She was the apple of their eyes. As an only daughter, Nabby enjoyed the special attentions of her father, who felt the need to protect her and pamper her. Abigail had always doted upon her, dressing her up in the latest fashions when she was little and counseling her when she was an adolescent. When Nabby grew up their relationship quickly evolved into a deep friendship. In spite of the devoted attentions of her parents, Nabby took it all in stride, never becoming spoiled or self-indulgent. She was even-handed, thick-skinned, and not afraid of responsibility— the daughter every parent dreamed of having.

When the War for Independence ended in 1783, Nabby was just seventeen years old, but she was in for an adventure. Congress appointed her father to serve as the first United States minister to England, and in 1785 the family crossed the Atlantic and took up residence in a house on Grosvener Square in London. They were immediately caught up in the social and political life of the world's greatest city, meeting King George III at court and other prominent politicians and attending the whirlwind of parties, meetings, banquets, and festivals common to the life of an ambassador.

For the first few months in London, Nabby was somewhat depressed, mostly because of homesickness because she had left behind a boyfriend who soon quit writing letters. Her mood caught her parents off guard—it was uncharacteristic of her—and they tried to reassure her that soon she would be feeling better. They were right. Soon Nabby had noticed a young man who was part of the American diplomatic staff in London. Colonel William Smith, a young veteran of the Continental Army and secretary to the American legation in London, had also noticed Nabby.

Smith was a dashing and handsome figure, racing around London in a two-seated carriage, something equivalent to a sports car today. He dressed well—a weakness for silk coats and shirts—and kept company with a variety of people in London's ex-patriot community, especially with Latin American liberals and radicals interested in securing independence from Spain. He was bold and impetuous, inspired by courage and limited by poor judgment. Because of his work with the American legation in London, and his role as secretary to Minister John Adams, Smith saw a great deal of the Adams family, and Nabby fell secretly in love with him. It was not long before he felt the same way, drawn to Nabby's beauty, grace, and intelligence. He proposed late in 1785 and they were married in June 1786, after a courtship which John and Abigail Adams felt was too short. They excused it because "a soldier is always more expeditious in his courtships than other men."

But Colonel William Smith was a soldier without a war, a dinosaur at the age of twenty-eight, and Nabby was in for a difficult life, an innocent victim of what her brother John Quincy called "fortune's treacherous game." Colonel Smith was not cruel. In fact, he always loved and cared for Nabby, and they had three children. With a stoicism that would have made the most devout Puritan proud, Nabby was more than willing to accept her financial fate and make a life for her family wherever Smith settled. The problem was that Smith never really settled down. He wasted his life away, always searching but never finding a place for himself, winning and losing political ap-

pointments, dabbling in Latin American *coup d'etats* and revolutions, dragging Nabby and the kids back and forth between New York and London trying to influence a new power broker or close another deal. He spent far more money than he ever earned, and Nabby was forever worrying about the bills and their reputation. By the early 1800s, Smith was trying to make his fortune in shady real estate schemes, hoping to profit from the desire of so many Americans to move west and get their own land, but he lost everything he had. He was bold but not shrewd enough for the life of an entrepreneur. In 1808, when Nabby first noticed the dimple, they were living on the edge of the frontier, in a small farmhouse along the Chenago River in western New York, where he spent the days behind an iron plow and a mule working a small plot of land. The Smiths were a long way, economically and geographically, from the heady world of Boston and London politics.

During the next year the dimple became more pronounced and more worrisome to Nabby, but it was not until late in 1809 that she felt a hard lump beneath the skin. Nabby Adams was an intelligent, well-informed woman, and throughout her adult life the Adams family had been close friends with Dr. Benjamin Rush, the country's most prominent physician. Breast cancer was as much the dreaded disease in the early 1800s as it is today, something educated women knew about and feared. Well-informed people had been aware of breast cancer for two thousand years, since Greek physicians first called it *karkinos* (carcinoma), or crab, because of its tenacious ability to hold on, to defy all attempts to cure it or cut it out. In fact, breast cancer in women was really the first cancer human beings ever identified, probably because it was more visible than other deadly tumors. And they knew breast cancer started with a hard lump. No records exist describing Nabby Smith's initial reaction to the lump in her breast, but it is safe to say that the intermittent, low-key concern about the dimple was instantly transformed into a chronic, persistent worry that would never quite go away.

Like so many women then and today, Nabby tried to ignore the lump, hoping that in the daily, busy routines of running a small farm and household she would not have time to think about it. But cancer has a way of asserting itself, finally obliterating even the most elaborate attempts at procrastination and denial. Nabby's cancer was no exception. The lump underwent an ominous growth, in spite of the efforts of local healers who prescribed a dizzying variety of external salves and potions. She wrote home to John and Abigail Adams in February 1811 that her doctor had discovered "a cancer in my breast." As soon as they received the letter, her parents began urging their daughter to come to Boston for medical advice. Some things do not change. Even today, people suffering from cancer often head to the major cities where comprehensive cancer centers can treat them.

In June 1811, with the lump now visible to the naked eye, a desperate Nabby returned to Massachusetts. As soon as she arrived in Quincy, Massachusetts, Nabby wrote to Benjamin Rush in Philadelphia, describing her condition and seeking his advice. When Abigail Adams first looked at her daughter's breast, she found the condition "alarming." The tumor was large enough to distend the breast into a misshapen mass. John and Abigail took Nabby to see several physicians in Boston—Drs. Holbrook and Welsh and Tufts and Johnson—and they were cautiously reassuring, telling her that the situation and her general health were "so good as not to threaten any present danger." They prescribed hemlock pills to "poison the disease."

Soon after that round of reassuring examinations, however, the Adams family received a more ominous reply from Dr. Benjamin Rush. In her initial letter, Nabby told the famous physician that the tumor was large and growing, but that it was "movable"—not attached to the chest wall. Rush found the news encouraging, as do most cancer specialists today. Malignant tumors which are "movable" are better candidates for surgery, since it is more likely that the surgeon can get what is termed a "clean margin"—a border of noncancerous tissue surrounding the tumor—reducing the chances that the cancer will recur or spread.

Knowing that Nabby had already traveled from western New York to Boston to seek more medical advice and to be cared for by her parents, Rush wrote a letter to John and Abigail Adams, telling them to gently break his news to Nabby. Dr. Rush wrote:

I shall begin my letter by replying to your daughter's. I prefer giving my opinion and advice in her case in this way. You and Mrs. Adams may communicate it gradually and in such a manner as will be least apt to distress and alarm her.

After the experience of more than 50 years in cases similar to hers, I must protest against all local applications and internal medicines for relief. They now and then cure, but in 19 cases out of 20 in tumors in the breast they do harm or suspend the disease until it passes beyond that time in which the only radical remedy is ineffectual. This remedy is the knife. From her account of the moving state of the tumor, it is now in a proper situation for the operation. Should she wait till it suppurates or even inflames much, it may be too late. . . . I repeat again, let there be no delay in flying to the knife. Her time of life calls for expedition in this business. . . . I sincerely sympathize with her and with you and your dear Mrs. Adams in this family affliction, but it will be but for a few minutes if she submit to have it extirpated, and if not, it will probably be a source of distress and pain to you all for years to come. It shocks me to think of the consequences of procrastination in her case.

Benjamin Rush knew that there were no home remedies or folk cures for breast cancer; Nabby Adams needed surgery—a mastectomy—and she needed it immediately.

Rush wrote to John and Abigail Adams, rather than replying directly to Nabby's inquiry, because he wanted them to break the news to her gently, to help her in overcoming the initial terror she was going to feel about going "under the knife." Surgery in the early nineteenth century was a brutal affair. Cutting instruments were crude and there was no such thing as anesthesia. Patients were wide awake during the operation, and they had to be belted down and restrained from moving or screaming. It was not at all uncommon for sick people to choose death rather than "the knife." And if they survived the surgery, they then faced the threat of massive infections. Nobody understood the principle of microscopic life, of germs which cause disease, or how careful, antiseptic procedures could prevent infections. Patients ran the risk of dying of massive infections within days of the operation. Surgery was always a last resort. But Benjamin Rush was convinced that Nabby's condition had reached the desperate point, and he wanted John and Abigail to talk her into it, to let her know that "the pain of the operation is much less than her fears represent it to be." Amputation of the diseased breast was her only chance.

They first had to convince their son-in-law. Fear of the "dread disease" had pushed William Smith into an advanced state of denial. When he learned of Rush's recommendation, he reacted indignantly, heading for libraries to learn whatever he could about the disease and its prognosis, hoping against hope to spare Nabby the operation. He talked and talked, trying to convince himself that maybe the tumor would just go away, that Nabby could probably live with it, that it was not so bad. Abigail Adams's mother had more faith in Rush and wrote to Smith: "If the operation is necessary as the Dr. states it to be, and as I fear it is, the sooner it is done the better provided Mrs. Smith can bring herself along, as I hope she will consent to it." She even asked her son-in-law, if Nabby agreed to the surgery, to be with "Nabby through the painful tryal." Smith finally acquiesced to Rush's opinion and Abigail's persistence. Nabby was also convinced that surgery was her only chance. They scheduled the operation for October 8, 1811.

There was nothing new about amputating a cancerous breast. Some surgeons in Europe had been performing the operation for more than a century, and the surgery was well known among Boston physicians. In 1728 Dr. Zabdiel Boylston

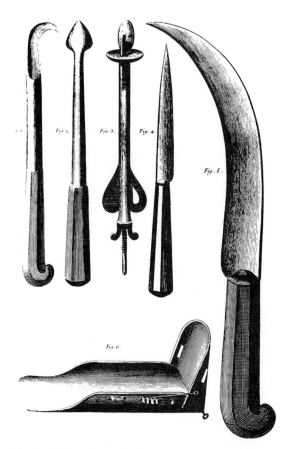

"State of the art" surgical instruments in the late eighteenth century.

amputated the breast of Sarah Winslow to remove a malignant tumor. The patient survived the surgery and lived another thirty-nine years, dying in 1767 of old age, and local physicians were convinced that the operation had brought about the cure. Amputation was not however, the treatment of choice for breast cancer in the late 1700s and early 1800s because the surgery itself was so harrowingly painful and the outcomes so problematic. Most patients undergoing surgery in the nineteenth century had to deal with the problem of massive, post-operative infections. Surgery was always a last resort.

Nabby and William Smith, along with their daughter Caroline, and Abigail Adams travelled from Quincy to Boston the day before the operation. Late in the afternoon, they met with John Warren, widely considered to be the city's most skilled surgeon. Warren gave Nabby a brief physical examination and told her what to expect. It was hardly reassuring. In fact, his description of the surgery, of what Nabby was about to go through, was nightmarishly terrifying, enough to make Nabby, William, Abigail, and Caroline rethink the decision. But Rush's warning—"It shocks me to think of the consequences of procrastination in her case"—reverberated through all of their minds. Nabby had no choice if she ever hoped to live to see her grandchildren.

The operation was as bad as they had feared. John Warren was assisted by his son Joseph, who was destined to become a leading physician in his own right, and several other doctors who had examined Nabby back in July. Warren's surgical instruments, laying in a wooden box on a table, were quite simple. One was a large fork with two six-inch prongs sharpened to a needle point. He also had a wooden-handled razor. A pile of compress bandages was in the box as well. In the corner of the room there was a small oven, full of red-hot coals, into which a flat, thick, heavy iron spatula had been inserted.

Nabby came into the room dressed for a Sunday service. She was a proper woman from the best family, and she felt obligated to act the part. The doctors were in professional attire—frock coats, with shirts and ties. Modesty demanded that Nabby unbutton only the top of her dress and slip it off her left shoulder, exposing the diseased breast but little else. She remained fully clothed. Since they knew nothing of bacteria in the early 1800s, there were no gloves or surgical masks, no need for Warren to scrub his hands or wash Nabby's chest before the operation or cover his own hair and beard. Warren had her sit down and lean back in a reclining chair. He belted her waist, legs, feet, and right arm to the chair and had her raise her left arm above her head so that the pectoralis major muscle would push the breast up. One of the physicians took Nabby's raised arm by the elbow and held it, while another stood behind her, pressing her shoulders and neck to the

chair. Warren told Nabby to shut her eyes, grit her teeth, and get ready. Abigail, Caroline, and William stood off to the side to witness the ordeal.

Warren then straddled Nabby's knees, leaned over her semi-reclined body, and began his work. Like a father carving a Thanksgiving turkey, he took the two-pronged fork and thrust it deep into Nabby's breast. With his left hand, he held onto the fork and raised up on it, lifting the breast from the chest wall. He reached over for the large razor and started slicing into the base of the breast, moving from the middle of her chest toward her left side. When the breast was completely severed, Warren lifted it away from Nabby's chest with the fork. But the tumor was larger and more widespread than he had anticipated. Breast cancer often spreads to regional lymph nodes, and Warren discovered that Nabby already had visible tumor tissue in the nodes of her axilla—under her left armpit. He took the razor in there as well and with his fingers pulled out nodes and tumor.

There was a real premium on speed in early nineteenth-century surgery. No wonder. Nabby was grimacing and groaning, flinching and twisting in the chair, with blood staining her dress and Warren's shirt and pants. Her hair was soon matted in sweat. Abigail, William, and Caroline had to turn their faces and eyes away from the gruesome struggle. With the patient writhing in pain and her family eyewitnessing the spectacle, Warren wanted to get the job done as quickly as possible. To stop the bleeding, he pulled the red-hot spatula from the oven and applied it several times directly to the wound, cauterizing the worst bleeding points. With each touch, steamy wisps of smoke hissed into the air and filled the room with the distinct smell of burning flesh. Warren then sutured the wounds together, bandaged them, stepped back from Nabby, and mercifully told her that it was over. The whole procedure had taken less than twenty-five minutes. Abigail and Caroline quickly went to the surgical chair and helped Nabby pull her dress back over her left shoulder. Modesty demanded it. William helped her out of the chair and they all walked outside to the carriage. The two-hour ride to

Quincy proved to be agony of its own for Nabby, with each bump in the road sending spasms of pain throughout her body.

Nabby had a long recovery from the surgery. Miraculously, she did not suffer from any serious post-surgical infections, but for months after the operation she was weak and feeble, barely able to get around. She could not use her left arm at all, and left it in a sling. Going back to the wilds of western New York was out of the question, so she stayed in Quincy with her mother, hoping to regain the strength she needed to return home. What sustained all of them during the ordeal of Nabby's recovery was the faith that the operation had cured the cancer. Within two weeks of the surgery, Dr. Benjamin Rush wrote John Adams congratulating him "in the happy issue of the operation performed upon Mrs. Smith's breast . . . her cure will be radical and durable. I consider her as rescued from a premature grave." Abigail wrote to a friend that although the operation had been a "furnace of affliction . . . what a blessing it was to have extirpated so terrible an enemy." In May 1812, seven months after the surgery, Nabby Adams felt well again. She returned home to the small farm along the Chenago River in western New York.

But Nabby Adams was not cured. Even today, breast cancer victims whose tumors have already spread to the lymph nodes do not have very good survival rates, even with modern surgery, radiation treatments, and chemotherapy. In Nabby's case, long before Dr. Warren performed the mastectomy, the cancer had already spread throughout her body. She was going to die, no matter what, and the horrific surgery in 1811 had served no purpose. Nabby suspected something was wrong within a few weeks of arriving home in New York. She began to complain of headaches and severe pain in her spine and abdomen. A local physician attributed the discomfort to rheumatism. The diagnosis relieved some of Nabby's anxiety, since she was already worried that the pain had something to do with cancer. Cancer patients grasp at straws, hoping against hope that there is an alternative explanation for

their distress, something simple and common, like a cold or the flu or rheumatism, anything but a recurrence of the dread disease.

For Nabby Adams, however, it was not the flu or "the rheumatism." The cancer was back. That became quite clear in 1813 when she suffered a local recurrence of the tumors. When Warren amputated her breast and excised tissues from her axilla, he thought he had "gotten it all," removing the visible tumor tissue. But cancer is a cellular disease and millions of invisible, microscopically tiny malignant cancers were left behind. Some of them had grown into tumors of their own by the spring of 1813—visible tumors below the scar where Nabby's breast had once been and on the skin as well. Nabby's doctor in New York then changed his diagnosis: her headaches and now excruciating body pains were not rheumatism. The cancer was back and had spread throughout her body. Nabby Adams was terminal. She was going to die in a matter of months.

Nabby declined steadily in the late spring, finally telling her husband that she "wanted to die in her father's house." William Smith wrote John and Abigail Adams in May that the cancer had returned and that Nabby wanted "to spend her state of convalescence within the vortex of your kindness and assiduities than elsewhere." The colonel was back into denial, refusing to voice the certainty that his wife was going to die. Since the country was in the midst of the War of 1812, Smith told his in-laws, he had to go to Washington D.C., to obtain a military appointment, and that he would return to Quincy, Massachusetts, as soon as the congressional session was over. John and Abigail prepared Nabby's room and waited for her arrival.

The trip was unimaginably painful—more than 300 miles in a carriage, over bumpy roads where each jolt meant stabbing pain. Her son John drove the carriage. When Nabby finally reached Quincy on July 26, she was suffering from grinding, constant, multiple-site pain. John and Abigail were shocked when they saw her. She was gaunt and thin, wracked by a deep cough, and her eyes had a moist, rheumy look to them. She groaned and sometimes screamed every time she moved. Huge, dark circles shadowed her cheeks, and a few minutes after she settled into bed, the smell of death was in the air. Cancer cells not only divide rapidly, they also die rapidly, and when a patient has a body full of tumors, the body is also full of an increasing volume of dead, necrotic tissue. Those tissues are rancid and rotten, full of bacteria, and they give off a foul odor. Scientists today call the condition "cachexia"—the body seems to be feeding on itself—but in the early 1800s it was known as "the odor of death."

Nabby's pain was so unbearable, and her misery so unmitigated, that Abigail went into a depression of her own, a depression so deep she could not stand even to visit her daughter's room. It was her husband John Adams, the second president of the United States, who ministered to his dying daughter, feeding her, cleaning her and seeing to her personal needs, combing her hair and holding her hand. He tried to administer several recommended pain killers, but nothing seemed to help, not until she lapsed into a pain-numbing coma. Her husband returned from Washington, D.C., and the death-watch began. On the morning of August 9, Nabby's breathing became more shallow and the passage of time between breaths more extended. The family gathered around her bedside. She took her last breath early in the afternoon. A few days later, in a letter to Thomas Jefferson, John Adams wrote: "Your Friend, my only Daughter, expired, Yesterday Morning in the Arms of Her Husband, her Son, her Daughter, her Father and Mother, her Husbands two Sisters and two of her Nieces, in the 49th. Year of Age, 46 of which She was the healthiest and firmest of Us all: Since which, She has been a monument to Suffering and to Patience."

Except for a chosen few victims, breast cancer was a death sentence in the early nineteenth century, and the surgical treatment for it was almost as bad as the disease. From the moment she first noticed the lump, Nabby was doomed. During the rest of the century, physicians learned about anesthesia, which dramatically eased the trauma of surgery. They also learned about bacteria and started washing their hands before putting the scalpel to a patient's breast. They discovered that all tissue was composed of tiny cells, and that cancer was a disease process involving those cells. Around 1900, when surgeons developed the radical mastectomy—a new surgical procedure for removing a cancerous breast—patient survival rates increased. Seventy-five years after Nabby Adams died of breast cancer, women with the disease had a better chance of survival.

But even today, nearly 200 years after Nabby's death, breast cancer remains a frighteningly unpredictable disease. More limited surgical procedures, radiation therapy, and chemotherapy provide new treatments, but nearly 50,000 American women die of breast cancer every year. According to statistics released in 2000, one out of nine American women—a total of nearly 15 million people—will develop breast cancer during their lifetime. And according to existing survival rates, approximately forty percent of them will die from it. The only real answer is early detection, hopefully from a mammogram examination when the cancer is tiny and curable. Nabby Adams did not have that option. We do.

Study Questions

1. What did Nabby Adams do when she first noticed the lump? What kind of medical attention did she get from her physicians in New York and Boston?

2. What did Dr. Benjamin Rush recommend and why did he give his advice to Nabby's parents rather than directly to her?

3. How did Nabby's husband, William Smith, react to the news of her illness and Dr. Rush's recommendation?

4. Why was Nabby Adams probably doomed to death from breast cancer no matter what she would have done after learning she had the disease?

5. How can a woman today greatly improve her chances of surviving breast cancer?

Bibliography

For an excellent description of Abigail "Nabby" Adams's marriage to William Smith, see Lida Mayo, "Miss Adams in Love," *American Heritage,* 16 (February 1965), 36–49, 80–89. Carl Binger's *Revolutionary Doctor, Benjamin Rush (1746-1813)* (1966) is a good introduction to the life of early America's most prominent physician. For the correspondence of Benjamin Rush with John and Abigail Adams, see L. H. Butterfield, *Letters of Benjamin Rush,* Vol. II: 1793–1813 (1951). The best biography of Abigail Adams is Phyllis Lee Levin's *Abigail Adams: A Biography* (1987). Also see Lynne Withay, *Dearest Friend: A Life of Abigail Adams* (1981). Also see Edith Belle Gelles, *Portia: The World of Abigail Adams* (1992). For recent histories, see David G. McCullough, *John Adams* (2001); Richard Brookhiser, *America's First Dynasty: The Adamses, 1735-1918* (2002); and John P. Diggins, *John Adams* (2003). On the history of breast cancer, see James S. Olson, *Bathsheba's Breast: Women, Cancer, and History* (2002).

READING 13

A Midwife's Tale

Laurel Thatcher Ulrich

While the founding fathers were busy fomenting the American Revolution, winning the War of American Independence, writing the U.S. Constitution, and forging a new government, less prominent Americans were going about their daily lives, making a living, raising families, and confronting a host of social, economic, and medical challenges. Martha Ballard was a midwife living in what is today southern Maine. In addition to her own domestic concerns, Ballard was as much of a physician as most people would ever see. She birthed their babies, attended their sick, and dressed their dead. The role midwives played in early America challenged male doctors and helped accelerate the development of professional, scientific medicine. In the following essay, Pulitzer Prize-winning historian Laurel Thatcher Ulrich describes the activities of a late eighteenth-century New England midwife.

Martha Ballard was a midwife—and more. Between August 3 and 24, 1787, she performed four deliveries, answered one obstetrical false alarm, made sixteen medical calls, prepared three bodies for burial, dispensed pills to one neighbor, harvested and prepared herbs for another, and doctored her own husband's sore throat. In twentieth-century terms, she was simultaneously a midwife, nurse, physician, mortician, pharmacist, and attentive wife. Furthermore, in the very act of recording her work, she became a keeper of vital records, a chronicler of the medical history of her town.

"Doctor Coney here. Took acount of Births & Deaths the year past from my minnits," Martha wrote on January 4, 1791. Surprisingly, it is her minutes, not his data, that have survived. The account she kept differs markedly from other eighteenth-century medical records. The most obvious difference, of course, is that it is a woman's record. Equally important is the way it connects birth and death with ordinary life. Few medical histories, even today, do that.

In June of 1787, as Martha's flax blossomed in the field beyond the mill pond, scarlet fever ripened in Hallowell. She called it the "canker rash," a common name in the eighteenth century for a disease that combined a brilliant skin eruption with an intensely sore, often ulcerated throat. The "Putrid Malignant Sore Throat," a New Hampshire physician called it. We know it as "strep," scarlet fever being one of several forms of infection from a particular type of streptococci. Although mild in comparison with the scourges of diphtheria that had swept through towns like Oxford earlier in the century, scarlet fever was dangerous. Martha reported five deaths in the summer of 1787, 15 percent of the canker rash cases she treated.

Six-month-old Billy Sewall, Henry and Tabitha's only child, was the first to die. "What an excellent thing is the grace of submission!" the young father wrote on the day of the baby's funeral. Had he been less certain of his own salvation, he might have interpreted the sickness in his family as a judgment of God upon him for his continuing quarrel with Mr. Isaac Foster, the Congregational minister of the town. But Henry Sewall was not given to that sort of self-doubt. "How happy to feel the temper of holy Job," he wrote. "Whom the Lord loveth he chasteneth."

The Lord loved the minister too. On July 28, when Sewall came to the Ballard mills to get a raft of slabs, Martha was in a neighbor's field digging cold water root to treat the minister, who was himself "very sick with the rash." By then a dozen families had someone ailing. Martha went back and forth across the river carrying remedies to feverish children, all the while watching for signs of illness in her own family. When a visiting nephew "seemed unwell," she swathed his neck with warmed tow and gave him hyssop tea. When Mr. Ballard and Dolly complained of feeling ill, she bathed their feet and brewed more tea, adding at the end of that day's entry, "I feel much fatagud my self."

At the height of the epidemic, the heat that lay over the Kennebec exploded in a cloudburst of hail. "I hear it broke 130 pains of glass in fort western," Martha told her diary in the August 4 passage. Sewall noted smugly that though the storm "broke all the windows the windward side of houses, mine I saved, chiefly by taking out the sashes." He weighed some of the hailstones and found they topped half an ounce. Two days later, fire struck at the Ballard sawmill. Martha watched it from the opposite side of the river where she had spent the night nursing four-year-old James Howard, whose sister, Isabella, had already died of the rash. "The men at the fort went over. Found it consumd together with some plank & Bords," she wrote.

For her there was little time to contemplate the loss of the mills. Through August she continued to nurse the sick, tracking their condition in her diary with formulaic phrases that went from "poorly" through "very ill," "very ill indeed," and "Exceeding Dangerously ill" to "seemingly Ex-

Laurel Thatcher Ulrich, *A Midwife's Tale: The Life of Martha Ballard, Based on Her Diary, 1785-1812* (New York: Alfred A. Knopf, 1990), 40-66.

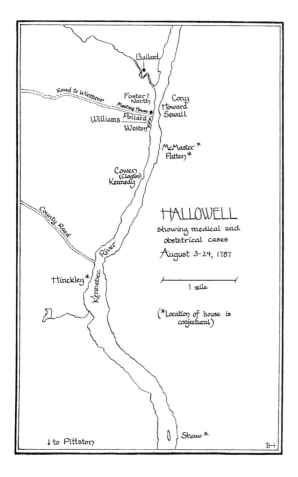

to stir, started home, stopping in at the Howards', where James was still "very Low," and at the Williamses', where "shee" (presumably the mother) was "very ill indeed." Although Martha was exhausted by the time she reached her house, she sat down to write in her journal: "William McMaster Expird at 3 O Clock this morn. Mrs Patin & I laid out the Child. Poor mother, how Distressing her Case, near the hour of Labour and three Children more very sick."

"Poor mother." That entry contains the one burst of emotion to appear in the diary all summer. Although Mrs. McMaster was not the only woman in Hallowell to lose a child nor the only mother with two or three children suffering from the rash, something about her situation had pierced Martha's literary reserve. Perhaps the three-day vigil had brought back that summer of 1769 when she was herself "near the hour of Labour" and diphtheria flourished like witch grass in Oxford. Hannah, the daughter born in the epidemic, turned eighteen on August 6, the day the sawmill burned. Martha remembered the birthday, but for some reason, during this summer of illness, she neglected her usual remembrance of the Oxford deaths. Her daily activities were enough of a memorial.

Not all the illness in Hallowell in the summer of 1787 can be attributed to scarlet fever. There were the usual accidents on farms or in the woods; Martha poulticed a swollen foot for one of the Foster boys in early June and in August, though she wasn't called to administer aid, noted that "Peter Kenny has wounded his Legg & Bled Excesivily." There were also those "sudden strokes" that twentieth-century physicians would attribute to cardiovascular causes. On July 12, 1787, Martha reported that "a man fell down dead in the Coart hous at Pownalboro," a fate that had overcome old James Howard a few months before.

Then there were the troubling deaths of Susanna Clayton and her infant. Martha had delivered the Clayton baby on August 16. The birth was uneventful, with no warning at all of the distressing news she would hear four days later as she was returning home from nursing Mrs. Hinkley, who

pireing" or in the opposite direction from "Dangirous" to "revived" or from "much as shee was yesterday" to "Easyer" and then "Comfortable." She recorded all the summer's events, her everyday work as well as the continuing evidence of God's chastening hand, in the same terse style. She "pulled flax," then bathed a child's cankered throat, "worked about house," then found a little boy "seemingly Expireing," picked saffron, then attended another child's funeral, drank tea, then laid out an infant in its mother's arms.

On August 11 she arrived at the McMaster house to find little William "very low." She sat with him all through the day on Sunday and into the night. At about three a.m. on Monday he died. With the help of Mrs. Patten she prepared the body for burial, then, as the neighborhood began lived in the southern part of the town opposite Bumberhook. James Hinkley had brought Martha upriver as far as Weston's landing, where she heard "that Mrs Clatons Child departed this life yesterday & that she was thot Expireing." Martha got back in the boat and went back down the river as far as the Cowen farm, where Susanna Clayton had given birth and was lying in.

She arrived in time to help with the last nursing and to lay out the baby in its mother's arms. These deaths brought no exclamation, no "Poor mother" (or "Poor husband"). The mere facts were enough to mark them as singular ("the first such instance I ever saw") and monumental ("the first woman that died in Child bed which I delivered"). Martha had seen newborn infants die, but in the more than 250 deliveries she had performed since coming to the Kennebec, no mother of hers had succumbed. Susanna Clayton's death appears in the diary as an inexplicable stroke of Providence, an event as unrelated to the canker rash as fire or hail. Martha could not have known that puerperal fever and scarlet fever grew from the same invisible seed—Group A hemolytic streptococci.

No one in the eighteenth century could have related the two phenomena. Not until the 1930s did scientists unravel the mysterious epidemiology of scarlet fever. Depending upon prior exposure, the same toxin that produces a sore throat and a rash in one person may produce a sore throat, a wound infection, a mild and fleeting illness, or no symptoms at all in others. Yet all these persons can spread the infection. Scarlet fever can even be transmitted through the milk of infected cows. It is not surprising, then, that Martha treated Isaac Hardin's son for an abscess as well as a rash, that Mrs. Kennedy had "a sweling under her arm" at the same time as her children were sick with the fever, or that puerperal infection and the canker rash both appeared at one house. Susanna Clayton was the daughter of Ephraim Cowen, the man who summoned Martha on August 23 to treat his younger daughters, "who are sick with the rash." She had given birth on her father's farm just upriver from the Kennedys',

where Martha had administered cold water tincture. Susanna Clayton was the only one of Martha's obstetrical patients to die, yet other women and their babies may have been infected. Mrs. McMaster, the "poor mother" of the August 13 entry, gave birth on September 8. Her infant, whom Martha described as "very weak and low," lived only two days, and by September 23 the mother was herself so ill that Dr. Cony was summoned. He apparently recommended some sort of laxative. "Mrs Cowen & I administred remdys that Doct Coney prescribd," Martha wrote, adding that when the "physic began to operate," she left to care for another patient. Fortunately, Mrs. McMaster survived.

Focusing on the progress of an epidemic, as we have done here, obscures the fact that most of those infected eventually recovered. Billy McMaster and his newborn brother died, but his mother got better. Saray and Daniel Foster, Polly Kennedy, and the younger Cowen girls were soon up and about, and little James Howard, a child "Exceeding Dangerously ill" in August, was once again "mending" in September. At the end of one of her diary packets, Martha tallied births and deaths for the six years 1785 through 1790. In eighteenth-century terms, Hallowell was a healthy place. Its death rate averaged fifteen per thousand, about what one would find in parts of southern Asia today, but only half of that recorded for eighteenth-century seaports like Salem or Boston. Just as important, in almost every year the town had four times as many births as deaths. Even in a sickly season, there was reason for hope as well as sorrow.

In western tradition, midwives have inspired fear, reverence, amusement, and disdain. They have been condemned for witchcraft, eulogized for Christian benevolence, and caricatured for bawdy humor and old wives' tales. The famous seventeenth-century English physician William Harvey dismissed the loquacious ignorance of midwives, "especially the younger and more meddlesome ones, who make a marvellous pother when they hear the woman cry out with her pains and implore assistance." Yet a popular obstetrical manual published in the same century dignified their work by arguing that Socrates's mother was a midwife and that "the Judges of old time did appoint a stipend for those women that did practice Physick well."

In the early years of settlement, some American colonies did in fact provide free land, if not stipends, for midwives. Yet the most famous midwife in early America is remembered for religious martyrdom rather than obstetrics. Boston ministers commended Anne Hutchinson for the "good discourse" she offered women in their "Childbirth-Travells," but when her teachings threatened to disrupt their authority, they condemned and banished her. The Puritans took their contradictions directly from the Bible. The Book of Exodus celebrates the courage of the Hebrew midwives who when told to destroy the male children of Israel "feared God, and did not as the king of Egypt commanded them." But the Apostle Paul, while acknowledging the good works of women who "relieved the afflicted," condemned those who wandered about from house to house, "speaking things which they ought not."

English midwifery guides also warned against impiety and gossip. "I must tell you, it is too common a Complaint of the modest Part of Womankind, against the Women-Midwives, that they are bold, and indulge their Tongues in immodest and lascivious Speeches," warned one author who styled himself a surgeon. Another echoed the language of the Apostle in arguing that a good midwife "ought to be *Faithful* and *Silent;* always on her *Guard* to conceal those Things, which ought not to be spoken of."

Samuel Richardson drew upon midwifery lore in creating the character of Mrs. Jewkes, the terrifying woman who holds the innocent Pamela captive in the novel that gave Martha Ballard's niece her name. Charles Dickens exploited the same body of myth to different effect in his comic portrait of Sairey Gamp in *Martin Chuzzlewit:*

She was a fat old woman, this Mrs. Gamp, with a husky voice and a moist eye. . . . She wore a very rusty black gown, rather the worse for snuff, and a shawl and bonnet to correspond. . . . Like most persons who have attained to great eminence in their profession, she took to hers very kindly; insomuch, that setting aside her natural predilections as a woman, she went to a lying-in or a laying-out with equal zest and relish.

Martha Ballard had at least one thing in common with Sairey Gamp—she was very fond of snuff. Yet in eighteenth-century Maine, it was not necessary to set aside one's "predilections as a woman" in order to perform what Martha once called "the last ofice of friendship." Her diary tames the stereotypes and at the same time helps us to imagine the realities on which they were based. Midwives and nurses mediated the mysteries of birth, procreation, illness, and death. They touched the untouchable, handled excrement and vomit as well as milk, swaddled the dead as well as the newborn. They brewed medicines from plants and roots, and presided over neighborhood gatherings of women.

Two nineteenth-century novels by New England women focus on the homely mysteries of village healers, coming closer to Martha's diary than most English literature. Sarah Josepha Hale's *Northwood,* published in 1827, was said to have been based on her own memories of a late-eighteenth-century New Hampshire town. Hale went out of her way to make clear that, though her gossipy healer Mrs. Watson was a fortune-teller, she was neither a witch nor a hag. No, she was "reputed one of the neatest women and best managers in the village. And many wondered how it happened that though she went abroad so much, she generally contrived to have her own work done in season, and quite as soon as her neighbors."

The central character of Sarah Orne Jewett's *Country of the Pointed Firs* is also a good housewife. In the opening pages of the book, Jewett describes a "queer little garden," green with balm and southerwood, presided over by Mrs. Todd. Some of her plants "might have belonged to sacred and mystic rites . . . but now they pertained only to humble compounds brewed at intervals with molasses or vinegar or spirits." Stopping to visit Mrs. Todd at her garden fence, the local physician "would stand twirling a sweet-scented sprig in his fingers, and make suggestive jokes, perhaps about her faith in a too persistent course of thoroughwort elixir."

Hale and Jewett idealized their New England villages—there is no diphtheria or canker rash in either book—yet they grounded their stories in a world Martha might have recognized. One of the central issues for her, as for Mrs. Watson, was how to get her work done at home while spending so much time with her neighbors. Her garden, though less romantic than Mrs. Todd's, also incorporated notions of healing handed down the centuries, and her diary reveals, as does Jewett's novel, the friendly distance between a "village doctor" and a "learned herbalist."

Later chapters will explore Martha Ballard's domestic economy. The remainder of this chapter will pursue Jewett's themes, reaching beneath the story of the August 1787 epidemic for clues to Martha's herbalism and to her relations with the town's other healers, male and female. Hallowell had several male physicians. In the last years of the eighteenth century, these included, in addition to Daniel Cony: Samuel Colman, who arrived at Fort Western in the 1780s; Benjamin Page, who set up practice at "the Hook" in 1791; and Benjamin Vaughan, an Edinburgh-educated doctor and heir to the Plymouth Company claims, who settled on the Kennebec in 1796, offering himself not as a competitor but as a gentlemanly mentor to the local doctors. In addition, several physicians from neighboring towns—Obadiah Williams, James Parker, and John Hubbard—occasionally treated Hallowell patients. (Martha's brother-in-law, Stephen Barton, practiced in Vassalboro from 1775 to 1787, but spent the next decade in Oxford and died shortly after returning to Maine.)

Martha was respectful, even deferential, toward the men's work, but the world she described was sustained by women—Mrs. Woodward, Mrs. Savage, Mrs. Vose, Old Mrs. Ingraham, Sally Fletcher, Lady Cox, Hannah Cool, Merriam Pollard, and dozens of others, the midwives, nurses, afternurses, servants, watchers, housewives, sisters, and mothers of Hallowell. The diary even mentions an itinerant "Negro woman doctor," who briefly appeared in the town in 1793. Female practitioners specialized in obstetrics but also in the general care of women and children, in the treatment of minor illnesses, skin rashes, and burns, and in nursing. Since more than two-thirds of the population of Hallowell was either female or under the age of ten, since most illnesses were "minor," at least at their onset, and since nurses were required even when doctors were consulted, Martha and her peers were in constant motion.

When Martha went to the field to dig cold water root on August 7, 1787, she was acting out the primary ritual of her practice, the gathering of remedies from the earth. Although she purchased imported laxatives and a few rare ingredients (myrrh, "dragon's blood," galbanum, spermaceta, and camphor) from Dr. Colman, she was fundamentally an herbalist. "Harvested saffron," "Cut the sage," "Gatherd seeds & Cammomile mint & hysop": such entries scattered throughout the diary tie her practice to English botanic medicine. Three-quarters of the herbs in the diary appear in Nicholas Culpeper's *The Complete Herbal,* published in London in 1649 (and reprinted many times in America). Almost all can be found in E. Smith, *The Compleat Housewife: OR, Accomplish'd Gentlewoman's Companion,* an early eighteenth-century English compendium. Martha administered herbs internally as teas, decoctions, syrups, pills, clisters, vapors, and smoke and externally in poultices, plasters, blisters, cataplasms, baths, ointments, and salves. "Find Dolly lame. Poultist her foot with sorril roasted," she wrote on October 11, 1787, and when Theophilus Hamlin came to the house feeling ill, she "made a bed by the fire & gave him some catnip tea." Presumably the warm drink and the fire would cure his cold by contraries. Sympathetic medicine also worked. When Martha used saffron to treat jaundice in newborn children, she was following the ancient doctrine of "signatures," the yellow plant being the obvious cure for yellow skin.

There is no evidence in the diary of direct borrowing—she never mentions reading a medical book—yet Martha's remedies obviously rested on a long accumulation of English experience. When she used dock root to treat "the itch" or applied burdock leaves to an aching shoulder, she was following Culpeper's practice whether she knew it or not. More difficult to determine is her attitude toward the astrological concepts that informed his herbal. She may not have been aware, when she gave a newly delivered woman feverfew tea, that "Venus has commended this herb to succour her sisters." But her quiet statement on July 26, 1788, "Dog Days begin this day," associates her with such ancient traditions. Since antiquity, the period in late summer when the Dog Star became visible in the heavens had been linked with illness. The almanacs, which had determined the very form of her diary, perpetuated such beliefs. In fact she had good reason for believing that dog days brought illness, for she consistently made more medical calls in late summer than at any other time of the year. Whether her neighbors were actually more sickly during August and September or simply more disposed to ask for help, we do not know.

Her remedies are even closer to those in Smith's book. Like the English woman, she accepted the medicinal as well as the culinary virtues of common garden plants like green beans, onions, and currants and of household staples like vinegar, soap, and flour. On October 14, 1790, for example, she was "Calld in great hast to see Mrs Hamlin who was in a fitt. I walkt there, applyd Vinagar to her Lips, temples, & hands & onions to her feet & shee revivd." And on another day, "Mr Ballard is unwell. Has taken some soap pills." There is hardly an ingredient in Martha's diary that does not appear in Smith's compendium. Both women routinely used camomile, sage, and tansy. Both employed cantharides and Elixir Proprietas. Both concocted that most famous of all cures—chicken soup. Yet compared to Smith's receipts, Martha's medicines *are* "simples." The most elaborate remedies described in her diary employ at most three or four plants. In contrast, Smith's recipe for "Lady Hewet's water" contains seventy-five separate plants, seeds, roots, and powders. Nor is there any hint in Martha's diary of the zoological inventiveness that led Smith to recommend setting a bottle of newly made cordial "into a hill of ants for amonth," to combine goose dung, ground snails, and earthworms with saffron, or to wet bandages in the spawn of frogs.

There is no indication that Martha used cow or sheep dung poultices, as did some New England healers, but she did believe in the curative powers of urine, as on September 23, 1786: "I was Calld Early this morn to see Lidia Savage who was very ill. Gave her some urin & honney & some Liquoris & put a plaster to her stomach. Went up afternoon. Find her Relievd." She also accepted the pervasive notion that cat's blood had healing power. When a Mr. Davis came to the house suffering from shingles, she "bled a Catt & applid the Blood which gave him Relief." She didn't say whether the cat she bled was pure black without a single white hair, as insisted on by some rural practitioners, but she did record one cure that clearly included the kind of detail which folklorists associate with magic. When her niece was suffering from consumption and all other remedies seemed to have failed, she tried a practice "recommended as very Beneficial by Mr Amos Page." The young woman rose from her sickbed "about an hour by sun in the morn went out & milkt the last milk from the cow into her mouth & swallowed it."

Even within Martha's practice, however, such cures were exotic. Herbs, wild as well as cultivated, were the true foundation of her practice. She wilted fresh burdock leaves in alcohol to apply to sore muscles, crushed comfrey for a poultice, added melilot (a kind of sweet clover) to hog's grease for an ointment, boiled agrimony, plantain, and Solomon's-seal into a syrup, perhaps following an old method that called for reducing the liquid by half, straining this decoction through a woolen cloth, then adding sugar to simmer to the thickness of new honey. Most of the wild plants she used had familiar English names, whether they were escapees from early gardens or New World varieties of Old World herbs. There are few distinctly American names in the diary. She mentioned poulticing wounds with basswood, a plant not found in the English herbals, but when she and a grandchild "went to the field and got sennakle root," they may have been gathering a local variety of sanicle, a plant Culpeper credited with the power to "stay women's courses" rather than Seneca snakeroot, an American native. (A later entry does, however, refer to "a decoction of snake root & saffron."

The root Martha dug during the scarlet fever outbreak of 1787 was an indigenous plant, however. According to a legend recorded in Rochester, Massachusetts (where Martha's brother, Jonathan Moore, was minister), a local man got cold water root from "an Indian named Nathan Hope" during an epidemic of diphtheria in 1754. Eventually it "developed into a wild herb common to all the region." Martha may have heard about the root and its uses from Jonathan. Just as likely, the plant had always been "common to all the region," in Oxford as in Rochester, though Indians may well have taught the first settlers how to use it. Its association with diphtheria is suggestive. If Martha had learned about cold water root in Oxford, it is difficult to imagine her preparing her sore throat "tincture" in Hallowell in 1787 without thinking of her own children and the epidemic of 1769.

The eclecticism of English medicine encouraged the incorporation of Indian or African cures. An aura of mystery, if not magic, attached to persons who were otherwise stigmatized in colonial society. Smith's recipe book included "The Negro Ceasars Cure for Poison" reprinted from *The Carolina Gazette,* and Hallowell patients sought out the "Negro doctoress" during her brief sojourn in the town. (Mrs. Parker even borrowed Martha's horse "to go and see the negro woman doctor.") There is no evidence that Martha was curious about Indian or Afro-American medicine, however. She noted the presence of the black healer but did not bother to record—or perhaps even to learn—her name. Such attitudes help to explain why her remedies are closer to Culpeper's seventeenth-century herbal than to James Thacher's *The American New Dispensatory,* an early-nineteenth-

century pharmacopoeia that attempted to evaluate and incorporate Indian physic.

In eighteenth-century terms, Martha was an "empiric," a person unconcerned with theory. Her own descriptions demonstrate that her most immediate concern was to make her patients feel better. "I gargled her throat which gave her great Ease," she wrote after preparing the cold water tincture for Polly Kennedy. The same remedy helped her own husband "find relief." The two phrases appear in the diary repeatedly. When one patient was suffering from dysentery, she "administerd a Clister which gave her Eas." When Hannah was ill, she gave her camomile and camphor and sent her "into a warm Bed. I hope it will relieve her." Beyond the physical comfort of hot tea or a soothing syrup was the comfort of an idea: Nature offered solutions to its own problems. Remedies for illness could be found in the earth, in the animal world, and in the human body itself. When Martha Ballard applied warmed tow to the neck of little Gideon Barton, she was doing more than assuaging pain, she was confirming the essential order of the universe.

It would be a mistake, however, to describe her as a fringe practitioner preserving ancient English remedies lost to professional medicine. Most of the therapies we now associate with "folk" medicine were still a part of academic practice in her time. One of the Kennebec's best-educated physicians, Dr. Moses Appleton of Waterville, Maine, left a manuscript collection of recipes that included, in addition to erudite Latin formulas, a cure for dropsy compounded of parsley roots, horseradish, and mustard seed and a treatment for "the malignant sore throat" that called for applying carded black wool wet with vinegar and salt, ear to ear. The most explicit reference to astrological (or, more precisely, lunar concepts) in Hallowell comes from Daniel Cony's family record. One Cony child, the doctor reported, was born on "the first day of the week, the first hour of the day and the first day of the moon," another on "the 5th day of the week, and the eleventh day of the moon."

The technological simplicity of early medicine meant that male doctors offered little that wasn't also available to female practitioners. The stethoscope had not yet been invented. Watches with second hands were so rare that no one as yet counted the pulse (though in a general way most practitioners observed it). Nor did the clinical thermometer exist. Even the simple technique of percussion (tapping the chest and abdomen to discover fluid or masses) was yet to come. A probate inventory taken after the death of Dr. Obadiah Williams included "A Quantity of Medicine & Bottles together with the Amputating Instruments." That brief sentence pretty well describes the medical arsenal available to an eighteenth-century physician—drugs and a few rudimentary surgical instruments. Williams *did* use his instruments. On March 5, 1789, Martha wrote, "There was a young man had his Legg Cutt off at Stirling by Doctor Williams. He brot it to Doctor Coneys & disected it." Martha didn't observe this dissection, but she did attend four autopsies in the course of her career, carefully recording the results in her diary (see Chapter Seven). That fact alone suggests that Hallowell's physicians considered midwives part of the broader medical community, a subordinate part no doubt (doctors dissected; midwives observed), but a part nonetheless.

Midwives and doctors shared a common commitment to what Martha would have called "pukes" and "purges." Early medicine merged the two meanings of *physic* as "knowledge of the human body" and as "a cathartic or purge." Because all parts of the body were related, laxatives treated the entire organism, not simply the gastrointestinal system. "I was calld to see Lidia White who has had fitts this day, but had left her before I arivd. Shee complaind of an opresion at her stomach and pain in her head, I left her a portion of senna and manna." Senna and manna were mild cathartics. When her daughter Dolly was ill, Martha noted that a combination of "Senna & manna with annis seed and Rhubarb . . . opperated kindly." She even used manna with infants.

The emphasis on expulsion derived from the ancient theory of humors, the notion that health was achieved by a proper balance of the four bodily fluids—blood, phlegm, choler (or yellow bile), and melancholy (or black bile). When Martha wrote that Lidia Bisbe was "sick of a bilious disorder" or that Mr. Savage's daughter "puked up a considerable quantity of phlegm," she was expressing that world view, as was Moses Appleton when he recommended black wool "to keep back the humors." The notion of humors had been greatly enlarged by the end of the eighteenth century, however. As one encyclopedist explained it, the term "humour, in medicine, is applied to any juice, or fluid part of the body, as the chyle, blood, milk, fat, serum." Writing of a "Child who had a bad humour on the head and feet, Martha was using the generic term. Yet the importance of fluids, their condition, quantity, and means of expulsion, remained central.

When Martha noted that a lanced abscess "discharged a Large quantity," she may have been commenting positively on the effectiveness of the cure rather than negatively on the seriousness of the infection. Festering was also a method by which the body expelled troublesome humors. The application of "blisters," local irritants designed to raise a watery discharge, imitated another of nature's remedies. "Calld to see Mrs Weston. Shee being very unwell I aplyd a Blister, Batht her feet, put on a Back Plaster," she wrote on November 14, 1786. Baths and plasters, like blisters, treated internal problems with external remedies. They cooled or heated, soothed or excited, according to temperature or contents.

Although theoretically a person might lose too much fluid, most remedies seem to have promoted expulsion. Constipation was dangerous, as was an unhealthy accumulation of bile. Menstruation, too, could prove troublesome if "obstructed," which is why Martha Ballard "prescribed the use of particullar herbs" for a young woman named Genny Cool. What those herbs were and whether they might also have been employed to induce abortion, we do not know. There is no mention in the diary of savine, the best-known English abortifacient, though Martha did gather tansy, a plant associated in some herbals with abortion. In her practice, however, tansy seems to have been employed as an *anthelmintic,* that is, an agent for expelling worms.

The most dramatic of the humoral therapies was bloodletting, a remedy Martha seldom mentioned and never employed. Along the Kennebec, the lancet was clearly a male implement. "Mr Stodard seemd to have more feavour," Martha wrote on February 16, 1795. "Doctor Page Bled him in the feet this morning. He has been bled, phisicked and Blistered before in his sickness." She noted that Dr. Colman bled one of her patients in the late stages of pregnancy, though it seems not to have been at her request. One home medical guide recommended bleeding "for pregnant women about the sixth, seventh or eighth month, who are plethoric and full of blood," but added that "children bear purging better than bleeding." Martha seems to have preferred purging for both groups. One of the few descriptions of bleeding in the diary involved a horse. "Mr Ballard went to Mr Browns for his mare," Martha wrote. "Had her Bled in the mouth. She bled all the way home & Continued to bleed an hour or two after coming home. We at length filld the incision with fur & it Ceast."

That male physicians leaned toward dramatic therapies was only to be expected. Their status—and fees—required as much. Dr. Cony used rhubarb and senna, as Martha did, but he also prescribed calomel, the mercurial compound Benjamin Rush called the "Samson of medicine." One historian concludes that in large doses calomel "did indeed slay great numbers of Philistines." The impressive salivation that followed its violent purging was in fact one of the symptoms of mercury poisoning. Hallowell's physicians also used laudanum (a liquid opiate), purple foxglove (digitalis), and the bark (quinine) therapies associated with a newer "solidistic" overlay on humoral therapy.

Unlike humoral therapy, which concentrated on bodily juices, solidistic medicine loosely followed Newtonian physics in attempting to regulate the mechanical properties of "solids," usually defined as blood vessels and nerves. Doctors employed tonics to stimulate bodily force, sedatives to induce relaxation. In practical terms, humoral and solidistic approaches overlapped, since both tried to control respiration, perspiration, and excretion. Thus, a physician might employ cathartics either to "flush out unbalanced humors" or "to relax the abnormal tensions which had constricted his patients' intestinal fibers." For the patient, the consequences were the same.

Whether or not Martha understood solidistic theory, she rejected some of the remedies associated with it. (Here she departed from Smith, who added laudanum to cough syrup and recommended "jesuits bark" for ague and fever.) Martha was dismayed when Dr. Page attempted to use laudanum in childbirth. She was also convinced that the use of "the bark" contributed to the death of Mrs. Pillsbury during another outbreak of the canker rash. Martha had been nursing the woman ("The Lady was in a fine persperation the most of the night") when an urgent call from another family took her away. When she returned two days later, she discovered Mrs. Pillsbury "in a kind of delirium; her raising had ceast and her mouth very dry. They informed me shee had been much so through the night past. It is my opinion the use of the Bark was in some measure the Cause." Martha seems to have interpreted the "raising"—that is, the rash itself—as a useful phenomenon, an indication that the sweating had been successful in expelling the ill humor. She did not say who had suggested the bark, though it may have been one of Hallowell's physicians. A published pamphlet on the "Putrid Malignant Sore Throat" argued that "the tonic as well as antiseptic powers of the Bark must render it a medicine not only proper, but highly necessary in this disorder." Martha disagreed. She seemed pleased when "Old Mrs Kenny Came and advised to giv her a syrrip of vinegar & onions and a decoction of Gold thread and shumake Berries. It was done and shee seemd revivd." The revival was temporary. Mrs. Pillsbury died.

Martha Ballard's dislike of the new remedies did not stem from a general mistrust of physicians—she was quite willing to call them to her own family in serious illness—but from an innate conservatism. She was most comfortable with the doctors when their ideas reinforced the old therapies and the long-standing social arrangements. When one of her own daughters fell ill, she walked to Dr. Colman's to get senna and manna, and when "shee soon became dilarious we sent for Doct Cony who approvd of what I had done— advised me to continue my medisin till it had opperation. She was siesd with a severe Puking soon." In the world of eighteenth-century medicine, midwives and doctors sought—and generally achieved—similar results.

In twentieth-century terms, the ability to prescribe and dispense medicine made Martha a physician, while practical knowledge of gargles, bandages, poultices, and clisters, as well as a willingness to give extended care, defined her as a nurse. In her world, such distinctions made little sense. She sometimes acted under the direction of a doctor. More frequently she acted alone, or with the assistance of other women. It is no accident that Daniel Cony's name appears only at the end of the August entries you have read. When scarlet fever broke out in Hallowell in June, he was in Boston attending the General Court. He was back on July 19 to deliver his sister, Susanna Church, of a son, but was soon off to the interior settlements on business. On July 26 Martha was summoned to *his* house to treat a servant, Peggy Cool, who was suffering from the rash.

Ironically, when the doctor did show up in the diary it was in the context of delivery. Martha's quiet entry for August 22, 1787—"Mrs Shaw has Doctor Coney with her"—suggests more than a casual interest in the doctor's whereabouts. Mrs. Shaw was then nine months pregnant, and perhaps in labor, or at least experiencing some of the signs of imminent delivery, when the doctor was called. Why she called him we do not know. Perhaps she was worried about possible complications, perhaps frightened by the recent death of Susanna Clayton. As it turned out, Martha delivered the baby. "Put [Mrs. Shaw] safe to Bed with a daughter at 10 O Clok this Evinng," she wrote on August 23, and on the next day added drily,

"Doctor Coneys wife delivrd of a dafter Last Evng at 10 O Clok"—that is, at exactly the same time as Mrs. Shaw. It would seem, then, that if his own child hadn't intervened, Cony might have delivered the Shaw baby. Still, whatever her original intent, Mrs. Shaw was apparently satisfied with her midwife: two years and one month later, she summoned Martha again.

Daniel Cony's presence at the bedside of Mrs. Shaw suggests that reverberations of the new scientific obstetrics had reached the Kennebec. Unlike the surgeons of an earlier era, who were called only in dire emergencies, usually to dismember and extract an irretrievably lost fetus, late-eighteenth-century physicians considered it appropriate to officiate at an ordinary delivery. Yet most of them limited their obstetrical practice to eight or ten cases a year, whatever they could conveniently fit into their practice. Significantly, Martha performed at least one delivery for Cony's sister Susanna Church and another for his sister-in-law Susanna Brooks.

Kennebec doctors were not only part-time midwives, they were part-time physicians. Daniel Cony was a land proprietor and politician as well as a physician—perhaps a politician most of all. A Portland associate complained after a visit, "He had not been in the house half an hour before my head turned round like a top with politics. I would not live in the same house with . . . Daniel Coney for ten thousand pounds per annum." Yet Cony knew how to use one specialty to reinforce another. In a letter to a Massachusetts congressman, he neatly dismissed his political opponents by offering a "chemical" analysis of their behavior. Such men, he wrote, "abound with 'vitriolic acid' with a certain proportion of 'aqua regia.' " He became a fellow of the Massachusetts Medical Society not so much because of his medical skills, which by the standards of his own time were ordinary, but because his election to the legislature put him in frequent contact with the gentlemen who ran such associations. He was also a justice of the peace, as were fellow doctors Moses Appleton of Waterville and Obadiah Williams of Vassalboro.

Samuel Colman, Hallowell's second physician, was less involved in public affairs, but almost as distracted. Still single when Martha's diary opened, he lived for a time at Fort Western, eventually opening a store where he sold scythes, hoes, and tobacco, as well as pharmaceuticals. Waterville's Harvard-educated doctor, Moses Appleton, had similar interests: a single entry in his daybook lists debits for an almanac, a half-yard of calico, and a gallon of vinegar; prescriptions for senna, camphor, and an unguent; and fees for sewing and dressing a wound. Dr. Page was more single-minded than the others (and the one most disposed to intrude on Martha's territory), but he too doubled as a trader. In 1796 he advertised "a very handsome assortment of Drugs and Medicine, among which is a variety of patent articles," including "Andersons, Hoopers, and Lockyers Pills, Bateman's Drops, Turlington's Balsam of Life, and Daffy's Elixer." He also sold smelling bottles, nutmegs, British oil, and cephalic snuff. That the region's most earnest prescriber of imported drugs was also its major supplier was a conflict of interest no one seems to have noticed—or at any rate been troubled by.

The most successful Kennebec physicians were Federalist gentlemen, organizers of agricultural societies, builders of bridges, incorporators of banks. Their involvement in medical organizations was part of this general commitment to voluntarism and civic betterment. (Colman, Appleton, and Page, like Cony, were members of the Massachusetts Medical Society, as well as promoters of regional organization.) They were successful practitioners not only because of their acknowledged status as learned gentlemen but because the town's other healers chose to defer to them in hard cases. There were no laws to prevent Martha or her neighbors from administering calomel or drawing blood, yet they did not do so. By custom and training, bonesetting, tooth-pulling, bloodletting, and the administration of strong drugs were reserved for self-identified male doctors. When Martha "misplaced a Bone in the Great toe of my right foot," she was grateful for the help of Dr. Page, but most of the time she and her family got along quite well without him. It was no doubt part of the men's strength that they supported neighborhood practitioners, offering chemical compounds and venesection only when tansy failed. Even their inaccessiblity was an advantage, a sign of their importance in the larger world.

Male physicians are easily identified in town records and, even in Martha's diary, by the title "Doctor." No local woman can be discovered in that way. Hallowell's female healers move in and out of sickrooms unannounced, as though their presence there were the most ordinary thing in the world—as it was. Historians have been dimly aware of this broad-based work, yet they have had difficulty defining it. Physicians who joined medical societies and adopted an occupational title can be recognized as professionals. But what shall we call the women? Persons who perambulated their neighborhoods hardly practiced *domestic medicine,* nor does *folk medicine* accurately describe the differences between them and male professionals. Other commonly employed categories are equally misleading. *Popular medicine* conveys the ferment of the nineteenth century, with its competing sects of herbalists, homeopaths, and hydropaths, but obscures the cooperative, if hierarchical, arrangements of eighteenth-century practice. *Lay medicine* connotes the lack of formal organization in female practice, but fails to suggest its complexity. A better label is *social medicine,* borrowing from the now familiar concept of social childbirth.

Professionals sought to be distinguished from the community they served (hence the need for the title "Doctor"). Social healers, on the other hand, were so closely identified with their public we can hardly find them. Professionals cultivated regional or cosmopolitan networks, joining occupational associations. Social healers developed personal affiliations and built local reputations. Professional training, even if only in the form of apprenticeship, was institutional, fixed in place and time. Social learning was incremental, a slow build-up of seemingly casual experience.

Florence Nightingale's famous statement that "every woman is a nurse" captures one element of social practice—its grounding in common duties—but it fails to convey the specialization that occurred even among female healers. Caring for the sick was a universal female role, yet several women in every community stood out from the others for the breadth and depth of their commitment. They went farther, stayed longer, and did more than their neighbors. It would be a serious mistake to see Martha Ballard as a singular character, an unusual woman who somehow transcended the domestic sphere to become an acknowledged specialist among her neighbors. She *was* an important healer, and without question the busiest midwife in Hallowell during the most active years of her practice, but she was one among many women with acknowledged medical skills. Furthermore, her strengths were sustained by a much larger group of casual helpers.

In the August 1787 passage, she named five persons who in some way shared the care of the sick during the canker rash epidemic. Hannah Cool was at the Williams house on August 7, Mrs. Pollard at Mrs. Howard's on August 9, "Capt Sewall & Lady" at the same house on August 10, and Mrs. Patten at the McMasters' on August 12. Although each person appears in the diary in much the same way, there were important differences between them.

Hannah Cool was living with Martha Ballard in the summer of 1787. She actually appears twice in the August segment: on August 6, when she "gott Mrs Norths web [of cloth] out at the Loome," and on August 7–8, when she was at Mrs. Williams's, where there was illness. Whether she was doing nursing or housework at the Williamses' we do not know, nor does it matter. In this period the occupations of nurse and maidservant overlapped. Hannah was probably a sister of Mrs. Williams, whose maiden name was Cool. Like most single women, she moved frequently between the homes of relatives and neighbors, performing whatever sort of work was needed. (Her sister Peggy died of the canker rash at Dr. Cony's, where she was also a servant.) Hannah was older and more skilled than most household helpers, however, capable of warping a loom as well as nursing. Living with Martha Ballard, she may have picked up some medical skills as well. In the spring of 1788, when Joseph

Williams was critically ill and "went to Dr Williams to be Doctered," Martha noted that "Hannah Cool went to be his nurse."

"Mrs Patin" and "Capt Sewall & Lady" were married folks fulfilling basic obligations of neighborliness. Sally Patten was the wife of Thomas Patten, the blacksmith. Martha Ballard had delivered their first child a year earlier. "Capt Sewall & Lady" were, of course, Henry and Tabitha, whom we have met before. In watching with little James Howard, they were returning the help they had received earlier that month when their own child was dying of the rash. Their obligation wasn't to Mrs. Howard in particular—she had been too busy nursing Isabella to have helped with the care of Billy—but to the common fund of neighborliness that sustained families in illness. Neither poverty nor wealth nor a recent bereavement excused one from helping where there was need. Henry's presence at the Howard house was somewhat unusual, however. Usually men sat with men, women with women or children. There is no entry in his diary for August 10, though he did note on August 14 that "Mr. McMaster buried a son, in his 4 year. It died of a canker rash."

Merriam Pollard represents a different form of social healing. The wife of Amos Pollard, the tavern and ferry keeper, she was the mother of at least seven children, most of whom were grown. She represents a group of perhaps ten women who served as general care-givers to the town. A frequent watcher at bedsides and attendant at deliveries, she was particularly skilled in laying out the dead. She was not a midwife, at least not yet, though she did deliver one child when Martha was delayed.

Seeing Hannah Cool, Sally Patten, and Merriam Pollard at a single instant, an experienced observer could easily have distinguished between them. One was simply a servant, the second a helpful neighbor, the third a recognized healer. The tasks that they performed were also distinct. Given the dominant therapies, Hannah Cool must have spent her time brewing tea, spooning gruel, and emptying chamber pots. Sally Patten had the most passive role. As a watcher, her job was to sit beside the patient, offering comfort or conversation, noting alterations in breathing, color, or demeanor, summoning help when it was needed. Merriam Pollard had more specialized tasks to perform. Like Martha Ballard, she knew how to swab swollen tonsils, change dressings, apply plasters, and administer a clister. She was also prepared, when the time came, to wash and dress the dead, easing eyelids and limbs into sleeplike dignity.

Yet each of these women could, over the course of a lifetime, encompass all these roles—and others besides. The social construction of healing allowed the free flow of information from one level to another. Administering a doctor's or midwife's prescription, feeding the fire under a bubbling syrup, shifting and turning a sister in bed, helping with the stitching on a child's shroud, watching, listening, soaking in attitudes of hand and eye, susceptible helpers found their callings. Martha Ballard probably started out very much like Hannah Cool, doing nursing as well as housework for her relatives or neighbors. Once married, she would have had less freedom for general nursing but more scope for perfecting the gardening and cookery that were so closely associated with herbal medicine. As a young matron she no doubt watched with sick neighbors and assisted at births, until in midlife, with her own child-rearing responsibilities diminished, she became a more frequent helper and eventually a healer and midwife. Midwives were the best paid of all the female healers, not only because they officiated at births, but because they encompassed more skills, broader experience, longer memory. "Mrs Patin with me." The social base of female medicine is apparent in the very casualness of the entry. A midwife was the most visible and experienced person in a community of healers who shared her perspective, her obligations, her training, and her labor.

There is no need to sentimentalize this "female world of love and ritual," to use Carroll Smith-Rosenberg's now famous phrase, to understand that birth, illness, and death wove Hallowell's female community together. Consider two

bland sentences from the entry for August 14, the day of William McMaster's funeral: "Mrs Patten here," and then later, "I drank Tea at Mr Pollards." Both visits—Sally Patten to Martha Ballard and Martha Ballard to Merriam Pollard—were continuations of meetings at the bedsides of gravely ill children. Recall that Merriam Pollard had "sett up" with Martha at the Howards' two days earlier, and that Sally Patten, who had come to the McMasters' to watch with Billy, had helped Martha prepare his body for burial. Since Merriam and Martha were old friends, their tea party is easily explained, but what of Sally Patten's visit to Martha? What led her up the path toward the mills? Presumably she had crossed the river to attend Billy McMaster's funeral, but Martha's house was three-quarters of a mile beyond the meeting house. Her visit cannot have been a casual one. Was it a practical errand that brought her there, or a deeper need to consolidate the experience she had shared a few hours before? Even for Martha, the nightwatch had been profoundly disturbing. What must it have meant for a young mother still new to the circle of matrons?

Eighteenth-century physicians, like twentieth-century historians, had difficulty distinguishing one social healer from another, yet they understood the power of their presence. William Smellie, who wrote an important English obstetrical treatise, displayed an acute consciousness of the female audience for any medical intervention. Cautioning young physicians not to do anything to make "the gossips uneasy," he explained the importance of reassuring both the patient and her "friends." The word "friends" appears repeatedly in doctors' writings from the mid-eighteenth to the mid-nineteenth century. The label is a telling one: female healers identified with the patients they served in ways that male physicians could not.

Little wonder that some physicians actively resented their presence. William Buchan, author of the immensely popular *Domestic Medicine,* published in London in 1769 and reprinted at least fifteen times in America, deplored the social dimensions of traditional childbirth:

We cannot help taking notice of that ridiculous custom which still prevails in some parts of the country, of collecting a number of women together on such occasions. These, instead of being useful serve only to crowd the house, and obstruct the necessary attendants. Besides they hurt the patient with their noise: and often, by their untimely and impertinent advice, do much mischief.

Here, as elsewhere, Buchan distinguished between what was "necessary" and what was merely customary. Like other eighteenth-century reformers, he wanted to simplify as well as improve contemporary practice. Groups of women cluttered a room with their ideas as well as their bodies.

In rural America, however, Buchan's ideas were just another strand in the dominant eclecticism. Doctors might mistrust the ubiquitous friends, but they could not easily do without them. Female healers performed the messy, time-consuming tasks of healing and at the same time validated male practice. As long as both sets of practitioners shared the same basic assumptions, and as long as physicians were content with the income available from part-time practice, there could be little competition between them.

Study Questions

1. Why would midwives inspire, as the author writes, "fear, reverence, amusement, and disdain"? Explain your answer and give examples.

2. What does the author mean by the statement, "Martha was respectful, even deferential, toward the men's work, but the world she described was sustained by women"?

3. Describe the medicines Ballard used in treating sick people. What does the author mean by the statement that when she used natural remedies, "she was confirming the essential order of the universe"?

4. What were the differences between the treatment methods of male doctors and female midwives? Explain your answer.

5. What was "bloodletting" and describe the medical theory behind it.

6. What does the author mean by the term "social medicine"?

Bibliography

For social life in colonial New England, see Bruce Colin Daniels, *Puritans at Play: Leisure and Recreation in Colonial New England* (1995) and John Demos, *Little Commonwealth: Family Life in Plymouth Colony* (1970). David Hackett Fisher's *Albion's Seed: Four British Folkways* (1990) brilliantly compares colonial regionalism. More general but equally informative are Jack P. Greene, *Pursuits of Happiness: The Social Development of Early Modern British Colonies and the Formation of American Culture* (1986); James A. Henretta and Gregory H. Nobles, *Evolution and Revolution: American Society, 1600-1820* (1987); *Women and Colonization* (1980) by M. Etienne and E. Leacock, eds. Another great work is by Laurel Ulrich, *A Midwife's Tale: The Life of Martha Ballard, Based on Her Diary, 1785-1812* (1990).

Merrill D. Smith's *Sex and Sexuality in Early America* (1998) is equally compelling, as is his *Breaking the Bonds: Marital Discord in Pennsylvania, 1730-1830* (1991). Among the best studies of gender in early America are Laura Ulrich Thatcher, *Good Wives: Image and Reality in the Lives of Women in Northern New England, 1650-1750* (1982) and Kathleen Brown, *Good Wives, Nasty Wenches, and Anxious Patriarchs: Gender, Race, and Power in Colonial Virginia* (1996). Also see Nancy F. Cott, *The Bonds of Womanhood: "Women's Sphere" in New England, 1780-1835* (1977) and Lyle Koehler, *A Search for Power: The "Weaker" Sex in Seventeenth Century New England* (1980). For especially relevant recent scholarship, see Deborah Meyers, *Common Whores, Vertuous Women, and Loveing Wives: Free Will Christian Women in Colonial Maryland* (2003).

READING 14

America's First Confrontation with the Muslim World

Uzal E. Ent

On September 11, 2001, when Muslim radicals flew two commercial airliners into the World Trade Center and killed more than three thousand people, the United States experienced a calamity of Pearl Harbor proportions. Ever since 1979, after Islamic fundamentalists seized the U.S. embassy in Tehran, Iran, Americans understood that Muslim extremists loathed the United States, but few realized the breadth of the contempt. Throughout the Muslim world, as the Twin Towers imploded, tens of millions of people celebrated what Americans considered a national tragedy. To a country used to considering itself a beacon of freedom in a troubled world, the reaction was, to say the least, very unsettling. The subsequent wars in Afghanistan and Iraq precipitated a political debate not seen since the Vietnam era.

But almost two centuries earlier, during the Jefferson administration, the United States collided for the first time with the Muslim world. Between 1785 and 1803, pirates operating in the Mediterranean, off the coast of Tripoli in North Africa, had captured twelve American merchant vessels and held the crews for ransom. When negotiations to end the practice failed, the United States deployed naval vessels and a contingent of Marines in what came to be known as the American-Tripolitan War. Newspapers suddenly printed stories about battles in exotic places like Mossouah and Bogom against exotic enemies like Yusuf Karamanli and Sheik el Tahib, and about the U.S. Marines, after a grueling march over five-hundred miles of desert, proclaiming victory and preserving freedom of the seas in the Mediterranean. In the following essay, Uzal E. Ent describes the war that inspired a line in the Marine Corps hymn, "From the Halls of Montezuma to the shores of Tripoli."

In 1801, the newly formed United States was compelled to go to war to protect its citizens and guarantee its freedom of the seas on the Mediterranean. Although little-remembered today, the American-Tripolitan War marked the first time that U.S. forces embarked on a land campaign on foreign soil. A line in the United States Marine Corps Hymn commemorates this conflict: "From the halls of Montezuma, to the shores of Tripoli . . ." The culminating military action of the war was the march to and storming of the Arab city of Derna in Tripoli (present-day Libya), on the North African coast in 1805.

The success of this march—over some five hundred miles of desolate land—and the subsequent capture of Derna by a polyglot, undependable force was attributable to the iron-willed determination of one man—William Eaton, American consul to Tunis. But he would not have been successful without the support of a United States Marine officer, seven enlisted Marines, and two United States Navy midshipmen. All the more remarkable is the fact that, in a time of fanatical religious division, most of the soldiers who made up the force were Muslims, yet leader Eaton was a Christian.

This is not just the story of a grueling desert march or a successful battle, but rather of a campaign that included both of these feats. More importantly, this campaign advanced the international prestige of the United States and helped to launch the well-earned and glorious military tradition of the United States Marine Corps.

For centuries prior to the creation of the United States, the corsairs of the Barbary States—Algiers, Tunis, Tripoli, and Morocco—had terrorized the Mediterranean, seizing ships and enslaving or holding for ransom their captives. European powers had come to uneasy terms with the pirates, and regularly paid them tribute in order to be free of their depredations. During its first years of independence, the United States had no such treaties.

Between 1785 and 1793 more than a dozen American merchant ships were captured by Barbary pirates and their crews taken for ransom. Among the captives were James Leander Cathcart and Richard O'Brien, both of whom would figure in later U.S. relations with the Barbary States.

In 1796 the United States signed treaties with Algiers, Tunis, and Tripoli at a cost of almost a million dollars, plus annual tribute in money and naval stores. The U.S. opened consulates in each of the city-states: Richard O'Brien was appointed consul to Algiers and consul-general for the entire Barbary Coast; James Cathcart, consul to Tripoli; and William Eaton, consul to Tunis.

Subsequently, as part of the tribute, the United States delivered three ships to the Dey (ruler) of Algiers. The Bashaw (Turkish civilian and military leader) of Tripoli, Yusuf Karamanli, learned of this and also demanded a ship. When none was forthcoming, he seized an American merchant vessel. On May 14, 1801, having received no "satisfactory" response from the United States for his demands, the Bashaw, as a declaration of war, had the flagpole of the American consulate in Tripoli chopped down.

Between 1801 and 1803, in the ensuing war, the United States maintained an on-again, off-again blockade of Tripoli. On October 31, 1803, while chasing a Tripolitan ship, the U.S. frigate *Philadelphia* ran aground near Tripoli. Her captain, William Bainbridge, after unsuccessfully attempting to refloat her, surrendered with 307 crewmen.

The Tripolitans later refloated the frigate, and, claiming possession, anchored her in Tripoli's harbor. Then, on February 16, 1804, Lieutenant Stephen Decatur, Jr., with a small band of sailors, boarded and burned the *Philadelphia* in a daring raid.

The ruthless Yusuf Karamanli had gained the throne of Tripoli by murdering his eldest brother, who had previously ruled, and then exiling his surviving older brother, Hamet. Early in the war, James Cathcart suggested that the United States attempt to install Hamet as ruler in his brother's place. Cathcart's plan was twofold: (1) The flagship of the blockading squadron would convey Hamet to Constantinople, capital of the Turkish Empire, to secure the sultan's recognition of Hamet as the rightful ruler of Tripoli. (The Bar-

Uzal W. Ent, "On the Shores of Tripoli," *American History Illustrated,* 20 (January 1986), 42–46, 48–49.

The exploits of the U.S. Marines at Tripoli quickly became legendary in American popular culture.

bary city-states were under the nominal suzerainty of the Turkish sultan, and paid him annual tribute.) (2) The United States would then support Hamet in a military expedition to oust Yusuf by attacking Tripoli from the sea.

Cathcart believed that these services would so deeply obligate Hamet to the United States that he would permanently protect American interests in his territory and secure free movement of American shipping in the Mediterranean.

In 1802 Yusuf offered Hamet the governorship of Derna, sixty miles east of Tripoli. Fearing a trap, William Eaton temporarily convinced him not to accept the offer. Hamet later changed his mind, however, went to Derna, and became governor. But Yusuf refused to return Hamet's wife and children, whom he had held captive during

the seven years of Hamet's exile. This led to inconclusive fighting between followers of the two brothers. After the capture of the *Philadelphia,* in 1803, Hamet lost his supporters and fled to Egypt.

William Eaton, meanwhile, had taken up Cathcart's plan, but could not win support from the American naval leaders in the Mediterranean. Eaton, once a captain in the United States Army, was ardently nationalistic, quick-tempered, combative, enterprising, adventurous, and blind to any but his own ideas. Although exasperated by the lack of cooperation from the Navy, he remained undeterred.

In 1803 Eaton returned to the United States and secured qualified governmental approval of the Cathcart plan. The Secretary of the Navy's instructions to Commodore Samuel Barron, as he departed in 1804 to take command of the U.S.

squadron in the Mediterranean with Eaton as his special assistant, read in part: "We have no objection to you availing yourself of [Hamet's] cooperation with you against Tripoli—if you . . . consider his cooperation expedient."

Although Barron was a reluctant participant, Eaton persuaded him to seek Hamet's cooperation. Accordingly, on November 26, 1804, the American brig *Argus,* with Eaton aboard, sailed into Alexandria, under orders from Commodore Barron to find Hamet and "convey him . . . to Derne [Derna] or such other place on the coast . . . determined most proper for co-operating with the [United States] naval force . . ." Barron also promised to support Hamet against his brother Yusuf and reestablish him as regent of Tripoli.

Eaton gained approval from the Turkish viceroy in Egypt for Hamet to leave the country. Then, accompanied by Lieutenant Presley Neville O'Bannon, commander of the Marine detachment aboard the *Argus,* he started up the Nile in search of Hamet, who was in hiding.

Not much is known about Lieutenant O'Bannon, except that he had come from the mountains of Virginia, and had a reputation among his Marine companions for military zeal, a thirst for glory, fiddle playing, and womanizing. Which of these activities he preferred most is not known, but his military zeal must have been outstanding, for he was to prove to be Eaton's most dependable and efficient subordinate in the ensuing campaign.

In establishing contact with Hamet, Eaton was aided by a Tyrolean soldier of fortune calling himself Eugene Leitensdorfer. Leitensdorfer had served in, and deserted from, four different European armies. He had also deserted at least two wives, and had engaged in an amazing variety of enterprises. Eaton gave him a letter to deliver to Hamet, telling of the Turkish viceroy's grant of amnesty and asking for a meeting. Leitensdorfer successfully delivered the letter, and a rendezvous was arranged.

Hamet accepted Eaton's proposal, and Derna was selected as the initial objective for the planned campaign. Hamet insisted on traveling overland to Derna, fearing that if he went by sea, his followers on shore would lose interest and disperse. He agreed to indemnify the United States

for supporting him against his brother by pledging to the U.S. the tribute to Tripoli from the Batavian Republic, Sweden, and Denmark; to release all American prisoners in Tripoli; to hold Yusuf and his family hostage, if captured; and to appoint Eaton "General," commanding the land forces during the campaign.

Eaton then set about raising an army, assembling it at Marabout, twelve miles southwest of Alexandria. The "army" was anything but inspirational in size, appearance, dependability, or composition. It included "General" Eaton, Lieutenant O'Bannon, Marine Sergeant Arthur Campbell and six Marine privates, and Midshipman Pascal Paoli Peck, all from the *Argus* (Eaton had asked Commodore Barron for one hundred Marines); a doctor whose name is unrecorded; an Englishman named Percival (or George) Farquhar; twenty-five cannoneers of mixed nationalities, commanded by one Selim Comb; Lieutenants Connant and Rocco, of whom little more is known; and thirty-eight Greeks, under Captain Luco Ulovix and Lieutenant Constantine.

Leitensdorfer was appointed adjutant and "chief of staff"—although there was no staff. Hamet's "suite" numbered seventy men. The Arab cavalry was commanded by Sheiks el Tahib and Mahomet. Footmen and camel drivers brought the total force to about four hundred men. The baggage train consisted of 107 camels and a few asses.

Commodore Barron's assignment of so few Marines to the expedition is inexplicable. The force requested by Eaton was reasonable and apparently close to attainable by using the various Marine contingents aboard ships of the Mediterranean squadron. What better use for these Marines, under the circumstances, is difficult to imagine. But Eaton persevered with the manpower he was given.

The ten Americans, Leitensdorfer, the doctor, Farquhar, the cannoneers, and the Greeks were all in what was referred to as the "Christian contingent" of the army. The remainder—over three hundred men—were all Muslims, who were diametrically opposed to Christians under normal circumstances.

From the outset, Eaton's monetary situation was bleak. When the account was found $1,350 short, he fired his treasurer.

Heading west toward Derna, the expedition set off from Marabout, Egypt, on March 6, 1805. On the second morning, General Eaton faced the first of many strikes by his camel drivers, who wanted to be paid in advance. His refusal and threat to abandon the enterprise ended this initial revolt.

Water and food supplies ran short early. A letter from Midshipman Peck to his father aptly described the situation: "We were frequently 24 hours without water, and once 47 hours without a drop. Our horses were sometimes three days without, and for the last twenty days [of the expedition] had nothing to eat except what they picked out of the sand."

The entire journey was made over a desolate wasteland. Peck described it as "a melancholy desert throughout . . . for the space of 450 miles [we] saw neither house nor tree, nor hardly anything green, except in one place, not a trace of a human being." Eaton, however, managed to move the group some twenty miles a day, until March 13, when they reached a landmark—a castle of Greek-style architecture.

That afternoon a messenger from Derna falsely informed Hamet that the city had rebelled and had thrown Yusuf's governor into jail. This touched off an enthusiastic display. Jubilant Arabs pranced their horses wildly about, wantonly discharging their muskets into the air. Arab footmen in the rear of the column, thinking the army had been attacked by Bedouins, rushed forward to join in the massacre of the Christians. They stopped, however, when the true reason for the commotion was explained to them. That night the party camped near deep wells, providing ample water.

On March 14 the army entered Tripolitan territory. Passing ruins of ancient forts, the group camped the next night in a ravine supplied with water from natural wells. High winds, along with heavy rain and thunder, kept the expedition in camp for a day, then drove it to higher ground. On the seventeenth, the camel drivers again refused to move without further payment. Eaton's promise of later payment temporarily won the day.

The army halted on the eighteenth near Massouah, an ancient castle 150 miles from Alexandria. Eaton now discovered, to his dismay, that Hamet had arranged for the carriers to go only as far as Massouah. He attempted to induce them to continue to Bomba, on the coast, where he had arranged to be resupplied by the *Argus.*

Eaton finally got them to agree to proceed for two more days—for a price. Using nearly all of his own money, he borrowed from the Marines, Greeks, and other Christians, raising a total of $673.50. He gave this to Hamet for the drivers. Nevertheless, that night all but forty of them deserted for Egypt, and the remainder refused to move forward.

Hamet suggested that the baggage be abandoned, and that the army should camp with tribes it met along the way. But Eaton, virtually bankrupt, refused to proceed destitute of provisions. The following night, the remaining carriers departed for Egypt.

On the nineteenth, a passing pilgrim, en route to Mecca, reported that a force of over eight hundred cavalry and many more infantry under Hassen Bey—commander of Yusuf's army—had been sent from Tripoli to reinforce Derna.

Hamet now suggested delay and caution. Eaton declared that, to the contrary, the news required even more haste in order to capture Derna before Yusuf's reinforcements arrived. In a stormy and protracted meeting, the two leaders could not agree.

Hamet and his followers, distrusting the Americans, decided to stay put until a runner could be sent to Bomba and return, to make sure that an American ship was actually waiting there. Angered, Eaton cut off rations to the Arabs and announced that he and the Christians would fortify themselves in the castle until he could summon a relief force of Marines from the American fleet. His determination won out, and the expedition prepared to continue. The next day fifty camel drivers returned, prepared to march for two more days.

On March 22 the column came upon a large camp of Bedouins friendly to Hamet. Here eighty mounted men, forty-seven families, and 150 more warriors joined the expedition. The army's horses were given good feed and water, although the soldiers still had only hard bread and rice to eat.

Eaton, on credit, hired ninety camels and drivers at $11 per camel to complete the trip to Bomba.

Then, Sheik el Tahib, one of the commanders of the Arab cavalry, incited mutiny among the newly hired camel drivers. Winning half of them to his side, he departed for Egypt. Eaton refused Hamet's request to try to induce their return, and he and the remainder of the army set out for Bomba on the morning of March 28. A few hours later a messenger from el Tahib caught up with the procession, announcing that the sheik wished to rejoin the expedition, declaring that Eaton's firm action had proved the influence he had over the Arabs.

The plague of desertions and threatened mutiny continued. Hamet himself grew more reluctant to proceed as he neared confrontation with Yusuf's army, seemingly grasping at any excuse for abandoning the enterprise. Demanding the return of some horses that he had loaned to Eaton's officers, he engaged in an angry exchange with the American, then started back toward Egypt. Eaton nevertheless continued forward with the Christian contingent and baggage, under Marine guard. Within two hours Hamet returned, expressing his admiration for their dedication to his cause.

That night, induced by the treacherous el Tahib, the Bedouins turned back. Hamet sent one of his officers after them.

The army camped all day on the twenty-ninth, hoping for recruits in response to a proclamation that Eaton had issued on behalf of Hamet, and awaiting the return of the wayward Bedouins. No recruits materialized, but the Bedouins rejoined the army on the thirtieth.

At the beginning of the expedition Hamet had given el Tahib $1,500, which he was to split with Sheik Mahomet, the other Arab cavalry commander. But he kept most of the money for himself, giving Mahomet only part of what was due him. When Mahomet discovered this treachery, he took his followers and started a rapid march back toward Egypt. This time Hamet himself, with a small escort, went after them.

In Hamet's absence, Sheik el Tahib attempted to wrest control from Eaton. Accompanied by five minor chiefs, he strode to Eaton's tent and de-

manded an increase in rations. Eaton refused, wrathfully denouncing the sheik for impeding the march. Because of el Tahib's obstructionism, the trek to Bomba, which should have been completed in two weeks, had already consumed twenty-five days and had covered only half the distance. Eaton also pointed out that el Tahib had brought only twenty-eight mounted Arabs instead of the four hundred he had promised.

El Tahib then threatened revolt: "Remember you are in a desert, and a country not your own. I am a greater man here than either you or the Bashaw [Hamet]."

At this, Eaton thundered, "Leave my tent, but mark! If I find a mutiny in camp during the absence of the Bashaw, I shall put you to instant death. . . ."

Hamet's treasurer, overhearing the altercation, persuaded the lesser chiefs to maintain peace until Hamet's return. That afternoon el Tahib apologized to Eaton and swore loyalty to him and the cause.

Hamet returned with Mahomet and his following the next day, April 2. Hamet had for once acted with resolution and courage, having ridden night and day nearly sixty miles in high winds and bone-chilling rain to overtake the withdrawing contingent.

That night Eaton met with the sheiks, reproving them for quarreling, and attempting to convince them that their strength was in unity. When the army set out the next morning, it had seven hundred fighting men, who, with families and attendants, made a body of twelve hundred.

On April 8, while the caravan refreshed itself at some cisterns, Eaton reconnoitered ahead. Returning at mid-morning, he was shocked to discover that Hamet had pitched camp and had sent a courier to Bomba to ensure that American ships were actually there. Although only a six-day supply of rice remained, placing the expedition in jeopardy, Hamet insisted that the travelers needed a rest. Eaton responded by cutting off rations for the Arabs.

Again the Arabs started to pack for a return to Egypt, but first they planned to seize the supplies in Eaton's possession. Learning of the plot, he drew up the Marines, Greeks, and other Christians around the supply tent. The Muslims confronted them in a stand-off for over an hour. Finally Hamet, seeing Eaton's determination, called off his men.

Eaton, unfortunately, then ordered the Marines to perform the manual of arms, intending this as a display of discipline. But believing that the Marines were about to open fire, the Arabs reformed, and about two hundred of them charged the Christians. Eaton, Lieutenant O'Bannon, and Midshipman Peck stood at the front of the defending line. The Muslim charge wheeled just before reaching them, and then withdrew a short distance. Then the Arabs brought their muskets as if to shoot, and someone actually ordered, "Fire!" But no one wanted to fire the first shot.

Eaton finally persuaded Hamet to restore order, and he secured the Arab's promise to continue to Bomba the following day in exchange for an issue of rice. Eaton later reported that "the firm and decided conduct of Mr. O'Bannon . . . did much to deter the violence of the savages by whom he was surrounded." The Bashaw, equally impressed with the young officer, called O'Bannon "the Brave American."

Hamet soon became ill, mutiny still threatened, and the Arab infantry became so worn out that it had to stop. Then a messenger brought the welcome news that American warships were indeed at Bomba.

But when the army arrived there late on the afternoon of April 15, they were dismayed to find no ships in sight. The Arabs accused the American of being a treacherous infidel. Eaton had signal fires lighted on the heights above the beach, and the following morning the *Argus* was sighted; she had prudently sailed well offshore for the night.

The coast at Bomba was not suited for landing provisions, but both a good harbor and good water were found twenty miles further west. Midshipman Peck now returned to the *Argus,* and Midshipman George Mann replaced him. Eaton arranged with Isaac Hull, captain of the *Argus,* for a joint land and sea attack on Derna. He also asked for two carronades from the ship, along with muskets and ammunition. On the twentieth, the schooner *Hornet* landed enough supplies to carry the army to Derna.

The march resumed on April 22. Two days later the army reached a lush valley of scattered barley fields, just five hours' march from Derna. A courier confirmed that Hassen Bey, with reinforcements from Tripoli, was nearing Derna and might arrive ahead of the Eaton-Hamet force. The expedition's Arab leadership, thrown into dismay and gloom by the news, convened a meeting, pointedly excluding Eaton.

When Eaton ordered the army to march early on the twenty-fifth, el Tahib and Mahomet rebelled once again and began to depart with their followers. The remaining Bedouins refused to break camp. Eaton, however, now had money, received from Hull. His cajoling and denunciations, along with $2,000, swayed the sheiks, and by early afternoon the army reached the heights overlooking Derna. That night a number of local sheiks rode out from town and pledged their support to Hamet, but also warned that the garrison numbered eight hundred men.

The march from Egypt had taken fifty days and covered 520 miles. In all that long, dangerous journey over forbidding desert, encumbered and outnumbered by sometimes hostile, always volatile Arab elements of his army, Eaton had brought the force through without a casualty—no deaths from any cause! It was a monumental feat of leadership by Eaton, who had been ably supported by O'Bannon and his small Marine detachment.

The area around Derna was lush and bountiful. The city overlooked a bay a mile from the sea, on a lowland point extending from the eastern end of *Jebel Akdar* (Green Mountain). A riverbed, the Wadi Derna, passed through the city and emptied into the harbor.

A water battery of eight nine-pounders formed the principal defense against attack from the sea. Breastworks and the walls of old buildings protected the northeast flank. Terraces and houses, with loopholes for guns, defended the southeast and waterfront. Governor Mustifa had mounted a ten-inch howitzer on the terrace of his palace, which stood on the western side of the wadi, across from the harbor fort.

The next day Eaton sent a message to Mustifa, stating that "the legitimate sovereign" accompanied him, asking for supplies in exchange for fair compensation, and pledging that Mustifa would remain governor. The Bey returned the note with the inscription, "My head or yours. Mustifa."

That afternoon the brig *Nautilus* arrived off Derna. The *Hornet* and *Argus* joined her on the twenty-seventh, the latter with the two requested cannons. So much time was consumed manhandling the first gun up an almost vertical cliff that Eaton, anxious to commence the attack, decided he could not wait for a second piece.

Later on the twenty-seventh, the American warships took station to bombard the fortifications. The *Hornet* anchored within a hundred yards of the water battery, the *Nautilus* and *Hornet* farther offshore. Firing began at 2:00 p.m., and within an hour the water battery was silenced and abandoned.

While the Navy deployed for its attack from the sea, Eaton divided his force into two wings, to attack the city from two directions by land. Hamet and about one thousand mounted Arabs formed the left wing, approaching from the south and southwest. They seized an old castle early in their advance, insuring some security if Hassen's army should arrive.

The main attack was carried out by the smaller Christian detachment and some lightly-armed Arab infantry, commanded by Lieutenant O'Bannon. General Eaton was in overall command.

O'Bannon commenced firing on the city just after the naval bombardment started. His single gun, served by the mercenaries, banged away. As the musketry and artillery fire continued, the defending lines were visibly reinforced by men from the now-deserted water battery.

Just as these enemy reinforcements arrived, Eaton's lone gun went out of action; its rammer, without which it was useless, had been accidentally fired out of the barrel.

The defenders' fire became increasingly effective, creating casualties and confusion in the attacking lines. Only the disciplined Marines remained undaunted. At this critical point Eaton ordered a charge. The blue-coated Marines led. "We rushed forward against a host of Savages," Eaton later wrote, "more than ten to our one."

The daring charge broke the Arab defense. A few defenders fired sporadically from palm tree to palm tree as they retired, but most broke and fled across the Wadi Derna.

At 3:30 p.m. Lieutenant O'Bannon and Midshipman Mann raised the American flag over the fortress—the first time in history that the flag of the United States had been raised in victory in a foreign land.

O'Bannon's men now discovered that the guns of the water battery were serviceable, and turned them on the remaining defenders of the city. The ships resumed fire, and Hamet's cavalry swept in from the south, cutting all avenues of escape. By 4:00 p.m., it was all over. O'Bannon's Christian battalion had suffered fourteen casualties. One Marine was killed and two others wounded, one mortally. And Eaton's left wrist had been shattered by a musket ball.

Hassen's army appeared outside Derna on May 1. On the thirteenth, it attacked the city and was bloodily repulsed. Another attack on June 10 was also turned back.

That same day, impressed by his loss of Derna and exaggerated reports of Hamet's strength, Yusuf signed a treaty with American representatives in Tripoli, providing for a "firm and lasting peace upon principles of reciprocal advantage." The American delegation, led by Tobias Lear, new consul-general at Algiers, in turn agreed to evacuate Derna; to persuade Hamet to withdraw; and to pay sixty thousand dollars in ransom for the release of the *Philadelphia*'s still-imprisoned crew. (Yusuf had originally demanded two hundred thousand dollars.)

Without doubt William Eaton's determination and leadership, along with the support of intrepid men like Lieutenant O'Bannon and his Marines, had combined to bring the venture to a successful conclusion. An impressive victory had been won, a peace treaty negotiated, and American prisoners were being set free.

In the uncompromising Eaton's view, however, the treaty amounted to little more than a sellout. He believed, with apparent justification, that he had been undercut by his fellow diplomats when further victories were within grasp, and that Yusuf

Karamanli could soon have been forced to submit to any terms the United States wished to dictate. Moreover, he deplored the treatment of the unfortunate Hamet and his followers, who, having been effectively abandoned by the United States, were again compelled to retire into exile.

Returning disillusioned and embittered to America, Eaton received only token recognition from a seemingly indifferent U.S. government for his bold and arduous service. Massachusetts was more grateful, notes an early historian: her legislature, "desirous to perpetuate a remembrance of heroic enterprise," gave Eaton ten thousand acres of land.

And Hamet, in recognition of Marine Lieutenant O'Bannon's courage and leadership, presented him with a sword with a Mameluke hilt. This blade became the pattern for the official sword of the United States Marine Corps, carried to this day by Marine officers on formal occasions.

Probably the most important consequence of Eaton's decisive land-sea campaign against Derna was that it proved to the world that the young United States would not tolerate interference with her right to freely sail the seas, and that she would fight to defend her citizens in foreign waters. In 1812, unfortunately, she would have to prove it all over again.

Study Questions

1. Why might some consider it a bit of an exaggeration to say that U.S. Marines won the war against Tripoli?

2. Provide a political, ethnic, and religious portrait of the American enemy—the so-called Barbary States.

3. Before the U.S. invasion, how had the United States handled the problem of ransom for kidnaped crews?

4. What does the term "freedom of the seas" mean?

5. What military tactics did the United States employ in the war?

Bibliography

For the larger context of Jeffersonian America, see Joseph Ellis, *Founding Brothers: The Revolutionary Generation* (2000) and Edmund S. Morgan, *The Meaning of Independence: John Adams, George Washington, and Thomas Jefferson* (1976). In *Empire of Liberty: The Statecraft of Thomas Jefferson* (1990), Robert W. Tucker describes Jefferson's political and world views, as does Peter S. Onuf in *Jefferson's Empire: The Language of American Nationhood* (2000). Theodore J. Crackel's *Mr. Jefferson's Army: Political and Social Reform of the Military Establishment, 1801–1809* (1987) analyzes the president's attempt to scale down and change the American military. For books dealing specifically with the American-Tripolitan War, see C. S. Forester, *The Barbary Pirates* (1975); A. B. C. Whipple, *To the Shores of Tripoli: The Birth of the U.S. Navy and Marine Corps* (2001); and Robert J. Allison, *The Crescent Obscured: The United States and the Muslim World, 1976–1815* (2000).

4

★ ★ ★

Adjusting to America

The nineteenth century was a time of extraordinary social and economic upheaval in the Western World, even though the historic forces were subtle and evolutionary in their impact. For a number of reasons—the absence of war in Europe after the Napoleonic era, improved sanitation and public health, the smallpox vaccine, and the dissemination of the potato and mass-produced grains—population growth was extraordinary. The European population exploded from 140 million people in 1750, to 260 million in 1850, to 400 million in 1914. Farm sizes dwindled, and younger sons and laborers began moving to cities to look for work. The industrial economy was also changing, destroying home production in favor of mass-produced factory goods. Traditional village lifestyles were altered forever. The Atlantic economy was slowly integrating America and Western Europe.

In the United States, a tremendous demand for labor attracted millions of the European peasants. Rapid industrialization, unprecedented economic growth, tremendous population increases, and steady expansion into the western territories created a dynamic society. At the same time, more and more workers were moving into the great American cities to labor on the assembly lines. Never before in human history had the way people made their livings undergone more dramatic change.

Within that larger economy, there were many distinct cultures of people trying to cope with the changes around them. Minority groups were especially vulnerable to social and economic change because they usually had little political power to control the forces affecting their lives. In the South, millions of black slaves were managing to develop a unique African-American culture that sustained them emotionally amidst gross discrimination and exploitation. They substituted cultural vitality for political power and succeeded in surviving psychologically and in ordering their lives. In the Southwest, acquired from Mexico in 1848, perhaps 80,000 Hispanics were engaged in a similar struggle, frustrated about being under Anglo power and struggling to retain their land and culture. Throughout the United States, women too were trying to cope with changing circumstances. People, confused by the social changes accom-

(a) Baron Biesele, upon his arrival in America (in German): "Hey, fellow countryman, where can we find a German tavern?" Countryman (in German): "Damme. Do you think I'm a no-good like you? I am an American."

(c) Baron Biesele, two weeks after arrival (in German): "Can you tell us—Hey, beautiful Marianel, isn't that you?" Marianel (in English): "You are mistaken. I don't talk Dutch."

(b) Baron Biesele, first week after arrival (in German): "Well, Marianel, how do you like it in America?" Marianel (in German): "Oh, Baron, the language, the language. I'll never learn it in all my life."

panying the Industrial Revolution, tried to preserve a sense of the mythical past by creating a "cult of domesticity" for women. In addition, hundreds of thousands of Native Americans were finding their way of life incompatible with the growth-oriented, materialistic economy of industrial America. For all these people, the changing nature of American society was an extraordinary challenge, one that required adjustment and accommodation.

READING 15

The Cult of True Womanhood: 1820-1860

Barbara Welter

In an interview with the Public Broadcasting System, American feminist Gloria Steinem was asked if her opinions about the women's movement had changed at all in the last twenty years. After reflecting for a moment, she remarked that over the years she had become increasingly aware that the problem of sexism was rooted more deeply than she had first assumed. One look at public policy debated in the United States during the 1990s confirms her belief. Most of the major domestic public policy questions in the United States today directly involve the place of women in society: wage discrimination, affirmative action and promotion, abortion and freedom of choice, Social Security and retirement benefits, child care, the Equal Rights Amendment, pornography and censorship, rape and sexual abuse, insurance and annuity rate differentials, divorce and child support, poverty and welfare, and gay rights. Virtually all of these problems have their roots in the gender stereotyping so common in American culture. Gender stereotyping is a residue from before the industrial and even modern eras when divisions of labor in society were directly tied to pregnancy, birthing, nursing, and child rearing. Although the economic institutions dictating such divisions of labor are now disappearing, the gender stereotypes have lives of their own, continuing to shape public expectations of men and women.

In "The Cult of True Womanhood: 1820–1860," historian Barbara Welter looks at the antebellum decades of the nineteenth century and describes an important stage in public expression of gender stereotypes. By making virtues of domesticity, submissiveness, passivity, and chastity for women, and leaving men free to exhibit a much wider range of behaviors, American culture hoped to promote industrialization while preserving some semblance of premodern values. The irony, of course, was that the relevance of the "cult of womanhood" declined in direct proportion to the pace of industrialization. Women gradually became confined to an increasingly unreal world of impossible expectations; the underside of domesticity and submissiveness, for many women, was anger, guilt, and extraordinary frustration. Even after the Nineteenth Amendment was ratified in 1920, the "cult of womanhood" still influenced American attitudes, and the modern feminist movement had to turn its attention to changing those attitudes as a prerequisite to realizing freedom and equality for both genders.

The nineteenth-century American man was a busy builder of bridges and railroads, at work long hours in a materialistic society. The religious values of his forebears were neglected in practice if not in intent, and he occasionally felt some guilt that he had turned this new land, this temple of the chosen people, into one vast countinghouse. But he could salve his conscience by reflecting that he had left behind a hostage, not only to fortune, but to all the values which he held so dear and treated so lightly. Woman, in the cult of True Womanhood presented by the women's magazines, gift annuals and religious literature of the nineteenth century, was the hostage in the home. In a society where values changed frequently, where fortunes rose and fell with frightening rapidity, where social and economic mobility provided instability as well as hope, one thing at least remained the same—a true woman was a true woman, wherever she was found. If anyone, male or female, dared to tamper with the complex virtues which made up True Womanhood, he was damned immediately as an enemy of God, of civilization and of the Republic. It was a fearful obligation, a solemn responsibility, which the nineteenth-century American woman had—to uphold the pillars of the temple with her frail white hand.

The attributes of True Womanhood, by which a woman judged herself and was judged by her husband, her neighbors, and society could be divided into four cardinal virtues—piety, purity, submissiveness, and domesticity. Put them all together and they spell mother, daughter, sister, wife—woman. Without them, no matter whether there was fame, achievement, or wealth, all was ashes. With them she was promised happiness and power.

Religion or piety was the core of woman's virtue, the source of her strength. Young men looking for a mate were cautioned to search first for piety, for if that were there, all else would follow. Religion belonged to woman by divine right, a gift of God and nature. This "peculiar susceptibility" to religion was given her for a reason: "the vestal flame of piety, lighted up by Heaven in the breast of woman" would throw its beams into the naughty world of men. So far would its candle power reach that the "Universe might be Enlightened, Improved, and Harmonized by WOMAN!!" She would be another, better, Eve, working in cooperation with the Redeemer, bringing the world back "from its revolt and sin." The world would be reclaimed for God through her suffering, for "God increased the cares and sorrows of woman, that she might be sooner constrained to accept the terms of salvation." A popular poem by Mrs. Frances Osgood, "The Triumph of the Spiritual Over the Sensual," expressed just this sentiment, woman's purifying passionless love bringing an erring man back to Christ.

Dr. Charles Meigs, explaining to a graduating class of medical students why women were naturally religious, said that "hers is a pious mind. Her confiding nature leads her more readily than men to accept the proffered grace of the Gospel." Caleb Atwater, Esq., writing in *The Ladies' Repository,* saw the hand of the Lord in female piety: "Religion is exactly what a woman needs, for it gives her that dignity that best suits her dependence." And Mrs. John Sandford, who had no very high opinion of her sex, agreed thoroughly: "Religion is just what a woman needs. Without it she is ever restless or unhappy. . . ." Mrs. Sandford and the others did not speak only of that restlessness of the human heart, which St. Augustine notes, that can only find its peace in God. They spoke rather of religion as a kind of tranquilizer for the many undefined longings which swept even the most pious young girl, and about which it was better to pray than to think.

One reason religion was valued was that it did not take a woman away from her "proper sphere," her home. Unlike participation in other societies or movements, church work would not make her less domestic or submissive, less a True Woman. In religious vineyards, said the *Young Ladies' Literary and Missionary Report,* "you

Barbara Welter, "The Cult of True Womanhood: 1820–1860"
In *American Quarterly,* Vol. 18 (Summer 1966): 151–174.
Copyright © The Johns Hopkins University Press. Reprinted by permission.

may labor without the apprehension of detracting from the charms of feminine delicacy." Mrs. S. L. Dagg, writing from her chapter of the Society in Tuscaloosa, Alabama, was equally reassuring: "As no sensible woman will suffer her intellectual pursuits to clash with her domestic duties," she should concentrate on religious work "which promotes these very duties."

The women's seminaries aimed at aiding women to be religious, as well as accomplished. Mt. Holyoke's catalogue promised to make female education "a handmaid to the Gospel and an efficient auxiliary in the great task of renovating the world." The Young Ladies' Seminary at Bordentown, New Jersey, declared its most important function to be "the forming of a sound and virtuous character." In Keene, New Hampshire, the Seminary tried to instill a "consistent and useful character" in its students, to enable them in this life to be "a good friend, wife and mother" but more important, to qualify them for "the enjoyment of Celestial Happiness in the life to come." And Joseph M. D. Matthews, Principal of Oakland Female Seminary in Hillsborough, Ohio, believed that "female education should be preeminently religious."

If religion was so vital to a woman, irreligion was almost too awful to contemplate. Women were warned not to let their literacy or intellectual pursuits take them away from God. Sarah Josepha Hale spoke darkly of those who, like Margaret Fuller, threw away the "One True Book" for others, open to error. Mrs. Hale used the unfortunate Miss Fuller as fateful proof that "the greater the intellectual force, the greater and more fatal the errors into which women fall who wander from the Rock of Salvation, Christ the Saviour. . . ."

One gentleman, writing on "Female Irreligion," reminded his readers that "Man may make himself a brute, and does so very often, but can woman brutify herself to his level—the lowest level of human nature—without exerting special wonder?" Fanny Wright, because she was godless, "was no woman, mother though she be." A few years ago, he recalls, such women would have been whipped. In any case, "woman never

looks lovelier than in her reverence for religion" and, conversely, "female irreligion is the most revolting feature in human character."

Purity was as essential as piety to a young woman, its absence as unnatural and unfeminine. Without it she was, in fact, no woman at all, but a member of some lower order. A "fallen woman" was a "fallen angel," unworthy of the celestial company of her sex. To contemplate the loss of purity brought tears; to be guilty of such a crime, in the women's magazines at least, brought madness or death. Even the language of the flowers had bitter words for it: a dried white rose symbolized "Death Preferable to Loss of Innocence." The marriage night was the single great event of a woman's life, when she bestowed her greatest treasure upon her husband, and from that time on was completely dependent upon him, an empty vessel, without legal or emotional existence of her own.

Therefore all True Women were urged, in the strongest possible terms, to maintain their virtue, although men, being by nature more sensual than they, would try to assault it. Thomas Branagan admitted in *The Excellency of the Female Character Vindicated* that his sex would sin and sin again, they could not help it, but woman, stronger and purer, must not give in and let man "take liberties incompatible with her delicacy." "If you do," Branagan addressed his gentle reader, "You will be left in silent sadness to bewail your credulity, imbecility, duplicity, and premature prostitution."

Mrs. Eliza Farrar, in *The Young Ladies' Friend,* gave practical logistics to avoid trouble: "Sit not with another in a place that is too narrow; read not out of the same book; let not your eagerness to see anything induce you to place your head close to another person's."

If such good advice was ignored the consequences were terrible and inexorable. In *Girlhood and Womanhood: Or Sketches of My Schoolmates,* by Mrs. A. J. Graves (a kind of mid-nineteenth-century *The Group*), the bad ends of a boarding school class of girls are scrupulously recorded. The worse end of all is reserved for "Amelia Dorrington: The Lost One." Amelia died in the almshouse "the wretched victim of depravity and intemperance" all because her mother had let her be "high-spirited not prudent." These girlish high spirits had been misinterpreted by a young man, with disastrous results. Amelia's "thoughtless levity" was "followed by a total loss of virtuous principle" and Mrs. Graves editorializes that "the coldest reserve is more admirable in a woman a man wishes to make his wife, than the least approach to undue familiarity."

A popular and often-reprinted story by Fanny Forester told the sad tale of "Lucy Dutton." Lucy "with the seal of innocence upon her heart, and a rose-leaf on her cheek" came out of her vine-covered cottage and ran into a city slicker. "And Lucy was beautiful and trusting, and thoughtless: and he was gay, selfish, and profligate. Needs the story be told? . . . Nay, censor, Lucy was a child—consider how young, how very untaught—oh! her innocence was no match for the sophistry of a gay, city youth! Spring came and shame was stamped upon the cottage at the foot of the hill." The baby died; Lucy went mad at the funeral and finally died herself. "Poor, poor Lucy Dutton! The grave is a blessed couch and pillow to the wretched. Rest thee there, poor Lucy!" The frequency with which derangement follows loss of virtue suggests the exquisite sensibility of woman, and the possibility that, in the women's magazines at least, her intellect was geared to her hymen, not her brain.

If, however, a woman managed to withstand man's assaults on her virtue, she demonstrated her superiority and her power over him. Eliza Farnham, trying to prove this female superiority, concluded smugly that "the purity of women is the everlasting barrier against which the tides of man's sensual nature surge."

A story in *The Lady's Amaranth* illustrates this dominance. It is set, improbably, in Sicily, where two lovers, Bianca and Tebaldo, have been separated because her family insisted that she marry a rich old man. By some strange circumstance the two are in a shipwreck and cast on a desert island, the only survivors. Even here, however, the rigid standards of True Woman-

hood prevail. Tebaldo unfortunately forgets himself slightly, so that Bianca must warn him: "We may not indeed gratify our fondness by caresses, but it is still something to bestow our kindest language, and looks and prayers, and all lawful and honest attentions on each other." Something, perhaps, but not enough, and Bianca must further remonstrate: "It is true that another man is my husband, but you are my guardian angel." When even that does not work she says in a voice of sweet reason, passive and proper to the end, that she wishes he wouldn't but "still, if you insist, I will become what you wish; but I beseech you to consider, ere that decision, that debasement which I must suffer in your esteem." This appeal to his own double standards holds the beast in him at bay. They are rescued, discover that the old husband is dead, and after "mourning a decent season" Bianca finally gives in, legally.

Men could be counted on to be grateful when women thus saved them from themselves. William Alcott, guiding young men in their relations with the opposite sex, told them that "Nothing is better calculated to preserve a young man from contamination of low pleasures and pursuits than frequent intercourse with the more refined and virtuous of the other sex." And he added, one assumes in equal innocence, that youths should "observe and learn to admire, that purity and ignorance of evil which is the characteristic of well-educated young ladies, and which, when we are near them, raises us above those sordid and sensual considerations which hold such sway over men in their intercourse with each other."

The Rev. Jonathan F. Stearns was also impressed by female chastity in the face of male passion, and warned woman never to compromise the source of her power: "Let her lay aside delicacy, and her influence over our sex is gone."

Women themselves accepted, with pride but suitable modesty, this priceless virtue. *The Ladies' Wreath,* in "Woman the Creature of God and the Manufacturer of Society," saw purity as her greatest gift and chief means of discharging her duty to save the world: "Purity is the highest beauty—the true pole-star which is to guide humanity aright in its long, varied, and perilous voyage."

Sometimes, however, a woman did not see the dangers to her treasure. In that case, they must be pointed out to her, usually by a male. In the nineteenth century any form of social change was tantamount to an attack on woman's virtue, if only it was correctly understood. For example, dress reform seemed innocuous enough and the bloomers worn by the lady of that name and her followers were certainly modest attire. Such was the reasoning only of the ignorant. In another issue of *The Ladies' Wreath* a young lady is represented in dialogue with her "Professor." The girl expresses admiration for the bloomer costume—it gives freedom of motion, is healthful and attractive. The "Professor" sets her straight. Trousers, he explains, are "only one of the many manifestations of that wild spirit of socialism and agrarian radicalism which is at present so rife in our land." The young lady recants immediately: "If this dress has any connection with Fourierism or Socialism, or fanaticism in any shape whatever, I have no disposition to wear it at all . . . no true woman would so far compromise her delicacy as to espouse, however unwittingly, such a cause."

America could boast that her daughters were particularly innocent. In a poem on "The American Girl" the author wrote proudly:

> Her eye of light is the diamond bright,
> Her innocence the pearl,
> And these are ever the bridal gems
> That are worn by the American girl.

Lydia Maria Child, giving advice to mothers, aimed at preserving that spirit of innocence. She regretted that "want of confidence between mothers and daughters on delicate subjects" and suggested a woman tell her daughter a few facts when she reached the age of twelve to "set her mind at rest." Then Mrs. Child confidently hoped that a young lady's "instinctive modesty" would "prevent her from dwelling on the information until she was called upon to use it." In the same vein, a book of advice to the newly married was ti-

tled *Whisper to a Bride.* As far as intimate information was concerned, there was no need to whisper, since the book contained none at all.

A masculine summary of this virtue was expressed in a poem "Female Charms":

> *I would have her as pure as the snow*
>   *on the mount—As true as the smile*
>   *that to infamy's given—As pure as*
>   *the wave of the crystalline fount,*
> *Yet as warm in the heart as the*
>   *sunlight of heaven.*
> *With a mind cultivated, not boastingly*
>   *wise,*
> *I could gaze on such beauty, with*
>   *exquisite bliss;*
> *With her heart on her lips and her soul*
>   *in her eyes—What more could I*
>   *wish in dear woman than this.*

Man might, in fact, ask no more than this in woman, but she was beginning to ask more of herself, and in the asking was threatening the third powerful and necessary value, submission. Purity, considered as a moral imperative, set up a dilemma which was hard to resolve. Woman must preserve her virtue until marriage and marriage was necessary for her happiness. Yet marriage was, literally, an end to innocence. She was told not to question this dilemma, but simply to accept it.

Submission was perhaps the most feminine virtue expected of women. Men were supposed to be religious, although they rarely had time for it, and supposed to be pure, although it came awfully hard to them, but men were the movers, the doers, the actors. Women were the passive, submissive responders. The order of dialogue was, of course, fixed in Heaven. Man was "woman's superior by God's appointment, if not in intellectual dowry, at least by official decree." Therefore, as Charles Elliott argued in *The Ladies' Repository,* she should submit to him "for the sake of good order at least." In *The Ladies' Companion* a young wife was quoted approvingly as saying that she did not think woman should "feel and act for herself" because "When, next to God, her hus-

Domesticity was considered a great virtue. The "true woman" was expected to stay at home and serve her family.

band is not the tribunal to which her heart and intellect appeals—the golden bowl of affection is broken." Women were warned that if they tampered with this quality they tampered with the order of the Universe.

The Young Lady's Book summarized the necessity of the passive virtues in its readers' lives: "It is, however, certain that in whatever situation of life a woman is placed from her cradle to her grave, a spirit of obedience and submission, pliability of temper, and humility of mind, are required from her."

Woman understood her position if she was the right kind of woman, a true woman. "She feels herself weak and timid. She needs a protector," declared George Burnap, in his lectures on *The Sphere and Duties of Woman.* "She is in a measure dependent. She asks for wisdom, constancy, firmness, perseverance, and she is willing to repay it all by the surrender of the full treasure of her affections. Woman despises in man every thing like herself except a tender heart. It is enough that she is effeminate and weak; she does not want another like herself." Or put even more strongly by Mrs. Sandford: "A really sensible woman feels her dependence. She does what she can, but she is conscious of inferiority, and therefore grateful for support."

Mrs. Sigourney, however, assured young ladies that although they were separate, they were equal. This difference of the sexes did not imply inferiority, for it was part of that same order of Nature established by Him "who bids the oak brave the fury of the tempest, and the alpine flower lean its cheek on the bosom of eternal snows." Dr. Meigs had a different analogy to make the same point; contrasting the anatomy of the Apollo of the Belevedere (illustrating the male principle) with the Venus de Medici (illustrating the female principle). "Woman," said the physician, with a kind of clinical gallantry, "has a head almost too small for intellect but just big enough for love."

This love itself was to be passive and responsive. "Love, in the heart of a woman," wrote Mrs. Farrar, "should partake largely of the nature of gratitude. She should love, because she is already loved by one deserving her regard."

Woman was to work in silence, unseen, like Wordsworth's Lucy. Yet, "working like nature, in secret" her love goes forth to the world "to regulate its pulsation, and send forth from its heart, in pure and temperate flow, the life-giving current." She was to work only for pure affection, without thought of money or ambition. A poem, "Woman and Fame," by Felicia Hemans, widely quoted in many of the gift books, concludes with a spirited renunciation of the gift of fame:

Away! to me, a woman, bring
Sweet flowers from affection's spring.

"True feminine genius," said Grace Greenwood (Sara Jane Clarke) "is ever timid, doubtful, and clingingly dependent; a perpetual childhood." And she advised literary ladies in an essay on "The Intellectual Woman"—"Don't trample on the flowers while longing for the stars." A wife who submerged her own talents to work for her husband was extolled as an example of a true woman. In *Women of Worth: A Book for Girls,* Mrs. Ann Flaxman, an artist of promise herself, was praised because she "devoted herself to sustain her husband's genius and aid him in his arduous career."

Caroline Gilman's advice to the bride aimed at establishing this proper order from the beginning of a marriage: "Oh, young and lovely bride, watch well the first moments when your will conflicts with his to whom God and society have given control. Reverence his *wishes* even when you do not his *opinions.*"

Mrs. Gilman's perfect wife in *Recollections of a Southern Matron* realizes that "the three golden threads with which domestic happiness is woven" are "to repress a harsh answer, to confess a fault, and to stop (right or wrong) in the midst of self-defense, in gentle submission." Woman could do this, hard though it was, because in her heart she knew she was right and so could afford to be forgiving, even a trifle condescending. "Men are not unreasonable," averred Mrs. Gilman. "Their difficulties lie in not understanding the moral and physical nature of our sex. They often wound through ignorance, and are surprised at having offended." Wives were advised to do their best to reform men, but if they couldn't, to give up gracefully. "If any habit of his annoyed me, I spoke of it once or twice calmly, then bore it quietly."

A wife should occupy herself "only with domestic affairs—wait till your husband confides to you those of a high importance—and do not give your advice until he asks for it," advised the *Lady's Token.* At all times she should behave in a manner becoming a woman, who had "no arms other than gentleness." Thus "if he is abusive, never retort." *A Young Lady's Guide to the Harmonious Development of a Christian Character* suggested that females should "become as little children" and "avoid a controversial spirit." *The Mother's Assistant and Young Lady's Friend* listed "Always Conciliate" as its first commandment in "Rules for Conjugal and Domestic Happiness." Small wonder that these same rules ended with the succinct maxim: "Do not expect too much."

As mother, as well as wife, woman was required to submit to fortune. In *Letters to Mothers* Mrs. Sigourney sighed: "To bear the evils and sorrows which may be appointed us, with a patient mind, should be the continual effort of our sex. . . . It seems, indeed, to be expected of us; since the passive and enduring virtues are more immediately within our province." Of these trials "the hardest was to bear the loss of children with submission" but the indomitable Mrs. Sigourney found strength to murmur to the bereaved mother: "The Lord loveth a cheerful giver." *The Ladies' Parlor Companion* agreed thoroughly in "A Submissive Mother," in which a mother had already buried two of her children and was nursing a dying baby and saw her sole remaining child "probably scalded to death. Handing over the infant to die in the arms of a friend, she bowed in sweet submission to the double stroke." But the child "through the goodness of God survived, and the mother learned to say 'Thy will be done.'"

Woman then, in all her roles, accepted submission as her lot. It was a lot she had not chosen or deserved. As *Godey's* said, "the lesson of submission is forced upon woman." Without comment or criticism the writer affirms that "To suffer and to be silent under suffering seems the great command she has to obey." George Burnap referred to a woman's life as "a series of suppressed emotions." She was, as Emerson said, "more vulnerable, more infirm, more mortal than man." The death of a beautiful woman, cherished in fiction, represented woman as the innocent victim, suffering without sin, too pure and good for this world but too weak and passive to resist its evil forces. The best refuge for such a delicate creature was the warmth and safety of her home.

The true woman's place was unquestionably by her own fireside—as daughter, sister, but most of all as wife and mother. Therefore domesticity was among the virtues most prized by the women's magazines. "As society is constituted," wrote Mrs. S. E. Farley, on the "Domestic and Social Claims on Woman," "the true dignity and beauty of the female character seemed to consist in a right understanding and faithful and cheerful performance of social and family duties. Sacred Scripture re-enforced social pressure: "St. Paul knew what was best for women when he advised them to be domestic," said Mrs. Sandford. "There is composure at home; there is something sedative in the duties which home involves. It affords security not only from the world, but from delusions and errors of every kind."

From her home woman performed her great task of bringing men back to God. *The Young Ladies' Class Book* was sure that "the domestic fireside is the great guardian of society against the excesses of human passions." *The Lady at Home* expressed its convictions in its very title and concluded that "even if we cannot reform the world

in a moment, we can begin the work by reforming ourselves and our households—It is woman's mission. Let her not look away from her own little family circle for the means of producing moral and social reforms, but begin at home."

Home was supposed to be a cheerful place, so that brothers, husbands, and sons would not go elsewhere in search of a good time. Woman was expected to dispense comfort and cheer. In writing the biography of Margaret Mercer (every inch a true woman) her biographer (male) notes: "She never forgot that it is the peculiar province of women to minister to the comfort, and promote the happiness, first, of those most nearly allied to her, and then of those, who by the Providence of God are placed in a state of dependence upon her." Many other essays in the women's journals showed woman as comforter: "Woman, Man's Best Friend," "Woman, the Greatest Social Benefit," "Woman, A Being to Come Home To," "The Wife: Source of Comfort and the Spring of Joy."

One of the most important functions of woman as comforter was her role as nurse. Her own health was probably, although regrettably, delicate. Many homes had "little sufferers," those pale children who wasted away to saintly deaths. And there were enough other illnesses of youth and age, major and minor, to give the nineteenth-century American woman nursing experience. The sickroom called for the exercise of her higher qualities of patience, mercy, and gentleness as well as for her housewifely arts. She could thus fulfill her dual feminine function—beauty and usefulness.

The cookbooks of the period offer formulas for gout cordials, ointment for sore nipples, hiccough and cough remedies, opening pills and refreshing drinks for fever, along with recipes for pound cake, jumbles, stewed calves head and currant wine. *The Ladies' New Book of Cookery* believed that "food prepared by the kind hand of a wife, mother, sister, friend" tasted better and had a "restorative power which money cannot purchase."

A chapter of *The Young Lady's Friend* was devoted to woman's privilege as "ministering spirit at the couch of the sick." Mrs. Farrar advised a soft voice, gentle and clean hands, and a cheerful smile. She cautioned against an excess of female delicacy. That was all right for a young lady in the parlor, but not for bedside manners. Leeches, for example, were to be regarded as "a curious piece of mechanism . . . their ornamental stripes should recommend them even to the eye, and their valuable services to our feelings." And she went on calmly to discuss their use. Nor were women to shrink from medical terminology, since "If you cultivate right views of the wonderful structure of the body, you will be as willing to speak to a physician of the bowels as the brains of your patient."

Nursing the sick, particularly sick males, not only made a woman feel useful and accomplished, but increased her influence. In a piece of heavy-handed humor in *Godey's* a man confessed that some women were only happy when their husbands were ailing that they might have the joy of nursing him to recovery "thus gratifying their medical vanity and their love of power by making him more dependent upon them." In a similar vein a husband sometimes suspected his wife "almost wishes me dead—for the pleasure of being utterly inconsolable."

In the home women were not only the highest adornment of civilization, but they were supposed to keep busy at morally uplifting tasks. Fortunately most of the housework, if looked at in true womanly fashion, could be regarded as uplifting. Mrs. Sigourney extolled its virtues: "The science of housekeeping affords exercise for the judgment and energy, ready recollection, and patient self-possession, that are the characteristics of a superior mind." According to Mrs. Farrar, making beds was good exercise, the repetitiveness of routine tasks inculcated patience and perseverance, and proper management of the home was a surprisingly complex art: "There is more to be learned about pouring out tea and coffee than most young ladies are willing to believe." *Godey's* went so far as to suggest coyly, in "Learning vs. Housewifery" that the two were complementary, not opposed: chemistry could be utilized in cooking, geometry in dividing cloth, and phrenology in discovering talent in children.

Women were to master every variety of needlework, for, as Mrs. Sigourney pointed out, "Needlework, in all its forms of use, elegance, and ornament, has ever been the appropriate occupation of woman." Embroidery improved taste; knitting promoted serenity and economy. Other forms of artsy-craftsy activity for her leisure moments included painting on glass or velvet, Poonah work, tussy-mussy frames for her own needlepoint or water colors, stands for hyacinths, hair bracelets, or baskets of feathers.

She was expected to have a special affinity for flowers. To the editors of *The Lady's Token,* "A woman never appears more truly in her sphere, than when she divides her time between her domestic avocations and the culture of flowers." She could write letters, an activity particularly feminine since it had to do with the outpourings of the heart, or practice her drawingroom skills of singing and playing an instrument. She might even read.

Here she faced a bewildering array of advice. The female was dangerously addicted to novels, according to the literature of the period. She should avoid them, since they interfered with "serious piety." If she simply couldn't help herself and read them anyway, she should choose edifying ones from lists of morally acceptable authors. She should study history since it "showed the depravity of the human heart and the evil nature of sin." On the whole, "religious biography was the best."

The women's magazines themselves could be read without any loss of concern for the home. *Godey's* promised the husband that he would find his wife "no less assiduous for his reception, or less sincere in welcoming his return" as a result of reading their magazine. *The Lily of the Valley* won its rights to be admitted to the boudoir by confessing that it was "like its namesake humble and unostentatious, but it is yet pure, and, we trust, free from moral imperfections."

No matter what later authorities claimed, the nineteenth century knew that girls *could* be ruined by books. The seduction stories regard "exciting and dangerous books" as contributory causes of disaster. The man without honorable intentions always provides the innocent maiden with such books as a prelude to his assault on her virtue. Books which attacked or seemed to attack woman's accepted place in society were regarded as equally dangerous. A reviewer of Harriet Martineau's *Society in America* wanted it kept out of the hands of American women. They were so susceptible to persuasion, with their "gentle yielding natures" that they might listen to "the bold ravings of the hard-featured of their own sex." The frightening result: "Such reading will unsettle them for their true station and pursuits, and they will throw the world back again into confusion."

The debate over women's education posed the question of whether a "finished" education detracted from the practice of housewifely arts. Again it proved to be a case of semantics, for a true woman's education was never "finished" until she was instructed in the gentle science of homemaking. Helen Irving, writing on "Literary Women," made it very clear that if women invoked the muse, it was as a genie of the household lamp. "If the necessities of her position require these duties at her hands, she will perform them nonetheless cheerfully, that she knows herself capable of higher things." The literary woman must conform to the same standards as any other woman: "That her home shall be made a loving place of rest and joy and comfort to those who are dear to her, will be the first wish of every true woman's heart." Mrs. Ann Stephens told women who wrote to make sure they did not sacrifice one domestic duty. "As for genius, make it a domestic plant. Let its roots strike deep in your house. . . ."

The fear of "blue stockings" (the eighteenth-century male's term of derision for educated or literary women) need not persist for nineteenth-century American men. The magazines presented spurious dialogues in which bachelors were convinced of their fallacy in fearing educated wives. One such dialogue took place between a young man and his female cousin. Ernest deprecates learned ladies ("A *Woman* is far more lovable than a *philosopher*") but Alice refutes him with the beautiful example of their Aunt Barbara who, "although she *has* perpetrated the heinous crime of writing some half dozen folios" is still "a model of

the spirit of feminine gentleness." His memory prodded, Ernest concedes that, by George, there was a woman: "When I last had a cold she not only made me a bottle of cough syrup, but when I complained of nothing new to read, she set to work and wrote some twenty stanzas on consumption."

The magazines were filled with domestic tragedies in which spoiled young girls learned that when there was a hungry man to feed, French and china painting were not helpful. According to these stories many a marriage is jeopardized because the wife has not learned to keep house. Harriet Beecher Stowe wrote a sprightly piece of personal experience for *Godey's,* ridiculing her own bad housekeeping as a bride. She used the same theme in a story "The Only Daughter," in which the pampered beauty learns the facts of domestic life from a rather difficult source, her mother-in-law. Mrs. Hamilton tells Caroline in the sweetest way possible to shape up in the kitchen, reserving her rebuke for her son: "You are her husband— her guide—her protector—now see what you can do," she admonishes him. "Give her credit for every effort: treat her faults with tenderness; encourage and praise whenever you can, and depend upon it, you will see another woman in her." He is properly masterful, she properly domestic and in a few months Caroline is making lumpless gravy and keeping up with the darning. Domestic tranquillity has been restored and the young wife moralizes: "Bring up a girl to feel that she has a responsible part to bear in promoting the happiness of the family, and you make a reflecting being of her at once, and remove that lightness and frivolity of character which makes her shrink from graver studies." These stories end with the heroine drying her hands on her apron and vowing that *her* daughter will be properly educated, in piecrust as well as Poonah work.

The female seminaries were quick to defend themselves against any suspicion of interfering with the role which nature's God had assigned to women. They hoped to enlarge and deepen that role, but not to change its setting. At the Young Ladies' Seminary and Collegiate Institute in Monroe City, Michigan, the catalogue admitted few of its graduates would be likely "to fill the learned professions." Still, they were called to "other scenes of usefulness and honor." The average woman is to be "the presiding genius of love" in the home, where she is to "give a correct and elevated literary taste to her children, and to assume that influential station that she ought to possess as the companion of an educated man."

At Miss Pierce's famous school in Litchfield, the students were taught that they had "attained the perfection of their characters when they could combine their elegant accomplishments with a turn for solid domestic virtues." Mt. Holyoke paid pious tribute to domestic skills: "Let a young lady despise this branch of the duties of woman, and she despises the appointments of her existence." God, nature and the Bible "enjoin these duties on the sex, and she cannot violate them with impunity." Thus warned, the young lady would have to seek knowledge of these duties elsewhere, since it was not in the curriculum at Mt. Holyoke. "We would not take this privilege from the mother."

One reason for knowing her way around a kitchen was that America was "a land of precarious fortunes," as Lydia Maria Child pointed out in her book *The Frugal Housewife: Dedicated to Those Who Are Not Ashamed of Economy.* Mrs. Child's chapter "How to Endure Poverty" prescribed a combination of piety and knowledge—the kind of knowledge found in a true woman's education, "a thorough religious *useful* education." The woman who had servants today, might tomorrow, because of a depression or panic, be forced to do her own work. If that happened she knew how to act, for she was to be the same cheerful consoler of her husband in their cottage as in their mansion.

An essay by Washington Irving, much quoted in the gift annuals, discussed the value of a wife in case of business reverses: "I have observed that a married man falling into misfortune is more apt to achieve his situation in the world than a single one . . . it is beautifully ordained by Providence that woman, who is the ornament of man in his happier hours, should be his stay and solace when smitten with sudden calamity."

A story titled simply but eloquently "The Wife" dealt with the quiet heroism of Ellen Graham during her husband's plunge from fortune to poverty. Ned Graham said of her: "Words are too poor to tell you what I owe to that noble woman. In our darkest seasons of adversity, she has been the angel of consolation—utterly forgetful of self and anxious only to comfort and sustain me." Of course she had a little help from "faithful Dinah who absolutely refused to leave her beloved mistress," but even so Ellen did no more than would be expected of any true woman.

Most of this advice was directed to woman as wife. Marriage was the proper state for the exercise of the domestic virtues. "True Love and a Happy Home," an essay in *The Young Ladies' Oasis,* might have been carved on every girl's hope chest. But although marriage was best, it was not absolutely necessary. The women's magazines tried to remove the stigma from being an "Old Maid." They advised no marriage at all rather than an unhappy one contracted out of selfish motives. Their stories showed maiden ladies as unselfish ministers to the sick, teachers of the young, or moral preceptors with their pens, beloved of the entire village. Usually the life of single blessedness resulted from the premature death of a fiancé, or was chosen through fidelity to some high mission. For example, in "Two Sisters," Mary devotes herself to Ellen and her abandoned children, giving up her own chance for marriage. "Her devotion to her sister's happiness has met its reward in the consciousness of having fulfilled a sacred duty." Very rarely, a "woman of genius" was absolved from the necessity of marriage, being so extraordinary that she did not need the security or status of being a wife. Most often, however, if girls proved "difficult," marriage and a family were regarded as a cure. The "sedative quality" of a home could be counted on to subdue even the most restless spirits.

George Burnap saw marriage as "that sphere for which woman was originally intended, and to which she is so exactly fitted to adorn and bless, as the wife, the mistress of a home, the solace, the aid, and the counsellor of that one, for whose sake alone the world is of any consequence to her." Samuel Miller preached a sermon on women: "How interesting and important are the duties devolved on females as wives . . . the counsellor and friend of the husband; who makes it her daily study to lighten his cares, to soothe his sorrows, and to augment his joys; who, like a guardian angel, watches over his interests, warns him against dangers, comforts him under trials; and by her pious, assiduous, and attractive deportment, constantly endeavors to render him more virtuous, more useful, more honourable, and more happy." A woman's whole interest should be focused on her husband, paying him "those numberless attentions to which the French give the title of *petits soins* and which the woman who loves knows so well how to pay . . . she should consider nothing as trivial which could win a smile of approbation from him."

Marriage was seen not only in terms of service but as an increase in authority for women. Burnap concluded that marriage improves the female character "not only because it puts her under the best possible tuition, that of the affections, and affords scope to her active energies, but because it gives her higher aims, and a more dignified position." *The Lady's Amaranth* saw it as a balance of power: "The man bears rule over his wife's person and conduct. She bears rule over his inclinations: he governs by law; she by persuasion. . . . The empire of the woman is an empire of softness . . . her commands are caresses, her menaces are tears."

Woman should marry, but not for money. She should choose only the high road of true love and not truckle to the values of a materialistic society. A story "Marrying for Money" (subtlety was not the strong point of the ladies' magazines) depicts Gertrude, the heroine, rueing the day she made her crass choice: "It is a terrible thing to live without love. . . . A woman who dares to marry for aught but the purest affection, calls down the just judgments of heaven upon her head."

The corollary to marriage, with or without true love, was motherhood, which added another dimension to her usefulness and her prestige. It also

anchored her even more firmly to the home. "My Friend," wrote Mrs. Sigourney, "If in becoming a mother, you have reached the climax of your happiness, you have also taken a higher place in the scale of being . . . you have gained an increase of power." The Rev. J. N. Danforth pleaded in *The Ladies' Casket,* "Oh, mother, acquit thyself well in thy humble sphere, for thou mayest affect the world." A true woman naturally loved her children; to suggest otherwise was monstrous.

America depended upon her mothers to raise up a whole generation of Christian statesmen who could say "all that I am I owe to my angel mother." The mothers must do the inculcating of virtue since the fathers, alas, were too busy chasing the dollar. Or as *The Ladies' Companion* put it more effusively, the father "weary with the heat and burden of life's summer day, or trampling with unwilling foot the decaying leaves of life's autumn, has forgotten the sympathies of life's joyous springtime. . . . The acquisition of wealth, the advancement of his children in worldly honor—these are his self-imposed tasks." It was his wife who formed "the infant mind as yet untainted by contact with evil . . . like wax beneath the plastic hand of the mother."

The Ladies' Wreath offered a fifty-dollar prize to the woman who submitted the most convincing essay on "How May An American Woman Best Show Her Patriotism." The winner was Miss Elizabeth Wetherell who provided herself with a husband in her answer. The wife in the essay of course asked her husband's opinion. He tried a few jokes first—"Call her eldest son George Washington," "Don't speak French, speak American"—but then got down to telling her in sober prize-winning truth what women could do for their country. Voting was no asset, since that would result only in "a vast increase of confusion and expense without in the smallest degree affecting the result." Besides, continued this oracle, "looking down at their child," if "we were to go a step further and let the children vote, their first act would be to vote their mothers at home." There is no comment on this devastating male logic and he continues: "Most women would follow the lead of their fathers and husbands," and the few who would "fly off on a tangent from the circle of home influence would cancel each other out."

The wife responds dutifully: "I see all that. I never understood so well before." Encouraged by her quick womanly perception, the master of the house resolves the question—an American woman best shows her patriotism by staying at home, where she brings her influence to bear "upon the right side for the country's weal." That woman will instinctively choose the side of right he has no doubt. Besides her "natural refinement and closeness to God" she has the "blessed advantage of a quiet life" while man is exposed to conflict and evil. She stays home with "her Bible and a well-balanced mind" and raises her sons to be good Americans. The judges rejoiced in this conclusion and paid the prize money cheerfully, remarking "they deemed it cheap at the price."

If any woman asked for greater scope for her gifts the magazines were sharply critical. Such women were tampering with society, undermining civilization. Mary Wollstonecraft, Frances Weight, and Harriet Martineau were condemned in the strongest possible language—they were read out of the sex. "They are only semi-women, mental hermaphrodites." The Rev. Harrington knew the women of America could not possibly approve of such perversions and went to some wives and mothers to ask if they did not want a "wider sphere of interest" as these nonwomen claimed. The answer was reassuring. "'NO!' they cried simultaneously, 'Let the men take care of politics, *we will take care of the children!*'" Again female discontent resulted only from a lack of understanding: women were not subservient, they were rather "chosen vessels." Looked at in this light the conclusion was inescapable: "Noble, sublime is the task of the American mother."

"Women's Rights" meant one thing to reformers, but quite another to the True Woman. She knew her rights,

The right to love whom others scorn,
The right to comfort and to mourn,
The right to shed new joy on earth,

The right to feel the soul's high
*   worth . . .*
Such women's rights, and God will bless
And crown their champions with
*   success.*

The American woman had her choice—she could define her rights in the way of the women's magazines and insure them by the practice of the requisite virtues, or she could go outside the home, seeking other rewards than love. It was a decision on which, she was told, everything in her world depended. "Yours it is to determine," the Rev. Mr. Stearns solemnly warned from the pulpit, "whether the beautiful order of society . . . shall continue as it has been" or whether "society shall break up and become a chaos of disjointed and unsightly elements." If she chose to listen to other voices than those of her proper mentors, sought other rooms than those of her home, she lost both her happiness and her power—"that almost magic power, which, in her proper sphere, she now wields over the destinies of the world."

But even while the women's magazines and related literature encouraged this ideal of the perfect woman, forces were at work in the nineteenth century which impelled woman herself to change, to play a more creative role in society. The movements for social reform, westward migration, missionary activity, utopian communities, industrialism, the Civil War—all called forth responses from woman which differed from those she was trained to believe were hers by nature and divine decree. The very perfection of True Womanhood, moreover, carried within itself the seeds of its own destruction. For if woman was so very little less than the angels, she should surely take a more active part in running the world, especially since men were making such a hash of things.

Real women often felt they did not live up to the ideal of True Womanhood: some of them blamed themselves, some challenged the standard, some tried to keep the virtues and enlarge the scope of womanhood. Somehow through this mixture of challenge and acceptance, of change and continuity, the True Woman evolved into the New Woman—a transformation as startling in its way as the abolition of slavery or the coming of the machine age. And yet the stereotype, the "mystique" if you will, of what woman was and ought to be persisted, bringing guilt and confusion in the midst of opportunity.

The women's magazines and related literature had feared this very dislocation of values and blurring of roles. By careful manipulation and interpretation they sought to convince woman that she had the best of both worlds—power and virtue—and that a stable order of society depended upon her maintaining her traditional place in it. To that end she was identified with everything that was beautiful and holy.

"Who Can Find a Valiant Woman?" was asked frequently from the pulpit and the editorial pages. There was only one place to look for her—at home. Clearly and confidently these authorities proclaimed the True Woman of the nineteenth century to be the Valiant Woman of the Bible, in whom the heart of her husband rejoiced and whose price was above rubies.

Study Questions

1. Summarize the "cult of true womanhood" and the behavioral expectations it imposed on American women.

2. Welter argues that the "cult of true womanhood" was an attempt to preserve premodern values in the industrial age. What does she mean? In what sense was industrialization incompatible with the "cult of true womanhood"? Why did the "cult of true womanhood" often leave nineteenth-century women feeling guilty?

3. To what extent was the "cult of true womanhood" an attempt by men in literary circles to prevent women from taking advantage of new opportunities provided by the rise of an industrial society? Was this a conspiracy or an unconscious cultural attempt to prevent change?

4. If the "cult of true womanhood" was indeed an attempt to retard modernization, what were people worried about? If they demanded domesticity, submissiveness, and chastity of women, why did they so fear professionalism, assertiveness, and sexual freedom?

Bibliography

For general histories of the women's movement in the United States, see Andrew Sinclair, *The Better Half* (1965) and Page Smith, *Daughters of the Promised Land* (1970). Important scholarly work has been done on the origins of the feminist movement in early American history. See Barbara J. Berg, *The Remembered Gate: Origins of American Feminism—The Woman and the City, 1800-1860* (1977); Ann Douglas, *The Feminization of American Culture* (1977); and Nancy F. Cott, *The Bonds of Womanhood: "Women's Sphere" in New England, 1780-1835* (1977). Ellen DuBois's *Feminism and Suffrage: The Emergence of an Independent Woman's Movement in America, 1848-1869* (1978) deals with the early years of the crusade for the right to vote and how this crusade led to a much broader demand for equality.

Philip Greven's *The Protestant Temperament* (1977) analyzes family roles and religious training in early America. Also see Barbara Leslie Epstein, *The Politics of Domesticity* (1981); M. P. Ryan, *Womanhood in America* (1983); and Nancy Woloch, *Women and the American Experience* (1984). Also see Harriet B. Apple White and Darlene G. Levy, eds., *Women and Politics in the Age of the Democratic Revolution* (1993); Thomas Dublin, *Women at Work: The Transformation of Work and Community in Lowell, Massachusetts, 1826–1860* (1979); John Mack Faragher, *Sugar Creek: Life on the Illinois Frontier* (1986); Paul E. Johnson and Sean Wilentz, *The Kingdom of Matthias: The Story of Sex and Salvation in Nineteenth-Century America* (1994); and Mary P. Ryan, *Cradle of the Middle Class: The Family in Oneida County, New York, 1790–1865* (1981). Deborah Gray White's *Ar'n't I a Woman?: Female Slaves in the Plantation South* (1985) demonstrates the way black slave women felt about their roles in society and in their families. Christine Stansell's *City of Women: Sex and Class in New York, 1789–1860* (1986) provides a look at the life of urban, working class women. So does Jeanne Boyston's *Home and Work: Housework, Wages, and the Ideology of Labor in the Early Republic* (1990). For the relationship between politics and social attitudes, see Joella Million, *Women's Voice, Women's Place: Lucy Stone and the Birth of Women's Rights* (2003).

READING 16

The Tragedy of Bridget Such-A-One

Peter Quinn

In the summer of 1844, when poor Irish peasants began to harvest their potato crop, they noticed that when exposed to the air, the potato rotted in a matter of hours, the victim of a killer fungus. The Irish soon began to die as well, starving to death by the hundreds of thousands. Since mass death stalked Ireland, it quickly dawned on millions of peasants that emigration was their only hope of survival. Between 1844 and 1860, more than two million Irish peasants emigrated, and most of them ended up in the United States, primarily in the cities of the Northeast, including Boston, New York, Philadelphia, and Baltimore. Their arrival precipitated controversy at every turn. Crowding into the poorest sections of the cities, they became America's first highly visible, ghetto minority, and most well-to-do Americans viewed them with contempt. As devout Roman Catholics, the Irish immigrants struck fear into many Protestants and inspired an anti-Catholic political movement. Finally, because they poured into the Democratic party, they invited the wrath of the Whigs and later the Republicans. It eventually took decades for the Irish to adjust to America and for America to adjust to them.

Walking through the woods outside Concord, Massachusetts, in the spring of 1846, amid his solitary experiment in living close to nature, Henry David Thoreau was driven by a sudden storm to find shelter in what he thought was an uninhabited hut. "But therein," Thoreau recounts in *Walden,* he found living "John Field, an Irishman, and his wife, and several children," and he sat with them "under that part of the roof which leaked the least, while it showered and thundered without."

Thoreau pitied this "honest, hard-working, but shiftless man," a laborer probably drawn to the area to lay track for the railroad and now reduced to clearing bogs for a local farmer. He also "purposely talked to him as if he were a philosopher, or desired to be one." "But alas," Thoreau lamented, "the culture of an Irishman is an enterprise to be undertaken with a sort of moral bog hoe."

Field "heaved a sigh" at Thoreau's suggestions that "if he and his family would live simply, they might go a-huckle-berrying in the summer for their amusement." Field's wife neither sighed nor spoke. A woman of "round greasy face," her breast exposed to suckle an infant, she "stared with arms a-kimbo" at the Yankee in their midst. The Fields left no account of this visit. Yet along with weighing the bewildering improbability of Thoreau's suggestion, it is probable that there were other matters on their minds.

By the spring of 1846 the condition of Ireland was well known. The country was on the edge. Hunger was widespread, and though the Fields may well have been illiterate, they must have shared with fellow immigrants a growing fear of what might happen if the potato failed again, as it had in 1845. Perhaps they had already received pleas from relatives still in Ireland who had sold their livestock or fishing nets to buy the American corn the government had imported. "For the honour of our lord Jasus christ and his Blessed mother," one contemporary letter writer to America cried, "hurry and take us out of this."

Peter Quinn, "The Trajedy of Bridget Such-A-One," *American Heritage,* 48 (December 1997), 36–51.

The Fields themselves were part of a steady stream of Irish who had been heading to North America for more than a century. The so-called Scotch-Irish—mostly Presbyterians from Ulster—were the first to come. They settled in large numbers in Canada and the American South, especially on the westward-moving edge of settlement, away from the low country with its established churches and plantation economy. By 1790 there were at least 250,000 Scotch-Irish in the United States.

After 1815 and the conclusion of the Napoleonic Wars, a steep fall in prices caused an agricultural depression in Ireland. At the same time, the start of widespread canal building in the United States (the Erie Canal was begun in 1817) and the laying of the groundwork for the country's industrial emergence drew more Irish Catholics, men whose sole marketable skill was their ability to wield a spade and whose religion, poverty, and numbers made them immediately suspect. The rough, brute work of canal building presaged the role that unskilled Irish labor would play in railroad construction, road building, and mining. Subject to cyclical employment and low wages, often living in shanties, the Irish were prized for their hard work and resented for what was seen as their proclivity to rowdiness and labor militancy.

The numbers of unskilled Irish in the cities along the Eastern seaboard grew. They lived where they worked, near the docks, foundries, and warehouses, in decaying housing that the former residents had fled or in flimsy, crowded structures erected to bring a maximum profit to their owners. By the early 1840s the increasing presence of the Catholic Irish helped prompt such prominent Americans as Samuel F. B. Morse, the inventor of the telegraph, and Lyman Beecher, progenitor of Harriet Beecher Stowe, to sound the tocsin against a supposed Catholic plot to subvert the liberties of native (i.e., white Protestant) Americans. A Boston mob attacked and burned a Catholic convent in Charlestown in 1834. In the spring of 1844 a nativist rally in Philadelphia ended in a three-day riot in which two Catholic churches, a convent, and a library were torched and a dozen people were left dead.

All this was prelude to the transformation that the Irish Famine brought. The famine represented the greatest concentration of civilian suffering and death in Western Europe between the Thirty Years' War and World War II. It rearranged the physical and mental landscape of Ireland, sweeping away a language and a way of life, and within a generation made a people steeped in rural traditions into the most urbanized ethnic group in North America.

Of the eight and a half million people in Ireland in 1845, a million perished from hunger and the fever and disease that stalked, jackal-like, in its wake. Between 1845 and 1855, in an unprecedented movement of people that was often less an organized migration than a panic, a mass unraveling, more than two million people left for England and Australia and the great majority for North America.

It was part of the continuum of the transatlantic movement of people, but the famine migration was also different and extraordinary. Particularly in the densely populated townlands of the south and west of Ireland, where the bonds of culture and community went deep, the famine broke the traditional ties of Irish society. More people left Ireland in the decade of the famine than had in the previous 250 years. The exodus from Cork, Tipperary, Kerry, Galway, Clare, Mayo, and Donegal became a self-perpetuating process of removal. It swept aside all the old reluctance of the people to let go of their one hope for survival—the land—and made emigration an expectation rather than an exception.

Just as the mass flight of the famine years dissolved the underpinnings of the Irish countryside, its impact on America was profound. From independence to 1845 the Republic had absorbed about 1.6 million immigrants, the great majority Protestants looking to settle on the land. The annual number of Irish arriving in the United States tripled between 1843 and 1846, from 23,000 to 70,000. By 1851 it had reached a peak of 219,000, almost ten times what it had been less than a decade before.

Between 1845 and 1855 Irish Catholic immigration approached that of all groups over the previous seventy years, and the condition of these Irish sometimes bore more resemblance to modern-day "boat people" than to the immigrants arriving from Germany and Scandinavia. In an 1855 address to the Massachusetts legislature, Gov. Henry J. Gardner went back to classical history to find a comparable event. The scale of Irish immigration and the inmates it had deposited in the commonwealth's prisons and asylums called to mind, the governor said, the "horde of foreign barbarians" that had overthrown the Roman Empire.

The cause of this influx was the blight that attacked the potatoes of Ireland in the late summer of 1845. It is estimated that the potato crop represented about 60 percent of Ireland's annual food supply. Almost three and a half million people relied on it for the biggest part of their diet. The dreadful implications of a sudden and universal threat to the potato, which were instantaneously clear to Irish laborers and government officials alike, threw into dramatic relief the precarious condition of large parts of the population even in the best of times.

A decade earlier, in 1835, Alexis de Tocqueville had made a tour of Ireland. "You cannot imagine," he wrote his father soon after landing, "what a complexity of miseries five centuries of oppression, civil disorder, and religious hostility have piled on this poor people." The poverty he subsequently witnessed was, he recorded, "such as I did not imagine existed in this world. It is a frightening thing, I assure you, to see a whole population reduced to fasting like Trappists, and not being sure of surviving to the next harvest, which is still not expected for another ten days." The same year as Tocqueville's visit, a German traveler in Kilkenny, in the relatively prosperous eastern part of the country, watched as a mother collected the skins of gooseberries that had been spit on the ground and fed them to her child.

Among the more unusual witnesses to the extent of Irish poverty was Asenath Nicholson, a widowed American temperance crusader and Protestant evangelist, who arrived from New York on the eve of the famine to distribute Bibles among the Catholic poor and stayed to become a one-woman relief expedition. Mrs. Nicholson told of giving a "sweet biscuit" to an obviously famished child, who held it in her hand and stared at it. "How is it," Mrs. Nicholson asked the child's mother, "she cannot be hungry?" The mother replied that the child had never seen such a delicacy before and "cannot think of parting with it." Mrs. Nicholson marveled that "such self-denial in a child was quite beyond my comprehension, but so inured are these people to want, that their endurance and self-control are almost beyond belief."

The anecdotes of visitors were confirmed by a commission of inquiry formed to study the extent of Irish poverty. Reporting in 1835, the commission noted that two-fifths of the population lived in "fourth-class accommodations"—one-room windowless mud cabins—and at least two and a half million people annually required some assistance in order to avoid starvation.

Although central to Irish life, the potato was a relatively recent ecological interloper. It is said to have been introduced in Cork in the 1580s by Sir Walter Raleigh, a principal in the plantation of both Ireland and the New World. Until the potato arrived, cattle and oats were the Irish mainstays. The land itself was divided among an amalgam of Gaelic and Norman-Gaelic lords, who were often feuding with one another. In the east a wedge of English-controlled territory—the Pale—had variously expanded and contracted since its conquest by the Normans.

The Atlantic explorations, the contest for overseas empire, and the bitter ideological divisions that accompanied the Reformation conferred on Ireland a new strategic importance. Beginning in the 1540s and extending through a long series of bloody wars and rebellions that ended in the defeat of the Catholic forces in 1691, Ireland was brought under the control of the English crown. Political power and ownership of the land were relentlessly concentrated in the hands of a Protestant ascendancy. The widespread dislocation caused by the long struggle for mastery of Ireland opened the way for the spread of the hardy, reliable, nutritionally rich potato, which not only

thrived in the cool, damp climate but yielded, per acre, three times the calories of grain.

Between 1700 and 1845, thanks in large part to the potato, a populace of less than three million grew to almost eight and a half million, to the point where Disraeli pronounced Ireland the most thickly peopled country in Europe. However, the population distribution was uneven. In pre-famine Ireland the general rule was: The worse the land, the more people on it. The greatest growth was in reclaimed bogs and on mountainsides. The number of small tenant farmers and laborers soared, particularly in the west, where the scramble for land drove an intense process of reclamation and subdivision.

The unit of Irish settlement was the *clachan* or *baile,* a cluster of cabins unlike the neatly laid-out village of school, shop, and church found throughout most of the British Isles. The *clachan* was a collection of families, often tied by friendship or blood, organized around a communal system of agriculture designed to ensure a fair distribution of the best land for tillage. The usually Irish-speaking culture of the *clachan* was carried on in the lives of the people, in storytelling, music, and dance, and in wakes, religious devotions, and fairs.

Like the potato, the fungus that destroyed it came from the Americas. In 1843 potato crops in the eastern United States were largely ruined by a mysterious blight. In June of 1845 the blight was reported in the Low Countries. In mid-September an English journal announced "with very great regret" that the blight had "unequivocally declared itself" in Ireland, then posed the question that anyone even passingly acquainted with the country knew must be faced: "Where will *Ireland* be, in the event of a universal potato rot?" The speed of the blight bewildered observers. Over and over they expressed amazement at how fields lush with potato plants could the next day be putrid wastelands. It was a generation before the agent of destruction was fingered as a spore-spreading fungus, *Phytophthora infestans,* and a generation after that before an antidote was devised.

Without prospect of a cure, Sir Robert Peel, the Tory prime minister, faced a crisis in Ireland. The appearance of the blight in late summer meant two-thirds of the potatoes had already been harvested, yet the near-total reliance of a sizable part of the population on a single crop left no doubt that extraordinary measures would have to be taken. Peel was an able administrator, knowledgeable about Ireland and its discontents. Responding quickly to the impending food crisis, he ordered the secret purchase of a hundred thousand pounds' worth of American corn to be held in reserve and released into the market when demand threatened to drive food prices out of control. This same supply was to be available for purchase, at cost, by local relief committees. Landlord-directed committees were set up to cooperate with the Board of Works in funding work schemes. The aim was to provide tenants and laborers with the chance to earn the money they needed to buy imported food and avoid direct government handouts that would encourage what was seen as the congenital laziness of the Irish.

In December 1845, in order to lower grain prices, Peel proposed repeal of the Corn Laws, import duties that protected British agriculture from foreign competition. He was convinced that increased competition would result in lowering the price of food for the British working classes, which it did. Cheap imports would not only lessen the immediate threat of mass hunger but help wean the poor from reliance on the potato and transform small tenants into landless, wage-earning laborers. As a result of Peel's relief measures, Ireland averted the worst consequences of the blight through the winter of 1845–46. The weather was unusually cold. The poorhouses began to fill up. The poor exhausted whatever reserves they may have had. But starvation was held at bay.

The repeal of the Corn Laws in June 1846 quickly precipitated the fall of Peel's government. Lord Russell, the new Whig prime minister, faced a more daunting challenge than had Peel. The return of the blight for a second year, and the devastation of three-quarters of the potato crop, drove thousands more on to the public works. In August 1846 the works were temporarily halted and overhauled along lines set down by Charles Trevelyan, the head permanent civil servant in the Treasury. The rules of employment were made stricter, and more of the cost was put on local landlords. By October the public works employed 114,000; three months later, in January 1847, more than 500,000; by March, 750,000. Reports of extreme suffering and death began to pour in from different parts of the country. In Skibbereen, County Cork, an artist sent by the *Illustrated London News* testified that neither pictures nor words could capture the horror of "the dying, the living, and the dead, lying indiscriminately upon the same floor, without anything between them and the cold earth, save a few miserable rags upon them."

The American temperance worker Asenath Nicholson got her first view of the worsening condition of Ireland in the outskirts of Dublin. In December 1846 a servant in a house where she was staying implored her to see a man nearby, the father of seven, who, though sick with fever and "in an actual state of starvation," had "staggered with his spade" to the public works. The servant brought in a human skeleton "emaciated to the last degree." Horrified as she was, Mrs. Nicholson would remember this as only "the *first* and the beginning of . . . dreadful days yet in reserve."

Daunted by the expense of the public works, the government decided to switch to soup kitchens, a form of relief introduced by the Quakers. The public works began to close in March. By midsummer of 1847 three million men, women, and children were being fed with soup. An indication of the government's capacity to restrain the ravages of hunger, the soup kitchens were the apogee of the relief effort—and its effective end.

Writing in *Blackwood's Magazine* in April 1847, a commentator complained of the expense being incurred to help the Irish. The famine was not an English problem, he wrote, and there was no need for wasting another shilling on a disaster "which the heedlessness and indolence of the Irish had brought upon themselves." A month earlier the *Times* of London had expressed a similar sense of the widespread frustration with the Irish, again connecting Ireland's agony to the innate defects of its people: "The Celt is less energetic, less independent, less industrious than the Saxon. This is the archaic condition of his race. . . . [England] can, therefore, afford to look with contemptuous pity on the Celtic cottier suckled in poverty which he is too callous to feel, and too supine to mend."

Since the abolition of the Dublin parliament in 1801, Ireland had theoretically been an integral part of the United Kingdom, its people entitled to the same protections and considerations as those of English shires. But as the famine made inexorably clear, Ireland remained a colony, one usually viewed as a turbulent, perplexing, intractable anomaly.

During the period immediately preceding the famine, Daniel O'Connell, who had led the agitation in the 1820s that won Catholics the right to sit in Parliament, had headed a movement to repeal the union with Britain and return a measure of self-rule to Dublin. The union was maintained, but now, in the face of Ireland's continuing distress, a tired, broken O'Connell told the House of Commons: "Ireland is in your hands. If you do not save her, she cannot save herself." His plea went unheeded. As framed by Sir Charles Wood, the chancellor of the exchequer, the challenge was no longer to help feed the Irish but "to force them into self-government . . . our song . . . must be—'It is your concern, not ours.'"

The potato didn't fail in the summer of 1847, yet the distress of the past two seasons had seriously curtailed the scale of plantings. Trevelyan, however, convinced that Ireland's problem wasn't inadequate food supplies but "the selfish, perverse and turbulent character of the people," pronounced the famine over. There would be no more extraordinary measures by the Treasury, not even when the potato failed again in 1848, 1849, and into the early 1850s. Irish needs would be met out of Irish resources.

The government's change of direction went beyond the withdrawal of desperately needed assistance. The passage in June 1847 of the Irish Poor Law Extension Act married racial contempt and providentialism—the prevalent conviction

Irish Women

among the British elite of God's judgment having been delivered on the Irish—with political economy. According to the theorists of the iron laws of economics, the great deficiencies of Ireland were a want of capital accumulation—the result of the maze of small tenancies—and the incurable lethargy of a people inured to indolent reliance on an inferior food. The famine provided an opportunity to sweep away the root causes of Ireland's economic backwardness.

The amendment of the Irish Poor Law made landlords responsible for the rates (taxes collected to support the workhouses) on all holdings valued under four pounds per year. Another provision—the Gregory Clause—denied relief to anyone holding more than a quarter-acre of land. This left many tenants with the choice of abandoning their holdings or condemning their families to starvation. Together these clauses were a mandate to clear the land of the poorest and most vulnerable. Entire villages were "tumbled." In one instance a newspaper reported that some of the evicted were found dead along the roadsides, "emitting green froth from their mouths, as if masticating soft grass." On the Mullet Peninsula in

Mayo, James Hack Tuke, a Quaker involved in the intensive relief effort undertaken by the Society of Friends, witnessed an entire settlement being razed: "Six or seven hundred people were evicted; young and old, mother and babe, were alike cast forth, without shelter and without means of subsistence! A fountain of ink (as one of them said) would not write half our misfortunes."

Asenath Nicholson traveled some of the same territory as Tuke and was horrified by the sheer scale of what she witnessed: "Village upon village, and company after company, have I seen; and one magistrate who was travelling informed me that at night-fall the preceding day, he found a company who had gathered a few sticks and fastened them into a ditch, and spread over what miserable rags they could collect . . . under these more than two hundred men, women, and children, were to crawl for the night . . . and not *one* pound of any kind of food was in the whole encampment."

Across much of Ireland the purgatory of the first two years of famine became a living hell. The workhouses, which the people had once done their best to avoid, were besieged by mobs clamoring to get in. The dead were buried coffinless in mass graves. The Reverend Francis Webb, a Church of Ireland rector in West Cork, published an account of dead children being left unburied and asked in anger and disbelief, "Are we living in a portion of the United Kingdom?" Asiatic cholera, carried from India in the bowels of British soldiers, eventually arrived and cut down thousands of those already weakened by hunger.

Emigration from Ireland became a torrent, no longer a quest for new opportunities but a question of life or death. The ports filled with people. Most sought passage to Liverpool, the former capital of the slave trade and now the entrepôt of emigration. From there they hoped to find a cheap fare to America. Jammed in the holds of coal barges and on the decks of cattle boats, three hundred thousand Irish sailed to Liverpool in 1847 alone.

The government made a pretense of enforcing regulations that prescribed medical inspection of all passengers and minimum space and rations for each. In reality emigrants, having scrambled how-

ever they could to put together the four pounds that passage to America typically cost, were at the mercy of a laissez-faire system that treated them more like ballast than like human beings. Dr. J. Custis, who served as a ship's surgeon on half a dozen emigrant vessels, published a series of articles that described their sailings: "I have been engaged during the worst years of famine in Ireland; I have witnessed the deaths of hundreds from want; I have seen the inmates of a workhouse carried by the hundreds weekly through its gates to be thrown unshrouded and coffinless into a pit with quicklime . . . and revolting to the feelings as all this was, it was not half so shocking as what I subsequently witnessed on board the very first emigrant ship I ever sailed on."

During a journey in steerage of anywhere from three to seven weeks, disease, seasickness, spoiled rations, hostile crews, and a lack of space and air—an experience one observer compared to "entering a crowded jail"—eroded whatever differences of region or accent or status once had divided the emigrants. By the time they landed, it was easy for nativists to lump them together as a race of feckless Paddies destined to be a permanent drain on American resources.

The reaction to the arrival of growing numbers of impoverished, famished immigrants wasn't long in coming. Congress tightened the regulations that governed passenger ships entering American ports and raised the fines on violators. Massachusetts began to enforce a law requiring that before any pauper or sick person was landed on its shores, the ship's master had to post a bond for every passenger. New York also required a bond and leveled a per person tax to cover the cost of those who became public charges. The net effect was that in the spring of 1847 a significant portion of the first wave of famine migrants left not for the United States but for British North America.

The demand for passage resulted in a hodgepodge of vessels being pressed into service. Poorly provisioned, devoid of medicines or sanitary facilities, crowded with hungry, fever-ridden passengers, they quickly developed a well-earned reputation as "coffin ships." In May 1847 the first of them arrived at a quarantine station, with a small hospital that had been set up on Grosse Île, in the St. Lawrence, thirty miles below Quebec. Out of a company of 240 passengers, 80 were down with typhus, and 9 already dead. By June nearly forty vessels were backed up for miles along the river, and 14,000 people awaited quarantine. The dead were buried in mass graves. By the end of the sailing season, the British government's conservative estimate was that of the 107,000 who had left for Canada from British ports, 17,500—one out of every six—had died.

Despite the barriers raised by American ports, the overwhelming majority of famine emigrants sought passage to the United States, for few wished to remain under British dominion. Even in 1847, as many as 25,000 immigrants arrived in Boston from British ports, and at least another 5,000 managed to find their way down from Canada. New York received the greatest number. Between 1845 and 1855, a million Irish—one-eighth of the country's population—landed on the wharves and piers around Manhattan. Many moved on. But many stayed, helping swell the city's population from 370,000 to 630,000 in a single decade.

The voyage to the United States wasn't characterized by the same catalogue of horrors as the emigration to Canada in 1847, but it was ordeal enough. Stephen de Vere, an Anglo-Irish gentleman with an interest in emigration, sailed to New York aboard the *Washington,* a well-built ship, in 1847. He watched the passengers in steerage being physically abused and denied the rations they were supposedly due. When he protested, the first mate knocked him to the deck. Taking his complaint to the captain, de Vere was threatened with the brig. Dysentery was rampant on the ship; a dozen children died from it. On landing, de Vere collected accounts of similar abuse aboard other ships and wrote a complaint to the emigration commissioners in London. In the end nothing was done.

One of the most compelling renderings of the emigrant trade in the famine era was by an American whose introduction to the sea was aboard a packet ship between Liverpool and New York. Herman Melville was nineteen when he made the voyage out and back in 1839. Ten years later, in 1849, he published *Redburn,* an account of his journey that is part fiction, part memoir, and part meditation on the changes that the mass descent of strangers was bringing to America. Though a novel, the book is alive with a real sense of the grandeur and misery of Liverpool and of the unromantic business of hauling five hundred emigrants across the Atlantic in a creaking, swaying, wind-driven ship.

The emigrants aboard Melville's fictional ship, the *Highlander,* were mostly Irish, and like many real emigrant ships, the *Highlander* wasn't built for passengers but was converted to that purpose. Triple tiers of bunks jerry-built along the ship's sides "looked more like dog-kennels than anything else" and soon smelled little different. "We had not been at sea one week," the protagonist, Wellingborough Redburn, observed, "when to hold your head down the fore hatchway was like holding it down a suddenly opened cesspool." Driven by hunger, some of the passengers stole a small pig, and "*him* they devoured raw, not venturing to make an incognito of his carcass." Fever struck. Emigrants began to die. Venturing down into steerage, Redburn encountered "rows of rude bunks, hundreds of meager, begrimed faces were turned upon us. . . . the native air of the place . . . was foetid in the extreme."

Docked at last on South Street, crew and passengers dispersed. As they left, young Redburn wondered at the fate of those who had survived the gauntlet of hunger and emigration but now seemed exhausted and broken: "How, then, with these emigrants, who, three thousand miles from home, suddenly found themselves, deprived of brothers and husbands, with but a few pounds, or perhaps but a few shillings, to buy food in a strange land?"

Other Americans shared such doubts, and for many the answer was that the Catholic Irish were a threat to the country's prosperity and liberty. Nativists focused on Irish poverty as a function of Irish character, a result of their addiction to "rum and Romanism." When the Irish banded together to form religious, fraternal, and labor organizations aimed at improving their lot, this was taken as proof of their conspiratorial clannishness. Near the end of the famine decade, in 1854, the American party, which was formed to halt the incursion of foreigners and Catholics, controlled the legislatures of most New England states as well as those of Maryland, Delaware, Kentucky, New Jersey, Pennsylvania, and California. For a time it was the most successful third-party movement in American history.

The poverty of the Irish, while only a part of the famine story, was not merely a figment of the nativist imagination. The cities of the Northeast faced problems of public order that wouldn't be repeated until after World War II. The newcomers didn't invent street gangs or rioting or machine politics—all pre-dated the arrival of the famine Irish—but the deluge of masses of disoriented, disorganized, unskilled alien labor raised an unprecedented sense of alarm. In 1851 it was estimated that one out of every six New Yorkers was a pauper. Of the 113,000 people residing in jails, workhouses, hospitals, or asylums or receiving public or private charity, three-quarters were foreign-born, the bulk of them Irish.

New York State formally opened its first immigrant depot in 1855 at Castle Garden, its purpose to bring order to the process of arrival. Three decades later, under federal control, the depot was moved to Ellis Island. Golden or not, the door America erected at its entryway was a legacy of the famine.

By the autumn of 1849, when Melville wrote of the travails of his company of tired and poor Irish immigrants, Asiatic cholera had arrived in New York. It spread as far west as St. Louis and took thousands of lives. At that same moment, two real-life immigrants reached American shores, and, for all their differences—one was an ex-policeman fleeing arrest, the other a young woman seeking work—they embodied much of the pain and the promise of the famine years.

Michael Corcoran was the son of an Irishman who had made a career in the Royal Army. In 1845, at the age of eighteen, Corcoran joined the Revenue Police, which, along with the Irish Constabulary, was organized along military lines. He was posted to Donegal to help suppress the trade in illicit liquor. The advent of the famine heightened the role of the constabulary and the army in Ireland, already the most policed and garrisoned part of the British Isles. By 1848 their combined total was at an all-time high of forty thousand—almost twice the size of the expeditionary force that the British government would soon send to the Crimea at a cost nine times what it spent on famine relief in Ireland.

Whether Corcoran, as a member of the Revenue Police, was called to the support of the army or constabulary is unknown. Both forces were active during the famine, especially in areas like Donegal. They helped distribute relief as well as guarantee the all-important rights of property. In the latter capacity they not only assisted in mass clearances but guarded the convoys that carried grain and beef to England throughout the famine. The image of those convoys became a touchstone of Irish bitterness in later years, alleged proof of the charge leveled by the Irish nationalist John Mitchel that "the Almighty indeed sent the potato blight, but the English created the Famine."

Over the course of the famine, more grain may have entered Ireland than left. But often the imports didn't reach the most distressed parts of the country, or were spoiled by the time they did. Unfamiliar with processing or cooking the yellow corn imported from America, people were made sick by it. The memory of soldiers and police guarding precious stores of food from the starving wasn't an invention. Mrs. Nicholson testified to the sight of well-fed, well-armed soldiers and "haggard, meagre, squalid skeletons . . . grouped in starving multitudes around them." In 1847—"Black '47," the Irish called it—two thousand people were transported to Australia for cattle stealing. On Spike Island, in Cork Harbor, three hundred adolescents were imprisoned for "taking bread while starving."

Whatever Corcoran witnessed or took part in as a policeman may have been part of what led him to break his oath to the Crown. In August 1849 he was "relinquished" from his duties on suspicion of belonging to one of the secret agrarian societies that were violently resisting evictions. Before he could be arrested, he slipped aboard an emigrant ship and escaped to New York. There was little to distinguish him from his fellow immigrants when he landed in October 1849. But he quickly made a name for himself. He got work in a tavern and became a district leader for Tammany Hall, which was just awakening to the potential of the Irish vote, and he was an early member of the Fenian Brotherhood, the secret Irish revolutionary society fueled by the burning intent to revenge the famine and overthrow British rule in Ireland.

Five years after he arrived, Corcoran was elected a captain in a heavily Irish militia unit, the 69th New York. Not long afterward he was commended for helping defend the quarantine station on Staten Island, which a mob had attempted to burn. In 1860 the Prince of Wales (the future Edward VII) paid the first visit by a member of the royal family to the United States. The militia was ordered to parade in the prince's honor; Corcoran, now the colonel of the 69th, refused to march his men for someone they called the "Famine Prince." He was court-martialed for what in many eyes confirmed the worst suspicions of Irish disloyalty to American institutions.

The outbreak of the Civil War saved Corcoran from being cashiered. He returned to his regiment, which he commanded at Bull Run, where he was badly wounded and captured. Freed a year later in a prisoner exchange, he returned to service as head of his own "Irish Legion." He again fell under an official cloud when he shot and killed an officer who had not only assaulted him, Corcoran said, but had called him "a damned Irish son of a bitch." Before any official judgment could be reached, Corcoran died—partly as the result of his wounds—and was given a hero's funeral in New York.

As with generations of immigrants to come, Irish and otherwise, Corcoran was eager for the opportunities that America had to offer and grateful when they proved real. He readily took on American citizenship and showed no hesitation about defending the Union. Yet he was equally unwilling to turn his back on the culture and people that had formed him. Fiercely loyal to his new homeland, he had no intention of abandoning his religion, disguising his ancestry, or detaching himself from the struggles of his native land. No one who observed Michael Corcoran could doubt that a powerful new element had been added to the American mix.

The month Michael Corcoran landed in New York, October 1849, Henry David Thoreau traveled to Cohasset, Massachusetts, to see the wreck of the *St. John,* a Boston-bound brig that had set sail from Ireland "laden with emigrants." It was one of sixty emigrant ships lost between 1847 and 1853. Thoreau walked the beach and inspected the bodies collected there: "I saw many marble feet and matted heads as the cloths were raised, and one livid, swollen and mangled body of a drowned girl,—who probably had intended to go out to service in some American family. . . . Sometimes there were two or more children, or a parent and child, in the same box, and on the lid would perhaps be written with red chalk, 'Bridget such-a-one, and sister's child.'"

Besides what Thoreau tells us of the drowned girl, we know only that she sailed from Galway, part of a legion of Bridget such-a-ones. It's possible that coming from the west, she was an Irish speaker; more than a third of the famine emigrants were. Perhaps she had relatives waiting for her. Perhaps not. Yet her corpse points to a larger story than the perils of the Atlantic crossing or the travails of a single season of immigrants. The dissolution of Irish rural life resulted in a bleak, narrow society of late marriage and of dowries carefully passed to single heirs, encouraging the young, especially girls, to emigrate. No other group of nineteenth-century immigrants had nearly the proportion of women as the Irish reached in the aftermath of the famine: more than 50 percent.

Encouraged, even expected, to make a contribution to the welfare of the parents and siblings they had left behind, Irishwomen worked in factories and mills. Irish maids became a fixture of bourgeois American life. Domestic service became so associated with the Irish that maids were often referred to generically as "Kathleens" or "Bridgets." The work could be demeaning as well as demanding. In 1845 the antislavery crusader Abby Kelley visited fellow abolitionists in Pennsylvania. Her hosts' Irish servant girl came to her in private and catalogued the work she had to perform for a dollar a week. "When I tried to console her and told her that we were trying to bring about a better state of things," Kelley wrote, "a state in which she would be regarded as an equal, she wept like a child."

Female employment was a source of independence and adaptation to American life, but above all, it was a wellspring of the money that poured back into Ireland, rescuing families from starvation and financing a self-perpetuating chain of emigration that would stretch across generations. At the height of the famine, Mrs. Nicholson marveled that "the Irish in America, and in all other countries where they are scattered, were sending one continued train of remittances, to the utter astonishment of the Postmasters." In the famine decade more than £8.4 million was remitted for passage out of the British Isles. The British colonial secretary was delighted that the outflow of Irish was being funded at no expense to the government and surprised to discover that "such feelings of family affection, and such fidelity and firmness of purpose, should exist so generally among the lower classes." In Massachusetts, Edward Everett Hale was struck by the generosity of the Irish but worried that their "clannish" spirit of sharing might drag them down together. "For example," he wrote, "it is within my own observation, that in the winter of 1850 to 1851, fourteen persons, fresh from Ireland, came in on the cabin hospitality of a woman in Worcester, because she was the cousin of one of the party."

The strains of adjustment to America were enormous. The itinerant work of railroad building, which many took part in, and high rates of disease, accidental death, and alcohol abuse put tremendous pressure on families. Irishwomen were more likely to be widowed or deserted than their American counterparts. But amid the epic transformation of potato-growing tenants into urban laborers, moving from the tightly woven fabric of Irish townlands to the freewheeling environment of American cities, what was most remarkable of all was the speed and scope with which the Irish reorganized themselves. Within little more than a generation they translated their numbers into control of the Democratic party in the major cities and turned municipal patronage into an immediate and pragmatic method for softening the ravages of boom-and-bust capitalism. Barred from the privileged circle of high finance, equipped with few entrepreneurial skills, suspicious through experience of theories that made capital accumulation a supreme good, the Irish spearheaded the rise of organized labor.

The greatest manifestation of their effort to regroup was the Catholic Church, which was elevated from an ingredient in Irish life to its center, the bulwark of a culture that had lost its language and almost disintegrated beneath the catastrophe of the famine. In America as well as Ireland, vocations to the priesthood and sisterhood soared. Catholic parishes became the defining institution of Irish neighborhoods. Catholic schools, hospitals, and asylums created a vast social welfare network. Catholic nuns founded protectories and orphanages that countered the placing-out system, which took hundreds of thousands of immigrant children and shipped them west to "Christian" (Protestant) homes. Eventually these institutions were influential in establishing the obligation of the state to the support of dependent children.

The Catholic Church was the strongest institutional link in the exodus from Ireland and adjustment to America. It was *the* enduring monument to the effects of the famine: to the sexual repression and religious devotionalism that followed it; to the quest for respectability amid jarring dislocation and pervasive discrimination; and to the discipline, cohesion, and solidarity that allowed the Irish to survive, progress, and eventually reach undreamed-of levels of success. Only after a century and a half, when the Irish had erased almost every trace of their once seemingly ineradicable status as outsiders, would the power of the church begin to wane.

For Irish Catholics in America, the famine was the forge of their identity, fire and anvil, the scattering time of flight and dissolution, and the moment of regathering that would one day make them an influential part of the world's most powerful democracy. The famine was rarely recalled in its specifics. There was no record made of its horrors or complexities. The blistering humiliations it inflicted and the divisions it exacerbated—the way it fell hardest on the landless Irish-speaking poor—were subsumed in a bitter and near-universal detestation of British rule in Ireland. Yet, unspoken, unexamined, largely lost to conscious memory, the famine was threaded into Irish America's attitudes, expectations, and institutions. The Irish-American film director John Ford said that he was drawn to making the movie version of *The Grapes of Wrath* because in the Depression-era saga of Okies evicted from the land and left to wander and starve he recognized the story of his own ancestors.

For America as well the famine was a time of testing. As Herman Melville saw it, the immigrants arriving unchecked on the docks of New York were a sign that America would be "not a nation, so much as a world." The greatness and genius of America wasn't in reproducing the ethnic sameness of Britain or France, he wrote. The world had no need of more pure-blooded tribes or xenophobic nationalities. Bereft of wealth or education or Anglo-Saxon pedigree, what Bridget such-a-one and all the other nameless, tired, hope-filled immigrants carried with them was the opportunity for America to affirm its destiny: "We are the heirs of all time, and with all nations we divide our inheritance. On this Western Hemisphere all tribes and people are forming into federated whole; and there is a future which shall see the estranged children of Adam restored as to the old hearth-stone in Eden."

Study Questions

1. Even before the onset of the potato famine, the economy of Ireland was in decline. Why?

2. The U.S. economy attracted Irish workers before the onset of the potato famine. Why?

3. How did native Americans respond to the Irish influx? Why?

4. How important was the potato in the Irish economy? Why was the potato fungus such a catastrophe for the Irish poor?

5. What was life like for the typical peasant in Ireland?

6. How did the British government respond to the potato famine?

7. How did many Americans explain the poverty of the Irish?

8. What did the term "Bridgets" or "Kathleens" mean and how did they come to be applied to the Irish?

Bibliography

The literature on antebellum immigration to the United States is extensive, but the scholarly work on Irish immigrants has been particularly rich. Among the best of these are Thomas B. Brown, *Irish-American Nationalism, 1870–1900* (1966); Dennis Clark, *The Irish in Philadelphia* (1973); Steven P. Erie, *Rainbow's End: Irish-Americans and the Dilemmas of Urban Machine Politics, 1840–1985* (1988); Andrew M. Greeley, *That Most Distressful Nation: The Taming of the American Irish* (1972); Lawrence McCaffery, *The Irish Diaspora in America* (1976); and Kirby A. Miller, *Emigrants and Exiles: Ireland and the Irish Exodus to North America* (1985). Also see Hasia Diner, *Erin's Daughters in America* (1983) and Noel Ignatiev, *How the Irish Became White* (1995). Also see Reginald Byron, *Irish America* (1999); Arthur Gribben, *The Great Famine and the Irish Diaspora in America* (1999); and J. Matthew Gilman, *Erin's Children: Philadelphia, Liverpool, and the Irish Famine Migration, 1845–1855* (2000).

READING 17

Folklore and Life Experience

Arnoldo De León and Saul Sanchez

Although Hispanic values are deeply rooted in American culture, more than three centuries of contact in the Southwest have produced little understanding between Anglos and their Spanish-speaking neighbors. A tenuous accommodation has replaced the violence of the nineteenth century, but an enormous gulf of suspicion, ignorance, and confusion still divides Anglos and Mexican Americans. Until recently, historians and anthropologists have reinforced the misunderstandings by giving ethnocentrism an intellectual legitimacy. Writing always from an Anglo perspective, albeit a liberal one, they have described Mexicans as a pleasant but inscrutable people, blessed with a love of life but cursed with a cultural malaise, a fatalism enabling them to survive tragedy but crippling any hope for triumph. Passive and childlike, ready to accept the course of history and quietly absorb stress, Mexicans were, according to the scholarly stereotype, unwilling and incapable of influencing their environment. Success, vertical mobility, and entrepreneurial opportunity were hopelessly beyond them.

But just as a new generation of historians have rewritten the African-American past, so too have young scholars taken another look at Mexican-American ethnicity. The foremost revisionary work was Arnoldo De León's *The Tejano Community, 1836–1900,* a study of Spanish-speaking people in nineteenth-century Texas. Combining the research techniques of history and anthropology with a Hispanic perspective, De León rejects the long-held notion of Mexican passivity and fatalism. Instead, he portrays a people who confidently exercised great control over their cultural and physical world through hard work, a vibrant folk culture and ethnoreligion, and strong extended families. These were hardly the hapless and helpless people of so many scholarly discourses. This selection from De León's work clearly illustrates the richness and vitality of Tejano culture.

Historians searching for the role of folklore in the lives of Tejanos confront serious difficulties. Generally speaking, Mexicanos, like other poor and illiterate classes, did not record their lore; historians who seek access to this oral tradition have to rely upon what Mexicanos related to inquisitive whites. Although these compilations are reliable, what Mexicans relayed to these collectors must be scrutinized rigorously. It is possible, for instance, that Mexicanos did not trust the interviewers and told them only what they wanted to hear. In addition, Tejanos may have been reluctant to relate tales that verged on the pornographic or those that revealed intimate feelings about race and other features of Mexican-American culture that they believed whites could not comprehend. The tales, moreover, surely lost something in the cultural and linguistic translation. Anglo folklorists could not have captured the teller's intonation, stress, chants, and mimicking, all of which are common to Mexican-American storytelling traditions.

Equally disturbing for the historian and folklorist is that these legends, myths, and other tales, collected in the twentieth century, forfeited the flavor of their nineteenth-century milieu. Yet, grouped together from different sources and different times, they give a clearer indication of the part folklore played in the belief system and world view that characterized nineteenth-century Mexican Americans.

In Texas, itinerants, historians, journalists, and other observers recorded the folklore of the state's Spanish-speaking community. But all historians owe a debt to the Texas Folklore Society for its indefatigable efforts in collecting Mexican-American materials. Organized in 1909, issuing its first volume in 1916, and continuing until the present, the Society regularly published scores of items relating to Tejano life. Long uninterpreted

From "Folklore and Life Experience" by Arnoldo De León and Saul Sanchez in *The Tejano Community, 1836–1900* by Arnoldo De León, pp. 156–171. Copyright © 1982 by the University of New Mexico Press. All rights reserved. Reprinted by permission.

or simply ignored, these and other collections reveal the views of a preindustrial folk as they came into contact with the predominantly agrarian society. They reveal not the behavior of a people living in the culture of poverty, but rather the culture of Tejanos who just happened to be poor. They identify the autonomous spirit of a community socialized, partly by choice, partly by force, as Mexican American.

Folklore provided an intrinsic survival tool for Tejanos; it identified them with the past and thus with an experience at once contiguous and familiar. It gave them a sense of history and thus the psychological affirmation necessary to endure in a setting that constantly reminded them that they came from practically nothing.

Because Tejano folklore was firmly planted in the Texas pre-Revolutionary War experience, it lent a profound sense of cultural continuity traceable to Mexico's colonial period. Legends about buried treasures, the naming of places, the origin of certain plants, miracles, and events involving the presence of Spaniards all related to Spanish themes, settings, characters, and the like.

No other aspects of folklore revealed the legacy of the Spanish experience as much as the legends about buried treasures. Spanish *entradas* into Texas and searches by Spanish Mexicans in later decades engendered a rich lore about mythical wealth and tales of hidden treasures. According to legends told by nineteenth-century Tejanos, Spaniards had hidden fortunes in moments of crises (usually Indian attacks) only to be prevented by some happenstance from returning at a later date to retrieve them. Thus, precious treasures lay hidden in diverse areas of the state from El Paso to East Texas. This folklore, passed on to Anglo Americans who migrated to the state in later generations, became part of the fantasy of the new arrivals.

The Spanish past manifested itself in many other ways. Such folktales as that of "Pedro de Urdemalas" for example, revealed the presence of Spanish characters. Border *corridos* (ballads) that appeared around the 1860s were a link to Spanish *romances,* although their subject matter and structure belonged to the New World, while the *tragedia* (a ballad of tragedy) tended to resemble the epics of Medieval France and Spain *(La Chanson de Roland* and *El Cantar de Mío Cid)* in origin and theme.

When Spanish domination ended for Tejanos in 1821, the post-Spanish experience threaded its way into folklore as had the colonial historical past. Thus an evolving and unfolding experience embraced tales of buried treasures left in Texas by Antonio López de Santa Anna or by *bandidos* and *rancheros.* For varied reasons associated with accidents, the law, or Indian attacks, Mexicans had left their goods at various points in McMullen County in hopes of returning some day. Tejanos related these legends to whites who themselves continued the search for the elusive treasure in following generations.

Also, folklore exposed Tejanos as the bicultural people they became after the Texas Revolution. On the one hand, it displayed the interest that Mexican Americans still retained in affairs that occurred in the mother country. Through songs, for example, they eulogized Mexican heroes: with the *coplas of los franceses,* Tejanos of the lower border hailed the exploits of Mexican president Benito Juárez in his struggle against the French imperialists of the 1860s. Corridos praised the victory of Texas-born Ignacio Zaragoza over the French at Puebla on May 5, 1862, and immortalized Catarino Garza for his revolution of 1891–1892 against Mexican President Porfirio Díaz. Social types, settings, traditions, and other elements similarly pointed to the Mexican cultural presence. On the other hand, as a folklore in flux, it displayed the Tejano's familiarity with the people who controlled Texas politics, economics, and society. Old legends about buried treasures, for one, showed a modification that included the presence of the *americanos.* In legends surrounding the battles of Palo Alto and Resaca de la Palma (May 8 and 9, 1846), the Mexican Army, pressed by Zachary Taylor's troops, lightened the retreat by burying its pay money and other valuables in the battlefield. Other tales had Anglos, rather than Spaniards or Mexicans, burying treasure and then, because of unforeseen contin-

gencies, never returning to retrieve it. Still others had the ghosts of white men guarding buried treasures, instead of the ghosts of Mexicans or Spaniards who had protected them before white men became part of the life experience of Tejanos.

Similarly, corridos reflected the Tejano adaptation to the American setting and their evolving nature as a bicultural people. While the corridos about Ignacio Zaragoza celebrated the exploits of a Mexican national hero, it also celebrated the fame of a native Tejano *(General de la frontera).* And surely, Mexicanos would not have eulogized the exploits of Ulysses S. Grant in song (or even have been aware of him) had they retained immutable ties to Mexico and repudiated all interest in the United States. Because those two corridos were sung during the same period, they indicated the familiarity of the border people with the significance of the two men and the fact that the Tejano mind naturally identified with both. Additionally, the corridos about the Catarino Garza revolution of 1891–1892 displayed a Tejano familiarity with both Texan and Mexican events. *El Corrido de los Pronunciados* eulogized the attack of Garza upon Mexican territory, while the *Corrido de Capitán Jol* depicted Texas Ranger Captain Lee Hall as a coward and an ineffective fighter compared to the *pronunciados* that defeated him. This type of ethnocentrism attested to a way of life on the border colored by the interaction between Mexican Americans and white Texans.

More aspects of folklore pointed to an experience of Tejanos well acquainted both with their past and their present. Folkloric themes indicated familiarity with time, featured settings, characters, and stylistic arrangements intimate to the narrator. Place names like Presidio, San Elizario, and San Antonio, ranchos belonging to well-to-do families, the Big Bend, and the *Chaparral* country of South Texas, local flora like *el cenizo* and the *guadalupana* vine, all permeated the folklore and thus revealed the Tejano's closeness to his environment. Allusions to personalities like the widow Doña Fidencia Ortega of San Elizario, Bartolo Mendoza of El Paso County, the Cantú family of South Texas, to the peasant José Días and to the rich Don

Pedro Carrasco, similarly reflected the reality of their daily experience. Descriptive detail, symbolism, and other stylistic forms added specificity and a localized frame of reference, more plausible characters, strength of purpose, and a more meaningful and convincing portrait to that folklore.

The benevolence of a Christian God, common to folklore universally, was also shown in the religious dimension of their folk stories. In their case, He was an altruistic God, seemingly an integral part of a world of disadvantaged people. A beneficent God took care of His people, intervened on their behalf in desperate moments, and fought off evil forces. He was a concerned God who intervened directly in order to give Tejanos relief from natural calamities. *Kineños* (residents of the King Ranch of South Texas), for example, related the story of a compassionate God bursting into tears that became the rain which brought relief to the drought-stricken countryside and His suffering people.

Also, folklore revealed a protective God who intervened in times of great desperation. Time after time, He had come to the assistance of the legendary Father Antonio Margil de Jesús, the ubiquitous folkloric figure. Nineteenth-century folklore credited Margil, accompanying the Domingo Ramón expedition in 1716, with working a miracle through the agency of prayer by turning an attacking "swarm of savages" near San Antonio into inoffensive deer. Then, as the expedition approached the city, Margil again rescued the thirsty party through another miracle that begot the San Antonio River. That same year, he delivered another thirsty missionary party from its plight near Nacogdoches by a miracle that produced a living stream of cool water from a site that came to be called the Holy Springs of Father Margil.

Folktales such as "El Cenizo" (which explained the creation of the cenizo shrub) and "La Guadalupana Vine" (which related how the *guadalupana* vine acquired its medicinal value) and the song "Nuestra Señora de los Dolores" (which recounted the powers of such a statue in Webb County) likewise revealed a faith, a moral uprightness, and a humility that testified to the privileged status and special relationship that Tejano vaqueros understood themselves to have with their Creator. In each, the miraculous intervention of the Divine warded off imminent catastrophe. In "El Cenizo," vaqueros arose on Ash (cenizo) Wednesday to rejoice over the desperately needed rain sent to them in response to their prayers. Likewise, the Virgen de Guadalupe had intervened directly to teach vaqueros that the guadalupana vine dipped in *mescal* had extraordinary medicinal values. And "Nuestra Señora de los Dolores," an old statue of the Virgin Mary kept at La Becerra Ranch in Webb County, invariably responded to the pleas of drought-stricken *rancheros* in the latter half of the century. During dry spells they carried the unprepossessing image in solemn procession while mothers marched praying the rosary and chanting "Nuestra Señora de los Dolores" (the song relating in ten assonantal *cuartetas* the affliction of the Virgin upon learning of the imminent crucifixion of the Lord). Legend had it that rain fell within days after marchers arrived at the drought-stricken ranch.

In each case, the Divine had intervened to bestow His blessings, not in behalf of one individual, but characteristically for the benefit of an entire community or group. In the legend of "La Guadalupana Vine" the Virgin intended the gift, in the form of the medicinal vine, for Mexicanos in general and the vaquero specifically. The wooden statue of the Virgin Mary ("of a dark color" and its paint "a kind of sticky-looking clay") to which Tejanos sang the verses of "Nuestra Señora de los Dolores," ostensibly represented God's people, the Mexicanos. In the legend of "El Cenizo," a considerate God delivered His blessings to *la gente* in the form of the rain.

A guardian God similarly defended His people from evil forces. In the legend of "The Devil's Grotto," a priest used the holy cross to overcome Satan and deliver the pagan people of Presidio, Texas, from the havoc wreaked upon them by the Devil. Converted to the Christian faith, the people thenceforth enjoyed good health, their crops grew abundantly, and they no longer feared Satan's evil designs. Similarly, a legend concerning the old Mission de Nuestra Señora de la Purísima Concepción de Acuña supposed that the Virgin, responding to the prayers of a supplicating *padre* seeing his neophytes retreating into the safety of the Mission with Comanches close on their heels, had interceded at the gates and somehow held back the "wild tribes" at the very lintel as the neophytes rushed into the safety of the Mission just as the gates closed behind them. In another legend, San Miguel, the patron saint of Socorro (in the El Paso Valley) came to the aid of the community when, during the Civil War, wild marauders from Major T. T. Teel's command commenced bombarding the old church at Socorro. San Miguel appeared in the tower waving a flaming sword and thus held them in check until the Major arrived from Ysleta to end the indiscriminate attack.

Likewise, Tejanos carried on their traditional world view that explained the mysteries of nature and the universe. *Kineños,* for example, employed folk yarns to explain astronomical phenomena. They borrowed freely from Catholic theology and their experiences as vaqueros at the King Ranch in giving subjective renditions of the arrangements of the heavenly bodies. For others, a similar world perception begot explanations of such things as the origin of the Earth's inhabitants, their place in the world order, their functions, and so on. Explanatory stories about birds especially followed such a scheme. Through folktales, Tejanos explained the mysteries in the *aves* (birds): the *paisano* (roadrunner) ran among the chaparral in order to hide his shame and disgrace after being punished for his vanity and arrogance; the owl called "Cú, Cú, Cú, Cú, Cú," as he searched for the Pájaro Cú who had become arrogant after receiving a coat of feathers from other birds that had clothed his naked body (the owl had posted bond that the Pájaro Cú would remain humble after receiving the coat); the male cardinal was beautiful while the female was a wonderful singer because the spirit of the plains could give only one gift to each; and the song of the dove was a sob because she never saw the Christ Child when all the other creatures of the world came to worship Him (the dove was so humble and unassuming that no one thought of telling her the wonderful news). Similarly, *la cigarra* (locust or *cicada*) achieved its ugly form when his wife called upon the eagle, the monarch

A strong of filial responsibility permeated nineteenth-century Mexican American life.

of all birds, to check the *cigarra's* roaming ways. The *cigarra's* eyes thus became popped and round and his colored wings turned an ashy gray (his wife, then wanting to be happy with the ugly creature, asked the eagle to make her like her husband).

Hence, by borrowing from their theology and everyday experiences and then combining that with their worldly wisdom, Tejanos rendered seemingly rational explanations of phenomena with which they had daily contact. Structured around such a prosaic framework, the explanations achieved credibility. Folklore provided a vehicle through which rational explanations untangled the supernatural, be it prairie lights, ghosts and spirits, mysterious lakes, physical ailments, or psychological states of mind. Thus, in explaining *la luz del llano,* that mysterious red light that appears at night on the prairie, which scientists believe is caused by peculiar atmospheric conditions, Kineño folklore held that it originated out of a covenant between an old woman and an old wizard. In exchange for food for her starving girls, the woman had agreed to surrender them to the wizard four years later. When the wizard took them the mother was so disconsolate that she set out searching for them, risking the wizard's warning that she not hunt for them on the penalty of immolation. Finally caught and burned alive, the old woman nevertheless kept up the search. Hence, *la luz del llano* was a bundle of fire held together by the spirit of the old woman who still traversed the llanos seeking her lost daughters. Unexplainable lights at night often were believed to indicate precious metals underground. Thus, legend held that the lights about Fort Ramírez (on Ramireño Creek in Nueces County) pointed to the money Ramírez had buried before Indians killed him in the early part of the century. Strange and unexplainable events such as those occurring at Rancho El Blanco, an old Spanish ranch in what is now Jim Hogg County, could be explained similarly—for ghosts and spirits in different forms haunted buried treasures. The appearance of a wraith at San Pedro's sparkling springs in San Antonio also signified the spirit of the tragic Francisco Rodríguez family that guarded the family's hidden treasure. Anyone daring to search for it confronted the specter of Don Francisco or his son or daughter, or the daughter's lover, who had, during Texas' colonial period, been part of a tragic scenario that had led to the treasure's burial. Likewise the feared presence at Espantosa (part of a multiplicity of pools—*tinajas*—and small lakes situated for many miles up and down the west side of the Nueces River and fifteen to twenty miles back) of huge alligators with a horn on their noses, was a result of God's wrath upon Mexican robbers who had once upon a time enticed the most beautiful señoritas to the lake's banks and kidnapped them. In his terrible vengeance, God created reptiles to prey on the children, the women, and the bandits. But after exterminating the band, the monsters still craved for human flesh and, hence, Tejanos in the 1870s still dreaded the Espantosa.

Tejanos also used folk tales as a means of explaining physical or psychological ailments. Such was the case concerning the robust young Eutiquio Holguín of nineteenth-century San Elizario who suffered from a strange malady that rendered him paralytic. After all remedies failed, it became obvious he was the victim of the local witch of Cenecú. Traumatized nightly by the *bruja* (witch), Eutiquio finally managed to grab her hand and struggle with her one night. He gradually recovered after that and, when fully recuperated, paid a visit to the *bruja.* Finding all her *monos* (figurines), he threw them into the fire, and with that the witch of Cenecú lost her powers.

And not illogically, a particularly distressing psychological state of mind caused by shock or tragedy found convenient explanation through folklore, as in the case of Elisa Valdez of San Antonio in 1888. A widow, she reluctantly consented to marry a second time. Still harboring feelings of guilt about infidelity to her dead husband, she had wandered away from the wedding festivity to be alone. Then she heard the musicians sing:

Toma el arpa con que canto Las hazañas de los
reyes y de amor las dulces leyes De tu imperio
seductor

At that moment she felt something pulling on her dress and, turning around, she saw a turkey. Frightened, the conviction forced itself upon her that the turkey was her dead husband coming to upbraid her for her forgetfulness and faithlessness to his memory. She knew then that her marriage could not be consummated, and, indeed, all Eliza did after that was wander around Mission Espada tending to her goat and her pet, the large turkey over which she sang Mexican love songs.

The strength, the durability, and the phenomenal endurance of the mortar of which the Mission de Nuestra Señora de la Purísima Concepción de Acuña in San Antonio consisted also found its explanation in folklore. It was as strong as brass and had resisted the effects of time because, according to legend, the priest had explained to the Indian workers that as the mission and church were to be erected in honor of the Virgin who was without sin, the mortar was to be mixed each day with fresh pure milk as a tribute to her purity. So also could the beneficent properties of particular plants that rendered Tejanos so much curative services be explained.

Stylized romantic tales and legends, ballads and *canciones* (songs), fables, and other folkloric stories focused on the notions Tejanos held about disenchantment with the opposite sex, filial responsibility, friendships, and other special relationships. The theme of love—especially between sweethearts—persisted in such tragic romances as the one involving María Morales and Alfonso Salinas. Legend held that María had defied her betrothal to a man of her father's choice by marrying Alfonso secretly. But as the newly wedded pair rowed along the San Antonio River, a deep whirlpool caught and swallowed them. So profound was their love that, when their lifeless bodies were found, they were clasped inseparably in each other's arms and had to be buried in the same casket. Similarly, nineteenth-century vaqueros and campesinos (farm workers) expressed their feelings of endearment toward special ladies in such canciones as "Adelita" and "La Trigueña."

Folklore also employed elements of the supernatural to show the power of love over evil. In the tale of "Blanca Flor," the gambler Juan had given his soul to the Devil in exchange for five years of good luck. At the end of the period, Juan went to the Devil's retreat at the Hacienda of Quiquiri-qui to fulfill his commands. While there he fell in love with the Devil's beautiful daughter, Blanca Flor, and through her help escaped his commitment to the Devil. Upon marrying Blanca Flor, the legend held, he renounced his former evil ways and both lived happily ever after. Love had redeemed the former gambler.

Tejanos expressed the intimacy of filial relationships through folklore as well. In the tale of "La Luz del Llano," the mother's love for her daughters had been so eternal that the spirit of the old woman in the form of "la luz del llano" still searched for her lost daughters. In contrast, the wrath of God visited the childbeater or unprincipled parent who abused little *inocentes* (innocents). In the "Devil on the Border," Tejanos related the story of a childbeating father who took his new born baby from his wife to starve it. She cursed the brute: "May the Devil get you." About midnight a terrific whirlwind enveloped the rancho; the smell of sulfur became suffocating, and a dust of ashes choked the people. At daylight, the people hurried toward the place where the father had taken the baby. There they found the dead child, a white dove hovering over its corpse. All that remained of the father was a heap of greenish yellow sulfur.

Filial responsibility necessarily included socializing the young, and nineteenth-century Tejano folklore contained abundant tales on morals, lessons, and good examples to be imitated by the young. Advice, counsel, and admonitions played prominent roles in these stories. Among the many tales told to impatient children was the story of King Solomon, the wise man who had discovered the secret of returning from death. Telling his most faithful servant that he would die on a certain day, he instructed him further on how to wrap his body, how to dig it up after three weeks, and how to unwrap it so that it would be resurrected. The servant was to tell no one. But people soon started wondering about Solomon's disappearance and threatened the servant with death. Realizing that if he talked, Solomon would never return but that, if he did not, both he and Solomon would be dead forever, the servant revealed the story. "They had not been patient with time, and just for that the secret of returning alive from death was lost forever."

Another didactic story concerned a little boy with three bad habits: aimlessness, asking about people's affairs, and not controlling his temper. One day while running away from home he encountered an old man who gave him three pieces of advice for his last three *pesos:* don't leave a highway for a trail; don't ask about things that don't concern you; and don't lose your temper. Leaving empty handed and feeling swindled, the boy soon encountered three crises to which the *viejito's* (old man) advice applied. By following it, he came into a thriving business and a lovely wife as rewards.

Other tales, such as "Baldheads," were intended to warn the young of certain deceptive types. A country boy had entrusted his money to a baldheaded man who owned a *Casa de Encargos,* which the boy thought to be a bank. Returning a few hours later, he was told that he had deposited nothing. To recover the money, his father designed a plan. He took a bag full of buttons and washers to the *Casa de Encargos* and as he arranged for its deposit, the son entered asking for his money. The clerk, fearing to lose the larger sum the old man possessed, returned the boy's cash. The father then revealed the plot and, turning to his son, advised him: "Keep an eye on baldheads."

And a tale of the Alamo sought to inculcate children with the value of courtesy by alerting them that someday they might meet the *"padre."* According to this legend, the *padre* rewarded courtesy with gifts.

As a cultural form, folklore defined the Tejano sense of values, ideals, and collective behavior. Those folktales that articulated the theme of retributive justice, for example, contained a repugnant, sometimes grotesque manifestation of supernatural evil that dramatized the consequences of unacceptable behavior. In the legend of "The Devil's Grotto," Satan arrived to bring all

manners of distress to the unconverted people of the Presidio, Texas, area and left them in peace only after they were converted. In the legend of "La Casa de la Labor," Doña Fidencia Ortega of San Elizario refused the parish priest Father Pedro a little wine to celebrate the feast of San Isidro and saw her beautiful ranch burn down the next day; the smouldering remains gave "testimony of the wrath of God." Shortly afterward she was seen "riding to the *laguna* on a bull that snorted fire" and plunged into the water never to be seen again. (More terrestrial though no less gruesome as symbols of punishment for bad behavior were "two slender hands" that drove Don Miguel mad for killing his lover's fiancé in the tale of "The Little White Dog." Similarly, in the tale "A Boom in Guarache Leather," a set of mean-looking bandits met their punishment at the hands of the destitute José Días, who, sharing their camp overnight, innocently placed an ugly devil's mask over his face as protection from the bitter night's cold.) Waking to find what they thought to be the very devil, the malefactors fled the campsite, scrambling over a cliff to their deaths.

Stories that dramatized the favorable outcome or retributive justice, as adduced by the rewards granted the obedient in recompense for their desirable behavioral traits, were as common. In "A Hanged Man Sends Rain," Bartolo Mendoza, a convict destined for execution on a day that "seemed to grow hotter with each moment that passed," repented of his crime before God and thus summoned Providence to send relief to drought-stricken San Elizario. Upon expiring on the gallows, he sent rain from Heaven. In a legend of the Big Bend country told by Natividad Luján in the early 1880s, his uncle Santiago had been killed by Indians sometime around mid-century and became "among the blessed who died for the Faith among the heathens" and his soul had journeyed to purgatory, there to be rescued by prayers said by his faithful descendants.

Folktales featuring the compensation of those who lived acceptably and the punishment of those who lived unacceptably were as frequent.

Juan Verdadero was one person whose exemplary behavior resulted in his being handsomely rewarded. According to the story, Juan never lied. But he became an innocent pawn between his *patrón* (boss) and a neighboring landowner who bet his farm that "any man under the urge of necessity will lie." Certain that Juan could be induced into a falsehood, the neighbor sent his daughter to Juan with an offer to exchange her valuable ring for the heart of the prize bull Juan herded. After an excruciatingly difficult decision, Juan killed the bull for the ring. As he approached the ranch house, his *patrón* queried:

"Juan Verdadero, how is the herd?" "Some fat, some poor, upon my word." "And the white and greenish-colored bull?" "Dead, señor, dead," replied Juan.

Juan had not lied, so his *patrón* made him the administrator of the new estate that the neighbor surrendered. But the case of Doña Carolina who lived in mid-century El Paso Valley was different. She was haughty and arrogant until she suffered a harrowing experience while searching for her absent husband. After the ordeal, she was no longer the supercilious woman of former days, and everyone noticed her new behavior. *Disobedientes* (disobedients), *malcridos* (ill-bred persons), *sinvergüenzas* (no 'counts) and other nonconformists received the severest castigations. Tejanos had little tolerance for culprits who abused their children or their spouses. One wife-beater was Don Paniqua, a magically powerful person everyone feared. One day his wife gave birth to a devil-baby who prophesied various horrors, both for the world and Don Paniqua. The raging Don Paniqua took the baby into the thicket and returned without it. No one knew what happened, but, when Don Paniqua died, the Kineños said, he became the foreman of the *infierno's* (hell) *corrida.* Other evil men, the Kineños maintained, went to work in Don Paniqua's outfit.

Brief and pithy animal tales that took the form of fables focused on deviant and unacceptable behavior. For being too proud, the mockingbird had

suffered the loss of part of his beautiful feathers; for being audacious in addressing his superiors as cousins, the *paisano* had been condemned to forget to fly and to feed on unclean things; for growing overbearing and cruel toward his ugly and less gifted wife, the male cardinal suffered the loss of his wife's respect; and for being a spirited adventurer who ignored his mate, the *cicada* incurred its repugnant appearance.

Like fables, corridos pointed to the Tejano value system. Lyrics often extolled the deeds of such great men as Ignacio Zaragoza, Ulysses Grant, and Catarino Garza, heroes who Tejanos looked upon as the personification of courage, liberty, and justice. The corridos not only exalted the adventures of those who challenged the powerful through defiance or confrontation, but they expressed delight in seeing the antagonist demeaned or denigrated—especially if he represented injustice and oppression.

Folktales also expressed a reality in which Tejanos could poke fun at the world, at its inhabitants, and at themselves. They ridiculed the Devil in a tale involving Pedro de Urdemañas (or Urdemalas), a well-traveled and much-experienced *caballero* who arrived in hell to regale the Devil with the wonders of Texas. Hastening to see the marvels of Texas firsthand, the Devil arrived in the state only to face a series of calamities with chili peppers, prickly pears, and an unruly cow. Returning swiftly to hell, he expelled Urdemañas who happily returned to Texas to pursue the lifestyle of his former days.

Also popular was the tale of Chano Calanche, who, for a bottle of wine, agreed to help some bandits rid themselves of a priest's body. Tricked by the killers into thinking that he had not buried the corpse—each time he returned to claim the bottle, he found the body of the *padrecito,* not knowing that the bandits had actually killed three priests—the drunken Chano finally decided to dispose of it once and for all. Lighting fire to the corpse, he stayed with it until he fell asleep. He awoke, however, to find the padrecito at his campfire; it was actually a traveling priest that happened to stop to warm his morning meal.

After the incident, the story held, Chano never claimed the wine and it was said that the prize occupied a place of esteem in the *cantina* (bar) for years after that and was never put up for sale.

In a tale with a more universal theme, Tejano common folks mocked female curiosity. "My wife is not inquisitive," retorted a husband to his friend's suggestion that "all women are curious." But, when his partner took a box to the first man's wife with instructions to keep it sealed, the wife could not resist her curiosity. Upon opening the box, she unwittingly allowed the bird inside to fly away, thereby ridiculing the husband and her own ineptness at keeping secrets.

And they could demean themselves, as in the song of "Coplas del payo," which portrayed in a jesting manner the general misfortune of their lives. In this story, an overseer encouraged a forlorn lover—an ordinary worker like the narrator—to jump over a cliff.

As poor and disadvantaged people, Tejanos employed folklore as a means of expressing wish fulfillment, wishful fantasizing, and ambitiousness. Such tales generally expressed expectations of winning against misfortune. One of those tales involved a poor, elderly couple who owned a miraculous dog capable of acting as a beast of burden, a hunter, and a racer. One day, a stranger arrived in a nearby town with a very swift horse that made short work of the local opposition. With a chance to make $10,000, the poor man matched his dog against the visiting steed. The dog won easily—in fact did not stop at the finish line but ran all the way to the moon—and the poor, elderly couple gained their ambition to be wealthy. Another tale involved a *conducta* (convoy) of weary, hungry men preparing to cook their meager meal at the end of the day. At that point Agapito Cercas spoke up: "Don't bother to cook anything. This very day a hog was slaughtered at my home. Just wait and I will bring you *carne adobada, chile con asadura,* and *tortillas calientes.*" He withdrew from the group, and, according to a witness, took off his clothes and disappeared. In a while, he called for his clothes and reappeared with the food he had promised. Some of the men started eating the appetizing meal they wished for, but others refused it suspecting the work of the supernatural.

As an ambitious people not fatalistically resigned to their lot, Tejanos used folklore to constantly question their social condition. They displayed confidence in themselves and showed that they regarded themselves to be as good as the next man and that, if granted more favorable circumstances, they could overcome their problems. Further revealed was the high regard Tejanos had of themselves: that they were good enough to outwit more formidable antagonists, whether it be a wily coyote, a rich *compadre* or a more fortunate neighbor.

This displayed itself conspicuously in several of the trickster tales. As a genre, these tales include the antagonistic forces of the weak (the underdog) and the strong (the opposer) with a scenario in which the weak used their wit to overcome the powerful. Such was the case of the innocent man outsmarted by a wily coyote who had rescued him from a snake; the man had originally rescued the snake from a trap whereupon the snake had turned on him because "to repay good with evil" was *la costumbre*—the custom. Beholden to the coyote, the man compensated the animal "with good" (contrary to custom). The man soon learned that he had been too generous, for the coyote kept increasing the payment. Tricking the coyote, he finally unleashed his dog upon the opportunist. "It isn't right to repay good with evil," called the outwitted coyote. "Perhaps," answered the man, "'*pero es la costumbre.*'"

Commonly, the antagonist was a compadre, for Tejanos spoke in terms of their own culture and social conditions as ordinary people. One tale involved two compadres—one rich and the other poor, and the former arrogant and snobbish toward the latter. One day the poor man was so desperate for survival that he schemed to extract money from his more affluent compadre. But his rich compadre grew so angry at his tricks that he finally sought to drown his nemesis by putting him in a bag and dumping him in the sea. But the poor compadre slyly escaped the bag and surfaced to report that he had recovered the rich man's lost pearls at the bottom of the water. Eager to retrieve more jewels, the rich compadre persuaded the poor man to tie him in a sack and dump him in the ocean—all his worldly goods would be put in trust to the poor man for the favor. The poor man did as his compadre wished and became wealthy and was held in great esteem by the people of the town for his innocent little pranks.

In a similar tale, a poor man sought to get even with a rich compadre who looked condescendingly upon him because of his poverty. He succeeded in convincing the rich man of the powers of a newly purchased cap. All that was necessary to obtain items at the store was to say *Debo de gorra* (put it on the cap, cuff). "What a marvelous cap," said the rich man, "Sell it to me for $30,000." Feigning reluctance, the poor man surrendered it. But when the rich man attempted to buy an expensive diamond necklace with it, he found himself in jail for failing to pay. The poor man went on to live a life of luxury, while the rich fellow wound up in the mad house.

A tale indicating the awareness Tejanos felt concerning social distance involved Don Pedro Carrasco, the owner of many cattle, and José Días, the owner of a single but fat and very productive cow. Jealous of José, Don Pedro tricked José into killing his only cow, telling him of the high price *guarache* leather was bringing in the neighboring town of Aldama. Disappointed at being tricked into killing his only cow (the price of leather at Aldama was rock bottom), José was making his way slowly homeward when he came upon some money left by bandits. Taking his newfound wealth, he arrived home to show the people the money which, he said, he had made off his cow. Don Pedro, thinking that the price of *guarache* leather was indeed high, killed his herd, only to find himself tricked by his sly compadre. Now José and his family became wealthy and gave money to the *santitos* (saints) and the poor. Such trickster tales allowed Tejanos to engage the enemy and triumph over him. It also permitted them psychic relief from oppressive conditions.

Nineteenth-century Texas folklore revealed an aspiring, scheming, dreaming, and changing people concerned with a multiplicity of things affecting them both as human beings and as an oppressed people. Like dependent classes elsewhere, Tejanos employed folklore to question their existence, to explain it, and to satisfy the mind as to the universe about them; but folklore was not limited to that. It also functioned as entertainment, as a way of eulogizing heroes and expressing discontent with "no 'counts", a means of expressing kinship, a vehicle for inculcating values and behavior patterns, a mode of teaching the lessons of acceptable ideals both to adults and the young, an art of poking fun at themselves, a manner of engaging in wishful fantasizing, and, much more importantly, a technique for passing on survival skills through fictionalized accounts where the weak could indeed triumph over powerful forces. Folklore, encompassing all these functions, acted not only to give identity and solidarity to a community that shared a similar experience, but it also provided them with a covert and subconscious form of resistance to oppression.

Folklore, of course, is a universal cultural feature among all classes, and it was present long before Tejanos met Anglos in the 1820s. It persisted as a vital force of the Tejano nineteenth-century experience, and it continued long after 1900. Indeed, it was in the first four or five decades of the twentieth century that the aforementioned Texas Folklore Society collected most of its materials. Primarily the tales and legends of Tejanos from the rural areas, that folklore, while manifesting the changes of the twentieth century, reflected themes, settings, and stylistic forms similar to the folklore of nineteenth-century agrarian Texas. It continued being a part of the intimate side of the Texas Mexican experience—like that of raising families, worshipping in particular ways, and maintaining a language. That folklore thrived meant it was part of an expressive culture defined from within but that also took and rejected from outside standards, observances, and patterns as it saw fit.

Study Questions

1. De León argues that Tejano culture was a fusion of Mexican and Anglo experiences. Do you agree? Why or why not?

2. Evaluate the traditional Anglo argument that Tejano culture was passive and fatalistic, with Tejanos taking a negative view of themselves and assuming they had little power over their own lives.

3. How did the Anglo view of Tejanos reinforce the existing social and economic institutions of nineteenth-century Anglo society?

4. Modern societies have increasingly distinguished between magic and formal religion. Can such distinctions be made for Tejano culture? Why or why not?

Bibliography

For portraits of Mexican Americans perceived as passive and fatalistic people, see William Madsen, *Mexican-Americans of South Texas* (1964) or Norman D. Humphrey, "The Cultural Background of the Mexican Immigrant," *Rural Sociology,* 13 (1948). More recent treatments of Mexican American history that employ liberal outrage over past discrimination as their major focus include Rodolfo Acuña, *Occupied America: The Chicano's Struggle for Liberation* (1972) and Carey McWilliams, *North from Mexico* (1968). For the best treatments of Mexican American ethnicity, which transcend the Anglo perspective, see Arnoldo De León, *The Tejano Community, 1836–1900* (1982); Leonard Pitt, *The Decline of the Californios: A Social History of Spanish-Speaking Californians, 1848–1890* (1966); and Louise Ano Nuevo Kerr, "Mexican Chicago: Chicago Assimilation Aborted, 1939–1952," in Melvin G. Holli and Peter d'A. Jones, *The Ethnic Frontier: Group Survival in Chicago and the Midwest* (1977). Also see James Officer, *Hispanic Arizona* (1987); David Montejano, *Anglos and Mexicans in the Making of Texas* (1987); and Douglas Monroy, *Thrown Among Strangers* (1990). Also see David J. Weber, *The Spanish Frontier in North America* (1992). For the best of the recent research on Hispanics in early America, see Andres Tijerina, *Tejanos and Texas Under the Mexican Flag, 1821–1836* (1994) and Ana Carolina Castillo Crimm, *De León: A Tejano Family History* (2003).

READING 18

★ ★ ★

Forgotten Forty-Niners

JoAnn Levy

Throughout the twentieth century, American popular culture and scholarly histories have maintained a keen interest in the frontier. Stories about explorers, mountain men, cowboys, buffalo hunters, gunslingers, Indians, and cavalry soldiers have captured the American imagination, and literally tens of thousands of books and movies have created nearly as many myths and stereotypes. No stereotypes have been more rigid, or more long-lived, than those involving women in the frontier West. They were either the stoic heroine mothers and wives of the John Wayne films or the heart-of-gold "dance hall girls" who populated the ubiquitous saloons of dusty frontier towns. The social structure of the American West was far more complicated than that. Millions of women settled the frontier, engaging in virtually every conceivable occupation and occupying every level of society. In the following essay, JoAnn Levy looks at the women who headed for California during the gold-rush days of the late 1840s and early 1850s.

If Concord, Massachusetts, is remembered for the "shot heard 'round the world," Sutter's Mill, in the foothills of California's Sierra Nevada, is remembered for the "shout heard 'round the world"—"Eureka!" As that cry reverberated across the globe in 1848 (and echoed into the 1850s), a flood of humanity converged on the land of golden opportunity. This human tide irrevocably changed the West, opening up the frontier as no other force in the nation's history has, before or since.

One of the most common assumptions about gold-rush-era California is that it was almost exclusively a male domain—and that such women as could be found there were prostitutes. As recently as 1983, a California historian asserted that "it was, literally, mankind which participated in the gold rush, for woman kind, at least of the 'proper' variety, was almost totally absent."

A careful study of surviving diaries, memoirs, newspapers, and census records from the period refutes this longstanding misperception, revealing that the vast wave of migration to California included thousands of "respectable" women— and numerous children, too.

Many of these adventurous women accompanied or followed their husbands, fathers, or brothers to the golden land; others arrived entirely on their own. Once in California, enterprising women engaged in almost every occupation and inhabited every level of society. They mined for gold, raised families, earned substantial sums by their domestic and entrepreneurial labors, and stayed on to help settle the land—contributing a facet of gold-rush history that until now has been largely overlooked or forgotten.

In actuality, so-called respectable women outnumbered prostitutes in California, even in 1850, by four to one. While 25 percent represents a large number, even if not in this instance a "respectable" one, it is far from a majority.

"Forgotten Forty-Niners" by JoAnn Levy. This article is reprinted from the January/February 1992 issue of *American History Illustrated* 26, pp. 38–49, with the permission of Cowles History Group, Inc. Copyright *American History Illustrated* magazine.

Before they could avail themselves of the opportunities afforded by the gold rush, women argonauts, like their male counterparts, had to undertake and survive the arduous journey to California. Many travelers chose the Cape Horn route, braving gale, storm, and shipwreck on a voyage that consumed from five to seven months; others shortened the ocean journey by making the difficult crossing of the Isthmus of Panama via small boat and mule. In 1849, more than twenty thousand gold-seekers arrived at San Francisco by sea, and nearly twenty-five thousand more followed in 1850. Many journals and letters mention the presence of women on these routes, which travelers generally regarded as being safer for families than the even more daunting overland crossings.

Despite the hardships and dangers involved, thousands of other wealth-seekers trekked overland by wagon or on foot, crossing plains, deserts, and forbidding mountain ranges while carrying with them—and then often abandoning for survival's sake—their worldly possessions. Trail-journal entries suggest that of the twenty-five thousand people traveling overland in 1849, at least three thousand were women and fifteen hundred children. Forty-four thousand people crossed the plains the following year, and, given California's census of 1850, about ten percent of these may be assumed to have been female. News of hardship, starvation, and cholera stemmed the tide of overland emigrants in 1851 to little more than a thousand, but in 1852 an estimated fifty thousand again surged across the continent. By July 13, 1852 the Fort Kearny register had tallied for that year alone the passage of more than seven thousand women and eight thousand children.

"The country was so level that we could see long trains of white-topped wagons for many miles," recorded one woman of her experiences on the eastern segment of the overland trail. "And, when we drew nearer to the vast multitude, and saw them in all manner of vehicles and conveyances, on horseback and on foot, all eagerly driving and hurrying forward, I thought, in my excitement, that if one-tenth of these teams and these people got [there] ahead of us, there would be nothing left for us in California worth picking up."

On June 28, 1849, the "Buckeye Rovers," a company of young men heading from Ohio to California's gold fields, camped near Independence Rock on the overland trail. One of the group, John Banks, wrote in his diary that night of seeing "an Irish woman and daughter without any relatives on the way for gold. It is said she owns a fine farm in Missouri." Two weeks later, on the banks of the Green River, their paths converged again: "Last night the Irish woman and daughter were selling liquor near us. . . . Fifty cents a pint, quite moderate."

Some distance beyond the Green River, near the Humbolt River, a woman named Margaret Frink recorded in her journal for August 12, 1850: "Among the crowds on foot, a negro woman came tramping along through the heat and dust, carrying a cast-iron bake oven on her head, with her provisions and blanket piled on top—all she possessed in the world—bravely pushing on for California."

Frink and her husband had begun their westward trek in Indiana. Along the way they stopped at the home of a Mr. and Mrs. McKinney near St. Joseph, Missouri. "Mrs. McKinney," wrote Margaret in her diary, "told me of the wonderful tales of abundance of gold that she had heard; 'that they kept flour-scoops to scoop the gold out of the barrels that they kept it in, and that you could soon get all that you needed for the rest of your life. And as for a woman, if she could cook at all, she could get $16.00 per week for each man that she cooked for, and the only cooking required to be done was just to boil meat and potatoes and serve them on a big chip of wood, instead of a plate, and the boarder furnished the provisions.' I began at once to figure in my mind how many men I could cook for, if there should be no better way of making money."

These vivid images of independent and determined women are strikingly at odds with the stereotypical picture of the long-suffering and sad-eyed pioneer wife peering wearily westward while a creaking covered wagon carries her even

farther from the comforts of home. Perhaps more startling is the departure from the perception of the gold rush as an exclusively male adventure.

All travelers endured hardships en route to California, but the lure of gold enticed and beckoned like a rainbow's promise. Upon reaching the golden ground, numbers of women, as eager as any male red-shirted miner, grubbed in the dirt and creekbeds for the glittering ore. Gold fever raged in epidemic proportions, and women were not immune.

The journal of schoolteacher Lucena Parsons, married but a year, reveals her infection's daily progress. On May 30, 1851, Parsons confessed to "a great desire to see the gold diggings"; she accompanied the men and watched them mine for gold. On May 31, she wrote: "This morning the gold fever raged so high that I went again with the rest but got very little gold. . . . " On June 2, "again went to the canion [*sic*] to find that bewitching ore"; and June 3, "a general turn out to the mines . . . we made 10 dollars to day." On June 4, she went again "and did very well."

Elizabeth Gunn, who had sailed around the Horn with four young children to join her prospecting husband in Sonora, observed to her family back East that "a Frenchman and his wife live in the nearest tent, and they dig gold together. She dresses exactly like her husband—red shirt and pants and hat."

The editor of the *Alta California* reported a similar sighting: "We saw last April, a French woman, standing in Angel's Creek, dipping and pouring water into the washer, which her husband was rocking. She wore short boots, white duck pantaloons, a red flannel shirt, with a black leather belt and a Panama hat. Day after day she could be seen working quietly and steadily, performing her share of the gold digging labor. . . . "

Many of the women who tried mining, however, found the prize unworthy of the effort it required. Eliza Farnham, famed for attempting to deliver one hundred marriageable women to California, wrote that she "washed one panful of earth, under a burning noon-day sun . . . and must frankly confess, that the small particle of gold, which lies this day safely folded in a bit of tissue paper . . . did not in the least excite the desire to continue the search."

Louisa Clapp, wife of a doctor at Rich Bar, concurred, writing to her sister in the East: "I have become a *mineress;* that is, if the having washed a pan of dirt with my own hands, and procured therefrom three dollars and twenty-five cents in gold dust . . . will entitle me to the name. I can truly say, with the blacksmith's apprentice at the close of his first day's work at the anvil, that 'I am sorry I learned the trade'; for I wet my feet, tore my dress, spoilt a pair of new gloves, nearly froze my fingers, got an awful headache, took cold and lost a valuable breastpin, in this my labor of love."

Mary Ballou, at the mining camp of Negro Bar, wrote her son Selden, left behind in New Hampshire, that she "washed out about a Dollars worth of gold dust . . . so you see that I am doing a little mining in this gold region but I think it harder to rock the cradle to wash out gold than it is to rock the cradle for Babies in the States."

The labor was indeed discouraging, and most gold-rushing women found it easier—and more profitable—to market their domestic skills in exchange for the glittering metal. As Margaret Frink had heard, if "a woman could cook at all," she could earn her living. Boasted one fiercely independent woman: "I have made about $18,000 worth of pies—about one third of this has been clear profit. One year I dragged my own wood off the mountain and chopped it, and I have never had so much as a child to take a step for me in this country. $11,000 I baked in one little iron skillet, a considerable portion by a campfire, without the shelter of a tree from the broiling sun. . . . "

Forty-niner Sarah Royce, who journeyed overland to California with her husband and three-year-old daughter, met a woman at Weaverville who "evidently felt that her prospect of making money was very enviable." The woman received one hundred dollars a month to cook three meals a day, was provided an assistant, and did no dishwashing.

In San Francisco, Chastina Rix supplemented the family income by ironing. In one week she noted that she had ironed sixty shirts, thirty-five starched and twenty-five plain, plus "hosts of other clothes & I have made twelve dollars by my labor." Her husband Alfred wrote to friends in the East that Chastina "is making money faster than half the good farmers in Peacham. She has just bought her another silk dress & lots of toggery & cravats & gloves for me and all the nice things & has quite a fund at interest at 3 percent a month."

Laundresses were in especially high demand in the gold fields: during the early days of the rush some desperate miners shipped their laundry to the Sandwich [Hawaiian] Islands and even to China, waiting for as long as six months for its return. Abby Mansur, at the Horseshoe Bar camp, wrote to her sister in New England about a neighbor who earned from fifteen to twenty dollars a month washing, "so you can see that women stand as good a chance as men[;] if it was not for my heart I could make a great deal but I am not stout enough to do it."

Whether washing or cooking, mining or ironing, women at work in frontier California toiled arduously. No labor, however, seemed more intimidating than keeping a boarding house. In 1850, about one out of every hundred persons gainfully employed in California ran some sort of hotel. Many were women, and none attested more eloquently to the labor involved than forty-niner Mary Jane Megquier, who had crossed the Isthmus from Winthrop, Maine to run a San Francisco boarding house.

"I should like to give you an account of my work if I could do it justice," Megquier wrote. "I get up and make the coffee, then I make the biscuit, then I fry the potatoes then broil three pounds of steak, and as much liver, while the [hired] woman is sweeping, and setting the table, at eight the bell rings and they are eating until nine. I do not sit until they are nearly all done . . . after breakfast I bake six loaves of bread (not very big) then four pies, or a pudding then we have lamb, for which we have paid nine dollars a quarter, beef, pork, baked, turnips, beets, potatoes, radishes, sallad [*sic*], and that everlasting soup, every day, dine at two, for tea we have hash, cold meat bread and butter sauce and some

Life in the California gold fields in the late 1840s was one of hard work and drudgery.

kind of cake and I have cooked every mouthful that has been eaten excepting one day and a half that we were on a steamboat excursion. I make six beds every day and do the washing and ironing[.] you must think that I am very busy and when I dance all night I am obliged to trot all day and if I had not the constitution of six horses I should [have] been dead long ago but I am going to give up in the fall whether or no, as I am sick and tired of work. . . ."

Although Megquier fails to mention how much she earned from these herculean exertions, another female forty-niner formerly of Portland, Maine earned $189 a week from her ten boarders, clearing $75 after expenses. The accommodations she shared with them were minimal, if not spartan:

"[We] have one small room about 14 feet square, and a little back room we use for a store room about as large as a piece of chalk. Then we have an open chamber over the whole, divided off by a cloth. The gentlemen occupy the one end, Mrs. H—and a daughter, your father and myself, the other. We have a curtain hung between

our beds, but we do not take pains to draw it, as it is of no use to be particular here. . . . We sleep on a cot without any bedding or pillow except our extra clothing under our heads."

California's inflated economy required that everyone work who could, as forty-niner Luenza Wilson, an overlander with her husband Mason and two young sons, vigorously affirmed: "Yes, we worked; we did things that our high-toned servants would now look at aghast, and say it was impossible for a woman to do. But the one who did not work in '49 went to the wall. It was a hand to hand fight with starvation at the first. . . ."

William Tecumseh Sherman, a gold-rush banker before history called him to greater fame as a Union general in the Civil War, confessed to a friend that keeping his wife Ellen in California ruined him financially: "No man should have a wife in California. . . . Unless she be a working woman, no man can by his own labor support her."

Many women like Ellen Sherman, accustomed to servants and unaccustomed to labor, gave up and returned east. Those willing to work, however, received substantial rewards in an economy where a washerwoman earned more than a United States congressman. Writing from San Francisco in 1850, one woman declared: "A smart woman can do very well in this country—true there are not many comforts and one must work all the time and work hard but [there] is plenty to do and good pay[.] If I was in Boston now and know what I now know of California I could come out here[.] If I had to hire the money to bring me out. It is the only country I ever was in where a woman received anything like a just compensation for work."

Many other gold-rushing women both affirmed the necessity to work and observed that there were "not many comforts." Those who had arrived via the overland trail, for example, often continued to make their beds in tents and wagons, like Mrs. John Berry, who protested: "Oh! you who lounge on your divans & sofas, sleep on your fine, luxurious beds and partake of your rich viands at every meal know nothing of the life of a California emigrant. Here are we sitting, on a pine block, a log or a bunk; sleeping in beds with either a quilt or a blanket as substitute for sheets, (I can tell you it is very aristocratic to have a bed at all), & calico pillow-cases for our pillows."

Harriet Ward, already a fifty-year-old grandmother when she journeyed overland, wrote happy descriptions of her roomy cabin and pine-stump furniture in remote Sierra Country. But of the beds she penned only, "Oh, such beds! I will say nothing of them!"

One report of a comfortable California bed does survive in the reminiscence of a guest at a celebrated gold-rush hostelry. The St. Francis boasted that it was the first San Francisco hotel to offer sheets on its beds. The lady confirmed that her bed there was "delightful." Two "soft hair mattresses" and "a pile of snowy blankets" hastened her slumbers. On this occasion, however, the California deficiency was not the bed, but the *walls:*

"I was suddenly awakened by voices, as I thought, in my room; but which I soon discovered came from two gentlemen, one on each side of me, who were talking to each other from their own rooms *through* mine; which, as the walls were

only of canvas and paper, they could easily do. This was rather a starting discovery, and I at once began to cough, to give them notice of my *interposition,* lest I should become an unwilling auditor of matters not intended for my ear. The conversation ceased, but before I was able to compose myself to sleep again . . . a nasal serenade commenced, which, sometimes a duet and sometimes a solo, frightened sleep from my eyes. . . ."

The walls of most early California habitations consisted of bleached cotton cloth stretched tightly and fastened to the dwelling's frame, then papered over. "These partitions look as firm and solid as they do made the usual way," noted Mrs. D. B. Bates, wife of a ship's captain, "but they afford but a slight hindrance to the passage of sounds."

California construction astonished Sarah Walsworth, a missionary's wife, who watched a house being built in Oakland: "Only a slight underpinning is laid on the ground, upon which rest the joists of the floor which is carefully laid down the *first thing.* This looked so odd to me at first, that I could but laugh[.] Give a carpenter a few feet of *lumber,* a few doors, & windows, a few pounds of nails & screws a few hinges; to a paperhanger, a few yards of cloth & a few rolls of paper—to them *both a good deal of gold* & you may have a house in 6 days—perhaps in less time. You will have no trouble with 'digging cellars,' laying wall, 'having a *raising*' nor with dirty 'masons'—but after it is all done it is but an improved speaking-trumpet[.]"

At Santa Cruz, forty-niner Eliza Farnham built her own house. "Let not ladies lift their hands in horror," she wrote, "[but] I designed supplying the place of journeyman carpenter with my own hands." She succeeded so well, she confessed, "that during its progress I laughed . . . at the idea of promising to pay a man $14 or $16 per day for doing what I found my hands so dexterous in."

While most women made do with tents, cabins, and flimsily constructed clapboard houses, a very few enjoyed luxurious surroundings. "See yonder house," wrote a San Francisco chronicler. "Its curtains are of the purest white lace embroidered, and crimson damask. . . . All the fixtures are of a keeping, most expensive, most voluptuous, most gorgeous. . . . " Upon the Brussels carpet "whirls the politician with some sparkling beauty," he added, "as fair as frail. . . . "

The house described is thought to have been that of Belle Cora, a beauty from Baltimore by way of New Orleans, who crossed the Isthmus in 1849 with gambler Charles Cora. Belle and a handful of other successful parlorhouse madams lived extravagantly, but such magnificence was the exception—even among California's demimonde population.

The first prostitutes to gold-rush California sailed from Valparaiso, Chile, where news of the gold discovery arrived in August 1848 via the Chilean brig *J.R.S.* Many of these women not only married argonauts, but enjoyed the luxury of choosing among their suitors.

Other Latin women, however, fared poorly. Hundreds, through indenture arrangements, were destined for fandango houses, the poor man's brothels. José Fernández, the first alcalde at San Jose under American rule, wrote: "They did not pay passage on the ships, but when they reached San Francisco the captains sold them to the highest bidder. There were men who, as soon as any ship arrived from Mexican ports with a load of women, took two or three small boats, or a launch, went on board the ship, paid to the captain the passage of ten to twelve unfortunates and took them immediately to their cantinas, where the newcomers were forced to prostitute themselves for half a year, during which the proprietors took the bulk of their earnings."

China, like Chile, received news of California's gold discovery in 1848. By 1854, San Francisco's burgeoning Chinatown included hundreds of Chinese girls imported for prostitution. Typically, agents took arriving Chinese girls to a basement in Chinatown where they were stripped for examination and purchase. Depending on age, beauty, and the prevailing market, they sold from $300 to $3,000.

American women were not exempt from similar exploitation, albeit more subtly executed. In late 1849 and early 1850, several prostitutes in the East received passage to California by signing contracts as domestics. Some unethical agencies subsequently adopted the ploy of advertising that "servants" were wanted in California and receiving exceptional wages. A number of girls innocently responded to these procurement fronts that masqueraded as employment offices.

France similarly pounced on the fortuitous discovery at Sutter's Mill. Recruiting agents, as well as the French government, assisted the emigration of French women, who arrived in California literally by the boatload. Testified one eyewitness: "They have done the wildest kinds of business you can imagine in San Francisco, such as auctioning off women in the public square. I got there when matters had settled down somewhat: a ship arrived with sixty French women, none of them had paid her passage, so they offered a girl to anyone who would pay what she owed. Next day they did not have a single one left."

A knowledgeable Frenchman noted that his countrywomen profitably hired themselves out to stand at gambling tables: "All in all, the women of easy virtue here earn a tremendous amount of money. This is approximately the tariff."

"To sit with you near the bar or at a card table, a girl charges one ounce ($16) an evening. She had to do nothing save honor the table with her presence. This holds true for the girls selling cigars, when they sit with you. Remember they only work in the gambling halls in the evening. They have their days to themselves and can then receive all the clients who had no chance during the night. . . . "

"Nearly all these women at home were streetwalkers of the cheapest sort. But out here, for only a few minutes, they ask a hundred times as much as they were used to getting in Paris. A whole night costs from $200 to $400."

Providing theatrical entertainment for lonesome miners offered a less notorious but equally profitable means of amassing California gold. Everywhere forty-niners could be found, from San Francisco's gilt-decorated theaters to the rough boards of a mining camp stage lit by candles stuck in whiskey bottles, actresses, dancers, singers, and musicians performed before appreciative audiences.

The pay varied as much as the venue. In Grass Valley, a black woman presented public piano concerts, charging fifty cents admission. The miners of Downieville bestowed $500 in gold on a young female vocalist who made them homesick by sweetly singing old familiar ballads. A Swiss organ-girl, by playing in gambling halls, accumulated $4,000 in about six months. A Frenchwoman who played the violin at San Francisco's Alhambra gambling hall earned two ounces of gold daily, about $32.

In 1850, three French actresses opened at San Francisco's Adelphi Theatre. A critic observed that two of them "have been on the stage for a long time (I was about to write too long a time), and . . . have never definitely arrived." The women succeeded despite the quality of the performances, for the critic noted that they "have not done badly from a financial point of view, as they now own the building, the lot, and the scenery."

Renowned female performers willing to try their fortunes in far-off California achieved enormous success. Soprano Catherine Hayes, a tall blonde woman of imposing appearance, introduced costumed operatic presentations to the San Francisco stage and was rumored to have departed from the golden state with an estimated quarter-million dollars. Lola Montez cleared $16,000 a week for performing her titillating spider dance.

California's free and open society also permitted women to pursue a variety of other employments normally deemed unacceptable for their gender. The editor of the *Alta California* welcomed a female doctor with a cheerfully delivered jibe: "So few ladies in San Francisco the New M.D. may attend them all. . . . No circumlocutions necessary. . . . Simply, as woman to woman: 'Saw my leg off!'"

The same newspaper advised "those wishing to have a good likeness are informed that they can have them taken in a very superior manner, by a real live lady, in Clay street, opposite the St. Francis Hotel, at a very moderate charge. Give her a call, gents."

The editor also boosted the business of a female barber with a shop on Commercial street by admitting that it was "not an unpleasant operation . . . to take a clean shave at the hands of a lady fair."

Advertising her own skills in the San Francisco paper was "Madame St. Dennis—Late of Pennsylvania," who could be "consulted on matters of love, law and business, from 8 a.m. to 8 p.m. Office second brown cottage from Union street, between Stockton and Dupont." Similarly self-promoting was the linguistically talented Madame de Cassins: "The celebrated diviner, explains the past and predicts the future. Can be consulted in English, French, Italian, Greek, Arabic, and Russian . . . No. 69 Dupont St." And, at the site of the future state capital, "Miss Chick begs to inform the inhabitants of Sacramento, that she has taken a suite of rooms . . . for the purpose of teaching all the new and fashionable dances."

California's early newspapers are a mother lode of rich and often surprising information about female gold-rushers; tidbits are as diverse as the experiences of these women.

Three women, for example, made one newspaper's December 14, 1850 listing of San Francisco's millionaires: Mrs. Elizabeth Davis, Mrs. Fuller, and Mrs. Wm. M. Smith. And in September 1850, noted another article, a fire destroyed the capacious dwelling house of Mrs. Jane Smith, "erected a few months since at an expense of $10,000."

At the opposite end of the spectrum, on March 10, 1852, the *Alta* reported the particulars of a washerwomen's meeting at which laundry fees were discussed and jointly agreed.

Newspapers also reported what we would term gossip-column material today, such as an item appearing in the September 14, 1852 *Alta:* "Forlorn: This was the charge written against Eliza Hardscrabble's name on the Recorder's docket. Unacquainted with the peculiar character of this offense, we referred to Webster, and found perhaps the proper definition, 'a lost forsaken, solitary person.' Yes, Eliza is one of 'em. Whether blighted affection, harrowing care, or an erring be the cause, she is now an incurable rum-drinker, and is no longer fit to take care of herself."

Quite able to take care of herself was Dorothy Scraggs. Nonetheless, she advertised in a Marysville newspaper that she wanted a husband. She advised that she could "wash, cook, scour, sew, milk, spin, weave, hoe, (can't plow), cut wood, make fires, feed the pigs, raise chicks . . . saw a plank, drive nails, etc." She added that she was "neither handsome nor a fright, yet an *old* man need *not* apply, nor any who have not a little more education than she has, and a great deal more gold, for there must be $20,000 settled on her before she will bind herself to perform all of the above."

Court records, too, provide intriguing glimpses into the lives of gold-rushing women. In July 1850 Mrs. Mary King testified in the Sacramento justice court that persons unknown had stolen from her two leather bags containing gold dust and California coin worth about $3,500.

According to the record of *People v. Seymour alias Smith,* Fanny Seymour was indicted on a charge of assault with intent to commit murder when she shot stage-driver Albert Putnam for refusing to pay for a bottle of wine.

In *People v. Potter,* Sarah Carroll's case against William Potter, whom she claimed stole $700 in gold coin from her trunk, was dismissed because she was black and Potter was white.

Equally interesting are the surviving letters, diaries, and reminiscences of men who encountered women during their California adventures. For instance, Enos Christman, a young miner, witnessed a bullfight in Sonora at which a "magnificently dressed" *matadora* entered the arena: "She plunged the sword to the hilt into the breast of the animal. She was sprinkled with crimson dye . . . and greeted with a shower of silver dollars."

In Weaverville, Franklin Buck, a trader, was smitten by a young woman who owned a train of mules by which she delivered flour to the distant mining community: "I had a strong idea of offering myself . . . but Angelita told me she had a husband somewhere in the mines . . . so I didn't ask."

Lawyer John McCrackan met a woman who, while en route to California, brought fresh produce from a Pacific island as a speculative venture: "She sold some pieces of jewelry . . . which cost her about twenty dollars at home [and] purchased onions which she sold on arriving here for eighteen hundred dollars, quite a handsome sum, is it not? . . . She also brought some quinces & made quite a nice little profit on them."

Most fascinating, however, are the women's own observations on life in the gold regions. Wrote Abby Mansur from Horseshoe Bar: "I tell you the women are in great demand in this country no matter whether they are married or not[.] You need not think [it] strange if you see coming home with some good looking man some of these times with a pocket full of rocks . . . it is all the go here for Ladys to leave there [*sic*] Husbands[.] two out of three do it."

In fact, the divorce rate in gold-rush California was startlingly high. One judge, growing impatient with incessant requests for divorces under California's permissive divorce law, sought to deter further applications to his court by publishing his negative decision in *Avery v. Avery* in the *Sacramento Daily Union.*

By the end of 1853, a contemporary historian estimated California's female population at more than sixty thousand, plus about half that many children. In San Francisco alone, women numbered about eight thousand.

By that time, energy and gold had transformed San Francisco from a city of tents into a booming metropolis. No longer a hamlet, the city reflected the changes taking place throughout the newly admitted state. Its people were no longer simply transient miners. Men were bankers and businessmen, lawyers and doctors, farmers and manufacturers. They intended to stay.

So did the women, as California pioneer Mallie Stafford later recalled. "Very few, if any, in those [first] days contemplated permanently settling in the country. . . . But as time wore on . . . they came to love the strange new country . . . and found that they were wedded to the new home, its very customs, the freedom of its lovely hills and valleys."

Thus tens of thousands of women, through choice, chance, or circumstance, found themselves in California during the "great adventure." And, after the gold fever eventually subsided, many of them remained to help settle the land. Although they are today a neglected part of gold-rush history, the "forgotten forty-niners" were there when history was being made—and they helped to make it.

Study Questions

1. What does the author say about the argument that the California gold rush was exclusively a "man's domain"?

2. In 1850, what percentage of women in California were prostitutes? Does this number surprise you? Why or why not?

3. Did women engage in mining? What does the author mean by the statement that women "found it easier—and more profitable—to market their domestic skills in exchange for the glittering metal"?

4. What were the "domestic skills" many women used to make a living?

5. What was life like for women in early California?

6. How did Hispanic and Chinese women immigrants fare in early California?

7. Were there more economic opportunities in frontier California for women than in other parts of the country? Why or why not?

Bibliography

An increasing volume of scholarly literature addresses the experiences of women in the West. Two books by Patricia Limerick are especially useful: *Desert Passages* (1985) and *The Legacy of Conquest* (1990). Also see Annette Kolodny, *The Land Before Her* (1984) and Joanna L. Stratton, *Pioneer Women* (1981). For works dealing with women in early California, see JoAnn Levy, *They Saw the Elephant: Women in the California Gold Rush* (1990); Louisa Clapp's *Shirley Letters from the California Mines, 1851–1852* (1983); and Sarah Royce, *A Frontier Lady: Recollections of the Gold Rush and Early California* (1977). For more recent accounts of the California gold rush, see Jean F. Blashfield, *The California Gold Rush* (2001) and Mary Hill, *Gold: The California Story* (1999). Also see Nan Alamilla Boyd, *Wide-Open Town: A History of Queer San Francisco to 1965* (2003).

PART
5

★ ★ ★

The Age of Imagination

For more than a century, historians have described the era of the 1830s and 1840s as "The Age of Jackson" or "The Age of Democracy." It was a propitious time for the young nation. A vast hinterland of apparently limitless resources beckoned to a generation of land-hungry settlers from both the Old World and the New. Two oceans protected them from the threats of foreign powers. With traditions vastly overwhelmed by expectations, it was the "age of imagination"—a time when Americans saw themselves as the hope of the world, and their country as the place where human potential would ultimately be fulfilled. Such vision translated into "Manifest Destiny," a slogan capturing the national imagination in the 1840s and justifying the march across the continent. A generation of Americans believed that God intended that they assume sovereignty over North America. It was also their intention to obliterate any vestige of aristocratic privilege, governmental oppression, or corporate hegemony. "Young America" glorified individual rights, common people, and popular sovereignty.

The origins of democratic individualism were buried deep in the European past and the American environment. From their English ancestors, the American colonists had inherited Lockean values—the belief that government was designed to protect individual rights, primarily life, liberty, and property. The settlers themselves were young, adventurous, ambitious, and unwilling to tolerate the status quo. Had they been otherwise, they would have stayed forever in the Old World. In America, they encountered the harsh frontier wilderness where individualism, self-reliance, and hard work were taken for granted. Unencumbered by aristocratic privilege and free to establish their own political institutions, the settlers of the United States accepted democratic individualism as the natural order of things.

Andrew Jackson personified the age of democracy. His humble roots in the Tennessee frontier gave poverty a certain social status, at least among politicians. In his assault on the Second Bank of the United States, Jackson stood as an enemy of economic privilege and as a friend of competition and laissez-faire. Impatient with those who prized wealth and social standing, Jackson inspired an unprecedented national infatuation with the democratic ideal. He was a politician of extraordinary charisma.

The national preoccupation with democracy also inspired a wide variety of reform movements during the 1830s and 1840s. Led by Horace Mann of Massachusetts, educational reformers campaigned for a public school system in which the future of democracy could be guaranteed by a literate electorate. Dorothea Dix led a crusade for mental health reform, primarily in the treatment of emotional illnesses. During the age of Andrew Jackson, the last property requirements for holding public office disappeared. William Ladd spearheaded a drive for international peace. Bible tract and temperance societies campaigned across the nation to purify society through the abolition of alcohol. And the great crusade of the antebellum period, led by people like William Lloyd Garrison and Theodore Dwight Weld, was the assault on slavery, a bitter issue that eventually tore the nation apart in a civil war. But that was only a distant threat in the 1830s and 1840s. Confidence and hope were the symbols of Jacksonian America.

READING 19

The Choice:
The Jackson-Dickinson Duel

William A. DeGregorio

For generations philosophers have debated the role of the individual in history—whether the force of historical events automatically produces "the great man or woman" or whether great individuals actually shape the course of history. Because they have traditionally worshipped at the altar of individualism and created a political culture to match, Americans have always preferred the latter interpretation, allowing great people to affect destiny. At best, historical greatness is an ephemeral blessing, frequently bestowed too quickly and always subject to the capricious mood of public opinion. Those who achieve it are usually lucky to have their personal skills tested by some great national crisis. Any list of the "great presidents" will include George Washington, Abraham Lincoln, and Franklin D. Roosevelt, primarily because they had to confront the founding of a new nation, a civil war, and a great depression and global war, respectively. Others who aspire to greatness may link their careers to some great event, such as Theodore Roosevelt and the charge up San Juan Hill in 1898 or John F. Kennedy and the exploits of PT-109. Carved out of an enormous, forbidding wilderness by restless immigrants assuming tremendous risks, American society has placed a great premium on individual determination, courage, and perseverance.

Andrew Jackson has also been considered a "great man," one whose character and resolve were tested in battle and crisis. In the 1820s and 1830s Jackson seemed the perfect person to lead a young nation. In his exploits against the British at the Battle of New Orleans, the Creek Indians in the frontier wars, and the National Bank during his presidency, Andrew Jackson had demonstrated an unrivaled determination to achieve whatever he wanted, regardless of the opposition. For a new youthful country preoccupied with its own destiny, Jackson seemed a "symbol for an age"—a man whose skills were complemented by the forces of history.

In the following essay, William A. DeGregorio closely examines Jackson's famous duel with Charles Dickinson. For his contemporaries, this event, as much as any other, attested to Jackson's courage and determination, and also his brutality and violent nature. And the glorification of the duel says much about the qualities that were admired in the mid-nineteenth century.

Gentlemen, are you ready?"

Andrew Jackson and Charles Dickinson squared off, facing each other eight paces (about twenty-four feet) apart. Each held a single-shot pistol at his side.

Dickinson, a handsome figure nattily dressed in a short blue coat and gray trousers, calmly replied, "Yes." Jackson, his spare, lanky frame concealed beneath a carelessly buttoned, full-length frock coat, fixed his icy blue eyes on his opponent and awaited the signal.

"Fire!"

Even before that Friday morning, May 30, 1806, news of the duel had swept Nashville. Residents placed bets furiously, with the smart money on Dickinson. At age twenty-seven, he was widely regarded as the best marksman in Tennessee. He was a rising attorney of some repute in the western part of the state, and had prospered by speculating in commodities, land, livestock, and slaves. Dickinson's arrogance and incessant bragging annoyed some, but his wit and charm allowed him to remain quite popular in Nashville.

Jackson, the man who nonetheless challenged this sharpshooter to a duel, had at age thirty-nine already served in both houses of Congress and as a judge in Tennessee's highest court, and held the rank of major general in the Tennessee militia. He had demonstrated many important leadership qualities—courage, vision, and an ability to motivate others. But there was a darker side to Jackson's character—a side he exposed during the events surrounding his duel with Dickinson.

Of course, those who knew Jackson well were aware that he had a visceral, forceful personality. He was combative, often stubborn, and had an explosive temper. His closest confidant and eventual presidential successor Martin Van Buren marveled at the way Jackson turned his anger on and off like a switch.

"The Choice" by William A. DeGregorio. This article is reprinted from the January/February 1990 issue, Volume XXIV/No. 7, pp.33–36, 72 of *American History Illustrated* with the permission of Cowles History Group, Inc. Copyright *American History Illustrated* magazine.

Some speculated that Jackson simply showed his temper for effect. Perhaps, but genuine rage often boiled within this rawboned veteran who, having been orphaned by age fourteen, had needed to grow up in a hurry, and who still bore the physical and emotional scars from his boyhood internment in a prisoner of war camp during the Revolution.

Thomas Jefferson observed Jackson regularly during the latter's brief Congressional career and was appalled at his inability to control his temper. "His passions are terrible," Jefferson said of Jackson. "When I was President of the Senate, he was senator, and he could never speak on account of the rashness of his feelings. I have seen him attempt it repeatedly, and as often choke with rage. His passions are, no doubt, cooler now; he has been much tried since I knew him, but he is a dangerous man."

"When Andrew Jackson hated," writes Robert V. Remini, Jackson's principal modern biographer, "It often became grand passion. He could hate with a Biblical fury and would resort to petty and vindictive acts to nurture his hatred and keep it bright and strong and ferocious. He needed revenge. He always struck back."

Especially in defense of his wife's honor.

When Jackson "married" Rachel Donelson Robards in 1791, neither realized that she was still legally wed to another man. Rachel thought she had been divorced, but because of a technicality that Jackson, though a lawyer, had somehow overlooked, the divorce was not yet finalized when she and Andrew exchanged vows. A few years later they discovered the error and were married in a second ceremony, this time legally. But whenever Jackson ran for office or was otherwise in the public spotlight, his adversaries and the opposition press hurled charges of adultery.

In October 1803, for example, Jackson was the target of a harsh verbal attack by former Tennessee governor John Sevier in a public confrontation on Knoxville's town square. "I know of no great service you have rendered the country," taunted Sevier, "except taking a trip to Natchez with another man's wife." A scuffle punctuated by gunshots ensued between the enraged Jackson and his bitter political rival; during the weeks that followed Jackson repeatedly challenged Sevier to duel and published charges that he was "a base coward and poltroon" who "will basely insult, but has not the courage to repair the wound." The satisfaction with arms that Jackson sought was barely averted at the last minute through the efforts of the two men's seconds.

Tradition credits the Jackson-Dickinson duel to similar circumstances: learning that Dickinson had made irreverent remarks about Rachel, the story goes, Jackson confronted the young lawyer. Dickinson apologized and blamed his loose tongue on too many drinks. Soon thereafter, however, Dickinson repeated the slanders, and escalating tempers eventually led to the dueling ground.

Although no authentic document survives to confirm that Dickinson besmirched the honor of Jackson's wife as legend and some historical accounts maintain, the degree of enmity Jackson felt toward Dickinson suggests this could well have been the case. But the sequence of events leading to the ultimate confrontation between the two men was far more complex than that, and it was set in motion by a wager over a horse race.

An avid horseman, Jackson owned a superb stallion named Truxton. In November 1805 Jackson and two partners arranged a $2,000 match race between Truxton and Ploughboy, a horse owned by Dickinson's uncle and partner, Captain Joseph Ervin. Ploughboy went lame before the appointed day, however, and Ervin and Dickinson canceled the race, paying Jackson the $800 forfeit in the form of promissory notes they held. A brief disagreement arose regarding whether the notes paid were the same as those presented when the race had been arranged, but the matter was settled amicably.

That would have been the end of the affair had not a third party—a young lawyer and newcomer to Nashville named Thomas Swann—meddled. Apparently seeking attention and notoriety, Swann incited both Dickinson and Jackson by repeating to each man inflammatory statements supposedly made by the other about the promis-

This grand statue of Jackson stands in Jackson Square in New Orleans; it is indicative of Jackson's reputation, and plays upon a romanticized view of militance, strength, and honor.

sory notes. Misunderstandings compounded and tempers flared. Finally, in a letter published in the Nashville newspaper *Impartial Review and Cumberland Repository,* Jackson charged Swann with being a "puppet and lying valet for a worthless, drunken, blackguard scounderal [*sic*]." Dickinson, replying publicly in the same newspaper, declared Jackson to be "a worthless scoundrel" and "a paltroon [*sic*] and a coward."

Jackson not unexpectedly responded by challenging Dickinson to duel. Although dueling was illegal in Tennessee, Jackson was prepared to defy the law to satisfy his passion. Nevertheless, for propriety's sake he and Dickinson agreed to meet outside of Tennessee—just across the state border in a popular forest clearing at Harrison's Mills, Kentucky, about thirty-five miles north of Nashville.

The day before the scheduled showdown, Jackson arose at 5 a.m., ate breakfast, and told his wife that he was leaving for a couple of days, adding parenthetically that he might have a bit of trouble to settle with Charles Dickinson. Rachel typically did not press him for details but easily could have surmised his mission. At 6:30 a.m. Jackson met his second in the duel, John Overton, and three other companions in Nashville; together they turned north toward Kentucky.

En route, Jackson was in a serious but talkative mood. Never hesitant to speak his mind on national affairs, Jackson criticized President Thomas Jefferson for not standing up to the British over the issue of impressment on the high seas, calling him "the best Republican in theory and the worst in practice." He criticized Aaron Burr, ironically in light of events about to unfold, for killing Alexander Hamilton in a duel two years earlier.

Jackson spoke little of his pending duel except to reveal his strategy of letting Dickinson shoot first. Jackson, only a fair shot himself, was aware of Dickinson's reputation as one of Tennessee's best marksmen. Some said Dickinson was capable of shooting apart a piece of string from eight yards away. Jackson reasoned that he had no chance to beat Dickinson to the draw, and that if he were to fire hastily, his aim was sure to be spoiled by the impact of Dickinson's bullet. Jackson was almost certain that he would be hit and believed that his only chance was to survive Dickinson's shot, then take careful aim.

Dickinson, his second, Dr. Hanson Catlett, and a half-dozen friends traveled ahead of the Jackson party in a carnival mood. Before setting off, Dickinson cheerily kissed his wife farewell and reassured her that he would return home safely the following evening. Boasting to all within earshot that he would shoot Jackson handily, he placed hundreds of dollars in wagers on himself in Nashville. Dickinson paused at times during the journey to demonstrate his marksmanship, delighting onlookers, and he repeated his vow to drop Jackson with one shot.

Before noon the Jackson party stopped for refreshments and a few hours' rest. Jackson had not had his usual morning ration of whiskey, wanting to keep a clear head for the business at hand, but did allow himself a single mint julep at the rest stop.

Later, at about 8 p.m., Jackson settled into David Miller's tavern near the site of the duel, displaying none of the jitters one would expect in a man about to put his life on the line. The prospect of the next morning's potentially fatal encounter disturbed neither his appetite nor his sleep. He enjoyed a full-course supper of fried chicken, sweet potatoes, waffles, and coffee. He then went out on the tavern porch to smoke his pipe for a bit and, at 10 p.m., went to bed. He was asleep in ten minutes. Throughout his life, Jackson was supremely confident of his ability to face any challenge—even a crack shot like Dickinson. Jackson slept so soundly that night that Overton had trouble rousing him at dawn.

Just after sunrise that morning the duelists stood ready in their positions with the seconds, Overton and Catlett, alert to gun down the opposing principal if either should fire prematurely.

Dickinson had won the toss for position, but because it was too early for the sun to break the horizon, this made little difference. Jackson had chosen the weapons—a pair of his own pistols with nine-inch barrels firing 70-caliber balls. Dickinson, therefore, had his pick of the two. Jackson won the right to have his second give the signal to fire.

Upon Overton's signal to "Fire!," Dickinson instantly raised his pistol and, as expected, got off the first shot. Kicking up dust from Jackson's coat as it entered, the bullet struck him full in the chest. Everyone watching knew that Jackson had been hit. Astonishingly, Jackson did not fall but remained standing, ramrod straight, though the ball had chipped off his breastbone, broken two ribs, plowed through chest muscle, and lodged so close to his heart that it could never be removed.

Jackson raised his left hand to the wound. Blood drained down his left leg and began to fill his boot, but except for a slight wince Jackson gave no outward appearance of how badly he had been hurt. His lips concealed how tightly he clenched his teeth.

Dickinson, dumfounded to see his gaunt target still erect, stumbled back off his mark and cried out, "Great God, have I missed him?" But he knew his aim had been sure; he had seen the bullet hit. Everyone there had seen it.

"Back to the mark, sir!" ordered Jackson's second, brandishing a gun. Dickinson had no honorable alternative but to return to the mark and await his fate. He was now at Jackson's mercy.

A man in Jackson's situation, if he did not believe himself to be mortally wounded, customarily raised his pistol, aimed it at his disarmed opponent, then pointed it at the sky and fired. Many present, especially Dickinson, no doubt anticipated this magnanimous, though not mandatory, gesture.

While Dickinson stood frozen at the mark, his arms folded across his chest, his eyes fixed on the ground, Jackson raised his pistol, took level aim— and pulled the trigger.

A harmless "click" followed. The hammer had mercifully failed to strike.

Jackson now had a second chance to consider his actions, to remind himself that Dickinson's wife was pregnant. Jackson had been born after his own father's death and so knew from experience the hardship of growing up fatherless on the frontier.

As Dickinson waited helplessly in place, Jackson carefully recocked his pistol and again took deliberate aim at his opponent. And for the second time he pulled the trigger. This time the weapon did not misfire.

The heavy bullet struck Dickinson in the abdomen, penetrating his intestines and leaving a gaping wound. Overton, satisfied that the figure writhing in agony on the ground would not survive the day, hurried over to Jackson and said, "He won't want anything more of you, General."

As the winning team strode off the field, Overton noted Jackson's left boot sloshing with blood and finally realized that his friend had been seriously wounded. "Oh, I believe that he pinked me," Jackson observed in typical understatement. "I don't want those people to know. Let's move on."

On examining the wound, the duelist's companions concluded that what had apparently saved Jackson was the set of his ill-fitting coat. With the frock hung askew, Dickinson had prob-

ably misjudged the location of his opponent's heart. But he had missed it by only an inch.

To those who wondered how Jackson had found the strength to remain standing and shoot Dickinson after having been so severely wounded, Jackson responded, "I should have hit him if he had shot me through the brain!"

Jackson showed no repentance for having shot Dickinson in cold blood. His notion of magnanimity was sending a bottle of wine to his victim and offering his surgeon's services. Dickinson's only comfort in his last hours was the lie friends told him: that Jackson was also on his deathbed, mortally wounded. At about 9 p.m. Dickinson asked, "Why did you put out the candles?" and died.

Throughout his career, Jackson never felt restrained to use the minimum force necessary to repel a threat. And in his encounter with Dickinson he felt fully justified in killing a man who had tried, albeit unsuccessfully, to kill *him*. No further excuse, he believed, was necessary; nor was any forthcoming. Jackson's apologists over the years have maintained that when he shot Dickinson he believed his own wound was fatal. If that is so, Jackson left no record of it.

The episode and the bullet Dickinson fired would haunt Jackson the rest of his life. The full ounce of lead was lodged so close to his heart that doctors never dared to attempt removing it. The bullet immobilized him for weeks. He recovered slowly and thereafter experienced sporadic chest pain that increased in frequency with old age.

Dickinson's funeral was one of the largest ever held in Nashville. A group of more than seventy angry mourners met after the services to petition the *Impartial Review* to run a memorial edition dedicated to Dickinson as an expression of regret for his death. When Jackson heard about this, he sent an angry letter to the editor demanding that the petitioners' names also be printed so that he would know who his enemies were. Confronted with such publicity, twenty-six people withdrew their names from the document, but the remainder, including some community leaders, agreed to take a public stand.

Erwin, the father of Dickinson's pregnant widow, publicly charged that Jackson, by pulling the trigger a second time after the pistol had jammed at half-cock, had violated the agreement governing the duel and therefore killed his opponent dishonorably. This accusation came to nothing, however; Catlett, Dickinson's second, joined Overton in a public statement attesting that the duel had been fought within the terms of the agreement.

Until he subsequently gained fame as "Old Hickory" during the War of 1812, Jackson remained something of a pariah in western Tennessee. Even after he became a national figure, the duel was occasionally dredged up and cited by political opponents as a good reason why Jackson should be denied public office.

Some saw the episode as part of a pattern of ruthless and belligerent behavior. Jackson's critics pointed out that the Dickinson shooting was not an isolated incident:

- In the 1803 fight previously noted, Jackson used his heavy walking stick to attack former Tennessee governor John Sevier on the steps of the Knoxville courthouse. The two men later met for a duel that was only narrowly averted before shots were exchanged.
- While preparing to defend New Orleans against imminent British attack during the War of 1812, Jackson executed deserters, imposed martial law on the city, dissolved the Louisiana legislature, suppressed free expression, and ignored a federal judge's writ of habeas corpus.
- In 1814 Jackson went gunning for Thomas Hart Benton in Nashville's City Hotel, but was shot in the back by Benton's brother, Jesse. The bullet tore Jackson's left shoulder and greatly reduced the mobility in that arm until the lead was removed nearly twenty years later.
- During the First Seminole War (1816–1818), Jackson occupied Spanish Florida without authorization from the administration in Washington, D.C. He also captured, court-martialed, and executed British citizens Alexander Arbuthnot and Robert Ambrister for having incited the Seminoles against the United States. The killings drew a sharp diplomatic rebuke from Britain.

During Jackson's first successful presidential campaign in 1828 the opposition compiled a résumé of brutality, the so-called Coffin Handbill, from such incidents. Under the bold, grim headline "Account of some of the Bloody Deeds of GENERAL JACKSON," it depicted clusters of caskets, eighteen in all, each with the name of an individual killed by Jackson's order and a brief narrative of how that person died.

Despite Jackson's vulnerability on what today is called the character issue, Americans twice elected him president and he went on to become perhaps the greatest chief executive in the half-century between Jefferson and Abraham Lincoln. Jackson was a founder of the modern activist presidency. He was the first to harness the latent powers of the office to implement his programs and thwart the will of the opposition. In so doing he vetoed more bills than all of his predecessors combined.

In the strictest sense, Jackson was the first common man to become president; his predecessors were either Virginia aristocrats or Boston lawyers. He was the first president to represent the interests of the burgeoning West. He destroyed the Bank of the United States, symbol to many of the moneyed interests' exploitation of the working class. And, in a showdown with South Carolina over its claimed right to nullify federal laws within its borders (1832–1833), Jackson stood firm and stamped out, at least temporarily, budding secessionist sentiment in the South.

The Dickinson episode, then, revealed some significant character flaws in Jackson, but these did not prove fatal to his presidency. Had voters focused on Jackson's temper and ruthless, unforgiving nature to the exclusion of his courage, integrity, tenacity, and unquestionable leadership ability, the nation would have been denied an outstanding president.

Study Questions

1. Why did Jackson and Dickinson get involved in a duel? Had these men been in-volved in other duels, and what circumstances prompted those confrontations?

2. Do the activities of the Southern "gentlemen" in this piece—especially the gam-bling, horse racing, and fighting—remind you of events described in an earlier reading in this text? What conclusions might you draw from the comparison?

3. What was a "second," and what role did he play in the elaborate protocol of duels?

4. Despite killing Dickinson in the duel described here, Andrew Jackson went on to become president of the United States and the most famous American of his era. In fact, some historians refer to the 1820-1840 period as the "Age of Jackson." Con-sidering the importance we currently place on the "character issue" in choosing our president, why do you think the majority of American voters not only elected a man with such a violent past to the White House, but considered him the living embodiment of the "American character" as well? Did Jackson display positive character traits which might have balanced out his violent temper?

Bibliography

The first place to go for superlative Jackson biography is Robert V. Remini, *Andrew Jackson and the Course of American Freedom, 1822-1833* (1981); and also by Rem-ini, *Andrew Jackson and the Course of American Democracy, 1833-1845* (1984). For an introduction to the Age of Jackson, see Glyndon G. Van Deusen, *The Jackson-ian Era, 1828-1848* (1959). Also see Edward Pessen, *Jacksonian America: Society, Personality, and Politics* (1978). A dated but still important interpretation of the phe-nomenon of Jacksonianism is Arther M. Schlesinger, Jr., *The Age of Jackson* (1945). Additionally, see John William Ward, *Andrew Jackson: Symbol for an Age* (1955) and Marvin Meyers, *The Jacksonian Persuasion* (1957) for analyses of the culture of Jack-sonian democracy. Finally, for the role of duels and the code of Southern "honor" see Bertram Wyatt-Brown, *Southern Honor: Ethics and Behavior in the Old South* (1982) and Edward L. Ayers, *Vengeance and Justice: Crime and Punishment in the Nineteenth-Century American South* (1984). Also see Andrew Burstein, *The Pas-sions of Andrew Jackson* (2003).

In Search of Davy's Grave

Randy Roberts and James S. Olson

Few events in United States history have so captured the American imagination as the Alamo. On March 6, 1836, General Antonio López de Santa Anna and his Mexican army overran the Alamo, killing all of its defenders and giving Texas a legion of martyrs. Among the defenders of the Alamo was Davy Crockett, already an iconic figure in the United States, whose death allowed most Americans to see Texas independence in the same way they viewed their own Revolution. But the question of just how Davy Crockett died—killing a slew of Mexican soldiers before being overwhelmed or being executed after surrendering or being captured—has become one of the most intriguing and controversial mysteries of American history. Texas patriots prefer a heroic death, like the one portrayed in Walt Disney's *Davy Crockett at the Alamo* or John Wayne's *The Alamo,* while those who see Crockett as a slave-owning, over-hyped buffoon take pleasure in a more humble, or humiliating, demise. In the following essay, historians Randy Roberts and James S. Olson examine the rise and fall of Davy Crockett and the subsequent controversy over how he died.

No one knows exactly when he got the idea, but it might have been that December night in 1833 at the Washington Theater. Congressman David Crockett of Tennessee had recently returned to the capital, exultant after his narrow re-election victory. Unlike in 1831, the forces aligned with President Andrew Jackson had failed to engineer Crockett's defeat, and his people were again his people, at least by a margin of 173 votes. But if it had been only by a single vote, what would it have mattered? He would still have been Congressman David Crockett, a man of importance, even though he struggled with debts, felt the limits of his meager education, and laid claim to few political or economic accomplishments. For Crockett, the position was significant. He yearned to be a respectable gentleman, trying to dress the part and associating with prominent Whigs. A seat in Congress put him in the same room, if not quite the same social circle, as Daniel Webster, Henry Clay, and John Quincy Adams. For a man born and raised in the hardscrabble poverty of the West, who married young only to discover that he was "better at increasing [his] family than [his] fortune," and whose primary talent was making other people like him, sitting close to Webster, Clay, and Adams would have to do—at least for the moment.

But something was changing in the United States. There was profound movement in the social and political landscape, some subtle shift that signaled the arrival of Crockett's moment—and not only Crockett's but that of a whole nation of Crocketts, white men from nowhere important who dreamed to be going somewhere and doing something. The change was acknowledged that cold December night at the theater. Crockett had gone to see actor James Hackett play the part of Colonel Nimrod Wildfire in James Kirke Paulding's play *The Lion of the West.* The part, as almost everyone knew, had been modeled on Crockett. Frontiersman Wildfire dressed in buckskin, wore a wildcat-skin hat, and spoke the patois of the

West—or at least what Easterners assumed was the patois of the West. Like the popular image of Crockett, Wildfire was known for his exaggerated boasts. In the play he claimed that he had "the fastest horse, prettiest sister, the quickest rifle, and the ugliest dog in the states," and that he could "jump higher, squat lower, dive deeper, and come up drier than any other fellow in the world." The play had opened in late 1831, had been performed across the country and in Great Britain, and had filled the house everywhere.

Crockett took his seat for the performance. No doubt pleased with himself, he looked at Hackett, who was ready to start his imitation of David Crockett. Hackett, dressed in his stage buckskin, saw Crockett, the real Crockett, then nodded to David and bowed. Crockett, dressed like a gentleman, nodded back, rose to his feet, and turned to acknowledge the other spectators, who by this time were clapping for Hackett, Crockett, and the sheer, pure theater of that moment. Crockett bowed, Hackett bowed, and an odd fusion took place. Legend and man, myth and reality, backwoodsman Davy Crockett and Congressman David Crockett—they had become one and interchangeable. If the word had existed in its modern meaning—which it did not until about 1850—Crockett would have realized that he had become a celebrity, famous not for anything he had actually accomplished but simply for being famous. He had become not so much a man of deeds as a figment of the American imagination, the sum total of the country's desires.

Maybe it was then that the glimmer of a thought became a fully formed idea. Why shouldn't he, David/Davy Crockett, get cut in for a piece of himself? Hackett and Paulding were making a small fortune from incantations of his life. So was Matthew St. Clair Clarke, who in January 1833 had published *Life and Adventures of Colonel David Crockett of West Tennessee,* an exaggerated portrait of Crockett, "that same David Crockett, fresh from the backwoods. . . . Half-horse, half-alligator, a little touched with snapping turtle." If Crockett did not understand that Paulding and Clarke had helped to make him a celebrity, he did

Randy Roberts and James S. Olson, *A Line in the Sand: The Alamo in Blood and Memory,* the Free Press, 2001.

*John Gadsby Chapman painted this portrait of
David Crockett in 1834.*

sense that he might become rich by selling an image of himself that Americans were hungry for. He went right to work writing his own account of himself, *A Narrative of the Life of David Crockett, of the State of Tennessee,* to which he appended, "by Himself." The autobiography appeared in March 1834 and was a great success, moving into its sixth printing within a few months and easing Crockett's debt. In the language of an American he told the story of an American, the great tale of democracy. Using phonetical spelling and frontier grammar, he told his story with great humor, demonstrating that while he was better than no other man, he was no worse either.

Unlike any autobiography before it, it was the story of a Jacksonian man, yearning for success in Jacksonian America. Unlike Benjamin Franklin, whose accomplishments merited an autobiography, Crockett wrote one simply because he could and because he gleaned a market for it. In a sense, it was not so much a record of his accomplishments as an accomplishment in itself, an announcement that he had arrived because he had written that he had arrived. And the beauty of his life, as he told it, was that it was so common, so down-home-Western common. He was born and raised honest, hunted bears and fought Indians, went to Congress, and became a toady for no man. That was about it—poverty, hunting, fighting, electioneering—representing the common man by being a common man. And he said it all in the language of the common man.

The language, the language was everything— words that followed no standards for spelling or usage. Words that were scattered in odd combinations and took on new meanings. Words that were as fresh and powerful and malleable as America itself, ever changing and mutating and transforming, always moving west on a vast mythical and physical landscape. Only a few years before the appearance of Crockett's autobiography, Frenchman Alexis de Tocqueville had toured America, studying the nature of Jacksonian democracy. He was shocked at the impact of democracy on language, suggesting that Americans believed that one person's use of a word was as good as the next's. "An author begins by a slight deflection of a known expression from its primitive meaning, and he adapts it. . . . A second writer twists the sense of the expression in another way; a third takes possession of it for another purpose." The end result is that words and expressions, like Jacksonian men, are self-made. Tocqueville analyzed and understood the process; David Crockett lived and was the process.

The autobiography had its desired effect, making Crockett even more famous, encouraging his Whig supporters to think of him as a potential presidential candidate. He just might be the Whig answer to Andrew Jackson. He just might be able to out-Jackson any politician the Democrats could throw at him. They had plans, important plans, for him; at least that was what Whig Party men indicated. Plans for a trip along the East Coast to broaden his political base, plans for speeches to show Americans the quality of him, plans for the White House, a symbolic place for a symbolic man. Congress was in session, but Crockett had bigger worlds to conquer. Texas, part of another country, was the furthermost thing from his mind.

In the spring of 1834, with dreams of the White House pushing him ahead, Crockett hit the road and traveled widely throughout the Northeast, drawing crowds and newspaper coverage at every stop, giving prospective voters a close look at a legend. But on May 13, 1834, he returned to Washington, D.C., tired and moody. David Crockett had grown tired of politics probably even before politics had grown tired of him.

The trip had gone passably well. Crockett had said all the right things, making people laugh when he wanted to and criticizing the administration of Andrew Jackson whenever the chance appeared. If he wanted to become the Whigs' presidential nominee in 1836, he had to become as familiar in Boston as he was in Nashville, as loved in Pennsylvania as in Tennessee, and the tour was designed for that purpose—that and to embarrass Jackson. But still, being all things to all people, even if the nomination hung in the balance, wearied an honest man in body and soul, and David Crockett, whatever people thought, was an honest man.

Congress now bored him. Too many speeches, too much hot air that was expended on blowing up grand balloons that always seemed to burst. Increasingly, he had stopped listening and left his seat, drifting out of the Capitol back to his boardinghouse or to a Washington watering hole. Although Congress was scheduled to adjourn on June 30, Crockett adjourned himself earlier, traveling to Philadelphia to pick up the finished rifle that had been promised to him during his spring tour. It was a beautifully crafted weapon with an alligator, a possum, and a deer etched in the silver plate on the stock. Along the barrel, in an inlaid gilded arrow, was Crockett's motto, *Go Ahead.* "Pretty Betsey," Crockett dubbed the fine rifle,

and he promised to use it in defense of America. As he said on the Fourth of July 1834, "I love my country." And he meant it. He may have developed a passionate dislike of Jackson and an itchy feeling sitting in Congress, but he had not lost his love of his country.

Back home in Tennessee, Democrats grumbled about Crockett's jaunts from Congress when he was paid $8 a day to be there looking after the interests of the people. But David knew that the $8 a day was not nearly enough to pay off the mountain of debt that he had accumulated. His only hope was to return to writing, following up the success of his *Narrative of the Life of David Crockett, of the State of Tennessee* with another account. During the fall and winter he labored on a narrative of his Northeastern trip, which was published in 1835 as *Col. Crockett's Tour to the North and Down East* and was not nearly as popular as his earlier work. But it helped to relieve some of the debt and encouraged him to believe that writing and politics might be his economic salvation.

That was the order—writing and politics. When Congress reconvened he spent more time preparing his book than he did tending to his congressional duties. And when he did attend a session and take the floor it was usually to attack Jackson or Martin Van Buren, the politician Democrats believed would be the next president of the United States. The thought of "Mr. *martin vanburen,*" all pink and clean, maneuvering his way into the White House infuriated Crockett. If that happened, he thought, he would pack up and leave the United States. "I will go to the wildes of Texas" and live under Mexican rule, Crockett wrote a friend.

In truth, the Crockett phenomenon was on the wane. In three terms in Congress he had failed to push through a single piece of legislation. As a political wag, his act was becoming repetitive and weary. The same stories, the same attacks on Jackson and Van Buren—it was wearing thin with both his Whig patrons and his Democratic friends. In the August 1835 congressional election against pro-Jackson Adam "Blackhawk" Huntsman, Crockett tried to explain away his failures and excuse his slightly amiss expense accounts. He could still speak the language of his backcountry constituents and he remembered how to make them laugh, but the combination of his turning on Jackson and Jackson turning on Crockett's home district was a distinct liability. Still, he fought a good fight, again proclaiming that a loss would not be the worst thing in the world. Texas was still west of Louisiana and south of Arkansas, and if by chance his people voted him out of office, by damn he would go to Texas.

By a thin margin Crockett lost his bid for a fourth term. He took it badly. In his own mind he had become some sort of heroic figure standing for truth and honesty against the most base tyranny; he had become a nineteenth-century version of Milton's Abdiel, the one true man in a crowd of false gods, transforming Jackson into Satan. He knew in his heart that he was right, but the mob had followed Jackson, or more precisely, followed Jackson's money. Now, like Abdiel, he would turn his back on them, turn his back on "those proud Tow'rs to swift destruction doom'd." Shortly after the election, he announced in the press that "I never expect to offer my name again to the public for any office."

When Crockett made the statement, he probably meant it, for defeat had never come easy to him. When he had tasted it previously, he had gone on a long hunt, forcing public affairs out of his mind and surrounding himself with friends whose loyalty was absolute. Now, more than ever, he needed nature, not society—friends, not political allies. For a decade his life had centered on politics and celebrity. He had drifted away from his family, his home in Tennessee, and perhaps even from himself. He had drunk too much, talked too much, and occupied too much of his time with things that didn't really matter. Over the years his Davy persona had hogtied and swallowed his David self.

The more he thought about Texas, the more the idea grew on him. Texas had wild game, good men like Sam Houston, and the promise of emotional, perhaps even political, regeneration. In Texas there were land and adventures and maybe even a future. It was certainly worth a look. In October he held a barbecue in his honor and spent the day drinking, eating, and talking, complaining about the past and speculating about the future. He was determined to go west and south.

On the first day of November 1835, the forty-nine-year-old Crockett, accompanied by his nephew William Patton and friends Lindsay Tinkle and Abner Burgin, set out for Texas. The news spread fast, and what started as a modest expedition began to swell and contract as men joined up with him for a day or a week or more and then left for home or to some other destination. At times as many as thirty men rode along, sharing stories and a jug with one another. They swept through Bolivar and Jackson, Tennessee, then turned southwest toward Memphis and the Mississippi River. All along his route people came out to gape and gawk and shake his hand. They wanted to meet Davy Crockett, wanted to hear him speak. "He was like a passing comet," noted an acquaintance, a perfect description for the year that Halley's comet tracked across the sky.

In Memphis he drank with friends—always with friends—at the Union Hotel and Neil McCool's saloon. Crockett's friends carried him on their shoulders and he made a speech standing on McCool's bar—the "Go to hell, I am going to Texas" speech. The next morning he crossed the Mississippi and set off overland to Little Rock. Along the way he shot game, which he toted with him. In Little Rock once again there were speeches to deliver, liquor to drink, and people to meet. Why was he going to Texas? In a letter to his brother-in-law penned before his departure from Tennessee, Crockett had written, "I want to explore Texas well before I return." In Little Rock he hinted that he had an interest in the revolutionary activities taking place there, and one reporter recalled that Davy said he would "have *Santa Anna's* head and wear it as a watch seal. . . ."

The dream of Texas gripped him tightly. There was simply so much of everything that a man could not help but be content there. He planned on becoming a land agent and attracting his friends to follow him. Texas, then, would be his financial salvation. Texas would get him out of debt and back on his feet. "I am rejoiced at my fate," he wrote. "I had rather be in my present situation than to be elected to a seat in Congress for life. I am in great hopes of making a fortune for myself and my family bad as has been my prospects."

Texas seemed as enthralled with Crockett as he was with it. He may have crossed over from the United States, but he had not passed beyond the border of his fame. He wrote his family that he had been "received by everyone with open arms of friendship, I am hailed with a hearty welcome to this country, a dinner and a party of Ladys [*sic*] have honored me with an invitation." Texans feted Crockett, and Davy told them what they wanted to hear in the language they wanted to hear it. Now he hardly needed to give a reason for his move. "To satisfy your curiosity at once as to myself, I will tell you all about it. I was, for some years, a member of Congress. In my last canvass, I told the people of my District, that, if they saw fit to re-elect me, I would serve them faithfull as I had done; but, if not, *They might go to hell, and I would go to Texas.* I was beaten, gentlemen, and here I am." It was still a story that never failed to bring whoops and hollers.

* * *

Texans turned out for him in Nacogdoches and San Augustine, listening to his stories and telling him their own grand tale, the narratives of Texas and Mexico and the dream of independence. They told how they defeated General Cos in Béxar and how they had won other skirmishes. In Nacogdoches in mid-January he took the "oath of the government"—insisting that the word "republican" be inserted into his oath as the type of future government he would support—and thought it likely that he would get elected as a member of the convention to form "the Constitution of the Provence [*sic*]." Others in San Augustine felt the same way. One citizen wrote Lieutenant Governor James Robinson that Crockett "is To Represent them in the Convention."

Without knowing exactly what he was getting into, he had been swept along. But into what?

Land speculation? Politics? War? Revolution? Treason? In Crockett's mind they were probably all tied together. To get into politics, he had to take the oath. To get land, he had to volunteer to fight. And the sum total of the politics and fighting was revolution and perhaps even treason. . . .

After March 6, 1836, Crockett's fate led to wild speculation. As the only national figure at the Alamo, he became more important than Travis or Bowie, rivaled in newspapers only by Santa Anna himself. In fact, newspapers transformed the fall of the Alamo into a perfect melodrama, complete with a noble, Byronic hero (Crockett), a ruthless, satanic villain (Santa Anna), and a fine cast of secondary characters. A poem in the *New York Star,* which was widely reprinted, captured the American story of Crockett:

*Tho' sad was his fate, and mournful
    the story,
The deeds of the hero shall never decay;
He fell in a cause dear to freedom and
    glory,
And fought to the last like a lion at bay.*

*When rang the loud call from a
    nation oppressed,
And her vallies with slaughter of
    brave men were red;
'Twas the pride of poor Crockett to
    help the distressed
And the watchword in Texas was
    heard, Go Ahead.*

*His death-dealing rifle no longer shall
    shower
Its unerring balls on the proud
    haughty foe.
Cut down in the spring-time of life's
    budding flower—
His tomb stone, alas, are the walls,
    Alamo.*

*Then may we not hope, since valor has
    crown'd him,
And o'er him bright fame her mantle
    has spread;*

*In the soul's parting hour good angels
      were round him,
Did his spirit arise to the skies "Go
      Ahead."*

In death Crockett became what he never was in life—a politician who transcended party squabbles and represented an American ideal. There were even some reports that Crockett had not died at all, though he had suffered near-mortal wounds. In late April, the *Cincinnati Whig* noted that a gentleman brought word from Texas "that Col. CROCKETT is still living. It is said, that he had been left for dead on the battle ground at San Antonio; but some acquaintances who happened to visit the scene of action, after the departure of the Mexicans, discovering that he still breathed, had him removed to comfortable quarters, where his numerous wounds were dressed; and he 'was doing well' when the gentleman in question . . . left San Antonio." But this report came to light after earlier stories of Crockett's death and the burning of all the corpses, and even the hopeful editor warned his readers to be cautious about the latest news.

Far more common were reports that Crockett died "fighting like a tiger." A story in the *New Orleans Bulletin* commented that Crockett's "conduct on this occasion was most heroic; having used his rifle as long as possible by loading and discharging, and the enemy crowding upon the walls, he turned the britch of his gun, and demolished more than twenty of the enemy before he fell." Along the same lines, the *Richmond Enquirer* reported that "David Crockett (now rendered immortal in glory) had fortified himself with sixteen guns well charged, and a monument of slain encompassed his lifeless body." In report after report, tales of Crockett's heroic fighting and epic glory escalated.

But there were also reports of surrenders and executions. Most papers [spoke of] seven rebels who gave up a lost cause, though there were different versions of what exactly happened. One widely reported version noted that the Texas garrison fought until only seven men remained alive, and that they "cried for quarters but were told

that there was no mercy for them—they then continued fighting until the whole were butchered." Another said that some men did surrender, only to be "dragged through hot embers, and their flesh cut off previous to being burnt in a pile." Occasionally reports said that Crockett was one of the last to die, and that he and a few of his comrades were the ones who asked for quarter, but when none was forthcoming they fought on to the death. The confusion offered fertile ground for an unsolvable mystery.

* * *

Some Texans were still searching for answers to several questions, the most important of which was what exactly had happened in the last moments of the battle of the Alamo. On the subject of David Crockett's death, they now had more witnesses. They had Santa Anna, as well as a number of his officers and men. After their defeat at San Jacinto, most of the Mexican soldiers were incarcerated on Galveston Island. There they waited while Burnet and the Texas cabinet negotiated final terms with Santa Anna, and their captors decided what to do with them. Many feared for their lives, and most nursed deep resentments toward Santa Anna, who may have become simultaneously the most unpopular man in Texas and Mexico. While on Galveston Island they passed their time like prisoners of war from other wars, chatting, engaging in wild speculations, reliving the past, and worrying about the future. In this uncertain, charged atmosphere, far-fetched stories grew into facts, and rumors blossomed into POW gospel. . . .

The story that received the most attention involved the Texans who had surrendered and been executed at the Alamo. The story itself was nothing new, of course; it had been passed on by word of mouth and in the newspapers for several months. What the Mexicans added was more details. George M. Dolson, an orderly sergeant who had joined the Texas army after San Jacinto, wrote to his brother in Detroit that he had been called upon to act as an interpreter for Colonel James Morgan, commandant of Galveston Island, in an interrogation of a Mexican prisoner. Dolson noted that Texas was in an agitated state. Rumors were circulating that Santa Anna had cut a deal for his own liberty and passage back to Mexico, and the news reached the army "like an electric shock." How, Dolson wondered, could such an evil tyrant—"a cold-blooded murderer, and worthy only of the sympathy of cowards and the scorn of great men"—be allowed to leave the very land he had "stained with blood"?

As proof of the dictator's evil, Dolson offered the Mexican officer's statement, given "according to a promise" (an intriguing phrase that is not explained). The officer stated that on the morning the Alamo was taken, General Manuel Fernández Castrillón discovered six Texans in a back room of the Alamo. They had fought bravely, but the battle was decided and continued bloodshed was useless. Castrillón offered them hope. Placing his hand on his chest, he said, "Here is a hand and a heart to protect you; come with me to the general-in-Chief, and you shall be saved." One of the men, the officer claimed, walked to the rear of the rest, "his arms folded, and appeared bold as the lion." Santa Anna's interpreter identified him as Crockett. When Castrillón presented the "brave prisoners" to Santa Anna, the dictator demanded, "Who has given you orders to take prisoners, I do not want to see those men living—shoot them." In a flash, "the hell-hounds of the tyrant" killed the six prisoners.

Dolson's letter, which appeared in the *Detroit Democratic Free Press* on September 2, 1836, and was reprinted in other newspapers, echoed another account, by an unidentified letter writer, that had appeared in the *Frankfort Commonwealth* on July 27. The details of the two letters, evidently, circulated widely among the Mexican prisoners and were undoubtedly picked up in several Mexican newspapers. Taken as a whole, the story conforms to the dictates of nineteenth-century melodrama. There is the valiant victim, Crockett; the noble victor, Castrillón; and the bloodthirsty fiend, Santa Anna. And since Crockett died at the Alamo, Castrillón fell at San Jacinto, and Santa Anna's word was without value, no one could really challenge the story. Throughout Texas, America, and Mexico, it played well and often.

* * *

In October 1975, Texas A&M University Press published a firsthand account of the Mexican campaign against Texas entitled *With Santa Anna in Texas: A Personal Narrative of the Revolution.* Written by José Enrique de la Peña, a lieutenant in the *zapadores* battalion, and translated by Carmen Perry, it recounted how Mexico lost Texas and, more specifically, who was responsible. De la Peña argued that Mexico had been betrayed by greedy, vicious, incompetent officers led by Generals Antonio López de Santa Anna, Vicente Filisola, and Joaquín Ramírez y Sesma, as well as officials in the war and treasury departments. As a whole the document is a product of the turmoil of late-1830s Mexico, an age of social decay, political chaos, and emotional unrest, a time of pointing fingers. Behind all of de la Peña's discussions of the strategy, logistics, and geography of war is the desire to affix blame for Mexico's sad condition.

Mexico's problems in the late 1830s were not even a fleeting American concern, and *With Santa Anna in Texas* would certainly have been ignored by everyone save a few historians if it had not been for one paragraph. After recounting the horrors of the attack on the Alamo, the senseless deaths and avoidable suffering, de la Peña turned his attention to Santa Anna. He noted that the general's victory speech lacked the "magic" of Napoleon, and that from his "crippled battalions" only a few icy *vivas* broke the silence. It was a grim scene—"an unbearable and nauseating odor," blackened faces contorted in death, friends searching through the dead for friends, groans of the wounded and dying. The best of the Mexican officers were surfeited with the fighting and dying. General Manuel Castrillón even disobeyed Santa Anna's order of no quarter and offered protection to seven Alamo survivors.

Among the seven, de la Peña wrote, "was one of great stature, well proportioned, with regular features, in whose face there was the imprint of adversity, but in whom one also noticed a degree of resignation and nobility that did him honor. He was the naturalist David Crockett, well known in

North America for his unusual adventures, who had undertaken to explore the country and who, finding himself in Béxar at the very moment of surprise, had taken refuge in the Alamo, fearing that his status as a foreigner might not be respected." Castrillón asked Santa Anna to show mercy on the survivors, but with a few words and a "gesture of indignation" the general ordered their executions. Instantly, several of Santa Anna's lackeys "thrust themselves forward, in order to flatter their commander, and with swords in hand, fell upon these unfortunate, defenseless men just as a tiger leaps upon his prey. Though tortured before they were killed, these unfortunates died without complaining and without humiliating themselves before their torturers. . . ."

De la Peña's brief aside on the death of David Crockett created an immediate controversy. No matter that rumors that Crockett surrendered—or was captured—and was then executed had begun within weeks of the end of the battle and were published in newspapers and books, and as late as the 1940s in the *Biographical Directory of the American Congress, 1774-1927*. No matter that the *Columbia Encyclopedia* continued to retread the rumors as if they were well-established fact. The de la Peña diary was harder to dismiss. . . .

Translated into English, *With Santa Anna in Texas* attracted immediate attention. "Students of American history and John Wayne fans take note," commented a journalist for the *Denver Post*. "The legendary story of the Alamo may need revision." "Has the King of the Wild Frontier been relieved of his coon-skin crown?" wondered a writer for the *Jackson* (Tenn.) *Sun*. "Naturally, it will be hard for a generation that grew up singing 'Born on a mountain-top in Tennessee' to accept the mental image of a cowardly Crockett groveling in the Alamo corner." Throughout America, de la Peña was news. *People* ran a story, complete with pictures of Carmen Perry and John Wayne and the headline DID CROCKETT DIE AT THE ALAMO? CARMEN PERRY SAYS NO. And the *Texas Monthly* presented the diary with one of its 1975 "Bum Steer" awards.

"We don't believe Davy Crockett ever surrendered," responded Mrs. Charles Hall, chair of the Alamo Committee of the Daughters of the Republic of Texas. "We feel he went down fighting. And by 'we' I mean all Texans." After publication of the book, Perry received angry phone calls and harassing anonymous letters condemning her efforts. But not all Texans stayed on the DRT's side of the line. The Sons of the Republic of Texas gave the book a prize, and the Movimiento Estudianil Chicanos de Aztlán of El Paso applauded it. Many people accepted it as a clear case of myth versus scholarship, Walt Disney and John Wayne versus dispassionate historical research. Commenting on the de la Peña controversy, Perry said, "People don't believe his account because they don't want to believe it. We prefer to live by legend."

Study Questions

1. Why might some say that Davy Crockett "was a legend in his own mind"?

2. Crockett was a legendary figure in the United States *before* his death. Describe the making of his celebrity.

3. In what ways was Crockett "a Jacksonian man"?

4. Why did Crockett go to Texas?

5. In what ways could Crockett have died on the morning of March 6, 1836? Was there any evidence that he surrendered? Is being executed after being captured any less heroic than "going down" fighting?

6. Exactly what did the de la Peña diary say about Crockett's death?

7. Why has the nature of his death intrigued Americans for so many years?

Bibliography

Texas history in general and the Alamo in particular have spawned a remarkably rich literature. For an excellent treatment of the Texas Revolution, see Paul Lack, *The Texas Revolutionary Experience: A Political and Social History* (1992). Stephen L. Hardin's *Texan Iliad: A Military History of the Texas Revolution* (1994) remains unrivaled. The classic book on the Alamo is Walter Lord's *A Time to Stand: The Epic of the Alamo* (1961). For books looking at the Alamo as an event and a memory, see Randy Roberts and James S. Olson, *A Line in the Sand: The Alamo in Blood and Memory* (2001) and Richard R. Flores, *Remember the Alamo: Memory, Modernity, and the Master Symbol* (2002). William C. Davis's *Three Roads to the Alamo: The Lives and Fortunes of David Crockett, James Bowie, and William Barret Travis* (1998) is exhaustively researched and clearly written. For a fictional account of the battle, see Stephen Harrigan, *The Gates of the Alamo* (2000). On Crockett specifically, see James Atkins Shackford, *Davy Crockett: The Man and the Legend* (1956) and Michael A. Lofaro, ed., *Davy Crockett: The Man, the Legend, the Legacy, 1786–1986* (1985).

READING 21

★ ★ ★

Anesthesia and the Politics of Pain

Martin S. Pernick

On October 6, 1846, the era of surgical anesthesia began when William Thomas Green Morton, a Boston dentist, employed ether to put a patient to sleep. Surgeon John C. Warren then removed a small facial tumor. Morton kept the patient unconscious for nearly thirty minutes, and Warren later commented, "A new era has opened on the operating surgeon. His visitations on the most delicate parts are performed . . . without the agonizing screams he has been accustomed to hear." The advent of anesthesia also opened the door to more radical surgical procedures and progress in curing disease and disability. But anesthesia also prompted a controversial debate about religion, gender, race, and class. In the age of Jacksonian democracy, Americans worried about the meaning of freedom and equality, and anesthesia raised the question of whether all people—regardless of income, skin color, sex, and religion—should enjoy access to the new technology. Did anesthesia thwart the power of God, in whose employ physical pain might achieve larger purposes? In the following essay, historian Martin S. Pernick examines that debate and its meaning for American society in the nineteenth century.

To Suffer Is to Live:
The Benefits of Pain

The hardest to comprehend and easiest to caricature of the arguments against anesthesia is the claim that pain might be necessary or even good. Such opinions usually get dismissed as stoic fatalism or as penitential masochism, when they have been noted at all. Yet a surprisingly broad segment of nineteenth-century opinion throughout the Western world held some version of the belief that physical pain had important benefits and that these benefits would be lost by the use of anesthesia. Such views were not limited to any one ideology or social group, nor did they constitute a unitary or even consistent set of arguments. They sometimes drew upon religious philosophies, ranging from the most radical perfectionism to the most rigid predestinarianism; yet others depended on no particular theological presuppositions. Some critics saw pain as a just and deserved punishment of human misdeeds; others saw it not as punishment at all, but as a functional aspect of normal human physiology. Such objections to anesthesia shed light on the wide range of nineteenth-century attitudes toward pain and suffering and on the complex interrelations of medicine, theology, and philosophy in the Western world.

PAIN AS FUNCTIONAL

By far the largest number of alleged drawbacks to anesthetic painlessness dealt with the supposed biological and psychological functions of pain, apart from any explicitly stated punitive function. On this view, pain was "natural" in the sense of "normal"; not a punishment for violation of divine or natural laws, but an essential part of the process of life.

Nineteenth-century physicians and laypeople had good reason to suspect that pain was integral to life, since the loss of sensation so often indicated conditions verging on death. The depth of insensibility achieved through anesthesia had previously been seen only in cases of coma or shock, following massive brain damage, severe poisoning, extensive blood loss, and similar portents of an impending demise. "The man seeming to suffer comparatively little during the operation—a circumstance which is generally considered rather unfavorable," recorded the attending physician at the New York Hospital, describing an amputation performed in about 1830. Conversely, pain was a sign of vitality, indicating a prompt recovery. "Painful . . . sensations all require sound and healthy organs," declared Felix Pascalis in 1826. "It is, therefore, our axiom, that the greater the pain, the greater must be our confidence in the power and energy of life."

Because of this long-observed association between insensibility and death, some physicians came to suspect that pain was integral to life. Any technique to suspend sensibility would therefore constitute a monstrous and foolhardy suspension of life itself. For the eminent French physiologist, François Magendie, pain was so basic to living that to be anesthetized was literally to be a "corpse." For Magendie, pain was "one of the prime movers of life." "It is not the particular agent, it is the condition of insensibility, however produced, that puts the patient into such peril," declared the *British Medical Journal* in 1858. A popular anesthesia textbook of 1865 quoted approvingly New York surgeon Frank H. Hamilton's observation, "The very annihilation of sensation itself impairs the health of the organs of the body." "The danger lies in the anesthesia rather than in the anesthetic," agreed another New York physician in 1870. "It has been well said that anaesthesia, whatever its form, is an assault upon the vital functions." As one pithy dentist summarized, "Anesthesia is death!"

Pain was equated not only with life in general but with healing and recovery in particular. The word "anesthesia" itself reflects an almost automatic association between the loss of sensibility and the lack of healing power. Since ancient times, the medical term "anesthesia" has desig-

From Martin S. Pernick, *A Calculus of Suffering: Pain, Professionalism, and Anesthesia in Nineteenth-Century America* (New York: Columbia University Press, 1985), 42–59, 148–57.

nated a potentially very serious pathological numbness in some or all parts of the body, such as might be caused by hereditary disease, nerve damage, or gangrene. Nineteenth-century physicians knew that the appearance of this type of anesthesia following a wound usually portended an injury that would heal poorly, if at all.

From this observed correlation between insensibility and poor healing, it was only a short step to the assumption that insensibility caused poor recovery and thus that pain must play a vital role in the healing process. As one worried dentist wrote to John Collins Warren, "If freedom from pain should continue the wound would not get well." "Pain is curative," declared AMA Vice President John P. Harrison in 1849; "—the actions of life are maintained by it—were it not for the stimulation induced by pain, surgical operations would more frequently be followed by dissolution." Because they believed the absence of pain indicated deficient healing power, many nineteenth-century surgeons refused to operate on patients who were in a coma or in shock until the subjects regained consciousness.

According to the common vitalist explanation, pain triggered the "system" to "react," that is, to revitalize and begin recuperation, in much the same way a slap on the rump supposedly got the "system" started at birth. An alternative explanation of the mechanism by which pain aided healing was based on the medical theory that one patient could not have two diseases simultaneously. Since pain was in one sense a disease and wound sepsis was also a disease, the presence of one drove out the other. As developed by the British surgeon John Hunter, this theory of "counterirritation" meant that therapy had to be painful in order to work. Benjamin Rush explained:

All evils cured by evil. Diseases cure each other, as gout and mania, dropsy, consumption, &c. Even remedies are nothing but the means of exciting new diseases. Whipping a dog prevents the effect of Nux Vomica. . . . What would be the effect of hot iron after swallowing poison?

Blistering the skin with chemical burns was a favorite technique of medical counterirritation; likewise the agony of surgery was thought essential to the proper healing of operative wounds. Several midcentury believers in this doctrine even attempted to use ether and chloroform, applied to the skin, in order to produce painful therapeutic burns.

Belief in the curative power of pain was not confined to the medically orthodox but was shared by the Thomsonian and Eclectic sects as well. Eclectic obstetrician John King recommended, as a substitute for anesthesia in controlling childbed convulsions, *"bastinadoing the soles of the feet."* "It may, at first sight, appear a rough measure, but the life of a human being is at stake."

The theory that pain is therapeutic reflected overtones of older beliefs—medicine must be painful to be effective because nothing of value can be attained without suffering. Pain constitutes one of the oldest measures of value, a connection still expressed by the dual connotations of words like "labor" and "painstaking." The word "indolent" now usually means "lazy," but in medical terminology it retains its original meaning, "painless." The doctrine of counter-irritation thus built upon a pervasive cultural tradition that anything which may be obtained without suffering is worthless.

Patients too, it was claimed, preferred painful remedies because they could *feel* them working. A medicine whose effects were immediately perceived inspired much more confidence than a remedy which did not produce any perceptible changes. "One who really desires to be cured of a disease, prefers an active nauseous dose to a more agreeable but ineffective one," explained Frederick Adolphus Packard in 1849.

Whatever mechanism they thought was involved, surgeons who viewed pain as essential to healing considered anesthetics a threat to recovery. Sir John Hall, inspector-general of hospitals and chief medical officer in the Crimea, "disparages chloroform, and lauds the lusty bawling of the wounded from the smart of the knife, as a powerful stimulant," according to a Confederate Virginia manual of military surgery. "Some of the older surgeons characterize the cries of the patient as music to the ear, and speak of it as an advantage to be courted, and not to be suppressed," the same handbook continued. A student at the University of Pennsylvania College of Medicine quoted another British authority for the view that "pain during surgical operations, is, in the majority of cases, . . . desirable; and, its prevention is for the most part, hazardous to the patient." The *New York Journal of Medicine* declared pain "an *essential* attendant on surgical operations" and "the natural incentive to reparative action." The author concluded that anesthesia could seriously retard or completely prevent proper healing by removing the pain essential to recovery.

Just as some surgeons concluded pain to be essential in the healing process, some obstetricians determined pain to be necessary in the process of giving birth. The association between the physical process of labor and the perceptual experience of suffering was so ingrained that the same word, "pains," was used for both the actual muscular contractions and their accompanying sensations. Not surprisingly, a few doctors concluded that both types of pains were equally necessary for delivery. "Pain—the psychical perception of pain—has its use. The abolition of pain has its danger," according to an article on obstetrics by Robert Barnes reprinted from the *Lancet* in the *American Journal of the Medical Sciences*.

According to Barnes' theory, the sensation of pain was caused by the pressure of the baby in the birth canal. This pain sensation in turn triggered the contractions. Thus, without the feeling of pain, there could be no contractions, and therefore normal delivery would be retarded. At the same time, obstetrical pain supposedly might also act as a safety valve—if the contractions became too forceful, the woman would scream, allowing air to escape, thus "reduc[ing] the pressure" and averting lacerations. "Pain," Samuel Gregory of Boston quoted the *Edinburgh Medical Journal*, "is the mother's safety, its absence her destruction."

In addition to physiological processes such as wound healing and birth contractions, pain allegedly played a vital role in emotional health, es-

pecially in the formation of appropriate sexual characteristics. For men, pain was necessary to the development of healthy masculine endurance. The most extreme advocates of this viewpoint, military surgeons, tended to lump painless surgery in the same category with the work of Dorothea Dix, Florence Nightingale, and Clara Barton, as products of misguided effeminate sentimentalism. Grizzled veteran medical officers on both sides of the Atlantic, men like Dr. Hall and Dr. Porter, scoffed at surgical anesthesia as a "mistaken philanthropy." A deep-rooted hostility toward "enthusiasm," "zeal," reformers, sentimentalism, and philanthropy pervaded their arguments. The military traditionally argued that philanthropic attempts to relieve suffering would only deprive the troops of a vital opportunity to become inured to the pains of battle and would thus actually worsen their suffering by causing the men to think about their miseries. Such opinions were not limited entirely to bullet-biting combat physicians. Perhaps the most extreme example was Benjamin Hill, a surgeon of the Eclectic sect. Hill encouraged his patients to submit to cauterization of cancers without anesthetics, in favor of the "moral medication" provided by pain:

I have not unfrequently had patients, after submitting, perhaps for an hour, to this "burning alive," without flinching or groaning, open their mouths for the first time, after I had got through, to express their fears that the operation had not been carried far enough, because they had felt it so much less than I had given them reason to expect. I have told them beforehand that, unless they had fortitude enough to bear to have their arm chopped off, inch by inch, on a block, or to hold it out like the Roman youth of old, while it burnt off on the altar, they need not expect to have their cancer cured—that its moral "final cause" was to develop such heroism in them!

Even confirmed sentimentalists like Samuel Gregory, the patriarch of the Boston Female Medical College, scorned surgical anesthesia, scoffing that

A Thomas Eakins potrait of an operation at the University of Pennsylvania in 1889.

"this suffocating one's self to avoid a trifling pain is no mark of prudence or courage."

If pain could anneal manly hardness, it could also refine womanly tenderness. The close and complex connection between pain and love was a preoccupation of midcentury sentimentalists. Suffering was "interesting"—a wonderful word meaning "capable of inspiring sublime emotions." Physician-poet Josiah Gilbert Holland wrote,

> *Hearts, like apples, are hard and sour,*
> *Till crushed by Pain's resistless power.*

As formulated by Emerson, the doctrine of "compensation" seemed to guarantee that all bodily pains carried with them their own spiritual rewards. Thus, Dr. Augustus K. Gardner, a prominent New York gynecologist, rhapsodized about the sufferings of his women patients, "I feel that these compensations are not limited to the mere physical strengthening of other . . . facilities; . . . this baptism of pain and privation has regenerated the individual's whole nature . . . by the chastening made but a little lower than the angels."

In particular many nineteenth-century obstetricians suspected that the pain of delivery was essential to promote normal and healthy maternal emotions. "The very suffering which a woman undergoes in labor is one of the strongest elements in the love she bears for her offspring," explained one such critic. In the effusive words of Dr. Edward R. Mordecai, a young Southern medical student at the University of Pennsylvania,

> *[T]he associations connected with the pangs of*
> *parturition may play an important part in*
> *framing the indissoluble link which binds a*

*parent to its offspring; in rearing the founda-
tion upon which rests no inconsiderable share
of the social happiness of this world. From such
a source springs, no doubt in part, that exhul-
tation with which a mother beholds for the
"first time her new-born babe," that soul-
stirring sympathy which weeps with it in sorrow, which smiles with it in prosperity; that un-
remitted affection which follows it from the
cradle to the grave.*

In the mouth of young Dr. Mordecai, such sentiments seem patronizing, but some Victorian fem-
inists used the same argument to prove that the
pain of childbirth made women morally superior
to men.

Some of the physicians who believed pain to
be an integral part of life did not attempt to spell
out the precise vital functions that suffering
might serve. After cataloging all the detailed physical and spiritual mechanisms by which bodily
torment benefited the sufferer, there remained a
strong residual feeling that pain was some thing
more elemental—something simply inherent in
the essential nature of human flesh. To lose the
ability to feel pain was to become less than
human, to be literally a vegetable or a brute.

Whereas most physiological explanations of
the value of pain depended on no particular theological assumptions, Philadelphia obstetrician
Dr. Charles D. Meigs in 1856 cautioned against
both surgical and obstetric anesthesia by noting
the morally "doubtful nature of any process that
the physicians set up to contravene the operation
of those natural and physiological forces that the
Divinity has ordained us to enjoy or to suffer." Unlike the perfectionist belief that God created nature so that only those who violated natural laws
would suffer, Meigs' Divinity created suffering itself as a natural law.

Although such criticism of anesthesia was
grounded for the most part in careful and intelligent argumentation, it would be wrong to overlook the influence of superstition, fear of change,
and an uneasy feeling that what had always been
was always meant to be. The belief that it was

"natural" to feel pain when cut with a scalpel paral-
leled the belief that obstetric pain was "natural"—
both drew upon the ethical fallacy that everything "natural" was both good and necessary.
"The pain attendant upon human parturition is a
physiological one, and is probably imposed upon
this particular function for a specific object, the
nature of which may to us be yet unknown," explained Dr. Edward H. Horner, a University of
Pennsylvania medical student. In one international example of the romantic era's penchant for
the naturalistic fallacy, Samuel Gregory quoted a
German report to the Royal Scientific Association,
on obstetric etherization: "These pains are natural
phenomena . . . and are therefore endured without detriment." The British obstetrician Francis
Ramsbotham summed up that argument as well as
anyone by declaring that women should be "contented to have children as it would seem, Nature
intended they should."

Belief in a physiological function for surgical or
obstetric pain is an empirically testable hypothesis, one that we might assume would have been
disproved by the rapidly accumulated evidence of
successful anesthetic procedures. Yet the same
institutional problems that impeded the precise
assessment of anesthesia's side effects kept alive
well into the 1880s the debate over the physical
functions of pain. The spiritual and psychological
functions of pain are even harder to test. Belief in
these emotional benefits of suffering has remained strong to the present day, especially in regard to childbirth.

PAIN AS PUNISHMENT

While some saw pain as biologically and emotionally functional, other critics of anesthesia portrayed physical suffering as punishment; in their
view anesthesia constituted an attempt to circumvent the chastisements inflicted by some Higher
Power. Today, such opinions are usually dismissed as the product of fundamentalist objections to the use of anesthesia in childbirth. Yet in
actuality these attacks were leveled against dental
and surgical anesthetics too and came from a diverse assortment of theological and scientific

viewpoints. Many nineteenth-century Americans agreed that pain was a just and beneficial discipline, but they disagreed over every detail of which pains were punishment, who or what was being punished, and by Whom.

Nineteenth-century Americans generally distinguished between physical pains whose immediate cause was a visible human agent, such as the agonies of dental or surgical operations, and those pains whose cause did not visibly involve human infliction, such as the throes of childbirth and disease. Both were seen as deserved punishments, but the arguments are best considered separately. Since birth and disease pains did not seem to depend directly on human infliction, they were easy candidates for attribution to the judgment of some higher purpose. But who was punishing whom for what? Was the infliction divine or natural? Did the guilt lie with the particular individual afflicted, the sufferer's entire community, the individual's immediate ancestors, or humanity's original ancestors? On these questions there was sharp debate.

The most familiar such argument pictured the pangs of childbirth as God's judgment on womankind for tempting Adam's Fall. Biblical literalism underlay a number of attacks on obstetric anesthesia throughout the nineteenth century, everywhere in the Western world. "I consider that *mothers* would consult their own happiness, to say nothing of health, by fulfilling the edict of bringing forth children 'in sorrow,' " warned a New York dentist in 1848. An American summary of a leading British textbook cited "the morality of pain" as one reason for the "impropriety of etherization" in childbirth. Biblical literalism in fact underlay many of the supposedly naturalistic functional explanations of birth pain. Thus the English obstetrician Ramsbotham believed labor pains to be functional but blamed this state of affairs on "an ordinance of the Deity" as punishment for the Fall.

But biblical literalists had no monopoly on the claim that obstetric anesthesia was an attempt to escape from a deserved punishment. Rather, it was the advocates of "natural healing," especially those inclined toward a perfectionist theology, such as hydropaths and vegetarians, who most loudly proclaimed that the pains of labor (and disease) were righteous chastisements. In this view, Nature, not God, was wielding the lash; and individual sins against natural law, not a universally shared original sin, was the provocation. Hydropath Dr. T. L. Nichols, for example scorned the literalist dogma that God intended for womankind to suffer, declaring it "an insult to Providence." "This world is the work of infinite power and benevolence," he continued. Perfect freedom from pain was both possible and intended for us in this world. "In a state of health no natural process is painful." "There is no more certain fact in physiology, than that the nerves of organic life, in a healthy condition, are not susceptible of pain," he concluded.

But if God is both benevolent and omnipotent, where do pain and disease come from? Pain for Nichols was unnatural, abnormal, pathological— the result of human free will contending against the beneficent laws of nature. Pains, declared the *Water Cure Journal,* "follow the sinner legitimately and unavoidably, the sure sum penalty of violated laws, as universal in their application and precise in their reference as any laws of nature." Physical suffering existed only because sinful humanity used its free will to violate natural law, but pain could be totally eradicated simply by following these laws—by adopting a pattern of life based on exercise, fresh air, cleanliness, virtue, and temperance. Childbirth was painful only to the precise extent that women lived unnatural lives.

Hydropaths therefore denounced obstetric anesthesia as an attempt to suspend the wise judgments of nature. For them, anesthesia was both an immoral escape from the retributive side of nature's punishment and also an unhealthy suspension of the deterrent and reformatory aspects of such penalties. Pain was nature's warning to change one's ways. If mothers used anesthesia to remove the pangs of childbirth without making fundamental changes in the unnatural habits that caused the pain, the result would be more serious pain and injury later on.

Hydropaths believed that human pain could be totally vanquished but only through adopting a way of life rigidly governed by the dictates of natural law. Their goal was not simply to eradicate pain but to revolutionize society according to nature's blueprint. Anesthesia threatened to subvert this revolution by deluding people into trying to eliminate pain without making any fundamental changes in their underlying unnatural behavior; it was a new opiate for the masses. Dr. Ellen Snow advised students at the New York Hydropathic Physiological School not to let the discovery of artificial painkillers divert them from their larger purpose. "By teaching mankind how to live, we can be far more serviceable to the world than we can by bending all our energies to invent some mode of subverting nature's laws, so as to relieve ourselves from suffering the penalty attached thereto." Orthodox medicine had discovered a way to make burning yourself painless, she told her audience; hydropathy taught you not to put your hand in the fire.

Compared to the biblical view that pain was an inescapable curse, the perfectionism of hydropathy offered unbounded hope. Contrary to strict Reformed theology, hydropaths taught that total freedom from pain was both moral and achievable. Pain could and should be eradicated—by the eradication of wrongdoing. But despite their differences, both perfectionists and predestinarians taught that pain was a righteous and deserved punishment for the existence of evil and therefore should not be anesthetized away.

Biblical literalism at least had offered the victim the solace of resignation and companionship— all were sinners, all would suffer. Strict Calvinists did not tantalize themselves with hopes of escape this side of heaven, nor did they impute particular individual guilt to the sufferer. Most early Reformed churches in colonial America, from Congregationalists to Quakers, viewed God's punishments as falling upon entire communities rather than simply upon the guilty individuals. Such theology accorded well with actual social conditions in pioneer New England and Pennsylvania. Accidents, diseases, famines, and disasters clearly did punish everyone, not merely the directly stricken. In small, isolated, highly interdependent communal societies, the incapacitation of a few individuals could easily threaten the well-being of all. Thus, breaking a leg or catching the ague do not necessarily imply that the victim was any more guilty or sinful than his or her neighbors. A member of the community of saints did not ask for whom the bell tolled.

But in the Erewhonian utopia of the hydropaths, where freedom from suffering was freely available to everyone, simply being in pain constituted *prima facie* evidence of individual moral guilt. "Sin, or violation of physical law, is the cause; and pain, sickness, and death in their largest signification, are its effects. To be sick, then, is sinful," proclaimed the *Water-Cure Journal*. Dr. Samuel Gridley Howe explained that mental retardation "*must* be the consequence of some violation of the *natural laws*,—that where there was so much suffering, there must have been sin." The victim was always to blame. If a mother suffered in labor, it proved her to be a moral and physiological failure.

Furthermore, these natural healers defined "natural" according to their own preferences. Those perverse, depraved beings who obstinately clung to different tastes in food, sex, clothing, religion, ethnic traditions, or politics would be stricken, and it served them right.

The major point of difference between biblical literalist like Ramsbotham or Charles Meigs and perfectionists like the hydropaths concerned whether birth pain was a universal or an individual punishment. For the literalists, birth pain was a universal law, built by God into the natural structure of female physiology, to punish all women. Hydropaths and other cosmic optimists rejected obstetric anesthesia on opposite grounds, that birth pain was an individual punishment, totally unnatural, nonnormal, hence pathological. Birth pain should be eliminated, but the only way to do it was through moral hygiene, not through drugs. Thus, although they were at opposite poles of nineteenth-century theology, both radical perfectionists and biblical literalists rejected obstetric anesthesia as an evil interference with a righteous punishment.

Although hydropathy claimed only a tiny handful of doctrinaire believers, many of its basic ideas were simply radical extensions of very widely held concepts. Their extreme perfectionism and individualism, their belief that every individual was independently capable of *total* obedience to natural law, won few adherents. But the concept that at least some pains were nature's punishment for poor hygiene and intemperate habits enjoyed the support of physicians, health reformers, educators, and other advocates of "natural healing," representing a broad segment of both sectarian and orthodox medical opinion. And their judgment that what is "natural" is "right" was shared by nineteenth-century romantics of all varieties.

Homeopaths declared, "Pain is the penalty we suffer for violating a physical law," according to an 1883 student at Hahnemann Medical College. "If you suffer," the homeopathically inclined Elizabeth Cady Stanton told mothers, "it is not because you are cursed of God, but because you violate his laws." Like the hydropaths too, homeopaths attacked all chemical pain relievers as artificial interference with nature's beneficial punishments. Long before anesthesia, Hahnemann himself had denounced opium and morphine. His views remained dogma to pure homeopaths through the end of the century.

Pain is the . . . true physician's best guide to the seat and character of cause of the pain. Deadening the nervous system by Morphine or any of its equivalents is virtually choking off Nature's voice . . . . thus leaving us to work in the dark.

Better let the patient suffer a while than complicate the trouble and retard the final recovery, or risk the patient's life by paralyzing the . . . . nervous system with Morphia.

Many homeopaths applied the same logic against anesthetics, when they were used for such "natural" pains as childbirth or disease. An 1868 student at Hahnemann declared obstetric etherization to be "one use of Anaesthetics by the Allopathic School, which we as Homoeopaths, most certainly should condemn."

We as students of Hahnemann, have been taught that all natural diseases (if I may call them such) can be so treated by the means of [homeopathic] remedies, properly given . . . . When therefore we are called upon to attend a case of labor, we do not expect to carry with us a bottle of Ether to make the patient insensible.

Both sects shared a commitment to natural healing; both held a deep suspicion that obstetric anesthesia constituted an immoral escape from nature's wise correction.

However, there were important differences between the two sects. Few homeopaths endorsed the hydropathic claim that perfect painlessness came exclusively through natural living. They regarded (homeopathic) drugs as invaluable aids to nature in eliminating pain. And most homeopaths doubted that a perfectly painless life was either possible or desirable.

To the extent that they shared a belief in natural healing, orthodox practitioners, as well as sectarians, criticized anesthesia as an immoral or unwise interference with nature's punishments. One young University of Michigan medical student unequivocally endorsed the most radical perfectionist position. "By leading a life in strict conformity with the requirements of physical laws man will live a life of absolute immunity from pain or suffering of any kind whatsoever."

Other advocates of natural healing rejected such perfectionism, regarding some pains as naturally avoidable and others as naturally necessary and beneficial. Samuel Gregory of Boston's Female Medical College reasoned that, if some birth pain was normal and some not, then those pains that were pathological should be prevented through hygiene and those pains that were natural should be endured as nature intended. "If women would, by activity and a proper course of life, preserve their health and vigor, and follow the dictates of reason in conception, pregnancy, and parturition, ether would be unnecessary, for they would experience no more pain than is actually favorable . . . no more suffering than is salutory."

Conservative physicians carefully balanced their commitments to Art and to Nature, avoiding an exclusive reliance on either. But to the extent they endorsed the basic concept of natural healing they shared its critique of anesthesia. Influential conservatives such as New York surgeon Frank H. Hamilton portrayed pain as the proper penalty for defiance of nature and regarded obstetric anesthesia as an unnatural form of interference. An anonymous newspaper clipping included in Dr. Hamilton's lecture notes (apparently by Hamilton himself) illustrates the influence of natural healing on the medical conservatives' view of pain.

THE USE OF PAIN—The power which rules the universe, this great tender power, uses pain as a signal of danger. Just, generous, beautiful. Nature never strikes a foul blow; . . . Patiently she teaches us her laws, plainly she writes her warnings, tenderly she graduates their force. . . .

And what do we do for ourselves? We ply whip and spur on the jaded brain as though it were a jibing horse. . . . We drug the rebellious body with stimulants, we hide the signal and think we have escaped the danger . . . .

At last, having broken Nature's laws, and disregarded her warnings, forth she comes . . . to punish us. Then we go down on our knees and whimper about it having pleased God Almighty to send this affliction upon us, and we pray him to work a miracle in order to reverse the natural consequences of our disobedience, or save us from the trouble of doing our duty. In other words, we put our finger in the fire and beg that it may not be hurt.

In summary, a wide variety of nineteenth-century healers concluded that the pains of childbirth and disease were deserved punishments, chastisements that it might be immoral and unhealthy to anesthetize away. A literal reading of the Bible did play a role in such opinion. However such arguments were derived more from the doctrines of natural healing than from the book of Genesis. And the most extreme exponents of such views were not strict predestinarians but such radical perfectionists as the hydropaths and Grahamites.

That the pains inflicted by surgery, dentistry, and similar professional ministrations might also be viewed as righteous chastisements seems hard to believe; yet a few nineteenth-century Americans apparently considered the *doctor* as much a part of their punishments as the *disease*. For a handful of the most rigid predestinarians, all the miseries of this life, including those medically inflicted, were punishments from God and could be taken away only by God. Infinitely depraved mankind deserved all the pain and more. As reported by *Harper's Magazine*, the city of Zurich (a wellspring of Reformed theology) banned all use of anesthetics, on the grounds that "pain was the natural and intended curse of the primal sin; therefore any attempt to do away with it must be wrong." In America, too, these extreme doctrines of predestination and human depravity may occasionally have lurked behind opposition to all forms of anesthesia, at least according to pro-anesthetic observers. Several Philadelphia surgeons reportedly called the use of ether "damnable."

Dr. William Henry Atkinson, an M.D. and first president of the American Dental Association, reportedly declared,

I think anesthesia is of the devil, and I cannot give my sanction to any Satanic influence which deprives a man of the capacity to recognize the law! I wish there were no such thing as anesthesia! I do not think men should be prevented from passing through what God intended them to endure.

Occasionally, physicians recorded cases in which patients refused surgical or dental anesthesia for reasons of religious belief.

Predestinarian denominations like the Hard Shell Baptists and Old School Presbyterians believed pain to be God's punishment of human depravity. Fallen mankind could not be saved without God's discipline; thus pain was a manifestation of God's love, evidence of His paternal concern for the proper upbringing of His children. "He who spares the rod hates his son" applied to the Heavenly Father, as well as to His earthly counterparts. However, even with proper punishments, true repentance was impossible without the aid of grace, a divine gift that most Reformed churches believed was sparingly bestowed. Thus, some portion of humanity would be subjected to God's chastisements, even though God had withheld from them the means of benefiting from their punishment. These miserable creatures existed for a higher purpose than simply to suffer. Their pains provide the fortunate with an opportunity to exercise benevolence. If the Lord caused some to suffer less than others, He expected the recipients of His favor to act as benevolent stewards on behalf of those less fortunate. Charity was a duty. However, there was no expectation that this benevolence could or should cure the pains of the afflicted. Despite all human efforts, the tormented, like the poor, would always be among us.

But in surgery, as in obstetrics, more opposition to anesthesia came from natural healers than from predestinarians. Many hydropaths and homeopaths denounced surgical anesthesia because they rejected surgery itself as an attempt to shortcut nature's punishment through human art. Surgery offered the illusion of cure without the necessary hygienic reforms; anesthesia only made the illusion more seductive. Even medically orthodox physicians and surgeons agreed that, by making cure seemingly painless, surgical anesthetics might tempt people to stray from the straight and narrow road of natural law.

Another common punitive justification of surgical pain derived from the medical theory of "counterirritation." Although overtly a purely scientific explanation of the natural function of pain, the doctrine that medicine must be painful to work was often expounded in frankly punitive metaphors. Such rhetoric reveals the extent to which many nineteenth-century Americans still saw the surgeon as God's enforcer, and regarded the doctor as part of the deserved punishment for

sin. In this view, medical therapy was part of the retribution for getting sick, just as sickness itself was a punishment. Painful medical treatment was simply substituting a controlled form of chastisement for a less controlled one. By punishing one's self with medicine, the necessity for punishment by disease might be eliminated. Only by doing medical penance could one expunge the sin that caused the illness. The same train of thought that led Rush to theorize that whipping might cure poisoning, led him to declare, "Punishment, therefore, of all kinds [is] benevolent." The physician to the Massachusetts State Prison in 1827 saw his job as the administration of "the severe, but needful physic, for the body and the soul." Such punishment could also be deterrent as well as retributive. By making the cure dreadful enough, maybe people would be discouraged from the sins that caused the disease. The Massachusetts prison physician used the specific example of venereal disease, which he claimed afflicted more than one-fifth of all his patients, to illustrate the utility of painful therapy as a deterrent. Thus, while only a minority of nineteenth-century Americans overtly criticized surgical anesthesia as sacrilegious, a wide variety of religious and medical viewpoints each led to the conclusion that surgical pains could have positive punitive value.

The Control of Anesthesia: Power and Its Abuse

Knowledge is power, noted Horace Mann, but power can be a force for evil as well as for good. Without the self-control and internalized discipline of a moral education, Mann warned, nineteenth-century scientific advances would produce only stronger and more ingenious knaves. In his summary report as superintendent of the common schools of Massachusetts, Mann repeatedly declared the need to keep technological prowess under moral restraint. He illustrated his point with the example of anesthesia. "A benefactor of the race discovers an agent which has the marvelous power to suspend consciousness, and take away the susceptibility of pain; a villain uses it to rob men or pollute women." Anesthetics conferred vast new power over pleasure and pain, and thus over rewards and punishments, even over consciousness itself. How and by whom would such awesome capabilities be controlled? While Mann believed moral self-discipline could prevent abuse, others feared the temptations might be too great.

THE MISUSE OF MEDICAL POWER

One fundamental anxiety of critics was that anesthetics gave physicians too much power over their patients. The new discovery threatened to overturn the vital checks and balances governing professional authority—restraints that had been built into the doctor-patient relationship since antiquity. One possible evil was the loss of the patient's supervisory power over the operation. The ability of the unanesthetized patient to observe the proceedings had a number of advantages. In many common operations, such as those for scrotal tumors, cataract, crossed-eyes, and bladder stones, doctors had come to depend on help from the subject to oversee the progress of the procedure and to prevent the operator from cutting too much. As late as 1862, it was not uncommon to find surgeons who "expected the patient to assist in small operations," such as probing wounds and removing bone fragments. But with an insensible client, complained A. C. Castle, a New York dentist, "the operator obtains no assistance whatever from the patient." In childbirth, too, a conscious patient could both assist the obstetrician and minimize medical mistakes.

Unanesthetized patients had the power to protect themselves against all sorts of medical carelessness, including the ability to make sure the right tooth, growth, or limb was being removed. "By rendering the patient insensible to pain, it [anesthesia] may throw the practitioner off his guard, and prevent that thorough examination . . . that would otherwise be made," a correspondent warned the AMA Committee on Obstetrics. Ether "presents an excellent cover for bungling mutilations in dentistical operations," declared Dr. Castle. A French cartoonist in 1847

gave voice to popular anxiety on this score in a drawing that depicted a patient awakening to find all his teeth had been pulled by mistake.

Even when there was little likelihood of medical error a few patients found satisfaction in knowing they had the authority to participate in what was being done to their bodies, especially (though not exclusively) in obstetrics. Until quite recently in Western history, many people seemingly preferred to be conscious when facing death, in order to prepare their temporal and spiritual affairs. The French physiologist Magendie thought it brutally dehumanizing to deprive someone of consciousness at such a critical hour; to carve a human being like so much meat. "I do not use any anesthetic of any kind," an Iowa physician declared bluntly, as late as 1887. "I want the patient to know what is going on."

The powerlessness of the anesthetized subject would lead not merely to carelessness and disrespect but also to involuntary surgery and to unnecessary and experimental operations, according to advocates of the cautious conservative approach to surgery, including even such anesthesia pioneers as Henry J. Bigelow. Bigelow worried that the availability of ether might provide an irresistible temptation for hack surgeons to perform unnecessary operations. The artist who portrayed "Furor Operativus" had no doubt that anesthesia left patients the helpless victims of knife-happy butchers.

* * *

Most nineteenth-century Americans and Europeans who paused to reflect on the subject believed that human beings differed widely in their sensitivity to and endurance of both natural and inflicted physical pain. "The causes which modify the external or internal sensations are innumerable: age, sex, temperament, the seasons, climate, habit, individual disposition," noted the renowned neurophysiologist François Magendie. Such an all-inclusive list of factors made cultural stereotypes and prejudices an integral part of professional judgments concerning which kinds of people were most susceptible to pain. Conversely, differences in pain sensitivity attributed to different individuals and groups provided scientific legitimacy for discriminatory treatment, both by the profession and by society at large. The belief that people varied widely in their ability to feel pain influenced almost every aspect of nineteenth-century social and professional life, including, of course, the use of anesthesia.

A Great Chain of Feeling

From the earliest history of empirical science to the present day, biomedical researchers have attempted to specify which types of people feel the most pain. Among the earliest efforts to generalize about variations in human sensitivity was Galen's doctrine of the four humors. Of the four types of "temperaments," fat, sluggish, "phlegmatic" people usually were assumed to feel the least pain; thin, excitable, "choleric" people the most.

But with the growing cultural and professional importance nineteenth-century Americans placed on accurately differentiating and categorizing detailed individual human differences, such broad rules of thumb no longer sufficed. A vast number of additional specific biological, social, and moral distinctions began to assume significance as predictors of human sensitivity to pain.

GENDER

Sex seemed to be one factor that clearly influenced the perception of pain. Several ancient societies possessed the notion that women felt pain much more severely than did men. In mid-nineteenth-century America, such traditional beliefs gained added significance as a result of the Victorian penchant for polarizing and dichotomizing sex roles in society.

"The nerves themselves are smaller, and of a more delicate structure" in women. "They are endowed with greater sensibility," explained one male physician. According to a standard midcentury American physiology textbook, all female "senses, as a general rule, are more acute." A leading American gynecology text declared woman to be "more delicate" in "her whole economy." Dr. Oliver Wendell Holmes marveled, "She is so

much more fertile in capacities of suffering than a man. She has so many varieties of headache." "In consequence of her greater sensitiveness to external impressions," declared Dr. Morrill Wyman of Cambridge, Massachusetts, "a blow of equal force produces a more serious effect" on a woman than on a man. Medical opinion that women possessed a low perceptual threshold for pain both drew upon and reinforced common Victorian cultural values. Romantic writers, from Edgar Allan Poe to Lydia H. Sigourney, saw feminine sensitivity to pain as a reflection of women's overall physical frailty and heightened spiritual "sensibility."

Conversely, traditional concepts of virility presumed a truly masculine man to be almost impervious to physical pain. Thomas Trotter, surgeon to the British fleet, warned physicians not to "confound the complaint of the slim soft-fibred man-milliner, with that of the firm and brawny ploughman." When a real man feels pain, it is serious. As the paragons of virility, soldiers and sailors exhibited masculine insensitivity to the fullest. Heroic manly fortitude, heightened by the "excitement" of battle, rendered soldiers insensitive to the pain of "almost any operation." At least such was the opinion of British military surgeon Rutherford Alcock, as quoted approvingly by American army surgeon John B. Porter. Even humanitarian reformers like Horace Mann agreed that "sensitiveness to bodily pain . . . impairs manliness," especially among soldiers.

AGE

Age, like sex, exerted a powerful influence on the perception of pain, according to most nineteenth-century theorists. Old age, it was generally agreed, diminished all perceptual acuity, including the ability to feel pain. But there the agreement ended. The degree of sensitivity in children proved an especially controversial issue. Dr. Abel Pierson of Massachusetts declared that infants could sleep insensibly even while undergoing surgery. Pierson, Henry J. Bigelow, and others who believed in infant insensibility, assumed that the ability to experience pain was related to intelligence, memory, and rationality; like the lower animals, the very young lacked the mental capacity to suffer. In contrast, others who felt children to be especially sensitive emphasized the feminine rather than the animal aspects of child nature. "The constitutions of children, in point of debility and irritability, approach to the female"; therefore, a child's "nervous power is . . . easily affected by stimuli," noted Dr. Trotter. As the idea that "women and children" comprised a single bio-social category gained popularity in Romantic Era America, the view that young children were extremely vulnerable to pain gradually came to predominate.

SOCIAL CONDITION

In addition to age and sex, social and economic class played a major role in determining which people were believed most sensitive to suffering. As explained by Tocqueville, the European pauper had become inured to perpetual misery and was hardly even aware of it. But, he declared, in the egalitarian United States, there were no such permanently degraded people (except for slaves). Everyone shared equally the extreme hypersensitivity of the middle classes. America's constantly fluctuating fortunes prevented anyone from becoming accustomed to the physical pains of poverty, while exposing everyone to the risk of having to undergo them.

Although Tocqueville could locate no hardened poor in white Jacksonian America, the wealthy Connecticut novelist John W. De Forest found them easily by 1863. "We waste unnecessary sympathy on poor people," he asserted. "A man is not necessarily wretched because he is cold & hungry and unsheltered; provided those circumstances usually attend him, he gets along very well with them; they are annoyances, but not torments."

Alcohol further hardened the poor to their lot, at least for the time they were actually drunk. But the chronic alcoholic, though insensible when intoxicated, became agonizingly hyperaesthetic when sober. "Mania a potu" resulted in a morbid sensibility of the nerves, whose painfulness rapidly drove the sufferer back to the bottle. Criminals too seemed highly insensitive to both physical and moral pain, according to one late-

nineteenth-century physical anthropologist. Immigrants, especially Germans and Irish, were also deemed less sensitive than were native Americans. Hydropath Thomas Low Nichols contrasted "our Teutonic friend's harder strung nerves, blunter sensation," with "the nicer sensibilities and consequent greater capacity of suffering of finer grained humanity."

And if poverty and degradation produced numbness, the combination of wealth, status, and femininity could breed a truly exquisite sensitivity. According to the Brothers Grimm, a genuine princess could invariably be distinguished from the ordinary herd by her royal hypersensitivity—even a pea hidden under many mattresses would produce pain. Such precious creatures were almost too sensitive to carry out normal bodily functions. Menstruation caused "almost all women in the better classes" to suffer pathological levels of pain, according to a midcentury obstetrics text. But "the nervous system of the poorer classes [of women] in our cities, fortified by constant exercise in the open air, and strengthened by frugal habits," was not subject to such "morbid action," in the opinion of the noted gynecologist Dr. Gunning S. Bedford. "Pain is in various proportions among women who are equally well formed," Dr. William Potts Dewees declared; "we generally find the women of the country more obnoxious to it, than those of cities."

Education and cultural refinement, factors closely correlated with class, comprised another influence long believed to alter human perception of pain. "For in much wisdom is much grief," warned Koheleth, the Preacher of Ecclesiastes; "and he that increaseth knowledge increaseth sorrow." From the story of Eve to the myth of Pandora the ancient teachings agreed—sensitivity to pain is the result of knowledge. Many nineteenth-century Americans took such concepts to heart. The leaders of the common school movement in particular stressed the importance of avoiding overcultivation of the intellect, lest public schooling produce a generation of overly sensitive children. Unlike Koheleth, Horace Mann did not conclude that all knowledge increased human suffering; yet he demanded that mental development proceed in step with physical education, to prevent excessive nervous sensitivity. Since women were already very sensitive, intellectual education for girls had to be especially circumscribed and carefully counteracted by physical exercise.

It was not just education, but culture and civilization itself that produced excessive sensibility. Nineteenth-century writers repeatedly contrasted the pain-free "natural" life of the savage with the hypersensitive nervous disorders of "artificial" civilized existence. The difference could be explained either theologically or naturalistically. Religious romantics called the savages' freedom from suffering a result of the primitives' almost prelapsarian innocence. Since pain was punishment for eating the fruit that gave knowledge of good and evil, those tribes still living in almost Edenic ignorance of moral responsibility were of course less subject to suffering. More naturalistic observers, like Dr. Dewees, rejected the notion that physical pain was punishment for original sin and that innocence could be any protection against the pain of violating natural laws. Dewees viewed the savage life as conferring freedom from pain simply because it was "natural"—because savages lived the way nature intended.

In *A View of the Nervous Temperament*, Thomas Trotter developed and expounded the idea that the spread of civilization "never fail[s] to induce a delicacy of feeling, that disposes alike to more accute pain, as to more exquisite pleasure." Writing in 1806, he introduced a concept that remained a source of concern throughout the nineteenth century when he warned that the growing "general effeminacy" of modern sensibility was leading to the self-destruction of civilization. American public health activists like Dr. John H. Griscom of New York agreed, blaming excessive "irritability of the nervous system" and the consequent "Degeneracy of the Human Race" on the poor ventilation and polluted air characteristic of civilized urban life. The morbid sensitivity produced by city life would lead to the self-induced fall of civilization. To avoid such a catastrophe, however, it was not necessary to abandon civilized living entirely, so long as city dwellers and

sophisticates could be lured back to the pure air, hard work, natural habits of life, and simple virtues of the yeoman farmer.

The effect of civilized living conditions on female sensitivity constituted a special threat to human survival, by making the function of reproduction unbearably painful. Dr. Dewees of Philadelphia, perhaps the foremost American obstetrician of the early nineteenth century, blamed "civilized life" for the fact that childbirth was "usually observed" to be "exceedingly painful . . . especially in the upper walks of life." Even domesticated animals suffered more exquisitely than did their wild sisters. The same sentiments were echoed at the other end of the century by Dr. Henry M. Lyman, professor at Chicago's Rush and Woman's Medical Colleges. "Really normal labor is not a painful process. . . . But in civilized society the majority of mankind are living under quite abnormal conditions. . . . Hence, in civilized society, it is the rule, rather than the exception, to find parturition attended with a high degree of suffering." Such opinions were not limited to male physicians. Even a homeopathically inclined feminist like Elizabeth Cady Stanton agreed that "refined, genteel, civilized" women suffered inordinate pain in childbearing.

While civilized women suffered excessively from pregnancy and childbirth, their savage sisters supposedly felt no pain at all. "Woman in a savage state . . . enjoys a kind of natural anaesthesia during labor," noted Dr. James Y. Simpson, the Scottish pioneer of artificial obstetric anesthesia. "Am I not almost a savage?" Stanton exulted, following her own painless delivery.

Concern over the implications of pain for the future of civilization heightened following the spread of Darwinian theory. The excessive sensibility produced by refined, artificial living clearly gave the uncivilized both an economic and reproductive advantage in the struggle for survival. But while evolutionary theory increased the frequency with which such fears were voiced, the basic idea, that civilization produced a self-destructive level of sensitivity to pain, remained unchanged throughout the entire nineteenth century. "There can be no question as to whether the nervous systems of highly cultivated and refined individuals among civilized peoples are more complex and refined in structure and delicate in susceptibility and action . . . than the nervous system of savages," declared a leading American neurologist in 1881. The distinguished founder of American neurology, Dr. Silas Weir Mitchell, agreed. "In our process of being civilized we have won, I suspect, intensified capacity to suffer. *The savage does not feel pain as we do.*"

RACE

Nineteenth-century white Americans viewed savagery and race as highly interrelated concepts. Both as a correlate of savagery and as an influence in its own right, race was believed to be crucially important in influencing human perception of pain. The archetype of savagery, the Indian, was believed almost incapable of feeling. "Every skin has its own natur'," the Pathfinder proclaimed to the sailor Master Cap. "Until you can find me a Chinaman, or a Christian man . . . who could sing . . . with [his] flesh torn with splinters and cut with knives . . . you cannot find a man with redskin natur'." Benjamin Rush asserted that Indian men could often "inure themselves to burning part of their bodies with fire, or cutting them with sharp instruments." Enlightenment America's foremost race theorist, the Reverend Mr. Samuel Stanhope Smith of Princeton, believed that no women suffered less from childbirth than American aborigines did. "We know that among Indians the squaws do not suffer in childbirth," Stanton lectured. "Among your red Indian and other uncivilized tribes," agreed Dr. Simpson, "the parturient female does not suffer the same amount of pain during labour, as the female of the white race."

The Negro constituted the Indian's closest rival for insensibility, according to a wide variety of observers on both sides of the Atlantic and all sides of the slavery issue. Early European voyagers to Africa noted black imperviousness to suffering. One medical explorer reported that blacks felt no pain even under the most radical surgery. "I have amputated the legs of many negroes who have held the upper part of the limb themselves," he asserted. The eighteenth-century English physician and expert on race, Dr. Charles White, cited such accounts as evidence for his contention that Negro immunity to pain resulted from the excessive thickness of black skin. Owing to their primitive "sensibilities," blacks could undergo, "with few expressions of pain, the accidents of nature which agonize white people," according to a West Indian plantation handbook.

But the most elaborate account of black insensibility came from an American—the controversial midcentury New Orleans physician Samuel A. Cartwright. Dr. Cartwright was the discoverer of "dysaesthesia Aethiopis," an hereditary disease of blacks, which caused such "obtuse sensibility of body" that its victims "seem to be insensible to pain when subjected to punishment." While few, even among slaveholders, adopted Cartwright's peculiar terminology, or his unscriptural conclusion that the Negro was a separate subhuman species, the basic "fact" of black insensibility won almost unquestioned Southern white acceptance. Dr. A. P. Merrill declared,

Nervous action in the negro is comparatively sluggish, but his senses of seeing, hearing, and smelling, are apt to be acute and active; those of touch and taste, obtuse. He requires less sleep than the white man; has greater insensibility to pain . . . .

They submit to and bear the infliction of the rod with a surprizing degree of resignation, and even cheerfulness. . . . They differ from their white masters in no one particular more than in this.

"What might be grievous misery to the white man, . . . is none to the differently tempered black," declared Virginia essayist George Frederick Holmes; "identity of sensibilities between the races of the free and the negroes" was preposterous.

Several Southern physicians performed excruciating experiments on black patients, in the clear belief that their victims lacked the ability to feel pain. America's most eminent gynecological surgeon, Dr. J. Marion Sims, explained that he carried out his lengthy and agonizing experimental operations on slave women, not because he could force slaves to submit to them, but because white women were too sensitive to pain. A Virginia physician experimented with a cure for pneumonia that involved pouring water "near the boiling point" over the bare back of the Negro subject; the treatment "seemed to arouse his sensibilities somewhat." A Georgia doctor trying the same experiment expressed genuine astonishment when the patient "leaped up instantly and appeared to be in great agony."

Even many opponents of slavery propagated the belief that blacks did not feel as much pain as did whites. Dr. Rush, one of the earliest American abolitionists, blamed the Negroes' morbid insensitivity on congenital leprosy (an explanation that also accounted for the blacks' supposedly distinctive odor). The cheerful demeanor of slaves, even "where the lash of the master" was at its cruelest, proved to Abraham Lincoln that black insensibility was evidence of God's compassion. Abolitionist Lydia Maria Child likewise praised the "merciful arrangement of Divine Providence, by which the acuteness of sensibility is lessened when it becomes merely a source of suffering." Tocqueville earlier had drawn the same conclusion, though he clearly recognized its moral ambiguity. "Am I to call it a proof of God's mercy, or a visitation of his wrath, that man, in certain states, appears to be insensible . . .? The Negro, plunged in this abyss of evils, scarcely feels his own calamitous situation." Fugitive slaves and freedmen like Henry Watson and Jermain Loguen agreed that bondsmen eventually became incapable of feeling.

Black women, like their Indian sisters, supposedly enjoyed racial immunity from the extreme sensitivity that characterized white womanhood. Negro mothers "were not subject to the . . . pain which attended women of the better classes in giving birth . . . ," according to the Southerners interviewed by Frederick Law Olmstead. Like black men, black women supposedly experienced little suffering, even from major surgery. "Negresses . . . will bear cutting with nearly, if not quite, as much impunity as dogs and rabbits," reported the *London Medical and Chirurgical Review* in 1817.

But while the "full-blooded" Negro was depicted as nearly without feeling, the "mulatto" was stereotyped as exceedingly sensitive. From the scientific-racist tracts of Alabama's Dr. Josiah C. Nott, to the most sentimental antislavery novels, nineteenth-century Americans unanimously declared the offspring of racial "amalgamation" to be almost as hypersensitive as white women. In *White-Jacket*, Melville's vignette, describing a "Head-bumping" contest between "a full-blooded 'bull-negro' " and a mulatto named "Rose-Water," assumes that the reader understands the two characters to be at virtually opposite poles of human sensibility. Melville, like the sentimentalist opponents of slavery, used the mulatto's almost feminine sensitivity to dramatize the injustice of a system that treated all nonwhites alike. Dr. Nott and the Southern apologists saw in the same phenomenon nothing but nature's ordained punishment for race-mixing.

Thus all living things might be arranged in a hierarchy of sensitivity, a great chain of feeling. Brute animals, savages, purebred nonwhites, the poor and oppressed, the inebriated, and the old, constituted the lower orders. The most sensitive included women; the rich, civilized, educated, and sophisticated; sober drunkards; and mulattoes. Children were usually considered feminine in sensitivity, though infants were sometimes believed not to feel. Occupying the virtuous middle ground were the sturdy yeoman farmers.

Study Questions

1. According to some Americans, what were the so-called "benefits" of pain for men and for women? Give examples.

2. What were the religious and theological dimensions of pain as punishment?

3. Compare and contrast hydropathic and homeopathic views on the use of anesthesia.

4. According to critics of anesthesia, in what ways would its use give physicians too much power over their patients?

5. How were social norms of femininity and masculinity reflected in the perception of pain?

6. Comment on the following: ". . . like lower animals, the very young lacked the mental capacity to suffer."

7. How did nineteenth-century Americans view the correlations between race and sensitivity to pain? Are there also twentieth-century examples of similar views?

Bibliography

In "A Historical-Phenomenological Study of Bodily Pain in Western Man," *Bulletin of the History of Medicine*, 48 (Winter 1974), 549–70, Daniel De Moulin examines the social and religious significance of pain in Western culture. Martin S. Pernick's *A Calculus of Suffering: Pain, Professionalism, and Anesthesia in Nineteenth-Century America* (1985) sees the issue in its American context. Ann Dally's *Women Under the Knife: A History of Surgery* (1991) deals with the interplay of gender, pain, and medicine. Also see Rhoda Truax, *The Doctors Warren of Boston: First Family of Surgery* (1968). Paul Starr's *The Social Transformation of American Medicine: The Rise of a Sovereign Profession and the Making of a Vast Industry* (1982) remains a brilliant history of American medicine.

READING 22

★ ★ ★

The Great Oneida Love-In

Morris Bishop

By the early nineteenth century, the Puritan impulse to change the world was still alive, but its energies were now dissipated in a multitude of crusades. One such crusade was the utopian movement. Blessed with few class distinctions or entrenched traditions, as well as with abundant land and space, America became a laboratory for dramatic social exchange. Periodically, utopian idealists consciously tried to start society anew—creating social institutions from scratch instead of dealing with normal conventions. Most of these proved to be feeble attempts destined for historical oblivion, but a few succeeded, not so much because they changed individual perceptions but because they managed to stimulate debate about fundamental American values. The most unique of the utopian experiments took place at Oneida Lake, New York, and it also provoked bitter controversy in American society.

Morris Bishop's "The Great Oneida Love-In" describes the dream and the reality of John Humphrey Noyes's utopian community. While American culture placed a premium on private property and individual progress, Noyes preached a socialistic gospel of group property and community progress. In a society worshiping monogamy and sexual propriety, Noyes called for "complex marriage" in which all men and women were united together sexually. In a country where religious sectarianism was the norm, Noyes worked for a "community of believers" without churches and denominational competition. Despite his dreams, Noyes failed to reform American society; indeed, American culture eventually transformed the Oneida community.

Sin, the conviction of sin, the assurance of punishment for sin, pervaded pioneer America like the fever and ague, and took nearly as many victims. Taught that in Adam's fall we had sinned all, threatened with hell-fire by revivalist preachers, tortured by the guilt of intimate offenses, earnest youths whipped themselves into madness and suicide, and died crying that they had committed the sin against the Holy Ghost, which is unforgivable, though no one knows quite what it is.

The year 1831 was known as the Great Revival, when itinerant evangelists powerfully shook the bush and gathered in a great harvest of sinners. In September of that year John Humphrey Noyes, a twenty-year-old Dartmouth graduate and a law student in Putney, Vermont, attended such a revival. He was in a mood of metaphysical despair, aggravated by a severe cold. During the exhortings the conviction of salvation came to him. Light gleamed upon his soul. "Ere the day was done," he wrote later, "I had concluded to devote myself to the service and ministry of God."

Noyes was a young man of good family. His father was a Dartmouth graduate, a successful merchant in Putney, and a congressman. John was a bookish youth, delighting in history, romance, and poetry of a martial character, such as lives of Napoleon or of the Crusaders or Sir Walter Scott's *Marmion.* He was red-haired and freckled, and thought himself too homely ever to consider marriage. But when he began preaching his face shone like an angel's: one of his sons later averred that "there was about him an unmistakable and somewhat unexpected air of spiritual assurance."

According to his phrenological analysis, his bumps of amativeness, combativeness, and self-esteem were large, his benevolence and philoprogenitiveness very large. His life confirmed these findings.

After his mystical experience in Putney, Noyes spent a year in the Andover Theological Seminary

"The Great Oneida Love-In" by Morris Bishop in *American Heritage,* February 1969. Reprinted by permission of *American Heritage* Magazine, a division of Forbes, Inc., © Forbes Inc., 1969.

(Congregational). He found his teachers and companions lukewarm in piety, and devoted himself to an intensive study of the New Testament, most of which he could recite by heart. A divine direction—"I know that ye seek Jesus which was crucified. He is not here"—sent him from Andover to the Yale Theological Seminary in New Haven. There he came in contact with the doctrine of perfectionism and was allured by it.

Perfectionism asserted that men may be freed from sin and attain in this life the perfect holiness necessary to salvation. It rejected therefore the consequences of original sin and went counter to the Calvinistic dogma of total depravity. Perfectionism took shape early in the nineteenth century and found lodgment among adventurous groups in New Haven, Newark, Albany, and in villages of central New York, "the burned-over district," where religion smote with a searing flame. Perfectionism was likely to develop into antinomianism, the contention that the faithful are "directly infused with the holy spirit" and thus free from the claims and obligations of Old Testament moral law. And antinomianism led readily to scandal, as when three perfectionist missionaries, two men and a sister of one of them, were tarred and feathered for sleeping together in one bed.

Though suspected of perfectionist heresy, Noyes was licensed to preach in August, 1833. At about the same time, he made a sensational discovery: Jesus Christ had announced that He would return during the lifetime of some of His disciples. Jesus could not have been mistaken; therefore the Second Coming of Christ had taken place in a.d. 70. The "Jewish cycle" of religious history then ended and a "Gentile cycle" began, in which the Church has improperly usurped the authority of the apostles. We live no longer in an age of prophecy and promise, but in an age of fulfillment. Perfect holiness is attainable in this life, as well as guaranteed deliverance from sin.

Noyes found this revelation by fasting, prayer, and diligent search of the Scriptures. At divine command he announced it in a sermon to the Free Church of New Haven on February 20, 1834. "I went home with a feeling that I had committed myself irreversibly, and on my bed that night I received the baptism which I desired and expected. Three times in quick succession a stream of eternal love gushed through my heart, and rolled back again to its source. 'Joy unspeakable and full of glory' filled my soul. All fear and doubt and condemnation passed away. I knew that my heart was clean, and that the Father and the Son had come and made it their abode."

This was all very well, but next day the word ran through New Haven, "Noyes says he is perfect!" with the inevitable corollary, "Noyes is crazy!" The authorities promptly expelled him from the seminary and revoked his license to preach. But the perfect are proof against imperfect human detractors. "I have taken away their license to sin, and they keep on sinning," said Noyes. "So, though they have taken away my license to preach, I shall keep on preaching." This he did, with some success. His first convert was Miss Abigail Merwin of Orange, Connecticut, with whom he felt himself sealed in the faith.

Nevertheless his way was far from smooth. He had yet to pass through what he called "the dark valley of conviction." He went to New York and wandered the streets in a kind of frenzy, catching a little sleep by lying down in a doorway, or on the steps of City Hall, or on a bench at the Battery. He sought the most ill-famed regions of the city. "I descended into cellars where abandoned men and women were gathered, and talked familiarly with them about their ways of life, beseeching them to believe in Christ, that they might be saved from their sins. They listened to me without abuse." Tempted by the Evil One, he doubted all, even the Bible, even Christ, even Abigail Merwin, whom he suspected to be Satan in angelic disguise. But after drinking the dregs of the cup of trembling he emerged purified and secure. He retreated to Putney for peace and shelter. His friends, even his sister, thought him deranged. But such was the power of his spirit that he gathered a little group of adepts, relatives, and friends to accept his revelation.

Miss Abigail Merwin, however, took fright, married a schoolteacher, and removed to Ithaca,

New York. Noyes followed her there—a rather ungentlemanly procedure. After a few months she left her husband, but not for Noyes's arms—only to return to her father in Connecticut.

Noyes was delighted with the pretty village of Ithaca, with his lodging in the Clinton House, and especially with the broad-minded printers, unafraid of publishing heresies and liberal with credit. On August 20, 1837, he established a periodical, the *Witness,* for a subscription rate of one dollar; or, if a dollar should be inconvenient, for nothing. The issue of September 23 reverberated far beyond the subscription list of faithful perfectionists. Noyes had written a private letter expressing his radical views on marriage among the perfect. By a violation of confidence, this had reached the free-thinking editor of a paper called the *Battle-Axe.* Noyes, disdaining evasion, acknowledged in the *Witness* his authorship of the letter and reiterated his startling conclusions. The essential of "the *Battle-Axe* letter" lies in the concluding words: "When the will of God is done on earth as it is in heaven, *there will be no marriage.* The marriage supper of the Lamb is a feast at which *every dish is free to every guest.* Exclusiveness, jealousy, quarreling, have no place there, for the same reason as that which forbids the guests at a thanksgiving dinner to claim each his separate dish, and quarrel with the rest for his rights. In a holy community, there is no more reason why sexual intercourse should be restrained by law, than why eating and drinking should be—and there is as little occasion for shame in the one as in the other. . . . The guests of the marriage supper may each have his favorite dish, each a dish of his own procuring, and that without the jealousy of exclusiveness."

Ungallant as this statement is in its characterization of women as dishes to pass, it states a reasonable protest against the egotisms of marriage. One may readily perceive in it also a secret resentment against the unfaithful Abigail Merwin. One may even interpret it as the erotic outburst of repressed impulse. Noyes, an impassioned, amorous type, was still a virgin.

Noyes was soon vouchsafed a sign, almost a miracle. When he was eighty dollars in debt to an

Ithaca printer, he received from a disciple in Vermont, Miss Harriet A. Holton of Westminster, a letter enclosing a gift of exactly eighty dollars. He paid his bill, returned to Putney, and after a decent interval, forgetting the perfectionist views of the *Battle-Axe* letter, proposed exclusive marriage to Miss Holton. The two were formally united in Chesterfield, New Hampshire, on June 28, 1838. For a honeymoon they drove to Albany to buy a second-hand printing press, with more of Harriet's money.

Thus began the Putney Community, which at first consisted only of Noyes and his wife, several of his brothers and sisters, and a small cluster of converts from the neighborhood. They lived in a group, sharing possessions and duties. Their chief occupations were spiritual exercises in pursuit of holiness and the printing of the *Witness* on their own press. Noyes had no great liking for sheer honest toil for its own sake; he wished to secure for all the freedom for spiritual development. The women prepared one hot meal a day—breakfast. Thereafter the hungry had to help themselves in the kitchen.

Noyes was restless in the monotonous peace of Putney. His wife inherited $9,000 in 1844; Noyes was provoked to fantastic visions. He wrote his wife: "In order to subdue the world to Christ we must carry religion into money-making." He proposed first a theological seminary for perfectionism, then agencies in Boston and New York to distribute their spiritual goods. "Then we must advance into foreign commerce, and as our means enlarge we must cover the ocean with our ships and the whole world with the knowledge of God. This is a great scheme, but not too great for God. . . . Within ten years we will plant the standard of Christ on the highest battlements of the world."

Though allured by such shimmering visions, he had to deal with present problems. An urgent personal problem was that of sex. His wife was pregnant five times in six years. She endured long agonies ending in four stillbirths. The only surviving child was Theodore, born in 1841. John Noyes suffered with his wife, and he protested against cruel nature, perhaps against God. Surely

women were not made to suffer so. Surely there was a better way. A perfectionist could not brook flagrant imperfection. Noyes's habit was to seek and find a better way, and then sanctify it. The better way turned out to be male continence.

Noyes had been trained in the Puritan ethic, which did not regard marital sex as unholy. Nevertheless the consequences of male egoism horrified him. "It is as foolish and cruel to expend one's seed on a wife merely for the sake of getting rid of it," he wrote, "as it would be to fire a gun at one's best friend merely for the sake of unloading it." After his wife's disasters he lived for a time chaste by her side. But chastity proving to be no solution at all; he embraced male continence, of which the definition embarrasses the chaste pen. When embarrassed, the chaste pen may decently quote. One of the community disciples, H. J. Seymour, thus defined the practice: "checking the flow of amative passion before it reaches the point of exposing the man to the loss of virile energy, or the woman to the danger of undesired childbearing." Or, with Latin decorum, *coitus reservatus;* or, more colloquially, everything but. This was not actually the beginning of birth-control advocacy. In 1832 a Boston physician, Charles Knowlton, published *The Fruits of Philosophy; or the Private Companion of Young Married People,* pointing to the menace of excessive childbearing and eventual overpopulation, and recommending contraception. Dr. Knowlton and his publisher were accused of blasphemy. Their case was carried to the Supreme Court, and they were condemned to several months in jail. Robert Dale Owen, the reformer of New Harmony, Indiana, supported by Miss Frances Wright, "the Priestess of Beelzebub," carried on the work. In his *Moral Physiology* (1836), Owen recommended *coitus interruptus,* which Noyes scored as substituting self-indulgence for self-control.

"Amativeness is to life as sunshine is to vegetation," wrote Noyes twelve years later in his *Bible Argument Defining the Relation of the Sexes in the Kingdom of Heaven.* "Ordinary sexual intercourse (in which the amative and propagative functions are confounded) is a momentary affair, terminating in exhaustion and disgust. . . . Adam and Eve . . . sunk the spiritual in the sensual in their intercourse with each other, by pushing prematurely beyond the amative to the propagative, and so became ashamed." In the future society, "as propagation will become a science, so amative intercourse will become one of the 'fine arts.' Indeed it will rank above music, painting, sculpture, &c.; for it combines the charms and the benefits of them all."

All this is very noble and high-minded; but we are trained to look for—and we usually find—a casuistical serpent in the gardens, who is able to transform impulse into ideals, even into new theologies. The serpent in this case was Mary Cragin, who with her husband, George, had joined Putney Community. Mary was a charmer, and, to put it baldly, sexy. (Do not condemn her; some are, some aren't. This is a well-known fact.) Noyes feared that she might "become a Magdalene" if he did not save her. One evening in the woods, Noyes and Mary discovered that they were united by a deep spiritual bond. "We took some liberty of embracing, and Mrs. George distinctively gave me to understand that she was ready for the full consummation." But Noyes insisted on a committee meeting with the respective spouses. "We gave each other full liberty, and so entered into marriage in quartette form. The last part of the interview was as amiable and happy as a wedding, and a full consummation . . . followed."

This was Noyes's first infidelity, according to the world's idiom. He found a more grandiloquent term for it—complex marriage, to contrast with the restrictiveness of simple marriage. Heaven beamed upon the participants. "Our love is of God; it is destitute of exclusiveness, each one rejoicing in the happiness of the others," said Mary. The Putney Community, in general, applauded; some, under direction, adopted the new cure for marital selfishness. It appears that some puritan wives, as well as husbands, were secretly weary of the "scanty and monotonous fare" provided by monogamy.

But righteous Putney soon had hints of goings-on and uprose in anger. On October 26, 1847, Noyes was arrested, charged with adultery, and released, pending trial, on $2,000 bail. Noyes de-

clared himself guiltless, insisting that in common law no tort has been committed if no one is injured. "The head and front and whole of our offense is communism of love. . . . If this is the unpardonable sin in the world, we are sure it is the beauty and glory of heaven." But in fear of mob violence from "the barbarians of Putney" he thought it well to jump bail, following the counsel of the highest authority: "When they persecute you in this city, flee ye into another."

A refuge awaited the persecuted saints in the burned-over district of central New York, a region familiar to Noyes. A group of perfectionists offered the Putneyans a sawmill and forty acres of woodland on Oneida Creek, halfway between Syracuse and Utica. It was a bland, fertile, welcoming country, suitable for an Eden. By good omen, the spot was the exact geographical center of New York, if one over-looked Long Island.

In mid-February of 1848, "the year of the great change," the pilgrims began to arrive. Defying the upstate winter, lodging in abandoned cabins, they set to with a will to build a community dwelling and workshops. Some of the neighbors looked at them askance; most welcomed these honest, pious, industrious newcomers, and some even were converted to perfectionism and threw in their lot with the colony.

The early years were the heroic age of Oneida. All worked together, cutting and sawing timber, digging clay for bricks, building simple houses, clearing land for vegetable gardens. Everyone took his or her turn at the household tasks. All work was held in equal honor, without prestige connotations. Noyes recognized that most American experiments in communal life had foundered because they were established on the narrow base of agriculture; his communism would live on industry. Thus Oneida marketed canned fruits and vegetables, sewing silk, straw hats, mop sticks, travelling bags, and finally, silver tableware. Its traps for animals, from rodents to bears, became famous as far as Alaska and Siberia. The cruelty of traps seldom occurred to the makers, who were frontiersmen as well as perfectionists. Sympathy with suffering beasts and the conservation of wildlife were

Members of the Oneida community standing outside of the Mansion House. This community home, with its towers, mansard roofs, and tall French windows, carried a message of security, peace, and material comfort.

concepts still underdeveloped. To a critic, Noyes replied that since God had covered the earth with vermin, Oneida simply had to cleanse it. Salesmen, known only as peddlers, were sent out to market the wares. On their return, they were given a Turkish bath and a sharp examination on faith and practice, a spiritual rubdown to expunge the stains of the unregenerate world.

The Oneida Community prospered. The numbers of the faithful rose. The great Mansion House, the community home, was begun in 1860 and completed a dozen years later. It is a far-wandering red-brick building or group of buildings, standing on a knoll amid magnificent fat trees. Harmoniously proportioned, with its towers, mansard roofs, and tall French windows, it is a superb example of mid-nineteenth-century architecture. Its message is security, peace, and material comfort. The interior is graced with fine woodwork and decorations. The parlors, the excellent library, the lovely assembly hall, are redolent with memories, jealously preserved and proudly recounted. Here live a number of descendants of the original Oneidans, together with

some lodgers, still regarded with kindly pity as "foreign bodies."

The memories, second-hand though they are, are all of a happy time, of a golden age long lost. John Humphrey Noyes, affectionately referred to by his grandchildren as "the Honorable John," was a cheerful person, and imposed happiness on his great family. The story is told of a visitor who asked her guide: "What is the fragrance I smell here in this house?" The guide answered: "It may be the odor of crushed selfishness." There was no money within the Oneida economy, no private possession, no competition for food and shelter, and hence little rivalry.

All worked and played together. Whenever possible, work was done on the "bee" system; thus a party of men and women would make handbags on the lawn, while a dramatic voice read a novel aloud. Classes were conducted in such recondite subjects as Greek and Hebrew. Dances and respectable card games, like euchre and whist, were in favor. Amateur theatricals were a constant diversion. The productions of the *The Merchant of Venice, The Merry Wives of*

Windsor, and especially of *H. M. S. Pinafore,* were famous as far as Utica and Syracuse. Music was encouraged, with an orchestra and much vocalization. Music, Noyes mused, was closely related to sexual love; it was an echo of the passions. However, music contained a menace; it gave rise to rivalries, jealousies, and vanities, to what Noyes reproved as "prima donna fever."

Noyes had strong views on dress. He called the contrast of men's and women's costumes immodest, in that it proclaimed the distinction of sex. "In a state of nature, the difference between a man and a woman could hardly be distinguished at a distance of five hundred yards, but as men and women dress, their sex is telegraphed as far as they can be seen. Woman's dress is a standing lie. It proclaims that she is not a two-legged animal, but something like a churn, standing on castors. . . . Gowns operate as shackles, and they are put on that sex which has most talent in the legs."

From the beginning at Oneida, a new dress for women was devised, loose skirts to the knee with pantalets below, thus approximating a gentleman's frock coat and trousers. Some visitors were shocked, some were amused; few were allured. Indeed the specimens remaining in the community's collections and the representations in photographs hardly seem beautiful. But the wearers rejoiced in their new freedom of movement. They cut their hair, in spite of Saint Paul. It was asserted they looked and felt younger.

For thirty years the community, a placid island amid the stormy seas of society, lived its insulated life. It numbered, at its peak, three hundred members. It was undisturbed, except by invasions of visitors brought on bargain excursions by the railroads. As many as a thousand appeared on a single day, picnicking on the grounds, invading the workshops and private quarters. They were welcomed; but on their departure all the Oneidans turned out in order to collect the scatterings, to scrub out the tobacco stains on the parquet floors.

The structure, the doctrine, the persistence of Oneida made a unique social phenomenon. It was consciously a family, with Noyes as father. As Constance Noyes Robertson says, it substituted "for the small unit of home and family and individual possessions the larger unit of group-family and group-family life." Its faith was "Bible Communism." Though it held aloof from all churches and deconsecrated the Sabbath, it was pietistic in demanding the regeneration of society by rejecting competition, a money economy, and private ownership, whether of goods or persons. But it was not Marxian, for it made no mention of class warfare, of a revolution to come, of proletarian dictatorship.

The internal organization of the community was loose and vague, depending largely on the will of Noyes. Justice and discipline were administered informally, if at all. To provide correction, Noyes trusted chiefly to a procedure known as mutual criticism. Saint Paul had said: "Speak every man truth with his neighbor; for we are members of one another"; and the Apostle James: "Confess your faults to one another." When an individual offered himself for criticism, or was designated from above, a committee prepared his "trial," but any member might join in the proceedings. The trial was a game, though a serious one. The subject was informed of his secret faults, of short-comings he had not suspected. He learned that his very virtues, on which he had flattered himself, were only disguised vices. The critics would pounce on an unpopular fellow-member with glee, seizing the opportunity to reveal to him some home truths, at the same time revealing their hidden rancors. A transcript of the proceedings was posted and often printed. The subject of this primitive psychoanalysis was likely to suffer dreadfully from his new self-knowledge. "I was shaken from center to circumference," said one. "I was metaphorically stood upon my head and allowed to drain until all the self-righteousness had dripped out of me." Afterward the subject felt enlightened, purified, happy. "Mutual criticism," said Noyes, "subordinates the I-spirit to the We-spirit." It also made the subjects, mostly brooding introspectives, for a time the center of interest and concern for the whole community. Mutual criticism, under the name "krinopathy," was even used as a therapeutic device to cure children's colds, with, it was said, remarkable success.

Of the various Oneida institutions, the most fascinating to the prudent observer is the organization of sex behavior. Since the community was a single great family, there could be within it no marrying and giving in marriage. Each was married to all, Noyes insisted; every man was husband and brother to every woman. Love, far from being a sin, was holy, a sacrament; in the sexual experience one escaped from egotism and self-hood into the ecstasy of communion. Every effort must be to "abound"—one of Noyes's favorite words. One must spend, not hoard. The human heart seldom realized its possibilities; it "is capable of loving any number of times and any number of persons; the more it loves the more it can love." One had only to look at surrounding society to recognize the evils of exclusive marriage, the chains binding unmatched natures, the secret adulteries, actual or of the heart, the hate-filled divorces, women's diseases, prostitution, masturbation, licentiousness in general.

Noyes maintained that sexual love was not naturally restricted to pairs, that second marriages were often the happiest. "Men and women find universally (however the fact may be concealed) that their susceptibility to love is not burned out by one honeymoon, or satisfied by one lover." The body should assert its rights; religion should make use of the senses as helpers of devotion. Sexual shame, the consequence of the fall of man, was fictitious and irrational. "Shame ought to be banished from the company of virtue, though in the world it has stolen the very name virtue. . . . Shame gives rise to the theory that sexual offices have no place in heaven. Anyone who has true modesty would sooner banish singing from heaven than sexual music." Beware, said Noyes, of one who proclaims that he is free from sexual desire, beware of religious teachers with fondling hands. Beware especially of Dr. Josiah Gridley of Southampton, Massachusetts, who boasts that he could carry a virgin in each hand without the least stir of passion. In short, "you must not serve the lusts of the flesh; if you do you will be damned. You must not make monks of yourself; if you do you will be damned."

One might suspect that these doctrines would have led to oughtright antinomianism and to general orgies. Nothing of the sort occurred, thanks to the watchful care of Noyes and thanks to the character of the Oneidans, devout and rather humorless seekers for perfection. The system of complex marriage, or pantagamy, begun in Putney, was instituted. A man might request the privilege of a private visit with a lady, or a lady might take the initiative, for "in all nature the female element invites and the male responds." The request was submitted to a committee of elders, headed by Noyes, who gave the final approval or disapproval. The mate besought had the right of refusal. It was recommended that older women initiate young men, and vice versa. Thus the young men were expertly guided in the practice of male continence, while the maturer men undertook without complaint the education of the maidens. The committee was also concerned to break up "exclusive and idolatrous attachments" of two persons of the same age, for these bred selfishness. We are assured that complex marriage worked admirably, and that for many life became a continuous courtship. "Amativeness, the lion of the tribe of human passions, is conquered and civilized among us." But the records are unwontedly reticent on the details of the system's operation. Only one scandal is remembered, when an unworthy recruit tried to force his attentions on the women, and was expelled through a window into a snowdrift. One suspects that in spite of all the spiritual training, there were heartaches and hidden anger, and much whispering and giggling at the sound of midnight footsteps on the stairs.

The flaw in the system of continence was the threatening sterilization of the movement—the fate of the Shakers. Noyes recognized the danger, and in his *Bible Argument* of 1848 had proposed scientific propagation to replace random or involuntary propagation. But the time was not yet ripe. In the difficult early years of Oneida, Noyes discouraged childbearing, and his docile followers produced only forty-four offspring in twenty years. Then increasing prosperity permitted him to take steps for the perpetuation of his community. Early in 1869, he proposed the inauguration of stirpiculture, or the scientific improvement of the human stock by breeding. "Every race-horse, every straight-backed bull, every premium pig tells us what we can do and what we must do for men." Oneida should be a laboratory for the preparation of the great race of the future.

The Oneidans, especially the younger ones, greeted the proposal with enthusiasm. Fifty-three young women signed these resolutions:

1. *That we do not belong to ourselves in any respect, but that we do belong to God, and second to Mr. Noyes as God's true representative.*
2. *That we have no rights or personal feelings in regard to childbearing which shall in the least degree oppose or embarrass him in his choice of scientific combinations.*
3. *That we will put aside all envy, childishness and selfseeking, and rejoice with those who are chosen candidates; that we will, if necessary, become martyrs to science, and cheerfully resign all desire to become mothers, if for any reason Mr. Noyes deem us unfit material for propagation. Above all, we offer ourselves "living sacrifices" to God and true Communism.*

At the same time thirty-eight young men made a corresponding declaration to Noyes:

The undersigned desire you may feel that we most heartily sympathize with your purpose in regard to scientific propagation, and offer ourselves to be used in forming any combinations that may seem to you desirable. We claim no rights. We ask no privileges. We desire to be servants of the truth. With a prayer that the grace of God will help us in this resolution, we are your true soldiers.

Thus began the first organized experiment in human eugenics. For several years Noyes directed all the matings, on the basis of physical, spiritual, moral, and intellectual suitability. In 1875 a committee of six men and six women was formed to

issue licenses to propagate. The selective process bore some bitter fruit. The eliminated males particularly were unhappy, unconsoled by the reflection that in animal breeding one superior stud may serve many females. Noyes relented in his scientific purpose so far as to permit one child to each male applicant. There was also some covert grumbling that Noyes, then in his sixties, elected himself to father nine children, by several mates. Eugenically, to be sure, he was entirely justified; there could be no doubt of his superiority.

The results of the stirpicultural experiment have not been scientifically studied, though an article by Hilda Herrick Noyes, prepared in 1921, offered some valuable statistical information. About one hundred men and women took part; eighty-one became parents, producing fifty-eight living children and four stillborn. No mothers were lost during the experiment; no defective children were produced. The health of the offspring was exceptionally good; their longevity has far surpassed the average expectations of life. The children, and the children's children, constitute a very superior group, handsome, and intelligent. Many have brilliantly conducted the affairs of their great manufacturing corporation; others have distinguished themselves in public service, the arts, and literature.

The integration of the children into the community caused some difficulties. The mother kept her child until he was weaned and could walk; then he was transferred to the Children's House, though he might return to his mother for night care. Noyes, with this ideal of the community family, disapproved of egotistic, divisive "special love"; the mothers were permitted to see their children only once or twice a week. The children were excellently educated in the nursery school, the kindergarten, and the grammar school, by teachers chosen for their competence and natural liking for the young. If the children cried for their mothers, they were severely reproved for "partiality" or "stickiness." One graduate of the Children's House remembered that when he was forbidden to visit his mother he went berserk. Another recalled her agony when she caught sight of her mother after a fortnight's enforced separation. The child begged her mother not to leave her— and her mother fled for fear of a penalty of an additional week's separation from her child.

The atmosphere of the Children's House was, in short, that of a friendly orphanage. If the disruption of the family units had any bad psychic effects on the children, they have not been recorded. Children accept their world as it is; they know no other. The memories of the Oneida boys and girls are mostly of happy schooldays under kind teachers, days of laughter, play, and delightful learning. The judgment of one eminent product, Pierrepont B. Noyes, is surely correct, that the community system was harder on the mothers than on the children.

The fathers were more remote from their children than were the mothers. Pierrepont Noyes admitted, "Father never seemed a father to me in the ordinary sense." The system reflected indeed the character of John Humphrey Noyes. He was the Father of his people, the semidivine begetter of a community, and he loved the community communally. He saw no reason to encourage family bonds, "partiality," among the faithful, at cost to the community spirit. He seems to have shown little personal affection for his sons after the flesh. No doubt a phrenologist would have noted that his bump of parental love was small. One is tempted to go further, to see in his disregard for his children a certain horror of paternity, a deep-implanted remembrance of his four stillborn babies, of his wife's sufferings and his own.

The rumors of strange sex practices roused the righteous and the orthodox, already angered by Oneida's nonobservance of the Sabbath and rejection of church affiliations. A professor at Hamilton College, John W. Mears, still the bogeyman of Oneida after a hundred years, began in 1873 a long campaign to destroy the community and its band of sinners. Though most of the inhabitants and newspaper editors of the region defended Noyes and his followers, though local justice could find no grounds for prosecution, the churches demanded action against "the ethics of the barnyard," and sought

enabling legislation from the state. The menace mounted until, in June, 1879, Noyes fled to Canada, as, thirty-one years before, he had fled from Vermont. From a new home in Niagara Falls, Ontario, he continued to advise and inspire his old companions until his death, on April 13, 1886.

With the Father's departure the community system collapsed. In August, 1879, complex marriage was abandoned. Most of the Oneidans paired off and married, to legitimize their children. There were distressing cases of mothers whose mates were already taken, of the children of Noyes himself, left high and dry. In the reorganization into conventional families, it was necessary to establish rights of private property. As Noyes had foreseen, the demons of greed, self-seeking, jealousy, anger, and uncharitableness invaded the serene halls of the Mansion House.

The Oneida industries were converted into a joint-stock company, the shares distributed to the members of the community. After a period of drifting and fumbling, the widely varied enterprises came under the inspired management of Pierrepont Noyes and became models of welfare capitalism, or the partnership of owners and workers. To the present day, high wages are paid, profits are shared, schools, country clubs, aids for home-building are provided. Oneida is the leading producer of stainless-steel flatware, the second largest producer of silver-plated ware in the United States. It has over three thousand employees in the Oneida plants, and many more in the factories in Canada, Mexico, and the United Kingdom. Its net sales in 1967 amounted to fifty-four million dollars, with net profits of two and a half million.

This outcome is not the least surprising feature of the Oneida story. Nearly all other communistic experiments in this country have long since disappeared leaving nothing more than a tumble-down barracks or a roadside marker. Oneida found a transformation into the capitalist world. It did so at the cost of losing its religious and social doctrines; but it has never lost the idealism, the humanitarianism, and the communitarian love of John Humphrey Noyes.

Study Questions

1. Some psychohistorians have argued that the early life of John Humphrey Noyes explains better than anything else the eccentric radicalism of his social philosophy. What is the basis for this argument? Do you agree? Why or why not?

2. Most Americans found Noyes's ideas to be outrageous at best and satanic at worst. Why? Is there any realistic hope that Noyes could have succeeded had he lived in our era? Why or why not?

3. Although Noyes set out to change America, his vision and community were eventually transformed by the environment. What went wrong with the Oneida experiment? What significance do you see in the change in Oneida from a socialist commune to a modern corporation?

Bibliography

The classic study of reform movements during the Jacksonian period is Alice Felt Tyler, *Freedom's Ferment* (1944). Also see Ronald G. Walter, *American Reformers, 1815–1860* (1978) and William G. McLoughlin, *Revivals, Awakenings, and Reform* (1978). Arthur Bestor's *Backwoods Utopias: The Sectarian and Owenite Phases of Communitarian Socialism in America, 1663–1829* (1950) remains an excellent survey. For sexual radicalism in early America, see Raymond Muncy, *Sex and Marriage in Utopian Communities* (1950). The best studies of John Humphrey Noyes and Oneida are M. L. Carden, *Oneida: Utopian Community to Modern Corporation* (1971) and R. D. Thomas, *The Man Who Would Be Perfect: John Humphrey Noyes and the Utopian Impulse* (1977). Also see Louis J. Kern, *An Ordered Love: Sex Roles and Sexuality in Victorian Utopias* (1981) and Lori D. Ginzberg, *Women and the Work of Benevolence: Morality, Politics, and Class in the Nineteenth-Century United States* (1990). For the best of the most recent work, see Robert P. Sutton, *Communal Utopias and the American Experience: Religious Communities, 1732–2000* (2003) and Phillip E. Wagner, *Imaginary Communities: Utopia, the Nation, and the Spatial Histories of Modernity* (2002).

READING 23

Gouge and Bite, Pull Hair and Scratch

Elliott J. Gorn

The tidewater aristocracy of Virginia enjoyed horse racing, "the sport of kings." If no kings could be found among the gentry, there was not lack of royal pretensions. Gentlemen raced their horses against other gentlemen, and at stake was more than just money or glory. Riding on the outcome was a gentleman's sense of self-worth. Robert "King" Carter, the most successful planter of his time, believed that if he lost a race, he lost face in the eyes of his peers. As T. H. Breen demonstrated in an earlier selection, gambling and horse racing provide the keys for unlocking the planters' attitudes toward themselves and life in general.

In the following essay, historian Elliott Gorn examines the brutal pastimes of the working-class men of the South and West. In particular, he focuses on gouging matches, in which the object was to pry the opponent's eye out of its socket using a thumb as the fulcrum. Like Breen, Gorn uses this activity as a means for understanding the world of working-class men in the southern and western backcountry. He uncovers a world in which violence was common, and "Indians, wild animals, lawless criminals, and natural forces threatened life." It was also a world in which work was physically hard and dangerous, and in which men spent more time in the company of other men than with women. In this environment, Gorn notes, "a man's role in the all-male society was defined less by his ability as a breadwinner than by his ferocity. . . . Violent sports, heavy drinking, and impulsive pleasure seeking were appropriate for men whose lives were hard, whose futures were unpredictable, and whose opportunities were limited."

I would advise you when You do fight Not to act like Tygers and Bears as these Virginians do—Biting one anothers Lips and Noses off, and *gowging* one another—that is, thrusting out one anothers Eyes, and kicking one another on the Cods, to the Great damage of many a Poor Woman." Thus, Charles Woodmason, an itinerant Anglican minister born of English gentry stock, described the brutal form of combat he found in the Virginia backcountry shortly before the American Revolution. Although historians are more likely to study people thinking, governing, worshiping, or working, how men fight—who participates, who observes, which rules are followed, what is at stake, what tactics are allowed—reveals much about past cultures and societies.

The evolution of southern backwoods brawling from the late eighteenth century through the antebellum era can be reconstructed from oral traditions and travelers' accounts. As in most cultural history, broad patterns and uneven trends rather than specific dates mark the way. The sources are often problematic and must be used with care; some speculation is required. But the lives of common people cannot be ignored merely because they leave few records. "To feel for a feller's eyestrings and make him tell the news" was not just mayhem but an act freighted with significance for both social and cultural history.

As early as 1735, boxing was "much in fashion" in parts of Chesapeake Bay, and forty years later a visitor from the North declared that, along with dancing, fiddling, small swords, and card playing, it was an essential skill for all young Virginia gentlemen. The term "boxing," however, did not necessarily refer to the comparatively tame style of bare-knuckle fighting familiar to eighteenth-century Englishmen. In 1746, four deaths prompted the governor of North Carolina

to ask for legislation against "the barbarous and inhuman manner of boxing which so much prevails among the lower sort of people." The colonial assembly responded by making it a felony "to cut out the Tongue or pull out the eyes of the King's Liege People." Five years later the assembly added slitting, biting, and cutting off noses to the list of offenses. Virginia passed similar legislation in 1748 and revised these statutes in 1772 explicitly to discourage men from "gouging, plucking, or putting out an eye, biting or kicking or stomping upon" quiet peaceable citizens. By 1786 South Carolina had made premediated mayhem a capital offense, defining the crime as severing another's bodily parts.

Laws notwithstanding, the carnage continued. Philip Vickers Fithian, a New Jerseyite serving as tutor for an aristocratic Virginia family, confided to his journal on September 3, 1774:

By appointment is to be fought this Day near Mr. Lanes two fist Battles between four young Fellows. The Cause of the battles I have not yet known; I suppose either that they are lovers, and one has in Jest or reality some way supplanted the other; or has in a merry hour called him a Lubber or a thick-Skull, or a Buckskin, or a Scotsman, or perhaps one has mislaid the other's hat, or knocked a peach out of his Hand, or offered him a dram without wiping the mouth of the Bottle; all these, and ten thousand more quite as trifling and ridiculous are thought and accepted as just Causes of immediate Quarrels, in which every diabolical Strategem for Mastery is allowed and practiced.

The "trifling and ridiculous" reasons for these fights had an unreal quality for the matter-of-fact Yankee. Not assaults on persons or property but slights, insults, and thoughtless gestures set young southerners against each other. To call a man a "buckskin," for example, was to accuse him of the poverty associated with leather clothing, while the epithet "Scotsman" tied him to the low-caste Scots-Irish who settled the southern highlands.

"Gouge and Bite, Pull Hair and Scratch: The Social Significance of Fighting in the Southern Backcountry" by Elliott J. Gorn in *American Historical Review*, Vol. 90, No. 1, pp.18–43, February 1985. Reprinted by permission of the author.

Fithian could not understand how such trivial offenses caused the bloody battles. But his incomprehension turned to rage when he realized that spectators attended these "odious and filthy amusements" and that the fighters allayed their spontaneous passions in order to fix convenient dates and places, which allowed time for rumors to spread and crowds to gather. The Yankee concluded that only devils, prostitutes, or monkeys could sire creatures so unfit for human society.

Descriptions of these "fist battles," as Fithian called them, indicate that they generally began like English prize fights. Two men, surrounded by onlookers, parried blows until one was knocked or thrown down. But there the similarity ceased. Where as "Broughton's Rules" of the English ring specified that a round ended when either antagonist fell, southern bruisers only began fighting at this point. Enclosed not inside a formal ring—the "magic circle" defining a special place with its own norms of conduct—but within whatever space the spectators left vacant, fighters battled each other until one called enough or was unable to continue. Combatants boasted, howled, and cursed. As words gave way to action, they tripped and threw, gouged and butted, scratched and choked each other. "But what is worse than all," Isaac Weld observed, "these wretches in their combat endeavor to their utmost to tear out each other's testicles."

Around the beginning of the nineteenth century, men sought original labels for their brutal style of fighting. "Rough-and-tumble" or simply "gouging" gradually replaced "boxing" as the name for these contests. Before two bruisers attacked each other, spectators might demand whether they proposed to fight fair—according to Broughton's Rules—or rough-and-tumble. Honor dictated that all techniques be permitted. Except for a ban on weapons, most men chose to fight "no holts barred," doing what they wished to each other without interference, until one gave up or was incapacitated.

The emphasis on maximum disfigurement, on severing bodily parts, made this fighting style unique. Amid the general mayhem, however, gouging out an opponent's eye became the sine qua non of rough-and-tumble fighting, much like the knockout punch in modern boxing. The best gougers, of course, were adept at other fighting skills. Some allegedly filed their teeth to bite off an enemy's appendages more efficiently. Still, liberating an eyeball quickly became a fighter's surest route to victory and his most prestigious accomplishment. To this end, celebrated heroes fired their fingernails hard, honed them sharp, and oiled them slick. "You have come off badly this time, I doubt?" declared an alarmed passerby on seeing the piteous condition of a renowned fighter. "'Have I,' says he triumphantly, shewing from his pocket at the same time an eye, which he had extracted during the combat, and preserved for a trophy."

As the new style of fighting evolved, its geographical distribution changed. Leadership quickly passed from the southern seaboard to up-country counties and the western frontier. Although examples could be found throughout the South, rough-and-tumbling was best suited to the backwoods, where hunting, herding, and semi-subsistence agriculture predominated over market-oriented, stable crop production. Thus, the settlers of western Carolina, Kentucky, and Tennessee, as well as upland Mississippi, Alabama, and Georgia, became especially known for their pugnacity.

The social base of rough-and-tumbling also shifted with the passage of time. Although brawling was always considered a vice of the "lower sort," eighteenth-century Tidewater gentlemen sometimes found themselves in brutal fights. These combats grew out of challenges to men's honor—to their status in patriarchal, kin-based, small-scale communities—and were woven into the very fabric of daily life. Rhys Isaac has observed that the Virginia gentry set the tone for a fiercely competitive style of living. Although they valued hierarchy, individual status was never permanently fixed, so men frantically sought to assert their prowess—by grand boasts over tavern gaming tables laden with money, by whipping and tripping each other's horses in violent quarter-races, by wagering one-half year's earnings on the flash of a fighting cock's gaff. Great planters and small shared an ethos that extolled courage bordering on foolhardiness and cherished magnificent, if irrational, displays of largess.

Piety, hard work, and steady habits had their adherents, but in this society aggressive self-assertion and manly pride were the real marks of status. Even the gentry's vaunted hospitality demonstrated a family's community standing, so conviviality itself became a vehicle for rivalry and emulation. Rich and poor might revel together during "public times," but gentry patronage of sports and festivities kept the focus of power clear. Above all, brutal recreations toughened men for a violent social life in which the exploitation of labor, the specter of poverty, and a fierce struggle for status were daily realities.

During the final decades of the eighteenth century, however, individuals like Fithian's young gentlemen became less inclined to engage in rough-and-tumbling. Many in the planter class now wanted to distinguish themselves from social inferiors more by genteel manners, gracious living, and paternal prestige than by patriarchal prowess. They sought alternatives to brawling and found them by imitating the English aristocracy. A few gentlemen took boxing lessons from professors of pugilism or attended sparring exhibitions given by touring exponents of the manly art. More important, dueling gradually replaced hand-to-hand combat. The code of honor offered a genteel, though deadly, way to settle personal disputes while demonstrating one's elevated status. Ceremony distinguished antiseptic duels from lower-class brawls. Cool restraint and customary decorum proved a man's ability to shed blood while remaining emotionally detached, to act as mercilessly as the poor whites but to do so with chilling gentility.

Slowly, then, rough-and-tumble fighting found specific locus in both human and geographical landscapes. We can watch men grapple with the transition. When an attempt at a formal duel aborted, Savannah politician Robert Watkins and United States Senator James Jackson resorted to gouging. Jackson bit Watson's finger to save his

eye. Similarly, when "a low fellow who pretends to gentility" insulted a distinguished doctor, the gentleman responded with a proper challenge. "He had scarcely uttered these words, before the other flew at him, and in an instant turned his eye out of the socket, and while it hung upon his cheek, the fellow was barbarous enough to endeavor to pluck it entirely out." By the new century, such ambiguity had lessened, as rough-and-tumble fighting was relegated to individuals in backwoods settlements. For the next several decades, eye-gouging matches were focal events in the culture of lower-class males who still relished the wild ways of old.

"I saw more than one man who wanted an eye, and ascertained that I was now in the region of 'gouging,'" reported young Timothy Flint, a Harvard educated, Presbyterian minister bound for Louisiana missionary work in 1816. His spirits buckled as his party turned down the Mississippi from the Ohio Valley. Enterprising farmers gave way to slothful and vulgar folk whom Flint considered barely civilized. Only vicious fighting and disgusting accounts of battles past disturbed their inertia. Residents assured him that the "blackguards" excluded gentlemen from gouging matches. Flint was therefore perplexed when told that a barbarous-looking man was the "best" in one settlement, until he learned that best in this context meant not the most moral, prosperous, or pious but the local champion who had whipped all the rest, the man most dexterous at extracting eyes.

Because rough-and-tumble fighting declined in settled areas, some of the most valuable accounts were written by visitors who penetrated the backcountry. Travel literature was quite popular during America's infancy, and many profit-minded authors undoubtedly wrote with their audience's expectations in mind. Images of heroic frontiersmen, of crude but unencumbered natural men, enthralled both writers and readers. Some who toured the new republic in the decades following the Revolution had strong prejudices against America's democratic pretensions. English travelers in particular doubted that the upstart nation—in which the lower class shouted its equality and the upper class was unable or unwilling to exercise proper authority—could survive. Ironically, backcountry fighting became a symbol for both those who inflated and those who punctured America's expansive national ego.

Frontier braggarts enjoyed fulfilling visitors' expectations of backwoods depravity, pumping listeners full of gruesome legends. Their narratives projected a satisfying, if grotesque, image of the American rustic as a fearless, barbaric, larger-than-life democrat. But they also gave Englishmen the satisfaction of seeing their former countrymen run wild in the wilderness. Gouging matches offered a perfect metaphor for the Hobbesian war of all against all, of men tearing each other apart once institutional restraints evaporated, of a heart of darkness beating in the New World. As they made their way from the northern port towns to the southern countryside, or down the Ohio to southwestern waterways, observers concluded that geographical and moral descent went hand in hand. Brutal fights dramatically confirmed their belief that evil lurked in the deep shadows of America's sunny democratic landscape.

And yet, it would be a mistake to dismiss all travelers' accounts of backwoods fighting as fictions born of prejudice. Many sojourners who were sober and careful observers of America left detailed reports of rough-and-tumbles. Aware of the tradition of frontier boasting, they distinguished apocryphal stories from personal observation, wild tales from eye-witness accounts. Although gouging matches became a sort of literary convention, many travelers compiled credible descriptions of backwoods violence.

"The indolence and dissipation of the middling and lower classes of Virginia are such as to give pain to every reflecting mind," one anonymous visitor declared. "Horse-racing, cock-fighting, and boxing-matches are standing amusements, for which they neglect all business; and in the latter of which they conduct themselves with a barbarity worthy of their savage neighbors." Thomas Anburey agreed. He believed that the Revolution's leveling of class distinctions left the "lower people" dangerously independent. Although An-

burey found poor whites usually hospitable and generous, he was disturbed by their sudden outbursts of impudence, their aversion to labor and love of drink, their vengefulness and savagery. They shared with their betters a taste for gaming, horse racing, and cockfighting, but "boxing matches, in which they display such barbarity, as fully marks their innate ferocious disposition," were all their own. Anburey concluded that an English prize fight was humanity itself compared to Virginia combat.

Another visitor, Charles William Janson, decried the loss of social subordination, which caused the rabble to reinterpret liberty and equality as licentiousness. Paternal authority—the font of social and political order—had broken down in America, as parents gratified their children's whims, including youthful tastes for alcohol and tobacco. A national mistrust of authority had brought civilization to its nadir among the poor whites of the South. "The lower classes are the most abject that, perhaps, ever peopled a Christian land. They live in the woods and deserts and many of them cultivate no more land than will raise them corn and cabbages, which, with fish, and occasionally a piece of pickled pork or bacon, are their constant food. . . . Their habitations are more wretched than can be conceived; the huts of the poor of Ireland, or even the meanest Indian wig-wam, displaying more ingenuity and greater industry." Despite their degradation—perhaps because of it—Janson found the poor whites extremely jealous of their republican rights and liberties. They considered themselves the equals of their best-educated neighbors and intruded on whomever they chose. The gouging match this fastidious Englishman witnessed in Georgia was the epitome of lower-class depravity:

We found the combatants . . . fast clinched by the hair, and their thumbs endeavoring to force a passage into each other's eyes; while several of the bystanders were betting upon the first eye to be turned out of its socket. For some time the combatants avoided the thumb stroke with dexterity. At length they fell to the ground, and in an instant the uppermost sprung up with his antagonist's eye in his hand!!! The savage crowd applauded, while, sick with horror, we galloped away from the infernal scene. The name of the sufferer was John Butler, a Carolinian, who, it seems, had been dared to the combat by a Georgian; and the first eye was for the honor of the state to which they respectively belonged.

Janson concluded that even Indian "savages" and London's rabble would be outraged by the beastly Americans.

While Janson toured the lower South, his countryman Thomas Ashe explored the territory around Wheeling, Virginia. A passage, dated April 1806, from his *Travels in America* gives us a detailed picture of gouging's social context. Ashe expounded on Wheeling's potential to become a center of trade for the Ohio and upper Mississippi valleys, noting that geography made the town a natural rival of Pittsburgh. Yet Wheeling lagged in "worthy commercial pursuits, and industrious and moral dealings." Ashe attributed this backwardness to the town's frontier ways, which attracted men who specialized in drinking, plundering Indian property, racing horses, and watching cockfights. A Wheeling Quaker assured Ashe that mores were changing, that the underworld element was about to be driven out. Soon, the godly would gain control of the local government, enforce strict observance of the Sabbath, and outlaw vice. Ashe was sympathetic but doubtful. In Wheeling, only heightened violence and debauchery distinguished Sunday from the rest of the week. The citizens' willingness to close up shop and neglect business on the slightest pretext made it a questionable residence for any respectable group of men, let alone a society of Quakers.

To convey the rough texture of Wheeling life, Ashe described a gouging match. Two men drinking at a public house argued over the merits of their respective horses. Wagers made, they galloped off to the race course. "Two thirds of the population followed:—blacksmiths, shipwrights, all left work: the town appeared a desert. The stores were shut. I asked a proprietor, why the warehouses did not remain open? He told me all good was done for the day: that the people would remain on the ground till night, and many stay till the following morning." Determined to witness an event deemed so important that the entire town went on holiday, Ashe headed for the track. He missed the initial heat but arrived in time to watch the crowd raise the stakes to induce a rematch. Six horses competed, and spectators bet a small fortune, but the results were inconclusive. Umpires' opinions were given and rejected. Heated words, then fists flew. Soon, the melee narrowed to two individuals, a Virginian and a Kentuckian. Because fights were common in such situations, everyone knew the proper procedures, and the combatants quickly decided to "tear and rend" one another—to rough-and-tumble—rather than "fight fair." Ashe elaborated: "You startle at the words tear and rend, and again do not understand me. You have heard these terms, I allow, applied to beasts of prey and to carnivorous animals; and your humanity cannot conceive them applicable to man: It nevertheless is so, and the fact will not permit me the use of any less expressive term."

The battle began—size and power on the Kentuckian's side, science and craft on the Virginian's. They exchanged cautious throws and blows, when suddenly the Virginian lunged at his opponent with a panther's ferocity. The crowd roared its approval as the fight reached its violent denouement:

The shock received by the Kentuckyan, and the want of breath, brought him instantly to the ground. The Virginian never lost his hold; like those bats of the South who never quit the subject on which they fasten till they taste blood, he kept his knees in his enemy's body; fixing his claws in his hair, and his thumbs on his eyes, gave them an instantaneous start from their sockets. The sufferer roared aloud, but uttered no complaint. The citizens again shouted with joy. Doubts were no longer entertained and bets of three to one were offered on the Virginian.

A REGULAR ROW IN THE BACKWOODS.

Men in the primitive southern backcountry used violence in sports, jokes, and talk as a means of release from life's hardships.

But the fight continued. The Kentuckian grabbed his smaller opponent and held him in a tight bear hug, forcing the Virginian to relinquish his facial grip. Over and over the two rolled, until, getting the Virginian under him, the big man "snapt off his nose so close to his face that no manner of projection remained." The Virginian quickly recovered, seized the Kentuckian's lower lip in his teeth, and ripped it down over his enemy's chin. This was enough: "The Kentuckyan at length *gave out,* on which the people carried off the victor, and he preferring triumph to a doctor, who came to cicatrize his face, suffered himself to be chaired round the ground as the champion of the times, and the first *rougher-and-tumbler.* The poor wretch, whose eyes were started from their spheres, and whose lip refused its office, returned to the town, to hide his impotence, and get his countenance repaired." The citizens refreshed themselves with whiskey and biscuits, and then resumed their races.

Ashe's Quaker friend reported that such spontaneous races occurred two or three times a week and that the annual fall and spring meets lasted fourteen uninterrupted days, "aided by the licentious and profligate of all the neighboring states." As for rough-and-tumbles, the Quaker saw no hope of suppressing them. Few nights passed without such fights; few mornings failed to reveal a new citizen with mutilated features. It was a regional taste, unrestrained by law or authority, an inevitable part of life on the left bank of the Ohio.

By the early nineteenth century, rough-and-tumble fighting had generated its own folklore. Horror mingled with awe when residents of the Ohio Valley pointed out one-eyed individuals to visitors, when New Englanders referred to an empty eye socket as a "Virginia Brand," when North Carolinians related stories of mass rough-and-tumbles ending with eyeballs covering the ground, and when Kentuckians told of battle-royals so intense that severed eyes, ears, and noses filled bushel baskets. Place names like "Fighting Creek" and "Gouge Eye" perpetuated the memory of heroic encounters, and rustic bombast reached new extremes with estimates from some counties that every third man wanted an eye. As much as the style of combat, the rich oral folklore of the backcountry—the legends, tales, ritual boasts, and verbal duels, all of them in regional vernacular—made rough-and-tumble fighting unique.

It would be difficult to overemphasize the importance of the spoken word in southern life. Traditional tales, songs, and beliefs—transmitted orally by blacks as well as whites—formed the cornerstone of culture. Folklore socialized children, inculcated values, and helped forge a distinct regional sensibility. Even wealthy and well-educated planters, raised at the knees of black mammies, imbibed both Afro-American and white traditions, and charismatic politicians secured loyal followers by speaking the people's language. Southern society was based more on personalistic, face-to-face, kin-and-community relationships than on legalistic or bureaucratic ones. Interactions between southerners were guided by elaborate rituals of hospitality, demonstrative conviviality, and kinship ties—all of which emphasized personal dependencies and reliance on the spoken word. Through the antebellum period and beyond, the South had an oral as much as a written culture.

Boundaries between talk and action, ideas and behavior, are less clear in spoken than in written contexts. Psychologically, print seems more distant and abstract than speech, which is inextricably bound to specific individuals, times, and places. In becoming part of the realm of sight rather than sound, words leave behind their personal, living qualities, gaining in fixity what they lose in dynamism. Literate peoples separate thought from action, pigeon-holing ideas and behavior. Nonliterate ones draw this distinction less sharply, viewing words and the events to which they refer as a single reality. In oral cultures generally, and the Old South in particular, the spoken word was a powerful force in daily life, because ideation and behavior remained closely linked.

The oral traditions of hunters, drifters, herdsmen, gamblers, roustabouts, and rural poor who rough-and-tumbled provided a strong social cement. Tall talk around a campfire, in a tavern, in front of a crossroads store, or at countless other meeting places on the southwestern frontier helped establish communal bonds between disparate persons. Because backwoods humorists possessed an unusual ability to draw people together and give expression to shared feelings, they often became the most effective leaders and preachers. But words could also divide. Fithian's observation in the eighteenth century—that seemingly innocuous remarks led to sickening violence—remained true for several generations. Men were so touchy about their personal reputations that any slight required an apology. This failing, only retribution restored public stature and self-esteem. "Saving face" was not just a metaphor.

The lore of backwoods combat, however, both inflated and deflated egos. By the early nineteenth century, simple epithets evolved into verbal duels—rituals well known to folklorists. Backcountry men took turns bragging about their prowess, possessions, and accomplishments, spurring each other on to new heights of self-magnification. Such exchanges heightened tension and engendered a sense of theatricality and display. But boasting, unlike insults, did not always lead to combat, for, in a culture that valued oral skills, the verbal battle itself—the contest over who best controlled the power of words—was a real quest for domination:

"I am a man; I am a horse; I am a team. I can whip any man in all Kentucky, by G—d!" The other replied, "I am an alligator, half man, half horse; can whip any man on the Mississippi, by G—d!" The first one again, "I am a man; have the best horse, best dog, best gun and handsomest wife in all Kentucky, by G—d." The other, "I am a Mississippi snapping turtle: have bear's claws, alligator's teeth, and the devil's tail; can whip any man, by G—d."

Such elaborate boasts were not composed on the spot. Folklorists point out that free-phrase verbal forms from Homeric epics to contemporary blues, are created through an oral formulaic process. The singer of epics, for example, does not memorize thousands of lines but knows the underlying skeleton of his narrative and, as he sings, fleshes it out with old commonplaces and new turns of phrase. In this way, oral formulaic composition merges cultural continuity with individual creativity. A similar but simplified version of the same process was at work in backwoods bragging.

A quarter-century after the above exchange made its way into print, several of the same phrases still circulated orally and were worked into new patterns. " 'By Gaud, stranger,' said he, do you know me?—do you know what stuff I'm made of? Clear steamboat, sea horse, alligator—run agin me, run agin a snag—jam up—whoop! Got the prettiest sister, and biggest whiskers of any man hereabouts—I can lick my weight in wild cats, or any man in all Kentuck!' " Style and details changed, but the themes remained the same: comparing oneself to wild animals, boasting of possessions and accomplishments, asserting domination over others. Mike Fink, legendary keelboatman, champion gouger, and fearless hunter, put his own mark on the old form and elevated it to an art:

"I'm a salt River roarer! I'm a ring tailed squealer! I'm a regular screamer from the old Massassip! Whoop! I'm the very infant that refused his milk before its eyes were open and called out for a bottle of old Rye? I love the women and I'm chockful o' fight! I'm half wild horse and half cock-eyed alligator and the rest o' me is crooked snags an' red-hot snappin' turtle. . . . I can out-run, out-jump, out-shoot, out-brag, out-drink, an' out-fight, rough-an'-tumble, no holts barred, any man on both sides the river from Pittsburgh to New Orleans an' back ag'in to St. Louiee. Come on, you flatters, you barger, you milk white mechanics, an' see how tough I am to chaw! I ain't had a fight for two days an' I'm spilein' for exercise. Cock-a-doodle-doo!"

Tall talk and ritual boasts were not uniquely American. Folklore indexes are filled with international legends and tales of exaggeration. But inflated language did find a secure home in America in the first half of the nineteenth century. Spread-eagle rhetoric was tailor-made for a young nation seeking a secure identity. Bombastic speech helped justify the development of unfamiliar social institutions, flowery oratory salved painful economic changes, and lofty words masked aggressive territorial expansion. In a circular pattern of reinforcement, heroic talk spurred heroic deeds, so that great acts found heightened meaning in great words. Alexis de Tocqueville observed during his travels in the 1830s that clearing land, draining swamps, and planting crops were hardly the stuff of literature. But the collective vision of democratic multitudes building a great nation formed a grand poetic ideal that haunted men's imaginations.

The gaudy poetry of the strapping young nation had its equivalent in the exaggeration of individual powers. Folklore placing man at the center of the universe buttressed the emergent ideology of equality. Tocqueville underestimated Americans' ability to celebrate the mundane, for ego magnification was essential in a nation that extolled self-creation. While America prided itself on shattering old boundaries, on liberating individuals from social, geographic, and cultural encumbrances, such freedom left each citizen frighteningly alone to succeed or fail in forging his own identity. To hyperbolize one's achievements was a source of power and control, a means of amplifying the self while bringing human, natural, and social obstacles down to size. The folklore of exaggeration could transform even the most prosaic commercial dealings into great contests. Early in the nineteenth century, legends of crafty Yankee peddlers and unscrupulous livestock traders abounded. A horse dealer described an animal to a buyer in the 1840s: "Sir, he can jump a house or go through a pantry, as it suits him; no hounds are too fast for him, no day too long for him. He has the courage of a lion, and the docility of a lamb, and you may ride him with a thread. Weight did you say? Why, he would carry the national debt and not bate a penny." The most insipid marketplace transactions were transfigured by inflated language, legends of heroic salesmanship, and an ethos of contest and battle.

The oral narratives of the southern backcountry drew strength from these national traditions yet possessed unique characteristics. Above all, fight legends portrayed backwoods men reveling in blood. Violence existed for its own sake, unencumbered by romantic conventions and claiming no redeeming social or psychic value. Gouging narratives may have masked grimness with black humor, but they offered little pretense that violence was a creative or civilizing force. Thus, one Kentuckian defeated a bear by chewing off its nose and scratching out its eyes. "They can't stand Kentucky play," the settler proclaimed, "biting and gouging are too hard for them." Humor quickly slipped toward horror, when Davy Crockett, for example, coolly boasted, "I kept my thumb in his eye, and was just going to give it a twist and bring the peeper out, like taking up a gooseberry in a spoon." To Crockett's eternal chagrin, someone interrupted the battle just at this crucial juncture.

Sadistic violence gave many frontier legends a surreal quality. Two Mississippi raftsmen engaged in ritual boasts and insults after one accidentally nudged the other toward the water, wetting his shoes. Cheered on by their respective gangs, they stripped off their shirts, then pummeled, knocked out teeth, and wore skin from each other's faces. The older combatant asked if his opponent had had enough. "Yes," he was told, "when I drink your heart's blood, I'll cry enough, and not till then." The younger man gouged out an eye. Just as quickly, his opponent was on top, strangling his adversary. But in a final reversal of fortunes, the would-be victor cried out, then rolled over dead, a stab wound in his side. Protected by his clique, the winner jumped in the water, swam to a river island, and crowed: "Ruoo-ruoo-o! I can lick a steamboat. My fingernails is related to a sawmill on my mother's side and my daddy was a double breasted catamount! I wear a hoop snake for a neck-handkerchief, and the brass buttons on my coat have all been boiled in poison."

The danger and violence of daily life in the backwoods contributed mightily to sanguinary oral traditions that exalted the strong and deprecated the weak. Early in the nineteenth century, the Southwest contained more than its share of terrifying wild animals, powerful and well-organized Indian tribes, and marauding white outlaws. Equally important were high infant mortality rates and short life expectancies, agricultural blights, class inequities, and the centuries-old belief that betrayal and cruelty were man's fate. Emmeline Grangerford's graveyard poetry—set against a backdrop of rural isolation shattered by sadistic clan feuds—is but the best-known expression of the deep loneliness, death longings, and melancholy that permeated backcountry life.

At first glance, boisterous tall talk and violent legends seem far removed from sadness and alienation. Yet, as Kenneth Lynn has argued, they grew from common origins, and the former allowed men to resist succumbing to the latter. Not passive acceptance but identification with brutes and brawlers characterized frontier legendry. Rather than be overwhelmed by violence, acquiesce in an oppressive environment, or submit to death as an escape from tragedy, why not make a virtue of necessity and flaunt one's unconcern? To revel in the lore of deformity, mutilation, and death was to beat the wilderness at its own game. The storyteller's art dramatized life and converted nameless anxieties into high adventure; bravado helped men face down a threatening world and transform terror into power. To claim that one was sired by wild animals, kin to natural disasters, and tougher than steam engines—which were displacing rivermen in the antebellum era—was to gain a momentary respite from fear, a cathartic, if temporary, sense of being in control. Symbolically, wild boasts overwhelmed the very forces that threatened the backwoodsmen.

But there is another level of meaning here. Sometimes fight legends invited an ambiguous response, mingling the celebration of beastly acts with the rejection of barbarism. By their very nature, tall tales elicit skepticism. Even while men identified with the violence that challenged them, the folklore of eye gouging constantly tested the limits of credibility. "Pretty soon I got the squatter down, and just then he fixed his teeth into my throte, and I felt my windpipe begin to loosen." The calculated coolness and understatement of this description highlights the outrageousness of the act. The storyteller has artfully maneuvered his audience to the edge of credulity.

Backwoodsmen mocked their animality by exaggerating it, thereby affirming their own humanity. A Kentuckian battled inconclusively from ten in the morning until sundown, when his wife showed up to cheer him on:

"So I gathered all the little strength I had, and I socked my thumb in his eye, and with my fingers took a twist on his snot box, and with the other hand, I grabbed him by the back of the head; I then caught his ear in my mouth, gin his head a flirt, and out come his ear by the roots! I then flopped his head over, and caught his other ear in my mouth, and jerked that out in the same way, and it made a hole in his head that I could have rammed my fist through, and I was just goin' to when he hollered: 'Nuff!'"

More than realism or fantasy alone, fight legends stretched the imagination by blending both. As metaphoric statements, they reconciled contradictory impulses, at once glorifying and parodying barbarity. In this sense, gouging narratives were commentaries on backwoods life. The legends were texts that allowed plain folk to dramatize the tensions and ambiguities of their lives: they hauled society's goods yet lived on its fringe; they destroyed forests and game while clearing the land for settlement; they killed Indians to make way for the white man's culture; they struggled for self-sufficiency only to become ensnared in economic dependency. Fight narratives articulated the fundamental contradiction of frontier life—the abandonment of "civilized" ways that led to the ultimate expansion of civilized society.

Foreign travelers might exaggerate and backwoods storytellers embellish, but the most neglected fact about eye-gouging matches is their actuality. Circuit Court Judge Aedamus Burke barely contained his astonishment while presiding in South Carolina's upcountry: "Before God, gentlemen of the jury, I never saw such a thing before in the world. There is a plaintiff with an eye out! A juror with an eye out! And two witnesses with an eye out!" If the "ring-tailed roarers" did not actually breakfast on stewed Yankee, washed down with spike nails and epsom salts, court records from Sumner County, Arkansas, did describe assault victims with the words "nose was bit." The gamest "gamecock of the wilderness" never really moved steamboat engines by grinning at them, but Reuben Cheek did receive a three-year sentence to the Tennessee penitentiary for gouging out William Maxey's eye. Most backcountrymen went to the grave with their faces intact, just as most of the southern gentry never fought a duel. But as an extreme version of the common tendency toward brawling, street fighting, and seeking personal vengeance, rough-and-tumbling gives us insight into the deep values and assumptions—the *mentalité*—of backwoods life.

Observers often accused rough-and-tumblers of fighting like animals. But eye gouging was not instinctive behavior, the human equivalent of two rams vying for dominance. Animals fight to attain specific objectives, such as food, sexual priority, or territory. Precisely where to draw the line between human aggression as a genetically programmed response or as a product of social and cultural learning remains a hotly debated issue. Nevertheless, it would be difficult to make a case for eye gouging as a genetic imperative, coded behavior to maximize individual or species survival. Although rough-and-tumble fighting appears primitive and anarchic to modern eyes, there can be little doubt that its origins, rituals, techniques, and goals were emphatically conditioned by environment; gouging was learned behavior. Humanistic social science more than sociobiology holds the keys to understanding this phenomenon.

What can we conclude about the culture and society that nourished rough-and-tumble fighting? The best place to begin is with the material base of life and the nature of daily work. Gamblers, hunters, herders, roustabouts, rivermen, and yeomen farmers were the sorts of persons usually associated with gouging. Such hallmarks of modernity as large-scale production, complex division of labor, and regular work rhythms were alien to their lives. Recent studies have stressed the premodern character of the southern uplands through most of the antebellum period. Even while cotton production boomed and trade expanded, a relatively small number of planters owned the best lands and most slaves, so huge parts of the South remained outside the flow of international markets or staple crop agriculture. Thus, backcountry whites commonly found themselves locked into a semisubsistent pattern of living. Growing crops for home consumption, supplementing food supplies with abundant game, allowing small herds to fatten in the woods, spending scarce money for essential staples, and bartering goods for the services of part-time or itinerant trades people, the upland folk lived in an intensely local, kin-based society. Rural hamlets, impassable roads, and provincial isolation—not growing towns, internal improvements, or international commerce—characterized the backcountry.

Even men whose livelihoods depended on expanding markets often continued their rough, premodern ways. Characteristic of life on a Mississippi barge, for example, were long periods of idleness shattered by intense anxiety, as deadly snags, shoals, and storms approached. Running aground on a sandbar meant back-breaking labor to maneuver a thirty-ton vessel out of trouble. Boredom weighed as heavily as danger, so tale telling, singing, drinking, and gambling filled the empty hours. Once goods were taken on in New Orleans, the men began the thousand-mile return journey against the current. Before steam power replaced muscle, bad food and whiskey fueled the gangs who day after day, exposed to wind and water, poled the river bottoms or strained at the cordelling ropes until their vessel reached the tributaries of the Missouri or the Ohio. Hunters, trappers, herdsmen, subsistence farmers, and other backwoodsmen faced different but equally taxing hardships, and those who endured prided themselves on their strength and daring, their stamina, cunning, and ferocity.

Such men played as lustily as they worked, counterpointing bouts of intense labor with strenuous leisure. What travelers mistook for laziness was a refusal to work and save with compulsive regularity. "I have seen nothing in human form so profligate as they are," James Flint wrote of the boatmen he met around 1820. "Accomplished in depravity, their habits and education seem to comprehend every vice. They make few pretensions to moral character; and their swearing is excessive and perfectly disgusting. Although earning good wages, they are in the most abject poverty; many of them being without anything like clean or comfortable clothing." A generation later, Mark Twain vividly remembered those who manned the great timber and coal rafts gliding past his boyhood home in Hannibal, Missouri: "Rude, uneducated, brave, suffering terrific hardships with sailor-like stoicism; heavy drinkers, course frolickers in moral sties like the Natchez-under-the-hill of the day, heavy fighters, reckless fellows, every one, elephantinely jolly, foul witted, profane; prodigal of their money, bankrupt at the end of the trip, fond of barbaric finery, prodigious braggarts; yet, in the main, honest, trustworthy, faithful to promises and duty, and often picaresquely magnanimous." Details might change, but penury, loose morality, and lack of steady habits endured.

Boatmen, hunters, and herdsmen were often separated from wives and children for long periods. More important, backcountry couples lacked the emotionally intense experience of the bourgeois family. They spent much of their time apart and found companionship with members of their own sex. The frontier town or crossroads tavern brought males together in surrogate brotherhoods, where rough men paid little deference to the civilizing role of women and moral uplift of the domestic family. On the margins of a booming, modernizing society, they shared an intensely communal yet fiercely competitive way of life. Thus, where work was least rationalized and specialized, domesticity weakest, legal institutions primitive, and the market economy feeble, rough-and-tumble fighting found fertile soil.

Just as the economy of the southern back country remained locally oriented, the rough-and-tumblers were local heroes, renowned in their communities. There was no professionalization here. Men fought for informal village and county titles; the red feather in the champion's cap was pay enough because it marked him as first among his peers. Paralleling the primitive division of labor in backwoods society, boundaries between entertainment and daily life, between spectators and participants, were not sharply drawn. "Bully of the Hill" Ab Gaines from the Big Hatchie Country, Neil Brown of Totty's Bend, Vernon's William Holt, and Smithfield's Jim Willis—all of them were renowned Tennessee fighters, local heroes in their day. Legendary champions were real individuals, tested gang leaders who attained their status by being the meanest, toughest, and most ruthless fighters, who faced disfigurement and never backed down. Challenges were ever present; yesterday's spectator was today's champion, today's champion tomorrow's invalid.

Given the lives these men led, a world view that embraced fearlessness made sense. Hunters, trappers, Indian fighters, and herdsmen who knew the smell of warm blood on their hands refused to sentimentalize an environment filled with threatening forces. It was not that backwoodsmen lived in constant danger but that violence was unpredictable. Recreations like cockfighting deadened men to cruelty, and the gratuitous savagery of gouging matches reinforced the daily truth that life was brutal, guided only by the logic of superior nerve, power, and cunning. With families emotionally or physically distant and civil institutions weak, a man's role in the all-male society was defined less by his ability as a breadwinner than by his ferocity. The touchstone of masculinity was unflinching toughness, not chivalry, duty, or piety. Violent sports, heavy drinking, and impulsive pleasure seeking were appropriate for men whose lives were hard, whose futures were unpredictable, and whose opportunities were limited. Gouging champions were group leaders because they embodied the basic values of their peers. The successful rough-and-

tumbler proved his manhood by asserting his dominance and rendering his opponent "impotent," as Thomas Ashe put it. And the loser, though literally or symbolically castrated, demonstrated his mettle and maintained his honor.

Here we begin to understand the travelers' refrain about plain folk degradation. Setting out from northern ports, whose inhabitants were increasingly possessed by visions of godly perfection and material progress, they found southern upcountry people slothful and backward. Ashe's Quaker friend in Wheeling, Virginia, made the point. For Quakers and northern evangelicals, labor was a means of moral self-testing, and earthly success was a sign of God's grace, so hard work and steady habits became acts of piety. But not only Yankees endorsed sober restraint. A growing number of southern evangelicals also embraced a life of decorous self-control, rejecting the hedonistic and self-assertive values of old. During the late eighteenth century, as Rhys Isaac has observed, many plain folk disavowed the hegemonic gentry culture of conspicuous display and found individual worth, group pride, and transcendent meaning in religious revivals. By the antebellum era, new evangelical waves washed over class lines as rich and poor alike forswore such sins as drinking, gambling, cursing, fornication, horse racing, and dancing. But conversion was far from universal, and, for many in backcountry settlements like Wheeling, the evangelical idiom remained a foreign tongue. Men worked hard to feed themselves and their kin, to acquire goods and status, but they lacked the calling to prove their godliness through rigid morality. Salvation and self-denial were culturally less compelling values, and the barriers against leisure and self-gratification were lower here than among the converted.

Moreover, primitive markets and the semi-subsistence basis of upcountry life limited men's dependence on goods produced by others and allowed them to maintain the irregular work rhythms of a precapitalist economy. The material base of backwoods life was ill suited to social transformation, and the cultural traditions of the past offered alternatives to rigid new ideals. Closing up shop in mid-week for a fight or horse race had always been perfectly acceptable, because men labored so that they might indulge the joys of the flesh. Neither a compulsive need to save time and money nor an obsession with progress haunted people's imaginations. The backcountry folk who lacked a bourgeois or Protestant sense of duty were little disturbed by exhibitions of human passions and were resigned to violence as part of daily life. Thus, the relative dearth of capitalistic values (such as delayed gratification and accumulation), the absence of a strict work ethic, and a cultural tradition that winked at lapses in moral rigor limited society's demands for sober self-control.

Not just unconverted poor whites but also large numbers of the slave-holding gentry still lent their prestige to a regional style that favored conspicuous displays of leisure. As C. Vann Woodward has pointed out, early observers, such as Robert Beverley and William Byrd, as well as modern-day commentators, have described a distinctly "southern ethic" in American history. Whether judged positively as leisure or negatively as laziness, the southern sensibility valued free time and rejected work as the consuming goal of life. Slavery reinforced this tendency, for how could labor be an unmitigated virtue if so much of it was performed by despised black bondsmen? When southerners did esteem commerce and enterprise, it was less because piling up wealth contained religious or moral value than because productivity facilitated the leisure ethos. Southerners could therefore work hard without placing labor at the center of their ethical universe. In important ways, then, the upland folk culture reflected a larger regional style.

Thus, the values, ideas, and institutions that rapidly transformed the North into a modern capitalist society came late to the South. Indeed, conspicuous display, heavy drinking, moral casualness, and love of games and sports had deep roots in much of Western culture. As Woodward has cautioned, we must take care not to interpret the southern ethic as unique or aberrant. The compulsions to subordinate leisure to productivity, to divide work and play into separate compartmentalized realms, and

to improve each bright and shining hour were the novel ideas. The southern ethic anticipated human evil, tolerated ethical lapses, and accepted the finitude of man in contrast to the new style that demanded unprecedented moral rectitude and internalized self-restraint.

The American South also shared with large parts of the Old World a taste for violence and personal vengeance. Long after the settling of the southern colonies, powerful patriarchal clans in Celtic and Mediterranean lands still avenged affronts to family honor with deadly feuds. Norbert Elias has pointed out that postmedieval Europeans routinely spilled blood to settle their private quarrels. Across classes, the story was the same:

Two associates fall out over business; they quarrel, the conflict grows violent; one day they meet in a public place and one of them strikes the other dead. An innkeeper accuses another of stealing his clients; they become mortal enemies. Someone says a few malicious words about another; a family war develops. . . . Not only among the nobility were there family vengeance, private feuds, vendettas. . . . The little people too—the hatters, the tailors, the shepherds—were all quick to draw their knives.

Emotions were freely expressed: jollity and laughter suddenly gave way to belligerence; guilt and penitence coexisted with hate; cruelty always lurked nearby. The modern middle-class individual, with his subdued, rational, calculating ways, finds it hard to understand the joy sixteenth-century Frenchmen took in ceremonially burning alive one or two dozen cats every Midsummer Day or the pleasure eighteenth-century Englishmen found in watching trained dogs slaughter each other.

Despite enormous cultural differences, inhabitants of the southern uplands exhibited characteristics of their forebears in the Old World. The Scots-Irish brought their reputation for ferocity to the backcountry, but English migrants, too, had a thirst for violence. Central authority was weak, and men reserved the right to settle differences for themselves. Vengeance was part of daily life. Drunken hilarity, good fellowship, and high spirits, especially at crossroads taverns, suddenly turned to violence. Traveler after traveler remarked on how forthright and friendly but quick to anger the backcountry people were. Like their European ancestors, they had not yet internalized the modern world's demand for tight emotional self-control.

Above all, the ancient concept of honor helps explain this shared proclivity for violence. According to the sociologist Peter Berger, modern men have difficulty taking seriously the idea of honor. American jurisprudence, for example, offers legal recourse for slander and libel because they involve material damages. But insult—publicly smearing a man's good name and besmirching his honor—implies no palpable injury and so does not exist in the eyes of the law. Honor is an intensely social concept, resting on reputation, community standing, and the esteem of kin and compatriots. To possess honor requires acknowledgement from others; it cannot exist in solitary conscience. Modern man, Berger has argued, is more responsive to dignity—the belief that personal worth inheres equally in each individual, regardless of his status in society. Dignity frees the evangelical to confront God alone, the capitalist to make contracts without customary encumbrances, and the reformer to uplift the lowly. Naked and alone man has dignity; extolled by peers and covered with ribbons, he has honor.

Anthropologists have also discovered the centrality of honor in several cultures. According to J. G. Peristiany, honor and shame often preoccupy individuals in small-scale settings, where face-to-face relationships predominate over anonymous or bureaucratic ones. Social standing in such communities is never completely secure, because it must be validated by public opinion whose fickleness compels men constantly to assert and prove their worth. Julian Pitt-Rivers has added that, if society rejects a man's evaluation of himself and treats his claim to honor with ridicule or contempt, his very identity suffers because it is based on the judgment of peers. Shaming refers to that process by which an insult or any public humilia-

tion impugns an individual's honor and thereby threatens his sense of self. By risking injury in a violent encounter, an affronted man—whether victorious or not—restores his sense of status and thus validates anew his claim to honor. Only valorous action, not words, can redeem his place in the ranks of his peer group.

Bertram Wyatt-Brown has argued that this Old World ideal is the key to understanding southern history. Across boundaries of time, geography, and social class, the South was knit together by a primal concept of male valor, part of the ancient heritage of Indo-European folk cultures. Honor demanded clan loyalty, hospitality, protection of women, and defense of patriarchal prerogatives. Honorable men guarded their reputations, bristled at insults, and, where necessary, sought personal vindication through bloodshed. The culture of honor thrived in hierarchical rural communities like the American South and grew out of a fatalistic world view, which assumed that pain and suffering were man's fate. It accounts for the pervasive violence that marked relationships between southerners and explains their insistence on vengeance and their rejection of legal redress in settling quarrels. Honor tied personal identity to public fulfillment of social roles. Neither bourgeois self-control nor internalized conscience determined status; judgment by one's fellows was the wellspring of community standing.

In this light, the seemingly trivial causes for brawls enumerated as early as Fithian's time—name calling, subtle ridicule, breaches of decorum, displays of poor manners—make sense. If a man's good name was his most important possession, then any slight cut him deeply. "Having words" precipitated fights because words brought shame and undermined a man's sense of self. Symbolic acts, such as buying a round of drinks, conferred honor on all, while refusing to share a bottle implied some inequality in social status. Honor inhered not only in individuals but also in kin and peers; when members of two cliques had words, their tested leaders or several men from each side fought to uphold group prestige. Inheritors of primal honor, the southern plain folk were quick to take offense, and any perceived affront forced a man either to devalue himself or strike back violently and avenge the wrong.

The concept of male honor takes us a long way toward understanding the meaning of eye-gouging matches. But backwoods people did not simply acquire some primordial notion without modifying it. Definitions of honorable behavior have always varied enormously across cultures. The southern upcountry fostered a particular style of honor, which grew out of the contradiction between equality and hierarchy. Honorific societies tend to be sharply stratified. Honor is apportioned according to rank, and men fight to maintain personal standing within their social categories. Because black chattel slavery was the basis for the southern hierarchy, slave owners had the most wealth and honor, while other whites scrambled for a bit of each, and bondsmen were permanently impoverished and dishonored. Here was a source of tension for the plain folk. Men of honor shared freedom and equality; those denied honor were implicitly less than equal—perilously close to a slave-like condition. But in the eyes of the gentry, poor whites as well as blacks were outside the circle of honor, so both groups were subordinate. Thus a herdsman's insult failed to shame a planter since the two men were not on the same social level. Without a threat to the gentleman's honor, there was no need for a duel; horsewhipping the insolent fellow sufficed.

Southern plain folk, then, were caught in a social contradiction. Society taught all white men to consider themselves equals, encouraged them to compete for power and status, yet threatened them from below with the specter of servitude and from above with insistence on obedience to rank and authority. Cut off from upper-class tests of honor, backcountry people adopted their own. A rough-and-tumble was more than a poor man's duel, a botched version of genteel combat. Plain folk chose not to ape the dispassionate, antiseptic, gentry style but to invert it. While the gentleman's code of honor insisted on cool restraint, eye gougers gloried in unvarnished brutality. In contrast to duelists' aloof silence, backwoods

fighters screamed defiance to the world. As their own unique rites of honor, rough-and-tumble matches allowed backcountry men to shout their equality at each other. And eye-gouging fights also dispelled any stigma of servility. Ritual boasts, soaring oaths, outrageous ferocity, unflinching bloodiness—all proved a man's freedom. Where the slave acted obsequiously, the backwoodsman resisted the slightest affront; where human chattels accepted blows and never raised a hand, plain folk celebrated violence; where blacks could not jeopardize their value as property, poor whites proved their autonomy by risking bodily parts. Symbolically reaffirming their claims to honor, gouging matches helped resolve painful uncertainties arising out of the ambiguous place of plain folk in the southern social structure.

Backwoods fighting reminds us of man's capacity for cruelty and is an excellent corrective to romanticizing premodern life. But a close look also keeps us from drawing facile conclusions about innate human aggressiveness. Eye gouging represented neither the "real" human animal emerging on the frontier, nor nature acting through man in a Darwinian struggle for survival, nor anarchic disorder and communal breakdown. Rather, rough-and-tumble fighting was ritualized behavior—a product of specific cultural assumptions. Men drink together, tongues loosen, a simmering of old rivalry begins to boil; insult is given, offense taken, ritual boasts commence; the fight begins, mettle is tested, blood redeems honor, and equilibrium is restored. Eye gouging was the poor and middling whites' own version of a historical southern tendency to consider personal violence socially useful—indeed, ethically essential.

Rough-and-tumble fighting emerged from the confluence of economic conditions, social relationships, and culture in the southern backcountry. Primitive markets and the semisubsistence basis of life threw men back on close ties to kin and community. Violence and poverty were part of daily existence, so endurance, even callousness, became functional values. Loyal to their localities, their occupations, and each other, men came together and found release from life's hardships in strong drink, tall talk, rude practical jokes, and cruel sports. They craved one another's recognition but rejected genteel, pious, or bourgeois values, awarding esteem on the basis of their own traditional standards. The glue that held men together was an intensely competitive status system in which the most prodigious drinker or strongest arm wrestler, the best tale teller, fiddle player, or log roller, the most daring gambler, original liar, skilled hunter, outrageous swearer, or accurate marksman was accorded respect by the others. Reputation was everything, and scars were badges of honor. Rough-and-tumble fighting demonstrated unflinching willingness to inflict pain while risking mutilation—all to defend one's standing among peers—and became a central expression of the all-male subculture.

Eye gouging continued long after the antebellum period. As the market economy absorbed new parts of the backcountry, however, the way of life that supported rough-and-tumbling waned. Certainly by mid-century the number of incidents declined, precisely when expanding international demand brought ever more upcountry acres into staple production. Towns, schools, churches, revivals, and families gradually overtook the backwoods. In a slow and uneven process, keelboats gave way to steamers, then railroads; squatters, to cash crop farmers; hunters and trappers, to preachers. The plain folk code of honor was far from dead, but emergent social institutions engendered a moral ethos that warred against the old ways. For many individuals, the justifications for personal violence grew stricter, and mayhem became unacceptable.

Ironically, progress also had a darker side. New technologies and modes of production could enhance men's fighting abilities.

"Birmingham and Pittsburgh are obliged to complete . . . the equipment of the 'chivalric Kentuckian,' " Charles Agustus Murray observed in the 1840s, as bowie knives ended more and more rough-and-tumbles. Equally important, in 1835 the first modern revolver appeared, and manufacturers marketed cheap, accurate editions in the coming decade. Dueling weapons had been costly, and Kentucky rifles or horse pistols took a full minute to load and prime. The revolver, however, which fitted neatly into a man's pocket, settled more and more personal disputes. Raw and brutal as rough-and-tumbling was, it could not survive the use of arms. Yet precisely because eye gouging was so violent—because combatants cherished maimings, blindings, even castrations—it unleashed death wishes that invited new technologies of destruction.

With improved weaponry, dueling entered its golden age during the antebellum era. Armed combat remained both an expression of gentry sensibility and a mark of social rank. But in a society where status was always shifting and unclear, dueling did not stay confined to the upper class. The habitual carrying of weapons, once considered a sign of unmanly fear, now lost some of its stigma. As the backcountry changed, tests of honor continued, but gunplay rather than fighting tooth-and-nail appealed to new men with social aspirations. Thus, progress and technology slowly circumscribed rough-and-tumble fighting, only to substitute a deadlier option. Violence grew neater and more lethal as men checked their savagery to murder each other.

Study Questions

1. In which areas of the United States did gouging matches take place? Which class of men were most likely to be involved in such matches?

2. Why did the men fight? What distinguished between fighting "for real" and fighting "for fun"?

3. How did foreign travelers regard the fighting?

4. What does the language of the men in the backcountry tell us about their culture and attitude toward life?

5. How do the gouging matches reflect backcountry life? How did the backcountry environment affect the settlers of the region?

6. Which characteristics of "manliness" were greatly valued by the backcountry settlers?

7. Why did the number of gouging matches eventually decline?

Bibliography

The work of modern social theorists is evident in Gorn's essay. Clifford Gretz, *The Interpretation of Culture* (1973); Norbert Elias, *The Civilizing Process* (1978); Richard G. Sipes, "War, Sports, and Aggression: An Empirical Test of Two Rival Theories," *American Anthropologist,* New Series, 75 (1973); and Peter Berger, et al., *The Homeless Man* (1973) present valuable insights. The nature of southern and western violence and society is discussed in Bertram Wyatt-Brown, *Southern Honor: Ethics and Behavior in the Old South* (1982); Arthur K. Moore, *The Frontier Mind* (1957); Sheldon Hackney, "Southern Violence," *American Historical Review,* 74 (1969); Richard Slotkin, *Regeneration Through Violence* (1973); James I. Robertson, Jr., "Frolics, Fights, and Firewater in Frontier Tennessee," *Tennessee Historical Quarterly,* 17 (1958); and James Leyburn, *The Scotch-Irish: A Social History* (1962). Also see Charles C. Bolton, *Poor Whites of the Antebellum South: Tenants and Laborers in Central North and Northeast Mississippi* (1994); Vernon Orville Burton, *In My Father's House Are Many Mansions: Family and Community in Edgefield, South Carolina* (1985); Lacy K. Ford, Jr., *Origins of Southern Radicalism: The South Carolina Upcountry, 1800–1860* (1988); Grady McWhiney, *Cracker Culture: Celtic Ways in the Old South* (1988); and *Confederates, Crackers, and Cavaliers* (2002).

6

★ ★ ★

Americans Divided

In the aftermath of General Andrew Jackson's victory over the British in New Orleans in 1815, Americans temporarily sounded a harmonious note. Nationalism was the order of the day. Americans sang a new national anthem and joined together in national enterprises. They built roads and dug canals to tie the country together; they protected fledgling northern industries with a tariff; they hailed the end of political strife; and they boldly issued sweeping foreign policy measures. Americans proudly watched as government agents pushed the flag of the Republic north, south, and west.

Nationalism, however, was short-lived. As early as the Panic of 1819, observers of the national scene noticed fundamental divisions within America. A year later, during the Missouri controversy, these lines of division became clearer. In 1820 Thomas Jefferson denounced the Missouri Compromise as an attempt to restrict the area where slavery could spread. It awoke him, he said, like "a fire-bell in the night" and sounded "the knell of the Union." If sectional tranquility was restored after the controversy, it lacked the optimism and giddiness of the earlier period.

Increasingly Northerners and Southerners found less common ground to stand on and more issues that divided them. In the winter of 1832–1833 a pall hung over the aristocratic festivities of Charleston, South Carolina. Led by the brilliant John C. Calhoun, South Carolina had nullified the tariffs of 1828 and 1832 and had forbidden the collection of customs duties within the state. The Union and the effectiveness of the Constitution swayed in balance. Again, however, the crisis passed. Politicians struck a compromise. But national unity was further weakened.

During the 1840s, Americans looked westward toward vast expanses of land. Some saw opportunity and moved toward it. Others saw a chance to escape persecution, and they too packed up their belongings and headed west. Indians and Mexicans, who occupied much of the land, came face to face with a movement of people who were unconcerned with their plight. "Make way, I say, for the young American Buffalo," cried one Democratic orator, "—he has not yet got land enough."

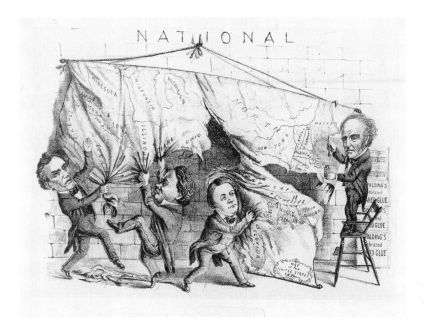

In the spring of 1846, the United States declared war on Mexico. It was a war that unified many Americans—but only for a brief time. The war brought new lands, and the new lands revived old questions. What would be the status of the new lands? Would the new territories and states, once formed, be free or slave? Who would decide the answers to these questions, and how would they decide them?

During the 1850s politicians struggled over these questions. Ultimately they lost the struggle. One solution after another failed. The South, which had contributed greatly to the victory in the Mexican War, demanded the right to move into the newly annexed regions with their "peculiar institution" intact. Northerners were just as determined that the lands would be settled by free labor. By the mid-1850s the subject dominated the national political arena. The issue destroyed one political party, split another, and created yet another. Political rhetoric became increasingly more strident and vitriolic. In 1861 the politicians passed the issue on to the generals.

READING 24

★ ★ ★

P. T. Barnum, Joice Heth, and Antebellum Spectacles of Race

Benjamin Reiss

In the years between the American Revolution and the Civil War, Americans found themselves coming to grips with the issues of "equality," "individual freedom," and "democracy," terms they bantered about confidently but rarely subjected to careful examination. They also confronted the issues of race and slavery, both of which served to undermine the very rhetoric of the democracy they so enthusiastically embraced. At the same time, the advent of widespread literacy, the penny press, and an improved transportation system gave rise to mass culture, in which more and more Americans consumed the same news and observed the same images. The stirring of modern medicine began to rob the human body of some of its mystery, leaving most people with an intense curiosity about life, health, death, and longevity. In the following essay, Benjamin Reiss examines the conjunction of Jacksonian democracy, mass culture, and modern medicine in antebellum America, via the case of Joice Heth, an African American slave who supposedly had helped raise George Washington. After Heth's death, P. T. Barnum took her body on national tours, selling tickets to spectators who would gawk at her remains and wonder, all at the same time, about history, slavery, health, and the true nature of democracy.

On 25 February 1836, P. T. Barnum orchestrated an event that would launch his career in show business and provide the nascent mass media one of its first great spectacles. Joice Heth, an aged African American woman whom Barnum had exhibited across the Northeast as the 161-year-old former nurse of George Washington, now lay dead on an operating table in New York's City Saloon. 1,500 spectators, including many of the most important editors in the city, paid fifty cents apiece to watch as Dr. David L. Rogers carved into her corpse. Rogers' "finding" that Heth was a fraud touched off an intense journalistic debate, in which the penny press—the first entirely commercial newspapers in the country—took the lead. Through this debate, a surprising number of improvisations on the themes of identity, authenticity, and essence were seemingly wrung from Heth's corpse. Alternately, she was still alive, dead but a fraud, the real thing and dead, an everlasting mystery, a waste of time, and about to embark on a tour of Europe as a phial of ashes; and the scientific inquiry into her death was authoritative, invasive, irrelevant, and fraudulent.

Reconstructing the Heth exhibit—in particular, its grisly aftermath—through its coverage in the media provides a microscopic view of some of the unsettling transformations that were shaping nineteenth-century culture. Providing a backdrop for and sometimes intruding directly into reporting of the affair were the issues of modernization that profoundly affected the lives of many who saw Heth: the new prestige of science, social atomization, the emergence of a commercial mass culture, rapid urbanization and the expansion of social roles, and a felt loss of communal, familial, and class-based traditions. Many of these transformations produced anxieties about status, authenticity, and identity: what was the basis of trust in a social interchange involving strangers? how could one be sure that an economic transaction was not fraudulent? How could

one truly "know" another? In several of its aspects, Heth's autopsy appears as a moment in which science—mediated by popular journalism and other mass media—faced some of the crises of legibility, authenticity, and recognition brought on by the process of modernization.

A related context for the exhibit was the changing meanings of "race" in the antebellum North. In early nineteenth-century America, racial distinction was a relatively loose set of discourses, practices, and ideas that separated and elevated one group from others, drawing on law, religion, and science with little internal consistency. The essential linkage between race and property rights, for example, would not become explicitly codified until the 1850s through legal decisions like Dred Scott and legislation like the Fugitive Slave Act; and notions of the biological determinism of race were only fully developed in later decades through the increased energies of anatomists and other scientists. Heth's itinerant exhibit reflects some of this loose structure, in that it was a free-floating, improvised racialist display, an open text that was given a wide range of readings in local media. These readings illuminate her various publics' notions of race, which were inevitably filtered through their differences of region, class, and ideology. But in death, the question of what she meant to her viewers and to readers became displaced by the more imperious question of who she was—or rather, who was behind her. The intensified focus on fixing her identity (which had always been a thread in reactions to her live exhibit), rather than interpreting her story, takes on an implicitly deterministic overtone when viewed within the context of scientific attempts to essentialize race in the antebellum period. The Heth autopsy—like other spectacular displays of race created by the emerging mass media—dramatized some of the new meanings of racial identity and provided an opportunity for whites to debate them (in a displaced register) as they gazed upon or read about her corpse. The episode thus offers the opportunity to construct an ethnographic miniature of white antebellum Northerners as they struggled

From Benjamin Reiss, "P. T. Barnum, Joice Heth, and Antebellum Spectacles of Race," *American Quarterly,* 51 (March 1999), 78–108.

to make sense of the interlocking issues of racial identification and modernization, and looked for symbolic resolution to those struggles in popular culture and the emerging mass media.

Freak Show, History Lesson, or Disgrace: Heth on Tour

The small scale and itinerancy of Heth's tour with Barnum mark it as an "early modern" entertainment—more consistent with the wandering performers, orators, and curiosities of the late eighteenth century than the urban spectacles of the mid- to late-nineteenth. Her first exhibitor was actually not Barnum but R. W. Lindsay, a hapless showman from Kentucky, who had exhibited her in towns and cities across the South, Ohio, and the mid-Atlantic states. Little is known about this early tour, but when Lindsay couldn't turn a profit, he sold his interest in the exhibit to Barnum, who was at the time working in a dry goods store in New York. Barnum thus became Heth's virtual owner and—with the assistance of a young lawyer named Levi Lyman—displayed her in taverns, inns, museums, railway houses, and concert halls across the Northeast for a period of seven months, until her death. Starting with an extended stay in New York, Heth, Barnum, and Lyman moved on to Providence, Boston, Hingham, Lowell, Worcester, Springfield, Hartford, New Haven, Bridgeport, Newark, Patterson, Albany and many towns in between, stopping back in New York several times. Wherever they went, newspapers reported Heth's comings and goings avidly, and crowds flocked to hear her tell about how she had witnessed the birth of "dear little George" and been the first to clothe him and even to breastfeed him, to hear her sing hymns she had supposedly taught him, and to ask questions about the upbringing of the father of the nation. Others came to judge for themselves the authenticity of her claims, which were supported by an impressive array of documents such as her birth certificate and bill of sale, as well as by the bodily signs of her old age; and to ponder the causes and implications of her extraordinary

longevity. Her debility was a draw, too, for many came to gaze on—even to touch—her marvelously decrepit body. Joice Heth was advertised as weighing only forty-six pounds; she was blind and toothless and had deeply wrinkled skin; she was paralyzed in one arm and both legs; and her nails were said to curl out like talons. Visitors regularly shook hands with her, scrutinized her, and sometimes even took her pulse. "Indeed," wrote one observer, "she is a mere skeleton covered with skin, and her whole appearance very much resembles a mummy of the days of the Pharaohs, taken entire from the catacombs of Egypt." Doctors and naturalists were fascinated. Well before she died—in fact, while some were predicting that she would *never* die—her autopsy was a greatly anticipated event.

Throughout her travels with Barnum and Lyman, a curious multivalence marked the exhibit of Joice Heth. Did her decrepitude mark her as a human oddity, to be marketed like the Chinese woman with "disgustingly deformed" bound feet, the Virginia dwarves, and the Siamese twins whose paths she often crossed on the touring circuit? Was it her scientific value as an embodiment of the different aging processes of the different races that merited her display? Was she an attraction because of her patriotic value as a living repository of memories of a glorious past? Because she was a storehouse of ancient religious practices? Or simply because she was a good performer? An advertisement for her exhibit at Niblo's Gardens in New York plays on all of these possibilities:

GREAT ATTRACTION AT NIBLO'S—
UNPARALLELED LONGEVITY. . . .
Joice Heth is unquestionably the most astonishing and interesting curiosity in the world! She was the slave of Augustine Washington (the father of Gen. Washington) and was the first person who put cloths [sic] on the unconscious infant who was destined to lead our heroic fathers on to glory, to victory, and to freedom. To use her own language when speaking of her young master, George Washington, "SHE

RAISED HIM!" Joice Heth was born in the is-land of Madagascar, on the coast of Africa, in the year of 1674, and has consequently now arrived at the astonishing age of ONE HUN-DRED AND SIXTY-ONE YEARS!!! She weighs but FORTY-SIX POUNDS, and yet is very cheerful and interesting. She retains her faculties in an unparalleled degree, converses freely, sings nu-merous hymns, relates many interesting anec-dotes of the boy Washington, the red coats, &c., and often laughs heartily at her own remarks, or those of the spectators. Her health is per-fectly good, and her appearance very neat. . . The appearance of this marvellous relic of an-tiquity strikes the beholder with amazement, and convinces him that his eyes are resting on the oldest specimen of mortality they ever be-fore beheld . . .

The tension in this advertisement between claims of Heth's historical importance ("SHE RAISED HIM!") and of her status as a monstrous wonder of nature ("she weighs but FORTY-SIX POUNDS") points to a tension between identification and objectification, exaltation and denigration, nostalgia and disgust that marked her visitors' responses. These vacilla-tions take on cultural significance when we con-sider the cultural politics behind differing repre-sentations of her body and her narrative.

Many newspapers across the North read Heth's exhibit primarily as a freak show. Displays of human curiosities, or *lusus naturae*—freaks of nature—were among the most popular traveling entertainments of the late eighteenth and early nineteenth centuries, but by the 1830s, the display of grotesquely embodied human forms was for some a populist carnivalesque entertainment, and for others an offense to genteel sensibilities. The contested meanings of Heth's extraordinary body reveal much about regional and class-based no-tions of race and cultural propriety, and point to-ward a larger struggle for cultural power in 1830s America. In New York, she was a favorite of the lively Jacksonian press, including the *Evening Star,* and the first three penny papers (the *Sun,* the *Transcript,* and the *Herald*.) These periodicals,

the first entirely commercial serial publications in America, were perhaps the most compelling voices of Jacksonian individualism. Their brash displays of hostility for the culture mavens of the upper classes (and for each other), their sympa-thies for the urban working and upwardly mobile classes, their freedom from political patronage, and their fierce egalitarianism for whites mixed with overt anti-black racism all marked their dis-tinctiveness from the more genteel "six-penny" pa-pers. For the most part, the Jacksonian press ped-dled images of Heth's debility, her great appetite and fondness for tobacco, and her grotesque ap-pearance. One article in the *Evening Star* men-tioned that "her nails are near an inch long, and the great toes horny and thick like bone and in-curvated, looking like the claws of a bird of prey," and the *Transcript*'s reporter was fascinated to find that her eyes "are entirely run out and closed." The popular New York "knowledge mag-azine" *Family* went so far as to report that al-though "food is administered to her regularly . . . evacuations occur but once in a fortnight."

Together, these New York papers and maga-zines were on the vanguard of mass culture, using new techniques in printing technology and distri-bution to publish more cheaply and to garner a wider audience than had previously existed for print ephemera. The frank ogling they encouraged—and performed—was a more risky business in New England, where the media were still dominated by the genteel classes, and where stage shows of any kind, let alone displays of human "curiosities," had only recently been toler-ated. Although some papers continued the kind of coverage Heth had received in New York, Bar-num and Lyman had to respond to a number of opprobrious reports. In Boston, the Whiggish *Atlas* complained of the onslaught of advertising for Heth. Begging her exhibitors to refrain from sullying their communication box with "puffs" for the show, the editors wrote that "a more inde-cent mode of raising money than by the exhibi-tion of an old woman—black or white—we can hardly imagine." The same city's *Courier* was more graphic in its disgust. Its protest expressed fear that viewers' morals would be corrupted by the display, but it also appealed to readers' sympathy for Heth herself:

Those who imagine they can contemplate with delight a breathing skeleton, subjected to the same sort of discipline that is sometimes exercised in a menagerie to induce the inferior animals to play unnatural pranks for the amusement of barren spectators, will find food to their taste by visiting Joice Heth. But Humanity sickens at the exhibition.

"Those" who so delighted in the display, one might infer, included the very editors who were challenging the genteel press' power in the cultural realm.

In response to these attacks, Barnum and Lyman wisely advertised Heth's cleanliness and her religiosity, rather than her freakishness, on the rest of her New England tour. According to a puff piece planted in the *Hartford Times*, "There is nothing in her appearance which can possibly be unpleasant to the minds of the most fastidious." Apparently to preempt further criticisms, they even printed a pamphlet biography of Heth, which stressed, in addition to her propriety, the roughness of her treatment in slavery and the humane qualities of her current exhibitors:

Some of the time since [her possession by the Washington family]. . . she has been very much neglected, laying for years in an outer building, upon the naked floor. In speaking of her past condition, she expresses great thankfulness, that Providence should so kindly provide the comforts of life, and make infinitely better her condition as she approaches towards the close of it.

Behind the differing representations of Joice Heth lay a radical disagreement about the role of the human body in public display, the stakes of which were connected to a wider argument about who controlled culture. Editors of the "penny-a-liners" typically saw themselves as cultural populists, providing what their upwardly

mobile readership wanted for the cheapest price possible. As James Gordon Bennett opined in the *Herald* in 1835, "Formerly no man could read unless he had $10 to spare for a paper. Now with a cent in his left pocket, and a quid of tobacco in his cheek, he can purchase more intelligence, truth, and wit, than is contained in such papers as the dull Courier & Enquirer, or the stupid Times for three months." Consumption was thus figured as a kind of empowerment; Bennett encouraged his readers to imagine that buying the papers transformed a struggling worker into a cultural superior. The genteel editors, on the other hand, viewed their role as guardians of an exalted realm, to be protected from the exploitations of "penny rascals" and other mercenary assaults on propriety. In protesting the Heth exhibit, the six-penny press' editors viewed its solicitation of voyeuristic interest as a kind of naked public aggression that threatened their moral guardianship of culture. When the *Courier* defended Heth's body from "the amusement of barren spectators," it posed as an embattled defender of an exalted cultural sphere, newly under siege from below. The final sentence of the piece expresses the enormity of the felt threat: "humanity"—not just those with money, taste, and morals—"sickens at the exhibition." The distaste of the Whiggish press for Heth's grotesque body can thus be read as a synecdochic rejection of all the rabble that were crowding into the public sphere, and fashioning, from the ground up, a mass public for the new mass culture.

The class-based cultural skirmishes over Heth's body fed as well on competing views of racial difference. Alexander Saxton has written that for the Whig coalition, as for the six-penny papers that were their central organs, maintaining class hierarchies was the primary ideological agenda. According to the genteel world-view, within the "spectrum of differences," racial difference was "simply one among many." In contrast, an emphasis on racial difference bolstered the group solidarity of the mechanics who comprised the bulk of the northern Jacksonian Democrats—and the bulk of the penny press' readers. Although this group perceived itself as united by class interests, it is tricky to define by the current lexicon of class terminology, for it included apprentices and journeymen laborers as well as established "master" craftsmen (blacksmiths, hatters, combmakers, etc.) and capitalist entrepreneurs who had risen from their ranks. If their interests were sometimes in conflict, the language of racial solidarity provided an imaginative category to reunite them, and images of a debased "other" reinforced the commonalty of whites.

Freak shows, perhaps more than any other popular antebellum practice, helped disseminate the lessons of racial solidarity because they acted as a hinge between scientific inquiries into racial essence and the popular desire for images of white domination. Exhibits typically highlighted the physical anomaly, grotesque features, extreme disability, or exotic racial or cultural difference of the displayed human object, and often more than one such quality at a time. For example, toward the end of the eighteenth century, Henry Moss, a black man afflicted with a disease that gave him spotted skin, exhibited himself in Philadelphia and became the subject of great popular attention, including that of Benjamin Rush, who concluded that Moss was undergoing a spontaneous "cure" of his blackness. This popular scientific interest was institutionalized in the next century by Barnum, who exhibited in his American Museum African Americans with vitiligo, albinism, and microcephaly, claiming that they were the "missing links" in an evolutionary chain extending from black to white and from monkey to man. The difference between the earlier and later exhibits is telling. Moss' control of his own exhibit in a major urban center would have been unthinkable in the following decades, as racial attitudes hardened in the North and as cultural entrepreneurs like Barnum, circus managers, and proprietors of dime museums began to corner the market on human curiosities. This increasing control of the freak's body was accompanied by the incorporation of freakishness into developing notions of racial science. Whereas Rush found that Moss blurred the distinctions between white and

black, the later displays tended to refine and enforce those distinctions: the "missing links" demonstrated the racialist implications of the new Darwinian theories. Finally, Rush's interest in Moss was simply one voice among many about the nature of "human curiosities," who were still often viewed in terms of religious wonder or the rituals of carnival that extended back to medieval Europe. By Barnum's time—starting with the Heth autopsy—science became the dominant discourse for interpreting the freak's body.

Not surprisingly, then, the papers that emphasized Heth's freakishness also debated her scientific value. Central to these discussions was the "fact" of her extraordinary old age, the significance of which was probed in the Jacksonian press when she grew ill toward the end of 1835. "Joice Heth goes South in about two or three weeks," the *New York Herald* announced. "She says she cannot spend the winter in the North, where the cold is so severe and the nights so long. The South is her native element." The *Herald* was here echoing a notion popular among early nineteenth-century scientists that, as one physician put it, "the African races are very susceptible of cold, and are as incapable of enduring a northern climate, as a white population are of supporting the torrid sun of Africa." This idea—most lucidly formulated by the English anatomist Robert Knox—took on the character of a racist ideologeme in the United States, as advocates of slavery argued that the South, with its semi-tropical climate, was as much a "natural" environment for blacks as Africa was. The *Evening Star* used Heth's old age to support this idea. Far from an anomaly, the paper argued, Heth's longevity was common among slaves in the South but almost unheard of in the North. Her sudden northern illness testified to the fact that "the calumniated climate of the South, which has been so decried for its marshes, stagnant streams, and pine barrens, is . . . admirably adapted for the African race." Amidst the swirling possibilities and anxieties attending modernization and urban life that these papers so brilliantly chronicled, race stood as an island of fixity: in this case, the laws of nature decreed that each race should remain in its proper place, and those laws could be read on or through the body.

If freaks were the image of denigration and difference, George Washington had become, by the early nineteenth century, the most exalted of national icons. Seen as a freak show, the Heth exhibit exaggerated stereotypical attributes of blacks: their grotesque materiality, their biological difference from white observers. But seen as a living relic of the age of Washington, Heth was sometimes an object of identification, even idolization. Audiences melted on hearing her sing the hymns she had taught him and tell stories of his youth; as a reporter for the *Providence Republican Herald* gushed,

when we heard her converse on subject or circumstance. . . connected with the birth, the infancy, and childhood of the immortal Washington—the mind was carried away by an intensity of interest, which no other object of curiosity has ever created in our breast.

"Somebody is raising money to build a monument to the memory of Washington," ran an item in the *New York Herald* on 25 November 1835.

What profanation! A monument has long since been built to the memory of Washington. Where is its foundation? In the breasts of free men in both Europe and America. Where is its highest pinnacle? Far beyond the brightest star in the heaven itself—in the bosom of Him who liveth for ever and ever.

As this article makes clear, Washington had passed beyond politics and into the realm of myth. From his death in 1799 until the outbreak of the Civil War, the mythic Washington was by far the most venerated figure in American history, and production of Washingtoniana one of the most profitable of patriotic industries. Artists by the dozen painted his portrait; monuments to his memory sprang up across the country (the *Herald*'s cries of profanation notwithstanding), and his face invested countless trinkets, walls,

and mantelpieces with a touch of nobility. Between 1800 and 1860, over four hundred books, essays, and articles on the life of Washington appeared in print, most of them outrageously flattering. (The most famous of these was—and continues to be—Mason Weems's 1809 *The Life of Washington,* whose famous cherry tree scene Heth claimed to have witnessed.) A clearly jealous John Adams wrote of the "idolatrous worship" accorded his colleague; he was deified "by all classes and nearly all parties of our citizens," who referred to him as " 'our Savior,' 'our Redeemer,' 'our cloud by day and our pillar of fire by night,' 'our star in the east,' 'to us a Son is born,' and 'our guide on earth, our advocate in heaven.' "

Such veneration served as a stabilizing force during a time of social upheaval. As the nation underwent its most rapid period of urbanization, widespread anxieties about loss of tradition surfaced in society and politics. In this context, legends of the "founding Fathers" presented the heroes of the glorious Revolutionary past as paternal role models on a national level. As George Forgie has written:

Society began to concern itself with child nurture as a political matter and to summon models from history at the same time that for essentially economic reasons actual fathers ceased to provide . . . automatic models of roles their sons would grow up to play. . . . At a time when expanding economic opportunity meant that boys were beginning to need a wider range of models than their surroundings were likely to provide, history stepped in to supply them in the form of the founding heroes.

And just as actual families were losing their cohesiveness, disunion on a broader scale was threatening the national "family": it began to look as though the North and the South could not live together as one nation. Amidst these anxieties, George Washington, as the father of all Fathers, stood as a figure of authority among squabbling sons. As such, he was subject not only to idolatry, but to the occasional "ritualistic acting out of patricidal fantasies."

Heth's exhibit was only one of many antebellum cultural productions that mingled nostalgia for the Revolutionary age with degrading images of blacks: stage plays, popular literature, and even minstrel shows often voiced longing for the glorious past most strongly through the mouths of simplistic African American characters. George Stevens's 1834 drama *The Patriot*, for instance, presents the character of Sambo, who claims he is descended from the servants of George Washington. When his master asks Sambo to take out the bust of Washington and dust it for the Fourth of July celebration, Sambo replies: "Yes Massa—de big Washington, me lub him massa! were he 'live, me would hug him massa, as him Sambo do—*dis*!", and then broke into the "Jim Crow" dance routine. William Andrews has argued that this antebellum trope of the ridiculous black patriot took shape in part because blacks were presumed incapable of progress (unless aided by whites) and therefore stood outside of history. In the words of Hegel, "Africa is a land of perpetual childhood" whose natives are "capable of no development or culture. . . . As we see them at this day, such have they always been." Stuck in the past, oblivious to the changes around them (one version of the Heth story has her blissfully ignorant of the identity of Andrew Jackson), Heth and Sambo were portrayed as developmentally stunted, but they were also inured from the present. These northern stagings of nostalgia—coming shortly after the final emancipation of slaves in northern states—thus expressed a conservative longing for a place and time in which blacks were perfectly in their place. Both the remembrance of Washington and its voicing in black (or blackface) dialect stood as a counterbalance to the changes wrought by modernization and those advocated by abolitionists.

Still, the past was not called forth without some "filial resentment." Heth's exhibit was an opportunity to pay respects to the memory of Washington, but the image of this freakish black woman having suckled "dear little George" (an image that caught on in popular discussion of the exhibit, though Heth herself usually claimed to have been a dry nurse) pointed to a monstrous perturbation in a culture-wide nostalgic idealization, a desire to see one's idols tainted by the grotesque. At times, the exhibit served to displace resentment toward Washington's impossibly grand historical example by directing it downward toward blacks. Heth was jeered in several papers for putting on airs and assuming the role of "lady Washington." (The *Providence Daily Journal,* for example, reported that she refused to eat chicken because "I'd tank you to understand dat I am Lady Washington, and want as good victuals as anyone.") Sometimes, too, the racial and patriotic meanings found in her exhibit clashed. If Joice Heth were truly who she claimed to be, then her exalted status was almost enough to erase the social fact of her blackness. This perspective occasionally made her marketing appear obscene, even in the world of the otherwise enthusiastic penny papers. During her initial performances in New York during August 1835, an indignant letter writer named Henry Cole asked in a letter to the *Sun*,

why SHE who nursed the "father of our country," the man to whom we owe our present happy and prosperous condition, should at the close of her life be exhibited as "our rarer monsters are." Is there not philanthropy enough in the American people to take care of her, although her skin be black?

This rare display of sympathy for Heth and her suffering body stretched but did not break the bounds of racist thinking: Cole saw the indignity taking place *despite* her being black. And even though Cole believed in her unique claim to historical importance, he was still comfortable viewing her as a piece of property, if not quite a commodity. He concluded by reminding the *Sun*'s readers that Joice Heth

is the common property of our country—she is identified with the history of the foundation, rise and progress of our government—she is the sole remaining tie of mortality which connects us to him who was "first in war, first in peace, first in the hearts of his countrymen"— and as such, we should protect and honor her, and not suffer her to be kept for a show, like a wild beast, to fill the coffers of mercenary men.

In contrast to Cole, the penny press's editors either scrutinized Joice Heth's freakish body for scientific significance or celebrated it in grotesque revelry, while the six-penny press sneered at it as a sign of filth bubbling up on the cultural landscape. However, Cole saw in the display not so much Heth's freakishness as the mythic history that passed through her body like breath. And yet this history seemed to have little to do with Heth herself, as its main function was to "connect us to him"—that is, white viewers to their symbolic father. (Could "us" include non-whites?) Cole sympathized with Heth by looking past her body rather than at it; beyond her body, he saw his own race's mythological kinship to Washington, and it was this that he wanted to protect from mercenaries. The mercenaries—Barnum as well as the penny press's editors—ultimately had their way.

Death, Dissection, and Cultural Commodification

A year before Joice Heth died, the body of George Washington was the focus of an interesting debate in Congress. The Senate and House had established a joint committee to plan a commemoration for the one-hundredth anniversary of George Washington's birth, and a proposal emerged to have his remains removed from Mount Vernon and placed in a tomb below the center of the U.S. Capitol Rotunda. Edward Everett, a senator from Massachusetts, spoke mainly for Northerners when he proclaimed that the procession of pallbearers would be a spectacle "unexampled in the history of the world . . . The sacred remains are . . . a treasure beyond all price, but it is a treasure of which every part of this blood-cemented Union has a right to claim its

share." Blood-cemented partners or no, Southerners resisted this Northerner's appeal to the "right" to move the body North; the plan faltered as southern congressmen lined up to keep the body in Mount Vernon, where it would emphasize Washington's southern roots. Cutting against the lofty symbolism of unity and spirituality that the idealized image of Washington invoked, his actual corpse exerted a downward drag, defacing his memory with the petty political interests of the disputants and, finally, with its own materiality.

If Washington's corpse was supposed to be free from the material interests of antebellum Americans, the corpse of his supposed nurse, who passed away on 21 February 1836, never had such a clear status. Instead of the spiritual and mythic values ascribed to Washington's corpse, Heth's remains were invested with overlapping and sometimes conflicting historical, scientific, commercial, and racial values. The first of these values made it a sanctified object, worthy of respect and protection; the others made it fit for rougher usage by anatomists and editors. The clash of these meanings, and the hay that the penny press made of them, reveal some unspoken but deeply felt beliefs and fantasies about what it meant to be white and to be black, what it meant to own oneself and to be owned.

In order to probe the riddles of her identity, the penny papers immediately began clamoring for an autopsy. The *Sun* provided the lone half-hearted note of dissent:

We were somewhat surprised that a public dissection of this kind should have been proposed, and were half inclined to question the propriety of the scientific curiosity which prompted it. We felt as though the person of poor old Joice Heth, should have been sacred from exposure and mutilation, not so much on account of her extreme old age, and the public curiosity which she had already gratified for the gain of others, as for the high honor with which she was endowed in being the nurse of the immortal Washington.

Consistent with Henry Cole's objection to Heth's exhibit in life, the *Sun* professed to view her autopsy not as an indignity for Heth herself, but as a mercenary assault on the memory of Washington. But this protest was disingenuous, for two days earlier, the same paper had encouraged the autopsy on the grounds that "the anatomy of very aged persons, affords one of the most curious and instructive studies in the science," and after the autopsy took place, the *Sun* never saw fit to impugn its propriety. As opposed to the historical value that was presumed to be embedded in Heth's body when she was alive, the *Sun* saw that her anatomical status was not only "curious and instructive," but potentially profitable as well, inasmuch as it touched on issues of race. As planned, Heth's autopsy was an early instance of the imperious gaze of anatomists, which made the racialized body a crossroads of science and popular culture. A precedent was set in 1815 with the death of Sartje Baartman (the "Hottentot Venus"), a native South African woman of the San tribe whose steatopygia—an excess of fatty tissue that gave her abnormally prominent buttocks—had made her an object of intense popular and scientific interest as she had been exhibited across Europe. When she died, the prominent French zoologist Georges Cuivier dissected her and presented to the scientific community a written report and her actual, excised genitals in a jar that still remains on a shelf in the *Musée de l'Homme* in Paris. The scrutiny of racial "types" that began with human curiosities like Baartman and Heth would become more thoroughgoing in the researches of the American School of anatomy, which dominated the field in the 1850s. Led by Samuel George Morton and Louis Agassiz, the American School sought to prove the African race's physiological uniqueness and mental inferiority through such means as measuring the cranial capacity and other physical features of large numbers of racially typed specimens. As with the story of Sartje Baartman in Europe, popular culture and racial science in the U.S. existed in a state of symbiosis. The popular press commented extensively on the "findings" of these scientists; popular exhibitors (led by Barnum) often called on scientists to authenticate their exhibits, and the exhibits themselves often led to further scientific research.

The *Sun*'s rationale for dissecting Heth was thus justified by scientific inquiries into racial difference (as was the autopsy of Baartman). It was also of a piece with wider cultural attitudes toward anatomists' work and toward the dead body. Ann Douglas has written that the corpse was imagined in the antebellum period as a spiritual object, a body that had found heavenly repose after a life of competition and ambition. But it is necessary to restrict this meaning to respectable white corpses, for those of blacks, the poor, and criminals usually met a different fate. Extending the stigma these bodies bore in life, they continued to be subjected to indignities in death—among them the anatomist's knife.

Autopsies were a crucial forum for medical research, but they were also a socially contested enterprise, charged with the conflicting meanings of science, religion, race, propriety, and commodification. Obvious as it sounds, white people's legal advantages over other races technically ended at death. The bodies of living white people in the antebellum period were a kind of quasi-property, which could not be sold or even given as a bequest. But at the moment of death, white bodies became in the eyes of the law—as Henry Cole wrote about Joice Heth—"the common property of our country." Body-snatching was in most states a misdemeanor offense, but the possession of stolen corpses was no crime at all—anatomists, surgeons, and medical students depended on the often-illicit traffic in corpses for their livelihood and the furtherance of knowledge. In a purely legal sense, death erased social difference by converting all bodies into raw materials for the potential researches of the scientific community. This stripping of privilege marked not only a limit to the advantages of whiteness, but it was in opposition to the exaltation of the corpse in the famously death-obsessed antebellum culture. As a result, sentiment against anatomists and acts of "burking" (grave-robbing for profit) ran high, and acts of vigilante justice against medical schools that trafficked in corpses were frequent throughout the first half of the nineteenth century. The racial politics of this "mob rule" were consistent with those of the great doctors' riot of New York in 1788. One later writer described the events that led to the disturbances:

Usually the [medical] students had contented themselves with ripping open the graves of strangers and negroes, about whom there was little feeling; but this winter they dug up respectable people, even young women, of whom they made an indecent exposure.

The ensuing riots and others like them in the early national period helped antebellum doctors and anatomists understand that their reputations and even security depended on producing an illusion of social distinctions between corpses that reproduced those between living bodies. Paupers, criminals, and blacks were most prone to be cut open, and, as Todd Savitt has shown, slaves provided the best material for morbid anatomy. Not only were their surviving kin powerless to raise trouble about the commodification of their corpses, but their bodies had been commodities to begin with. The protection of white corpses from desecration and commodification inscribed one of the dominant social meanings of race onto the dead. As Priscilla Wald and Cheryl Harris have shown, the maintenance of racial distinction hinged on conceptions of property rights: whites were the only group that had an inalienable right to own property, including most importantly a Lockean property in the self. Blacks were at the other extreme, since they not only possessed no such right, but could be bought and sold as commodities. Within the racial hierarchy of antebellum possessive individualism, white corpses had an uncanny status. They were clearly the same objects as the once-living bodies that had occupied a position of privilege and had been exempt from commodification, but they were now stripped of this legal protection. The popular outcry against the abuse of white corpses reveals a collective fantasy about the metaphysics of racial demarcation: that whites would own themselves in perpetuity, even after death.

As Barnum and the penny press' editors saw, the cluster of social meanings adhering to Heth's corpse made it an object of considerable value. Its connection to Washington made it a curiosity in its own right; and it was prized material for scientists because of its rarity (the remains of medical curiosities usually generated top dollar in the market for corpses) and because of its significance in the loaded debates about race, biology, and region. In addition, Heth's blackness exempted those responsible for her autopsy from the clamor against human dissection and turned them into actors in a scene of white domination. Finally, popular interest in racial science translated her scientific value into commercial value.

Soon after Heth died, Barnum contacted Dr. David L. Rogers, a respected New York surgeon who had expressed a desire to perform an autopsy on her when she expired. Barnum took Rogers up on his offer, rented the City Saloon in New York, converted its exhibition room into a makeshift operating theater, and opened the doors to the public. Despite the steep fifty-cent admission price, fifteen-hundred spectators showed up, netting a large profit for Barnum. The spectacle also provided a windfall for the commercial press. The *Sun* was first on board, reporting the spectacle of her dismemberment in clinical detail:

On dissecting the heart [Dr. Rogers] found the cardinary [coronary] artery not at all ossified, nor were the valves in general; and it was only at the arch of the aorta. . . that even the slightest degree of ossification was present.

On examining the lungs he found very extensive adhesions to the left side. . . and also many tubercles in the lobe, which he presumed to have been the cause of death. On opening the head he found the brain healthy, and the sutures of the skull not only quite distinct, but easily separable with the hand: phenomena, never before observed in very old subjects.

On the strength of these findings, Rogers pronounced that Heth could have been no more than eighty years old and that the whole exhibit had therefore been a hoax.

But was the corpse even hers? The uncanny aspects of corpses that made them such curious objects in antebellum culture were multiplied in Joice Heth's case by a kind of extended cultural and commercial play that set in after the autopsy. Two days after the dissection, Barnum and Lyman paid a visit to James Gordon Bennett, the notorious editor of the *New York Herald* (the *Sun*'s main competitor among the penny dailies), and convinced him that Heth was still alive and well and living in Connecticut. The body on the table, they explained, was actually that "of a respectable old negress called AUNT NELLY, who has lived many years in a small house by herself, in Harlaem." The Aunt Nelly theory, published in the *Herald* the next day, ignited a journalistic free-for-all, with the *Sun,* the *Herald,* and several fledgling penny papers all claiming to have the true story. Though Bennett bought the claim that Heth was still alive, he persisted in calling her a humbug; the *Sun* clung to its original story based on the autopsy; the *Transcript* ran a long piece by another surgeon who had been present, which rebutted Rogers' findings on scientific grounds (the absence of signs of aging in Heth was taken as evidence that the aging process developed differently in her than in other subjects); and the *Sunday Morning News* thought that nothing was yet certain. Hoping to have the last word, the *Sun* reported that Barnum and Lyman confessed to their imposture and were preparing to take Heth's ashes with them on a tour of Europe, where, accompanied by "an old male negro who is to rejoice in the name of Joice's husband, and to swear he is 180 years old," they would begin their humbug over again. Predictably, the other papers denounced this story as yet another of Barnum and Lyman's hoaxes, with the *Sun*'s editor as the dupe; each paper charged the others with fraud, idiocy, perversity, and charlatanism.

The multiplicity of responses to the autopsy obscures the fact that a fundamental reduction in the scope of interpretation was taking place. Earlier newspaper accounts had addressed Heth's spirituality, her place in history, and the propriety of her display, but here the focus was exclusively on her authenticity, which was reduced to a set of material facts: whether the body on the table was even her; if it was, whether it possessed the scientific or historical value ascribed to it, and how one could know. Amidst the smoke screens and deceptions thrown up by Barnum and the editors, the task had become to divine Heth's essence rather than to interpret her narrative or place her within a larger narrative of history. This task of divination was not explicitly *about* race, but the structure of the event was conditioned by wider scientific and popular inquiries into racial essence. Michael O'Malley has charted the rise of racial essentialism in the nineteenth century against the backdrop of rapid urbanization and free-market liberalism. As the economy dilated and as social roles for whites grew more varied and unstable, essentialized notions of race served as ballast for anxieties about the shifting grounds of identity, status, and authenticity. In attempting to fix Heth's identity, the new mass media appealed to white readers who looked both to racial science and to popular culture for signs of their own mastery in a time of social and economic instability.

Exposure and Mastery

In attempting to "expose" the Heth fraud, the editors found a way to push product while playfully addressing their readers' anxieties about the deceptions latent in capitalist culture—a theme the commercial press was in a unique position to address. As Karen Halttunen has put it, "the proliferation of moveable wealth, especially negotiable paper, in the early nineteenth century, and the growing confusion and anonymity of urban living, had made possible for the first time a wide variety of swindles, frauds, forgeries, counterfeiting activities, and other confidence games." The series of exposés—and exposés of exposés—that followed Heth's autopsy offered numerous variations on this theme of counterfeiture, providing an array of deceptions for readers to work through, always promising a final resolution, but always holding out. The epistemological process of reading the unfolding story—peeling off the layers of hoax to arrive at "the truth"—provided symbolic compensation for the struggles of many of the penny papers' readers. In contrast to the increasing illegibility of the social world, in the genre of the exposé (which was a favorite of the penny papers and which was to become perhaps the most popular genre of literature in the mid-nineteenth century), the darkest secrets could always be penetrated, mastered, and possessed, if only in the cultural realm.

Seven months after Barnum and Lyman duped Bennett with the Aunt Nelly theory, Lyman granted the *Herald* an exclusive interview, in which he promised finally to deliver the real story behind Heth's exhibit. What followed was "the Joice Heth Hoax," a month-long serialized account of the entire episode. This exposé to end all exposés was itself an example of the thing it purported to expose, for in it Lyman—who seven months earlier had convinced Bennett that Heth was still alive—duped Bennett once again. The reporting of the hoax served as a half-joking version of the *Herald*'s many serialized exposés of notorious frauds, swindlers, and "stock-jobbers." From the first installment, it cast the self-making northern confidence man or swindler as an emblem of Yankee ingenuity, rather than of threatening inauthenticity. An unnamed "gentleman from New England" (presumably Barnum) visits a Kentucky plantation and is struck by the appearance of an extraordinarily old-looking slave woman. Thinking "hard and steady," the New Englander formulates a plan to turn this decaying matter into profit by exhibiting her as a curiosity; he offers the Kentuckian owner "an interest in the speculation," which the Kentuckian accepts. The story goes on to detail the New Englander's successive money-making schemes with his new bogus commodity, who calls him "massa." First he dreams up the George Washington story and drills it into his subject; then, when she begins to object to performing for him, he contrives to addict her to whiskey, so that he can have some leverage in compelling her to act; he also pulls out all her teeth in order to make her look older (using liberal doses of whiskey to drown her curses and protests). In this way, the northern master becomes an even more shrewd exploiter of the slave's body than his southern counterpart—he is the true exemplar of the master race, for he can compel black bodies to work to the point of death, and beyond. This is because he understands that labor is not the only basis of value, that the northern economies of "speculation" and entertainment provide novel opportunities to invest in the raw materials, even the waste, of the South. Joice Heth becomes, in his hands, not just a commodity, but an example of capitalist alchemy: value produced out of nothing—an ingenious counterfeit bill.

The serialized "Joice Heth Hoax" cuts off abruptly after seven installments—well before the spectacular autopsy is narrated—when Bennett apparently realized that Lyman was pulling his leg again. (Barnum had of course not "discovered" Heth on a Kentucky plantation, nor had he invented her story; as he later admitted, she was exhibited first by R. W. Lindsay.) But in casting the Barnum-figure as a cultural hero for the same sorts of manipulations of value and confidence that the penny press elsewhere denounced so thoroughly, the *Herald* voiced its ambivalent relation to capitalist culture. As the first purely commercial journalistic enterprise, the penny press was itself an important part of the capitalist expansion whose excesses it exposed. In keeping with this ambivalence, the penny press portrayed Barnum as that liminal figure who was symbolic of both the dangers and possibilities of capitalist culture: the confidence man. The essence of social mobility, the confidence man was in early mass culture either vilified as an impostor or lionized as an emblem of self-making. Neither role, however, was to be afforded African Americans: in the overlapping realms of science, law, and popular culture, their nature and identity were generally seen to be "fixed"—their supposedly inferior status rendered them incapable of the self-making that whites both feared and aspired to. As Saidiya Hartman has argued, one of the purposes of exhibitions of African Americans in popular entertainments both in the South and the North was to demonstrate "the possession of the captive's body by the owner's intentions." In the same story that cast Barnum as the ultimate confidence man, Heth herself was made to seem a blank slate whom the white man animated with his schemes. Her role in the deception was displaced entirely onto the will of this strange northern "master."

This displacement became more severe but also more anxious in a series of mock-confessional texts written by Barnum himself over the following decades. As Bluford Adams has related the story, shortly after Barnum's triumph with Heth came the financial panic of 1837, and Barnum found himself "at the bottom round of fortune's ladder." He worked for several years with small circuses and variety acts touring the U.S. and Canada, then found himself selling blacking, waterproof paste, cologne, and bear's grease back in the Bowery of New York. Finally, he got a job writing articles for a new commercial paper, the *Atlas,* and used the opportunity to reclaim the spotlight. It is not surprising, as Adams notes, that he used the opportunity to resuscitate his great humbug of five years earlier. In a serialized novella or mock-autobiography called *Adventures of an Adventurer, Being Some Passages in the Life of Barnaby Diddleum,* Barnum trumpeted his own (lightly fictionalized) rise in an aggressive, vernacular voice that was the hallmark of the Jacksonian Yankee, a shrewd aspiring merchant who uses his wiles to achieve upward mobility. In this text he retold the exposé of "The Joice Heth Hoax" from a particularly egomaniacal perspective: "Crown me with fame—erect a monument to my memory—decree me a roman triumph—I deserve all—I stand alone—I have no equal, no rival—I am the king of Humbugs—the king among princes," begins the first chapter on his involvement with Heth. Here the discovery of Heth in Kentucky is given a menacing new spin. Barnaby Diddleum (for "diddle 'um") has heard of the "remarkably old negro woman" who "was swindling my friend by her disgusting pertinacity to cling to life at his expense," and he goes to visit master and slave:

> "You want to get rid of aunt Joice?" said I.
> "I do."

> "I'll do it. What will you give me?"
> "Oh!" he said laughingly, "she must die a natural death.
> "To be sure," said I, "and be as well or better taken care of than now. I have a crochet in my head by which I may probably make something out of her. At all events, I'll take her off your hands if you give me something handsome."

The Kentuckian readily assents, agreeing to pay Diddleum half of what Aunt Joice would cost him if she were to languish another year on his plantation. This jovial linking of Diddleum's plan for profit to the murder of Joice Heth reveals an aggression and a will for power over his touring companion that continues throughout the text. "Adventures" repeats scenes from the "Joice Heth Hoax" in which the new master dreams up the Washington story, yanks out her teeth, and uses whiskey as a means of control—all now told from the first person.

> I soon got Joyce [sic] into training, and from a devil of a termagant, converted into a most docile creature, as willing to do my bidding as the slave of the lamp was to obey Aladdin. I discovered her weak point. . . . WHISKEY. Her old master, of course, would indulge an old bedridden creature in no such luxury, and for a drop of it, I found I could mould her to anything.

Written two decades after the final abolition of slaves in the North, the story's emphasis on Diddleum's absolute possession of his performer's will reads like a Yankee wish-fulfillment—Diddleum achieves his northern glory by appropriating and reworking materials (both human property and narrative) from southern slavery. But the story also betrays a hint of unease about the tractability of slaves; Diddleum's insistence on the absolute emptiness of Heth is in tension with her continued backstage swearing and her occasional complicity in the scheme (at one point, Diddleum refers to her as "a very good actor"). In a text similar to "Adventures of an Adventurer" called "The Autobiography of Petite Bunkum," published in pamphlet form in 1855, the whiskey that cements her dependence comes back to haunt the master. "In fact," Barnum (or "Bunkum") writes, "the old lady occasionally used to get drunk; and in one instance she bestowed upon me the compliment of a black eye, by a blow of her crutch, because I refused to 'come down' with another half pint." The story of Joice Heth (referred to as "Judy Heath") drunkenly braining "Bunkum" with her crutch serves as a mock uprising, one that accords with the dynamics of the story as a whole. Earlier in the same text, Bunkum overhears a conversation between Heath and her owner, leading up to their arrangement for this human property to tour with the would-be showman:

*"How are you today, aunty?" inquired
Mr. Shelby, kindly.*

*"Bless de Lord, massa," mumbled the old
woman—"I is alive. When is massa goin' to let
de poor ole nigger go to de free States, so dat
she may die and go to glory a free woman?"*

*"Well, well; we'll see about it soon,"
answered Mr. Shelby, carelessly; and then,
turning to me, he continued, in a low tone—*

*"The poor creature has taken a strange
fancy to die in the free States. She appears to
believe that if she dies a slave, she can not go
to heaven. I would instantly set her free and
send her North, were it not on account of the
certainty of her coming to suffering and want."*

Playing to the kindly affections of this "good master," Bunkum, a Yankee, offers to take the slave woman off his hands and fulfill her dreams of dying in a free state. In the story that follows, though, her dream is endlessly deferred; their life on the road becomes a battle of wills, in which the northern master always has the upper hand and always pockets the money. When she dies, writes Bunkum, "I shed tears upon her humble grave not of sorrow for her decease—but of regret on account of my having lost a valuable and profitable property."

Exposing Heth's sham story of connection to Washington had been for the penny papers an exercise in unraveling Barnum's mind, but Heth's own role in the imposture was left unexamined.

So, too, these later texts made her a blank slate, but not without some trouble: she is shown struggling, resisting, even lashing out in violence, and she must be broken, taught to voice her master's will. Negating the urgency of this comic resistance is the fact that she is impelled not by an ongoing secret desire for freedom, but by her enslavement to a stronger master than Bunkum—whiskey.

The troubling notion of a slave's resistance to white control that these texts laughed off was a recurrent preoccupation for the penny papers and in much antebellum popular culture in the North. During the 1830s, in the wake of the Nat Turner rebellion, newspapers across the North were fascinated with slave uprisings and conspiracies. Penny press readers' insatiable appetite for even rumors of such distant events reflects the ambiguous mixture of envy and anxiety that, according to Eric Lott, also characterized the appeal of blackface minstrelsy. Lott shows that for working-class whites, the black insubordination on display on the minstrel stage could be read metaphorically—the idea of slave's transgression was often made to articulate the resentments of "class difference, intentionally or not, by calling on the insurrectionary resonances of black culture." Mirroring the relation of minstrel audience to performers, the scene of white workers consuming images of black rebels during the volatile labor situation of the 1830s and 1840s in New York has more than a whiff of "insurrectionary resonance." And just as the comforting filter of grease and cork allowed minstrelsy's audiences to dismiss the transgressive behavior of the minstrel-blacks as an evening's antic fun, the editors of the penny press exposed slave uprisings, the supreme evidence of slaves' calculated fury, only to reveal them as hollow. The *Herald*—and to a lesser degree, the *Sun*—pulled off an extraordinary trick by reporting slave uprisings in a manner that completely undercut the motive and intelligence behind them, and they displaced that intelligence and motive onto the figure of ingenious if dastardly white men. In the seven months' run of the *Herald* and the *Sun* during the time when Joice Heth's story was reported, there are four reports of uprisings. One of them, in Farmington, Tennessee, turned out to have been instigated by "some white man, who refused to tell [the rebel slaves] his name"; the other three, readers would be relieved and intrigued to learn, were not uprisings at all, but were elaborate hoaxes. One of these involved a southern speculator who wanted to create panic in the markets so that he could profit from the ruins. In these reports, the papers performed the disciplinary function of exposing the fraud—and even more comfortingly, revealing that the transgression was not instigated by those who had the highest stake in upsetting the social order. As Michael Rogin has written, "the wish for basic trust that obliterates the autonomy of the other brings with it anxiety over vengeance." If the penny press openly addressed (and profited from) readers' nervousness about the manipulations of untrustworthy capitalist speculators above them, they assured them that blacks, at least, were not autonomously capable of plotting from below.

The goal of the various exposures of the Heth hoax was not to discern how she had come to gull thousands of white viewers and readers, but who was behind her; and it was comforting to find that it was a Yankee, one whose own story of upward mobility white northern working-class readers could identify with. During Heth's exhibition, many of her visitors had delighted in her animation, her quick responses to questions, and her improvised responses as well as her well-rehearsed routine; but in her mass-cultural afterlife, she was a drunken, swearing negro who spoke nothing but her master's words on stage, and whose attempts at resistance were laughable. In recycled legends of the Heth story, Barnum was both a capitalist confidence man and a breaker of slaves, a trader in bogus commodities and an emblem of white mastery.

Conclusion and Postscript: The Dark Subject

As the Joice Heth episode progressed from itinerant road show to urban spectacle, from wondrous display of human curiosity to medical specimen, from historical relic to fraudulent commodity, it traversed many of the geographical and conceptual spaces of the modernizing antebellum North. Her living display had been given a range of readings contingent on the regional and ideological interests of her visitors. Her autopsy, in contrast, shows mass media and science converging on the black body in search of a fixed text in a fluxional world: if Barnum's deceptions—like the text of modern life—were hard to read, Heth's body was not. In this sense the autopsy anticipates the work of racial anatomists, like one Dr. Caldwell, whose "personal examination of dissection of the entire negro anatomy," led him to conclude that it is easier to "distinguish an African from a Circassian skeleton" than that of a dog from a hyena, a tiger from a panther, or a horse from an ox. This type of work established racial difference as a zone of distinct legibility and fixed boundaries; this essential fixity, when reported in the popular press, was a dialectical counterweight to the popular fascination with hoaxes, confidence games, and conspiracy theories that grew out of modern anxieties of authenticity, status, trust, and recognition. The autopsy can also help us perceive the links between nascent racial essentialism and the grotesque popular essentialism of the freak show and minstrelsy, which were beginning to emerge as dominant mass cultural representations of blacks in the modernizing, urbanizing North. Scientific ideas about the biological nature of racial difference provided a conceptual framework for popular images of degraded, deformed, and otherwise humiliated blacks on stage. As these links suggest, the shifting and sometimes conflicting meanings found in the Heth display, the autopsy, and the various exposures do not simply constitute a paratactic sequence of sometimes contradictory interpretations. Rather, they illustrate that her exhibit was a profoundly overdetermined event whose major themes continued to fascinate scientists and purveyors of mass culture through the mid-nineteenth century, and whose minor ones appear now as roads not taken.

Barnum himself circled back in his writings to the Heth exhibit several more times throughout a long and varied career. In his 1855 autobiography, he finally gave away the secret that he had not dreamed up the Heth act, but had seen Lindsay's exhibit of her in Philadelphia and decided to purchase her and continue the tour himself. "The question naturally arises," he wrote,

if Joice Heth was an impostor, who *taught her these things? and how happened it that she was so familiar, not only with ancient psalmody, but also with the minute details of the Washington family? To all this, I unhesitatingly answer,* I do not know. *I taught her none of these things. She was perfectly familiar with them all before I ever saw her, and she taught me many facts in relation to the Washington family with which I was not before acquainted.*

In what was to prove the penultimate "final" exposure of the Heth story, Barnum reversed course by suggesting that he was not Heth's absolute master—that he had in fact been gulled by Heth as much as any visitor had been. Despite this disarming admission, Barnum took pains to show that he had still been firmly in control of the exhibit, dreaming up ever more complex schemes of deception—such as passing her off as an automaton and averting abolitionist protests of the exhibit by claiming that proceeds of the exhibit went toward freeing slaves—that culminated in the autopsy itself. But in the next edition of his autobiography, in 1869, he retold the story with something like shame. Barnum had by this time remade himself from a Jacksonian Democrat into a Republican politician; in 1867, he ran an unsuc-

cessful campaign for Congress, and he went on to become Mayor of Bridgeport in 1875. Ever the opportunist, he enthusiastically endorsed the Republican platform, including the granting of franchise for the newly freed slaves, and he now cast himself as a defender of African American freedoms. In looking back on his own potentially embarrassing career as a northern slaveowner, he wrote that the Joice Heth exhibit was "the least deserving of my efforts in the show line . . . a scheme in no sense of my own devising." And as to the identity of Heth, he claimed to be as ignorant as anyone else. All he could say about the results of the autopsy, whose mystification he had spent months producing, was that "the doctors disagreed, and this 'dark subject' will probably always be shrouded in mystery." As for the dark subject's story, he wrote, "I honestly believed it to be genuine; something, too, which . . . I did not seek, but which by accident came in my way and seemed to compel my agency." This turnabout owes much to the rhetorical demands of the situation Barnum found himself in, but his denial exceeds those demands. Not only was his role in the exhibit an "accident," but "it"—or Joice Heth herself—"seemed almost to compel my agency." Entrepreneurs of culture in the antebellum North had borrowed images from the slave-owning South to construct fantasies of northern white mastery, in which the slave's body was subjected to the modern disciplines of scientific and mass-cultural scrutiny. In the process, the slave's mind had been repressed; but now it returned, after the war, to haunt the northern master.

Study Questions

1. Who was Joice Heth and why did so many Americans find her so intriguing?

2. How does the case of Joice Heth reveal America's changing ideas about race in the nineteenth century?

3. In what ways was P. T. Barnum pulling off a fraud in his exploitation of Joice Heth?

4. Why does Reiss argue that the widespread display of Heth's body exposed differences in class in American society? Give an example.

5. What role did the "penny press" play in the event and why was that important?

6. What criticisms did many Americans offer about Barnum's tour?

7. What is an autopsy and what role did it play in the Heth case?

8. Who was P. T. Barnum, and what is his significance in American history?

9. How did southerners treat the tour?

Bibliography

For a look at fraud, spectacle, and taste in American history, see Karen Halttunen, *Confidence Men and Painted Women: A Study of Middle-Class Culture in America* (1982) and John Kasson, *Rudeness and Civility: Manners in Nineteenth-Century America* (1990). Andie Tucher's *Froth and Scum: Truth, Beauty, Goodness and the Ax Murder in America's First Mass Medium* (1994) examines the role of the penny press in promoting popular culture in early America. The best biographies of P. T. Barnum include A. H. Saxon, *P. T. Barnum: The Legend and the Man* (1989) and Bluford Adams, *E Pluribus Barnum: The Great Showman and the Making of U.S. Popular Culture* (1997). Robert Bogdan's *Freak Show: Presenting Human Oddities for Amusement and Profit* (1988) is considered a pioneering work. Also see Rosemary Garland Thomson, *Freakery: Cultural Spectacles of the Extraordinary Body* (1996).

READING 25

The Slave Warehouse
from Uncle Tom's Cabin

Harriet Beecher Stowe

On meeting Harriet Beecher Stowe during the Civil War, President Abraham Lincoln remarked, "So this is the lady who made this big war!" To be sure, Stowe did not cause the Civil War, but her novel, *Uncle Tom's Cabin,* aroused Northerners and angered Southerners. She portrayed slavery as a great moral evil—not at all the benign institution presented by southern apologists. Unlike the abstract writings of some of her contemporaries, Stowe confirmed the reality of slavery to Northerners who had never seen a slave or ventured below the Mason-Dixon line. The novel gave northern abolitionists a new rhetoric to use in condemning slavery, and it helped convince the South that the North was bent on destroying the southern way of life. State after state in the South banned the sale of the book, and southern postmasters routinely intercepted and destroyed all copies of the book mailed from northern book distributors.

Published in 1852, *Uncle Tom's Cabin* became a runaway bestseller, a literary success on both sides of the Atlantic. Stowe's characters—Uncle Tom, Eliza, Simon Legree, and Little Eva—were hailed as universal types. In the following selection, "The Slave Warehouse," good-hearted Christian slaves are purchased at a slave auction by Simon Legree.

A slave warehouse! Perhaps some of my readers conjure up horrible visions of such a place. They fancy some foul, obscure den, some horrible *Tartarus "informis, ingens, cui lumen ademptum."* But no, innocent friend; in these days men have learned the art of sinning expertly and genteelly, so as not to shock the eyes and senses of respectable society. Human property is high in the market; and is, therefore, well fed, well cleaned, tended, and looked after, that it may come to sale sleek, and strong, and shining. A slave warehouse in New Orleans is a house externally not much unlike many others, kept with neatness; and where every day you may see arranged, under a sort of shed along the outside, rows of men and women, who stand there as a sign of the property sold within.

Then you shall be courteously entreated to call and examine, and shall find an abundance of husbands, wives, brothers, sisters, fathers, mothers, and young children, to be "sold separately, or in lots, to suit the convenience of the purchaser;" and that soul immortal, once bought with blood and anguish by the Son of God, when the earth shook, and the rocks were rent, and the graves were opened, can be sold, leased, mortgaged, exchanged for groceries or dry goods, to suit the phases of trade, or the fancy of the purchaser.

It was a day or two after the conversation between Marie and Miss Ophelia, that Tom, Adolph, and about half a dozen others of the St. Clare estate, were turned over to the loving kindness of Mr. Skeggs, the keeper of a depot on——street, to await the auction next day.

Tom had with him quite a sizable trunk full of clothing, as had most others of them. They were ushered, for the night, into a long room, where many other men, of all ages, sizes, and shades of complexion, were assembled, and from which roars of laughter and unthinking merriment were proceeding.

"Ah, ha! that's right. Go it, boys—go it!" said Mr. Skeggs, the keeper. "My people are always so merry! Sambo, I see!" he said, speaking approvingly to a burly Negro who was performing tricks of low buffoonery, which occasioned the shouts which Tom had heard.

As might be imagined, Tom was in no humor to join these proceedings; and, therefore, setting his trunk as far as possible from the noisy group, he sat down on it, and leaned his face against the wall.

The dealers in the human article make scrupulous and systematic efforts to promote noisy mirth among them, as a means of drowning reflection, and rendering them insensible to their condition. The whole object of the training to which the Negro is put, from the time he is sold in the northern market till he arrives south, is systematically directed towards making him callous, unthinking, and brutal. The slave-dealer collects his gang in Virginia or Kentucky, and drives them to some convenient, healthy place—often a watering-place,—to be fattened. Here they are fed full daily; and, because some incline to pine, a fiddle is kept commonly going among them, and they are made to dance daily; and he who refuses to be merry—in whose soul thoughts of wife, or child, or home, are too strong for him to be gay—is marked as sullen and dangerous, and subjected to all the evils which the ill-will of an utterly irresponsible and hardened man can inflict upon him. Briskness, alertness, and cheerfulness of appearance, especially before observers, are constantly enforced upon them, both by the hope of thereby getting a good master, and the fear of all that the driver may bring upon them, if they prove unsalable.

"What dat ar nigger doin' here?" said Sambo, coming up to Tom, after Mr. Skeggs had left the room. Sambo was a full black, of great size, very lively, voluble, and full of trick and grimace.

"What you doin' here?" said Sambo, coming up to Tom, and poking him facetiously in the side. "Meditatin', eh?"

"I am to be sold at the auction, to-morrow!" said Tom, quietly.

"Sold at auction—haw! haw! boys, an't this yer fun? I wish't I was gwin that ar way!—tell ye, wouldn't I make 'em laugh? but how is it—dis yer

"The Slave Warehouse" from *Uncle Tom's Cabin* by Harriet Beecher Stowe. New York, 1852.

whole lot gwine to-morrow?" said Sambo, laying his hand freely on Adolph's shoulder.

"Please to let me alone!" said Adolph, fiercely, straightening himself up, with extreme disgust.

"Law, now, boys! dis yer's one o' yer white niggers—kind o' cream-color, ye know, scented!" said he, coming up to Adolph and snuffing. "O Lor! he'd do for a tobaccershop; they could keep him to scent snuff! Lor, he'd keep a whole shop agwine—he would!"

"I say, keep off, can't you?" said Adolph, enraged.

"Lor, now, how touchy we is—we white niggers! Look at us, now!" and Sambo gave a ludicrous imitation of Adolph's manner; "here's de airs and graces. We's been in a good family, I specs."

"Yes," said Adolph; "I had a master that could have bought you all for old truck!"

"Laws, now, only think," said Sambo, "the gentlemens that we is!"

"I belonged to the St. Clare family," said Adolph, proudly.

"Lor, you did! Be hanged if they aren't lucky to get shet of ye. Spects they 's gwine to trade ye off with a lot o' cracked teapots and sich like!" said Sambo, with a provoking grin.

Adolph, enraged at this taunt, flew furiously at his adversary, swearing and striking on every side of him. The rest laughed and shouted, and the uproar brought the keeper to the door.

"What now, boys? Order—order!" he said, coming in and flourishing a large whip.

All fled in different directions, except Sambo, who, presuming on the favor which the keeper had to him as a licensed wag, stood his ground, ducking his head with a facetious grin, whenever the master made a dive at him.

"Lor, Mas'r, 't an't us—we 's reg'lar stiddy—it's these yer new hands; they's real aggravatin'—kinder pickin' at us, all time!"

The keeper, at this, turned upon Tom and Adolph, and distributing a few kicks and cuffs without much inquiry, and leaving general orders for all to be good boys and go to sleep, left the apartment.

While this scene was going on in the men's sleeping-room, the reader may be curious to take a peep at the corresponding apartment allotted to the women. Stretched out in various attitudes over the floor, he may see numberless sleeping forms of every shade of complexion, from the purest ebony to white, and of all years, from childhood to old age, lying now asleep. Here is a fine bright girl, of ten years, whose mother was sold out yesterday, and who tonight cried herself to sleep when nobody was looking at her. Here, a worn old Negress, whose thin arms and callous fingers tell of hard toil, waiting to be sold to-morrow, as a cast-off article, for what can be got for her; and some forty or fifty others, with heads variously enveloped in blankets or articles of clothing, lie stretched around them. But, in a corner, sitting apart from the rest, are two females of a more interesting appearance than common. One of these is a respectably dressed mulatto woman between forty and fifty, with soft eyes and a gentle and pleasing physiognomy. She has on her head a high-raised turban, made of a gay red Madras handkerchief, of the first quality, and her dress is neatly fitted, and of good material, showing that she has been provided for with a careful hand. By her side, and nestling closely to her, is a young girl of fifteen—her daughter. She is a quadroon, as may be seen from her fairer complexion, though her likeness to her mother is quite discernible. She has the same soft, dark eyes, with longer lashes, and her curling hair is of a luxuriant brown. She also is dressed with great neatness, and her white, delicate hands betray very little acquaintance with servile toil. These two are to be sold to-morrow, in the same lot with the St. Clare servants; and the gentleman to whom they belong, and to whom the money for their sale is to be transmitted, is a member of a Christian church in New York, who will receive the money, and go thereafter to the sacrament of his Lord and theirs, and think no more of it.

These two, whom we shall call Susan and Emmeline, had been the personal attendants of an amiable and pious lady of New Orleans, by whom they had been carefully and piously instructed and trained. They had been taught to read and write, diligently instructed in the truths of religion, and their lot had been as happy an one as in their condition it was possible to be. But the only son of their protectress had the management of her property; and, by carelessness and extravagance, involved it to a large amount, and at last failed. One of the largest creditors was the respectable firm of B. & Co., in New York. B. & Co. wrote to their lawyer in New Orleans, who attached the real estate (these two articles and a lot of plantation hands formed the most valuable part of it), and wrote word to that effect to New York. Brother B., being, as we have said, a Christian man, and a resident in a free state, felt some uneasiness on the subject. He didn't like trading in slaves and souls of men—of course, he didn't; but, then, there were thirty thousand dollars in the case, and that was rather too much money to be lost for a principle; and so, after much considering, and asking advice from those that he knew would advise to suit him, Brother B. wrote to his lawyer to dispose of the business in the way that seemed to him the most suitable, and remit the proceeds.

The day after the letter arrival in New Orleans, Susan and Emmeline were attached, and sent to the depot to await a general auction on the following morning; and as they glimmer faintly upon us in the moonlight which steals through the grated window, we may listen to their conversation. Both are weeping, but each quietly, that the other may not hear.

"Mother, just lay your head on my lap, and see if you can't sleep a little," says the girl, trying to appear calm.

"I haven't any heart to sleep, Em; I can't, it's the last night we may be together!"

"Oh, mother, don't say so! perhaps we shall get sold together—who knows?"

"If 't was anybody's else case, I should say so, too, Em," said the woman; "but I'm so 'feared of losin' you that I don't see anything but the danger."

"Why, mother, the man said we were both likely, and would sell well."

Susan remembered the man's looks and words. With a deadly sickness at her heart, she remembered how he had looked at Emmeline's hands, and lifted up her curly hair, and pronounced her a first-rate article. Susan had been trained as a Chris-

tian, brought up in the daily reading of the Bible, and had the same horror of her child's being sold to a life of shame that any other Christian mother might have; but she had no hope—no protection.

"Mother, I think we might do first-rate, if you could get a place as cook, and I as chambermaid or seamstress, in some family. I dare say we shall. Let's both look as bright and lively as we can, and tell all we can do, and perhaps we shall," said Emmeline.

"I want you to brush your hair all back straight, to-morrow," said Susan.

"What for, mother? I don't look near so well, that way."

"Yes, but you'll sell better so."

"I don't see why!" said the child.

"Respectable families would be more apt to buy you, if they saw you looked plain and decent, as if you wasn't trying to look handsome. I know their ways better'n you do," said Susan.

"Well, mother, then I will."

"And, Emmeline, if we shouldn't ever see each other again, after to-morrow—if I'm sold way up on a plantation somewhere, and you somewhere else—always remember how you've been brought up, and all Missis has told you; take your Bible with you, and your hymnbook; and if you're faithful to the Lord, he'll be faithful to you."

So speaks the poor soul, in sore discouragement; for she knows that to-morrow any man, however vile and brutal, however godless and merciless, if he only has money to pay for her, may become owner of her daughter, body and soul; and then, how is the child to be faithful? She thinks of all this, as she holds her daughter in her arms, and wishes that she were not handsome and attractive. It seems almost an aggravation to her to remember how purely and piously, how much above the ordinary lot, she has been brought up. But she has no resort but to *pray;* and many such prayers to God have gone up from those same trim, neatly arranged, respectable slave-prisons—prayers which God has not forgotten, as a coming day shall show; for it is written, "Whoso causeth one of these little ones to offend, it were better for him that a millstone were hanged about his neck, and that he were drowned in the depths of the sea."

The soft, earnest, quiet moonbeam looks in fixedly, marking the bars of the grated windows on the prostrate, sleeping forms. The mother and daughter are singing together a wild and melancholy dirge, common as a funeral hymn among the slaves:—

"Oh, where is weeping Mary?
Oh, where is weeping Mary?
'Rived in the goodly land.
She is dead and gone to heaven;
She is dead and gone to heaven;
'Rived in the goodly land."

These words, sung by voices of a peculiar and melancholy sweetness, in an air which seemed like the sighing of earthly despair after heavenly hope, floated through the dark prison-rooms with a pathetic cadence, as verse after verse was breathed out—

"Oh, where are Paul and Silas?
Oh, where are Paul and Silas?
Gone to the goodly land.
They are dead and gone to heaven;
They are dead and gone to heaven;
'Rived in the goodly land."

Sing on, poor souls! The night is short, and the morning will part you forever!

But now it is morning, and everybody is astir; and the worthy Mr. Skeggs is busy and bright, for a lot of goods is to be fitted out for auction. There is a brisk lookout on the toilet, injunctions passed to every one to put on their best face and be spry; and now all are arranged in a circle for a last review, before they are marched up to the Bourse.

Mr. Skeggs, with his palmetto on and his cigar in his mouth, walks around to put farewell touches on his wares.

"How's this?" he said, stepping in front of Susan and Emmeline. "Where's your curls, gal?"

The girl looked timidly at her mother, who, with the smooth adroitness common among her class, answers—

"I was telling her, last night, to put up her hair smooth and neat, and not havin' it flying about in curls; looks more respectable so."

"Bother!" said the man, peremptorily, turning to the girl; "you go right along, and curl yourself real smart!" He added, giving a crack to a rattan he held in his hand, "And be back in quick time, too!"

"You go and help her," he added, to the mother. "Them curls may make a hundred dollars difference in the sale of her."

Beneath a splendid dome were men of all nations, moving to and fro, over the marble pave. On every side of the circular area were little tribunes, or stations, for the use of speakers and auctioneers. Two of these, on opposite sides of the area, were now occupied by brilliant and talented gentlemen, enthusiastically forcing up, in English and French commingled, the bids of connoisseurs in their various wares. A third one, on the other side, still unoccupied, was surrounded by a group, waiting the moment of sale to begin. And here we may recognize the St. Clare servants—Tom, Adolph, and others; and there, too, Susan and Emmeline, awaiting their turn with anxious and dejected faces. Various spectators, intending to purchase, or not intending, as the case might be, gathered around the group, handling, examining, and commenting on their various points and faces with the same freedom that a set of jockeys discuss the merits of a horse.

"Hulloa, Alf! what brings you here?" said a young exquisite, slapping the shoulder of a sprucely dressed young man, who was examining Adolph through an eye-glass.

"Well, I was wanting a valet, and I heard that St. Clare's lot was going. I thought I'd just look at his"—

"Catch me ever buying any of St. Clare's people! Spoilt niggers, every one. Impudent as the devil!" said the other.

"Never fear that!" said the first. "If I get 'em, I'll soon have their airs out of them; they'll soon find that they've another kind of master to deal with than Monsieur St. Clare. 'Pon my word, I'll buy that fellow. I like the shape of him."

"You'll find it'll take all you've got to keep him. He's deucedly extravagant!"

"Yes, but my lord will find that he *can't* be extravagant with *me*. Just let him be sent to the calaboose a few times, and thoroughly dressed down! I'll tell you if it don't bring him to a sense of his ways! Oh, I'll reform him, up hill and down—you'll see. I buy him that's flat!"

Tom had been standing wistfully examining the multitude of faces thronging around him, for one whom he would wish to call master. And if you should ever be under the necessity, sir, of selecting, out of two hundred men, one who was to become your absoulte owner and disposer, you would, perhaps, realize, just as Tom did, how few there were that you would feel at all comfortable in being made over to. Tom saw abundance of men—great, burly, gruff men; little, chirping, dried men; long-favored, lank, hard men; and every variety of stubbed-looking, commonplace men, who pick up their fellow-men as one picks up chips, putting them into the fire or a basket with equal unconcern according to their convenience; but he saw no St. Clare.

A little before the sale commenced, a short, broad, muscular man, in a checked shirt considerably open at the bosom, and pantaloons much the worse for dirt and wear, elbowed his way through the crowd, like one who is going actively into a business; and, coming up to the group, began to examine them systematically. From the moment that Tom saw him approaching, he felt an immediate and revolting horror at him, that increased as he came near. He was evidently, though short, of gigantic strength. His round, bullet-head, large, light-grey eyes, with their shaggy, sandy eyebrows, and stiff, wiry, sunburned hair, were rather unprepossessing items, it is to be confessed; his large, coarse mouth was distended with tobacco, the juice of which, from time to time, he ejected from him with great decision and explosive force; his hands were immensely large, hairy, sunburned, freckled, and very dirty, and garnished with long nails, in a very foul condition. This man proceeded to a very free personal examination of the lot. He seized Tom by the jaw, and pulled open his mouth to inspect his teeth; made him strip up his sleeve, to show his muscle; turned him round, made him jump and spring, to show his paces.

"Where was you raised?" he added, briefly, to these investigations.

"In Kintuck, Mas'r," said Tom, looking about, as if for deliverance.

"What have you done?"

"Had care of Mas'r's farm," said Tom.

"Likely story!" said the other, shortly, as he passed on. He paused a moment before Dolph; then spitting a discharge of tobacco-juice on his well-blacked boots, and giving a contemptuous umph, he walked on. Again he stopped before Susan and Emmeline. He put out his heavy, dirty hand, and drew the girl towards him; passed it over her neck, and bust, felt her arms, looked at her teeth, and then pushed her back against her mother, whose patient face showed the suffering she had been going through at every motion of the hideous stranger.

The girl was frightened, and began to cry.

"Stop that, you minx!" said the salesman; "no whimpering here—the sale is going to begin." And accordingly the sale began.

Adolph was knocked off, at a good sum, to the young gentleman who had previously stated his intentions of buying him; and the other servants of the St. Clare lot went to various bidders.

"Now, up with you, boy! d' ye hear?" said the auctioneer to Tom.

Tom stepped upon the block, gave a few anxious looks round; all seemed mingled in a common, indistinct noise—the clatter of the salesman crying off his qualifications in French and English, the quick fire of French and English bids; and almost in a moment came the final thump of the hammer, and the clear ring on the last syllable of the word "*dollars,*" as the auctioneer announced his price, and Tom was made over. He had a master.

He was pushed from the block; the short, bullet-headed man, seizing him roughly by the shoulder, pushed him to one side, saying in a harsh voice, "Stand there, *you!*"

Tom hardly realized anything; but still the bidding went on—rattling, clattering, now French, now English. Down goes the hammer again— Susan is sold! She goes down from the block,

Families endured forced separation at slave auctions like the one depicted above; here a mother and child are being sold. Contrary to popular belief, slave markets were usually well-tended warehouses. Slaves were fattened and groomed before auctions in order to bring better prices.

stops, looks wistfully back—her daughter stretches her hands towards her. She looks with agony in the face of the man who has bought her—a respectable, middle-aged man, of benevolent countenance.

"Oh, Mas'r, please do buy my daughter!"

"I'd like to, but I'm afraid I can't afford it!" said the gentleman, looking, with painful interest, as the young girl mounted the block, and looked around her with a frightened and timid glance.

The blood flushes painfully in her otherwise colorless cheek, her eye has a feverish fire, and her mother groans to see that she looks more beautiful than she ever saw her before. The auctioneer sees his advantage, and expatiates volubly in mingled French and English, and bids rise in rapid succession.

"I'll do anything in reason," said the benevolent-looking gentleman, pressing in and joining with the bids. In a few moments they have run beyond his purse. He is silent; the auctioneer grows warmer; but bids gradually drop off. It lies now between an aristocratic old citizen and our bullet-headed acquaintance. The citizen bids for a few turns, contemptuously measuring his opponent; but the bullet-head has the advantage over him, both in obstinacy and concealed length of purse, and the controversy lasts but a moment; the hammer falls—he has got the girl, body and soul, unless God help her.

Her master is Mr. Legree, who owns a cotton plantation on the Red River. She is pushed along into the same lot with Tom and two other men, and goes off, weeping as she goes.

The benevolent gentleman is sorry; but, then, the thing happens every day! One sees girls and mothers crying, at these sales, *always!* it can't be helped, etc.; and he walks off, with his acquisition, in another direction.

Two days after, the lawyer of the Christian firm of B. & Co., New York, sent on their money to them. On the reverse of that draft, so obtained, let them write these words of the great Paymaster, to whom they shall make up their account in a future day: *"When he maketh inquisition for blood, he forgetteth not the cry of the humble!"*

"Thou art of purer eyes than to behold evil, and canst not look upon iniquity: wherefore lookest thou upon them that deal treacherously, and holdest thy tongue when the wicked devoureth the man that is more righteous than he?"—*Hab.* i. 13.

On the lower part of a small, mean boat, on the Red River, Tom sat—chains on his wrists, chains on his feet, and a weight heavier than chains lay on his heart. All had faded from his sky—moon and star; all had passed by him, as the trees and banks were now passing, to return no more. Kentucky home, with wife and children, and indulgent owners; St. Clare home, with all its refinements and splendors; the golden head of Eva, with its saint-like eyes; the proud, gay, handsome, seemingly careless, yet ever-kind St. Clare; hours of ease and indulgent leisure—all gone! and in place thereof, *what* remains?

It is one of the bitterest apportionments of a lot of slavery, that the Negro, sympathetic and assimilative, after acquiring, in a refined family, the tastes and feelings which form the atmosphere of such a place, is not the less liable to become the bond-slave of the coarsest and most brutal—just as a chair or table, which once decorated the superb saloon, comes, at last, battered and defaced, to the bar-room of some filthy tavern, or some low haunt of vulgar debauchery. The great difference is, that the table and chair cannot feel, and the *man* can; for even a legal enactment that he shall be "taken, reputed, adjudged in law, to be a chattel personal," cannot blot out his soul, with

its own private little world of memories, hopes, loves, fears, and desires.

Mr. Simon Legree, Tom's master, had purchased slaves at one place and another, in New Orleans, to the number of eight, and driven them, handcuffed, in couples of two and two, down to the good steamer Pirate, which lay at the levee, ready for a trip up the Red River.

Having got them fairly on board, and the boat being off, he came round, with that air of efficiency which ever characterized him, to take a review of them. Stopping opposite to Tom, who had been attired for sale in his best broadcloth suit, with well-starched linen and shining boots, he briefly expressed himself as follows:

"Stand up."

Tom stood up.

"Take off that stock!" and, as Tom, encumbered by his fetters, proceeded to do it, he assisted him, by pulling it, with no gentle hand, from his neck, and putting it in his pocket.

Legree now turned to Tom's trunk, which, previous to this, he had been ransacking, and taking from it a pair of old pantaloons and a dilapidated coat, which Tom had been wont to put on about his stable-work, he said, liberating Tom's hands from the handcuffs, and pointing to a recess in among the boxes—

"You go there, and put these on."

Tom obeyed, and in a few moments returned.

"Take off your boots," said Mr. Legree.

Tom did so.

"There," said the former, throwing him a pair of course, stout shoes, such as were common among the slaves, "put these on."

In Tom's hurried exchange, he had not forgotten to transfer his cherished Bible to his pocket. It was well he did so; for Mr. Legree, having refitted Tom's handcuffs, proceeded deliberately to investigate the contents of his pockets. He drew out a silk handkerchief, and put it into his own pocket. Several little trifles, which Tom had treasured, chiefly because they amused Eva, he looked upon with a contemptuous grunt, and tossed them over his shoulder into the river.

Tom's Methodist hymn-book, which, in his hurry, he had forgotten, he now held up and turned over.

"Humph! pious, to be sure. So, what's yer name—you belong to the church, eh?"

"Yes, Mas'r," said Tom, firmly.

"Well, I'll soon have *that* out of you. I have none o' yer bawling, praying, singing niggers on my place; so remember. Now, mind yourself," he said, with a stamp and a fierce glance of his gray eye, directed at Tom, "*I'm* your church now! You understand—you've got to be as I say."

Something within the silent black man answered *No!* and, as if repeated by an invisible voice, came the words of an old prophetic scroll, as Eva had often read them to him, "Fear not! For I have redeemed thee. I have called thee by my name. Thou art MINE!"

But Simon Legree heard no voice. That voice is one he never shall hear. He only glared for a moment on the downcast face to Tom, and walked off. He took Tom's trunk, which contained a very neat and abundant wardrobe, to the forecastle, where it was soon surrounded by various hands of the boat. With much laughing, at the expense of niggers who tried to be gentlemen, the articles very readily were sold to one and another, and the empty trunk finally put up at auction. It was a good joke, they all thought, especially to see how Tom looked after his things, as they were going this way and that; and then the auction of the trunk, that was funnier than all, and occasioned abundant witticisms.

This little affair being over, Simon sauntered up again to his property.

"Now, Tom, I've relieved you of any extra baggage, you see. Take mighty good care of them clothes. It'll be long enough 'fore you get more. I go in for making niggers careful; one suit has to do for one year, on my place."

Simon next walked up to the place where Emmeline was sitting chained to another woman.

"Well, my dear," he said, chucking her under the chin, "keep up your spirits."

The involuntary look of horror, fright, and aversion with which the girl regarded him, did not escape his eye. He frowned fiercely.

"None o' your shines, gal! you's got to keep a pleasant face, when I speak to ye—d' ye hear? And you, you old yellow poco moonshine!" he said, giving a shove to the mulatto woman to whom Emmeline was chained, "don't you carry that sort of face! You's got to look chipper, I tell ye!"

"I say, all on ye," he said, retreating a pace or two back, "look at me—look at me—look me right in the eye—*straight,* now!" said he, stamping his foot at every pause.

As by a fascination, every eye was now directed to the glaring greenish gray eye of Simon.

"Now," said he, doubling his great, heavy fist into something resembling a blacksmith's hammer, "d' ye see this fist? Heft it!" he said, bringing it down on Tom's hand. "Look at these yer bones! Well, I tell ye this yer fist has got as hard as iron *knocking down niggers.* I never see the nigger, yet, I couldn't bring down with one crack," said he, bringing his fist down so near to the face of Tom that he winked and drew back. "I don't keep none o' yer cussed overseers; I does my own overseeing; and I tell you things *is* seen to. You's every one of ye get to toe the mark, I tell ye; quick—straight—the moment I speak. That's the way to keep in with me. Ye won't find no soft spot in me, nowhere. So, now, mind yerselves; for I don't show no mercy!"

The women involuntarily drew in their breath, and the whole gang sat with downcast, dejected faces. Meanwhile, Simon turned on his heel, and marched up to the bar of the boat for a dram.

"That's the way I begin with my niggers," he said, to a gentlemanly man, who had stood by him during his speech. "It's my system to begin strong—just let 'em know what to expect."

"Indeed!" said the stranger, looking upon him with the curiosity of a naturalist studying some out-of-the-way specimen.

"Yes, indeed. I'm none o' yer gentlemen planters, with lily fingers, to slop round and be cheated by some old cuss of an overseer! Just feel of my knuckles, now; look at my fist. Tell ye, sir, the flesh on't has come jest like a stone, practising on niggers—feel on it."

The stranger applied his fingers to the implement in question, and simply said,

" 'Tis hard enough; and, I suppose," he added, "practice has made your heart just like it."

"Why, yes, I may say so," said Simon, with a hearty laugh. "I reckon there's as little soft in me as in any one going. Tell you, nobody comes it over me! Niggers never gets round me, neither with squalling nor soft soap—that's a fact."

"You have a fine lot there."

"Real," said Simon. "There's that Tom, they told me he was suthin uncommon. I paid a little high for him, 'tendin' him for a driver and a managing chap; only get the notions out that he's larnt by being treated as niggers never ought to be, he'll do prime! The yellow woman I got tookin in. I rayther think she's sickly, but I shall put her through for what she's worth; she may last a year or two. I don't go for savin' niggers. Use up, and buy more, 's my way—makes you less trouble, and I'm quite sure it comes cheaper in the end;" and Simon sipped his glass.

"And how long do they generally last?" said the stranger. "Well, donno; 'cordin' as their constitution is. Stout fellers last six or seven years; trashy ones gets worked up in two or three. I used to, when I fust begun, have considerable trouble fussin' with 'em, and trying to make 'em hold out—doctorin' on 'em up when they's sick, and given' on 'em clothes and blankets, and what not, tryin' to keep 'em all sort o' decent and comfortable. Law, 't wasn't no sort o' use; I lost money on 'em, and 't was heaps o' trouble. Now, you see, I just put 'em straight through, sick or well. When one nigger's dead, I buy another; and I find it comes cheaper and easier, every way."

The stranger turned away, and seated himself beside a gentleman, who had been listening to the conversation with repressed uneasiness.

"You must not take that fellow to be any specimen of southern planters," said he.

"I should hope not," said the young gentleman, with emphasis.

"He is a mean, low, brutal fellow!" said the other.

"And yet your laws allow him to hold any number of human beings subject to his absolute will without even a shadow of protection; and, low as he is, you cannot say that there are not many such."

"Well," said the other, "there are also many considerate and humane men among planters."

"Granted," said the young man; "but, in my opinion, it is you considerate, humane men, that are responsible for all the brutality and outrage wrought by these wretches; because, if it were not for your sanction and influence, the whole system could not keep foothold for an hour. If there were no planters except such as that one," said he, pointing with his finger to Legree, who stood with his back to them, "the whole thing would go down like a mill-stone. It is your respectability and humanity that licenses and protects his brutality."

"You certainly have a high opinion of my good nature," said the planter, smiling; "but I advise you not to talk quite so loud, as there are people on board the boat who might not be quite so tolerant to opinion as I am. You had better wait till I get up to my plantation, and there you may abuse us all, quite at your leisure."

The young gentleman colored and smiled, and the two were soon busy in a game of backgammon. Meanwhile, another conversation was going on in the lower part of the boat, between Emmeline and the mulatto woman with whom she was confined. As was natural, they were exchanging with each other some particulars of their history.

"Who did you belong to?" said Emmeline.

"Well, my Mas'r was Mr. Ellis—lived on Levee Street. P'r'aps you've seen the house."

"Was he good to you?" said Emmeline.

"Mostly, till he tuk sick. He's lain sick, off and on, more than six months, and been orful oneasy. 'Pears like he warn't willin' to have nobody rest, day nor night; and got so curous, there couldn't nobody suit him. 'Pears like he just grew crosser, every day; kep me up nights till I got farly beat out, and couldn't keep awake no longer; and 'cause I got to sleep, one night, Lors, he talk so orful to me, and he tell me he'd sell me to just the hardest master he could find; and he'd promised me my freedom, too, when he died."

"Had you any friends?" said Emmeline.

"Yes, my husband—he's a blacksmith. Mas'r gen'ly hired him out. They took me off so quick, I didn't even have time to see him; and I's got four children. Oh, dear me!" said the woman, covering her face with her hands.

It is a natural impulse, in every one, when they hear a tale of distress, to think of something to say by way of consolation. Emmeline wanted to say something, but she could not think of anything to say. What was there to be said? As by a common consent, they both avoided, with fear and dread, all mention of the horrible man who was now their master.

True, there is religious trust for even the darkest hour. The mulatto woman was a member of the Methodist Church, and had an unenlightened but very sincere spirit of piety. Emmeline had been educated much more intelligently, taught to read and write, and diligently instructed in the Bible, by the care of a faithful and pious mistress; yet, would it not try the faith of the firmest Christians to find themselves abandoned, apparently, of God, in the grasp of ruthless violence? How much more must it shake the faith of Christ's poor little ones, weak in knowledge and tender in years.

The boat moved on—freighted with its weight of sorrow—up the red, muddy, turbid current, through the abrupt, tortuous windings of the Red River; and sad eyes gazed wearily on the steep red-clay banks, as they glided by in dreary sameness. At last the boat stopped at a small town, and Legree, with his party, disembarked.

Study Questions

1. How does Stowe convey the inhumanity of the slave auction?

2. How does Tom accept his fate?

3. How does Stowe portray the evil of Legree?

4. What reactions do you believe Stowe was trying to arouse in her readers?

Bibliography

For studies of *Uncle Tom's Cabin* and Harriet Beecher Stowe, see Charles A. Foster, *The Wrungless Ladder* (1954); Chester E. Jorgensen, ed., *Uncle Tom's Cabin as Book and Legend* (1952); Forrest Wilson, *Crusader and Crinoline* (1941); and Edmund Wilson, *Patriotic Gore* (1962). Anne Fields, *Life and Letters of Harriet Beecher Stowe* (1898), contains useful information on *Uncle Tom's Cabin,* and Herbert Ross Brown, *The Sentimental Novel in America 1789-1860* (1940), puts the novel into its literary perspective. For more recent examinations of *Uncle Tom's Cabin,* see Robert S. Levine, *Martin Delaney, Frederick Douglass, and the Politics of Representative Identity* (1997) and Barbara Anne White, *The Beecher Sisters* (2003).

READING 26

The Southampton Slave Revolt

Henry F. Tragle

The need for some form of involuntary servitude seemed inevitable in the American South. Land was abundant and cheap, but labor was limited and expensive. Unlike the situation in England, American settlers found it fairly easy to acquire land of their own but practically impossible to find people to work it. If Southerners were going to get the most out of their land, they needed labor; if no volunteers were available, slavery seemed a viable alternative. They found their workers in West Africa, importing the first group of slaves to Virginia in 1619. By the time of the Civil War, that handful of blacks had grown to four million people.

Southern life was full of ambiguities, but none of them was more ironic than the role of those four million slaves. Whites needed slaves to plant their land, harvest their crops, clean their houses, cook their food, and suckle their children. Whites needed slaves in order to thrive and prosper, so they imported more and more Africans, making slaves a permanent, visible fixture in southern life.

But the arrival of more and more slaves made southern whites nervous. Despite the prevailing rationale that slavery benefited all concerned, whites knew instinctively that the Africans resented their bondage and yearned to be free. Rumors of slave rebellions were rampant in the nineteenth century. Whites became paranoid about their slaves; they were always on guard, always searching for conspiracies, always afraid of a slave uprising. Then, on the morning of August 22, 1831, their worst nightmares came true in Southampton, Virginia. There Nat Turner led a group of slaves on a bloody rampage through white farms and plantations. When the orgy of violence was over, sixty whites were dead, hacked apart by axes wielded by slaves. The South would never be the same.

The voluminous histories of this country written in the nineteenth century, while admirable in many respects, are of little value to a student today who seeks reliable information on the institution of American slavery. Concerned primarily with slavery as a political question, or with its economic, social, and cultural impact on the white population, the historians rarely made any attempt to understand the black man as a human being.

One of the persistent themes pursued by those who have written recently on the subject of American slavery has been to ask why the slave was willing to tolerate his lot. Why, when in many sections of the South the slave population considerably outnumbered the white, was there no more evidence of unrest?

Actually, there was considerable. But one must look beyond the writings of the most respected of the nineteenth-century historians in order to perceive this. The works of James Schouler, John Fiske, Hermann von Holst, John W. Burgess, James Ford Rhodes, and John Bach McMaster simply did not deal with the available evidence on this question. Satisfied to accept the stereotype of the American black man as docile, ignorant, and inherently inferior, they saw no reason to probe very deeply. Fiske did find that the absence of any insurrectionary spirit was, in itself, "one of the remarkable facts of American history," and Schouler, when considering the same question, wrote that American Negroes were "a black servile race, . . . brutish, obedient to the whip."

Yet, in order to see that all was not "sweetness and light" in the Southern states one can find countless instances of individual unrest and resistance, and a few uprisings organized on a sufficient scale to be called insurrections or revolts. The contemporary press and the historical archives of the states that were part of the slave-holding South are the best sources of such information. Despite the tendency of Southern newspapers to play down these stories, the black files of any such paper for the period from 1800 up to the time of the Civil War will reveal numerous accounts of homes or barns burned, of property damaged or destroyed, and instances of white masters beaten, or even murdered by their own slaves. A summary prepared by the state auditor of Virginia in 1831 shows that, between 1820 and 1831, the state paid out a total of $124,785 for 313 slaves who were either executed as criminals or were "transported" out of the state for acts judged to be criminal. Since, under existing law, the state was required to reimburse an owner for a slave executed or transported, and since neither of these actions could be taken without benefit of trial in a court of law, it can be assumed that the 313 slaves on the list had been judged guilty of serious crimes.

Three well-authenticated attempts at organized slave revolt took place in the first third of the nineteenth century. In 1800 there was the so-called "Gabriel's Insurrection" in Richmond. While the details of the plot have never been fully known, it is clear that a group of slaves living in and near the Virginia capital developed a plan to burn and sack the city and destroy its white inhabitants. Although discovered before any blow was actually struck, the conspiracy caused great excitement. Those believed to be the ringleaders were executed, the laws governing the conduct of slaves as well as of free black people were applied more severely, and the governor, James Monroe, wrote a special report on the matter for the Virginia Legislature.

In 1822 in Charleston, South Carolina, occurred what has come to be known as the "Denmark Vesey Plot." Vesey, who had been the slave of a sea-captain, had traveled abroad with his master and had learned to read and write. After purchasing his freedom, he became a respected black artisan in Charleston. In a plot that was revealed through slave informers, Vesey was accused along with a number of other black men, slave and free, of planning an insurrection and was executed. Again, no actual uprising took

"The Southampton Slave Revolt" by Henry F. Tragle. This article is reprinted from the November 1971 issue of *American History Illustrated* 6, pp. 4–11, 44–47, with the permission of Cowles History Group, Inc. Copyright *American History Illustrated* magazine.

place, but it seems clear that plans had been laid to organize a black rebellion which would have extended well into the interior of the state.

The most famous instance of this sort, and the only one which actually resulted in the deaths of a sizable number of white people, took place in an obscure backwater of Virginia, Southampton County, in August of 1831. Generally referred to as "The Southampton Insurrection," or "the servile insurrection of 1831," it has been called by one historian the "single instance of sustained revolt of slaves against their masters in American history." Whether this description is justified or not depends on the criteria one uses, but there is no question that the revolt led by the slave Nat Turner had a powerful and lasting effect on the institution of slavery throughout the entire South.

Interest in Turner as an individual has recently been intensified by a highly successful fictionalized version of his exploits, as well as by the growing interest in serious study of the culture and history of the American black man as a hitherto neglected aspect of the American heritage. Nat Turner, as symbol and folk hero, has figured frequently in fiction, poetry, and drama in the 140 years since 1831. Harriet Beecher Stowe, in her novel, *Dred,* which she published in 1856, used what little was known of Turner in shaping her principal character, and included as an appendix to her book a portion of the "Confession" which he is supposed to have made while awaiting trial in the Southampton jail. George Payne Rainsford James, a prolific novelist of the nineteenth century and Historiographer Royal to King William IV of England, published a novel in 1853 which he called *The Old Dominion.* The plot is based on what had taken place in Southampton County some twenty years earlier, and Nat Turner emerges as a kind of black mystic. James had served for a short time as British Consul in Norfolk, Virginia, and it is possible that during this period he heard the actual event discussed.

It is possible to reconstruct from contemporary records and the news stories of the time a reasonably accurate account of what happened during the period August 21 through November 11, 1831, on which date Nat Turner was executed. But we know little about the man himself and even less about his basic motivation. He was born the slave of Benjamin Turner on October 2, 1800. The Turner home, located about fifteen miles southwest of Jerusalem, the county seat of Southampton, was characteristic of the style of life which prevailed in that part of Virginia. Most of Southampton's white male citizens farmed small holdings, and only a handful of its most prosperous citizens owned more than twenty-five slaves. In 1830 its population totaled 16,074 of which 6,573 were white and 9,501 black. Jerusalem, the main town, had but 175 inhabitants. The county was unusual in one particular: a relatively high proportion of its black population, 1,745, were what were then known as "free men (or women) of color." This exception from the prevailing pattern in Southside Virginia was due in large part to the activity of the Quakers and the Emancipating Baptists, both of which sects had flourished in the area in the years following the Revolutionary War. Both had taken strong stands against slavery. Little is known about these free black people and their way of life, but it is safe to assume that their existence was marginal at best. Of the fifty persons eventually tried on suspicion of having taken part in the revolt, five of those arraigned were free black men.

Since blacks lived under a legal system which made it a felony to teach a slave to read or write, it is not surprising that illiteracy among them was almost universal. Yet Nat Turner was not only literate, he was known, by black and white alike, for his profound knowledge of the Bible. As surprising as the possession of these skills is the fact that he avoided attracting the serious attention of white members of the community, whose suspicion and animosity could be readily aroused by any signs of intelligence or ability on the part of a slave. Yet the lawyer who recorded his "Confessions," Thomas R. Gray, wrote this evaluation in the concluding lines of his account:

It has been said that he was ignorant and cowardly, and his object was to murder and rob for the purpose of obtaining money to make his escape. It is notorious that he was never known to have a dollar in his life, to swear an oath, or drink a drop of spirits. As to his ignorance, he certainly never had the advantages of an education, but he can read and write (it was taught him by his parents) and for natural intelligence and quickness of apprehension, is surpassed by few men I have ever seen.

There is no evidence that Nat Turner was a pampered house servant, or that, except for the austerity of his personal life and his habit of reading the Bible in every free moment, he was outwardly much different from any other able-bodied male slave in the county. After the revolt he was characterized in news stories as a "Black Preacher," but white persons in the neighborhood who knew him denied that he had even attended church regularly. When Benjamin Turner died in 1810, Nat passed into the ownership of a younger brother, Samuel, and at his death in 1822, was sold to a neighbor, one Thomas Moore. In his "Confessions," he speaks of having revelations from Heaven, and is quoted as saying, "these confirmed me in the impression that I was ordained for some great purpose in the hands of the Almighty." Speaking further to Gray of the influence he realized that he had obtained over the minds of his fellows in bondage, he said, "I now began to prepare them for my purpose, by telling them that something was about to happen that would terminate in fulfilling the great promise that had been made to me." But he makes it clear that at this point he himself was not aware of the nature of his mission.

Finally, according to his account, he had a vision on May 12, 1828, in which he "heard a loud noise in the heavens, and the Spirit instantly appeared to me and said . . . the time was fast approaching when the first should be last and the last should be first." In the same vision he was told that "until the first sign appeared, I should conceal it from the knowledge of men."

In the meantime, the ordinary round of life went on in Southampton County. Nat Turner's third owner, Thomas Moore, died in 1828 and his nominal ownership passed to Moore's nine-year-old son, Putnam. Within two years the Widow Moore married a local wheelwright, Joseph Travis, who moved into her house and set up his business on the place.

On February 12, 1831, there occurred an eclipse of the sun, and this came to Nat Turner as the sign he had been awaiting. In his words, "the seal was removed from my lips, and I communicated the great work laid out for me to do, to four in whom I had the greatest confidence, (Henry, Hark, Nelson and Sam)." Slaves, of course, had no patronymic. Because many shared the same given name, they generally used the last name of their owner, and when they changed owners, they usually changed names. Hark (who had also belonged to Thomas Moore) subsequently was spoken of as Hark Travis. Yet Nat Turner seemed always to remain Nat Turner. Also, in the trials that eventually ensued, the arraignment usually read "Hark, or Sam, or Jack, a man slave belonging to" so and so. Nat Turner was arraigned as "Nat, alias Nat Turner." He was even mentioned in one news story in a Richmond paper (and not in a facetious manner) as "Mr. Turner."

The first date chosen for the beginning of his "mission of work" was July 4, 1831, but he tells in his "Confessions" that this date had to be abandoned because "I fell sick." Then on August 13 there occurred a day-long atmospheric phenomenon, during which the sun was seen but faintly and appeared to be of a greenish hue. This occurrence, which caused wide-spread consternation in many places in the eastern United States, was accepted by Nat Turner as a direct communication from God. After alerting those whom he had originally chosen as his primary lieutenants, and recruiting two more, he arranged a meeting for Sunday, August 21, deep in the woods near the Travis homestead at a place called Cabin Pond.

The followers met first and roasted a pig and drank brandy. Later in the day Nat Turner appeared and explained the nature of his mission. It is significant that he is also quoted in the "Confessions" as saying, "we expected . . . to concert a plan, as we had not yet determined on any." This, and the fact that no physical preparations, such as the prior secreting of weapons or supplies had been undertaken, gives the impression that Turner saw himself purely as an instrument acting for a higher power which would provide all that was necessary when the time came.

The gist of the plan which emerged was nothing less than the destruction of every white person within reach; again in the words of the "Confessions," "we should commence at home (Mr. J. Travis') on that night, and until we had armed and equipped ourselves, and gathered sufficient force, neither age nor sex was to be spared. . . . "

Beginning at about two o'clock on the morning of Monday, August 22, the plan became reality. Leaving the site of the meeting, the group made its silent way through the woods to the Travis farm. Nat Turner ascended to a second-story window by means of a ladder, opened the door to the others, and they quickly disposed of Mr. and Mrs. Travis, their young child, Nat Turner's legal master, Putnam Moore, and a young apprentice, Joel Westbrook. Thus began the gory crusade, which was to lead in a long, S-shaped path toward the county seat. Having dispatched their first victims with axes and hatchets, they acquired weapons and horses as they went. By dawn, they had visited half a dozen homes and had killed more than twenty men, women, and children. Mounted now, they moved swiftly from house to house, gaining recruits as they went. But, probably to their surprise, many slaves on neighboring places either had to be forced at gunpoint to join them, and subsequently had to be guarded almost as hostages, or escaped and gave the alarm. When shortly after daybreak they began to find homes deserted, they realized that a warning had been spread.

The bloody details of the slayings which took approximately sixty lives were described at length in the Richmond and Norfolk newspapers in the days that followed. The stories appear to agree on several aspects which surprised the surviving white community; insofar as was ever known, no female victim was sexually molested, no wanton torture was inflicted, no buildings were burned, and—except for horses and weapons—relatively little in the way of personal property was taken.

At about nine o'clock they arrived at the home of Captain Thomas Barrow, a veteran of the War of 1812. Disdaining to flee, the Captain held off the entire band long enough to permit his wife to escape. According to a local legend, Captain Barrow's determined resistance so impressed his slayers that, having finally killed him by cutting his throat, they wrapped the body in a quilt and placed a plug of tobacco on his chest.

From the gateway of his farm, Barrow had built a road eastward for about five miles to a junction with the highway that ran south from Jerusalem to the North Carolina line. Still known locally as Barrow Road (and officially as County Highway 658), this was one of the few real roads in the county. Nat Turner and his men now followed it eastward, sowing death as they went. They probably numbered between forty and fifty at their peak, and all were mounted. If there is a monument to the Southampton Revolt, it is the Barrow Road itself.

Apples were a principal product of the county, and almost every homestead had its own still where brandy was made. As the day wore on, this potent spirit took its toll of some, but it seemed not to affect the determination of the eight or ten leaders who are responsible for most of the killing. One of the recruits who had joined while still at the Cabin Pond, Will, appears to have been the principal executioner. Most of his victims were decapitated by a razor-sharp axe. Strangely, according to Nat Turner's subsequent "Confessions," he dealt the death blow only once, and that to the young daughter of a Travis neighbor, Margaret Whitehead.

At Levi Waller's, the master of the house saw the band approaching and was able to conceal himself in a nearby field from which he watched the murder of his wife, his children, and a number of other children who attended a school at his homeplace. In all, eleven died at that one home, and their bodies were heaped in one room together. Levi Waller survived to appear as a witness at Nat Turner's trial. At William Williams' after killing the man of the house and his two children, the band caught Mrs. Williams and forced her to lie beside her dead husband, and then shot her. At Jacob Williams' house one of the original group, Nelson, was cheated of his intent to destroy his master, who was away from home, but Mrs. Williams, their two children, the wife of their overseer, Mrs. Caswell Worrell, and her child, as well as a visitor, Edwin Drewry, were left dead.

The final home visited, just about noontime, was that of Mrs. Rebecca Vaughan. Pleading vainly for her life, she was quickly dispatched, as were her niece, Eliza, her young son, Arthur, and their overseer. Although she did not know it, her older son, George, had fallen victim to the band when they encountered him earlier on the road leading to the Thomas Barrow homestead.

The Vaughan house lay close to the junction of the Barrow Road with the highway leading to the county seat, and again, in the words of Nat Turner's "Confessions," we learn that "here I determined on starting for Jerusalem." Presumably his goal was the local armory where weapons, powder, and shot were stored in abundance. In the aftermath, it was frequently speculated that Nat Turner intended to lead his band into the almost impenetrable fastness of the Dismal Swamp, some thirty miles distant; but this is never stated in his "Confessions."

Turning northeast at the crossroads, they rode toward Jerusalem. About half a mile from the junction lay the entrance to James Parker's farm. Some of the participants had friends here, who they thought would join them, and they probably also thought that weapons, and possibly additional brandy, could be obtained there. Apparently against his better judgment, Nat Turner had the party divide, some going toward the Parker house, from which the family had fled, while a small group including Turner himself stayed at the entrance to the farm.

Suddenly a detachment of militia rode into view. They had been tardily assembled when the alarm reached Jerusalem, and here, in Parker's cornfield, the first armed confrontation took place between the slaves in revolt and their embattled masters. Apparently there were no fatalities on either side, and after an exchange of shots, and a few wounds being inflicted, they broke off contact. But Nat Turner realized that the road to Jerusalem was effectively barred. His force was thrown into confusion by the encounter, was reduced in numbers, and now was much harder to manage. He resolved to try a crossing of the Nottaway River, which lay between him and the town, at a point to the east, Cypress Bridge, but a quick reconnaissance showed it to be well guarded.

Gathering the remnants of his force he turned south, seeking recruits. Discouraged by the obvious evidence that the countryside was now alarmed, he turned north again, crossed the path he had followed earlier, and holed up for the night, with a force of forty or fewer, near the Ridley plantation. During the night a false alarm scared off more than half of his remaining followers.

At dawn on Tuesday, August 23, the last blow of the revolt was struck. Probably believing that the residents had already fled "Belmont," the home of Dr. Simon Blunt, the band entered the lane leading from the main road. Close to the house they were met with withering fire from the doctor, his son, the overseer, and three white neighbors, who, rather than fleeing, had barricaded themselves in the house. At least one of Turner's men fell dead, and several including his principal lieutenant, Hark, were wounded. Blunt's own slaves, having hidden in an out-building, now rallied to the defense of their master and aided in the capture of the wounded and the unhorsed. Nat Turner escaped with a handful of the faithful.

Deciding to return to the vicinity of their starting point, they were met by militia along the Barrow Road. One or more were killed and by late afternoon, Nat Turner found himself alone, a fugitive pursued not only by the aroused citizenry of the county but by a horde of vigilantes from adjoining Virginia and North Carolina counties and by various military forces which had begun to arrive in response to appeals for help.

On Monday, when word of the trouble in the southwestern part of the county reached

Jerusalem, the postmaster, James Trezevant, sent a letter by express rider to the mayor of Petersburg, some fifty miles away. This was relayed to Governor John Floyd in Richmond, who received it in the early morning hours of Tuesday, the 24th. He quickly ordered armed militia units to the scene, and arranged for weapons and supplies to be sent as rapidly as possible. Floyd, a veteran of the War of 1812 and a brigadier general in the militia, immediately considered the possibility that what was happening in Southampton could be the prelude to a general slave uprising. For this reason, together with others related to the prestige of the State, he refrained from asking for help from the Federal forces stationed at Fort Monroe, just across Hampton Roads from Norfolk.

However, word of what was happening had reached Norfolk by means of the regular stagecoach, and the mayor, backed by the city council, decided to call for Federal help. No possibility existed for communication with the state authorities in Richmond, so very soon a request had gone to Colonel House at Fort Monroe, to the commander of the United States Naval yard, and to two ships of war lying in the Roads. Within a matter of hours, a joint force of regular army troops, marines, and sailors was alerted and on their way to Southampton. As it turned out, the revolt was quelled before any of the Federal forces could participate and most were turned around and returned to their stations without reaching the site of the action. Governor Floyd, eventually learning of the precipitate action by Norfolk's mayor, was furious. He felt that the psychological impression which the call-out had created was bad. He also pointed out that, had the uprising been of a general character, drawing off the available Federal force from Fort Monroe would have left the area on the north bank of the James River, including numerous plantations and settlements where the blacks outnumbered the whites, entirely without possibility of reinforcement.

But the lot of the innocent blacks in Southampton County itself might have been better if Federal forces had taken charge. As it was, once the scare was over and the true nature of the

Nat Turner's 1831 revolt, be it just or unjust, had a significant impact on slavery throughout the South, and brought the issue of slavery to the attention of the nation.

threat ascertained, the life of every black person in the country was threatened. The spirit of revenge and retaliation ran wild. The editor of one Richmond newspaper, who went as a member of a militia troop of cavalry to the scene, wrote:

It is with pain we speak of another feature of the Southampton Rebellion; for we have been most unwilling to have our sympathies for the sufferers diminished or affected by their misconduct. We allude to the slaughter of many blacks, without trial, and under circumstances of great barbarity.

The militia commander placed in charge by Governor Floyd, Brigadier General Richard Eppes, finally found it necessary to threaten to invoke the Articles of War to halt the indiscriminate slaughter.

Most of those involved were either killed or rounded up. In the meantime, the fear of an uprising had spread to neighboring counties in Virginia and North Carolina. It is impossible to estimate how many innocent blacks paid with their lives for no more than the merest suspicion. For example, a group of citizens from Sampson County in North Carolina, wrote to the governor to report that they had "ten or fifteen Negroes in Jail," and in passing noted that "the people of Duplin County have examined ten or fifteen Negroes, and found two guilty, and have put them to death." It was not even suggested that any of those jailed or executed were known to have participated in any type of threatening action.

Trials began in the Southampton Court of Oyer and Terminer on August 31 and continued into November. During this period more than twenty slaves, including one woman and three boys of less than fifteen years, were convicted and sentenced to death. Some of the sentences were subsequently reduced by the governor to transportation out of the state. All of those who had been part of Nat Turner's original band were either killed in the aftermath of the revolt, or were subsequently executed. Estimates of the number who were killed without trial run to more than one hundred. In many instances, the only witnesses for the prosecution were fellow-slaves of the accused, some of whom were subsequently to go to the gallows.

Through all this, the question remained, "What had become of Nat Turner?" Despite search by several thousand militiamen, augmented by volunteer vigilantes from all over the area, the leader eluded capture. There were almost daily reports that he had been sighted; by one mail, the governor was informed that he had been taken prisoner in Washington; a few days later he was reported to have drowned while trying to escape capture in the western part of the state. On September 14, Floyd proclaimed a reward of $500 for his capture, and persons in the area increased this by another $600. Yet all this time "General Nat," as the papers frequently called him, was hiding no more than a mile from the place of original assembly at Cabin Pond. Having secured a small stock of food, he scratched a tiny "cave" under a pile of fence rails where he remained concealed for more than four weeks. Later, after two frightened slaves had stumbled onto this hiding place, he concealed himself in a haystack and then moved to the shelter of a hole beneath the branches of a fallen pine tree.

Finally, on October 30, when most of his companions had already been executed or shipped out of the state, he was discovered by a local white man, Benjamin Phipps. Armed only with a small sword, he surrendered and was turned over to the Southampton County jailor the next day. It was while awaiting trial that he agreed to talk with Thomas R. Gray. These "Confessions," which Gray is supposed to have taken down verbatim, were recorded on the 1st, 2nd, and 3rd of November. Gray is frequently referred to as Nat Turner's counsel at his trial, which took place on November 5. Actually he had no official connection with the case. It seems more likely that, as a local lawyer who had served as court-appointed counsel for some of those tried earlier, and who was familiar with all that had happened, he saw the considerable commercial possibilities in converting Nat Turner's story into a pamphlet. This is what he did, and very speedily. The twenty-three page document, authenticated by a certificate of the justices of the court, and containing lists of the white people who had been killed and all of the persons tried up to that time, was copyrighted by Gray in Washington on November 10, just one day before Nat Turner was, according to the sentence of the court, "taken by the Sheriff to the usual place of execution, and there . . . hanged by the neck until he be dead."

About ten days later the pamphlet was published in Baltimore, and the accuracy of Gray's estimate of public interest in the matter can be gauged by the fact that several other editions were subsequently printed, and it is said to have sold more than 40,000 copies. Yet today copies of the original pamphlet are very rare. A Norfolk newspaper wrote that a "portrait painter" of that town had made a likeness of Nat Turner while in jail. Pictures purporting to depict Nat Turner have been published, but it has never been established that any of these were drawn from life.

Governor Floyd was convinced, despite the lack of any real evidence, that the revolt was part of a larger plot which extended to many areas of the South. He also felt that the relative freedom which had been accorded black preachers as well as such abolitionist writings as Garrison's *Liberator* and Walker's *Appeal* had been part of the root cause. A resident of western Virginia, he favored the abolition of slavery, provided it was coupled with a removal of all black people from the state. His sentiments were not so much an expression of humanitarian feelings, as they were a conviction that Virginia could make no real economic progress while burdened with "the peculiar institution."

From letters to the newspapers during the fall of 1831, it can be readily seen that Floyd's views were widely shared. During November he wrote in his diary, "Before I leave this Government, I will have contrived to have a law passed gradually abolishing slavery in the State. . . ." Yet the message which he sent to the newly assembled legislature on December 6 contained no such proposal. Instead, after a lengthy review of the revolt and an analysis of what he believed to be its causes, he proposed the enactment of extremely stern laws which would apply to all of the state's black people, slave and free alike.

Between December 1831 and February 1832, the whole question of slavery was hotly debated by the legislature, and a resolution supporting emancipation failed by a very narrow margin. This debate, which engaged some of the best minds of the state, and which attracted wide attention, has been called the last free and uninhibited discussion of the question of slavery in any Southern legislative body. But once the vote was taken, those who had favored emancipation seemed to fade away. Floyd's biographer, Charles Ambler, explains the Governor's attitude in this way:

Absorbed as he was in national affairs, Floyd was perfectly willing to turn the whole subject of the state's proper policy regarding negro slavery over to the solution of a master who was at hand in the person of Thomas R. Dew of William and Mary College. . . . The able defense and justification of the institution of negro slavery which followed was accepted by Floyd and most other Virginians of whatever section as final.

In the end we are left with the question of the net effect of Nat Turner's actions on the institution of slavery itself. Did it hasten or retard the thrust toward emancipation? Herbert Aptheker, one of those who has written much on the subject concludes that "The Turner Revolt may be summed up by the one word accelerator." Probably the best assessment is that of John W. Cromwell, a black historian and lawyer, who saw the final results in this fashion:

Whether Nat Turner hastened or postponed the day of the abolition of slavery . . . is a question that admits of little or much discussion in accordance with opinions concerning the law of necessity and free will in national life. Considered in the light of its immediate effects upon its participants, it was a failure, an egregious failure, a wanton crime. Considered in its relation to slavery and as contributory to making it a national issue by deepening and stirring of the then weak local forces, that finally led to the Emancipation Proclamation and the Thirteenth Amendment, the insurrection was a moral success and Nat Turner deserves to be ranked with the great reformers of his day.

Study Questions

1. Nat Turner was not a "typical" Virginia slave. In what ways was he different?

2. In what ways was the black population of Southampton County unique? How might those unique demographic circumstances have contributed to white and black attitudes about slavery there?

3. In your opinion, was Nat Turner "crazy"? Explain your answer.

4. What was the white reaction to the slave uprising? How did the uprising affect the lives of the rest of the blacks—slave and free—in Southampton County?

5. Why did the slave uprising create an intense debate in Virginia about freeing all of the slaves? Why, in your opinion, did that emancipation movement fail?

Bibliography

William Styron's *The Confessions of Nat Turner* (1968), a novel based on Turner's confession to Thomas Gray, remains a highly readable, if controversial, account of the 1831 rebellion. For a history of the rebellion, see Stephen B. Oates, *The Fires of Jubilee: Nat Turner's Fierce Rebellion* (1975). For general histories of slave rebellions, see the highly polemical *American Negro Slave Revolts* (1943) by Herbert Aptheker and the more balanced *From Rebellion to Revolution: Afro-American Slave Revolts in the Making of the Modern World* (1979) by Eugene D. Genovese. Also see Gerald Mullin, *Flight and Rebellion: Slave Resistance in Eighteenth-Century Virginia* (1972). Some of the best descriptions of slavery come from slaves themselves. See Charles T. Davis and Henry Louis, *The Slave's Narrative* (1985) and Paul D. Escott, *Slavery Remembered: A Record of Twentieth-Century Slave Narratives* (1979). Also see John Blassingame, *The Slave Community* (1979); Eugene Genovese, *Roll, Jordan, Roll: The World the Slaves Made* (1974); Randolph B. Campbell, *An Empire for Slavery: The Peculiar Institution in Texas, 1821–1865* (1989); Paul Kolchin, *American Slavery, 1619–1877* (1993). For the most recent contributions to the literature of the Southampton rebellion, see Mary Kemp Davis, *Nat Turner Before the Bar of Judgment: Fictional Treatments of the Southampton Slave Insurrection* (1999) and Kenneth S. Greenburg, *Nat Turner: A Slave Rebellion in History and Memory* (2003).

READING 27

Notes on Mormon Polygamy

Stanley S. Ivins

Upstate New York in the 1820s was a "burned-over district" according to one historian because of all the "hell-fire and damnation" preaching going on by competing Protestant denominations. Religion was a topic dear to most people's hearts as they contemplated the salvation or damnation of souls. Near Palmyra, New York, a confused young man, troubled by religious contention, decided to ask God for direct and complete answers to his questions about religion. After offering such a prayer, fourteen-year-old Joseph Smith, Jr., claimed to have been visited by two angelic beings. Identifying themselves as God the Father and Jesus Christ, they told him to join none of the churches and to wait for further instruction. Three years later Smith said he had been visited by an angel who had left him responsible for translating a historical record, engraved on golden plates, of the ancient inhabitants of the American continent. That translation was published in 1829 as the *Book of Mormon,* and the Church of Jesus Christ of Latter-day Saints was organized in 1830.

Under the charismatic leadership of Joseph Smith, the young church grew rapidly in the 1830s and 1840s, and encountered persecution in direct proportion to its success. Their internal cohesiveness and tendency to vote as a bloc usually embittered their neighbors, and the practice of polygamy, introduced by Joseph Smith in the late 1830s, enraged American society. Driven from Ohio and Missouri, the Mormons settled in southern Illinois in 1839. When Joseph Smith was assassinated in 1844, Brigham Young assumed leadership of the Mormons, and in 1846–1847 he led them on an extraordinary journey across the continent to the valley of the Great Salt Lake in present-day Utah. Free of persecution, the Mormons thrived, accepting tens of thousands of converts and colonizing new regions in southern Utah, Nevada, southern California, Idaho, Arizona, and Wyoming.

But for the next half-century, the practice of polygamy created a national uproar as well as a crusade against the Mormons involving an invasion of Utah by the United States Army in 1857, federal antipolygamy laws, and mass jailings of Mormon leaders. In the process, a series of myths about the Mormon practice of polygamy became firmly entrenched in the public mind. In "Notes on Mormon Polygamy," Stanley Ivins describes polygamous marriages in Utah during the nineteenth century.

Time was when, in the popular mind, Mormonism meant only polygamy. It was assumed that every Mormon man was a practical or theoretical polygamist. This was a misconception, like the widespread belief that Mormons grew horns, for there were always many of these Latter-day Saints who refused to go along with the doctrine of "plurality of wives." It was accepted by only a few of the more than fifty churches or factions which grew out of the revelations of the prophet Joseph Smith. Principal advocate of the doctrine was the Utah church, which far outnumbered all other branches of Mormonism. And strongest opposition from within Mormondom came from the second largest group, the Reorganized Church of Jesus Christ of Latter-day Saints, with headquarters at Independence, Missouri.

This strange experiment in family relations extended over a period of approximately sixty-five years. It was professedly inaugurated on April 5, 1841, in a cornfield outside the city of Nauvoo, Illinois, with the sealing of Louisa Beeman to Joseph Smith. And it was brought to an official end by a resolution adopted at the seventy-fourth Annual Conference of the Utah church, on April 4, 1904. Since that time, those who have persisted in carrying on with it have been excommunicated. But the project was openly and energetically prosecuted during only about forty years. For the first ten years the new doctrine was kept pretty well under wraps, and it was not until the fall of 1852 that it was openly avowed and the Saints were told that only those who embraced it could hope for the highest exaltation in the resurrection. And during the fifteen years prior to 1904, there were only a few privately solemnized plural marriages. So it might be said that the experiment was ten years in embryo, enjoyed a vigorous life of forty years, and took fifteen years to die.

The extent to which polygamy was practiced in Utah will probably never be known. Plural marriages were not publicly recorded, and there is lit-tle chance that any private records which might have been kept will ever be revealed.

Curious visitors to Utah in the days when polygamy was flourishing were usually told that about one-tenth of the people actually practiced it. Since the abandonment of the principle this estimate has been revised downward. A recent official published statement by the Mormon church said: "The practice of plural marriage has never been general in the Church and at no time have more than 3 percent of families in the Church been polygamous." This estimate was apparently based upon testimony given during the investigation into the right of Reed Smoot to retain his seat in the United States Senate. A high church official, testifying there, referred to the 1882 report of the Utah Commission, which said that application of the antipolygamy laws had disfranchised approximately 12,000 persons in Utah. The witness declared that, since at least two-thirds of these must have been women, there remained no more than 4,000 polygamists, which he believed constituted less than 2 percent of the church population. The error of setting heads of families against total church membership is obvious. Using the same report, Senator Dubois concluded that 23 percent of Utah Mormons over eighteen years of age were involved in polygamy. Later on in the Smoot hearing the same church official testified that a careful census, taken in 1890, revealed that there were 2,451 plural families in the United States. This suggests that, at that time, 10 percent or more of the Utah Mormons might have been involved in polygamy.

Of more than 6,000 Mormon families, sketches of which are found in a huge volume published in 1913, between 15 and 20 percent appear to have been polygamous. And a history of Sanpete and Emery counties contains biographical sketches of 722 men, of whom 12.6 percent married more than one woman.

From information obtainable from all available sources, it appears that there may have been a time when 15, or possibly 20, percent of the Mormon families of Utah were polygamous. This leaves the great majority of the Saints delinquent in their obligation to the principle of plurality of wives.

"Notes on Mormon Polygamy" by Stanley S. Ivins in *Western Humanities Review,* X (Summer 1956), pp. 229–39. Reprinted by permission of *Western Humanities Review.*

While the small proportion of Mormons who went into polygamy may not necessarily be a true measure of its popularity, there is other evidence that they were not anxious to rush into it, although they were constantly reminded of its importance to their salvation.

A tabulation, by years, of about 2,500 polygamous marriages, covering the whole period of this experiment, reveals some interesting facts. It indicates that, until the death of prophet Joseph Smith in the summer of 1844, the privilege of taking extra wives was pretty well monopolized by him and a few of his trusted disciples. Following his death and the assumption of leadership by the Twelve Apostles under Brigham Young, there was a noticeable increase in plural marriages. This may be accounted for by the fact that, during the winter of 1845–1846, the Nauvoo Temple was finished to a point where it could be used for the performance of sacred rites and ordinances. For a few weeks before their departure in search of a refuge in the Rocky Mountains, the Saints worked feverishly at their sealings and endowments. As part of this religious activity, the rate of polygamous marrying rose to a point it was not again to reach for ten years. It then fell off sharply and remained low until the stimulation given by the public announcement, in the fall of 1852, that polygamy was an essential tenet of the church. This spurt was followed by a sharp decline over the next few years.

Beginning in the fall of 1856 and during a good part of the following year, the Utah Mormons were engaged in the greatest religious revival of their history. To the fiery and sometimes intemperate exhortations of their leaders, they responded with fanatical enthusiasm, which at times led to acts of violence against those who were slow to repent. There was a general confession of sins and renewal of covenants through baptism, people hastened to return articles "borrowed" from their neighbors, and men who had not before given a thought to the matter began looking for new wives. And, as one of the fruits of the Reformation, plural marriages skyrocketed to a height not before approached and never again

to be reached. If our tabulation is a true index, there were 65 percent more of such marriages during 1856 and 1857 than in any other two years of this experiment.

With the waning of the spirit of reformation, the rate of polygamous marrying dropped in 1858 to less than a third and in 1859 to less than a fifth of what it was in 1857. This decline continued until 1862, when Congress, responding to the clamor of alarmists, enacted a law prohibiting bigamy in Utah and other territories. The answer of the Mormons to this rebuke was a revival of plural marrying to a point not previously reached except during the gala years of the Reformation.

The next noticeable acceleration in the marriage rate came in 1868 and 1869 and coincided with the inauguration of a boycott against the Gentile merchants and the organization of an anti-Mormon political party. But this increased activity was short-lived and was followed by a slump lasting for a dozen years. By 1881 polygamous marrying had fallen to almost its lowest ebb since the public avowal of the doctrine of plurality.

With the passage of the Edmunds Act of 1882, which greatly strengthened the antipolygamy laws, the government began its first serious effort to suppress the practice of polygamy. The Mormons responded with their last major revival of polygamous activity, which reached its height in 1884 and 1885. But, with hundreds of polygamists imprisoned and most of the church leaders driven into exile to avoid arrest, resistance weakened and there was a sudden decline in marriages, which culminated in formal capitulation in the fall of 1890. This was the end, except for a few undercover marriages during the ensuing fifteen years, while the experiment was in its death throes.

* * *

If there is any significance in this chronicle of polygamous marrying, it is in the lack of evidence that the steady growth of the Utah church was accompanied by a corresponding increase in the number of such marriages. The story is rather one of sporadic outbursts of enthusiasm, followed by relapses, with the proportion of the Saints living in polygamy steadily falling. And it

Fleeing persecution, Mormons traveled west and settled in Utah. By the 1850s Mormons could no longer afford draft animals; nevertheless, they crossed the prairies and the Rockies drawing two-wheeled handcarts.

appears to be more than chance that each outbreak of fervor coincided with some revivalist activity within the church or with some menace from without. It is evident that, far from looking upon plural marriage as a privilege to be made the most of, the rank and file Mormons accepted it as one of the onerous obligations of church membership. Left alone, they were prone to neglect it, and it always took some form of pressure to stir them to renewed zeal.

The number of wives married by the men who practiced polygamy offers further evidence of lack of enthusiasm for the principle. A common mistaken notion was that most polygamists maintained large harems, an idea which can be attributed to the publicity given the few men who went in for marrying on a grand scale. Joseph Smith was

probably the most married of these men. The number of his wives can only be guessed at, but it might have gone as high as sixty or more. Brigham Young is usually credited with only twenty-seven wives, but he was sealed to more than twice that many living women, and to at least 150 more who had died. Heber C. Kimball had forty-five living wives, a number of them elderly ladies who never lived with him. No one else came close to these three men in the point of marrying. John D. Lee gave the names of his nineteen wives, but modestly explained that, "as I was married to old Mrs. Woolsey for her soul's sake, and she was near sixty years old when I married her, I never considered her really a wife. . . . That is the reason that I claim only eighteen true wives." And by taking fourteen wives, Jens Hansen earned special mention in the *Latter-day Saint Biographical Encyclopedia,* which said: "Of all the Scandinavian brethren who figured prominently in the Church Bro. Hansen distinguished himself by marrying more wives than any other of his countrymen in modern times." Orson Pratt, who was chosen to deliver the first public discourse on the subject of plural marriage and became its most able defender, had only ten living wives, but on two days, a week apart, he was sealed for eternity to more than two hundred dead women.

But these men with many wives were the few exceptions to the rule. Of 1,784 polygamists, 66.3 percent married only one extra wife. Another 21.2 percent were three-wife men, and 6.7 percent went as far as to take four wives. This left a small group of less than 6 percent who married five or more women. The typical polygamist, far from being the insatiable male of popular fable, was a dispassionate fellow, content to call a halt after marrying the one extra wife required to assure him of his chance at salvation.

Another false conception was that polygamists were bearded patriarchs who continued marrying young girls as long as they were able to hobble about. It is true that Brigham Young took a young wife when he was sixty-seven years old and a few others followed his example, but such marriages were not much more common with Mormons than among other groups. Of 1,229 polygamists, more than 10 percent married their last wives while still in their twenties, and more than one half of them before arriving at the still lusty age of forty years. Not one in five took a wife after reaching his fiftieth year. The average age at which the group ceased marrying was forty years.

There appears to be more basis in fact for the reports that polygamists were likely to choose their wives from among the young girls who might bear them many children. Of 1,348 women selected as plural wives, 38 percent were in their teens, 67 percent were under twenty-five and only 30 percent over thirty years of age. A few had passed forty and about one in a hundred had, like John D. Lee's old Mrs. Woolsey, seen her fiftieth birthday.

There were a few notable instances of high-speed marrying among the polygamists. Whatever the number of Joseph Smith's wives, he must have married them all over a period of thirty-nine months. And Brigham Young took eight wives in a single month, four of them on the same day. But only a few enthusiasts indulged in such rapid marrying. As a rule it proceeded at a much less hurried pace. Not one plural marriage in ten followed a previous marriage by less than a year. The composite polygamist was first married at the age of twenty-three to a girl of twenty. Thirteen years later he took a plural wife, choosing a twenty-two-year-old girl. The chances were two to one that, having demonstrated his acceptance of the principle of plurality, he was finished with marrying. If, however, he took a third wife, he waited four years, then selected another girl of twenty-two. The odds were now three to one against his taking a fourth wife, but if he did so, he waited another four years, and once more chose a twenty-two-year-old girl, although he had now reached the ripe age of forty-four. In case he decided to add a fifth wife, he waited only two years, and this time the lady of his choice was twenty-one years old. This was the end of his marrying, unless he belonged to a 3 percent minority.

Available records offer no corroboration of the accusation that many polygamous marriages were incestuous. They do, however, suggest the source of such reports, in the surprisingly common practice of marrying sisters. The custom was initiated by Joseph Smith, among whose wives were at least three pairs of sisters. His example was followed by Heber C. Kimball, whose forty-five wives included Clarissa and Emily Cutler, Amanda and Anna Gheen, Harriet and Ellen Sanders, Hannah and Dorothy Moon, and Laura and Abigail Pitkin. Brigham Young honored the precedent by marrying the Decker sisters, Lucy and Clara, and the Bigelow girls, Mary and Lucy. And John D. Lee told how he married the three Woolsey sisters, Agatha Ann, Rachel, and Andora, and rounded out the family circle by having their mother sealed to him for her soul's sake. Among his other wives were the Young sisters, Polly and Lovina, sealed to him on the same evening. The popularity of this custom is indicated by the fact that of 1,642 polygamists, 10 percent married one or more pairs of sisters.

While marrying sisters could have been a simple matter of propinquity, there probably was some method in it. Many a man went into polygamy reluctantly, fully aware of its hazards. Knowing that his double family must live in one small home, and realizing that the peace of his household would hinge upon the congeniality between its two mistresses, he might well hope that if they were sisters the chances for domestic tranquility would be more even. And a wife, consenting to share her husband with another, could not be blamed for asking that he choose her sister, instead of bringing home a strange woman.

* * *

The fruits of this experiment in polygamy are not easy to appraise. In defense of their marriage system, the Mormons talked much about the benefits it would bring. By depriving husbands of an excuse for seeking extramarital pleasure, and by making it possible for every woman to marry, it was to solve the problem of the "social evil" by eliminating professional prostitution and other adulterous activities. It was to furnish healthy tabernacles for the countless spirits, waiting anxiously to assume their earthly bodies. It was to build up a "righteous generation" of physically and intellectually superior individuals. It was to enhance the glory of the polygamist through a posterity so numerous that, in the course of eternity, he might become the god of a world peopled by his descendants. And there was another blessing in store for men who lived this principle. Heber C. Kimball, Brigham Young's chief lieutenant, explained it this way:

I would not be afraid to promise a man who is sixty years of age, if he will take the counsel of brother Brigham and his brethren, that he will renew his age. I have noticed that a man who has but one wife, and is inclined to that doctrine, soon begins to wither and dry up, while a man who goes into plurality looks fresh,

young and sprightly. Why is this? Because God loves that man, and because he honors His work and word. Some of you may not believe this; but I not only believe it—I also know it. For a man of God to be confined to one woman is small business; for it is as much as we can do now to keep up under the burdens we have to carry; and I do not know what we should do if we had only one wife apiece.

It does appear that Mormon communities of the polygamous era were comparatively free from the evils of professional prostitution. But this can hardly be attributed to the fact that a few men, supposedly selected for their moral superiority, were permitted to marry more than one wife. It might better be credited to the common teaching that adultery was a sin so monstrous that there was no atonement for it short of the spilling of the blood of the offender. It would be strange indeed if such a fearful warning failed to exert a restraining influence upon the potential adulterer.

There is, of course, nothing unsound in the theory that a community of superior people might be propagated by selecting the highest ranking males and having them reproduce themselves in large numbers. The difficulty here would be to find a scientific basis for the selection of the favored males. And there is no information from which an opinion can be arrived at as to the results which were obtained in this respect.

When it came to fathering large families and supplying bodies for waiting spirits, the polygamists did fairly well, but fell far short of some of their dreams. Heber C. Kimball once said of himself and Brigham Young: "In twenty-five or thirty years we will have a larger number in our two families than there now is in this whole Territory, which numbers more than seventy-five thousand. If twenty-five years will produce this amount of people, how much will be the increase in one hundred years?" And the *Millennial Star* reckoned that a hypothetical Mr. Fruitful, with forty wives, might, at the age of seventy-eight, number among his seed 3,508,441 souls, while his monogamous counterpart could boast of only 152.

With such reminders of their potentialities before them, the most married of the polygamists must have been far from satisfied with the results they could show. There is no conclusive evidence that any of Joseph Smith's many plural wives bore children by him. Heber C. Kimball, with his forty-five wives, was the father of sixty-five children. John D. Lee, with only eighteen "true wives," fell one short of Kimball's record, and Brigham Young fathered fifty-six children, approximately one for each wife.

Although the issue of the few men of many wives was disappointing in numbers, the rank and file of polygamists made a fair showing. Of 1,651 families, more than four-fifths numbered ten or more children. Half of them had fifteen or more and one-fourth, twenty or more. There were eighty-eight families of thirty or more, nineteen of forty or more, and seven of fifty or more. The average number of children per family was fifteen. And by the third or fourth generation some families had reached rather impressive proportions. When one six-wife elder had been dead fifty-five years, his descendants numbered 1,900.

While polygamy increased the number of children of the men, it did not do the same for the women involved. A count revealed that 3,335 wives of polygamists bore 19,806 children, for an average of 5.9 per woman. An equal number of wives of monogamists, taken from the same general group, bore 26,780 for an average of eight. This suggests the possibility that the overall production of children in Utah may have been less than it would have been without the benefit of plurality of wives. The claim that plurality was needed because of a surplus of women is not borne out by statistics.

There is little doubt that the plural wife system went a good way toward making it possible for every woman to marry. According to Mormon teachings a woman could "never obtain a fullness of glory, without being married to a righteous man for time and all eternity." If she never married or was the wife of a Gentile, her chance of attaining a high degree of salvation was indeed slim. And one of the responsibilities of those in official church positions was to try to make sure that no woman went without a husband. When a widow or a maiden lady "gathered" to Utah, it was a community obligation to see to it that she had food and shelter and the privilege of being married to a good man. If she received no offer of marriage, it was not considered inconsistent with feminine modesty for her to "apply" to the man of her choice, but if she set her sights too high she might be disappointed. My grandmother, who did sewing for the family of Brigham Young, was fond of telling how she watched through a partly open doorway while he forcibly ejected a woman who was too persistent in applying to be sealed to him. Her story would always end with the same words: "And I just couldn't help laughing to see brother Brigham get so out of patience with that woman." However, if the lady in search of a husband was not too ambitious, her chances of success were good. It was said of the bishop of one small settlement that he "was a good bishop. He married all the widows in town and took good care of them." And John D. Lee was following accepted precedent when he married old Mrs. Woolsey for her soul's sake.

As for Mr. Kimball's claims concerning the spiritual uplift to be derived from taking a fresh, young wife, what man is going to quarrel with him about that?

* * *

The most common reasons given for opposition to the plural wife system were that it was not compatible with the American way of life, that it debased the women who lived under it, and that it caused disharmony and unhappiness in the family. To these charges the Mormons replied that their women enjoyed a higher social position than those of the outside world, and that there was less contention and unhappiness in their families than in those of the Gentiles. There is no statistical information upon which to base a judgment as to who had the better of this argument.

In addition to these general complaints against polygamy, its critics told some fantastic stories about the evils which followed in its wake. It was said that, through some mysterious workings of the laws of heredity, polygamous children were born with such peculiarities as feeblemindedness, abnormal sexual desires, and weak and deformed bodies.

At a meeting of the New Orleans Academy of Sciences in 1861, a remarkable paper was presented by Dr. Samuel A. Cartwright and Prof. C. G. Forshey. It consisted mainly of quotations from a report made by Assistant Surgeon Robert Barthelow of the United States Army on the "Effects and Tendencies of Mormon Polygamy in the Territory of Utah." Barthelow had observed that the Mormon system of marriage was already producing a people with distinct racial characteristics. He said:

The yellow, sunken, cadaverous visage; the greenish-colored eye; the thick, protuberant lips; the low forehead; the light, yellowish hair, and the lank, angular person, constitute an appearance so characteristic of the new race, the production of polygamy, as to distinguish them at a glance. The older men and women present all the physical peculiarities of the nationalities to which they belong; but these peculiarities are not propagated and continued in the new race; they are lost in the prevailing type.

Dr. Cartwright observed that the Barthelow report went far "to prove that polygamy not only blights the physical organism, but the moral nature of the white or Adamic woman to so great a degree as to render her incapable of breeding any other than abortive specimens of humanity—a new race that would die out—utterly perish from the earth, if left to sustain itself."

When one or two of the New Orleans scientists questioned the soundness of parts of this paper, the hecklers were silenced by Dr. Cartwright's retort that the facts presented were not so strong as "those which might be brought in

proof of the debasing influence of abolitionism on the moral principles and character of that portion of the Northern people who have enacted personal liberty bills to evade a compliance with their constitutional obligations to the Southern States, and have elevated the Poltroon Sumner into a hero, and made a Saint of the miscreant Brown."

Needless to say there is no evidence that polygamy produced any such physical and mental effects upon the progeny of those who practiced it. A study of the infant mortality rate in a large number of Mormon families showed no difference between the polygamous and monogamous households.

It is difficult to arrive at general conclusions concerning this experiment in polygamy, but a few facts about it are evident. Mormondom was not a society in which all men married many wives, but one in which a few men married two or more wives. Although plurality of wives was taught as a tenet of the church, it was not one of the fundamental principles of the Mormon faith, and its abandonment was accomplished with less disturbance than that caused by its introduction. The Saints accepted plurality in theory, but most of them were loath to put it into practice, despite the continual urging of leaders in whose divine authority they had the utmost faith. Once the initial impetus given the venture had subsided it became increasingly unpopular. In 1857 there were nearly fourteen times as many plural marriages for each one thousand Utah Mormons as there were in 1880. Left to itself, undisturbed by pressure from without, the church would inevitably have given up the practice of polygamy, perhaps even sooner than it did under pressure. The experiment was not a satisfactory test of plurality of wives as a social system. Its results were neither spectacular nor conclusive, and they gave little justification for either the high hopes of its promoters or the dire predictions of its critics.

Study Questions

1. List the basic myths surrounding the Mormon practice of polygamy and then describe the social reality of each idea.

2. Ivins feels that the practice of polygamy was really not that popular among the Mormons. What evidence does he use to support that idea?

3. How important was polygamy as a religious principle among the Mormons? What was the relationship between the "Reformation" and the practice of polygamy?

4. What did Mormons believe about the social and spiritual benefits of polygamy?

5. How did the non-Mormon public in the nineteenth century view polygamy? What did they believe about the consequences of polygamy? Why did they have such attitudes?

Bibliography

The classic study of Mormon settlement in the Intermountain West is Leonard Arrington, *Great Basin Kingdom: An Economic History of the Latter-day Saints, 1830–1900* (1958). An early sociological study of the Mormon faith is Thomas F. O'Dea, *The Mormons* (1957). The best survey history of the Mormon Church is James B. Allen and Glen M. Leonard, *The Story of the Latter-day Saints* (1976). For background material to the founding of the Mormon Church, see Whitney Cross, *The Burned-over District* (1950). For biographies of Joseph Smith, see Fawn Brodie, *No Man Knows My History: The Life of Joseph Smith, the Mormon Prophet* (1946) and Donna Hill, *Joseph Smith, The Mormon Prophet* (1977). The drama of the Mormon trek west is described in Wallace R. Stegner, *The Gathering of Zion: The Story of the Mormon Trail* (1964). Robert Flanders, *Nauvoo: Kingdom on the Mississippi* (1965) and Leonard Arrington, *Brigham Young: American Moses* (1984) are excellent sources. Also see Richard Bushman, *Joseph Smith and the Beginnings of Mormonism* (1984). For treatments of Mormon polygamy, see B. Caron Hardy, *The Mormon Polygamous Passage* (1992); Lawrence Foster, *Religion and Sexuality: The American Communal Experiments of the Nineteenth Century* (1981); and Sarah Gordon Barringer, *The Mormon Question: Polygamy and Constitutional Conflict in Nineteenth Century America* (2002). Also see Todd Compton, *In Sacred Loneliness: The Plural Wives of Joseph Smith* (1997) and Richard S. Van Wagoner, *Mormon Polygamy: A History* (1992).

READING 28

★ ★ ★

God's Angry Man

Stephen B. Oates

John Brown was a man given to excess. He fathered twenty children, and in thirty-five years he engaged in more than twenty different businesses. When he was fifty-five, he radically changed professions. He became, in his mind and in the minds of his devoted followers, a visionary and a modern-day prophet. His crusade and reason for living was the abolition of slavery. An utterly fearless man of action, he left talking to others and took matters into his own hands. On the night of May 24, 1856, John Brown, four of his sons, a son-in-law, and two other men left their blood imprint on history. At Pottawatomie Creek, in Kansas, they murdered and mutilated five proslavery settlers. The action, Brown said, had been "decreed by Almighty God, ordained from Eternity."

In October 1859, Brown and a larger group of followers made a more daring raid. They were determined to capture the federal arsenal at Harpers Ferry, Virginia, and from there, to move South and liberate the slaves. The action failed and Brown was captured, tried, and executed. As historian Stephen B. Oates shows in the following essay, Brown's raid on Harpers Ferry illustrated how far the North and South had grown apart and how much northern as well as southern whites were alienated from slaves. In the North, the dead Brown became a sainted martyr. In the South, he became a symbol of bloodthirsty northern aggression. By the late 1850s, the two regions were speaking different languages as they marched toward civil war.

God sees it," John Brown said with tears in his fierce gray eyes. His son Jason nodded in solemn agreement. They were standing on the bank of the Marais des Cygnes, watching the free-state settlement of Osawatomie smoke and blaze against the Kansas sky. Yes, God saw it, the old man said: the homes of his friends going up in flames; the body of his son Frederick lying in the road near the Adairs' place; and the Missouri raiders riding up and down the smoke-filled streets looting buildings and stampeding cattle with shouts and gunfire. It was August 30, 1856, and the Missourians were sacking Osawatomie in retaliation for Brown's own violent work some three months before, when he and his antislavery band, seeking revenge for numerous proslavery atrocities and hoping to create "a restraining fear," had taken five proslavery men from their cabins along Pottawatomie Creek and hacked them to death with broadswords.

An eye for an eye and a tooth for a tooth—that was the war cry of both sides in Bleeding Kansas— and now Osawatomie lay in flames, Brown himself had narrowly escaped capture, and one of his own sons lay in the Kansas dirt with a proslavery bullet in his heart. The old man trembled with grief and rage. "I have only a short time to live—only one death to die," he told Jason, "and I will die fighting for this cause. There will be no more peace in this land until slavery is done for. I will give them something else to do than to extend slave territory. I will carry the war into Africa."

On September 7, Brown rode into free-state Lawrence with his gun across his saddle and his eyes burning more fiercely than ever. For many days he came and went, his mind busy with plots. He was hiding out somewhere in or near Lawrence when Governor John W. Geary, head of the peace party in Kansas, led a cavalry force out to end the "fratricidal strife" in the Lawrence vicinity and drive the Missourians out of the territory. In early October, hearing rumors that Geary would arrest him, Brown and three of his sons—

Stephen B. Oates, "God's Angry Man," *American History Illustrated*, 20 (January 1986), 10–21.

Jason, Owen, and John, Jr.—rode out of Kansas and headed east. For already the old man was obsessed with visions of "God-fearing men, men who respect themselves," fighting in mountain passes and ravines for the liberation of the slaves. Already he believed that God was calling him to a greater destiny than the skirmishes he had been waging against slavery in Kansas. What was it the Prophet had said? "That it might be fulfilled which was spoken of the Lord by the prophet saying, 'Out of Egypt have I called my son.' " And John Brown of Osawatomie was ready now, after all these years of trial, to answer the call of his God.

At fifty-six, Brown was lean and hard as stone, with coarse, iron-gray hair and a head that seemed too small for his five-foot-nine-inch frame. If he was extremely religious, he could also be dictatorial and self-righteous, with an imperious manner that made him intolerant and unappreciative of others, especially his own sons. As a businessman, he could be inept and self-deluded. He could become obsessed with a single idea—now slavery, now land speculation, now a wool crusade in Massachusetts—and pursue his current project with unswerving zeal.

Yet he could be kind and gentle, extremely gentle. He could rock a baby lamb in his arms. He could stay up several nights caring for a sick child, or his ailing father, or his afflicted first wife. He could hold children on both knees and sing them the sad, mournful refrains of his favorite hymn, "Blow ye the trumpet, blow." He could stand at the graves of four of his children who had died of dysentery, weeping and praising God in an ecstasy of despair. He could teach his children to fear God and keep the Commandments—and exhibit the most excruciating anxiety when the older ones began questioning the value of religion. All his life he could treat America's "poor, despised Africans" as his equals—a significant trait in view of the anti-Negro prejudice that prevailed in North and South alike in his time. And he could feel an almost paralyzing bitterness toward bondage itself—that "sum of villainies"—and toward all those in the United States who sought to preserve and perpetuate it.

He was born in 1800 in a stark, shutterless farmhouse in West Torrington, Connecticut. His father, a cobbler and tanner who soon moved the family to Ohio's Western Reserve, taught the boy to fear an austere Calvinist God who demanded the most exacting obedience from the frail, wretched sinners He placed on trial in this world. Brown's father also instructed him from earliest childhood to oppose slavery as "a great sin against God." The boy's mother died when he was eight, a tragedy that left him devastated with grief. When his father remarried, young John refused to accept his stepmother emotionally and "pined after his own mother for years."

He grew into an arrogant and contentious young man who ordered others about, said a brother, like "a King against whom there is no rising up." Although he dropped out of school at an early age, he read the Bible and committed its entire contents to memory, taking pleasure in correcting anyone who quoted it wrongly. In 1816, he aspired to become a minister and traveled east

to study. But an eye inflammation and want of funds forced him to abandon his plans.

Back in Ohio, he built his own tannery and married pious and plain Dianthe Lusk. Dianthe bore seven children, whom Brown rigorously disciplined with a rod in one hand and the Bible in the other. In western Pennsylvania, where they lived for ten years, he organized an Independent Congregational Society and frequently preached in a makeshift sanctuary on the second floor of his tannery. He reminded his flock that they were all "poor dependent, sinning, and self-condemned mortals" who looked to God as a constant, directive presence in their lives.

In the late 1820s, Brown entered a bitter season of trial. Dianthe showed symptoms of deep-rooted emotional troubles, and then she and two of their children died. He soon remarried, his new wife a large, reticent sixteen-year-old named Mary Ann Day. Mary gave him thirteen children, seven of whom died in childhood. There were tragedies in his worldly concerns too: he was wiped out in the Panic of 1837, declared bankrupt in 1842. Caught up in the reckless, go-ahead spirit of the age, Brown recouped his fortunes and plunged into another business venture, and another. Each ended in failure.

As he grew older, Brown became more self-righteous and fixed in his convictions than ever. He lectured his children about Providential interposition and their trial on earth, beseeching them to suffer the word of exhortation. At the same time, he became increasingly distressed about the oppression of Negroes in the North as well as the South. He worked on the Underground Railroad in Ohio and publicly opposed the state's "black laws." He even tried to integrate a Congregational Church he attended there, only to be expelled for his effort. After that, he grew more violent in his denunciations of slavery. He would gladly lay down his life for the destruction of that institution, because "death for a good cause," he told a friend, was "glorious."

While living in Springfield, Massachusetts, Brown not only chided Negroes for passively submitting to white oppression, but devised a secret scheme to run slaves out of the South through a "Subterranean Pass Way." He told Frederick Douglass, the great Negro abolitionist, that he wanted to arm the black men he liberated, because using guns would give them "a sense of manhood." In 1851 Brown exhorted Negroes to kill any Southerner or federal officer who tried to enforce the fugitive slave law, and enlisted forty-four Springfield blacks into a mutual-defense organization called the "Branch of the United States League of Gileadites," based on the story of Gideon in the Book of Judges.

But to Brown's despair, the curse of slavery seemed to be spreading. On May 30, 1854, President Franklin Pierce signed the Kansas-Nebraska Bill, which overturned the old Missouri Compromise line and decreed that henceforth the citizens of each territory would vote on whether or not to have slavery. Until they did so, Southerners were free to take their slaves into most of the western territories. At once, antislavery Northerners decried the act as part of a Southern conspiracy to seize the frontier—and maybe the North as well. The first step in the plot was to occupy the new territory of Kansas in the western heartland. "Come on, gentlemen of the slave States," cried Senator William H. Seward of New York: "Since there is no escaping your challenge, I accept it in behalf of the cause of freedom. We will engage in competition for the virgin soil of Kansas, and God give the victory to the side that is stronger in numbers as it is in right."

In response, hundreds of pioneers, mostly from the northwestern states, started for Kansas to make new lives for themselves on a "free-soil" frontier. Among them were five of Brown's sons. In the spring of 1855, border Missourians invaded Kansas, voted illegally in elections there, and vowed to exterminate "every Goddamned abolitionist in the Territory." Brown's sons wrote him that an armed struggle between freedom and despotism was about to commence in Kansas, and they urged him to join them with plenty of weapons.

Brown had already decided to migrate to Kansas for purposes of business and settlement.

But when he received his sons' letters, he gathered an arsenal of guns and broadswords and headed for Kansas to help save it from "Satan's legions." Violence broke out several months after he arrived, as Missourians again crossed the border to kill free-state men and terrorize free-state settlements. Brown flung himself into the struggle with uninhibited fury, riding to meet the Philistine slaveholders as Gideon had gone after the Midianites. The result was the shocking Pottawatomie murders, then open civil war, the sacking of Osawatomie, and the killing of Brown's son Frederick. The Kansas civil war must have made it all clear to him now. God was at last calling him to a special destiny ("in all thy ways acknowledge Him & He shall direct thy paths") and had chosen this terrible conflict, including the death of his own son, to show Brown what must be done to avenge the crimes of this "slave-cursed" land.

But to accomplish his "mission," as he called it, Brown needed to raise money and guns, an army, and the support of influential men. In early 1857 he launched a fund-raising campaign across the Northeast that had all the fervor of a religious revival. Standing one wintry night in the Town House in Concord, Massachusetts, with Ralph Waldo Emerson, Henry David Thoreau, and other eminences in his audience, Brown recounted the Kansas civil war blow by blow, telling how the Border Ruffians had murdered innocent God-fearing people—people like his own son. What Kansas needed, Brown contended, was men who would fight—and it needed money, too, a great deal of money. He went on to speak of his family sufferings, of how his wife and daughters were living in near-destitution, in a farmhouse in the Adirondacks of upstate New York, while he and his sons fought God's war against slavery and the evil forces that sought to spread it. His vow that he and his remaining sons would never stop fighting until the war was won brought enthusiastic applause from the townspeople, who pledged a modest sum of money before filing into the chill night convinced that Brown was "the rarest of heroes," as Emerson put it, "a true idealist, with no by-ends of his own."

But Brown's talk of continuing the fight in Kansas was a blind for something far larger, something he actually hinted at in a conversation with Emerson. Brown told him that he believed in two things—the Bible and the Declaration of Independence—and that it was "better that a whole generation of men, women and children should pass away by a violent death than that a word of either should be violated in this country." Emerson stared at him for a moment—obviously the Bible and the Declaration had been repeatedly violated in this country. Finally the essayist nodded his approval: he thought the old man was speaking symbolically, as Emerson liked to do himself. But Brown meant every word he said—as much as he had ever meant anything in his life.

A few days later Brown talked to a forge-master in Collinsville, Connecticut, ordering a thousand pikes "for our free-state settlers in Kansas," and agreeing to make a down payment of $500 with a promise of an additional $450 on delivery. The forge-master was more than happy to have Brown's business. But he was puzzled. Brown had implied during their conversation that Kansas was full of re-volvers and Sharps rifles. What could settlers skilled in the use of firearms want with a thousand pikes? Also, why should Brown want a Connecticut forge-master to make them when a blacksmith in Iowa or Kansas could do it just as well?

Back in Kansas again, at a campsite on the prairie near Topeka, Brown piled wood on a smoking campfire as November winds howled out of the night. Around him sat four young men, all veterans of the Kansas civil war—they were the initial recruits for Brown's guerrilla company. Among them was an Ohio schoolteacher named John Henry Kagi, who was to become Brown's trusted lieutenant and whose abolitionism was as deeply principled as it was intractable.

The four men spoke to Brown with a deep respect, for they regarded him as a brave and high-minded warrior who would lay down his life to save Kansas from the "Slave Power." But they wanted to know what specific plans he had made. They all knew he had other recruits. Where was it he wanted them to serve?

Brown would only say that they were going back east to drill, since Kansas was now quiet and it was too cold to do much campaigning out here. His sons and several others would go along. Then he gave one of his recruits a draft for $82.68 and said, "Get that cashed in Lawrence tomorrow. We'll meet again at Tabor in Iowa. Then I'll tell you what we are going to do. If you want hard fighting you'll get plenty of it."

At Tabor, Brown gathered nine recruits around him. "Our ultimate destination," he said with a look of grim determination, "is Virginia."

In February 1858 Brown was at Gerrit Smith's mansion in Peterboro, New York, holding intense discussions with Smith, a wealthy reformer, and young Franklin Sanborn, a Concord school-teacher and secretary of the Massachusetts State Kansas Committee. Brown argued that it was too late to settle the slave question through politics or any other peaceful means. The Southern defense of slavery as "a positive good," the proslavery policies of the Buchanan administration, the infamous Dred Scott decision—all had convinced Brown that bondage had become too entrenched in American life ever to be expunged except by revolutionary violence. There was no recourse left to the black man, he said, but in God and a massive slave uprising in which the blood of slaveholders would be spilled. This was a terrible thing, but slavery was a terrible wrong, the same as murder, and the unrepentant Southerners deserved to be violently punished for it.

It was God's will, Brown continued, that *he* should incite this insurrection—by a forced march on Virginia, the queen of the slave states, with a guerrilla contingent he was already raising. And even if the insurrection failed, it would nevertheless congeal Northern hatred of slavery and thus provoke a crisis, perhaps a civil war, in which the North would break the black man's chains on the battlefield.

But Brown needed financial support if his war for slave liberation was to succeed. Would Smith and Sanborn help? While Smith seemed willing, Sanborn raised objections. But Brown's convic-tion, and the fiery obstinacy that burned in his eyes, won Sanborn over in the end. "I expect to effect a mighty conquest," Brown assured him, "even though it be like the last victory of Samson."

In March, Brown traveled to Boston, where he revealed his plan to Theodore Parker and Thomas Wentworth Higginson, two eminent Unitarian ministers; to George Luther Stearns, a prominent businessman; and to Samuel Gridley Howe, a dashing physician and reformer. Though Brown undoubtedly mentioned Virginia in their conversations, none of them knew exactly where he intended to strike his blow. Nevertheless, they formed a secret committee of six, including Smith and young Sanborn, and raised a considerable sum of money for him. They all realized that the attempted insurrection might fail. But even so, as Brown had repeatedly argued, it might ignite a sectional powder keg that would explode into civil war in which slavery would be destroyed.

With the support of the Six, Brown now felt free to work with both hands. In May, he appeared in Chatham, Canada, where he held a secret meeting in a Negro schoolhouse with eleven whites and thirty-four blacks. He told them that slaves all over Dixie were ready for revolt. At the first sign of a leader who wanted to liberate them, "they would immediately rise all over the Southern states." And John Brown of Osawatomie was that leader. He explained that he would invade Virginia, in the region of the Blue Ridge Mountains, and march into Tennessee and northern Alabama. As he moved, thousands of slaves would rally to his standard. They would then wage war upon the plantations on the plains west and east of the mountains, which would serve as their base of operations.

"But what if troops are brought against you?" someone asked.

Brown waved aside all doubts. A small force trained in guerrilla warfare could easily defend those Thermopylae ravines against Southern militia or the U.S. Army. He believed that "all the free negroes in the Northern states" would also rally to his cause once the invasion began.

Brown went on to read a constitution he had drawn up that would create a new state once the slaves were freed, with Brown as commander in chief and John Henry Kagi as secretary of war. The preamble of Brown's document actually declared war against slavery, which was itself "a most barbarous, unprovoked, and unjustifiable War" of one portion of American citizens upon another.

The Negroes enthusiastically endorsed the sentiments in Brown's constitution, but they were not so sure about joining his army of liberation. The thought of going back to the South must have terrified them. And the plan of invasion itself sounded fantastic—almost mad. They had already risked their lives, had suffered much hardship, to get to Canada and freedom. Were they willing to abandon that now? Were they willing to follow Brown and some boys back to that Gibraltar of slavery and possibly a horrible death in a carnage of racial violence? Furthermore, was Brown really an instrument of God to free the slaves? Or was he just a poor self-deluded old man?

An irritating delay arose when a drillmaster Brown had enlisted in his company defected and told part of what he knew to a U.S. senator and other politicians. Most of Brown's backers were panic-stricken and voted to send him back to Kansas until things cooled off. The old man was not happy about their decision, but when they offered him an additional $2,000 or $3,000 if he would leave, Brown grudgingly rode back to the Territory. That December he executed a bold and bloody slave-running expedition into Missouri, one that almost started another civil war along the smoldering western border. When told that President Buchanan himself had denounced the raid and put a price of $250 on his head, Brown retorted with a price of $2.50 on the head of the president.

But it was all a diversion to keep him associated with Kansas in the public mind. In the spring of 1859, suffering from an old case of malaria and "a terrible gathering" in his head, Brown made his way back to Boston, where he warned his secret backers that there would be no more postponements. In June, he went to Connecticut to expedite the shipment of pikes and later turned up in Ohio to gather a hidden cache of guns. "Now is the time to help in the movement, if ever," Sanborn wrote Higginson, "for within the next two months the experiment will be made."

Brown planned to launch his "experiment" at a town called Harpers Ferry, situated on a narrow neck of land at the confluence of the Shenandoah and Potomac rivers in the Blue Ridge Mountains of northern Virginia. His prime military target there was a federal arsenal and armory works whose store of guns he desperately needed for his guerrilla army. With an advance agent already in town, Brown rented a delapidated two-story farmhouse about seven miles away on the Maryland side of the Potomac, giving his name as "Smith" and telling neighbors that he was a cattle buyer from New York. With him were sons, Oliver and Owen, and a young Kansan who vowed "to make this land of liberty and equality shake to the centre."

While the commander in chief cultivated a beard and studied books on guerrilla warfare, a handful of additional volunteers trickled in. One was Brown's son Watson, who had left a young wife and a newborn child in the Adirondacks. Another was a freed mulatto named Dangerfield Newby, who at forty-eight was the oldest raider and who hoped to liberate his wife and seven children from a plantation at Brentville, Virginia.

As they awaited more recruits, Brown gathered his men upstairs and finally disclosed his plans in full. Up to this point some of them thought they were going on a large slave-running expedition, but now the old man was saying things that astonished them. They were going to attack Harpers Ferry itself, gather up the guns in the federal armory, and hold the town until the slaves from the surrounding area joined them. Then they would strike southward, spreading terror throughout Dixie.

As Brown spoke, first one recruit and then his own sons strenuously objected to an attack on Harpers Ferry, arguing that it was suicidal for a mere handful of men to try to capture and hold an entire town against militia and possibly federal troops. Kagi, proud and impressive with his dark beard and large, alert eyes, actually favored the plan, as did some of the others. But the malcontents were as immovable as their fierce-eyed chief. Twice there was a threat of mutiny. In a show of anger, Brown resigned as commander in chief—a calculated move that warded off revolt and brought them all back to his side.

Still, he knew that the cramped quarters and fear of discovery frayed everyone's nerves. If he did not attack soon, they might all break under the strain. Where were the pikes anyway? And all the volunteers he had expected from New England, Pennsylvania, and Kansas? He had sent urgent pleas to his friends there as well as to his Negro allies in Canada. Where were the Negroes? They had more of a stake in this than any of the whites. And there was the money problem. The money from the secret committee had melted away in expenses; Sanborn and Howe had sent an additional $205, but that was not nearly enough to sustain him in an all-out war. There were so many obstacles and delays . . . Could it be that his plans were wrong, that God intended some other way?

But the old man had put too much into this enterprise to believe that now. He prayed for guidance. He must continue to believe that he was an instrument in God's hands, that the Almighty would hurl him like a stone into the black pool of bondage and that He alone would determine the outcome.

Late in September there were propitious signs: the 950 pikes came in from Chambersburg, and Osborn P. Anderson, a brave young Negro, arrived from Canada asserting that he was ready for war. The last obstacles to the attack—and any lingering doubts Brown may have had about his destiny—disappeared when three late recruits reached the farm in mid-October. One even contributed six hundred dollars in gold. For Brown, that gold was an unmistakable sign that God wanted him to move. At dawn on Sunday, October 16, Brown gathered his little army—sixteen whites and five Negroes—for a final worship service. At 8 P.M., leaving a rear guard at the farm, the old man climbed into a wagon loaded with guns and pikes, and led his men two-by-two into a damp moonless night.

When the town lights came into view, two raiders took off through the woods to cut telegraph lines. Then Brown flung his little army across the covered railroad and wagon bridge that led into Harpers Ferry, deploying Newby, Oliver Brown, and others to guard the Potomac and Shenandoah bridges. Except for a few figures strolling in the streets, the town showed little sign of life. The raiders darted up Potomac Street and took the watchman at the government works by surprise, pinning him against the gate and securing both the armory and the arsenal. To the frightened watchman, Brown must have seemed an apparition, with his glaring eyes and flowing gray beard. "I came here from Kansas," the old man said; "I want to free all the negroes in this State . . . if the citizens interfere with me I must only burn the town and have blood."

So far everything was going perfectly. Kagi and two of the Negroes manned Hall's Rifle Works above the armory on Shenandoah Street. By now, Owen Brown, one of the rear guard, should have moved to the schoolhouse near the farm where slaves from Maryland were to report; Brown's advance agent had assured him that they would swarm in like bees.

Around midnight a detachment of raiders brought three hostages into the armory yard— among them Colonel Lewis W. Washington, a wealthy planter and a great-grandnephew of the first president—with their slaves and their household weapons, including a magnificent sword of Washington's that Frederick the Great had allegedly given his illustrious relative. In the glare of torches, Brown armed the slaves with pikes and ordered them to guard the prisoners. He was admiring the sword—a fine symbol for the revolution that had begun this night—when a raider reported that the telegraph lines east and west of town had been cut. Now, as soon as Owen came with the slaves, Brown would garrison the town, take more hostages, and move on.

At about 1:30 in the morning, Brown heard gunshots in the direction of the bridges. His sentinels there were firing on men from a train that had just arrived from Wheeling. Then there was another crack of gunfire. In the darkness and confusion, Brown's men had mortally wounded a free Negro who worked at the station as a baggage master. The first real blood in Brown's war against slavery had been spilled.

By now the gunfire and unusual commotion around the arsenal had aroused the townspeople; they gathered in the streets with knives, axes, squirrel rifles, with any weapon they could pick up. What was it? What was happening? A slave insurrection, someone said: hundreds of them with some Yankee abolitionists murdering and looting around the armory. Panic-stricken, the townsmen fled with their families to the heights in back of town. But in all the confusion and hysteria they seemed not to notice the very Negroes they dreaded cowering in their midst, as terrified as they were.

Down in town the bell on the Lutheran Church was tolling the alarm, calling to farmers all over the countryside: *Insurrection, Insurrection,* tolling on into the mist-swept morning. By that time the alarm was also spreading to other towns, as two villagers galloped madly along separate roads yelling at the top of their lungs: Insurrection at Harpers Ferry! Slaves raping and butchering the streets! The thing all Southerners had dreaded since Nat Turner's terrible uprising in 1831 was now upon them like a black plague. Soon church bells were tolling in towns and villages throughout the area, and shouting militiamen were on the march. At the same time, Brown had allowed the express train to push on; and it was carrying the alarm to Monocacy and Frederick. From Monocacy, the news would tick over the telegraphs to Richmond and Washington, D.C., and would soon be blazing in headlines throughout the South and East.

By eleven o'clock that Monday morning a general battle was raging at Harpers Ferry, as armed farmers and militiamen poured into town and laid down a blistering fire on both the rifle works and the fire-engine house of the armory where Brown and a dozen of his men were gathered. The speed with which the countryside had mobilized surprised Brown completely. To Osborn P.

Anderson, he seemed "puzzled" as he watched the bustle of armed men in the streets and searched the gray sky beyond, perhaps hoping for a sign from Providence.

As the old man waited at the armory, militiamen over-ran the bridges, driving the sentinels off with rifles blazing. Oliver Brown and another sentinel made it back to the armory, but Dangerfield Newby fell from a sniper's bullet, the first of the raiders to die and the last hope of his slave wife. "Oh dear Dangerfield," read a letter from her in his pocket, "come this fall without fail, money or no money I want to see you so much: that is one bright hope I have before me." Newby lay in the street until somebody dragged him into the gutter and sliced his ears off as souvenirs.

As the townsmen now swarmed off the heights and joined in the fighting, Brown had to admit that he might be trapped, that he could not wait for white or slave reinforcements. The only thing he could do, cut off as he was from Kagi at the rifle works and from the rear guard in Maryland, was to negotiate for a cease-fire, offering to release his hostages if the militia would let him and his men go free. He sent a raider named Will Thompson out under a truce flag, but the excited crowd grabbed Thompson and took him off at gunpoint. Brown grew desperate. Gathering the remnants of his force and the hostages in the fire-engine house at the front of the armory, he sent his son Watson and another raider out under a second white flag. But the mob gunned them both down. Watson managed to crawl back to the engine house, where he doubled up in agony at his father's feet.

By late afternoon the town was in chaos as half-drunken and uncontrolled crowds thronged the streets. Hearing their shouts from behind the trestlework below the armory, kindly old Fontaine Beckham, the mayor of Harpers Ferry, was distressed at what was happening to his town. In his agitation he kept venturing out on the railroad between some freight cars and the water station, trying to see what was going on around the beleaguered armory. Inside the engine house, a raider named Edwin Coppoc, a Quaker

boy from Iowa, drew a bead on Beckham from the doorway: Coppoc fired, missed, fired again, "and the dark wings again brushed the little town" as Mayor Beckham—the best white friend the Negroes had in the county—slumped to the timbers. In his Will Book the mayor had provided for the liberation upon his death of Negro Isaac Gilbert, his slave wife and three children. The Quaker's shot had freed them all.

In retaliation, a group of furious men dragged Will Thompson kicking and screaming down to the Potomac, where they shot him in the head with revolvers and flung him into the water. According to one writer, Thompson "could be seen for a day or two after, lying at the bottom of the river, with his ghostly face still exhibiting his fearful death agony."

By now, Brown's situation in the fire-engine house had become even more acute. A newly arrived militia company had rushed through the armory yard from the rear, thus cutting off his last means of retreat. A party of whites had also over-run the rifle works, annihilating Kagi in a crossfire and mortally wounding one black raider and capturing the other; only the intervention of a local physician kept whites from lynching him. More reinforcements stormed into town that evening; and rifle fire and drunken shouts punctuated the drizzly darkness.

Inside the engine house, it was painfully cold and pitch dark as Brown, four uninjured raiders, and eleven prisoners watched the night drag by. One raider lay dead; Watson and Oliver Brown, who had also been wounded, lay side by side on the floor, both choking and crying in intense pain. The old man, distraught and exhausted, paced back and forth muttering to himself and fingering Washington's sword. He paused, listening to the clank of arms outside, then started pacing again. Oliver, one of the prisoners remembered, begged his father "again and again to be shot, in the agony of his wound." But Brown turned on him. "If you must die, die like a man." Then he turned to the prisoners in despair. "Gentlemen, if you knew of my past history you would not blame me for being here. I went to Kansas a peaceable man, and the proslavery people hunted me down like a wolf. I lost one of my sons there." He stood trembling for a moment, then called to Oliver. There was no answer. "I guess he is dead," the old man said, and started pacing again.

When the first gray light of morning spread through the high windows of the engine house, Brown and the remaining raiders took their places at the gun holes they had dug out of the walls. Brown could only wince at what he saw in the streets outside: a company of United States Marines under Army Colonel Robert E. Lee, dispatched from Washington by President Buchanan himself, had arrived during the night, and was now deployed in front of the engine house with bayonets and sledgehammers, while two thousand spectators looked on from sidewalks and buildings as far as Brown could see. He had the doors barricaded and loopholed, but he knew they would not hold against sledgehammers, he knew that this was the end for him and the young men who stood by his side. Yet his face wore an expression of awakened resolution. Brown "was the coolest and firmest man I ever saw," Colonel Washington said. "With one son dead by his side, and another shot through, he felt the pulse of his dying son with one hand and held his rifle with the other, and commanded his men with the utmost composure, encouraging them to sell their lives as dearly as they could."

But the Marines did not attack. Instead a tall, bearded trooper named Jeb Stuart approached under a flag of truce. Brown cracked the door, and with his rifle aimed at Stuart's head took a note from his outstretched hand. The note summoned Brown to surrender unconditionally, with assurances that he would be protected from harm and handed over to the proper authorities.

Brown handed the note back with his eyes on Stuart's. He would surrender, he said, only on terms that would allow him and his men to escape. At that some of the prisoners begged Stuart to ask Colonel Lee himself to come and reason with Brown. But Stuart replied that Lee would agree only to the terms offered in the note. Then suddenly Stuart jumped away from the door and

waved his cap. With the spectators cheering wildly, storming parties rushed the engine house and started battering at the thick oak doors.

The raiders fired back desperately, powder smoke wreathing out of the gun holes and cracks in the building. But it was no use. The Marines tore down one of the doors with a heavy ladder and swarmed inside, pinning one raider to the wall with a bayonet and running another through as he crawled under a fire engine. Colonel Washington then pointed to Brown, who was kneeling with his rifle cocked, and said, "This is Osawatomie." Lieutenant Israel Green struck Brown with his light dress sword before the old man could fire, and then tried to run him through with a savage thrust that almost lifted him off the floor, but the blade struck either a bone or Brown's belt buckle and bent double. Had Green been armed with his heavy battle sword, which he had left in the barracks in all the excitement, he would probably have killed Brown with that thrust. As the old man fell, Green beat him on the head with the hilt of his dress sword until Brown was unconscious. When Green at last got control of himself, he had Brown and the other dead and wounded raiders carried outside and laid on the grass. Colonel Lee inspected Brown himself and when he regained consciousness the colonel had a doctor tend to his wounds.

Thirty-six hours after it had begun, Brown's war for slave liberation had ended in dismal failure. No uprisings had taken place anywhere in Virginia or Maryland, because the slaves there, lacking organization and leadership, having little if any knowledge of what was going on, and fearing white reprisals, had been both unable and unwilling to join him. The raid had cost a total of seventeen lives. Two slaves, three townsmen, a slaveholder, and one Marine had been killed, and nine men had been wounded. Ten of Brown's own recruits, including two of his sons, had been killed or fatally injured. Five raiders had been captured and the rest had escaped, some for a few days, some for good.

Brown himself, "cut and thrust and bleeding and in bonds," found himself lodged in the paymaster's office of the armory, where he appeared cool and indomitable even as a lynch mob outside cried for his head. That afternoon, while he lay on a pile of old bedding, the governor of Virginia and a retinue of officers, U.S. congressmen, and reporters questioned him for a full three hours. Brown refused to implicate anybody else in his war against slavery, blamed only himself for its failure. How could he possibly justify his acts? asked one interrogator. "I pity the poor in bondage that have none to help them," he said, with one eye on the martyrdom that was nearly his now; "that is why I am here: not to gratify any personal animosity, revenge or vindictive spirit. It is my sympathy with the oppressed and the wronged, that are as good as you and as precious in the sight of God." Then he addressed the entire gathering—and a divided nation beyond. "I wish to say, furthermore, that you had better—all you people of the South—prepare yourselves for a settlement of that question that must come up for settlement sooner than you are prepared for it . . . You may dispose of me very easily; I am nearly disposed of now; but this question is still to be settled—this negro question I mean—the end of that is not yet."

While a bitter debate over Brown's raid was taking shape between the South and antislavery Northerners, the old man stood trial in a crowded courtroom in nearby Charlestown. On November 2, the court sentenced him to die on the gallows for murder, treason against the state of Virginia, and conspiring with slaves to rebel.

"Let them hang me," Brown rejoiced. "I am worth inconceivably more to hang than for any other purpose."

On December 2, on his way to the gallows, he handed one of his guards a last message he had written to his countrymen: "I John Brown am now quite *certain* that the crimes of this guilty, land; will never be purged *away;* but with Blood. I had *as I now think:* vainly flattered myself that without *very much* bloodshed; it might be done."

As it turned out, Brown was prophetic. For Harpers Ferry polarized the country as no other event had done; it set in motion a spiral of accusation and counteraccusation between North and South that bore the country irreversibly toward secession and the beginning of a civil war in which slavery itself would perish—the very thing the old man had hoped and prayed would be the ultimate consequences of his Harpers Ferry raid.

His friends and family brought his body home to North Elba in the Adirondacks, where they buried him by a large boulder near the Brown farmhouse. As they lowered him into the earth, four members of a Negro family sang "Blow ye the trumpet, blow," the hymn Brown had loved so: "O, happy is the man who hears. Why should we start, and fear to die. With songs and honors sounding loud. Ah, lovely appearance of death." Apart from his impact on the country, all that remained of John Brown now was a silent grave in the stillness of the mountains.

Study Questions

1. Describe John Brown's background and his personality.

2. Describe the process by which Brown's attitudes about slavery developed.

3. In what ways was the raid on Harpers Ferry a poorly planned, tactical disaster?

4. How did Brown finance the raid on Harpers Ferry, and why did that financing further strain relations between the North and South?

5. Did the death sentence he received change Brown's thinking about slavery and the future of the country? Why or why not?

6. In your opinion, was John Brown insane? Why or why not?

Bibliography

John Brown has not been forgotten—at least not by historians. In the 1970s, for example, he was the subject of four biographies. The most balanced biography of Brown is Stephen B. Oates, *To Purge This Land with Blood: A Biography of John Brown* (1970). Two older works that are also valuable are James C. Malin, *John Brown and the Legacy of Fifty-Six* (1942) and Garrison Villard, *John Brown, 1800-1859: A Biography Fifty Years After* (1910). James W. Davidson and Mark H. Lytle attempt a psychological interpretation of Brown in "The Madness of John Brown: The Uses of Psychohistory," *After the Fact: The Art of Historical Detection* (1982). James A. Rawley, *Race and Politics: "Bleeding Kansas" and the Coming of the Civil War* (1969) presents a fine introduction to the section where Brown acquired his initial fame. Students interested in psychohistory should consult Robert J. Lifton, ed., *Explorations in Psychohistory* (1974) and Bruce Mazlish, *Psychoanalysis and History* (1971). Also see Bruce Levine, *Half Slave and Half Free: The Roots of the Civil War* (1992); John Stauffer, *The Black Hearts of Men: Radical Abolitionists and the Transformation of Race* (2002); Merrill D. Petersen, *John Brown: The Legend Revisited* (2002); and Chester G. Hearn, *Six Years of Hell: Harpers Ferry During the Civil War* (1996).

★ ★ ★

Civil War and Reconstruction

It seemed impossible. Threats and rumors of civil war, rebellion, and secession had circulated throughout the 1850s, but most Americans had confidently assumed they were just talk, not descriptions of what really could come to pass. But when South Carolina military forces fired on Union vessels trying to resupply Fort Sumter in 1861, the rumors suddenly became reality. War was at hand—a war few people wanted. With an attempt at optimism, many assumed the rebellion would be a short-run affair, decided quickly in the first major military engagement. The Confederate victory at the first battle of Bull Run dashed those hopes. Four years later, the Civil War would prove to have been the bloodiest, most costly conflict in American history.

The sectionalism that brought on the Civil War was evident from the very beginning of the republic. Southerners were devoted to slavery as a source of cheap labor. Southerners also saw slavery as an institution of social control, a way of managing a large, alien black population. To protect their economy and society, Southerners preached a loyalty to laissez-faire and states' rights.

As long as the nation was confined east of the Appalachian Mountains, the North and South were able to coexist peacefully because the two sections were relatively isolated from each other. But early in the nineteenth century, tens of thousands of Americans began pouring into the western territories each year, forcing new issues on the political system. After the War of 1812, a balance of power existed in the United States Senate between free states and slave states, but each time a new territory applied for statehood, its permanent status as a "slave state" or "free state" had to be decided. Most Northerners came to oppose the expansion of slavery into the territories; Southerners believed the survival of their way of life depended on its expansion. Between 1820 and 1860, the country debated this fundamental issue repeatedly. The debate ultimately splintered the nation. Primarily because of their opposition to the expansion of slavery, the Republicans were anathema to the South, and when Abraham Lincoln won the presidency in 1860, the secession movement began.

Although the Civil War was not started as a crusade against slavery, it ended that way. The Emancipation Proclamation and the Thirteenth Amendment to the Constitution ended legal human bondage in the United States, and during Reconstruction Republicans worked diligently to extend full civil rights to former slaves. The Civil Rights Act of 1866 and the Fourteenth and Fifteenth Amendments to the Constitution were designed to bring the emancipated slaves into the political arena and build a respectable Republican party in the South.

Both goals were stillborn. When Congress removed the troops from the last Southern states in 1877, the old planter elite resumed control of Southern politics. They disenfranchised blacks and relegated them to second-class citizenship. The South became solidly Democratic.

As Reconstruction was coming to an end, another era was beginning. Out west, ambitious farmers were rapidly settling the frontier, while cattlemen were forging their own empire by supplying the eastern demand for beef. Civilization was again replacing a wilderness mentality with familiar political, economic, and social institutions. America was trying to forget about the divisions of the past and get on with the business of building a new society.

READING 29

Gettysburg

Joseph Glathaar

General Robert E. Lee returned north for the last time in 1863, taking his Army of Northern Virginia up the Shenandoah Valley, across the Potomac River, and into Pennsylvania. A Confederate victory there might have convinced Great Britain and France to join the rebellion. Union General George Meade's Army of the Potomac met up with Lee at Gettysburg, Pennsylvania, where the Civil War's most memorable battle took place. The two armies came at one another repeatedly during three days of fighting from July 1–3, culminating in Pickett's charge on Cemetery Ridge. Hoping to break through the Union lines, Lee ordered 15,000 Confederates to attack Cemetery Ridge across nearly a mile of open ground. During the assault, Union artillery and rifle fire shredded Confederate lines. Nearly 8,000 Confederate soldiers never even got close to Cemetery Ridge. One Union artillery commander remembered that "we could not help hitting them at every shot." Bodies piled up all along the line of the assault. "Yankee artillery," one Confederate recalled, "hit us with fearful effect, sometimes as many as ten men being killed and wounded by . . . a single shell." So many Confederates fell that one soldier remembered "my boots and pants becoming drenched in blood, not from any wound of my own but from stomping through pools and puddles of blood." A Union soldier recalled, "I tried to ride over the field but could not, for dead and wounded lay too thick to guide a horse through." In the following essay, Professor Joseph Glathaar examines the battle that left more than 50,000 men dead or wounded, turned the tide of the Civil War, and inspired the most famous speech in American history.

In one of the most misinterpreted statements in the Civil War, Confederate General Robert E. Lee once explained his command style to Prussian military observer Justus Schiebert. "I think and work with all my powers to bring my troops to the right place at the right time." Once he had completed that, Lee continued, "I leave the matter up to God and the subordinate officers," because to interfere "does more harm than good." Lee was not abdicating responsibility for the course of battle, as some scholars have suggested; rather, he was merely concurring with Union generals Ulysses S. Grant and William Tecumseh Sherman that a commander's ability to influence combat was finite. Success on the battlefield depended on subordinate officers' capacity to command, and soldiers' ability to fight. In short, Lee could bring his forces together at the proper location and the precise moment, but the army, its officers and its men, had to execute for victory.

In historical examinations of the Battle of Gettysburg, the emphasis has been misplaced. Military leaders and subsequent scholars have devoted far too much attention to command decisions and paid far too little notice to the performance of "common soldiers." In the literature of Gettysburg, scholars have posed the proper central questions: "Why did the Union hold?" and "Why did the Confederate attack fail?" Unfortunately, they generally look for answers in the wrong areas. They wonder how George G. Meade contributed to the Federal victory; why Richard Ewell did not storm Cemetery Hill on the first day; what prompted James Longstreet to delay on the second day; whether Lee should have swung around Big and Little Round Top, instead of assailing the Union center; and what impact the absence of Stuart's cavalry had on the battle's outcome. Thus, issues of high command have dominated the debate.

"Gettysburg," from Joseph T. Glathaar, "The Common Soldier's Gettysburg Campaign," in Gabor S. Boritt, ed., *The Gettysburg Nobody Knows* (New York: Oxford University Press), pp. 3–29.

Perhaps the answer to those fundamental questions of why the Union won and why the Confederacy lost at Gettysburg, though, lies with the common soldiers of the Union and Confederate armies. Over the course of a month-long campaign, and three of the most savage days of combat in the war, some 160,000 men endured the hardships, suffered the privations, thrilled to the exhilaration, bore the sorrow, and fought that battle. Their story is truly the Gettysburg nobody knows.

Since the Confederate victory at Fredericksburg in December 1862, when weather and road conditions deterred a follow-up offensive, Gen. Robert E. Lee's "desire" to raid enemy territory "haunted" him. Once before, that September, his Army of Northern Virginia had surged across the Mason–Dixon Line. Having driven the invaders from Confederate Virginia that summer, Lee intended on sustaining the initiative by campaigning in Maryland and Pennsylvania throughout the fall, hoping to influence the Northern elections and enable Virginia farmers to harvest their crops unmolested. Unfortunately for the Confederates, a lost campaign order compelled him to contract operations prematurely, and straggling and heavy casualties at the Battle of Antietam brought the expedition to an early close.

This time, Lee had the luxury of ample time to plan the raid carefully. In February 1863, he took the first step by asking Lt. Gen. Thomas Jonathan Jackson to order his expert map maker, Jedediah Hotchkiss, to sketch the road network of central Pennsylvania all the way to Philadelphia. Later that spring, Lee requested that authorities in Richmond repair the Virginia Central Railroad, to draw critical supplies for any advance into Maryland and beyond, and he commenced the tedious task of accumulating the necessary wagons to support his command.

Lee had multiple objectives for launching the invasion. A campaign into the North could influence Confederate operations as far west as the Mississippi River by drawing Union troops eastward. It could also spare Southern farmers and ease commissary burdens by enabling the Confederate government to feed its largest army on

Bloated corpes on the "killing fields" of Gettysburg.

Northern grain and livestock. And like everyone else in the Army of Northern Virginia, Lee sought an opportunity to defeat the Federal army far away from the works around Washington or the naval gunboats of the Atlantic fleet, where he could follow up his victory with repeated attacks and extinguish the Army of the Potomac.

Supply problems, however, postponed the implementation of his plans. Confederates had great difficulty obtaining long forage to strengthen their animals for a lengthy march, and the need to draw artillery ammunition from the Deep South taxed the railroads. In early February, an explosion and fire killed forty-three employees and closed the Richmond Arsenal for two months. The Army had a sufficient supply of shot and shells on hand to support a battle, but a lengthy campaign would require much more ammuni-

tion. Authorities had to redirect carload after carload of case shot and shells northward from Charleston and Augusta, to accumulate a stockpile. Meanwhile, the ammunition consumed valuable cargo space on trains, which could have hauled the necessary forage.

Despite the ensuing delays, Lee hoped to "assume the aggressive by the 1st of May," sweeping Federals from the Shenandoah Valley and turning the giant Union Army of the Potomac out of Virginia, to some position north of the Potomac River. Maj. Gen. Joseph Hooker, commander of the Army of the Potomac, refused to cooperate.

In late April, Hooker's mammoth command rumbled forward, forcing its way across the Rappahannock and Rapidan Rivers and sandwiching Lee's Army between its two wings. Undermanned with a pair of Longstreet's divisions on detached service, two choices confronted Lee. He could select the safe option, fall back to a strong defensive position, and abandon hope of a raid northward until late summer or autumn. Or, Lee could stand and fight, defeat Hooker's command, and follow up his triumph by pressing on into Maryland and Pennsylvania. A gambler to the core, Lee chose to stand and fight.

The Battle of Chancellorsville was the single most costly engagement up to that point in the war. In driving Hooker's army back across the Rappahannock River, the Confederates inflicted 17,000 casualties on the Union, while suffering a staggering 13,000 themselves. Among the fallen was Lee's most able lieutenant, Stonewall Jackson. "I have heard such sounds, & seen such sights, as make my flesh almost crawl when I think of them," described a Confederate. After gazing at a train of wounded soldiers creaking rearward, a New Yorker recorded, "how little do the folks at home know the miseries of war. May they never witness its horrors, as I have." Several days after the battle, a North Carolinian still could not write properly from the prolonged stress. "I have Got the trimbles," he confessed to his wife. Descriptive words failed a Massachusetts man. He could only utter in dismay, "What a life we lead, and all for $13 a month."

Confederates taunted Yankees, especially their failed commander. " 'Fighting'—*fainting*—fleeing" Joe Hooker had an appealing ring among Rebel circles. Yet the heavy losses cut deeply into the ranks. And Jackson was irreplaceable. "General Lee is a far greater General than 'Old Stonewall,' " conceded a Georgian, "but he can never excite the enthusiasm which this old war horse did with his old faded coat and cap and his sun burnt cheek,—*'Requiescat in Pace.' "*

With Jackson gone, Lee restructured the army by creating three corps instead of two. Ewell and A. P. Hill now joined Longstreet as corps commanders. Once Longstreet and his two divisions arrived from southeast Virginia, the Army of Northern Virginia numbered just under 80,000 men. By then, Lee had gathered sufficient wagons and supplies, and he was ready for his long-awaited advance.

In the aftermath of the Battle of Chancellorsville, Union troops held their heads low. "The roads and fields are filled with troops going back to their old camps," moped a sergeant, "but a more disheartened set of fellows I never saw. All because we were ordered to retreat." In the minds of soldiers in the Army of the Potomac, leadership at the top snatched defeat from the jaws of victory.

Morale did not suffer for long, at least among cavalrymen. In early June, while on a mission to determine whether Lee had begun to shift his army, Federal horsemen surprised J. E. B. Stuart's mounted troops at Brandy Station (or Beverly Ford). The two-pronged attack penetrated Stuart's screen and ascertained that Lee had maneuvered his army to the northwest, perhaps as a springboard for a northern raid. Equally important, Union cavalrymen had surprised Stuart and his men. Confederate infantry-men rushed to the aid of their stunned comrades, adding more in the way of emotional support than actual firepower, and Rebel horsemen eventually drove the Yankees back across the Rappahannock River. But the Federals had shattered the aura of invincibility that Confederate cavalry had earned, and Stuart took a beating in the press for his lack of preparedness. "The battle at Beverly Ford had stiffened up the troopers wonderfully, increasing their morale and confidence," assessed a Yankee officer. "A new era began to dawn upon our hitherto somewhat disorganized cavalry force, for it was seen that the Confederate cavalry, with its easily accumulated prestige, was now slightly on the wane, more especially because they could no longer rely upon blooded remounts." A member of Stuart's staff pithily summed up the affair when he noted that the Battle of Brandy Station "*made the Federal cavalry.*"

While the Confederate horse soldiers endured a taste of humility, the rest of the Army of Northern Virginia rode a wave of conviction. "I am sure there can never have been an army with more confidence in its commander than that army had in Gen. Lee," recalled the multi-talented Edward Porter Alexander. "We looked forward to victory under him as confidently as to successive sunrises." Barely a month and a half ago, they had bested a massive Union force without two of Longstreet's division. With their return, nothing could stop them.

Certainly, they had lost Jackson. He was irreplaceable. But the Dick Ewell–Jubal Early combination seemed to measure up well as a substitute. At the Battle of Second Winchester, in mid-June, Ewell's troops crushed a Federal command, inflicting heavy losses and capturing well over three thousand Yankees. A Union officer claimed that the Confederates had lied about Jackson's death. Referring to Early's flank attack, he insisted, "there was no officer in either army that could have executed that movement but 'Old Jack.' " Richmond newspapers, too, joined the chorus, proclaiming Ewell the Second Jackson. Troops rejected such labels as hyperbole, yet his handling of the affair impressed most soldiers and boded well for the war effort.

On the march northward, troops stirred up clouds of dust that coated clothing and hair and caked on faces. Everyone, it seemed, had doused their hair, eyebrows, and eyelashes with white. Only streams of perspiration disrupted the uniform pale facial mask, creating a macabre appearance. "A demon or ghost could not have looked worse," a soldier jotted down. Mile after mile they trudged, as scorching June heat and choking dirt particles sucked energy from the men in gray.

The Potomac River offered an opportunity to cleanse themselves of Virginia soil. In a frolicsome event, thousands of buck-naked men hoisting clothing and accouterments aloft, plunged into the brisk, waist-deep river, "yelling & screaming like school children." The crossing shattered the monotony and refreshed the body-weary. When they emerged on the opposite bank, soldiers occupied Maryland soil.

Plundering among resource-scarce soldiers had already become a problem. In mid-June, Ewell had warned his corps that "this plundering must be repressed or our discipline is gone." Three days later, when the provost marshal entered Martinsburg, "there was a mob breaking open stores," committing all sorts of depredations.

While local citizens huddled in their homes "nearly frightened to death," according to an officer, "the streets were crowded with hundreds of drunken men as there are any number of bar rooms & distilleries in town." Across the Potomac in Sharpburg, "our boys have nearly all supplied themselves with articles of some use or necessity." Whether troops liberated items is unclear, but a soldier did admit, "The stores have been opened & the prices have been to us 'Dixie boys' remarkably moderate."

Although Maryland had remained in the Union, it was a sister slave state, and many Confederates believed that Northerners coerced Marylanders into retaining their loyalty to the old Constitution. Pennsylvania lay above the Mason–Dixon Line. It was the undisputed land of the enemy, and Lee's troops eagerly anticipated an opportunity to cross over into Pennsylvania and invade the North. For two years, nearly all fighting by Lee's Army had taken place in Virginia. It had been Virginia homes invaded, Virginia livestock confiscated, Virginia fences dismantled, and Virginia fields trampled. Now, it was time to exact some retribution. "The wrath of southern vengeance will be wreaked upon the pennsilvanians & all property belonging to the abolition horde which we may cross," vowed a soldier. "We will try & pay them for what they have been doing to the innocent & helpless in our good southern land."

As Confederates pushed on into Pennsylvania, the countryside startled them. For most, this was their first trip to the North, and the natural beauty of the region and the level of opulence among northern farmers shocked these southern boys. They had accepted unquestioningly arguments about the superiority of slave labor. What they saw, however, belied those tales. Soldier after soldier wrote home of stunning landscape, with hardwood forests atop hills and lush pastureland and tidy fields scattered along the gentle slopes and valley floors. In Pennsylvania, the soil was rich and the livestock fat. Impressive stone homes and enormous barns dotted the panorama. Evidently, these middle-class farmers in a free labor society did quite well for themselves.

Not nearly as impressive were the local inhabitants. Typical was the comment of a private, who wrote to his sister, "We passed through some of the prettiest country that I ever saw in my life they has [some] of the finest land in it in the world and some of the ugliest women that I ever saw." Soldiers usually treated the residents respectfully, except when locals were a bit too forceful in their support of the Union. One Pennsylvania woman, adorned with a miniature flag affixed to her blouse, cast contemptuous glances at Confederate troops as they marched past. Finally, a Texan had enough. Pointing his finger at the woman, he announced, "Take care, madam, for Hood's boys are great at storming breastworks when the Yankee colors is on them." She retreated into her home.

It was Lee's intention to disperse his forces, drawing on the local population for foodstuffs, fresh horses and fodder, and any other equipment that his army might need. Plundering was unacceptable behavior. He directed officers to pay Northerners for goods, and those who refused to sell would have the necessary property confiscated and a receipt issued to them. Any citizen who attempted to conceal or remove food or useful equipment would have the property seized and their name submitted to headquarters. Clearly, Lee wanted no mob activity.

Instead, deprivation, temptations, and hostility toward Northerners bred misconduct. Quartermasters and soldiers alike took all they could carry or consume, stretching Lee's directives to the breaking point. "There was, in short, a good deal of lawlessness," confessed an officer, "but not as much as might have been expected under the circumstances." Another soldier declared that he and his comrades "enjoyed ourselves finely." He went on to admit that "although positive orders were issued prohibiting soldiers from disturbing private property, they paid no attention to any order of the kind, and took everything they could lay their hands on in the eating line."

Pennsylvanians, like Southerners in Georgia and the Carolinas in the face of William T. Sherman's march, tried their best to conceal livestock and other items. Despite their ingenuity, efforts failed. "They were hidden in most extraordinary places," explained a Carolinian. "Some in upper stories of barns & others in cellars of houses. Some even in haystacks all of which was very ludicrous."

Troops plundered abandoned buildings and occasionally took items from civilians. "Numbers of our soldiers exchanged hats with citizens to day, without a willingness on part of citizens," a soldier confessed. "Some of them who were bare footed made citizens pull off shoes and boots." Quartermasters, commissary personnel, and individual troops scoured the region for horses, mules, and cows, impressing all they could lay their hands on. Officers indulged their men and even joined in the process. Almost everyone seized what they wanted. "In short, we killed, captured, and destroyed everything that came our way," boasted a Rebel.

For many Confederates, it was simply a matter of giving Pennsylvanians a taste of real conflict. "They have Known nothing of the war heretofore," justified a Virginian, "and I believe unless we do bring it home to them in this manner they would be willing to carry it on indefinitely." Another Virginian, writing to his father, expressed similar sentiments: "I hope these people may be taught the horrors of war—may be made to feel its deep effects both upon their pockets and persons."

The repercussions of such conduct were subtle, yet grave. For two years, Confederates in the Virginia Theater had repulsed overwhelming Union forces. While superior leadership had been an instrumental factor, victory demanded more. It required tenacious fighting. Beyond their ramshackle look, the men in the Army of Northern Virginia were an aggressive, disciplined, focused, seasoned combat command. That ability to execute in battle had saved them time after time. They carried critical works, held on to key pieces of terrain, delayed their opponents at vital moments, and laid down their lives at pivotal junctures in order to win. In time, they developed an unflagging confidence in themselves and their officers.

Yet it was more than merely a belief in their capacity to fight. Confederates tapped into an extra incentive by battling in defense of their civil rights and for the protection of their loved ones and homes. This additional motivation provided unusual direction. It instilled in them an ability to focus deeply on the problem at hand. Amid the external jollity, these troops possessed a capacity to concentrate, a mental keenness that enabled them to endure untold hardships and execute in the face of unusual adversity. On numerous fields, the margin for victory was slim. That focus provided them with just enough edge to triumph in battle after battle.

On the raid into Pennsylvania, foraging and plundering dulled their edge. The campaign adopted a festive tone, as discipline slipped and concentration lapsed. In essence, the Army of Northern Virginia lost that focus. The excitement of invading the North, the necessity of roaming the countryside and rummaging through homes for essentials, and the opportunity to seize goods that sacrificing soldiers and their loved ones at home had done without for so long was too much for the troops. Officers succumbed to the wishes of the men and their own desires. "Stringent orders have been issued against such conduct by our generals," recorded a company-level officer, "though it is rather a hard matter to restrain our troops when they remember the devastated plains of Virginia and the conduct of the Federals in other portions of our country." In enemy territory, with novel experiences and unusual distractions, Confederate troops needed to elevate their level of concentration, to strengthen their fix on the campaign and its execution. Instead, it dwindled.

Hooker, for his part, responded slowly to Lee's advance. Stuart's cavalry disguised Rebel movements temporarily, and his raid northward further confused the picture from the Union perspective. The Union army commander also seemed a bit reluctant to lock swords with Lee. More than anyone else, Hooker had failed at the Battle of Chancellorsville. He had designed an excellent plan, and executed well initially, but at the critical moment he lost courage in himself, his scheme, and to some extent his army. Lee exploited the opening, and Hooker and his command, beaten by vastly inferior numbers, withdrew to safety.

Fortunately for the North, morale suffered only a brief decline among Union troops. In their minds, they had not lost at Chancellorsville—their generals had. Faith in one another and their cause remained unshaken. And they chastised those at home whose belief wavered. "Mother, you said you was down harted," private Jerome Farnsworth penned, "now ma I just tell you that you must not get discouraged for Every thing will be Well." He reminded her that all her sons in the army were alive and in good health and urged her, "remember that they are a fighting for to put this Horrible Rebellion down and to Save our Country."

The thrill of soldiering had vanished long ago; warfare was serious business. As Union troops began their sluggish pursuit northward, a veteran from the Iron Brigade spotted some men from the 22nd Corps, garrison soldiers for the Washington defenses, all attired in fresh, clean uniforms. He and his comrades admired the new garb, "But those days of 'fancy soldiering' had long since passed away and we were now on a real military campaign loaded with dust, our clothes appearing as if we had never used a brush on them, and we careing little how we appeared."

In late June, as the Union army pursued tentatively, troops received some good news. Hooker had locked horns repeatedly with General in Chief Henry W. Halleck and Secretary of War Edwin M. Stanton over strategy and other military policies, and when he offered his resignation, authorities in Washington accepted it. His replacement as commander of the Army of the Potomac was Maj. Gen. George G. Meade.

Meade was a West Point graduate and a topographical engineer in the Old Army. A bright, hard-working man and an excellent tactician, Meade had an explosive temper that earned him the nickname "Old Snapping Turtle." He had risen steadily from brigade to corps commander based on his accomplishments. Unlike many general officers in the Army of the Potomac, Meade refused to play politics or criticize superiors. He concentrated on his job, performed it well, and won the respect of officers and men alike. "Meade was our corps general," a captain commented to his mother after the selection. "You may know perhaps,—a grumpy, stern, severe, and admirable soldier."

With Meade at the helm, pursuit suddenly took on a sense of mission and urgency. He had orders to target Lee's army, all the while shielding Baltimore and Washington. At Pipe Creek, some twenty miles southeast of Gettysburg, Meade laid out a strong defensive position, in case his army had to retire, and then pushed beyond it. Skillfully, he fanned his forces out in all directions in search of the enemy, always keeping his seven corps in support of one another. On June 29, the 1st Corps marched thirty miles in mid-summer heat. "About half the corps fell out," recorded a New York private, "many of them coming up afterwards." The next day, early morning rain created hot and muggy weather. Again it was a long, fatiguing jaunt for the Federals. By the morning of July 1, Meade's corps were anywhere from five to twenty-five miles from Gettysburg, and he had instructed Maj. Gen. John Reynolds to take charge of the three forward corps and be prepared for offensive or defensive operations.

On crossing north into Pennsylvania, a transformation took place among the soldiers in the Army of the Potomac. No longer were they in enemy territory or a state like Maryland, where slavery existed and support for the Union cause was mixed. In Virginia, the women "are our bitterest enemies, where they never look on us except with contempt and never speak but in derision," noted a soldier. Guerrillas infested the countryside, and soldiers always had to be on their guard. Anyone who wandered away from camp carelessly did so at his peril. Maryland was not nearly so dangerous, but soldiers had to act cautiously there, too. In Pennsylvania, they were among friends. Soldiers could concentrate exclusively on the Confederate army.

More important, they gained a psychological boost by campaigning in Pennsylvania. Now, they were fighting to drive an invader from their own soil, to protect their own hearths and homes. The notion gave added impetus to their spirit and strengthened their will to defeat Lee's army. As the 41st Pennsylvania crossed into its home state near midnight on July 1, "The col[onel] Halted us at the line and the boys gave 3 cheers for old Pa[.] and we vowed never to leave the state until we had driven the rebels out," explained Edwin Benedict. "We all felt enthused and showed our determination by increasing our speed." He concluded by reporting, "There is no nonsense about us." Crowds gathered outside shops and homes to cheer on their defenders. In reply, "Many a fervent 'God bless you!' and 'Good for you!' were uttered by the tired and weary soldiers, and many, too, forgot their weariness and their loads, feeling that for such they could fight and endure any hardship without grumbling," a Minnesotan penned home. A fellow named Russ Allen then called out to his buddies, "Boys, who wouldn't fight for such as these?" The commitment of the troops firmed. "Just that little expression," recorded a witness, "and the way it was expressed, seemed to put new life into all of us, and we resolved, if possible, to give them yet more pleasure by driving the invaders from their soil." Days later, Allen gave his life in the attempt.

Federal soldiers perceived a major battle in Pennsylvania as a great opportunity for them. With the Confederates such a long distance from home, a decisive victory and a vigorous pursuit by Union forces could devastate the primary secessionist field command. "We hope to capture or so cripple the confederate army here on northern soil that the south will give up the contest and an honorable peace restored," an optimistic Connecticut soldier jotted down in his diary. "But," came the great caveat, "time will determine." In the recesses of their minds, many Federals sought to end the war here, as did their Confederate counterparts.

The Battle of Gettysburg was an encounter engagement. Neither side anticipated a large-scale fight there. It began almost by accident, with some skirmishing on June 30 and full-fledged combat the following day. Confederates in Maj. Gen. Harry Heth's Division of A. P. Hill's Corps trudged into town in search of plunder; Federal cavalry under Brig. Gen. John Buford opposed them. Once the two sides exchanged fire, reinforcements poured into the area, deploying and joining the fray without any specific plan in mind, merely to take advantage of visible openings.

Heth parcelled his two lead brigades on either side of the Chambersburg Pike. Buford's men, supported by some artillery, fought aggressively and held their position until infantry supplanted them. The weary horsemen then passed rearward through town.

Federals in the 1st Corps arrived on the scene and filtered through cavalry lines. Among those forces, the famed Iron Brigade of Wisconsin, Michigan, and Indiana troops caused the greatest impact. These men crashed through some woods and overwhelmed James J. Archer's Brigade of Tennesseans and Alabamians in front and flank, capturing a sizeable portion of the command, including Archer. On the other side of the Chambersburg Pike, where New York and Pennsylvania troops had their hands full against Joseph R. Davis's Brigade of Mississippians and North Carolinians, the 6th Wisconsin of the Iron Brigade dealt the heavy blow. Ordered to " 'move to the right' and 'go like hell,' " these Badgers waded through a withering fire and stormed a railroad cut to dislodge those "kowardly sons of bitches." In the end, they seized the prized ground and a few hundred Confederates along with it. The price, however, was immense. The names of over one-third of the 6th Wisconsin appeared on the casualty list.

To the north, Maj. Gen. Robert Rodes's division of Ewell's Corps suddenly materialized on Oak Hill. One of Lee's premier division commanders, Rodes had received orders the previous day to withdraw from Carlisle and concentrate at Cashtown. With the fight well underway, he deployed three brigades in front and two in support and pressed forward without skirmishers. The troops on Rodes's right helped to clear the railroad cut and drive the Federals back to a gentle slope near town. The Rebels east of the road attacked feebly and fell back rapidly, thus opening the door for a Union concentration on the middle brigade.

After the Yankee 1st Corps, men from the 11th Corps arrived on the scene. They secured Cemetery Hill south of town with their artillery and rushed to the sounds of gunfire, forming part of an L-shaped position that shielded Gettysburg on the north and west sides. As Brig. Gen. Alfred Iverson's North Carolinians in Rodes's center advanced, Union troops who had opposed the weak attack east of the Mummasburg Road swung around and concealed themselves along a stone wall directly on Iverson's left flank. The Tar Heels stepped right into the trap. Federals rose up and poured a devastating fire into the Confederates. The next morning, a Rebel artilleryman recorded the tragic sight. Seventy-nine North Carolinians lay dead in a perfectly straight line, apparently killed by a single volley. Other victims were scattered across the field. The scene was "perfectly sickening" and "would have satiated the most blood-thirsty and cruel man on God's earth," he moaned. It was a turkey shoot with human targets. "Great God!" he recorded in exasperation, "When will this horrid war stop?"

With Rodes's Division stalled, victory on the first day seemed within Union grasp, until a Confederate division under Jubal Early rolled around the Federal right wing. Down the road from Heidlersburg, northeast of Gettysburg, Early's troops pressed, penetrating the Yankee rear and threatening to cut off the retreat route through the town. Panic gripped thousands of bluecoats from the 11th Corps, who broke ranks and raced rearward. That compelled soldiers of the 1st Corps to flee also. In the confusion, a Wisconsin man was knocked down and trampled by his comrades. Some Federals passed through town to safety, while others were cut off or tried to hide. Many, though, were not so fortunate. A Confederate thought they "draged as many as five hundred from the cellars." All told, over three thousand Yankees fell into Confederate hands that day.

South of town, Federals formed a new line, anchored at Cemetery Hill. One month earlier at Chancellorsville, it had been men from the 11th Corps who had buckled under Jackson's flank attack. For some time after the event, Yankees jeered members of the 11th Corps, calling them "Coward" or "Flying Dutchman" in reference to its large number of German regiments. Now, they had done it again. As soldiers emerged from the town, an officer directed them by corps positions. When a man with a German accent asked for the 11th Corps, some embittered soldier shouted over the voice of the directional officer, "1st Corps to the right & 11th Corps go to *hell*."

That evening and throughout the night, Federal forces streamed into the Gettysburg area, anchoring the right and extending along a ridge to form a fishhook-shaped position. Amid the darkness, soldiers on their own initiative piled logs, branches, and stones to form barricades or exploited existing walls as protection against Confederate advances. The lucky ones caught a few hours of sleep, but many rested little more than an hour. By sunrise, five of the seven Union corps, along with the army commander, were on the scene.

Although Lee arrived in the vicinity of Gettysburg in mid-afternoon, he could not organize his army well enough to strike again before nightfall. Losses were so severe that regiments and, in a few cases, brigades almost dissolved. Confederate units had converged from the west, north, and northeast on the Yankee position, and, in the rout, commands got mixed up. Structure disintegrated as units searched house to house. Soldiers uncovered pockets of resistance, crushed them, and gathered and escorted prisoners to the rear. Even worse, Confederates continued their pillaging activities. Many broke into shops and homes and appropriated so many items that a soldier boasted, "I assure you that city is well plundered. The Louisianians left nothing that human hands could destroy." Other Confederates complained about how their comrades dropped out of ranks to rob Yankees killed and wounded. A Maryland man grumbled, "Very often you could see some of our boys go down on a dead yank and take his money out of his pocket." An officer on Early's staff scanned the battlefield and was disgusted with what he saw. "The Yankee dead were stripped, almost to utter nakedness," he wrote with shame. "It seems strange that the champion of liberty, can be the prostitute of avarice. Yet such is the case." He went to state, "The hand that

shoots from the front rank of battle is frequently the first to find the pockets of the dead and this pilfering of the fallen is by no means confined to the skulkers, & followers in the rear." Thus, casualties, chaos, a breakdown of discipline, and darkness prevented the Confederates from mounting a strong attack that evening on the new position.

As the sun rose, Union soldiers observed their commander, Meade, surveying the line. With the eye of a topographical engineer, Meade examined it carefully. The position his forces had laid out impressed him. One soldier heard him utter, "We may fight it out here just as well as anywhere else." Meade's decision to stand and fight complimented the army. By implication, it indicated his belief in their ability to slug it out with Lee's troops.

On the Confederate side, Stuart's cavalry, on its grandiose raid around the Union command, was still unaccounted for, but most of Lee's army had concentrated the night before. Early the next morning, after a reconnaissance indicated that the Union had neglected to secure its south wing, Lee ordered two of Longstreet's divisions to swing around to the south and roll up the Federal left flank. To position themselves properly for a surprise attack, Confederate troops began the march and had to backtrack, wasting all morning and much of the afternoon. The lengthy trek under a roasting sun and stifling humidity drained the attackers of precious energy. By 4 P.M., when the attack finally began, Longstreet's troops were tired.

In defense, Maj. Gen. Daniel Sickles, commander of the Federal 3rd Corps, had foolishly projected his forces out from the original line to occupy some high ground where locals had planted peach trees. The new bow in the Union position doubled the length of his defense, forcing him to commit all his reserves and to pull troops away from a natural southern anchor, Little Round Top, to maintain a contiguous line. Meade's Chief Engineer, Gouverner K. Warren, noticed the problem, and a division from the 5th Corps raced over to secure the position as the assault began.

On the Confederate right flank, Hood's men rumbled through difficult terrain just to reach Union lines. At Devil's Den, a rocky outcropping guarded by huge boulders several hundred yards north of Little Round Top, Union guns poured such an effective fire into the attackers that it drew front-line and follow-on units like a magnet. Eventually, Confederates carried Devil's Den, but carefully positioned artillery and infantry to the rear prevented the attackers from exploiting the gain. The resistance, moreover, detracted from the strength of the extreme Confederate right by drawing away two Alabama regiments from the initial assault and a brigade of Georgians who composed the second wave.

Over at Little Round Top, Alabamians and Texans attempted to seize the position by storm. They had carried such difficult places before; this time, they failed. Disorganized from the cut-up terrain, and fatigued by a long day in a broiling sun, these Rebel attackers launched several assaults late that afternoon. Lacking reinforcements, they were too few in number and too weary in body and spirit to wrest the position from the Federals. Even had they gained Little Round Top, Federal reinforcements approaching the area most likely would have snuffed out the penetration, as they did elsewhere on the field that day. So exhausted and demoralized were these Confederates that four hundred of them surrendered to a counterattack by perhaps two hundred men with fixed bayonets.

Aiding the defenders, too, was a severe water shortage among the troops from Alabama and Texas. The exhausting march in intense heat sapped liquids from their bodies, and as soldiers ripped apart cartridges with their teeth, the gunpowder sponged up all moisture in their mouths. The brigade commander later admitted his men "suffered greatly for water," believing it "contributed largely to our failure." Yet it was not simply a matter of thirst that injured the attacker's cause. Without water, Confederates could not clean their weapons of the black powder residue that caked the inside of their rifle barrels. After firing a dozen rounds, the grimy buildup prevented them from ramming down charges. Armed with unusable muskets, their weary bodies drained of fluids, and spirits flagging, they were nearly defenseless against the Union counterattack.

Much credit has gone to Col. Joshua Chamberlain of the 20th Maine for his leadership in the valiant defense of Little Round Top. Yet it was Chamberlain, a historian with exceptional writing skills, who prepared the dramatic report. Soldiers in the regiment who wrote home immediately after the battle scarcely mentioned Chamberlain. It was his troops who stood tall that day, resisting the Confederate onslaught superbly. Amid the smoke, noise, and fright, few in the regiment probably noticed their colonel. The men in the 20th Maine, like so many other Union soldiers that day, reached deep within themselves and found the character and fortitude to do what was necessary for victory. When ammunition ran out, soldiers remained at their post, rather than fall back. Chamberlain may have ordered them to fix bayonets, but evidently the critical counterassault was either spontaneous or directed by a subordinate officer.

Elsewhere on the field that day, Union and Confederate forces battled with similar results. Several times Confederates pierced the Federal line, only to falter at the critical moment. Tired from the prolonged delays, drained by the heat, and lacking that sharp edge of focus and discipline that had sustained its charges in the past, Confederate columns fought aggressively at first, but failed to exploit the advantage. Casualties and straggling soldiers eroded the power of their assault, and lacking the mental toughness to see the attack through as they had done so many times in Virginia, Federals hurled them back. Lee's army suffered some 6,500 losses that day, all in vain.

Despite being overwhelmed at the initial point of attack, Union troops fought an inspired battle on July 2. Two days earlier, Meade had requested subordinates explain to the troops "the immense issues involved in the struggle" and that "The whole country now looks anxiously to this army to deliver it from the presence of the foe." He believed the Army of the Potomac "will fight more desperately and bravely than ever if it is addressed in fitting terms." The men responded. Before Brig. Gen. John Gibbon's division entered combat, officers read Meade's circular to the troops, reminding them what was at stake and urging them to do their duty. One of Gibbon's soldiers, in the 1st Minnesota, applauded the decision, insisting "one thing our armies lack is enthusiasm, and no efforts are made to create it, when, in many cases, it would accomplish more than real bravery or bull dog courage." That day, the 262 men who composed the 1st Minnesota suffered 82 percent casualties, but drove back Cadmus Wilcox's Alabama Brigade in a desperate fight. Genuine enthusiasm and bulldog courage marked their conduct.

No other Yankee units endured the losses of the 1st Minnesota, and perhaps none accomplished as much with such limited manpower, but the Army of the Potomac had never fought better. Some 9,500 Federals fell on July 2. Nevertheless, the Union troops had held, despite some generals' blunders. That day, they were a focused, motivated combat force. Often in the past, with their line shattered, they had fled to the rear. This time, they battled desperately, fell back and regrouped, and fought again. On several occasions, at critical moments, determined bluecoats repelled superior numbers of Lee's troops. They reached deep within themselves and discovered the courage, fortitude, and sheer force of will to bend, but not break.

After moments of indecision on the night of July 2, Meade elected to remain right there and slug it out with the Confederates the next day. Again, he had made a statement to the troops that he believed in them.

The entire affair had frustrated Lee. It was an encounter engagement on a field not of his choosing. Despite great success on July 1, his army had not completed its work. The Confederates had squandered too much daylight on the second day, and had failed to exploit opportunities. He could withdraw in the face of an undefeated enemy, a risky proposition at best that would most likely end the campaign, or he could attempt one more desperate fight. Audacious to the core, Lee placed his faith in the Army of Northern Virginia to win the next day.

Lee's plan for the third day was to place pressure on the two Union flanks and crack through the Federal center. Near success in the middle of the Union line convinced Lee that Meade had weakened the center to fortify the wings. Ewell's Corps, on the northern end, would strike at Culp's and Cemetery Hills. Stuart's cavalry, which had only reached Gettysburg on the afternoon of July 2, would swing around both Big and Little Round Top and threaten Meade's rear. An extensive bombardment, followed by a massive assault, would rupture the Yankee line.

At 1. P.M., the Confederates fired a signal salvo, followed by a barrage of shot and shell. One hundred thirty-eight guns under the command of Brig. Gen. Porter Alexander blasted away at the Union defenses, sustaining a tremendous fire for nearly three hours. Federal artillery replied vigorously at first, but gradually tapered off to conserve ammunition. A Mississippian recalled that "the smoke was so thick that I could not see our battery horses between our lines and the guns." Nor could the troops tell the difference between the reverberation of Rebel guns and the explosion of Yankee shells. Both shook the ground terribly.

From Culp's Hill, a Connecticut soldier reported, "All at once it seemed as though all the artillery in the universe had opened fire and was belching forth its missiles of death and destruction." The thunderous sound, recorded a Yankee officer, reminded him of Niagara Falls. Soldiers along Cemetery Ridge hunkered down as best they could, to shield themselves from the deadly projectiles. Solid shot struck among the Federals or in front and bounced through the lines, as Rebel gunners intended. But exploding shells, the ammunition that Confederates depended on for success, failed them. Only those shells that struck well up in the trees rained chards and chunks of lead on the defenders. According to a Minnesotan, the enemy "tried to explode their shells directly over us, but fortunately, most of them just went far enough to clear us." Although some Federals were killed or wounded in the bombardment, no one in his regiment suffered an injury. "Many more were killed in the rear than in the front," he insisted, "though their fire was directed at the front line and batteries nearly altogether." Wagons, rear-area personnel, and Meade's headquarters, hundreds of yards behind the front line, endured a blistering fire, while the Confederates had neglected to soften up the Union defenders. Smoke and clouds of dirt obscured the view. The attackers did not know that the greatest bombardment since the origin of mankind had not fulfilled its designs.

As his ammunition began to run out, Alexander sent word to open the assault. Soldiers rose to their feet and aligned. Eleven brigades joined in the attack, led by troops in George Pickett's and J. J. Pettigrew's Divisions. Alexander supported them as best he could with the artillery, but problems with premature explosion of shells negated any hope of indirect cannon fire to assist them.

"I never was scard as bad in my life," confessed a Mississippian in Pettigrew's Division. Over several fences and up and down gentle slopes elegant formations of Confederates marched. Union rounds carved gaping holes in these ranks, only to have them close up rapidly. The various angles of approach and the different distances that the attackers had to cover began to disrupt formations. At a range of approximately 250 yards, Union infantry opened fire. Rather than continue the charge, pockets of Confederates halted in open ground and exchanged rifle fire, exposing themselves horribly and detracting from the power of the assaulting waves.

On the Confederate left, brigades converged on the target area. Gradually, however, strength on the wing withered away. Federals concentrated effective fire on the outer flank of the attackers, first compelling Brockenbaugh's Virginians to fall back, then Davis's Mississippians. As the remainder of Pettigrew's Division struck the principal Federal line, Yankees poured fire from two and sometimes three directions. The Confederate left buckled. "Suddenly the column gave way," described an Ohioan, "the sloping landscape appeared covered, all at once, with the scattered and retreating foe. A withering sheet of missiles swept after them, and they were torn and tossed and prostrated as they ran. It seemed as if not one would escape."

Among the defenders, a New Yorker "thought that our line would give way as I noticed the uneasiness of some of the men." At a critical moment,

"some of the men began to cheer and the spirit was soon spread along the line." Within seconds, "cheer on cheer rent the air and we all fought with increased vigor and the ranks of the foe became confused and broken and they were forced back."

The stalwart Union defense, accompanied by a devastating fire on the flank and even rear, demoralized many attackers. "Rebels laid down their arms & came in and no one to make them," described a Federal soldier. His regiment alone claimed five Confederate flags that day. One of the heroes, his brother Morris, led a party of ten Union troops who counterattacked and seized the 14th North Carolina's flag. Morris received a Medal of Honor for his efforts.

In the center and on the Confederate right, miscommunication caused serious problems. Pickett's brigades angled sharply to the left, while Wilcox's Alabamians and Perry's Brigade of Floridians charged directly ahead, splitting the assault columns. Some Vermonters seized the opening. On orders from their brigade commander, they struck Pickett's men on the flank and damaged that attack. Then, the 16th Vermont pivoted and poured a wicked fire on Wilcox's and Perry's Brigades, shattering their charge.

Led fearlessly by their brigade commanders, the bulk of Pickett's troops rushed onward. With a shout, they raced at the double quick toward the works. Blasts of canister and volley after volley of Federal rifle fire struck down Confederates by the hundreds. Some halted in the open field and blazed away at the Yankees, and then continued the advance. Others dropped to the earth, shielding themselves from the hail of lead. To them, the situation was hopeless; the risk was too great.

Yet, somehow, a portion of the wave pressed on. At twenty yards from the wall they endured a burst, recoiled, and then surged forward. The sight of this seemingly irresistible mass panicked the defenders. Suddenly, some Pennsylvanians broke and raced rearward, leaving a handful of their comrades to repel the onslaught. Several hundred intrepid Confederate souls crashed over a low stone wall and penetrated the Union works. Remnants of the Pennsylvania regiments battled them with rifle butts and bayonets, as if they were warring for sacred ground, but the Northerners were outmanned.

In reality, the Rebels were too few in number, and too far from support, for this small band to have held the break for long. To an unlikely hero like Lieut. Frank Haskell, however, the situation appeared perilous. A Wisconsin volunteer on Gibbon's staff, Haskell coaxed adjacent brigades into lending support, and then helped rally the troops for a counterattack. With Haskell in the thick of it, Yankee reinforcements smashed into the Southerners. The struggle lasted just a few minutes. These Confederates fought brilliantly, but their numbers were too small. Many fell right there; others yielded to the Federals. And some foolishly attempted to run the gauntlet back to Confederate lines, where they made easy targets.

Lee's attack had failed. Bodies littered the field, and those who had broken or laid down now had to race back across "no man's land." Union riflemen and artillery picked them off as they worked their way rearward. As one soldier described, "many noble spirits who had passed safely through the fiery ordeal of the advance and charge, now fall on the right and on the left." A few Confederates backed their way out, fearing the mortification of their family had they been shot in the back while retreating. Thousands lay still or groaning with wounds. As Pickett rode off the field, tears rolled down his cheeks. "Taylor," he sobbed to a staff officer, "we've lost all our friends."

A few weeks after the battle, tests undertaken by the Confederate Ordnance Department indicated some problems that may have been an influential factor in the outcome of the fight on July 3. Complaints of the premature explosion of some shells during the Battle of Chancellorsville led to an investigation of ammunition produced at all Confederate arsenals. From mid-July through January the next year, disturbing results trickled in: There was a lack of regularity in the performance of artillery shells and fuses. When artillerists fired shells and case shot, they cut the fuses a particular length. The blast that hurled the projectile forward also ignited the fuse, which burned down and caused the shell or case shot to explode over the enemy position. Fuses produced in Charleston, Atlanta, and Augusta, however, usually burned slower and performed more inconsistently than those made in Richmond. Confederate artillerists simply assumed a level of uniformity in manufacture, that all fuses burned at roughly the same rate. As experienced gunners, they had estimated the distances correctly. Although some batteries may have cut the fuses a bit longer, to protect themselves against premature explosions, in most instances they employed fuses for the proper length of shells manufactured in Richmond. But because many of the shells and fuses had come from the other arsenals in the aftermath of the Richmond Arsenal explosion, the fuses burned more unevenly—often slower—and the explosive projectiles carried far beyond the Union line before they burst. Clouds of smoke and dirt obscured visual confirmation of the gunners' accuracy, but the explosion of Yankee caissons and damage to Federal guns by solid shot convinced them that they had determined the range properly.

As darkness settled over the battlefield, Union forces engaged in the horrible task of attending to the dead and wounded. On Culp's Hill, where fighting had begun before sunrise and lasted into the early afternoon, Federal troops built fires to light up the field. They buried gray and blue alike and carried the injured to hospitals. "The groans and moans of the wounded were truly sadning," recorded a Connecticut soldier.

Over the next few days, soldiers gazed at the battlefield in utter shock and dismay. "Such a sight I never want to see again," insisted a man from New Hampshire. "The men had turned black, their eyes had sweled out of their head and they were twice the natural size and the stench of the field was awful and dead men were thick. You may as well believe," he concluded, "I had rather go in to a fight than to see the effects of it." A New Yorker confirmed the horror when he penned his sister, "The look of their bloated, blackened corpses was a thing to murder sleep." The aftermath of battle haunted him.

Confederates, too, had no immunity from such visions. "Part of the field, across which I had occasion to ride twice, presented a horrible spectacle," recorded Campbell Brown. "Corpses so monstrously swollen that the buttons were broken from the loose blouses & shirts, & the baggy pantaloons fitted like a skin—so blackened that the head looked like an immense cannon ball, the features being nearly obliterated."

Soldiers initiated the search for friends and loved ones. The heartbreak was nearly unbearable. An officer and his buddy went searching for two friends, presumed killed in action. "We did not look long," he explained to his mother, "it was too sad and horrid a piece of business."

Physicians poured into the Gettysburg area to lend a hand. They had no idea what awaited them. The foul odors and ungodly sights prompted many to lie down and vomit. Without adequate facilities, wounded lay on the field for days and even weeks, until doctors and nurses could care for them. In many cases, the situation was hopeless. "I went to bid good bye to Capt. Barré—of our regiment, but he was unconscious, and died in half an hour after I saw him." Barré lived near family friends and had a wife and two children. Soldiers knew him for a beautiful singing voice. Balls shattered his leg and arm and two more lodged near his spine. For a moment, he awoke and sang, " 'I wish I were a child again, just for tonight.' " Soldiers around him on the ground, wounded and healthy alike, "cried like babies."

Suffering from pain, and slowly expiring, soldiers made amends to their God. A few also had the privilege of jotting some final words to loved ones. "I am here a prisoner of war & mortally wounded," an Alabamian wrote his mother. "I can live but a few hours more at the farthest—was shot fifty yards [from] the enemy's lines. They have been exceedingly kind to me." After expressing the hope that he would live long enough to hear Confederate shouts of victory, he called on his mother, "Do not mourn my loss. I had hoped to have been spared, but a righteous God has ordered it otherwise and I feel prepared to trust my case in his hands." He concluded with the words, "Farewell to you all. Pray that God may receive my soul. *Your unfortunate son John.*" He was buried in an unmarked grave on the outskirts of Gettysburg. Born with an identity, he rests in oblivion.

After the repulse on July 3, Lee expected to continue the battle. He waited a day, hoping the Yankees would come out of their works and offer an open-field fight. Meade refused to take the bait, and by nightfall Lee began the evacuation.

On July 4, Federal forces had much to celebrate. It was the anniversary of the day of the nation's birth, and they had just won their first true victory in the war. Soldiers felt good about themselves and also their commander. The leaders "are now practicing war not theorizing it," exclaimed a Yankee. Meade did not throw them into battle piecemeal. He let the army fight as an army.

But as they dawdled, and Lee's army escaped, Union troops became more and more disillusioned with their leader. "We do not understand why we do not start in pursuit," wrote a soldier in dismay several days after the battle. "Meade was no longer equal to the situation," concluded a New Yorker. As it became more and more apparent that Lee's damaged army was escaping, soldiers became downright hostile. "The Prisoners that come in this morning say that we might have took their whole army just as well as not," complained an annoyed soldier, "it is just as I expected Mead was very fraid of A little rain and laid over 24 hours to long and they sliped away from him evry Solgier is growling about it because we might just as well had him as not and now they will march us like light[n]ing to catch him again but Shit let it go." Soldiers would pay the penalty for Meade's mistake. They would have to fight more campaigns.

For many Federals, the unsatisfactory pursuit placed the Battle of Gettysburg in clearer perspective. Senior leadership had not won there; they had. Never before had the Army of the Potomac fought so well. Campaigning in defense of Union soil had compelled these men to reach deep within themselves, to draw more on their courage, experience, discipline, and commitment than they had ever done before. It aided them just enough to win all the critical engagements within the larger battle. They now knew what it would take to defeat Lee's army, and they felt confident in their ability to replicate that level of focus and performance.

By the time Lee's army returned to Virginia soil, the Confederate troops were absolutely exhausted. It had been a long and demanding campaign, with a merry entrance into the North, a calamitous battle, and a hasty retreat. "We had a nice time going into Pa.," a veteran wrote a friend in early August, "but comeing out was quite to the contrary." Another soldier insisted this was easily the most demanding expedition of the war. "I thought I knew it all, but this last campaign exceeds in hardships anything I ever experienced. I have been cold, hot, wet, dry, ragged, dirty, hungry & thirsty, marched through clouds of dust, waded mud knee deep & suffered from fatigue & loss of sleep." He was glad to be "home," on Confederate soil.

In evaluating the campaign and its results, some refused to acknowledge defeat. They equated victory with driving the opposing forces from the field. Since the Confederates retreated voluntarily, they had not lost. "The truth about Gettysburg is that we were *repulsed* at the *final* position of the enemy, & that the *want* of *success* was a *terrible calamity*; but we were *not defeated*," inisted Robert Stiles. "Our men were very much mortified at the result—but say they can whip the Yanks—have done so and can whip them still," justified another soldier. "At no time during the engagement were our men panic stricken or routed." Gettysburg was merely a setback on the road to independence—nothing more.

Yet in their state of exhaustion, quite a number of troops admitted to dissatisfaction, verging on demoralization. With food and rest, however, spirits revived. Others took "french leave"—unauthorized absence—or threatened to do so, but with time to recuperate, they returned to their commands or realized how foolish their thoughts had been. Morale recovered.

Some Rebels blamed their failure on the strength of the Union position. "The Enemy occupied a Gibralter of a position," commented brigade commander Dodson Ramseur. "It was a second Fredericksburg affair," asserted a perceptive captain, "only the wrong way." They chided their leaders for their conduct of the battle. "The insanity of our Generals led them to attack," argued an Alabama officer. Confederate tactics at Gettysburg made no sense. The Yankees "are as mere chaff before the wind when ever they come out in the open country and this but makes the policy of attacking them when they are entrenched more criminal." Another soldier called it a "sin" to kill experienced troops in such numbers because "his place could not be filled."

For the first time since he took command in early June 1862, criticism spilled over on Lee, although most of it was indirect. Soldiers grumbled that the loss was at the general's level, or that "I don't think we made much by going into Pennsylvania." When they did target Lee specifically, it was done so gently. They now admitted that the campaign proved Lee was "*human*." Even those who were more direct in their objections to the way he handled the battle expressed them gingerly. "Gen. Lee was too confident in his men—," conceded a soldier, "expecting them to overcome difficulties too great." Lee himself corroborated that opinion. Assuming full responsibility for the failure of the campaign, he stated in his official report, "More may have been required of them than they were able to perform." In fairness to Lee, however, his army had always carried the critical positions. No doubt, he believed they could crack the Union line.

The attack on July 3 may have been unwise, but Confederate troops had certainly seized more difficult positions than those they attacked on July 2. Part of the explanation for failure, as one soldier pointed out, was that "the enemy had the advantage over them in position, & supplies, and were encouraged to fight, because we were invading their soil." Yet a more determined foe was not the sole reason for the repulse. Another factor rested with the Confederate troops. Throughout the campaign, the distractions of invasion—amid a hostile populace and novel surroundings, living off the countryside and plundering Yankee households—may have stripped the Confederate troops of their fighting edge. The distractions and festivities of the raid eroded their discipline and focus. As one Confederate pinpointed in a letter home, "I felt[,] when I saw how our men were going on[,] that nothing but disaster would follow and in truth I was associated with an armed mob with the broadest license and not with a disciplined army such as General Lee has had under his command." Walter Taylor, Lee's aide-de-camp, employed different words to ratify the same argument, that the soldiers fought better in Virginia than in Pennsylvania. "I will not hide one truth—that our men are better satisfied on this side of the Potomac," he divulged to his brother. "They are not accustomed to operating in an enemy country where the people are inimical to them & certainly every one of them is today worth twice as much as he was three days ago."

For two years, Confederates had dominated the war in Virginia. Time after time, they had pulled out victories, despite overwhelming Union advantages in men and matériel, by drawing on peerless leadership and superiority in battle. There was a focus, a level of concentration, and eventually a confidence among Confederate troops that Federals lacked. But in the Gettysburg Campaign, roles reversed. Fighting on Northern soil, Union troops exhibited an un-usual degree of commitment and tenacity, which enabled them to hold on during the most desperate moments of the battle, to win the critical fights within the fight. And for the first time in the war, Confederates lost those decisive encounters. Distracted by the complexities, hazards, and temptations of invasion, and the ensuing slippage of discipline that widespread foraging and plundering wrought on them, detracted just enough from the fighting effectiveness of Lee's troops to swing the outcome of the battle to the Federals.

For all the casualties, the impact of Gettysburg was more dramatic for Federal soldiers than for Confederates. In a series of major engagements, Lee's army had won all except one, and in that instance the Federals had failed to drive them from the field. No one doubted they would win again. But for the Union troops, the victory at Gettysburg was more important. For the first time, they had bested Lee's army in a campaign. The triumph provided proof positive for soldiers' claims that they were "good stuff" from which to build an army. With proper army leadership, they could defeat the Army of Northern Virginia. This newfound confidence, born of experience, helped to sustain them through that last, decisive year of war.

Study Questions

1. What did Robert E. Lee mean when he said, "I leave the matter up to God and the subordinate officers . . . [to interfere] does more harm than good"?

2. Professor Glathaar contradicts Lee's statement. How?

3. Describe General Lee's objectives in attacking Union forces at Gettysburg.

4. How did Confederate soldiers react when they marched into Pennsylvania? Why did it raise questions among some of them about the virtues of slave labor? How did Confederate troops behave as they arrived in Pennsylvania?

5. Describe the personalities of Robert E. Lee and George G. Meade.

6. Why did the battle result in such horrific numbers of casualties?

7. Describe the significance of the Battle of Gettysburg.

Bibliography

Gettysburg continues to haunt Americans. In 1863, more than 50,000 soldiers were killed or wounded there, and President Abraham Lincoln's speech later consecrated their sacrifice. The literature about Gettysburg has always been rich, no more so than in recent years. For books about Lincoln's speech, see Gary Wills, *Lincoln at Gettysburg: The Words That Remade America* (1992) and Philip B. Kunhardt, *A New Birth of Freedom: Lincoln at Gettysburg* (1983). The classic book on Gettysburg is Bruce Catton's *The Battle of Gettysburg* (1963). For a recent, riveting account of the battle, see Stephen W. Sears, *Gettysburg* (2003). Historians have also taken keen interest in how the battle of Gettysburg has been remembered by Americans. For three excellent books, see Edward Tabor Lilienthal, *Sacred Ground: Americans and Their Battlefields* (1991); Carol Reardon, *Pickett's Charge in History and Memory* (1992); and Jim Weeks, *Memories, Market, and an American Shrine* (2003).

READING 30

John Wilkes Booth and the Politics of Assassination

James W. Clarke

"Right or wrong, God judge me, not man. For be my motive good or bad, of one thing I am sure, the lasting condemnation of the North." So began a letter John Wilkes Booth wrote shortly before his abortive attempt to abduct President Abraham Lincoln. When he later assassinated Lincoln, he was guaranteed the condemnation of the North and most of the South as well. John Wilkes Booth is America's most famous assassin. Hundreds of books and articles have been written about Booth, the assassination, and his motives. Was he a failed actor looking for theatrical immortality by playing a role of his own twisted invention? Were his motives rooted in some childhood trauma or in the need to compensate for some gnawing sense of inferiority? Or were his motives anchored in the external events of his life—the bloody Civil War, the hatred and opposition of Lincoln, the fear of emancipation?

In his book *American Assassins: The Darker Side of Politics,* James W. Clarke argues that not all assassinations can be dismissed simply as the actions of deranged men and women who had easy access to handguns and rifles. Often assassins are motivated by the political context of their age. In the following essay Clarke examines the political context of the Lincoln assassination.

It is commonly assumed that President Lincoln's assassin, John Wilkes Booth, killed to achieve the fame that had eluded him in a floundering career as an actor. Booth's stage career, it is reasoned, had never achieved the distinction of his famous father, the English-born tragedian Junius Brutus Booth, or his older brother Edwin. Realizing this in 1864, and confronted with a bronchial condition that threatened his ability to perform, Booth, in a classically compensatory manner, supposedly decided to resolve his personal disappointments and failures and achieve lasting fame by striking a dramatic political blow for the Confederate cause. Probably the most widely respected and quoted proponent of this view is Stanley Kimmel in his *The Mad Booths of Maryland.*

Drawing upon Kimmel, Booth has been dismissed elsewhere in even less qualified language as merely a deluded, acrobatic, noisy, and alcoholic actor. Other secondary work has imposed a rather strained psychoanalytic interpretation on this general explanation that goes even further in stressing Booth's neurotic motives. Yet even in Kimmel's carefully researched work, numerous facts appear that raise doubts about his interpretation.

The most important qualification of Kimmel's explanation, however, is that it virtually ignores the political context of the assassination: facts such as Lincoln's unpopularity in the North as well as the South, the vicious opposition within his cabinet and the Congress, and the controversy surrounding his re-election in 1864. To ignore the political circumstances and events of the Civil War era is to miss the most important element in Booth's motives. And virtually every account of the assassination that shares Kimmel's conclusion about Booth does just that.

In most cases, the omission is a result of the erroneous assumption that the nation's esteem and affection for Lincoln preceded his death. The fact is that until Appomattox, a week before his

death, Lincoln was one of the most criticized and vilified presidents in American history, commonly referred to as "the baboon, the imbecile, the wet rag, the Kentucky mule." Although winning re-election in 1864 by a convincing margin (55 percent of the popular vote), that victory can be best understood, not in terms of Lincoln's personal popularity, but rather in terms of the ineffectiveness and confusion of the opposition—both within his own party as well as among his Democratic opponents—and a final reluctant resignation of party leaders to the principle that in time of war it is best not to change horses in midstream. When considered in this political context, the facts of Booth's life—both his upbringing and his career—suggest a different view of the man and his motives.

Youth and Career

John Wilkes Booth was born on May 10, 1838 near Baltimore. He was almost twenty-seven years of age when he shot himself in a burning barn surrounded by soldiers on April 26, 1865. Of the ten children born to Junius Brutus Booth and his second wife, Mary Ann Holmes Booth, John Wilkes, or "Johnny" as he was called, was their favorite. A beautiful child with shiny black hair and classically sculpted features, he exuded the brightness and exuberance of a happy childhood. His mother and his older sister Asia adored his kind and gentle ways, while his tempestuous but doting father admired his fiery spirit and athletic ability. As we will see, this positive view of Booth was shared by virtually everyone who ever knew him. He made friends easily and was loyal and generous to a fault. Even after he had achieved fame as an actor, Booth did not forget his childhood friends. Throughout his life his friendships endured, uncontaminated by his success, and they would span a sociological range from stable boys and clerks to debutantes and high-ranking public officials.

As a youth, Booth attended private schools where he studied history and the classics, reading Milton, Byron, and Shakespeare, and committing much of the latter to memory in preparation for a stage career virtually assured by family tradition. He also played the flute. He learned to ride early and well, and his sister later remembered fondly their spirited gallops together chasing imaginary villains through the wooded Maryland countryside. A lover of the outdoors, Booth's respect for living creatures prevented him from becoming the hunter and angler so encouraged by the culture of nineteenth-century America. Rather his interest ran toward botany and geology; he was an observer rather than a conqueror of nature. His sister described him as "very tender of flowers, and of insects and butterflies; lightning bugs he considered as 'bearers of sacred torches' and would go out of his way to avoid injuring them."

An unusually articulate youth, Booth's gaiety and exuberance for life had a contagious quality that partly explains his popularity with those who knew him. Often his activities were punctuated with melodramatic exclamations that delighted his friends. His sister recorded one occasion where he exclaimed:

Heaven and Earth! How glorious it is to live! how divine! to breathe this breath of life with a clear mind and healthy lungs! Don't let us be sad. Life is so short—and the world is so beautiful. Just to breathe is delicious.

Booth was fourteen when his famous father died in 1852. During his lifetime, the elder Booth had become the most famous Shakespearean actor in America. Although his career kept him away from home frequently during his son's formative years, there was no question of his love for the handsome boy who had inherited so much of the old man's spirit and flamboyance. Edwin, Booth's talented but more taciturn older brother, had spent a youthful stage apprenticeship with his father and thus logically assumed many of the roles and much of the acclaim previously enjoyed by the elder Booth. The oldest brother, Junius Brutus, Jr., was also an actor, but being some seventeen years older than John Wilkes, a sibling rivalry, which often placed strains on the relationship between the two younger brothers, never developed between them.

When Booth began his acting career at the age of seventeen, three years after his father's death, there is no question that some rivalry developed with respect to his by-now-famous older brother Edwin. No doubt both were intent on carrying on the proud and highly successful tradition their father had established. What is less clear, however, is the familiar contention that Booth fared less well in the views of audiences and critics than did Edwin—the basic premise of the argument upon which so many have explained the Lincoln assassination.

The evidence appears to support the premise only for the first three years of John's career, when his inexperience was acknowledged in his reviews. The sense of inferiority Kimmel claims Booth experienced during these early years of apprenticeship, performing in the shadow of a late and lamented father and an older brother, was no doubt justified. The fact that Booth had himself billed as "J. Wilkes" rather than invoking the renown of the Booth name attests to that fact. It also suggests Booth's desire to make a reputation on his own merits rather than capitalizing on the fame of his father and brother. Determined in this respect, Booth took his critical knocks, as most young actors do, as an obscure "J. Wilkes" before emerging triumphantly on the Richmond stage in the autumn of 1858 where he delighted audiences and was proclaimed then and until his death as the handsomest actor on the American stage.

The argument that Booth's sympathies for the Confederacy had their origins in the applause of Southern audiences and the critical disdain he received in the North has no basis in fact. After his first three apprenticeship years, Booth was never to receive a bad review—North or South. He was a star, a matinee idol whose talents approximated those of Edwin, while his physical attractiveness and flair on stage exceeded his older brother's and placed him in a position of undeniable ascendancy in the American theater. In fact, the only reservations about his abilities cited by Kimmel are those expressed by Edwin in private correspondence. Contrary to Edwin's assessment, Booth's reviews across the country were sufficiently enthusiastic to trigger professional envy from an older brother. Consider the following representative critical comments taken from Booth's reviews:

An artist of the highest order.
[Richard III, New York, January 1862]

. . . the most brilliant [Richard III]
ever played in the city.
[Chicago, January–February 1862]

In Baltimore, his performances were thought superior to Edwin's. Even in New York where Edwin was a special favorite of theater audiences, complementary comparisons were made. His performances also cut through the typical Bostonian reserve of the *Daily Advertiser,* which allowed that with some reservations about "proper treatment of the voice," it was "greatly pleased" by his Richard III. When he returned to Boston in January 1863 for an appearance in *The Apostate* with brother Edwin in the audience, he was "wildly cheered."

In February of the same year, Booth played Macbeth at the Arch Street Theater in Philadelphia where one of his first appearances as a fledgling actor had been poorly received. Nearby at the Chestnut Street Theater, Edwin Forrest, perhaps America's first matinee idol, was performing in the same role. In a convincing demonstration of his great appeal, audiences ignored Forrest and lined up to see the handsome new star of the American stage—John Wilkes Booth. And reviews indicate that they were not disappointed. Advanced billings for Booth's April appearance as Richard III in Washington described him as "a star of the first magnitude." Reviewers later acknowledged that he had established himself as a reigning favorite in the capital. Attracted by such reviews, President Lincoln saw Booth perform in *The Marble Heart* on November 9, 1863. Later that month, the Washington *Daily National Intelligencer* praised his performance of Romeo in the Shakespearean drama as "the most satisfactory of all renderings of that fine character."

Recognition of Booth's talents were not limited to audiences and critics only. Established professionals in the theater acknowledged his superior talents. John Ellsler, Director of the respected Cleveland Academy of Music, who knew and admired all the Booths, observed that John Wilkes had "more of (his famous father's) power in one performance than Edwin can show in a year." He went on to predict that John Wilkes Booth would become "as great an actor as America can produce."

Such appraisals continued as long and wherever Booth performed. At a March 1864 appearance in New Orleans, he gave an emotional performance before a typically appreciative audience in the same role and on the same stage where his father had given his last performance. Similar praise followed his engagements in Boston later that year, where crowds waited after the performance outside the stage exit hoping for another glimpse of the handsome actor as he left the theater. On November 25, 1864, he appeared for the first and last time with his brothers Edwin and Junius in *Julius Caesar* before an ecstatic audience of over two thousand "Bravo"-shouting New Yorkers who crowded the Winter Garden Theater for a command performance. Again, it should be emphasized that from 1858 through his last performance at Ford's Theater less than a month before the assassination, there is *no* evidence that Booth received other than the most complimentary reviews of his work.

In the context, it is surprising that he remained so well-liked by his peers in the acting profession. Although numerous young women succumbed to Booth's dashing good looks and personal charm, he remained a discrete and invariably kind and sensitive Lothario. Such refinement set him apart from the typical nineteenth-century American male; women found him irresistible. Clara Morris, a contemporary of Booth's on the American stage, described him as "so young, so bright, so gay, so kind." Recalling an incident where Booth, hurrying from the stage door of the theater, inadvertently knocked over a small child, the actress described how Booth picked up the little street urchin and carefully wiped the tears from his grimy face. Then satisfied that the child was not injured, Booth kissed him and pressed a pocketful of change into his hand before dashing off. The significance of the act was that it was so characteristic of Booth:

He knew of no witness to the act. To kiss a pretty clean child under the approving eyes of mamma might mean nothing but politeness, but surely it required the prompting of a warm and tender heart to make a young and thoughtful man feel for and caress such a dirty, forlorn bit of babyhood as that.

Nor was Booth's kindness and generosity confined to star-struck young women and children. He remained a close and loving son and brother to his mother and sister Asia. More interesting, however, is that men from seemingly all walks of life valued the friendship of the engaging young actor. Even male peers within his competitive and egocentric profession genuinely seemed to like and admire Booth. A fellow actor, Sir Charles Wyndham, described him as "a man of flashing wit and magnetic manner. He was one of the best raconteurs to whom I ever listened." Another actor who knew Booth explained that he was liked because of his quick good humor, his love of fun, and his unassuming ease with people regardless of social rank. He never permitted his celebrity status to become a barrier to old friends. He was also generous with his money.

Thus an accurate view of John Wilkes Booth—the view of his contemporaries—represents a stark contrast to the image of a frustrated, highly neurotic actor obsessed with achieving fame. Booth's character emerged out of a childhood of great love and affection—a beautiful, self-confident child who never knew unkindness or hardship. Raised in the cultured, if eccentric, environment of a theatrical aristocracy, the transition to the stage was swift, smooth, and highly successful. The acclaim denied to so many in the acting profession was well within grasp by his twenty-first year. By the time of his death, some six years later, his reputation as a fine actor and matinee idol was established. Booth's popularity and success

John Wilkes Booth is infamous in American history because he assassinated President Abraham Lincoln.

were reflected in his income: in 1862, he wrote that he was averaging 650 dollars per week for his performances—an extraordinary sum for that period. At the time of his death, even after he had cut his performances drastically because of his war-related activities, he wrote that he was earning "more than twenty-thousand dollars a year."

To bolster the unconvincing explanation that professional jealously and an obsessive "greed for fame" motivated Booth, the argument, as previously observed, has also been made that he was threatened with a loss of his voice due to a recurring bronchial condition. Recognizing that his career was limited, he then supposedly turned to political extremism only as a means of eclipsing a loathesome brother's theatrical ascendancy. While this argument cannot be substantiated or denied in the absence of medical evidence, it is true that Booth's sixth performance in New Orleans in March, 1864 was cancelled because of a "cold." But there is simply no other evidence attesting to the alleged seriousness or chronic nature of this problem as Kimmel suggests. Rather it is *assumed* that Booth had permanently damaged his voice and was thus forced to acknowledge that his acting career was over. It is further *assumed* that this circumstance heightened his "neurotic sense of inferiority." Such is the highly questionable basis of the Kimmel explanation.

The Political Context

Political events in 1864, rather than assumptions about chronic laryngitis and sibling rivalry, provide a more accurate context in which to assess Booth's motives. Nearing the completion of his first term in office, Abraham Lincoln enjoyed none of the esteem accorded to him after his death. Lincoln had been elected president, a minority candidate of an upstart new party, with less than 40 percent of the popular vote. He had won only because the Democratic party had divided ranks with two candidates, J. C. Breckenridge and Stephen A. Douglas, splitting 47.5 percent of the vote while the remaining 12.6 percent went to Constitutional Union party candidate John Bell. Undaunted by his lack of a popular mandate, Lincoln quickly embarked upon a course of action with a single overriding purpose in mind—the restoration of the Union between the North and South.

Needless to say, Lincoln was hated in the rebellious states. Not so obvious in history texts, however, was his unpopularity in the North, where growing opposition to the war required drastic—some would say dictatorial—executive actions to control the festering and volatile dissent. Lincoln quickly, and on his own initiative, suspended the constitutionally guaranteed writ of *habeas corpus* and authorized the arbitrary arrest of any suspected opponents of his war policies. In 1863, for example, some 38,000 persons were arrested in the North and imprisoned without trial for suspected anti-war activities. Soon after the first shots were fired at Fort Sumter, he had—

without Congressional approval—called up the militia and expanded the size of the regular army. He arbitrarily, and again without congressional approval, transferred some two million dollars to Union agents in New York for assistance in stifling the anti-war movement. Ignoring Congress, he instituted unpopular conscription in 1862 by executive order. He aggressively appointed and removed a succession of politically ambitious Union generals before finding a satisfactory commander in Grant. He issued the Emancipation Proclamation, freeing the slaves in the rebellious states without consulting Congress. He issued executive orders establishing provisional courts in conquered states and appointed military governors in Arkansas, Louisiana, and Tennessee without Congressional approval or clear constitutional authority. In general, President Lincoln ignored the Congress and the Constitution during his first term in office and dramatically exploited his executive authority.

A nation averse to strong central government, sympathetic to states' rights, and embued with notions of Jacksonian democracy did not respond kindly to this unimpressive-looking, obscure midwesterner who was presiding over the bloodiest war in American history with the iron hand of a despot—a war that would kill and maim over a million American boys, many of them drafted as reluctant participants in what had become an All-American holocaust. Such negative public sentiments were reflected most vigorously in the Congress, where Lincoln was especially reviled by members of his own party. He was also condemned and ridiculed by his own cabinet appointees. Prominent and influential newspaper editors charged him with abuses ranging from incompetence to war profiteering. On one side, Democrats blasted him for waging an unconstitutional war against political self-determination; on the other, radical Republicans condemned his restraint in prosecuting the war. By 1864, it was difficult to identify any important segment of support for the President. Strong criticism had developed in the North in response to costly military defeats at Southern hands, racist opposition to emancipation, and resistance to the draft in an exceedingly bloody war to free Negroes most Northerners considered less than human.

Opposition to Lincoln and the draft was particularly vigorous in New York and Philadelphia, as well as smaller towns on the eastern seaboard and Ohio, Kentucky, and Wisconsin in the Midwest, not to mention the strong Southern sympathy in the marginally loyal Border States. Following on the heels of New York Governor Horatio Seymour's denunciation of Lincoln in a July Fourth speech in 1863, draft resisters rioted in New York City, attacking blacks and abolitionists in a murderous three-day rampage.

By early 1864, many prominent Union supporters considered Lincoln's presidency an unqualified failure; it was certain that his renomination would be challenged. As the peace movement grew in 1864, influential newspapers in New York and Philadelphia attacked the use of black soldiers and condemned the Emancipation Proclamation. Moreover, Lincoln's vilification was not confined to this country: London papers also sneered at his manners and ridiculed his homeliness while condemning his policies.

A discouraged Lincoln anticipated defeat in 1864 and prepared a memorandum on the transition as serious challenges to his re-nomination were mounted by Salmon P. Chase, his Treasury Secretary, and former general and "Great Pathfinder" John C. Fremont, as well as another general, Benjamin Butler. Largely as a result of the fragmented quality of his opposition, rather than his own popularity, Lincoln was finally renominated in Baltimore by an unenthusiastic party amid feelings of sullen resentment. Prominent Union supporters such as William Cullen Bryant, Theodore Tilton, and Horace Greeley considered Lincoln a failure as president but saw no acceptable alternative.

Undoubtedly, the curious nomination and party platform of opposition Democrats contributed importantly to the beleaguered Lincoln's subsequent re-election. The Democrats nominated another former general, George McClellan, as a candidate committed, like Lincoln, to an un-

compromising military solution to the war. They then saddled the general with an incongruous peace platform written by chief anti-war advocate and vice-presidential nominee Clement L. Vallandigham—a man who had been arrested and deported to the South by a military court for his treasonous Confederate sympathies. Confronted with a choice between such a contradiction or the unpopular Lincoln, the electorate held its nose and voted for the incumbent, giving him an unanticipated impressive victory.

Lincoln's surprising re-election and mandate signaled an ominous message for the South. Given Lincoln's unpopularity in the North and the growing anti-war sentiment in that part of the country, many war-weary Southerners had prayed for his defeat and a negotiated end to the war that would recognize, as many Northern papers advocated, an independent Confederacy. The loss of life on both sides during Grant's Wilderness Campaign in May and June 1864 was staggering—an estimated 90,000 casualties. Lincoln, like another president a hundred years and a different war later, was widely blamed for this carnage that many, anticipating a shorter, less costly war, now considered unnecessary. For the South, his re-election meant that the destructive war of attrition Grant was now conducting would grind on toward its humiliating ultimate objective—unconditional surrender. It was a time of desperation in the South. Lincoln, as Commander in Chief of the Union armies now intent on destroying men, not merely capturing territory, was intensely hated throughout the South. The *Richmond Examiner* asked: "What shall we call him? Coward, assassin, savage, murderer of women and babies? Or shall we consider them all embodied in the word of fiend, and call him Lincoln the Fiend."

Booth's Politics and Plan

Few persons loved the South and hated Abraham Lincoln more than John Wilkes Booth. From the beginning of the war, Booth had made his Southern sympathies clear in the most outspoken and unequivocal manner. His hatred for the President was both personal and political, and it grew more intense as the conflict dragged on. He held Lincoln responsible for a bloody and unnecessary war and, as a man of some refinement, he was contemptuous of what he saw as Lincoln's personal coarseness of style and manner. In Booth's eyes, Lincoln was not qualified by birth or training to be president.

As a performer, Booth was permitted to travel throughout the country—North and South—during the war. He used this privilege to smuggle quinine and other war-related material, as well as information, into the South at every opportunity. As prospects for a Southern victory began to dim after Lee's defeat at Gettysburg in 1863, Booth's activities intensified. By 1864, he was preoccupied with the war effort, severely curtailing his professional commitments—not because of bad reviews or throat problems—but because his priorities were now elsewhere.

It is worth noting that Booth's theatrical tours regularly took him to areas of the most intense opposition to the President. In addition to Southern cities, Booth regularly toured New York, Philadelphia, and Baltimore, not to mention the capital itself where the anti-war movement was very strong. It is little wonder that he correctly viewed himself as participating in a widely popular cause.

In September 1864, the same month that Lincoln was renominated for a second term, Sherman's forces swept through Atlanta burning and pillaging as they went. To the north, Lee's army was being forced into a last stand outside Richmond. The situation for the Confederates was desperate. It was at this time that Booth became part of a plan to abduct the President so that subsequently Lincoln could be ransomed for the release of Confederate prisoners of war who were sorely needed to restore Lee's badly depleted ranks. In October, Booth went to Montreal on the first of many trips he would make across the border over the next few months to meet with Confederate agents. While there, he opened a bank account and packed his theatrical wardrobe and paraphernalia in a trunk for future shipment to Richmond. Any doubts about the plan were put aside with Lincoln's November re-election. It was now evident that drastic measures would be required to prevent Southern defeat.

Various alternatives were discussed by Confederate agents: plots to sabotage government ships and buildings; raids from Canada on cities such as Buffalo, Detroit, and New York: attacks on prisoner of war camps to release Confederate soldiers; a plot to burn New York City; and a plan to distribute clothes infested with yellow fever, smallpox, and other contagious diseases in Washington—all desperate measures to stem the tide of a war going very badly.

In this context, the plan to abduct the President seems less bizarre. Earlier in April 1864, General Grant had refused a Confederate proposal for a prisoner exchange; a successful abduction could possibly achieve that end. In any case, it was worth the gamble. In November, Booth initiated actual preparations to carry out the abduction. He began to recruit among old friends and acquaintances for persons willing to assist in the operation. He also made trips into southern Maryland to plan the route by which the handcuffed president would be transported across Southern lines. During the year, Booth had spent large sums of his own money in such espionage activities.

Intent on having his purpose and motives for the abduction clearly understood, Booth drafted a sealed letter of explanation and left it with his sister Asia's husband, John Sleeper Clarke, for safekeeping. The letter, which remained unopened until it was discovered after the assassination, reveals the scope and depth of Booth's feeling and his rationale for his anticipated crime:

My Dear Sir:

You may use this as you think best. But as some may wish to know when, who and why, and as I know not how to direct, I give it (in the words of your master).

To whom it may concern,

Right or wrong, God judge me, not man. For be my motive good or bad, of one thing I am sure, the lasting condemnation of the North.

I love peace more than life. Have loved the Union beyond expression. For four years I have waited, hoped and prayed for the dark clouds to break, and for the restoration of our former sunshine. To wait longer would be a crime. All hope for peace is dead. My prayers have proved as idle as my hopes. God's will be done. I go to see and share the bitter end.

I have ever held the South were right. The very nomination of Abraham Lincoln, four years ago, spoke plainly war—war upon Southern rights and institutions. His election proved it. Await an overt act. Yet, till you are bound and plundered. What folly! The South was wise. Who thinks of argument or patience when the finger of his enemy presses the trigger? In a foreign war, *I too, could say, country right or wrong. But in a struggle such as* ours *where the brother tries to pierce the brother's heart, for God's sake, choose the right. When a country like this spurns* justice *for her side, she forfeits the allegiance of every honest free man, and should leave him untrammelled by any fealty soever, to act as his own conscience may approve.*

People of the North, to hate tyranny, to love liberty and justice, to strike at wrong and oppression, was the teaching of our fathers. The study of our early history will not let me forget it and may it never.

This country was formed for the white man and not for the black. And looking upon African slavery *from the same standpoint as held by the noble framers of our Constitution, I, for one, have ever considered it one of the greatest blessings for themselves and for us that God ever bestowed upon a favored nation. Witness heretofore our wealth and power; witness their elevation and enlightenment above their race elsewhere. I have lived among it most of my life, and have seen less harsh treatment from master to man than I have beheld in the North from father to son. Yet heaven knows that* no one *would be more willing to do more for the negro race than I, could I but see a way to* still better their condition.

But Lincoln's policy is only preparing the way to their total annihilation. The South are not nor have they been fighting for the continuance *of slavery. The first battle of Bull Run did away with that idea. The causes since for war have been as* noble, and greater far than those that urged our fathers on. Even though we should allow that they were wrong at the beginning of this contest, cruelty and injustice *have made the wrong become the right, and they now stand before the wonder and admiration of the world, as a noble band of patriotic heroes. Hereafter reading of* their deeds, *Thermopylae will be forgotten.*

When I aided in the capture and execution of John Brown who was a murderer on our western border, who was fairly tried and convicted *before an impartial judge and jury, of treason, and who by the way, has since been made a god, I was proud of my little share in the transaction, for I deemed it my duty, and that I was helping our common country to perform an act of justice. But what was a crime in poor John Brown is now considered by themselves as the greatest and only virtue of the Republican party. Strange transmigration. Vice is to become a virtue, simply because more* indulge *in it.*

I thought then, as now, *that the Abolitionists* were the only traitors *in the land, and that the entire party deserved the same fate as poor old Brown, not because they wish to abolish slavery, but on account of the means they have endeavored to use to effect that abolition. If Brown were living, I doubt whether he himself* would set slavery against the Union. Most, or many in the North do, and openly curse the Union, if the South are to return and attain a single right *guaranteed to them by every tie which we once* revered as sacred. *The South can make no choice. It is either extermination or slavery for* themselves *worse than death to draw from. I know* my *choice.*

I have also studied hard to discover upon what grounds the right of a state to secede has been denied, when our name, United States and Declaration of Independence, both provide for secession. But this is no time for words. I write in haste. I know how foolish I shall be deemed for undertaking such a step as this, where on one side I have my friends and every thing to make me happy, where my profession alone has gained me an income of more than *twenty thousand dollars a year, and where my great personal ambition in my profession has such a great field of labor. On the other hand the South have never bestowed upon me one kind word, a place where I have no friends except beneath the sod: a place where I must either become a private soldier or a beggar.*

To give up all the former *for the* latter, *besides my mother and sisters whom I love so dearly, although they differ so widely in opinion, seems insane; but God is my judge. I love* justice *more than a country that disowns it; more than fame and wealth; heaven pardon me, if wrong, more than a happy home. I have never been upon the battle field, but, O my countrymen, could all but see the* reality *or effects of this horrid war, as I have seen them in every state* save Virginia, *I know you would think like me, and would pray the Almighty to create in the Northern mind a sense of* right and justice *even should it possess no seasoning of mercy, and then he would dry up this sea of blood between us, which is daily growing wider. Alas, poor country, is she to meet her threatened doom? Four years ago I would have given a thousand lives to see her as I have always known her, powerful and unbroken. And even now I would hold my life as naught, to see her what she was. O, my friends, if the fearful scenes of the past four years had never been enacted or if what had been done were but a frightful dream from which we could now awake with over-flowing hearts, we could bless our God and pray for his continued favor. How I have loved the old flag* can never be known.

A few years since the world could boast of none so pure and spotless. But of late I have been seeing and hearing of the bloody deeds *of which she has been* made the emblem, *and would shudder to think how changed she has grown. Oh, how I have longed to see her break*

from the midst of blood and death that circles round her folds, spoiling her beauty and tarnishing her honor! But no: day by day she has been dragged deeper into cruelty and oppression, till now in my eyes her once bright red striped look [like] bloody gashes *on the face of heaven.*

I look now upon my early admiration of her glories as a dream.

My love as things stand today is for the South alone. Nor do I deem it a dishonor in attempting to make for her a prisoner of this man to whom she owes so much misery. *If success attends me, I go penniless to her side. They say she has found that last ditch which the North has so long derided and been endeavoring to force her in, forgetting they are our brothers, and it is impolite to goad an enemy to madness. Should I reach her in safety and find it true, I will proudly beg permission to triumph or die in that same ditch by her side.*

A Confederate doing duty on his own responsibility.

J. Wilkes Booth

Booth coolly and rationally recruited five men (all of whom he had known earlier) to assist him: John Surratt, a Confederate spy and a person well acquainted with the geography of southern Maryland; David Herold, a simple-minded but extremely loyal person who also knew the country; George Atzerodt, an experienced boatman who was familiar with the river crossings that would be required; Lewis Payne,[1] a burly, physically powerful ex-Confederate soldier familiar with firearms; and finally, another ex-Confederate soldier, an old boyhood friend, Samuel Arnold. The qualifications of all but possibly Herold, who had only his loyalty to recommend him, suggest Booth's choices were not as ill-considered as some have made them out to be. A number of other persons were indirectly involved in the conspiracy (and theories abound about those who

---

[1]Variously known as Lewis Powell or Lewis Paine.

were not involved but were aware of the plot), but these were the main actors.

The plan was to abduct Lincoln on his way to the play, "Still Waters Run Deep," which was being performed at the Soldier's Home on the outskirts of Washington. On either March 16 or 20[2], 1865, the conspirators prepared for the abduction. They hoped to stop the President's carriage, overpower him and any aides (he was rarely escorted by more than one), then drive the handcuffed chief executive south where fresh horses would carry the group beyond to the protection of the Confederate lines.

The plan failed, however, because Lincoln did not appear. Rather, he had asked Treasury Secretary and political adversary Salmon P. Chase to go in his place. The carriage of a startled Chase was stopped by a group of riders, who, seeing the President was not on board, then galloped off.

Military events soon made it clear that abduction was no longer a viable strategy. Lee's army could not hold its positions at Petersburg much longer without an enormous sacrifice of life; surrender appeared inevitable. But on April 4, Confederate President Jefferson Davis, fearing the terms of surrender, urged a continuation of the war as guerrilla campaign "operating in the interior . . . where supplies are more accessible, and where the foe will be far removed from his own base." He went on to ask the South for a renewed commitment to "render our triumph certain."

Lee, closer to the suffering of his troops than the truculent Davis, saw no reason to continue a senseless slaughter. On April 7, he asked for terms, and two days later he formally surrendered his army. Desperate, Davis continued to press for a continuation of the war west of the Mississippi. With General Joe Johnston's Confederate army still in the field blocking Sherman's way north, he reasoned, perhaps there was a way out yet. Davis, the Southern zealot, was grasping for straws. So was Booth.

---

[2]The exact date remains uncertain.

The Assassination

After the abduction plot had failed, Booth began to consider other more drastic measures that could throw the Union war effort into disarray permitting the South to regroup militarily long enough, at least, to enhance the possibility of a negotiated settlement rather than an unconditional surrender dictated by the despised Lincoln. The plan that evolved was to strike down by assassination key government and military leaders, thus producing complete chaos in Washington. The targets: the President, Vice President Andrew Johnson, Secretary of State William H. Seward (who would become President in the event of the death of a succeeding Vice President), and General Ulysses S. Grant, commander of the Union army. In so doing, the conspirators hoped to eliminate in one stroke the government's formal political and military leadership.

On April 14, after learning of the President's theater plans with General Grant, a determined Booth decided that this was the opportunity he had been awaiting. It was time to strike. He again wrote a letter to explain what he was about to do and gave it to a fellow actor, John Matthews, in a sealed envelope instructing him to deliver it personally to the publisher of the *National Intelligencer* the next day. An unnerved Matthews tore open the letter after the assassination, then fearing the consequences of having it in his possession, destroyed it. He recalled the closing paragraph, however:

The moment has at length arrived when my plans [to abduct] must be changed. The world may censure me for what I am about to do, but I am sure posterity will justify me.

To this Booth signed his name and those of fellow conspirators Payne, Atzerodt, and Herold. Reserving for himself the President and General Grant, who was expected to accompany the President, Booth assigned Atzerodt to kill Vice President Johnson and Payne to kill Secretary of State Seward with Herold's assistance.

Why did Booth choose a public theater for the act? And why the leap to the stage after the fatal shot, unless it was for recognition? Booth's choice of Ford's Theater was in part fortuitous, but it was also a very rational, calculating decision. As a famous actor, he had unlimited access to Ford's. This meant that he could enter and leave the theater when and where he pleased without questions. Thus, he could enter and climb the stairs to the President's box without suspicion. He leaped to the stage after the shooting because that was the quickest, most direct way out of the crowded theater. To go back down the stairs and through the lobby would have meant almost certain capture. This is not to suggest that Booth was averse to the publicity. As his letters and diaries indicate, he was convinced that what he was doing was right and that public opinion would support the elimination of this "tyrant" who had ruled the country and had conducted the bloodiest war in American history. But the desire for notoriety, in this case, was a distinctly secondary consideration—neither necessary nor sufficient as a motive for his act.

Except for whatever fleeting personal satisfaction Booth may have derived from Lincoln's death, the plan was a failure: Payne's attempt to kill Seward ended bloody but unsuccessful; Atzerodt could not bring himself to execute a man he did not know: he made no attempt on the Vice President's life. Grant had declined the President's theater invitation because of plans to visit a daughter in New Jersey. Thus, only the President died.

The conspirators, except for John Surratt, were quickly arrested, although much controversy surrounded the investigation of the conspiracy and many questions remained about its thoroughness and the possibility of other conspirators.[3] If it hadn't been for Booth's broken leg, which he suffered in his leap to the stage, he and the ever faithful Davy Herold, who accompanied him on his flight toward an anticipated sanctuary in Virginia, might have escaped.

Booth's diary records his despair after the event as he realized that his act was poorly timed and misunderstood. The Nation was tired of killing after four long years of war. North and South, a war-weary nation welcomed Appomattox. A year earlier, the result may have been different, but except for zealots like Jefferson Davis and Booth, Americans were ready to lay down their arms and return to their homes and farms. Now in great pain, making his way through the Maryland swamps, Booth wrote:

April, 13, 14, Friday, The Ides
Until today nothing was ever thought of sacrificing to our country's wrongs. For six months we have worked to capture. But our cause being almost lost, something decisive and great must be done. But its failure was owing to others who did not strike for their country with a heart. I struck boldly, and not as the papers say. I walked with a firm step through a thousand of his friends, was stopped but pushed on. A colonel was at his side. I shouted Sic semper before I fired. In jumping I broke my leg. I passed all his pickets. Rode sixty miles that night, with the bone of my leg tearing the flesh at every jump.

I can never repent it, though we hated to kill. Our country owed all our troubles to him, and God simply made me the instrument of his punishment.[4]

The country is not what it was. This forced union is not what I have loved. I care not what becomes of me. I have no desire to outlive my country. This night [before the deed] I wrote a long article and left it for one of the editors of the National Intelligencer, *in which I fully set*

---

[3]David Herold, George Atzerodt, Lewis Payne, and Mary Surratt (the latter in a highly questionable judgement) were hanged on July 7, 1865. Other conspirators not directly involved, Samuel Arnold, Samuel Mudd, Edward Spangler, and Michael O'Laughlin were given prison sentences. John Surratt escaped to Europe. After his capture in Cairo in November 1866, he was returned to the country for trial. He was released in August 1867 after the jury failed to reach a verdict.

---

[4]The final phrase of this sentence is often cited out of context as evidence of Booth's alleged delusion of divine inspiration.

forth our reasons for our proceedings. He or the Gov't. . . . (the entry ends)[5]

A week later, a depressed Booth laments that his act has been misunderstood:

Friday 21

After being hunted like a dog through swamps, woods, and last night being chased by gunboats till I was forced to return wet, cold, and starving, with every man's hand against me, I am here in despair. And why? For doing what Brutus was honored for—what made Tell a hero. And yet I, for striking down a greater tyrant than they ever knew, am looked upon as a common cut-throat. My action was purer than either of theirs. One hoped to be great.[6] *The other had not only his country's, but his own, wrongs to avenge. I hoped for no gain. I knew no private wrong. I struck for my country and that alone. A country that groaned beneath this tyranny, and prayed for this end, and yet now behold the cold hand they extend me. God cannot pardon me if I have done wrong. Yet I cannot see my wrong, except in serving a degenerate people. The little, the very little, I left behind to clear my name, the government will not allow to be printed (the letter he had left with John Matthews). So ends all. For my country I have given up all that makes life sweet and holy, brought misery upon my family, and am sure there is no pardon in the Heaven for me, since man condemns me so. I have only heard of what has been done (except what I did myself), and it fills me with horror. God, try and forgive me, and bless my mother. Tonight I will once more try the river with the intent to cross. Though I have a greater desire and almost a mind to*

---

[5]In the last incomplete sentence, Booth probably intended to express his frustration that "he [John Matthews] or the Gov't" suppressed his letter of explanation.
[6]The sentence, "One hoped to be great" is also cited out of context as evidence of Booth's alleged desire for fame, despite the fact that the reference is clearly to another earlier assassin.

return to Washington, and in a measure clear my name—which I feel I can do. I do not repent the blow I struck. I may before my God, but not to man. I think I have done well. Though I am abandoned, with the curse of Cain upon me, when, if the world knew my heart, that one blow would have made me great, though I did desire no greatness.

Tonight I try to escape these blood-hounds once more. Who, who can read his fate? God's will be done. I have too great a soul to die like a criminal. O, may He, may He spare me that, and let me die bravely.

I bless the entire world. Have never hated or wronged anyone. This last was not a wrong, unless God deems it so, and it's with Him to damn or bless me. And for this brave boy with me, who often prays (yes, before and since) with a true and sincere heart—was it crime in him? If so, why can he pray the same?

I do not wish to shed a drop of blood, but "I must fight the course." Tis all that's left me.

Given the tone and intensity of Booth's remarks, it is difficult to take seriously an often-quoted subsequent remark he allegedly made to a farm girl, who, unaware of who he was, said to him that she thought Lincoln's assassin had killed for money. Booth was said to have replied that in his opinion "he wasn't paid a cent, but did it for notoriety's sake."

Had Booth been seeking the fame he already possessed, it is likely that he would have welcomed a well-publicized trial where he could have spoken with the dramatic persuasiveness of the skilled actor he was in his own defense. He could have given expression to the many eloquent political statements he had penned in letters and diary. Rather, he chose to die alone "bravely." With that in mind, as he leaned heavily on a crutch, surrounded by Union troops who had encircled his refuge in a barn, he shouted back when asked to surrender:

Captain, I know you to be a brave man, and I believe you to be honorable: I am a cripple. I have got but one leg; if you withdraw your men in "line" one hundred yards from the door, I will come out and fight you.

When the officer-in-charge replied that it was his intention to take him and Herold prisoners, Booth shouted back: "Well, my brave boys, prepare a stretcher for me." He then negotiated with the soldiers to permit his panicked companion to surrender alone. Soon after Herold left the barn, it was set afire by the soldiers. Seeing no other honorable alternative, Booth raised his pistol and fired a shot behind his right ear, smashing instead his spinal column and leaving him paralyzed but conscious to die a slow agonizing death. Throughout an ordeal so painful that he pleaded to be killed, he did not recant on his principles. Shortly before he died, he whispered to a soldier bending over him, "Tell mother I die for my country."

Conclusions

Much of the misunderstanding about Booth and his motives has been the result of the failure to consider the political context of his actions. It has been assumed that Lincoln was the revered leader in life that he became after his death: the fact that his assassination is frequently referred to as a martyrdom attests to this point. Thus, it has been further assumed that only a deranged person could have killed so noble a human being. Consequently, writers have interpreted virtually every aspect of Booth's life from this incorrect perspective. As I have indicated, it is unlikely that a "ham" actor would have received the consistently good reviews that Booth did. It is also unlikely that a person consumed with the egocentric and anxiety-induced needs for acclaim attributed to Booth would have had so very many friends and admirers from all walks of life.

Booth was wrong, obviously, on moral grounds; moreover, he was wrong politically, as subsequent events illustrated. But he was not deranged, nor did he kill for neurotic compensatory or nihilistic reasons. His motives were more akin to those of the German officers who conspired and attempted to kill Hitler to end the madness of World War II than they were to a deranged person. Such a conclusion is difficult to accept because it conflicts so directly with the mythology surrounding a slain national hero. But during most of his presidency, Abraham Lincoln was viewed by many Americans, especially in the South, as a cruel, despotic man. As a more restrained but still bitter Jefferson Davis wrote some years later about Lincoln, "[The South] could not be expected to mourn" an enemy who had presided over such misery.

Study Questions

1. Discuss Booth's background. Was there anything in his early life that would suggest psychological troubles?

2. Was Booth an unsuccessful actor? Did his career play a part in his assassination of Lincoln?

3. Describe the political climate in America in 1864 and early 1865. How do political tensions help to explain Booth's actions?

4. How did Booth support the Confederacy during the Civil War? What do Booth's letter and diary entries indicate about his personality and motives?

5. How rational were Booth's plans to abduct and then to assassinate Lincoln?

6. What was Booth's motive for assassinating Lincoln?

Bibliography

The literature on Abraham Lincoln and his assassination is enormous. The Library of Congress lists more books on Lincoln than any other individual save Jesus and William Shakespeare. The best place to begin to examine the circumstances surrounding Lincoln's assassination is William Hanchett, *The Lincoln Murder Conspiracies* (1983). Harold M. Hyman, *With Malice Toward Some: Scholarship (or Something Less) on the Lincoln Murder* (1978) is also outstanding. Stanley Kimmel, *The Mad Booths of Maryland* (1969) presents the thesis that Booth's actions were psychologically motivated. Jim Bishop, *The Day Lincoln Was Shot* (1955) presents a popularized account of the assassination. Margaret Leech, *Reveille in Washington, 1861–1865* (1945) describes the feelings toward Lincoln during the Civil War. For the most recent contributions to the literature, see Leonard F. Guttage, *Dark Union: The Secret Web of the Profiteers, Politicians, and Booth Conspirators That Led to Lincoln's Death* (2003); Edward Steers, *Blood on the Moon: The Assassination of Abraham Lincoln* (2001); and Corinne J. Naden, *Civil War Ends: Assassination, Reconstruction, and the Aftermath* (2000).

READING 31

Knights of the Rising Sun

Allen W. Trelease

The Civil War, which started in 1861 and ended in 1865, was like a nightmare come true for most Americans. More than 600,000 young men were dead, countless others wounded and permanently maimed, and the South a prostrate ruin. For the next twelve years, northern Republicans tried to "reconstruct" the South in a chaotic crusade mixing retribution, corruption, and genuine idealism. Intent on punishing white Southerners for their disloyalty, northern Republicans, especially the Radicals, tried to extend full civil rights—via the Fourteenth and Fifteenth Amendments—to the former slaves. For a variety of reasons, the attempt at giving equality to southern blacks failed, and by 1877 political power in the South reverted to the white elite.

A major factor in the failure of Radical Republicans to "reconstruct" the South was the rise of the Ku Klux Klan. Enraged at the very thought of black political power, Klansmen resorted to intimidation and violence, punishing southern blacks even suspected of sympathizing with Radicals' goals for the South. In "The Knights of the Rising Sun," historian Allen W. Trelease describes Klan activities in Texas during the late 1860s. Isolated from the main theaters of the Civil War, much of Texas remained unreconstructed, and the old white elite, along with their Klan allies, succeeded in destroying every vestige of black political activity and in eliminating the Republican party from the political life of the state.

Large parts of Texas remained close to anarchy through 1868. Much of this was politically inspired despite the fact that the state was not yet reconstructed and took no part in the national election. In theory the Army was freer to take a direct hand in maintaining order than was true in the states which had been readmitted, but the shortage of troops available for this duty considerably lessened that advantage. At least twenty counties were involved in the Ku Klux terror, from Houston north to the Red River. In Houston itself Klan activity was limited to the holding of monthly meetings in a gymnasium and posting notices on lampposts, but in other places there was considerable violence.

By mid-September disguised bands had committed several murders in Trinity County, where two lawyers and both justices of the peace in the town of Sumter were well known as Klansmen. Not only did the crimes go unpunished, but Conservatives used them to force a majority of the Negroes to swear allegiance to the Democratic party; in return they received the familiar protection papers supposedly guaranteeing them against further outrage. "Any one in this community opposed to the Grand Cyclops and his imps is in danger of his life," wrote a local Republican in November. In Washington County the Klan sent warning notices to Republicans and committed at least one murder. As late as January 1869 masked parties were active around Palestine, shaving heads, whipping, and shooting among the black population, as well as burning down their houses. The military arrested five or six men for these offenses, but the Klan continued to make the rounds of Negroes' and Union men's houses, confiscating both guns and money. Early in November General J. J. Reynolds, military commander in the state, declared in a widely quoted report that "civil law east of the Trinity river is almost a dead letter" by virtue of the activities of Ku Klux Klans and similar organizations. Republicans had been publicly slated for assassination and forced to flee their homes, while the murder of Negroes was too common to keep track of. These lawless bands, he said, were "evidently countenanced, or at least not discouraged, by a majority of the white people in the counties where [they] are most numerous. They could not otherwise exist." These statements did not endear the general to Conservative Texans, but they were substantially true.

The worst region of all, as to both Klan activity and general banditry, remained northeast Texas. A correspondent of the Cincinnati *Commercial* wrote from Sulphur Springs early in January 1869:

Armed bands of banditti, thieves, cut-throats and assassins infest the country; they prowl around houses, they call men out and shoot or hang them, they attack travellers upon the road, they seem almost everywhere present, and are ever intent upon mischief. You cannot pick up a paper without reading of murders, assassinations and robbery. . . . And yet not the fourth part of the truth has been told; not one act in ten is reported. Go where you will, and you will hear of fresh murders and violence. . . . The civil authority is powerless—the military insufficient in number, while hell has transferred its capital from pandemonium to Jefferson, and the devil is holding high carnival in Gilmer, Tyler, Canton, Quitman, Boston, Marshall and other places in Texas.

Judge Hardin Hart wrote Governor Pease in September to say that on account of "a regularly organized band which has overrun the country" he could not hold court in Grayson, Fannin, and Hunt counties without a military escort.

Much of this difficulty was attributable to outlaw gangs like those of Ben Bickerstaff and Cullen Baker, but even their activities were often racially and politically inspired, with Negroes and Union men the chief sufferers. Army officers and soldiers reported that most of the population at Sulphur Springs was organized into Ku Klux clubs affiliated with the Democratic party and some of

---

the outlaws called themselves Ku Klux Rangers. At Clarksville a band of young men calling themselves Ku Klux broke up a Negro school and forced the teacher to flee the state.

White Conservatives around Paris at first took advantage of Klan depredations among Negroes by issuing protection papers to those who agreed to join the Democratic party. But the marauding reached such proportions that many freedmen fled their homes and jobs, leaving the crops untended. When a body of Klansmen came into town early in September, apparently to disarm more blacks, some of the leading citizens warned them to stop. The freedmen were not misbehaving, they said, and if they needed disarming at a later time the local people would take care of it themselves. Still the raiding continued, and after a sheriff's posse failed to catch the culprits the farmers in one neighborhood banded together to oppose them by force. (Since the Klan had become sacred among Democrats, these men claimed that the raiding was done by an unauthorized group using its name. They carefully denied any idea of opposing the Klan itself.) Even this tactic was ineffective so far as the county as a whole was concerned, and the terror continued at least into November. The Freedmen's Bureau agent, Colonel DeWitt C. Brown, was driven away from his own farm thirty miles from Paris and took refuge in town. There he was subjected to constant threats of assassination by Klansmen or their sympathizers. From where he stood the Klan seemed to be in almost total command.

The Bureau agent at Marshall (like his predecessor in the summer) suspected that the planters themselves were implicated in much of the terrorism. By driving Negroes from their homes just before harvest time the Klan enabled many landowners to collect the crop without having to pay the laborers' share.

Jefferson and Marion County remained the center of Ku Klux terrorism, as the Cincinnati reporter pointed out. A garrison of twenty-six men under Major James Curtis did little to deter violence. Bands of hooded men continued to make nocturnal depredations on Negroes in the surrounding countryside during September and October as they had for weeks past. "Whipping the freedmen, robbing them of their arms, driving them off plantations, and murdering whole families are of daily, and nightly occurrence," wrote the local Bureau agent at the end of October, "all done by disguised parties whom no one can testify to. The civil authorities never budge an inch to try and discover these midnight marauders and apparently a perfect apathy exists throughout the whole community regarding the general state of society. Nothing but martial law can save this section as it is at present. . . . " Inside town, Republicans hardly dared go outdoors at night, and for several weeks the county judge, who was afraid to go home even in the daytime, slept at the Army post. The local Democratic newspapers, including the *Ultra Ku Klux*, encouraged the terror by vying with one another in the ferocity of their denunciations of Republicans.

Major Curtis confirmed this state of affairs in a report to General Reynolds:

Since my arrival at the Post . . . [in mid-September] I have carefully observed the temper of the people and studied their intentions. I am constrained to say that neither are pacific. The amount of unblushing fraud and outrage perpetrated upon the negroes is hardly to be believed unless witnessed. Citizens who are esteemed respectable do not hesitate to take every unfair advantage. My office is daily visited by large numbers of unfortunates who have had money owing them, which they have been unable to obtain. The moral sense of the community appears blunted and gray headed apologists for such men as Baker and Bickerstaff can be met on all the street corners. . . . The right of franchise in this section is a farce. Numbers of negroes have been killed for daring to be Radicals, and their houses have so often been broken into by their Ku Klux neighbors in search of arms that they are now pretty well defenceless. The civil officers cannot and will not punish these outrages. Calvary armed with double barrelled shotguns would

*soon scour the country and these desperadoes
be met on their own ground. They do not fear
the arms that the troops now have, for they
shoot from behind hedges and fences or at
night and then run. No more notice is taken
here of the death of a Radical negro than of a
mad dog. A democratic negro however, who
was shot the other day by another of his stripe,
was followed to his grave through the streets of
this city by a long procession in carriages, on
horseback, and on foot, I saw some of the most
aristocratic and respectable white men in this
city in the procession.*

On the same night that Curtis wrote, the new
Grand Officers of the Knights of the Rising Sun
were installed in the presence of a crowd of 1,200
or 1,500 persons. "The town was beautifully illu-
minated," a newspaper reported, "and the Seymour Knights and the Lone Star Club turned out
in full uniform, with transparencies and burners,
in honor of the occasion." Sworn in as Grand
Commander for the ensuing twelve months was
Colonel William P. Saufley, who doubled as chairman of the Marion County Democratic executive
committee. Following the installation "able and
patriotic speeches" were delivered by several no-
tables, including a Democratic Negro.

As usual, the most hated Republican was the
one who had the greatest Negro following. This
was Captain George W. Smith, a young Union
army veteran from New York who had settled in
Jefferson as a merchant at the end of the war. His
business failed, but the advent of Radical Reconstruction opened the prospect of a successful political career; at the age of twenty-four Smith was
elected to the state constitutional convention by
the suffrage of the Negro majority around Jefferson. At the convention, according to a perhaps
overflattering posthumous account, he was recognized as one of the abler members. "In his daily
life he was correct, almost austere. He never
drank, smoked, chewed, nor used profane language." However, "he was odious as a negro
leader, as a radical, as a man who could not be
cowed, nor scared away." Smith may also have

alienated his fellow townspeople by the strenuous efforts he made to collect debts they owed
him. Even a few native Republicans like Judge
Charles Caldwell, who was scarcely more popular
with Conservatives, refused to speak from the
same platform with him. As his admirer pointed
out, Smith "was ostracized and his life often
threatened. But he refused to be scared. He sued
some of his debtors and went to live with colored
people." One day, as he returned from a session
of the convention, his carpetbag—perhaps
symbolically—was stolen, its contents rifled, and
a list of them published in a local newspaper.

The beginning of the end for Smith came on
the night of October 3, after he and Anderson
Wright, a Negro, had spoken at a Republican
meeting. As he opened the door of a Negro cabin
to enter, Smith was fired upon by four men outside including Colonel Richard P. Crump, one of
Jefferson's leading gentry. Smith drew his revolver and returned the fire, wounding two of
the assailants and driving them away. He then
went to Major Curtis at the Army post. Here
Crump, with the chief of police and others, soon
arrived bearing a warrant for his arrest on a
charge of assault. The attackers' original intention to kill Smith now assumed greater urgency
because he and several Negroes present had recognized their assailants. Smith objected strenuously to their efforts to get custody of him,
protesting that it was equivalent to signing his
death warrant. Nevertheless Curtis turned him
over to the civil authorities on their assurance of
his safety. Smith was taken off to jail and a small
civilian guard was posted around it. The major
was uneasy, however, and requested reinforcements from his superior, but they were refused.

The next day there were signs in Jefferson of
an assembling of the Knights of the Rising Sun.
Hoping to head off a lynching, Curtis dispatched
sixteen soldiers (the greater part of his command)
to help guard the jail. At 9 P.M., finally, a signal
was sounded—a series of strokes on a bell at the
place where the Knights held their meetings.
About seventy members now mobilized under
the command of Colonel Saufley and proceeded

to march in formation toward the jail; they were in disguise and many carried torches. The jail building lay in an enclosed yard where at that time four black men were confined for a variety of petty offenses. One of the prisoners was Anderson Wright, and apparently the real reason for their being there was that they had witnessed the previous night's attempt to murder Smith; they may even have been fellow targets at that time. When the Knights reached this enclosure they burst through it with a shout and overpowered the guard, commanded by a young Army lieutenant. The invaders then turned to the Negro prisoners and dragged them into some adjoining woods. Wright and a second man, Cornelius Turner, managed to escape from them, although Wright was wounded; the other two prisoners were shot nearly to pieces. As soon as Major Curtis heard the shooting and firing he came running with his remaining soldiers; but they too were quickly overpowered. Repeatedly the major himself tried to prevent the mob from entering the jail building in which Smith was confined, only to be dragged away from the door each time. They had no trouble unlocking the door, for city marshall Silas Nance, who possessed the key, was one of the conspirators.

At first Smith tried to hold the door shut against their entry. Eventually failing at this, he caught the foremost man, pulled him into the room, and somehow killed him. "It is common talk in Jefferson now," wrote a former Bureau agent some months later, "that Capt. Smith killed the first man who entered—that the Knights of the Rising Sun afterward buried him secretly with their funeral rites, and it was hushed up, he being a man from a distance. It is an established fact that one Gray, a strong man, who ventured into the open door, was so beaten by Capt. Smith that he cried, 'Pull me out! He's killing me!' and he was dragged out backward by the leg." All this took place in such darkness that the Knights could not see their victim. Some of them now went outside and held torches up to the small barred window of Smith's cell. By this light they were able to shoot

him four times. "The door was burst open and the crowd surged in upon him as he fell, and then, man after man, as they filed around fired into the dying body. This refinement of barbarity was continued while he writhed and after his limbs had ceased to quiver, that each one might participate in the triumph."

Once the mob had finished its work at the jail it broke up into squads which began patrolling the town and searching for other Republican leaders. County Judge Campbell had anticipated trouble earlier in the evening and taken refuge as usual at Major Curtis' headquarters. Judge

Caldwell was hated second only to Smith after his well-publicized report as chairman of the constitutional convention's committee on lawlessness. Hearing the shooting around the jail, he fled from his home into the woods. In a few moments twenty-five or thirty Knights appeared at the house, looking for him. Some of the party were for killing him, and they spent two hours vainly trying to learn his whereabouts from his fifteen-year-old son, who refused to tell. Another band went to the house of G. H. Slaughter, also a member of the convention, but he too escaped.

The next day the few remaining white Republicans in town were warned by friends of a widely expressed desire to make a "clean sweep" of them. Most of them stayed at the Haywood House hotel the following night under a military guard. Meanwhile the KRS scoured the city looking for dangerous Negroes, including those who knew too much about the preceding events for anyone's safety. When Major Curtis confessed that the only protection he could give the white Republicans was a military escort out of town, most of them decided to leave. At this point some civic leaders, alarmed at the probable effects to the town and themselves of such an exodus under these circumstances, urged them to stay and offered their protection. But the Republicans recalled the pledge to Smith and departed as quickly as they could, some openly and others furtively to avoid ambush.

White Conservatives saw these events—or at least their background and causes—in another light. They regarded Smith as "a dangerous, unprincipled carpet-bagger" who "lived almost entirely with negroes, on terms of perfect equality." Whether there was evidence for it or not, they found it easy to believe further that this "cohabitation" was accompanied by "the most unbridled and groveling licentiousness"; according to one account he walked the streets with Negroes in a state of near-nudity. For at least eighteen months he had thus "outraged the moral sentiment of the city of Jefferson," defying the whites to do anything about it and threatening a race war if they tried. This might have been overlooked if he had

not tried repeatedly to precipitate such a collision. As head of the Union League he delivered inflammatory speeches and organized the blacks into armed mobs who committed assaults and robberies and threatened to burn the town. When part of the city did go up in flames earlier in the year Smith was held responsible. Overlooking the well-attested white terrorism which had prevailed in the city and county for months, a Democratic newspaper claimed that all had been peace and quiet during Smith's absence at the constitutional convention. But on his return he resumed his incendiary course and made it necessary for the whites to arm in self-defense.

According to Conservatives the initial shooting affray on the night of October 3 was precipitated by a group of armed Negroes with Smith at their head. They opened fire on Crump and his friends while the latter were on their way to protect a white man whom Smith had threatened to attack. Democrats did not dwell over-long on the ensuing lynching, nor did they bother to explain the killing of the Negro prisoners. In fact the affair was made deliberately mysterious and a bit romantic in their telling. According to the Jefferson *Times,* both the soldiers and the civilians on guard at the jail characterized the lynch party as "entirely sober and apparently well disciplined." (One of the party later testified in court that at least some of them had put on their disguises while drinking at a local saloon.) "After the accomplishment of their object," the *Times* continued, "they all retired as quietly and mysteriously as they came—none knowing who they were or from whence they came." (This assertion, it turned out, was more hopeful than factual.)

The *Times* deplored such proceedings in general, it assured its readers, but in this case lynching "had become . . . an unavoidable necessity. The sanctity of home, the peace and safety of society, the prosperity of the country, and the security of life itself demanded the removal of so base a villain." A month later it declared: "Every community in the South will do well to relieve themselves [*sic*] of their surplus Geo. Smiths, and others of like ilk, as Jefferson rid herself of hers. This is not a healthy locality for such incendiaries, and no town in the South should be." Democratic papers made much of Judge Caldwell's refusal to appear publicly with Smith—which was probably inspired by his Negro associations. They claimed that Smith's fellow Republicans were also glad to have him out of the way, and noted that the local citizens had assured them of protection. But there was no mention of the riotous search and the threats upon their lives which produced that offer, nor of their flight from the city anyway.

The Smith affair raises problems of fact and interpretation which appeared in almost every Ku Klux raid across the South. Most were not so fully examined or reported as this, but even here it is impossible to know certainly where the truth lay. Republican and Democratic accounts differed diametrically on almost every particular, and both were colored by considerations of political and personal interest. But enough detailed and impartial evidence survives to sustain the Republican case on most counts. Negro and Republican testimony concerning the actual events in October is confirmed by members of the KRS who turned state's evidence when they were later brought to trial. Smith's prior activities and his personal character are less clear. Republicans all agreed later that he was almost puritanical in his moral code and that he was hated because of his unquestioned social associations and political influence with the blacks. He never counseled violence or issued threats to burn the town, they insisted; on the contrary, the only time he ever headed a Negro crowd was when he brought a number of them to help extinguish the fire which he was falsely accused of starting.

As elsewhere in the South, the logic of some of the charges against Smith is not convincing. Whites had a majority in the city and blacks in the county. Theoretically each could gain by racial violence, offsetting its minority status. But Conservatives always had the advantage in such confrontations. They were repeatedly guilty of intimidating the freedmen, and in case of an open collision everyone (including Republicans) knew they could win hands down. Democrats were certainly sincere in their personal and political detestation of Smith; almost as certainly they were sincere in their fears of his political activity and what it might lead to. From their viewpoint an open consorter with and leader of Negroes was capable of anything. It was easy therefore to believe the worst and attribute the basest motives without clear evidence. If some Negroes did threaten to burn the town—often this was a threat to retaliate for preceding white terrorism—it was easy to overlook the real cause and attribute the idea to Smith. The next step, involving hypocrisy and deliberate falsehood in some cases, was to charge him with specific expressions and activities which no other source substantiates and which the logic of the situation makes improbable. Men who practiced or condoned terrorism and murder in what they conceived to be a just cause would not shrink from character assassination in the same cause.

Interestingly enough, most of the character assassination—in Smith's case and generally—followed rather than preceded Ku Klux attacks. This did not arise primarily from a feeling of greater freedom or safety once the victim was no longer around to defend himself; some victims, unlike Smith, lived to speak out in their own behalf. Accusations after the fact were intended rather to rationalize and win public approval of the attack once it had occurred; since these raids were the product of at least semisecret conspiracy there was less need to win public approval beforehand. Sometimes such accusations were partially true, no doubt, and it was never easy for persons at a distance to judge them; often it is no easier now. Democrats tended to believe and Republicans to reject them as a matter of course. The *Daily Austin Republican* was typical of Radical papers in its reaction to Democratic newspaper slurs against Smith after his death: "We have read your lying sheets for the last *eighteen* months, and this is the first time you have made any such charges. . . . " It was surely justified in charging the Democratic editors of Texas with being accessories after the fact in Smith's murder.

The military authorities had done almost nothing to stop KRS terrorism among the Negroes before

Smith's murder, and this violence continued for at least two months afterward. Similar conditions prevailed widely, and there were too few troops—especially cavalry—to patrol every lawless county. But the murder of a white man, particularly one of Smith's prominence and in such a fashion, aroused officials to unwonted activity. The Army recalled Major Curtis and sent Colonel H. G. Malloy to Jefferson as provisional mayor with orders to discover and bring to justice the murderers of Smith and the two freedmen killed with him. More troops were also sent, amounting ultimately to nine companies of infantry and four of cavalry. With their help Malloy arrested four of Jefferson's leading men on December 5. Colonel W. P. Saufley, whom witnesses identified as the organizer of the lynching, would have been a fifth, but he left town the day before on business, a Democratic newspaper explained, apparently unaware that he was wanted. (This business was to take him into the Cherokee Indian Nation and perhaps as far as New York, detaining him so long that the authorities never succeeded in apprehending him.) That night the KRS held an emergency meeting and about twenty men left town for parts unknown while others prepared to follow.

General George P. Buell arrived soon afterward as commandant, and under his direction the arrests continued for months, reaching thirty-seven by early April. They included by common repute some of the best as well as the worst citizens of Jefferson. Detectives were sent as far as New York to round up suspects who had scattered in all directions. One of the last to leave was General H. P. Mabry, a former judge and a KRS leader who was serving as one of the counsel for the defense. When a soldier revealed that one of the prisoners had turned state's evidence and identified Mabry as a leader in the lynching, he abruptly fled to Canada.

The authorities took great pains to recover Anderson Wright and Cornelius Turner, the Negro survivors of the lynching, whose testimony would be vital in the forthcoming trials. After locating Wright, General Buell sent him with an Army officer to find Turner, who had escaped to New Orleans. They traveled part of the way by steamboat and at one point, when the officer was momentarily occupied elsewhere, Wright was set upon by four men. He saved himself by jumping overboard and made his way to a nearby Army post, whence he was brought back to Jefferson. Buell then sent a detective after Turner, who eventually was located, and both men later testified at the trial.

The intention of the authorities was to try the suspects before a military commission, as they were virtually sure of acquittal in the civil courts. Defense counsel (who consisted ultimately of eleven lawyers—nearly the whole Jefferson bar) made every effort to have the case transferred; two of them even went to Washington to appeal personally to Secretary of War Schofield, but he refused to interfere. R. W. Loughery, the editor of both the Jefferson *Times* and the *Texas Republican* in Marshall, appealed to the court of public opinion. His editorials screamed indignation at the "terrible and revolting ordeal through which a refined, hospitable, and intelligent people are passing, under radical rule," continually subject to the indignity and danger of midnight arrest. He also sent requests to Washington and to Northern newspapers for intercession against Jefferson's military despotism. The prisoners, he said, were subject to brutal and inhuman treatment. Loughery's *ex parte* statement of the facts created a momentary ripple but no reversal of policy. In reality the prisoners were treated quite adequately and were confined in two buildings enclosed by a stockade. Buell released a few of them on bond, but refused to do so in most cases for the obvious reason that they would have followed their brothers in flight. Although they seem to have been denied visitors at first, this rule was lifted and friends regularly brought them extra food and delicacies. The number of visitors had to be limited, however, because most of the white community regarded them as martyrs and crowded to the prison to show their support.

After many delays the members of the military commission arrived in May and the trial got under way; it continued into September. Although it proved somewhat more effective than the civil courts in punishing Ku Klux criminals, this tribunal was a far cry from the military despotism depicted by its hysterical opponents. The defense counsel presented their case fully and freely. Before long it was obvious that they would produce witnesses to swear alibis for most or all of the defendants. Given a general public conspiracy of this magnitude, and the oaths of KRS members to protect each other, this was easy to do; and given the dependence of the prosecution by contrast on Negro witnesses whose credibility white men (including Army officers) were accustomed to discounting, the tactic was all too effective. The results were mixed. At least fourteen persons arrested at one time or another never went to trial, either for lack of evidence or because they turned state's evidence. Seventeen others were tried and acquitted, apparently in most cases because of sworn statements by friends that they were not present at the time of the lynching. Only six were convicted. Three of these were sentenced to life terms, and three to a term of four years each in the Huntsville penitentiary. General Reynolds refused to accept the acquittal of Colonel Crump and three others, but they were released from custody anyway, and the matter was not raised again. Witnesses who had risked their lives by testifying against the terrorists were given help in leaving the state, while most of the defendants returned to their homes and occupations. The arrests and trials did bring peace to Jefferson, however. The Knights of the Rising Sun rode no more, and the new freedom for Radicals was symbolized in August by the appearance of a Republican newspaper.

Relative tranquillity came to northeast Texas generally during the early part of 1869. Some Republicans attributed this to the election of General Grant, but that event brought no such result to other parts of the South. Both Ben Bickerstaff and Cullen Baker were killed and their gangs dispersed, which certainly helped. The example of military action in Jefferson likely played a part; it was accompanied by an increase of military activity throughout the region as troops were shifted here from the frontier and other portions of the state. Immediately after the Smith lynching in October, General Reynolds ordered all civil and military officials to "arrest, on the spot any person wearing a mask or otherwise disguised." Arrests did increase, but it was probably owing less to this order than to the more efficient concentration of troops. In December the Bureau agent in Jefferson had cavalry (for a change) to send out after men accused of Ku Klux outrages in Upshur County. Between October 1868 and September 1869 fifty-nine cases were tried before military commissions in Texas, chiefly involving murder or aggravated assault; they resulted in twenty-nine convictions. This record was almost breathtaking by comparison with that of the civil courts.

The Texas crime rate remained high after 1868. Organized Ku Klux activity declined markedly, but it continued in sporadic fashion around the state for several years. A new state government was elected in November 1869 and organized early the next year under Republican Governor E. J. Davis. In his first annual message, in April 1870, Davis called attention to the depredations of disguised bands. To cope with them he asked the legislature to create both a state police and a militia, and to invest him with the power of martial law. In June and July the legislature responded affirmatively on each count. The state police consisted of a mounted force of fewer than 200 men under the state adjutant general; in addition, all county sheriffs and their deputies and all local marshals and constables were considered to be part of the state police and subject to its orders. In November 1871 a law against armed and disguised persons followed. Between July 1870 and December 1871 the state police arrested 4,580 persons, 829 of them for murder or attempted murder. Hundreds of other criminals probably fled the state to evade arrest. This activity, coupled with occasional use of the governor's martial law powers in troubled localities, seems to have diminished lawlessness by early 1872. There still remained the usual problems of prosecuting or convicting Ku Klux offenders, however, and very few seem to have been punished legally.

Study Questions

1. Why was Klan terrorism so rampant in Texas? Did the federal government possess the means of preventing it?

2. What was the relationship between the Ku Klux Klan in Texas and the Democratic party?

3. How did well-to-do white planters respond to the Ku Klux Klan?

4. What were the objectives of the Ku Klux Klan in Texas?

5. Who were the white conservatives? How did they interpret Klan activities?

6. Why did the state government try to curtail Klan activities in the early 1870s? Did state officials succeed?

Bibliography

The book that created two generations of stereotypes by vindicating the South and indicting the North is William A. Dunning's *Reconstruction, Political and Economic* (1907). The first major dissent came from W. E. B. DuBois's classic *Black Reconstruction in America, 1860–1880* (1935). It was not until the civil rights movement of the 1960s that historians engaged in a fresh look at Reconstruction. John Hope Franklin's *Reconstruction After the Civil War* (1961) took Dunning to task, as did Kenneth Stampp in *The Era of Reconstruction* (1965). For a look at political corruption during the era of Reconstruction, see Mark W. Summers, *The Era of Good Stealings* (1993). Since its inception in the 1870s, the Ku Klux Klan rose and fell, then rose and fell again, and then resurrected again, waxing and waning in rhythm with American debates over race, immigration, and ethnicity. Allan Trelease's *White Terrorism: The Ku Klux Klan Conspiracy and Southern Reconstruction* (1971) is a good place to begin a study of the early Klan. Also see Stanley F. Horn, *Invisible Empire: The Story of the Ku Klux Klan, 1866–1871* (1969). For general histories of the Klan, see Wyn Craig Wade, *Fiery Cross: The KKK in America* (1986) and Mark David Chalmers, *Hooded Americanism: The History of the Ku Klux Klan* (1981). For the recent history of the Klan, see Mark David Chalmers, *Backfire: How the KKK Helped the Civil Rights Movement* (2003).

READING 32

A Road They Did Not Know

Larry McMurtry

The battle remains even today, over 125 years later, shrouded in mystery and a pop culture fog. The great Sioux warrior chiefs—Crazy Horse and Sitting Bull—took on one of the United States Army's most flamboyant officers, and when the dust settled, all of the white soldiers, including Lt. Col. George Armstrong Custer, were dead, killed in a tactical blunder of epic proportions. The death of Custer and the troops in his 7th Cavalry captured the American imagination in the 1870s; and since then, it has continued to inspire curiosity, awe, and inquiry. It has spawned a scholarly literature and a mythology unequaled in United States history. In the following article, one of America's most gifted novelists—Larry McMurtry—deciphers exactly what happened on June 25-26, 1876, at the Battle of the Little Big Horn, why it happened, and what it has meant to Americans.

By the summer of 1875 a crisis over the Black Hills of South Dakota could no longer be postponed. Lt. Col. George Armstrong Custer had made a grand announcement that there was gold in the hills, and it caught the nation's attention. After that miners could not be held back. The government was obviously going to find a way to take back the Black Hills, but just as obviously, it was not going to be able to do so without difficulty and without criticism. The whites in the peace party were vocal; they and others of various parties thought the government ought to at least *try* to honor its agreements, particularly those made as solemnly and as publicly as the one from 1868 giving the Sioux the Black Hills and other lands. So there ensued a period of wiggling and squirming, on the part of the government and the part of the Sioux, many of whom had become agency Indians by this time. The free life of the hunting Sioux was still just possible, but only in certain areas: the Powder River, parts of Montana, and present-day South Dakota west of the Missouri River, where the buffalo still existed in some numbers.

By this time most of the major Indian leaders had made a realistic assessment of the situation and drawn the obvious conclusion, which was that their old way of life was rapidly coming to an end. One way or another they were going to have to walk the white man's road—or else fight until they were all killed. The greatest Sioux warriors, Crazy Horse and Sitting Bull, were among the most determined of the hostiles; two others, Red Cloud and Spotted Tail, rivals at this point, both had settled constituencies. They were administrators essentially, struggling to get more food and better goods out of their respective agents. As more and more Indians came in and enrollment lists swelled, this became a full-time job, and a vexing and frustrating one at that.

There were of course many Indians who tried to walk a middle road, unwilling to give up the old ways completely but recognizing that the presence of whites in what had once been their country was now a fact of life. Young Man Afraid of His Horses, son of the revered Old Man Afraid of His Horses, was one of the middle-of-the-roaders.

The whites at first tried pomp and circumstance, bringing the usual suspects yet again to Washington, hoping to tempt them—Red Cloud, Spotted Tail, anyone—to sell the Black Hills. They would have liked to have had Sitting Bull and Crazy Horse at this grand parley, or even a moderate, such as Young Man Afraid of His Horses, but none of these men or any of the principal hostiles wanted anything to do with this mini-summit. Red Cloud and Spotted Tail had no authority to sell the Black Hills, or to do anything about them at all, a fact the white authorities should have realized by this time. There were still thousands of Sioux on the northern plains who had not given their consent to anything. The mini-summit fizzled.

Many Indians by this time had taken to wintering in the agencies and then drifting off again once the weather improved. Thousands came in, but when spring came, many of them went out again.

Crazy Horse, who was about thirty-five years old, enjoyed in 1875–76 what was to be his last more or less unharassed winter as a free Indian. How well or how clearly he realized that his time was ending, we don't know. Perhaps he still thought that if the people fought fiercely and didn't relent, they could beat back the whites, not all the way to the Platte perhaps, but at least out of the Powder River country. We don't really know what he was thinking and should be cautious about making him more geopolitically attuned than he may have been. At this juncture nobody had really agreed to anything, but as the spring of 1876 approached, the Army directed a number of its major players toward the northern plains. To the south, on the plains of Texas, the so-called Red River War was over. The holdouts among the Comanches and the Kiowas had been defeated and their horse herd destroyed. Ranald S. Mackenzie and Nelson A. Miles both distinguished themselves in the Red River War and were soon sent north to help subdue the Cheyennes and the northern Sioux. Gen. George Crook was already in the field, and Col. John Gib-

Larry McMurtry, "A Road They Did Not Know," *American Heritage,* 50 (February–March 1999), 52–65.

Sitting Bull

Lt. Col. George Armstrong Custer

bon, Gen. Alfred Terry, and, of course, George Armstrong Custer were soon on their way.

By March of 1876 a great many Indians were moving north, toward Sitting Bull and the Hunkpapa band of Sioux, ready for a big hunt and possibly for a big fight with the whites, if the whites insisted on it, as in fact they did. The Little Bighorn in eastern Montana was the place chosen for this great gathering of native peoples, which swelled with more and more Indians as warmer weather came.

General Crook—also known as Three Stars, or the Grey Fox—struck first. He located what the scout Frank Grouard assured him was Crazy Horse's village, made a dawn attack, captured the village, destroyed the ample provender it contained (some of which his own hungry men could happily have eaten), but killed few Indians. Where Crazy Horse actually was at this time is a matter much debated, but the camp Crook destroyed seems not to have been his. For Crook the encounter was more vexation than triumph. The Sioux regrouped that night and got back most of their horses, and the fight drove these peace-seeking Indians back north toward Sitting Bull. Crook continued to suppose that he had de-

stroyed Crazy Horse's village; no doubt some of the Indian's friends were there, but the man himself was elsewhere.

A vast amount had been written about the great gathering of Indians who assembled in Montana in the early summer of 1876. It was to be the last mighty grouping of native peoples on the Great Plains of America. For the older people it evoked memories of earlier summer gatherings—reunions of a sort—such as had once been held at Bear Butte, near Crazy Horse's birthplace. Many of these Indians probably knew that what was occurring was in the nature of a last fling; there might be no opportunity for such a grand occasion again. Most of the Indians who gathered knew that the soldiers were coming, but they didn't care; their numbers were so great that they considered themselves invincible. Many Indians, from many tribes, remembered it as a last great meeting and mingling, a last good time. Historically, from this point on, there is a swelling body of reminiscence about the events of the spring and summer of 1876. Indeed, from the time the armies went into the field in 1876 to the end of the conflict, there is a voluminous memoir literature to be sifted through—most of it military memoirs written by whites.

Much of this found its way into the small-town newspapers that by then dotted the plains. These memoirs are still emerging. In 1996 four letters written by the wife of a captain who was at Fort Robinson when Crazy Horse was killed were discovered and published. The woman's name was Angie Johnson. It had taken more than a century for this literature to trickle out of the attics and scrapbooks of America, and it is still trickling. Of course it didn't take that long for the stately memoirs of Generals Sheridan and Sherman and Miles and the rest to be published.

Though the bulk of this memoir literature is by white soldiers, quite a few of the Sioux and the Cheyennes who fought at the Little Bighorn managed to get themselves interviewed here and there. It is part of the wonder of the book *Son of the Morning Star* that Evan S. Connell has patiently located many of these obscurely published reminiscences from both sides of the fight and placed them in his narrative in such a way as to create a kind of mosaic of firsthand comment. These memoirs don't answer all the questions, or even very many of them, but it is still nice to know what the participants *thought* happened, even if what we're left with is a kind of mesquite thicket of opinion, dense with guessing, theory, and speculation. Any great military conflict—Waterloo, Gettysburg, et cetera—leaves behind a similar confusion, a museum of memories but an extremely untidy one. Did the general say that or do this? Was Chief Gall behind Custer or in front of him or nowhere near him? The mind that is troubled by unanswered and possibly unanswerable questions should perhaps avoid military history entirely. Battles are messy things. Military historians often have to resort to such statements as "it would at this juncture probably be safe to assume. . . ." Stephen E. Ambrose is precisely right (and uncommonly frank) when he says plainly that much of the fun of studying the Battle of the Little Bighorn is the free rein it offers to the imagination. Once pointed toward this battle, the historical imagination tends to bolt; certainly the field of battle that the Indians called the Greasy Grass has caused many imaginations to bolt.

What we know for sure is that when June rolled around in 1876, there were a great many Indians, of several tribes, camped in southern Montana, with a fair number of soldiers moving west and north to fight them. Early June of that year may have been a last moment of confidence for the Plains Indians: They were many, they had meat, and they were in *their* place. Let the soldiers come.

This buildup of confidence was capped by what was probably the best-reported dream vision in Native American history—namely, Sitting Bull's vision of soldiers falling upside down into camp. This important vision did not come to the great Hunkpapa spontaneously; instead it was elaborately prepared for. Sitting Bull allowed a friend to cut one hundred small pieces of flesh from his arms, after which he danced, staring at the sun until he fainted. When he came out of his swoon, he heard a voice and had a vision of soldiers as numerous as grasshoppers falling upside down into camp. There were some who were skeptical of Sitting Bull—he could be a difficult sort—but this vision, coming as it did at the end of a great Sun Dance, convinced most of his people that if the soldiers did come, they would fall. (It is worth mentioning that Sitting Bull had mixed luck with visions. Not long before his death a meadowlark, speaking in Sioux, told him that his own people would kill him—which is what occurred.)

Shortly after this great vision of soldiers falling had been reported and considered, some Cheyenne scouts arrived with the news that General Crook was coming from the south with a lot of soldiers and a considerable body of Crow and Shoshone scouts. This was a sign that Sitting Bull had not danced in vain, although Crook never got very close to the great encampment, because Crazy Horse, Sitting Bull, and a large force immediately went south to challenge him on the Rosebud Creek, where the first of the two famous battles fought that summer was joined.

When the Indians attacked, Crook's thousand-man force was very strung out, with soldiers on both sides of the river, in terrain that was broken and difficult. Crow scouts were the first to spot the great party from the north; by common agreement the Crows and Shoshones fought their hearts out that day, probably saving Crook from the embarrassment of an absolute rout. But Crazy Horse, Black Twin, Bad Heart Bull, and many others were just as determined. Once or twice Crook almost succeeded in forming an effective battle line, but Crazy Horse and the others kept dashing right into it, fragmenting Crook's force and preventing a serious counterattack. There was much close-quarter, hand-to-hand fighting. In a rare anticipation of women in combat, a Cheyenne woman rushed in at some point and saved her brother, who was surrounded. (The Cheyennes afterward referred to the Battle of the Rosebud as the Battle Where the Girl Saved Her Brother.) Crook struggled all day, trying to mount a strong offensive, but the attackers were so persistent that they thwarted him. Finally the day waned, and shadows began to fall across the Rosebud. The Indians, having enjoyed a glorious day of battle, went home. They had turned Three Stars back, allowing him nowhere near the great gathering on the Little Bighorn.

Because the Indians left the field when the day was over, Crook claimed a victory, but nobody believed him, including, probably, himself. The Battle of the Rosebud was one of his most frustrating memories. It was indeed a remarkable battle between forces almost equally matched; in some ways it was more interesting than the fight at the Little Bighorn eight days later. Neither side could mount a fully decisive offensive, and both sides suffered unusually high casualties but kept fighting. The whites had no choice, of course; their adversaries in this case fought with extreme determination. The body count for the two sides varies with the commentator. Among historians who have written about the battle, George Hyde puts Crook's loss as high as fifty-seven men, a number that presumably includes many Crows and Shoshones who fell that day. Stephen Ambrose says it was twenty-eight men; Stanley Vestal says it was ten; and Robert Utley and Evan Connell claim it was nine. The attacking Sioux and Cheyennes may themselves have lost more than thirty men, an enormous casualty rate for a native

force. Accustomed as we are to the wholesale slaughter of the two world wars, or even of the Civil War, it is hard to keep in mind that when Indian fought Indian, a death count of more than three or four was unusual.

At the end of the day, General Crook at last accepted the advice his scouts had offered him earlier, which was that there were too many Indians up ahead for him to fight.

Had the full extent of Crook's difficulties on the Rosebud been known to the forces moving west into Montana, the sensible officers—that is, Gibbon and Terry—would have then proceeded with extreme caution, but it is unlikely that any trouble of Crook's would have slowed Custer one whit. Even if he had known that the Indians had sent Crook packing, it is hard to imagine that he would have proceeded differently. He had plenty of explicit—and, at the last, desperate—warnings from his own scouts, but he brushed these aside as he hurried the 7th Cavalry on to its doom. He plainly did not want to give his pessimistic scouts the time of day. He refused the offer of extra troops and also refused a Gatling gun, for fear that it might slow him down and allow the Indians to get away. It was only in the last minutes of his life that Custer finally realized that the Indians were fighting, not running. Custer was convinced that he could whip whatever body of Indians he could persuade to face him. He meant to win, he meant to win alone, and he meant to win rapidly, before any other officers arrived to dilute his glory.

Custer, that erratic egotist, has been studied more than enough; he has even been the subject of one of the best books written about the West, Evan Connell's *Son of the Morning Star*. Historians have speculated endlessly about why he did what he did at the Little Bighorn on the twenty-fifth of June, 1876; and yet what he did was perfectly in keeping with his nature. He did what he had always done: push ahead, disregard orders, start a fight, win it unassisted if possible, then start another fight. He had seldom done otherwise, and there was no reason at all to expect him to do otherwise in Montana that summer.

It may be true, as several writers have suggested, that he was covertly running for President that summer. The Democratic National Convention was just convening; a flashy victory and a timely telegram might have put him in contention for the nomination. Maybe, as Connell suggests, he thought he could mop up on the Sioux, race down to the Yellowstone River, hop on the steamer *Far West,* and make it to the big opening of the Philadelphia Centennial Exposition on July 4. So he marched his men most of the night and flung them into battle when—as a number of Indians noted—they were so tired their legs shook as they dismounted. As usual, he did only minimal reconnaissance, and convinced himself on no evidence whatever that the Indians must be running away from him, not toward him. The highly experienced scouts who were with him—the half-breed Mitch Bouyer and the Arikara Bloody Knife and the Crow Half Yellow Face—all told Custer that they would die if they descended into the valley where the Indians were. None of them, in all their many years on the plains had ever seen anything to match this great encampment. All the scouts knew that the valley ahead was for them the valley of death. Half Yellow Face, poetically, told Custer that they would all go home that day by a road they did not know. The fatalism of these scouts is a story in itself. Bouyer, who knew exactly what was coming, sent the young scout Curly away but then himself rode on with Custer, to his death.

Whatever they said, what wisdom they offered, Custer ignored. It may be that he *was* running for President, but it is hard to believe that he would have done anything differently even if it had been an off year politically. Maj. Marcus Reno and Capt. Frederick Benteen, whom he had forced to split off, both testified much later that they didn't believe Custer had any plan when he pressed his attack. He was—and long had been—the most aggressive general in the American army. It didn't matter to him how many Indians there were. When he saw an enemy, he attacked, and would likely have done so even if he had had no political prospects.

In the week between the fight on the Rosebud and the one at the Little Bighorn, Crazy Horse went back to the big party. The great General Crook had been whipped; the Indians felt invincible again. Everyone knew that more soldiers were coming, but no one was particularly concerned. These soldiers could be whipped in turn.

Some commentators have suggested that a sense of doom and foreboding hung over the northern plains during this fatal week; Indian and soldier alike were said to feel it. Something dark and terrible was about to happen—and yet it was high summer in one of the most beautiful places in Montana, the one time when that vast plain is usually free of rain clouds or snow clouds. But this summer, Death was coming to a feast, and many felt his approach. On the morning of the battle, when most of the Sioux and Cheyennes were happily and securely going about their domestic business, never supposing that any soldiers would be foolish enough to attack them, Crazy Horse, it is said, marked a bloody hand in red pigment on both of his horse's hips and drew an arrow and a bloody scalp on both sides of his horse's neck. Oglala scouts had been keeping watch on Custer, following his movements closely. Crazy Horse either knew or sensed that the fatal day had come.

The Battle of the Little Bighorn, June 25 and 26, 1876, is one of the most famous battles in world history. I doubt that any other American battle—not the Alamo, not Gettysburg—has spawned a more extensive or more diverse literature. There are books, journals, newsletters, one or another of which has by now printed every scrap of reminiscence that has been dredged up. Historians, both professional and amateur, have poured forth voluminous speculations, wondering what would have happened if somebody— usually the unfortunate Major Reno—had done something differently, or if Custer hadn't foolishly split his command, or if and if and if. Though the battle took place more than 120 years ago, debate has not much slackened. In fact the sudden rise in Native American studies has resulted in increased reprinting of Indian as opposed to white reminiscences; now the Sioux and the Cheyennes are pressing the debate.

A number of white historians have argued that one or another Indian leader made the decisive moves that doomed Custer and the 7th; for these historians the battle was decided by strategy and generalship, not numbers. Both Stephen Ambrose and Mari Sandoz have written many pages about the brilliance of Crazy Horse in flanking Custer and seizing the high ground—today called Custer Hill—thus ending Custer's last hope of establishing a defensive position that might have held until reinforcements arrived. Others argue for their favorite chief, whether Gall, Two Moon, or another. Evan Connell, in his lengthy account of the battle, scarcely mentions Crazy Horse's part in it. All these arguments, of course, depend on Indian memory, plus study of the battleground itself. To me they seem to be permanently ambiguous, potent rather than conclusive. It is indeed an area of study where historians can give free rein to their imaginations; what Stephen Ambrose doesn't mention is that the Sioux and the Cheyennes, in remembering this battle, might be giving *their* imaginations a little running room as well. A world in which all whites are poets and all Indians sober reporters is not the world as most of us know it.

We are likely never to know for sure who killed Custer. He had his famous hair short for this campaign; had it still been long, many Indians might have recognized him. It is as well to keep in mind that as many as two thousand horses may have been in motion during this battle; between the dust they raised and the gun smoke, the scene would have become phantasmagorical; it would have been difficult for anyone to see well, or far. It is thus little wonder that no one recognized Custer. At some sharp moment Custer must have realized that his reasoning had been flawed. The Indians he had assumed were running away were actually coming to kill him, and there were a lot of them. Whether he much regretted his error is doubtful. Fighting was what Custer did, battle thrilled him, and now he was right in the dead thick of the biggest Indian fight of all. He may have enjoyed himself right up to the moment he fell.

For his men, of course, it was a different story. They had been marching since the middle of the night; a lot of them were so tired they could barely lift their guns. For them it was dust, weariness, terror, and death.

No one knows for certain how many Indians fought in this battle, but two thousand is a fair estimate, give or take a few hundred. Besides their overpowering numbers they were also highly psyched by the great Sun Dance and their recent victory over Crook. When Major Reno and his men appeared at the south end of the great four-mile village, the Indians were primed. Reno might have charged them and produced, at least, disarray, but he didn't; the Indians soon chased him back across the Little Bighorn and up a bluff, where he survived, just barely. A lucky shot hit Bloody Knife, the Arikara scout, square in the head; Major Reno, standing near, was splattered with his brain matter. Some think this gory accident undid Major Reno, but we will never know the state of his undoneness, if any. Gall, the Hunkpap warrior, who, by common agreement, was a major factor in this battle, soon had fifteen hundred warriors mounted and ready to fight. If Reno *had* charged the south end of the village, he might have been massacred as thoroughly as Custer.

Exactly when Crazy Horse entered the battle is a matter of debate. Some say he rode out and skirmished a little with Reno's men; others believe he was still in his lodge when Reno arrived and that he was interested only in the larger fight with Custer. Most students of the battle think that when it dawned on Custer that he was in a fight for survival, not glory, he turned north, toward the high ground, hoping to establish a defensive redoubt on the hill, or rise, that is now named for him. But Crazy Horse, perhaps at the head of as many as a thousand warriors himself, flanked him and seized that high ground, sealing Custer's doom while, incidentally, making an excellent movie role for Errol Flynn and a number of other leading men.

So Crazy Horse may have done it, but it was Gall and *his* thousand or so warriors who turned back Reno and then harried Custer so hard that the

7th Cavalry—the soldiers who fell into camp, as in Sitting Bull's vision—could never really establish *any* position. If Crazy Horse did flank Custer, it was of course good quarter-backing, but it hardly seems possible now to insist that any one move was decisive. Gall and his men might have finished Custer without much help from anyone; Gall had lost two of his wives and three of his children early in the battle and was fighting out his anger and his grief.

From this distance of years the historians can argue until their teeth rot that one man or another was decisive in this battle, but all these arguments are unprovable now. What's certain is that George Armstrong Custer was very foolish, a glory hound who ignored orders, skipped or disregarded his reconnaissance, and charged, all but blindly, into a situation in which, whatever the quality of Indian generalship, he was quickly overwhelmed by numbers.

What I think of when I walk that battleground is dust. Once or twice in my life I rode out with as many as thirty cowboys; I remember the dust that small, unhurried group made. The dust of two thousand milling, charging horses would have been something else altogether; the battleground would soon have been a hell of dust, smoke, shooting, hacking; once the two groups of fighting men closed with each other, visibility could not have been good. Custer received a wound in the breast and one in the temple, either of which would have been fatal. His corpse was neither scalped nor mutilated. Bad Soup, a Hunkpapa, is said to have pointed out Custer's corpse to White Bull. "There he lies," he said. "He thought he was going to be the greatest man in the world. But there he is."

Most of the poetic remarks that come to us from this battle are the work of writers who interviewed Indians, or those who knew Indians, who thought they remembered Bad Soup saying something, or Half Yellow Face making (probably in sign) the remark about the road we do not know, or Bloody Knife staring long at the sun that morning, knowing that he would not be alive to see it go down behind the hills that evening. All we can conclude now is that Bloody Knife and Bad Soup and Half Yellow Face were

right, even if they didn't say the words that have been attributed to them.

Hundreds of commentators, from survivors who fought in the battle to historians who would not be born until long years after the dust had settled in the valley of the Little Bighorn, have developed opinions about scores of issues that remain, in the end, completely opaque. Possibly Crazy Horse fought as brilliantly as some think—we will never really know—but he and Sitting Bull and Two Moon survived the battle and Custer didn't. General Grant, no sentimentalist, put the blame for the defeat squarely on Custer, and said so bluntly. The Indians made no serious attempt to root out and destroy Reno, though they could have. Victory over Long Hair was enough; Custer's famous 1868 dawn attack on the Cheyenne chief Black Kettle was well avenged.

The next day, to Major Reno's vast relief, the great gathering broke up, the Indians melting away into the sheltering vastness of the plains.

What did the Sioux and Cheyenne leaders think at this point? What did they feel? Several commentators have suggested that once the jubilation of victory subsided, a mood of foreboding returned. Perhaps the tribes recognized that they were likely never to be so unified again, and they were not. Perhaps the leaders knew that they were likely never to have such a one-sided military victory again either—a victory that was thrown them because of the vainglory of one white officer.

Or perhaps they didn't think in these terms at all—not yet. With the great rally over, the great battle won, they broke up and got on with their hunting. Perhaps a few did reckon that something was over now, but it is doubtful that many experienced the sense of climax and decline as poetically as Old Lodge Skins in Thomas Berger's novel *Little Big Man:* "Yes, my son," he says, "it is finished now, because what more can you do to an enemy than beat him? Were we fighting red men against red men—the way we used to, because that is a man's profession, and besides it is enjoyable—it would now be the turn of the other side to whip us. We would fight as hard as ever and perhaps win again, but they would definitely start with an advantage, because that is the *right* way.

There is no permanent winning or losing when things move, as they should, in a circle. . . .

"But white men, who live in straight lines and squares, do not believe as I do. With them it is everything or nothing: Washita or Greasy Grass. . . . Winning is all they care about, and if they can do that by scratching a pen across a paper or saying something into the wind, they are much happier. . . ."

Old Lodge Skins was right about the Army's wanting to win. Crook's defeat at the Rosebud had embarrassed the Army, and the debacle at the Little Bighorn shamed it. The nation, of course, was outraged. By August of 1876 Crook and Terry were lumbering around with a reassuring force of some four thousand soldiers. Naturally they found few Indians. Crazy Horse was somewhere near Bear Butte, harrying the miners in the Black Hills pretty much as the mood struck him. There was a minor engagement or two, of little note. The Indians were not suicidal; they left the massive force alone. Crook and Terry were such respecters now that they were bogged down by their own might.

In the fall of that year, the whites, having failed to buy the Black Hills, simply took them, with a travesty of a treaty council at which the Indians lost not only the Black Hills but the Pow-der River, the Yellowstone, the Bighorns. By the end of what was in some ways a year of glory, 1876, Crazy Horse had to face the fact that his people had come to a desperate pass. It was a terrible winter, with subzero temperatures day after day. The Indians were ragged and hungry; the soldiers who opposed them were warmly clothed and well equipped. The victories of the previous summer were, to the Sioux and the Cheyennes, now just memories. They had little ammunition and were hard pressed to find game enough to feed themselves.

During this hard period, with the soldiers just waiting for spring to begin another series of attacks, Sitting Bull decided to take himself and his people to Canada. Crazy Horse perhaps considered this option and then rejected it because in Canada the weather was even colder, or maybe he just didn't want to leave home. But in early May of 1877, he had eleven hundred people with him, and more than two thousand horses, when he came into Red Cloud agency at Fort Robinson in northwestern Nebraska. Probably neither the generals nor Crazy Horse himself ever quite believed that a true surrender had taken place, but this august event, the surrender of "Chief" Crazy Horse was reported in *The New York Times* on May 8, 1877.

Study Questions

1. What happened to Native Americans on the Great Plains in the nineteenth century and why did so many Indian leaders feel that they had no choice but to "either walk the white man's road" or die fighting?

2. Describe Crazy Horse and Sitting Bull.

3. What role did General George Crook play in the events leading up to Little Big Horn?

4. Why, in early June 1876, did the Indians consider themselves invincible in face of the invading white army?

5. Describe the personality of Lieutenant Colonel George Armstrong Custer.

6. When Custer's troops went into battle, what disadvantages did they face? How did Custer's personality contribute to their problems? What miscalculations did Custer make just prior to the battle?

7. What happened to the Sioux and to the Black Hills after the battle?

Bibliography

For general surveys of the "conquest" of the American West, see Patricia Nelson Limerick, *The Legacy of Conquest: The Unbroken Past of the American West* (1987) and *"It's Your Misfortune and None of My Own": A History of the American West* (1991). Excellent studies of the Plains Indians include Morris W. Foster, *Being Comanche: A Social History of an American Indian Community* (1991) and Catherine Price, *The Oglala People, 1841–1879* (1996). For biographies of the major figures involved in the Battle of the Little Big Horn, see John G. Neihardt, *Black Elk Speaks: Being the Life Story of a Holy Man of the Oglala Sioux* (1961); Mari Sandoz, *Crazy Horse: The Strange Man of the Oglalas* (1961); Robert M. Utley, *Cavalier in Buckskin: George Armstrong Custer and the Western Military Frontier* (1988) and *The Lance and the Shield: The Life and Times of Sitting Bull* (1993). Patricia Limerick's *The Legacy of Conquest: The Unbroken Promise of the American West* (1987) is perhaps the most influential of the "New Western History" literature. Also see Gregory Nobles, *American Frontiers: Cultural Encounters and Continental Conquest* (1997) and David K. Richter, *Facing East from Indian Country: A Native History of Early America* (2001).

Credits

3 Attributed to John Foster, *Mr. Richard Mather,* woodcut printed after 1700. MHS Image number 1860. The Massachussetts Historical Society

8 Stock Montage, Inc./Historical Picture Service

19 © Bettmann/Corbis

43 Thomas A. Heinz/Corbis

54 Library of Congress

67 Library of Congress

74 American Antiquarian Society

84 Bibliothèque Nationale de France, Paris

92 *The Maryland Gazette,* May 17, 1745

119 Copyright Yale University Art Gallery, Trumbull Collection

123 Stock Montage, Inc.

135 Benjamin Blyth, "Abigail Adams," *c.*1766. Courtesy of the Massachusetts Historical Society, MHS Image number 73

150 Culver Pictures, Inc.

173 Naval Historical Foundation

181 Collection of the New-York Historical Society

187 Brooklyn Museum of Art, Dick S. Ramsay Fund (57.68)

202 Staten Island Historical Society, Alice Austen Collection (D81)

214 Security Pacific National Bank Photograph Collection/Los Angeles Public Library

226 © Bettmann/Corbis

233 Shearson Lehman Hutton Collection

236 Historic New Orleans Collection

243 John Gadsby Chapman, "Davy Crockett," date unknown. Art Collection, Harry Ransom Humanities Research Center, The University of Texas at Austin (Negative number 65.349)

255 H. Armstrong Roberts/Corbis

274 Oneida Community Collection/George Arents Research Library at Syracuse University

286 American Antiquarian Society

299 Library of Congress

324 Missouri Historical Society

335 Library of Congress

342 "Handcart Pioneers" by CCA Christensen, © by Intellectual Reserve, Inc. Courtesy of Museum of Church History and Art, used by permission

349 Boston Athenaeum

361 National Archives and Records Administration

364 New York Public Library

384 Brown Brothers

399 Hayes Presidential Center, Negative number 369

407 (left) © Corbis

407 (right) © Medford Historical Society Collection/Corbis